America's
Best Cheap Sleeps

Open Road *is* Travel!

Comfortable Budget Accommodations Anywhere in the U.S. For $50 or Less Per Night

About the Author

Tracy Whitcombe, a native of Washington State, is an avid and seasoned traveler. He has traveled extensively throughout the United States and Canada, mostly along two-lane, blue highways. Mr. Whitcombe is also a member of the Extra Miler Club, an organization whose members' common goal is to visit every county in the United States. Mr. Whitcombe makes his home in Edmonds, Washington.

America's
Best Cheap Sleeps

Open Road *is* Travel!

TRACY WHITCOMBE

Open Road Publishing

Open Road Publishing

We offer travel guides to American and foreign locales. Our books tell it like it is, often with an opinionated edge, and our experienced authors always give you all the information you need to have the trip of a lifetime. Write for your free catalog of all our titles.

Open Road Publishing
P.O. Box 284, Cold Spring Harbor, NY 11724
E-mail: Jopenroad@aol.com

Library of Congress Control No. 2004100024
ISBN 1-59360-013-5

ACKNOWLEDGMENTS

America's Best Cheap Sleeps is the product of many long hours of work at the computer and on the telephone, but it would not have been possible without a few special people in my life: my friends Beth and Shari who listened when I needed a friendly ear, my parents whose belief in me nourished my dreams, my dear friend Gary whose strength, maturity and wisdom has illuminated even the darkest path, and my great-grandmother Maggie — I never knew a more gentle, loving and unselfish person. These pages are for all of you.

The author has made every effort to be as accurate as possible, but neither he nor the publisher assumes responsibility for the services provided by any business listed in this guide; for any errors or omissions; or any loss, damage, or disruptions in your travel for any reason.

Contents

OVERVIEW

THE STATES

America's Best Cheap Sleeps

OVERVIEW

INTRODUCTION

In the summer of 1996, when I set out on a road trip from my home in Seattle to the Midwest, I brought along the most comprehensive and detailed accommodations guides known to me at the time. As I rolled into town each night on my trip, I began my routine of seeking out a place to stay for the night by scanning these guides. Since I was traveling alone on a budget, I used a yardstick of $40 or less per night for gauging the best deals. I felt confident that I could stay within my budget, knowing that I was traveling through places where there would be a wide selection of economy motels, motor hotels and inns. I soon discovered, however, that there weren't a lot of lodgings listed in these guides that met my budget criteria.

Determined not to pay more than what I had budgeted for the night, I then drove around town looking for affordable motels. In every such situation, I found what I was looking for. I always managed to find a clean, comfortable and inexpensive place to stay which was *not* listed in any of my guides. I thought it odd since most of these inexpensive places were every bit as comfortable, clean and safe as the more expensive places I found in my travel guides. So I decided to write a travel guide for cost-conscious car travelers, the first of its kind.

When you consider the relative costs of travel (airfare, car rental, gasoline, meals, tolls/admissions, postcards, souvenirs, etc.), you will quickly note that what you pay for a place to sleep each night accounts for the largest portion of your travel budget. And if you are traveling by car, what you pay in lodging expenses typically comes out to more than all your other relative travel expenses combined. While airfares and car rental rates have declined during the past fifteen years or so, the cost of accommodations has not. What we pay for a place to sleep has maintained a fairly steady growth rate over the same period of time. Now more than ever, travelers need to be aware of and access the bargains out there—to find those places which offer rooms at reasonable rates. *America's Best Cheap Sleeps* was put together with this goal in mind: to provide travelers with options for affordable lodgings and to help keep money in their pockets while they explore the country by car.

I know that you'll find this book a helpful companion as you make your way around the country by car. The next time you hit the open road, you'll know that your money is being well spent on a clean, safe place to stay — *and* you'll have money left over to eat!

There are approximately 200,000 miles of asphalt in the old federal highway system and nearly 43,000 miles of interstate to be explored. What better way to experience the richly diverse American roadscape than by car? One word of advice: get off the interstates whenever possible and take the two-lane federal and state highways. Though less direct than the interstate system, the federal and state highways are far more interesting and scenic. So break out your road atlas and plot your course for the open highway. Freedom awaits you!

ROOM RATES

Rates in this directory are quoted for single-occupancy accommodations. Although rates for additional persons vary from place to place, the average is $5.00 per person. Rates shown are those which were in effect at the time of publication. They have been rounded off to the nearest dollar and do not include local taxes. Please note that these rates are not guaranteed—they are subject to change at the discretion of the property owner/manager. This is something you should be aware of and keep in mind when using this guide—rates fluctuate and change from time to time. The best way to guarantee a room rate is to call ahead and find out what the room is going for, and, if the price falls within an acceptable range for you, make the reservation. If the rates do increase from those quoted in this directory, they most likely will increase by only a few dollars.

In some cases, low occupancy may force property owners to lower their standard room rate in order to attract business. In addition, many motel owners offer special "limited" promotions in order to entice travelers into staying at their property. As a result, you may at times find that room rates are actually cheaper than those quoted in this directory.

2Also, rates can fluctuate from season to season. Generally, summertime or "peak season" rates will be higher than off-season rates. The opposite is true in the sunbelt states, such as Florida and Arizona, where winter is the peak season. Rates can also increase on weekends or during special events and holidays. Typically, more will be charged for a room on Fridays and Saturdays. Care has been taken in this directory to note when you can expect such rate fluctuations. To be sure of what the rate is at any time of year, take the time to call ahead and verify what rooms are going for at your motel of choice.

ALTERNATIVES TO MOTEL TRAVEL

Although this guide focuses primarily on budget motels, lodges, motor hotels and inns, these are by no means the only inexpensive lodging options available to the frugal car traveler. There *are* a few other cheap alternative lodging options: campgrounds, youth hotels and RV travel. As a rule of thumb, there is an inverse relationship between low-cost lodging and comfort level. The less you pay for a night's stay, the more likely it is that your stay will not have the usual comforts and amenities of home. For the money, the budget motel is perhaps the best all-around value, which is why I have chosen it as the principal focus of this book. For those of you who don't mind doing without a few basic comforts, other inexpensive lodging options are explored briefly below.

YOUTH HOSTELS

Don't be fooled by the name. You do NOT need to be 18 years old and fresh out of high school in order to stay at a youth hostel. Youth hostels are open to people of all ages and offer a surprisingly broad array of amenities for your money. You can expect to pay anywhere from $8 to $35 for a night's stay (a typical night's stay is around $16). Unlike hotels and motels which charge a nominal fee for each additional person in your party, youth hotels charge the same rate for each individual traveler regardless of party size. If you are unfamiliar with the type of lodging offered by youth hostels, you should know that rooms are almost always dormitory-style. Usually, you will have to share a room with two or three other people. Some hostels have even larger rooms sleeping 10 or more people. If you are traveling with a companion of the opposite sex, you will have to sleep in separate rooms. Also, some youth hostels require that you bring your own bed linens, but most provide these for you if you come without them (either free or for a small rental fee). By cutting back on overhead and keeping their costs down this way, youth hostels can afford to offer lodgings at such reasonable rates. If you are determined to stay overnight in the heart of a large city, such as New York or San Francisco, and not spend more than $50 for the night, you will no doubt find that your only options will be youth hotels or YMCAs.

Of course, youth hostels are just as varied in what they offer as motels are. Some offer private rooms which you can rent for a little more money, while others do not. Some youth hostels have 24-hour access, while others have restricted hours for check-in and check-out. Some are open year-round while others close up for the winter. You might even find a youth hostel which offers breakfast or guided tours or even bike rentals. Most hostels do have kitchens, linen rentals, a TV room and laundry facilitics. Smokers and pet owners beware: youth hostels do not allow smoking or pets inside their facilities. If privacy is important to you, hostelling may not be your best option, unless you opt for one of the private rooms.

Although not required to stay at a youth hostel, you can purchase a Hostelling International annual membership card for $25.00. The cost for senior citizens (over 55) is a mere $15.00. These memberships can be purchased at nearly all participating Hostelling International facilities or at an American Youth Hostel Council office. (For more information, write to **American Youth Hostels**, 733 15th Street N.W., Suite 840, Washington, DC 20005 or call 202.783.6161). There are certain advantages to becoming a Hostelling International member:

- You are automatically entitled to the standard nightly rate charged for a bed. Non-members are required to pay an additional $3.00 for their bed.
- As a member, you are given priority in allocating beds for the night over non-members. Beds are allocated on a first-come, first-served basis. You can call ahead and reserve a bed if you like, but you take a chance during peak season by just showing up at the end of the day and requesting a bed, particularly if you are a non-member. Your Hostelling International membership will serve you well if you are vying for a bed with others who are non-members.
- Your membership is valid not only at participating hostels in the United States, but at any International Youth Hostel facility around the world.

There are perhaps 500 different youth hostels in the United States and Canada, only a few of which are featured in this book. If you would like a more comprehensive youth hostel directory, you can obtain a copy of *The Hostel Handbook for the U.S.A. and Canada* by writing to:

Sugar Hill Hostel
c/o Jim Williams
722 St. Nicholas Avenue
New York, NY 10031

The cost of the directory is $3.00 ($2.00 for the directory, plus a dollar for postage). If you are writing from Canada, the cost is $4.00.

CAMPGROUNDS

The United States abounds with thousands of campgrounds. Next to sleeping in your car in a parking lot (which I do not recommend for safety reasons), this is perhaps your least-expensive overnight option. Campgrounds charge a very modest fee, usually $5-15 per night, for a small tenting site. Most campgrounds are equipped with showers and toilets, and some even have public telephones. Going this route, you *will* have to give up some of the creature comforts, such as a private bath, a television and climate control (heat and A/C). Also, camping is a very seasonal activity. You are not likely to pitch a tent in the dead of winter or even during a heavy rainstorm (unless you are an avid enthusiast of the outdoors and are well-prepared for camping out in inclement weather). Nevertheless, pitching a tent for the night can be an inexpensive and fun proposition under the right conditions.

RV TRAVEL

Unless you already own one, RV travel may not make the most economic sense. You will need to either purchase or rent one. Purchasing an RV will require a significant outlay of cash to the tune of tens of thousands of dollars. You might be able to pick up a used RV for less money, but it will still involve a painful parting of cash from your wallet. If you do decide to purchase a used RV, you will most likely end up putting a lot of money into maintenance and repairs.

The rental option, although cheaper than purchasing one outright, is still far less attractive than all the other options. Consider this: The average weekly rental rate of a motorhome is $900-1100 during peak season and $700-900 during the off-season—and that's not the end of it. RV rental companies will give you anywhere from 50 to 100 free miles per day, but after that, they charge between 30¢ and 35¢ per mile. At the end of the day, you will still need to find a place to settle for the night. RV parks typically charge anywhere from $10-25 per night. That can really add up. So, if you travel, say, 250 miles per day during peak season with an RV you rented for $900/week and 100 free miles, and stay in a reasonably priced RV park, your daily cost, not including gas, is $182—way above the $45-or-less target that is the subject of this book.

TRAVEL CLUB MEMBERSHIPS

American Automobile Association

It pays to become a member of AAA. If you are already a member, terrific! As a member, you already know about the many benefits and services you get with your membership. If you are not a member of AAA, you should seriously consider signing up. Annual dues for a Primary Membership are $51.00, and if you know someone who is already a member of AAA, you can have them sponsor you for an Associate Membership at $27.00. What you get with your membership more than pays for the annual dues, particularly if you are planning to travel around a bit. Not only do you get free maps, customized travel itineraries and emergency towing insurance, you automatically qualify for discounts at thousands of hotels, motels, lodges, resorts and inns across the United States and Canada. AAA discounts are generally good for *at least* 10% off the standard room rates wherever your membership is honored. Many of the businesses listed in this directory offer discounts for AAA memberships. If you are traveling on a budget, your membership will make it easier for you to travel farther for your money.

Super 8 VIP Membership

You can obtain a special *Super 8 VIP* membership card from Super 8 Motels, Inc. by calling 1.800.800.8000 or by stopping in at any Super 8 Motel. Enrollment is a one-time fee of $4.00. Your membership will never expire. You will receive a Super 8 Motels VIP card which entitles you to a 10% discount on the standard room rates at all Super 8 Motels in the United States and Canada. This is an exceptionally good deal for you, considering that you will likely make up the $4.00 enrollment fee the very first time you use your membership. Super 8 Motels are categorized as budget-oriented, so their room rates are fairly reasonable, even without the discount. Your Super 8 VIP membership makes your stay even more affordable.

Knights Inn Royalty Club

Knights Inn, a nationwide budget lodgings chain with over 200 locations, offers discounts to a variety of travelers. Seniors will enjoy a 10% discount on all rooms. AARP members can take advantage of their 15-30% room rate discount. Plus, there is a 10% discount for AAA members and business travelers.

Hospitality International's INNcentive Card

Hospitality International, parent company of Scottish Inns, Red Carpet Inns, Passport Inns and Downtowner Inns, offers a free membership card which entitles you to a 10% discount at participating motels. To become a member, call 1.800.247.4677 between the hours of 8:30 a.m. and 5:30 p.m. (Eastern Time) or visit their website at *www.bookroomsnow.com* and order your free INNcentive Card online.

GETTING THE BEST ROOM RATE

Despite outward appearances, advertised room rates are not etched in stone. Unlike other commodities you may purchase, a night's stay in a hotel or motel does not necessarily have a single price tag on it. Many motels have varying rate structures, *even for the same room*. The standard room rate, also known in the trade as the "rack" rate, is the rate you will be quoted if you were to just walk in and ask what they are charging for a room. The following are suggestions for bringing down the cost of a night's stay at a given hotel or motel.

- Ask if they offer a **discount for AAA members**. Most places do, but still many do not. This directory lists and designates a number of properties which will extend a discount to you for your AAA membership, but don't assume that a motel or hotel will not offer you a discount just because it is not indicated as such in this directory. You will be surprised at how many places will extend a discount to you, even if they normally do not honor AAA memberships. Always be sure to ask.
- If you are 55 years or older, be sure to ask if they offer **senior citizen discounts**. Most places do offer discounts for senior citizens, but some businesses, such as Motel 6, require that you belong to the American Association of Retired Persons (AARP) and that you present your membership card for verification in order to get a discount.
- If you are unsatisfied with the standard room rate and are unable to get a discount otherwise, ask for the "corporate" rate. Many places offer a **corporate rate** in order to attract business travelers. This is the rate reserved for businesspeople and is typically a few dollars less than the standard room rate, but not usually more than 10%. Non-business travelers, don't be discouraged! Even if you are not traveling on business, you can still take advantage of this rate merely by requesting it when you check in or when you call to make reservations. Generally, motel and hotel clerks will not ask you to prove that you are traveling on business (the very idea is preposterous!), but some may ask to see a business card. If you have a business card, be sure to bring a few along for your trip, just in case.
- Rodeway Inn and Econo Lodge now offer a 30% discount to business travelers over the age of 50.
- Many places offer discounts to government employees, truck drivers and military personnel, so if you are a member of any of these groups, be sure to let them know.
- Ask if they are running any **promotions or specials**. You may not be able to get a discount on the rack rate, but some motels and hotels offer special deals in connection with other local businesses. For

example, you might get a coupon for a 99¢ breakfast at a nearby restaurant, free admission to an area attraction or even gambling tokens for a local casino. These perks might translate into an overall savings for you on the cost of renting a room for the night, even without a discount on the standard rate.

COUPONS

Exit Information Guide, Inc. (EIG), a company based in Gainesville, Florida, puts out the *Traveler's Discount Lodging Guide*, a booklet which contains an amazing number of coupons good for significant discounts at hotels and motels in 35 states. These guides are published on a seasonal basis by AATAA (the Auto and Air Travelers Association of America) and are available for individual states and groups of states around the country. Copies of the *Traveler's Discount Lodging Guide* are FREE and can be found at more than 11,000 locations nationwide. You will find copies of these guides at welcome centers, highway rest areas, restaurants (Denny's, for example), and at gas stations and convenience stores located along major roads and highways.

If you would like advance copies of the *Traveler's Discount Lodging Guide*, you can call EIG to order them at 1.800.332.3948. There is a small postage and handling fee ($3 for the first guide and $1 for each additional guide). Major credit cards are accepted. If you would like to order them by mail, you can write to:

Exit Information Guide, Inc.
4205 N.W. 6th Street
Gainesville, FL 32609

You need to allow 2 to 3 weeks for delivery, so be sure to order early. EIG also has a website: *www.travelerdiscountguide.com* or *www.roomsaver.com*.

PETS

Many motels in this guide offer rooms to travelers with pets. However, some are more restrictive than others in their policies. For example, some motel owners will only allow small dogs or may even have a strict "no cats" policy. When you check in, don't try to smuggle your pet into your room with you. Even though it may be indicated in this guide that pets are allowed, you should always be sure to request permission for your pet from the front desk. If the motel staff discover you have a pet in your room without first getting approval, you could be asked to leave. For those motels which are pet-friendly, some will require a nominal daily fee for your pet, while others will require both a daily fee and refundable deposit. Some motels will even provide a kennel for your dog. Be aware that it is quite common for motels to allot only a certain number of rooms for people traveling with pets, so it is wise to reserve your room in advance.

6 P.M. AND NO RESERVATIONS?

If you are arriving in town at 6:00 p.m. without motel reservations, do not worry. At 6:00 p.m., many places check their reservations file and then promptly make available any non-guaranteed rooms (i.e., rooms not held with a major credit card or rooms held to only 6:00 p.m.). This is your opportunity to secure a room for yourself (and, if you have them, present any discount coupons to the front desk clerk). The longer after 6:00 p.m. you wait to check in, the scarcer the availability, so be sure to arrive early enough to get your room, optimally just after 6:00 p.m.

BIG CITY TRAVEL

If you are headed to one of the big cities (Boston, New York, San Francisco, Washington DC, Philadelphia, Miami, Chicago, Los Angeles, Seattle, Miami, Detroit or Baltimore), you should know in advance that finding inexpensive accommodations will be difficult, if not impossible. I have provided some information in this guide for locating the accommodations of relative affordability for each of these cities. It is always a good idea to call ahead to make reservations if you *are* planning to stay in any of these major cities—last-minute availability is harder to come by in the big cities than it is in the suburban and rural areas of the country.

1-800 NUMBERS FOR BUDGET MOTEL CHAINS

A number of properties listed in this directory belong to one of the many budget-oriented hotel/motel chains across the country. In addition to the local phone numbers listed with each property, below are the 1-800 reservation numbers of the various budget-oriented hotel/motel chains. Use these numbers when requesting rate information or when making reservations and save a few pennies in long distance charges.

If you call one of the 1-800 numbers and are quoted a rate higher than you had expected, or are told that there are no rooms available at your motel of choice, try calling the motel at their local number. The 1-800 reservation services are allocated only a certain number of motel rooms at certain rates, while the local motels try to keep rooms on hand for last-minute local arrivals. Also, if you have a discount coupon you would like to use, you may need to call the motel at their local number in order to get the discount. Although some 1-800 reservation services *do* honor these coupons, most do not.

MOTEL CHAIN AND WEBSITE	RESERVATION NO. AND REGION
Budget Host Inns *www.budgethost.com*	1.800.BUDHOST Nationwide
Best Value Inns *www.bestvalueinns.com*	1.800.315.2378 Nationwide
Cross Country Inn *www.crosscountryinns.com*	1.800.621.1429 Midwest
Days Inn *www.daysinn.com*	1.800.DAYSINN Nationwide
Econo Lodge *www.econolodge.com*	1.800.55ECONO Nationwide
Howard Johnson/HoJo Inn *www.hojo.com*	1.800.446.4656 Nationwide
Inns of America *www.innsamerica.com*	1.800.826.0778 CA, Southeast
Knights Inns/Courts *www.knightsinn.com*	1.800.843.5644 Nationwide
Masters Economy Inns *www.mastersinn.com*	1.800.633.3434 Southeast
Microtel Inns & Suites *www.microtelinn.com*	1.888.771.7171 Nationwide
Motel 6 *www.motel6.com*	1.800.4MOTEL6 Nationwide
National 9 Inns	1.800.524.9999 West
Passport Inn *www.bookroomsnow.com*	1.800.251.1962 Southeast
Ramada Limited *www.ramada.com*	1.800.272.6232 Nationwide
Red Carpet Inn *www.bookroomsnow.com*	1.800.251.1962 Nationwide
Red Roof Inns *www.redroof.com*	1.800.843.7663 Midwest/East
Rodeway Inns *www.rodeway.com*	1.800.228.2000 Nationwide

Scottish Inns *www.bookroomsnow.com*	1.800.251.1962 Nationwide
Super 8 Motels *www.super8.com*	1.800.800.8000 Nationwide
Travelodge/Thriftlodge *www.travelodge.com*	1.800.578.7878 Nationwide
Vagabond Inn *www.vagabondinns.com*	1.800.522.1555 West
Villager Lodge *www.villager.com*	1.800.328.7829 Nationwide

SAFETY TIPS

Contrary to popular conception, not all motels are fleabags and unsafe. By and large, motels are not only safe places to spend the night, but they offer comfort and cleanliness at a reasonable price. Having said that, you should not just throw caution to the wind and suspend your common sense. It is always prudent to take extra precautions to ensure safety wherever you travel. Below are a few guidelines you might want to consider when checking in for the night.

- It goes without saying that you should ALWAYS lock your door. Most motels and hotels have doors which are always locked from the outside. Don't just assume this to be the case every time. You should check just to be sure. Check any windows or sliding doors which may be part of your room. Also, if a deadbolt or chain is provided, be sure to engage it for extra security.
- If your room is on the ground floor, or if the motel has exterior corridors, be sure to draw the curtains or blinds completely closed on any windows in your room, especially at night.
- Don't leave valuables in your car. At night, your car is more vulnerable to burglary than your room.
- After dark, if you go out for dinner from your motel room, be sure to turn on the television and leave the lights on in the room. From the outside, it will appear as if someone is in the room and it will serve as a powerful deterrent to any would-be burglars.
- Don't flaunt your cash or jewelry while standing at the reservation desk and avoid leaving your room key out in the open, particularly if your room number is printed on it.
- If someone knocks on your door unexpectedly, ask who they are before opening the door. Most motels and hotels have installed peepholes in the doors for your safety. If you are at all suspicious about the person at your door, call the front desk immediately and report it. If

they say they were sent by the front desk, and you are still suspicious, call anyway to verify their story.

•Trust your gut-level instincts. If you find yourself in what feels like an unsafe situation, get out of it.

HOW TO INTERPRET LISTINGS

All accommodations found in this book are first listed alphabetically by state and then by city. After the business name, rates, address and phone number, you will find information on the following: number of units, pets, meals, amenities and services, wheelchair accessibility, discounts offered and credit cards accepted. Below is an example of a typical listing:

Super 8 Motel
$45
305 Hwy. 49N • 478.956.3311
57 Units, pets OK ($10 dep. req.). Continental breakfast. Pool. Laundry facility. Rooms come with phones and cable TV. Some rooms have microwaves, jacuzzis and refrigerators. AAA/senior discount. Credit cards accepted: AE, CB, DC, DS, MC, V.

Rates. The rate listed is the lowest rate which was quoted at the time of publication for a single room, one person. Not all single rooms, however, will fetch the same rate. Some motels and hotels have both single rooms with king-sized beds and single rooms with double beds. Generally, the rooms with double beds are going to be cheaper than the rooms with king-sized beds, so be sure to ask for the cheapest room. Rates are sometimes listed as a range of prices. This is because they can fluctuate according to season or availability, or the motel or hotel may offer single rooms with varying amenities. If rates climb higher than $40/ night for a single room during a particular season or event, it will be noted just after the primary rate information.

Units. This tells you how many units are in the motel or hotel and gives you some idea of its size relative to others.

Pets. This tells you whether or not the motel or hotel allows pets on the premises. Some places which allow pets, do so for a fee and/or deposit. Whenever possible, that information has been included with each listing.

Meals. Some motels and hotels have restaurants on the premises and still more offer a complimentary continental breakfast as part of your room rate. A continental breakfast may consist of as little as coffee and doughnuts, or it may consist of a more complete menu of bagels, fruit, cold cereal, pastries and juice.

Amenities and Services. Almost every motel and hotel in the country offers some kind of amenity, whether it be a phone in the room or cable TV. Most places, however, offer a little more than just a phone and cable TV. Among the many amenities you might find at a given motel or hotel are a swimming pool, a jacuzzi, a sauna, laundry facilities, meeting rooms and dataports for business travelers, playgrounds for children or picnic tables. Some motels and hotels even offer rooms which come equipped with refrigerators, microwaves and kitchenettes for extended stays. Fax and copy services as well as airport shuttle services are offered by some innkeepers.

Wheelchair Accessibility. Wherever possible, wheelchair accessibility has been noted for the various listings in this directory.

Discounts. Senior and AAA discounts are listed immediately after amenities and services. If you do not see a discount noted with the motel you are interested in, be sure to ask at check-in or when making reservations. If a discount is not noted for a particular motel, it does not necessarily mean that you can't get one upon request.

Credit Cards. Almost all motels and hotels accept credit cards as payment for your room. Here's how to interpret the abbreviations you will find in this section:

AE = American Express
CB = Carte Blanche
DC = Diners Club
DS = Discover
JCB = Japan Credit Bureau
MC = Master Card
V = Visa

FEEDBACK

There are over 4,600 lodgings in this book, but there are undoubtedly numerous other motels, hotels, lodges and inns offering rooms at $50 or less which were not featured in this guide. If you know of any and would like to see them included in next year's publication, please send me your comments and/or information. Likewise, if you discover a printed error in this publication, please let me know so that it can be corrected for next year's edition. Please also give me your feedback on any portions of this book you especially liked or disliked. Your comments are important and are the driving force that will shape the content and approach of this directory in future publications.

If you'd like to contact me, write to *amcheapsleeps@hotmail.com*. Thank you for your interest in *America's Best Best Cheap Sleeps* and happy travels!

alabama

ABBEVILLE

Best Western—Abbeville Inn
$40-50
Jct. US 431 & SR 27 • 334.585.5060
40 Units, pets OK. Continental breakfast. Pool. Meeting rooms. Rooms come with phones and cable TV. Some rooms have refrigerators, jacuzzis and microwaves. Credit cards: AE, CB, DC, DS, JCB, MC, V.

ALBERTVILLE

Kings Inn
$32-55
7080 US 431N • 256.878.6550 or 800.490.8589
32 Units, pets OK. Restaurant on premises. Pool. Rooms come with phones and cable TV. Senior discount. Major credit cards.

ANNISTON — see also Oxford

Mid Town Inn
$39
1407 Quintard Avenue • 256.237.7564
55 Units, no pets. Rooms come with phones and cable TV. Senior and AAA discount. Major credit cards.

Super 8 Motel
$45-59
6220 McLellan Blvd. • 256.820.1000
44 Units, pets OK. Continental breakfast. Pool. Laundry facility. Rooms come with phones and cable TV. Wheelchair accessible. Senior discount. Credit cards: AE, CB, DC, DS, MC, V.

Villager Inn
$29-40
1015 Hwy. 431N, I-20, Exit 185
256.237.2525
64 Units, no pets. Laundry facility. Jacuzzi. Rooms come with phones and cable TV. Senior discount. Major credit cards.

ATHENS

Bomar Inn
$31
1101 Hwy. 315 • 256.232.6944
81 Units, pets OK. Pool. Restaurant on premises. Meeting room. Rooms come with phones and cable TV. Senior discount. Major credit cards.

Travelodge
$34-46
I-65, Exit 351 (1325 US 72E)
256.233.1446
60 Units, no pets. Continental breakfast. Laundry facility. Rooms come with phones and cable TV. Some rooms have refrigerators and microwaves. AAA/Senior discount. Credit cards: AE, CB, DC, DS, JCB, MC, V.

ATTALLA

Ramada Limited
$49
915 E. Fifth Avenue • 256.570.0117
48 Units, pets OK. Continental breakfast. Rooms come with phones and cable TV. AAA/Senior discount. Major credit cards.

AUBURN — *see also OPELIKA*

Heart of Auburn Inn & Suites
$45
333 S. College Street • 334.887.3462
101 Units, pets OK. Continental breakfast. Pool. Fitness facility. Rooms come with phones and cable TV. Laundry facility. Senior discount. Major credit cards.

BESSEMER

Masters Economy Inn
$34
I-20/I-59 & Academy Drive (Exit 108)
205.424.9690
122 Units, pets OK ($5). Continental breakfast. Pool. Rooms come with phones and cable TV. Senior discount. Major credit cards.

Motel 6
$34-36
1000 Shiloh Lane • 205.426.9646
121 Units, pets OK. Pool. Laundry facility. Data ports. Rooms come with phones, A/C and cable TV. Wheelchair accessible. Credit cards: AE, CB, DC, DS, MC, V.

BIRMINGHAM — *see also Bessemer, Moody, Fultondale and Homewood*
Microtel
$34-51
251 Summit Pkwy. • 205.945.5550 or 800.275.8047
102 Units, pets OK. Continental breakfast. Rooms come with phones and cable TV. Wheelchair accessible. AAA/Senior discount. Major credit cards.

Red Roof Inn
$46-56
151 Vulcan Road • 205.942.9414
96 Units, pets OK. Rooms come with phones and cable TV. AAA discount. Major credit cards.

Super 8 Motel — Airport
$43
1813 Crestwood Blvd. • 205.956.3650
142 Units, no pets. Pool. Rooms come with phones and cable TV. Senior discount. Major credit cards.

Villager Lodge Civic Center
$33-60
1313 Third Avenue N. • 205.323.8806
150 Units, no pets. Laundry facility. Restaurant on premises. Meeting rooms. Rooms come with phones and cable TV. Senior discount. Major credit cards.

BOAZ
Boaz Inn
$28-35
2656 Hwy. 431 N • 256.593.2874
60 Units, pets OK. Rooms come with phones and cable TV. Some rooms have kitchenettes. Senior discount. Major credit cards.

Rodeway Inn
$38
751 Hwy. 431 S • 256.593.8410
116 Units, pets OK. Continental breakfast. Pool. Rooms come with phones and cable TV. Wheelchair accessible. Senior discount. Major credit cards.

BREWTON
Colonial Manor
$33
219 Hwy. 31S • 251.867.5421
70 Units, pets OK. Restaurant on premises. Pool. Jacuzzi. Rooms come with phones and cable TV. Some rooms have kitchenettes. Senior discount. Major credit cards.

CLANTON
Days Inn
$43
2000 Big M Blvd., I-65, Exit 205
205.755.0510
100 Units, pets OK ($5). Pool. Meeting rooms. Rooms come with phones and cable TV. Some rooms have refrigerators and microwaves. Senior discount. Major credit cards.

Shoney's Inn
$42-47
946 Lake Mitchell Road, I-65, Exit 208
205.280.0306
74 Units, pets OK ($20 dep. req.). Restaurant on premises. Pool. Laundry facility. Meeting rooms. Rooms come with phones and cable TV. AAA discount. Major credit cards.

COLLINSVILLE
Howard Johnson Inn
$46-50
I-59, Exit 205 • 256.524.2114
32 Units, pets OK. Pool. Rooms come with phones and cable TV. Some rooms have microwaves and refrigerators. Major credit cards.

CULLMAN
Days Inn
$42-48
1841 4th Street S.W. • 256.739.3800
120 Units, pets OK ($4). Restaurant on premises. Continental breakfast. Pool. Rooms come with phones and cable TV. AAA/Senior discount. Credit cards: AE, CB, DC, DS, JCB, MC, V.

DALEVILLE
Daleville Inn
$30-55
108 N. Daleville Avenue • 334.598.4451
150 Units, pets OK. Restaurant on premises. Pool. Rooms come with phones and cable TV. Some rooms have kitchenettes. Senior discount. Major credit cards.

Green House Inn & Lodge
$33-50
761 S. Daleville Avenue • 334.598.1475
74 Units, pets OK ($4). Pool. Jacuzzi. Laundry facility. Rooms come with phones and cable TV. Some rooms have refrigerators and microwaves. Senior discount. Credit cards: AE, CB, DC, DS, MC, V.

DAPHNE
Eastern Shore Motel
$50
29070 Hwy. 98 • 334.626.6601
63 Units, pets OK. Continental breakfast. Rooms come with phones and cable TV. Senior discount. Major credit cards.

DAUPHIN ISLAND
Gulf Breeze Motel
$50
1512 Cadillac Avenue • 251.861.7344 or 800.286.0296
38 Units, pets OK. Laundry facility. Rooms come with phones and cable TV. Some rooms have kitchenettes. Major credit cards.

DECATUR — see also Priceville
Knights Inn
$33-40
3429 Hwy. 31S • 256.355.0190
85 Units, pets OK. Continental breakfast. Pool. Laundry facility. Rooms come with phones and cable TV. Senior discount. Major credit cards.

DEMOPOLIS
Days Inn
$51
1005 Hwy. 80E • 334.289.2500
42 Units, no pets. Continental breakfast. Pool. Laundry facility. Rooms come with refrigerators, microwaves, phones and cable TV. Senior discount. Credit cards: AE, CB, DC, DS, JCB, MC, V.

Riverview Inn
$40-50
1301 N. Walnut • 334.289.0690
25 Units, pets OK ($3). Boat dock. Meeting rooms. Laundry facility. Rooms come with refrigerators, microwaves, phones and cable TV. Senior discount. Credit cards: AE, CB, DC, DS, MC, V.

Windwood Inn
$41-50
628 Hwy. 80E • 334.289.1760 or 800.233.0841
94 Units, no pets. Pool. Rooms come with phones and cable TV. Some rooms have kitchenettes. Senior discount. Major credit cards.

DOTHAN
Motel 6
$30
2907 Ross Clark Circle SW • 334.793.6013
101 Units, pets OK. Pool. Laundry facility. Data ports. Rooms come with phones, A/C and cable TV. Wheelchair accessible. Credit cards: AE, CB, DC, DS, MC, V.

Travelodge & Baywood Suites
$30-50
2901 Ross Clark Circle • 334.793.5200
99 Units, no pets. Pool. Meeting rooms. Rooms come with phones and cable TV. Senior discount. Major credit cards.

EUFALA
Best Western Inn
$43-48
1335 Hwy. 431 S. • 334.687.3900
42 Units, pets OK. Continental breakfast. Pool. Rooms come with phones and cable TV. Some rooms have microwaves and refrigerators. AAA discount. Major credit cards.

Lakeside Motor Lodge
$35
1010 N. Eufaula Avenue (Hwy. 431N) 334.687.2477
48 Units, no pets. Pool. Rooms come with phones and cable TV. Some rooms have kitchenettes. Senior discount. Major credit cards.

EUTAW
The Western Inn Motel
$40-45
I-20/59, Exit 40 • 205.372.9363
63 Units, no pets. Restaurant on premises. Pool. Rooms come with phones and cable TV. Senior discount. Major credit cards.

EVERGREEN
Days Inn
$45
On SR 63, I-65, Exit 96 • 251.578.2100
40 Units, pets OK ($5). Continental breakfast. Data ports. Rooms come with phones and cable TV. Senior discount. Major credit cards.

Evergreen Inn
$38-50
I-56 & Hwy. 83 • 251.578.5500
100 Units, no pets. Rooms come with phones and cable TV. Senior discount. Major credit cards.

FAIRHOPE
Barons "On the Bay" Inn
$39-50
701 S. Mobile Avenue • 251.928.8000
24 Units, pets OK. Restaurant on premises. Meeting rooms. Rooms come with phones and cable TV. Senior discount. Major credit cards.

FLORENCE
Super 8 Motel
$44-54
Hwys. 72 & 43E • 256.757.2167
34 Units, pets OK ($5 and $20 dep. req.). Pool. Laundry facility. Boat ramp. Rooms come with phones and cable TV. Some rooms have refrigerators, jacuzzis and microwaves. AAA/Senior discount. Credit cards: AE, CB, DC, DS, MC, V.

FORT PAYNE
Red Carpet Inn
$39-60
1412 Glenn Blvd. S.W. • 256.845.4013
79 Units, no pets. Continental breakfast. Pool. Meeting rooms. Laundry facility. Rooms come with phones and cable TV. Some rooms have microwaves and refrigerators. Senior discount. Major credit cards.

FULTONDALE
Super 8 Motel
$50
624 Decatur Hwy. • 205.841.2200
126 Units, no pets. Continental breakfast. Pool. Laundry facility. Picnic area. Rooms come with phones and cable TV. Wheelchair accessible. Senior discount. Major credit cards.

GADSDEN
Gadsden Inn & Suites
$41-50
200 Albert Raines Blvd. • 256.543.7240
83 Units, no pets. Continental breakfast. Laundry facility. Fitness facility. Rooms come with phones and cable TV. Some rooms have refrigerators, jacuzzis and microwaves. AAA/Senior discount. Credit cards: AE, CB, DC, DS, MC, V.

Super 8 Motel
$40
2110 Rainbow Drive • 256.547.9033
42 Units, pets OK. Continental breakfast. Pool. Rooms come with phones and cable TV. Senior discount. Wheelchair accessible. Major credit cards.

GREENVILLE
Econo Lodge
$45-55
946 Fort Dale Road, I-65, Exit 130
334.382.3118
39 Units, pets OK ($3). Continental breakfast. Rooms come with phones and cable TV. AAA/Senior discount. Major credit cards.

Thrifty Inn
$39-44
105 Bypass • 334.382.6671
47 Units, pets OK. Rooms come with phones and cable TV. Senior discount. Major credit cards.

GROVE HILL
Windwood Inn
$40-42
Hwy. 43N • 251.275.4121 or 800.233.0841
43 Units, no pets. Pool. Rooms come with phones and cable TV. Senior discount. Major credit cards.

GULF SHORES
Island Oasis Motel
$39*
807 E. Canal Drive • 251.968.6561
10 Units, no pets. Pool. Rooms come with phones and cable TV. Some rooms have

kitchenettes. Major credit cards.
*Rates as high as $74/night.

GUNTERSVILLE
Holiday Lodge Motel
$35-45
3233 Hwy. 79S • 256.582.5677
22 Units, no pets. Rooms come with phones and cable TV. Some rooms have kitchenettes. Senior discount. Major credit cards.

Overlook Mountain Inn
$35-45
13045 Hwy. 431 • 256.582.3256
33 Units, pets OK. Pool. Rooms come with phones and cable TV. Some rooms have kitchenettes. Senior discount. Major credit cards.

HARTSELLE
Express Inn
$38-47
1601 Hwy. 31 S.W. • 256.773.3000
33 Units, no pets. Pool. Rooms come with phones and cable TV. Senior discount. Major credit cards.

HEFLIN
Howard Johnson Express
$35-45
I-20 & Hwy. 9 • 256.463.2900
32 Units, pets OK ($5). Continental breakfast. Rooms come with phones and cable TV. Some rooms have jacuzzis. Credit cards: AE, CB, DC, DS, MC, V.

HOMEWOOD
Super 8 Motel
$39
140 Vulcan Road • 205.945.9888
102 Units, no pets. Meeting room. Rooms come with phones and cable TV. Wheelchair accessible. Senior discount. Credit cards: AE, CB, DC, DS, MC, V.

HUNTSVILLE
Alabama Inn
$27-33
2524 N. Memorial Pkwy • 256.852.9200
80 Units, no pets. Pool. Restaurant on premises. Rooms come with phones and cable TV. Major credit cards.

Days Inn—North
$40-55
2201 N. Memorial Pkwy • 256.536.7441
98 Units, no pets. Continental breakfast. Pool. Wading pool. Meeting rooms. Rooms come with phones and cable TV. Some rooms have refrigerators and microwaves. Credit cards: AE, CB, DC, DS, MC, V.

Kings Inn
$38
11245 S. Memorial Pkwy • 256.881.1250
112 Units, no pets. Restaurant on premises. Pool. Meeting room. Rooms come with phones and cable TV. Some rooms have kitchenettes. Senior discount. Major credit cards.

Motel 6
$34-36
8995 Hwy. 20W (I-565/Exit 8) 256.772.7479
90 Units, pets OK. Pool. Laundry facility. Data ports. Rooms come with phones, A/C and cable TV. Wheelchair accessible. Credit cards: AE, CB, DC, DS, MC, V.

Super 8 Motel
$44
3803 University Drive • 256.539.8881
80 Units, no pets. Pool. Rooms come with phones and cable TV. Some rooms have refrigerators. Senior discount. Credit cards: AE, CB, DC, DS, MC, V.

JACKSON
Jackson Motel
$37-56
3680 N. College • 251.246.2405
45 Units, no pets. Pool. Rooms come with phones and cable TV. Some rooms have kitchenettes. Major credit cards.

JACKSONVILLE
University Inn
$40-45
1530 Pelham Road S. • 256.435.3300
66 Units, pets OK. Pool. Rooms come with phones and cable TV. Senior discount. Major credit cards.

JASPER
Travel-Rite Inn
$26-39

200 Mallway • 205.221.1161
60 Units, pets OK. Meeting rooms. Rooms come with phones and TV. Major credit cards.

LANETT
Super 8 Motel
$46
2314 S. Broad Avenue • 334.644.8888
30 Units, no pets. Continental breakfast. Pool. Rooms come with phones and cable TV. Senior discount. Major credit cards.

LEESBURG
Leesburg Lodge
$36-56
5915 Weiss Lake Blvd. • 256.526.7378
36 Units, pets OK. Laundry and fitness facility. Rooms come with phones and cable TV. Senior discount. Major credit cards.

LIVINGSTON
The Western Inn Motel
$39
On SR 38E • 205.652.9751
60 Units, no pets. Pool. Rooms come with phones and cable TV. Senior discount. Major credit cards.

LOXLEY
Wind Chase Inn
$50
13156 N. Hickory Street • 251.964.4444 or 800.401.4181
60 Units, pets OK. Meeting rooms. Rooms come with phones and cable TV. Senior discount. Major credit cards.

MADISON
Motel 6
$36-49
8995 Hwy. 20 • 256.772.7479
92 Units, pets OK. Pool. Rooms come with phones, A/C and cable TV. Wheelchair accessible. Credit cards: AE, CB, DC, DS, MC, V.

MOBILE
Days Inn of Mobile
$39-50
5550 I-10 Service Road • 251.661.8181
100 Units, pets OK ($5). Pool. Laundry facility. Rooms come with phones and cable TV. Some rooms have refrigerators. Credit cards: AE, CB, DC, DS, JCB, MC, V.

Family Inns
$43-48
900 S. Beltline Hwy. • 251.344.5500 or 800.251.9752
83 Units, no pets. Continental breakfast. Pool. Rooms come with phones and cable TV. Some rooms have kitchenettes. Senior discount. Major credit cards.

Motel 6—North
$34-40
400 S. Beltline Hwy. (Southbound I-65, Exit 4A, Northbound I-65, Exit 3B) 251.343.8448
93 Units, pets OK. Pool. Laundry facility. Data ports. Rooms come with phones, A/C and cable TV. Wheelchair accessible. Credit cards: AE, CB, DC, DS, MC, V.

Motel 6—West
$34-40
5488 Inn Road (I-10 Service Road) 251.660.1483
98 Units, pets OK. Pool. Laundry facility. Data ports. Rooms come with phones, A/C and cable TV. Wheelchair accessible. Credit cards: AE, CB, DC, DS, MC, V.

Red Roof Inn
$35-48
33 S. Beltline (I-65, Exit 4) • 251.476.2004
108 Units, pets OK. Rooms come with phones and cable TV. AAA discount. Major credit cards.

MONROEVILLE
Knights Inn
$32-38
Rte. 3, Box 227 (in town) • 251.743.3154 or 800.553.2666
40 Units, pets OK. Restaurant on premises. Continental breakfast. Pool. Jacuzzi. Laundry facility. Rooms come with phones and cable TV. AAA/Senior discount. Major credit cards.

Royal Inn
$28-36
3236 S. Alabama Avenue • 251.575.3177
53 Units, no pets. Restaurant on premises.

Pool. Meeting rooms. Rooms come with phones and cable TV. Major credit cards.

MONTGOMERY
Best Western Montgomery Lodge
$42-60
977 W. South Blvd. • 334.288.5740
100 Units, pets OK. Pool. Laundry facility. Rooms come with phones and cable TV. Credit cards: AE, CB, DC, DS, MC, V.

Capitol Inn
$32-44
205 N. Goldthwaite St. • 334.265.3844
94 Units, pets OK. Restaurant on premises. Pool. Meeting room. Rooms come with phones and cable TV. Senior discount. Major credit cards.

Econo Lodge
$45-48
4135 Troy Hwy. • 334.284.3400
45 Units, pets OK ($8). Continental breakfast. Pool. Rooms come with phones and cable TV. Major credit cards.

Motel 6
$38-44
1051 Eastern Bypass (I-85/Exit 6)
334.277.6748
102 Units, pets OK. Pool. Laundry facility. Data ports. Rooms come with phones, A/C and cable TV. Wheelchair accessible. Credit cards: AE, CB, DC, DS, MC, V.

Wynfield Inn
$40-47
1110 Eastern Blvd. • 334.272.8880
64 Units, no pets. Rooms come with phones and cable TV. Senior discount. Credit cards: AE, CB, DC, DS, MC, V.

MOODY
Super 8 Motel
$50
2451 Moody Parkway • 205.640.7091
50 Units, no pets. Continental breakfast. Rooms come with phones and cable TV. Wheelchair accessible. Senior discount. Credit cards: AE, CB, DC, DS, MC, V.

NORTHPORT
Best Western Catalina Inn
$45-50
2015 McFarland Blvd. • 205.339.5200
37 Units, pets OK. Continental breakfast. Pool. Rooms come with phones and cable TV. Some rooms have microwaves and refrigerators. AAA/Senior discount. Major credit cards.

ONEONTA
Super 8 Motel
$43
120 High School Street • 205.625.3961
44 Units, no pets. Continental breakfast. Meeting rooms. Laundry facility. Rooms come with phones and cable TV. Some rooms have refrigerators and microwaves. Credit cards: AE, CB, DC, DS, MC, V.

OPELIKA — *see also AUBURN*
Knights Inn
$25-30
1105 Columbus Parkway • 334.749.8377 or 800.843.5644
95 Units, no pets. Pool. Rooms come with phones and cable TV. Some rooms have kitchenettes. AAA/Senior discount. Major credit cards.

Motel 6
$28-30
1015 Columbus Pkwy. • 334.745.0988
78 Units, pets OK. Pool. Laundry facility. Data ports. Rooms come with phones, A/C and cable TV. Wheelchair accessible. Credit cards: AE, CB, DC, DS, MC, V.

Travelodge
$37-40
1002 Columbus Pkwy. • 334.749.1461
100 Units, pets OK ($7). Continental breakfast. Heated pool. Jacuzzi. Rooms come with phones and cable TV. Some rooms have refrigerators. AAA/Senior discount. Credit cards: AE, CB, DC, DS, MC, V.

OPP
Travel Inn
$42-47
Junction of US 331 S and US 84 W
334.493.3551
49 Units, pets OK. Continental breakfast. Pool. Rooms come with phones and cable TV. Major credit cards.

OXFORD
Motel 6
$32-36
202 Grace Street • 256.831.5463
115 Units, pets OK. Pool. Data ports. Rooms come with phones, A/C and cable TV. Wheelchair accessible. Credit cards: AE, CB, DC, DS, MC, V.

Red Carpet Inn
$29-36
1007 Hwy. 21S • 256.831.6082
40 Units, no pets. Rooms come with phones and cable TV. Senior discount. Major credit cards.

OZARK
Best Western Ozark Inn
$47
On US 231 at Deese Rd. • 334.774.5166
62 Units, pets OK. Continental breakfast. Pool. Rooms come with phones and cable TV. AAA/Senior discount. Credit cards: AE, CB, DC, DS, MC, V.

PHENIX CITY — *see also Columbus (GA)*
Colonial Inn
$30
905 E. 280 Bypass • 334.298.9361
143 Units, no pets. Pool. Restaurant on premises. Rooms come with phones and cable TV. Major credit cards.

PRATTVILLE
Super 8 Motel
$45
639 Malwest Drive, I-65, Exit 181
334.365.7250
50 Units, pets OK. Continental breakfast. Pool. Rooms come with phones and cable TV. Senior discount. Major credit cards.

SCOTTSBORO
Days Inn
$42-55
1106 John Reid Pkwy. • 256.574.1212
83 Units, pets OK. Continental breakfast. Pool. Laundry facility nearby. Rooms come with phones and cable TV. Wheelchair accessible. Senior discount. Major credit cards.

Scottish Inn
$25-43
902 E. Willow Street • 256.574.1730
33 Units, no pets. Restaurant on premises. Laundry facility nearby. Rooms come with phones and cable TV. Senior discount. Credit cards: AE, DS, MC, V.

SELMA
Budget Inn
$35-49
601 Highland Avenue • 334.872.3451
55 Units, pets OK. Pool. Rooms come with phones and cable TV. Senior discount. Major credit cards.

SHEFFIELD
Regal Inn Express
$30-50
4301 Jackson Hwy. • 256.383.1114
35 Units, no pets. Restaurant on premises. Pool. Rooms come with phones and cable TV. Senior discount. Major credit cards.

STEVENSON
Budget Host Inn
$30-35
42973 US 72 • 256.437.2215
30 Units, pets OK ($4). Laundry facility. Rooms come with phones and cable TV. Some rooms have microwaves and refrigerators. AAA/Senior discount. Credit cards: AE, DS, MC. V.

SYLACAUGA
Super 8 Motel
$42
40770 US Hwy. 280 • 256.249.4321
110 Units, pets OK. Pool. Rooms come with phones and cable TV. Some rooms have refrigerators and microwaves. AAA discount. Credit cards: AE, CB, DC, DS, MC, V.

THOMASVILLE
Days Inn
$34-38
424 Hwy. 43N • 334.636.5467
21 Units, pets OK. Continental breakfast. Rooms come with microwaves, refrigerators, phones and cable TV. Wheelchair accessible. Major credit cards.

Econo Lodge
$39-49
1431 Hwy. 43N • 334.636.0123
67 Units, no pets. Meeting rooms. Fitness facility. Rooms come with microwaves, refrigerators, phones and cable TV. AAA/ Senior discount. Credit cards: AE, DC, DS, MC, V.

TROY
Scottish Inn
$35-55
186 Hwy. 231N • 334.566.4090 or 800.251.1962
44 Units, pets OK. Rooms come with phones and cable TV. Senior discount. Major credit cards.

TUSCALOOSA — see also Northport
Masters Economy Inn
$36-56
3600 McFarland Blvd. • 205.556.2010
152 Units, pets OK. Pool. Rooms come with phones and cable TV. Some rooms have kitchenettes. Senior discount. Major credit cards.

Motel 6
$30-38
4700 McFarland Blvd. E. • 205.759.4942
124 Units, pets OK. Pool. Laundry facility. Data ports. Rooms come with phones, A/C and cable TV. Wheelchair accessible. Credit cards: AE, CB, DC, DS, MC, V.

Super 8 Motel
$42-50
4125 McFarland Blvd. E. • 205.758.8878
62 Units, no pets. Rooms come with phones and cable TV. Wheelchair accessible. Senior discount. Credit cards: AE, CB, DC, DS, MC, V.

YORK
Days Inn
$44
17700 SR 17, I-59/20, Exit 8
205.392.9675
50 Units, pets OK ($10). Continental breakfast. Rooms come with phones and cable TV. Some rooms have microwaves and refrigerators. Wheelchair accessible. Senior discount. Major credit cards.

alaska

Traveler Advisory: Almost all goods and services in Alaska are more expensive than their counterparts in the lower 48, including accommodations. If you are planning to make your way up to the 49th State, be aware that you will need more than $50 per night for lodging, unless you are camping out or staying at youth hostels. You would be very fortunate to find accommodations anywhere in Alaska for less than $60/night during peak summer season. Generally, the more remote the destination, the higher the room rate. To help you get the best deals, here are a few recommendations to suit your budget:

(Price ranges represent high and low season rates)

Anchorage
Anchor Arms Motel ($49-79)
520 E. 4th Avenue • 907.272.9619

EconoLodge ($40-$65)
642 E. 5th Avenue • 907.274.1515

Days Inn ($79-$100)
321 E. Fifth Avenue • 907.276.7226

Denali
Denali Dome Home B&B ($60-$110)
P.O. Box 262 • 907.683.1239

White Moose Lodge ($70-$90)
Open May 15-September 15 •
P.O. Box 68 • 800.481.1232

Fairbanks
Alaska Fairbanks B&B ($45-$65)
902 Kellum Street • 907.452.4967

Golden North Motel ($49-$69)
4888 Old Airport Way • 907.479.6201 or 800.447.1910

Ranch Motel ($55-$90)
2223 S. Cushman Street • 907.452.4783 or 888.452.4783

Haines
Fort Seward Lodge ($50-$95)
P.O. Box 307 VP • 907.766.2009 or 800.478.7772

Mountain View Motel ($55-$89)
Edge of Fort Seward • 907.766.2900 or 800.478.2900

Homer
Alaska's Pioneer Inn ($55-$99)
244 W. Pioneer Avenue • 907.235.5670 or 800.STAY.655

Driftwood Inn ($40-$58)
135 W. Bunnell Avenue • 907.235.8019

Juneau
The Driftwood Lodge ($62-$104)
435 Willoughby Avenue • 907.586.2280 or 800.544.2239

Super 8 Motel ($59-$80)
2295 Trout Street • 907.789.4858

Travelodge ($75-$105)
9200 Glacier Hwy. • 907.789.1969

Ketchikan
Captain's Quarters B&B ($59-$90)
325 Lund Street • 907.225.4912

The Gilmore Hotel ($65-$110)
P.O. Box 6814 • 907.225.9423

Kodiak
Shelikof Lodge ($70-$85)
211 Thorsheim • 907.486.4141

Nome
Nugget Inn ($89-$99)
Center & Front Streets • 907.443.2323

Petersburg
Tides Inn ($75-$85)
307 Dolphin Street N. • 907.772.4288

Water's Edge B&B ($70-$95)
P.O. Box 1201 • 907.772.3736

Seward
"The Farm" B&B ($45-$65)
P.O. Box 305 • 907.224.5691

Trail Lake Lodge ($79-$109)
P.O. Box 69 • 907.288.3101

Sitka
Hannah's B&B ($75-$85)
504 Monastery Street • 907.747.8309

Helga's B&B ($60-$95)
P.O. Box 1885 • 907.474.5497

Skagway
At the White House ($65-$106)
P.O. Box 41 • 907.983.9000

Golden North Hotel ($65-$120)
Third and Broadway Streets • 907.983.2294

Wind Valley Lodge ($75)
Open April 15 - September 30 • 22nd E. State Street • 907.983.2236

Tok
Snowshoe Motel & Gift Shop ($47-$68)
1314 Alaskan Hwy. • 907.883.4511 or 800.478.4511

Young's Motel ($55-$76)
1313 Alaskan Hwy. • 907.883.4411

Valdez
Glacier Sound Inn ($69-$109)
210 Egan Drive • 907.835.4485

Note: If you will be driving the Alaska Highway, you should check out The Milepost ($25.95). It is perhaps the most comprehensive guide available on food, gas, camping, attractions and lodging along the entire route of the Alaska Highway.

ANCHORAGE
Hostelling International
$16
700 "H" Street • 907.276.3635
95 Beds, Hours: 8 am - midnight
Facilities: equipment storage area, information desk, kitchen, laundry facilities, lockers/baggage storage, linen rental, limited street parking, wheelchair accessible. Private rooms available. Open year-round. Reservations recommended May 15 through September 15. Credit cards: MC, V.

FAIRBANKS
College Inn
$40-50
700 Fairbanks Street • 907.474.3666
100 Units, no pets. Laundry facility. Rooms have phones and color TVs. Major credit cards.

KETCHIKAN
Hostelling International
$12
Grant and Main • 907.225.3319
19 Beds (sleeping bags allowed), Hours: 7-9 am & 6-11 pm
Facilities: information desk, linen rental, kitchen, on-site parking at night only. Closed August 31 through June 1. Reservations not essential. Credit cards not accepted.

SITKA
Hostelling International
$11
303 Kimsham Street • 907.747.8356
20 Beds (bring a sleeping bag)
Hours: 8-10 am & 6-11 pm
Facilities: on-site parking. Closed September through May. Reservations recommended. Credit cards not accepted.

arizona

AJO
Marine Motel
$38-55 (55-65)*
1966 2nd Avenue • 520.387.7626
21 Units, pets OK. Rooms come with A/C, phones and cable TV. Some rooms have refrigerators. AAA/Senior discount. Major credit cards.
*Higher rates effective February through mid-April.

APACHE JUNCTION
Apache Junction Motel
$38-47 (54-60)*
1680 W. Apache Trail • 480.982.7702
15 Units, pets OK. Rooms come with phones and cable TV. Some rooms have microwaves and refrigerators. AAA discount. Credit cards: AE, DS, MC. V.
*Higher rates mid-January through March.

BENSON
Motel 6
$40-50
637 S. Whetstone Commerce Drive
I-10, Exit 302 • 520.586.0066
63 Units, pets OK. Pool. Laundry facility. Rooms come with phones, A/C and cable TV. Credit cards: AE, CB, DC, DS, MC, V.

Super 8 Motel
$42-53
855 N. Ocotillo Road • 520.586.1530
40 Units, pets OK ($10). Heated pool. Rooms come with phones and cable TV. AAA/Senior discount. Credit cards: AE, DS, MC, V.

BULLHEAD CITY
Best Western Bullhead City Inn
$44
1126 Hwy. 95 • 928.754.3000
88 Units, pets OK ($10 and $25 dep. req.). Continental breakfast. Heated pool. Laundry facility. Jacuzzi. Meeting rooms. Rooms come with phones and cable TV. AAA/Senior discount. Major credit cards.

Lodge on the River
$26-54
1717 Hwy. 95 • 928.758.8080
64 Units, pets OK ($20 dep. req.). Heated pool. Laundry facility. Rooms come with phones and cable TV. Some rooms have microwaves and refrigerators. Senior discount. Credit cards: AE, CB, DC, DS, MC, V.

Super 8 Motel
$35
1616 Hwy. 95 • 928.763.1002
118 Units, pets OK. Pool. Rooms come with phones, A/C and cable TV. Wheelchair accessible. Credit cards: AE, CB, DC, DS, MC, V.

CAMP VERDE
Comfort Inn
$45-49
340 N. Industrial Drive, I-17, Exit 287
520.567.9000
85 Units, pets OK ($15). Heated Pool. Jacuzzi. Laundry facility. Meeting rooms. Data ports. Rooms come with phones and cable TV. AAA/Senior discount. Major credit cards.

CASA GRANDE
Motel 6
$30-50
4965 N. Sunland Gin Rd. • 520.836.3323
97 Units, pets OK. Restaurant on premises. Pool. Laundry facility. Rooms come with phones, A/C and cable TV. Credit cards: AE, CB, DC, DS, MC, V.

COTTONWOOD
Cottonwood Pines Motel
$39-55
920 S. Camino Real • 928.634.9975
14 Units, pets OK. Rooms come with phones, cable TV, refrigerators and microwaves. AAA/Senior discount. Credit cards: AE, D, MC, V.

The View Motel
$36-48
818 S. Main Street • 928.634.7581
34 Units, pets OK ($3-5). Heated pool. Jacuzzi. Rooms come with phones and TV. Some rooms have A/C. Credit cards: AE, DS, MC, V.

DOUGLAS
Motel 6
$34
111 16th Street • 520.364.2457
98 Units, pets OK. Pool. Laundry facility. Rooms come with phones, A/C and cable TV. Credit cards: AE, CB, DC, DS, MC, V.

ELOY
Super 8 Motel
$40-44 (54)*
3945 W. Houser Road • 520.466.7804
42 Units, pets OK. Heated pool. Laundry facility. Rooms come with phones and cable TV. Wheelchair accessible. AAA/Senior discount. Major credit cards.
*Higher rates effective February and March.

FLAGSTAFF
Budget Host Saga Motel
$38-46*
820 W. Hwy. 66 • 928.779.3631
30 Units, no pets. Heated pool. Picnic area and playground. Laundry facility. Rooms come with phones and TV. Credit cards: AE, DC, DS, MC, V.
*Higher rate first week of May through first week of September.

Motel 6
$33-50
2010 E. Butler Avenue • 928.774.1801
150 Units, pets OK. Pool. Laundry facility. Rooms come with phones, A/C and cable TV. Credit cards: AE, CB, DC, DS, MC, V.

Motel 6
$30-50
2440 E. Lucky Lane (I-40, Exit 198)
928.774.8756
103 Units, pets OK. Pool. Rooms come with phones, A/C and cable TV. Wheelchair accessible. Credit cards: AE, CB, DC, DS, MC, V.

Motel 6
$33-50
2745 S. Woodlands Vill. • 928.779.3757
150 Units, pets OK. Pool. Laundry facility. Rooms come with phones, A/C and cable TV. Wheelchair accessible. Credit cards: AE, CB, DC, DS, MC, V.

Rodeway Inn
$29-55
2650 E. Rte. 66 • 928.526.2200
89 Units, pets OK. Continental breakfast. Rooms come with phones, A/C and cable TV. AAA/Senior discount. Credit cards: AE, CB, DC, DS, JCB, MC, V.

GILA BEND
Yucca Motel
$43
836 E. Pima • 928.683.2211
20 Units, pets OK. Pool. Rooms come with A/C, phones and cable TV. Some rooms have microwaves and refrigerators. Senior discount. Major credit cards.

GLOBE
El Rancho Motel
$25
1300 E. Ash Street • 928.425.5757
22 Units, pets OK. Rooms come with phones and cable TV. Major credit cards.

El Rey Motel
$23-27
1201 E. Ash Street • 928.425.4427
23 Units, no pets. Picnic area. Rooms come with phones and cable TV. Major credit cards.

GRAND CANYON — *see Flagstaff and Williams*

HOLBROOK
Best Inn
$36-52
2211 E. Navajo Blvd. • 928.524.2654 or 800.551.1923
40 Units, pets OK ($25 dep. req.). Continental breakfast. Rooms come with phones, refrigerators and cable TV. AAA/Senior discount. Major credit cards.

Budget Host Holbrook Inn
$20-26
235 W. Hopi Drive • 928.524.3809
26 Units, pets OK ($4). Laundry facility. Rooms come with phones and cable TV. Some rooms have microwaves and refrigerators. AAA/Senior discount. Credit cards: AE, CB, DC, DS, MC, V.

Motel 6
$30
2514 Navajo Blvd. • 928.524.6101
124 Units, pets OK. Pool. Laundry facility. Rooms come with phones, A/C and cable TV. Wheelchair accessible. Credit cards: AE, CB, DC, DS, MC, V.

KEARNY
General Kearny Inn
$42
301 Alden Road • 520.363.5505
47 Units, pets OK. Restaurant on premises. Pool. Meeting rooms. Rooms come with phones, A/C and cable TV. Wheelchair accessible. Major credit cards.

KINGMAN
Motel 6 - East
$30
3351 E. Andy Devine Avenue
1-40, Exit 53 • 928.757.7151
118 Units, pets OK. Pool. Rooms come with phones, A/C and cable TV. Wheelchair accessible. Credit cards: AE, CB, DC, DS, MC, V.

Motel 6 - West
$36-40
424 W. Beale Street • 928.753.9222
80 Units, pets OK. Restaurant on premises. Pool. Laundry facility. Rooms come with phones, A/C and cable TV. Wheelchair accessible. Credit cards: AE, CB, DC, DS, MC, V.

Ramblin' Rose Motel
$26-32
1001 E. Andy Devine • 928.753.5541
35 Units, no pets. Pool. Rooms come with phones and cable TV. Some rooms have microwaves and refrigerators. AAA/Senior discount. Credit cards: AE, DS, MC, V.

Silver Queen Motel
$25-50
3285 E. Andy Devine • 928.757.4322
146 Units, pets OK. Restaurant on premises. Pool. Rooms come with phones and cable TV. Wheelchair accessible. Major credit cards.

LAKE HAVASU CITY
Inn at Tamarisk
$45-49
3101 London Bridge Rd. • 928.764.3033
17 Units, no pets. Heated pool. Laundry facility. Rooms come with phones, A/C and cable TV. AAA/Senior discount. Major credit cards.

Super 8 Motel
$36-46*
305 London Bridge Rd. • 928.855.8844
60 Units, no pets. Heated pool and spa. Rooms come with phones and cable TV. Wheelchair accessible. Senior discount. Credit cards: AE, CB, DC, DS, MC, V.
*October rates higher ($85/night).

MESA
Motel 6
$38-50
336 W. Hampton Ave. • 480.844.8899
162 Units, pets OK. Heated pool. Laundry facility. Rooms come with phones, A/C and cable TV. Wheelchair accessible. Credit cards: AE, CB, DC, DS, MC, V.

Motel 6
$38-50
1511 S. Country Club Dr. • 480.834.0066
91 Units, pets OK. Heated pool. Rooms come with phones, A/C and cable TV. Wheelchair accessible. Credit cards: AE, CB, DC, DS, MC, V.

Motel 6
$38-50
630 W. Main Street • 480.969.8111
102 Units, pets OK. Heated pool. Rooms come with phones, A/C and cable TV. Wheelchair accessible. Credit cards: AE, CB, DC, DS, MC, V.

MONUMENT VALLEY — *see Bluff (UT) and Blanding (UT)*

NOGALES
Motel 6
$36-38
141 W. Mariposa Road • 520.281.2951
79 Units, pets OK. Pool. Laundry facility. Rooms come with phones, A/C and cable TV. Wheelchair accessible. Credit cards: AE, CB, DC, DS, MC, V.

Super 8 Motel
$45-50
547 W. Mariposa Road • 520.281.2242
116 Units, pets OK. Restaurant on premises. Heated pool. Jacuzzi. Laundry facility. Fitness facility. Rooms come with phones, cable TV and refrigerators. AAA discount. Major credit cards.

PAGE
Economy Inn Budget Host
$35-59
121 S. Lk. Powell Blvd. • 928.645.2488
63 Units, pets OK ($20 dep. req.). Heated pool. Rooms come with phones, A/C and

cable TV. AAA/Senior discount. Major credit cards.

Motel 6
$33-50 (60)*
637 S. Lk. Powell Blvd. • 928.645.5888
111 Units, pets OK. Pool. Laundry facility. Rooms come with phones, A/C and cable TV. Wheelchair accessible. Credit cards: AE, CB, DC, DS, MC, V.
*Higher rate effective July and August.

PARKER
Kofa Inn
$41-50
1700 California Avenue • 928.669.2101 or 800.742.6072
41 Units, no pets. Pool. Rooms come with phones, A/C and cable TV. AAA discount. Credit cards: AE, DS, MC, V.

Motel 6
$35-50
604 California Avenue • 928.669.2133
40 Units, pets OK. Laundry facility. Rooms come with phones, A/C and cable TV. Wheelchair accessible. Credit cards: AE, CB, DC, DS, MC, V.

PAYSON
Motel 6
$40-50 (60)*
101 W. Phoenix Street • 928.474.4526
39 Units, pets OK. Rooms come with phones, A/C and cable TV. Wheelchair accessible. Credit cards: AE, CB, DC, DS, MC, V.
*Higher rate effective weekends May through August.

PHOENIX — *see also Apache Junction, Mesa, Tempe and Youngtown*
Motel 6 - Airport
$40-50 (56)*
214 S. 24th Street (I-80, Exit 148)
602.244.1155
61 Units, pets OK. Pool. Rooms come with phones, A/C and cable TV. Wheelchair accessible. Credit cards: AE, CB, DC, DS, MC, V.
*Higher rate effective winter weekends.

Motel 6
$38-50
4130 N. Black Canyon Hwy. (I-17, Exit 202) • 602.277.5501
351 Units, pets OK. Pool. Laundry facility. Spa. Rooms come with phones, A/C and cable TV. Wheelchair accessible. Credit cards: AE, CB, DC, DS, MC, V.

Motel 6 - East
$40-50*
5315 E. Van Buren St. • 602.267.8555
80 Units, pets OK. Pool. Rooms come with phones, A/C and cable TV. Wheelchair accessible. Credit cards: AE, CB, DC, DS, MC, V.
*Higher rate mid-January through mid-April.

Motel 6
$40-50
2735 W. Sweetwater Avenue, I-17S, Exit 210 or I-17N, Exit 209 • 602.942.5030
130 Units, pets OK. Pool. Laundry facility. Rooms come with phones, A/C and cable TV. Wheelchair accessible. Credit cards: AE, CB, DC, DS, MC, V.

Motel 6 – West Phoenix
$40-50
1530 N. 52nd Drive, I-10, Exit 139
602.272.0220
147 Units, pets OK. Pool. Rooms come with phones, A/C and cable TV. Wheelchair accessible. Credit cards: AE, CB, DC, DS, MC, V.

Motel 6
$40-52
2330 W. Bell Road, I-17, Exit 212A
602.993.2353
139 Units, pets OK. Pool. Laundry facility. Rooms come with phones, A/C and cable TV. Wheelchair accessible. Credit cards: AE, CB, DC, DS, MC, V.

Motel 6—North
$40-52
8152 N. Black Canyon Hwy., I-17, Exit 206
602.995.7592
142 Units, pets OK. Pool. Laundry facility. Rooms come with phones, A/C and cable TV. Wheelchair accessible. Credit cards: AE, CB, DC, DS, MC, V.

PINETOP
Forest House Motel
$43
2990 W. White Mountain Blvd. 520.368.6628 or 888.440.2220
17 Units, pets OK. Laundry facility. Rooms

come with phones, A/C, refrigerators, microwaves and cable TV. Major credit cards.

PRESCOTT
Motel 6
$36-46
1111 E. Sheldon Street • 928.776.0160
79 Units, pets OK. Pool. Laundry facility. Rooms come with phones, A/C and cable TV. Wheelchair accessible. Credit cards: AE, CB, DC, DS, MC, V.

Pine View Motel
$35-45
510 Copper Basin Road • 928.445.4660
9 Units, pets OK. Airport transportation. Rooms come with phones, A/C and cable TV. Credit cards: AE, MC, V.

Wheel Inn Motel
$39-49
333 S. Montezuma St. • 928.778.8346 or 800.717.0902
10 Units, no pets. Rooms come with phones, A/C and cable TV. Wheelchair accessible. Credit cards: AE, DS, MC, V.

SAFFORD
EconoLodge
$42
225 E. Hwy. 70 • 928.348.0011
39 Units, pets OK. Pool. Laundry facility. Rooms come with phones and cable TV. Major credit cards.

ST. JOHNS
Budget Inn
$43
75 E. Commercial St. • 928.337.2990
31 Units, pets OK. Rooms come with phones and cable TV. Wheelchair accessible. Senior discount. Credit cards: AE, CB, DC, DS, MC, V.

SCOTTSDALE
Motel 6
$42-48 (60-64)*
6848 E. Camelback Rd. • 480.946.2280
122 Units, pets OK. Restaurant on premises. Heated pool. Spa. Laundry facility. Rooms come with phones, A/C and cable TV. Wheelchair accessible. Credit cards: AE, CB, DC, DS, MC, V.
*Higher rates effective winter months.

SEDONA
Village Lodge
$45-59
78 Bell Rock Blvd. • 928.284.3626
17 Units, pets OK. Rooms come with phones and cable TV. Some rooms have refrigerators. AAA/Senior discount. Major credit cards.

SELIGMAN
Historic Route 66 Motel
$47-57
500 W. Hwy. 66 • 520.422.3204
15 Units, pets OK ($25 dep. req.). Rooms come with phones and cable TV. AAA/Senior discount. Major credit cards.

SHOW LOW
Kiva Motel
$40-42
261 E. Deuce of Clubs • 928.537.4542
20 Units, pets OK. Sauna. Jacuzzi. Rooms come with phones and cable TV. Some rooms have microwaves and refrigerators. AAA/Senior discount. Major credit cards.

Motel 6
$40-45
1941 E. Deuce of Clubs • 928.537.7694
42 Units, pets OK. Laundry facility. Rooms come with phones, A/C and cable TV. Wheelchair accessible. Credit cards: AE, CB, DC, DS, MC, V.

SIERRA VISTA
Motel 6
$35
1551 E. Fry Blvd. • 520.459.5035
103 Units, pets OK. Pool. Laundry facility. Rooms come with phones, A/C and cable TV. Wheelchair accessible. Credit cards: AE, CB, DC, DS, MC, V.

SPRINGERVILLE
Super 8 Motel
$43
138 W. Main Street • 928.333.2655
41 Units, pets OK ($20 dep. req.). Rooms come with phones, A/C and cable TV. Some rooms have microwaves and refrigerators. Major credit cards.

SUN CITY — *see Youngtown*

TAYLOR
Silver Creek Inn
$45-48*

825 Main Street • 928.536.2600
42 Units, pets OK ($10). Continental breakfast. Sauna. Jacuzzi. Rooms come with phones, A/C and cable TV. AAA/Senior discount. Major credit cards.
*AAA discounted rates.

TEMPE
Knights Inn
$50
1915 E. Apache Blvd. • 480.736.1700
58 Units, no pets. Continental breakfast. Pool. Jacuzzi. Rooms come with phones, A/C and cable TV. Wheelchair accessible. Major credit cards.

Motel 6
$38-50
1720 S. Priest Drive • 480.968.4401
131 Units, pets OK. Heated pool. Laundry facility. Rooms come with phones, A/C and cable TV. Wheelchair accessible. Credit cards: AE, CB, DC, DS, MC, V.

Motel 6
$38-50
513 W. Broadway Rd. • 480.967.8696
60 Units, pets OK. Heated pool. Rooms come with phones, A/C and cable TV. Wheelchair accessible. Credit cards: AE, CB, DC, DS, MC, V.

Motel 6
$40-50
1612 N. Scottsdale Rd. • 480.945.9506
101 Units, pets OK. Heated pool. Rooms come with phones, A/C and cable TV. Wheelchair accessible. Credit cards: AE, CB, DC, DS, MC, V.

TOMBSTONE
Larian Motel
$49
410 Fremont Street • 520.457.2272
9 Units, pets OK. Rooms come with phones and cable TV. Credit cards: MC, V.

Trail Riders Inn
$35
13 N. 7th Street • 520.457.3573
13 Units, no pets. Rooms come with phones and cable TV. AAA discount. Credit cards: MC, V.

TUCSON
Econo Lodge I-10
$29-39*
3020 S. 6th Avenue • 520.623.5881
88 Units, no pets. Continental breakfast. Heated pool. Indoor jacuzzi. Laundry facility. Rooms come with phones and cable TV. Credit cards: MC, V.
*Rates increase to $70-75 late January through mid-February.

Knights Inn
$30-35*
720 W. 29th Street • 520.624.8291
94 Units, no pets. Continental breakfast. Pool. Laundry facility. Rooms come with phones, A/C and cable TV. Some rooms have microwaves and refrigerators. Credit cards: AE, MC, V.
*Rates higher January through April.

Motel 6 - Airport
$36-50
1031 E. Benson Hwy., I-10, Exit 262
520.628.1264
146 Units, pets OK. Restaurant on premises. Pool. Laundry facility. Rooms come with phones, A/C and cable TV. Wheelchair accessible. Credit cards: AE, CB, DC, DS, MC, V.

Motel 6
$32-50
960 S. Freeway (I-10, Exit 258)
520.628.1339
111 Units, pets OK. Restaurant on premises. Pool. Laundry facility. Rooms come with phones, A/C and cable TV. Wheelchair accessible. Credit cards: AE, CB, DC, DS, MC, V.

WILLCOX
Days Inn
$45-49
724 N. Bisbee Avenue • 520.384.4222
73 Units, pets OK. Continental breakfast. Pool. Laundry facility. Rooms come with phones and cable TV. Some rooms have microwaves and refrigerators. AAA/Senior discount. Major credit cards.

Motel 6
$35
921 N. Bisbee Avenue • 520.384.2201
106 Units, pets OK. Restaurant on premises. Pool. Laundry facility. Rooms come with phones, A/C and cable TV. Wheelchair accessible. Credit cards: AE, CB, DC, DS, MC, V.

WILLIAMS
Budget Host Inn
$20-50
620 W. Rte. 66 • 928.635.4415
26 Units, pets OK. Airport transportation. Laundry facility. Rooms come with phones and TV. AAA/Senior discount. Wheelchair accessible. Credit cards: AE, CB, DC, DS, MC, V.

Motel 6 - East
$30-52
710 W. Bill Williams Ave. • 928.635.4465
48 Units, no pets. Rooms come with phones and cable TV. Senior discount. Major credit cards.

WINSLOW
Motel 6
$41-51
520 Desmond Street • 928.289.9581
55 Units, pets OK. Indoor pool. Rooms come with phones, A/C and cable TV. Wheelchair accessible. Credit cards: AE, CB, DC, DS, MC, V.

Super 8 Motel
$38-54
1916 W. 3rd Street • 928.289.4606
46 Units, pets OK with permission. Continental breakfast. Area transportation available. Rooms come with phones and cable TV. Wheelchair accessible. AAA/ Senior discount. Credit cards: AE, CB, DC, DS, MC, V.

YOUNGTOWN
Motel 6
$42-50 (60)*
11133 Grand Avenue • 623.977.1318
62 Units, pets OK. Heated pool. Rooms come with phones, A/C and cable TV. Wheelchair accessible. Credit cards: AE, CB, DC, DS, MC, V.
*Higher rate effective winter weekends.

YUMA
Interstate 8 Inn
$27-40
2730 S. 4th Avenue • 928.726.6110 or 800.821.7465
120 Units, pets OK. Pool. Spa. Rooms come with phones, A/C and cable TV. Credit cards: AE, CB, DC, DS, MC, V.

Motel 6
$30-48
1640 S. Arizona Avenue • 928.782.6561
151 Units, pets OK. Pool. Laundry facility. Rooms come with phones, A/C and cable TV. Wheelchair accessible. Credit cards: AE, CB, DC, DS, MC, V.

Motel 6 - East
$30-50
1445 E. 16th Street • 928.782.9521
123 Units, pets OK. Pool. Laundry facility. Rooms come with phones, A/C and cable TV. Wheelchair accessible. Credit cards: AE, CB, DC, DS, MC, V.

arkansas

ALMA
Days Inn
$45-55
I-40, Exit 13 • 479.632.4595
48 Units, no pets. Continental breakfast. Pool. Laundry facility. Rooms come with phones and cable TV. Wheelchair accessible. Major credit cards.

ARKADELPHIA
Days Inn
$48-52
On Hwy 67N (I-30, Exit 78)
870.246.3031
53 Units, pets OK. Pool. Jacuzzi. Rooms come with phones and cable TV. Wheelchair accessible. Major credit cards.

Super 8 Motel
$45-55
118 Valley Street, I-30, Exit 78 870.246.8585
50 Units, no pets. Continental breakfast. Jacuzzi. Laundry facility. Rooms come with phones, microwaves, refrigerators and cable TV. AAA discount. Major credit cards.

BALD KNOB
Scottish Inn
$32-38
3505 US 167 • 501.724.3204
34 Units, pets OK. Restaurant on premises. Pool. Rooms come with phones and cable TV. Some rooms have refrigerators. Senior discount. Major credit cards.

BATESVILLE
Super 8 Motel
$44
1287 N. St. Louis Street • 870.793.5888
49 Units, no pets. Continental breakfast. Rooms come with phones and cable TV. Major credit cards.

BEEBE
Oxford Inn
$46
100 Tammy Lane, US 67/167, Exit 28
501.882.2008
41 Units, pets OK ($10). Continental breakfast. Pool. Laundry facility. Data ports. Rooms come with phones and cable TV. Some rooms have microwaves and refrigerators. Wheelchair accessible. AAA/ Senior discount. Credit cards: AE, DC, DS, MC, V.

BENTON
Best Western Inn
$44
17036 I-30 • 501.778.9695
68 Units, pets OK. Pool. Playground. Game room. Laundry facility. Rooms come with phones and cable TV. Some rooms have refrigerators and jacuzzis. Credit cards: AE, CB, DC, DS, MC, V.

Days Inn
$46
17701 I-30 (I-30, Exit 118)
501.776.3200
117 Units, pets OK ($5). Continental breakfast. Pool. Laundry facility. Data ports. Rooms come with phones and cable TV. Some rooms have refrigerators. Senior discount. Major credit cards.

Econo Lodge
$32-40
1221 Hot Springs Road, I-30, Exit 117
501.776.1515
43 Units, pets OK ($5). Data ports. Rooms come with phones and cable TV. Some rooms have refrigerators. AAA/Senior discount. Credit cards: AE, CB, DC, DS, MC, V.

BENTONVILLE
Hartland Motel of Bentonville
$40
1002 S. Walton Blvd. • 479.273.3444
31 Units, pets OK ($10 dep. req.). Rooms come with phones and cable TV. Major credit cards.

BLYTHEVILLE
Best Western
$48-51
3700 S. Division, I-55, Exit 63 870.762.5200
40 Units, no pets. Pool. Laundry facility. Rooms come with phones and cable TV. AAA/Senior discount. Credit cards: AE, CB, DC, DS, MC, V.

BRINKLEY
Super 8 Motel
$41
I-40 & US 49N • 870.734.4680
100 Units, pets OK. Continental breakfast. Pool. Laundry facility. Meeting rooms. Rooms come with phones and cable TV. Wheelchair accessible. AAA/Senior discount. Major credit cards.

BRYANT
Super 8 Motel
$43-47
201 Dell Drive, I-30, Exit 123
501.847.7888
33 Units, pets OK ($50 dep. req.). Continental breakfast. Data ports. Rooms come with phones and cable TV. Some rooms have microwaves and refrigerators. AAA/Senior discount. Major credit cards.

CABOT
Days Inn
$45-55
1114 W. Main Street, US 67/167, Exit 19
501.843.0145
42 Units, pets OK ($5). Pool. Rooms come with phones and cable TV. Some rooms have microwaves and refrigerators. AAA/Senior discount. Major credit cards.

CLARKSVILLE
Days Inn
$40-50
2600 W. Main Street • 479.754.8555
47 Units, pets OK. Restaurant on premises. Pool. Rooms come with phones and cable TV. Some rooms have kitchens and refrigerators. Wheelchair accessible. Credit cards: AE, CB, DC, DS, MC, V.

Super 8 Motel
$41
1238 Rogers Avenue • 479.754.8800
57 Units, pets OK. Pool. Laundry facility. Rooms come with phones and cable TV. Some rooms have microwaves, jacuzzis and refrigerators. Credit cards: AE, DC, DS, MC, V.

CLINTON
Super 8 Motel
$41
On US 65S • 501.745.8810
44 Units, pets OK. Continental breakfast. Meeting rooms. Rooms come with phones and cable TV. Wheelchair accessible. Senior discount. Major credit cards.

CONWAY
Howard Johnson Inn
$49
1090 Skyline Drive, I-40, Exit 125
501.329.2961
108 Units, pets OK ($10). Restaurant on premises. Pool. Sauna. Laundry facility. Jacuzzi. Fitness facility. Meeting rooms. Rooms come with phones and cable TV. AAA/Senior discount. Major credit cards.

Kings Inn
$40
126 Oak Street • 501.329.5653
32 Units, no pets. Pool. Rooms come with phones and cable TV. Wheelchair accessible. AAA/Senior discount. Major credit cards.

Motel 6
$30-38
1105 Hwy. 65N (1-40, Exit 125)
501.327.6623
88 Units, pets OK. Pool. Laundry facility. Data ports. Rooms come with phones, A/C and cable TV. Wheelchair accessible. Credit cards: AE, CB, DC, DS, MC, V.

DARDANELLE
Economy Inn
$36
From I-40, Exit 81, 7 miles south on US 7 (at jct. of Hwys. 7, 22 & 27) • 479.229.4118
46 Units, pets OK ($5). Pool. Rooms come with phones and cable TV. AAA/Senior discount. Credit cards: AE, DS, MC, V.

EL DORADO
Days Inn
$40
301 W. Hillsboro Street • 870.862.6621
90 Units, no pets. Continental breakfast. Pool. Rooms come with phones and cable TV. Senior discount. Major credit cards.

EUREKA SPRINGS
Dogwood Inn
$30-48
On US 23, 0.3 miles south of junction with Hwy. 62 • 479.253.7200
33 Units, pets OK ($10). Continental breakfast. Pool. Playground. Rooms come with phones and cable TV. Credit cards: AE, DS, MC, V.

Super 8 Motel
$34-43
Hwy. 62 & Passion Play Rd.
479.253.5959
44 Units, no pets. Continental breakfast. Pool. Meeting room. Rooms come with phones and cable TV. Wheelchair accessible. Senior discount. Credit cards: AE, DC, DS, MC, V.

Travelers Inn
$28-48
One mile south of town on US 62E
479.253.8386
60 Units, pets OK. Continental breakfast. Heated pool. Picnic area. Meeting rooms. Playground. Data ports. Rooms come with phones and cable TV. Some rooms have kitchens, microwaves and refrigerators. AAA/Senior discount. Credit cards: AE, DC, DS, MC, V.

FAYETTEVILLE
Motel 6
$36-37
2980 N. College Avenue • 479.443.4351
98 Units, pets OK. Pool. Laundry facility. Data ports. Rooms come with phones, A/C and cable TV. Wheelchair accessible. Credit cards: AE, CB, DC, DS, MC, V.

FORREST CITY
Comfort Inn
$45-50
115 Barrow Hill Road • 870.633.0042
76 Units, no pets. Continental breakfast. Pool. Laundry facility. Rooms come with phones, microwaves, refrigerators and cable TV. AAA discount. Major credit cards.

Luxury Inn
$35-39
315 Barrow Hill Road • 870.633.8990
42 Units, pets OK ($5). Rooms come with phones and cable TV. Some rooms have microwaves and refrigerators. Senior discount. Credit cards: AE, DS, MC, V.

FORT SMITH
Days Inn
$38-44
1021 Garrison Avenue • 479.783.0548
53 Units, pets OK ($5). Continental breakfast. Pool. Laundry facility. Airport transportation. Data ports. Rooms come with phones and cable TV. Some rooms have microwaves and refrigerators. AAA/Senior discount. Major credit cards.

Motel 6
$35-40
6001 Rogers Avenue • 479.484.0576
109 Units, pets OK. Pool. Laundry facility. Data ports. Rooms come with phones, A/C and cable TV. Wheelchair accessible. Credit cards: AE, CB, DC, DS, MC, V.

Super 8 Motel
$40-45*
3810 Towson Avenue • 479.646.3411
52 Units, pets OK ($5). Restaurant on premises. Continental breakfast. Airport transportation. Pool. Jacuzzi. Fax service. Rooms come with phones and cable TV. Wheelchair accessible. AAA/Senior discount. Credit cards: AE, CB, DC, DS, MC, V.
*Rates may increase slightly during weekends, holidays and special events.

HARRISON
Family Budget Inn
$30-34
401 S. Main Hwy. 65B • 870.743.1000
54 Units, pets OK ($3). Continental breakfast. Pool. Playground. Rooms come with phones and cable TV. Some rooms have kitchens. AAA/Senior discount. Credit cards: AE, DS, MC, V.

Super 8 Motel
$36-45
1330 Hwy 62/65N • 870.741.1741
50 Units, pets OK ($5). Continental breakfast. Pool. Laundry facility. Jacuzzi. Airport transportation. Rooms come with phones and cable TV. Some rooms have kitchens. AAA/Senior discount. Credit cards: AE, DC, DS, MC, V.

HAZEN
Super 8 Motel
$50
I-40 (Exit 193) • 870.255.3563
44 Units, no pets. Pool. Laundry facility. Rooms come with phones and cable TV. Senior discount. Credit cards: AE, CB, DC, DS, MC, V.

HEBER SPRINGS
Colonial Motor Inn
$32-42
2949 Hwy. 25B • 501.362.5846
38 Units, pets OK. Restaurant adjoining.

Heated pool. Sauna. Meeting room. Picnic area. Rooms come with phones, A/C and cable TV. Major credit cards.

HOPE
Best Western of Hope
$45-49
I-30 & US 278, I-30, Exit 30
870.777.9222
74 Units, pets OK. Continental breakfast. Pool. Laundry facility. Airport transportation. Data ports. Rooms come with phones and cable TV. Some rooms have microwaves and refrigerators. AAA/Senior discount. Major credit cards.

Relax Inn & Suites
$31-46
I-30 & SR 29 • 870.777.0777
54 Units, pets OK ($5). Continental breakfast. Rooms come with phones and cable TV. Some rooms have microwaves and refrigerators. AAA/Senior discount. Major credit cards.

HOT SPRINGS NATIONAL PARK
Knights Inn
$29-49
1871 E. Grand Avenue, US 70, Exit 3
501.623.1192
50 Units, no pets. Restaurant on premises. Pool. Laundry facility. Rooms come with refrigerators, phones and cable TV. Wheelchair accessible. Major credit cards.

Travelier Motor Lodge
$31-56*
1045 E. Grand Avenue • 501.624.4681
56 Units, pets OK. Continental breakfast. Pools. Rooms come with phones and cable TV. Some rooms have microwaves and refrigerators. Senior discount. Credit cards: AE, CB, DC, DS, MC, V.
*AAA discounted rates.

Vagabond Motel
$35-39
4708 Central Avenue • 501.525.2769
23 Units, no pets. Pool. Picnic area. Rooms come with phones and TV. Some rooms have kitchenettes. AAA discount. Major credit cards.

JACKSONVILLE
Comfort Inn
$44
1850 John Harden Drive • 501.982.9219
58 Units, no pets. Continental breakfast. Pool. Jacuzzi. Laundry facility. Data ports. Rooms come with phones and cable TV. Some rooms have microwaves and refrigerators. Senior discount. Major credit cards.

Days Inn
$45-50
1414 John Harden Dr.
US 67/167, Exit 10B • 501.982.1543
40 Units, pets OK ($5). Rooms come with phones and cable TV. Some rooms have microwaves and refrigerators. Senior discount. Major credit cards.

JONESBORO
Best Western
$45-49
2901 Phillips Drive • 870.932.6600
60 Units, pets OK. Continental breakfast. Pool. Meeting rooms. Rooms come with phones and cable TV. Some rooms have jacuzzis, microwaves and refrigerators. AAA/ Senior discount. Credit cards: AE, CB, DC, DS, MC V.

Motel 6
$30-35
2300 S. Caraway Road • 870.932.1050
80 Units, pets OK. Pool. Laundry facility. Data ports. Rooms come with phones, A/C and cable TV. Wheelchair accessible. Credit cards: AE, CB, DC, DS, MC, V.

Super 8 Motel
$35-39
2500 S. Caraway Road • 870.972.0849
68 Units, pets OK ($10). Laundry facility. Rooms come with phones and cable TV. Some rooms have microwaves and refrigerators. AAA/Senior discount. Credit cards: AE, CB, DC, DS, MC, V.

LITTLE ROCK — *see also North Little Rock*
Days Inn South
$32-38
2600 W. 65th Street • 501.562.1122
82 Units, pets OK. Restaurant on premises. Pool. Meeting rooms. Airport transportation. Laundry facility. Rooms come with phones and cable TV. AAA discount. Credit cards: AE, CB, DC, DS, MC, V.

Masters Economy Inn
$35
I-30 at 6th & 9th Street (Exit 140)

501.372.1732
170 Units, no pets. Restaurant on premises. Pool. Game room. Fax service. Meeting rooms. Rooms come with phones and cable TV. AAA/Senior discount. Major credit cards.

Motel 6—Southeast
$35-36
7501 I-30 • 501.568.8888
128 Units, pets OK. Pool. Laundry facility. Data ports. Rooms come with phones, A/C and cable TV. Wheelchair accessible. Credit cards: AE, CB, DC, DS, MC, V.

Motel 6—West
$38
10524 W. Markham St. • 501.225.7366
146 Units, pets OK. Pool. Laundry facility. Data ports. Rooms come with phones, A/C and cable TV. Wheelchair accessible. Credit cards: AE, CB, DC, DS, MC, V.

Red Roof Inn
$37-53
7900 Scott Hamilton Dr. • 501.562.2694
108 Units, pets OK. Rooms come with phones and cable TV. AAA discount. Credit cards: AE, CB, DC, DS, MC, V.

MALVERN
Super 8 Motel
$43
Hwy. 270W & I-30 • 501.332.5755
75 Units, no pets. Continental breakfast. Pool. Rooms come with phones and cable TV. Senior discount. Major credit cards.

MARKED TREE
Travel Inn
$36
201 Hwy. 63S • 870.358.2700
42 Units, pets OK. Restaurant on premises. Meeting room. Rooms come with phones and cable TV. AAA discount. Credit cards: AE, DC, DS, MC, V.

MENA
Ozark Inn
$33-39
2102 US 71S • 479.394.1100
35 Units, pets OK. Pool. Rooms come with phones and cable TV. AAA discount. Credit cards: AE, DS, MC, V.

MORRILTON
Days Inn
$34-44
1506 N. Hwy. 95 • 501.354.5101
53 Units, pets OK. Pool. Jacuzzi (in season). Rooms come with phones and cable TV. AAA discount. Credit cards: AE, CB, DC, DS, JCB, MC, V.

Scottish Inn
$40-44
356 Hwy. 95 & I 40 • 501.354.0181
55 Units, pets OK. Restaurant on premises. Pool. Laundry facility. Meeting rooms. Rooms come with phones and cable TV. Some rooms have microwaves and refrigerators. AAA/Senior discount. Credit cards: AE, CB, DC, DS, JCB, MC, V.

MOUNTAIN HOME
Super 8 Motel
$50
865 Hwy. 62E • 870.424.5600
41 Units, no pets. Continental breakfast. Rooms come with phones and cable TV. Major credit cards.

NEWPORT
Days Inn
$40-50
101 Olivia Drive • 870.523.6411
40 Units, pets OK. Continental breakfast. Pool. Rooms come with phones and cable TV. Credit cards: AE, CB, DC, DS, MC, V.

NORTH LITTLE ROCK
Masters Economy Inn
$30-34
2508 Jacksonville Hwy. • 501.945.4167
150 Units, pets OK ($5). Airport transportation. Laundry facility. Rooms come with phones and cable TV. Some rooms have microwaves and refrigerators. Senior discount. Major credit cards.

Motel 6
$30-37
400 W. 29th Street • 501.758.5100
118 Units, pets OK. Pool. Laundry facility. Rooms come with phones, A/C and cable TV. Wheelchair accessible. Credit cards: AE, CB, DC, DS, MC, V.

Super 8 Motel
$44-48
1 Gray Rd., I-40, Exit 157 • 501.945.0141
75 Units, pets OK. Continental breakfast. Laundry facility. Rooms come with phones

and cable TV. AAA/Senior discount. Major credit cards.

OZARK
Oxford Inn
$34-36
305 N. 18th Street • 479.667.1131
32 Units, pets OK ($5). Pool. Rooms come with phones and cable TV. Wheelchair accessible. Credit cards: AE, CB, DC, DS, MC, V.

PINE BLUFF
Economy Inn
$40
4600 Dollarway Road • 870.534.4510
90 Units, no pets. Rooms come with phones and cable TV. Major credit cards.

POCAHONTAS
Scottish Inn
$33-42
1501 Hwy. 67N • 870.892.4527
40 Units, pets OK. Restaurant on premises. Pool. Rooms come with phones and cable TV. Senior discount. Major credit cards.

PRESCOTT
Econo Lodge
$35-45
1703 Hwy. 371W • 870.887.6641
48 Units, no pets. Continental breakfast. Pool. Rooms come with phones and cable TV. Major credit cards.

ROGERS
Super 8 Motel
$40*
915 S. 8th Street • 501.636.9600
82 Units, pets OK. Continental breakfast. Copy and fax service. Rooms come with phones and cable TV. Wheelchair accessible. Senior discount. Credit cards: AE, CB, DC, DS, MC, V.
*Rates may increase slightly during special events.

RUSSELLVILLE
Knights Inn
$30-44
504 W. Birch Street • 479.968.1450
98 Units, no pets. Continental breakfast. Pool. Boat ramp. Laundry facility. Meeting rooms. Rooms come with phones and cable TV. Some rooms have refrigerators. Wheelchair accessible. Senior discount. Credit cards: AE, DC, DS, MC, V.

Motel 6
$30-32
215 W. Birch Street • 479.968.3666
79 Units, pets OK. Pool. Laundry facility. Data ports. Rooms come with phones, A/C and cable TV. Wheelchair accessible. Credit cards: AE, CB, DC, DS, MC, V.

Econo Lodge
$39-52
154 E. Aspen Lane, I-40, Exit 81
479.968.7200
67 Units, no pets. Continental breakfast. Laundry facility. Rooms come with phones and cable TV. Some rooms have refrigerators. Wheelchair accessible. Major credit cards.

SEARCY
Honey Tree Inn of Searcy
$35
3211 E. Race Street • 501.268.9900
56 Units, no pets. Rooms come with phones and cable TV. Major credit cards.

SPRINGDALE
Scottish Inns & Suites
$39-49
1219 S. Thompson St. • 479.751.4874
50 Units, pets OK. Restaurant on premises. Pool. Laundry facility. Rooms come with phones and cable TV. Some rooms have jacuzzis. Senior discount. Major credit cards.

STUTTGART
Super 8 Motel
$40-50
701 W. Michigan Street • 870.673.2611
48 Units, pets OK. Continental breakfast. Laundry facility. Rooms come with phones and cable TV. Senior discount. Major credit cards.

TEXARKANA — *see also Texarkana (TX)*
Knights Inn
$30-50
200 Realtor Road, I-30, Exit 223A
870.774.3151
100 Units, no pets. Continental breakfast. Pool. Laundry facility. Rooms come with phones and cable TV. Some rooms have refrigerators. AAA/Senior discount. Credit cards: AE, CB, DC, DS, MC, V.

Super 8 Motel
$40-50
325 E. 51st Street, I-30 & US 59 and 71

870.774.8888
44 Units, pets OK. Continental breakfast. Game room. Rooms come with phones and cable TV. Wheelchair accessible. Senior discount. Credit cards: AE, CB, DC, DS, MC, V.

VAN BUREN
Motel 6
$36-37
1716 Fayetteville Road • 479.474.8001
92 Units, pets OK. Pool. Laundry facility. Data ports. Rooms come with phones, A/C and cable TV. Wheelchair accessible. Credit cards: AE, CB, DC, DS, MC, V.

Super 8 Motel
$45-48
106 North Plaza Ct. • 479.471.8888
46 Units, pets OK ($25 dep. req.). Heated pool. Jacuzzi. Laundry facility. Rooms come with phones and cable TV. Some rooms have microwaves and refrigerators. AAA/Senior discount. Major credit cards.

WEST MEMPHIS
Econo Lodge
$34
2315 S. Service Road • 870.732.2830
153 Units, pets OK ($20 dep. req.). Local transportation available. Rooms come with phones and cable TV. Some rooms have refrigerators. Senior discount. Credit cards: AE, DC, DS, MC, V.

Howard Johnson
$44-50*
2411 S. Service Road, I-40, Exit 279A
870.732.9654
39 Units, no pets. Fitness facility. Data ports. Rooms come with phones, A/C and cable TV. Some rooms have jacuzzis. AAA/Senior discount. Major credit cards.
*Request the "SA3" rate for 10-20% discount.

Motel 6
$34-40
2501 S. Service Road • 870.735.0100
85 Units, pets OK. Pool. Laundry facility. Data ports. Rooms come with phones, A/C and cable TV. Wheelchair accessible. Credit cards: AE, CB, DC, DS, MC, V.

WHEATLEY
Ramada Limited
$40-50
129 Lawson Road, I-40, Exit 221
870.457.2202
101 Units, pets OK ($50 dep. req.). Continental breakfast. Pool. Rooms come with phones and cable TV. AAA/Senior discount. Credit cards: AE, CB, DC, DS, MC, V.

california

ADELANTO
Days Inn
$44-55
11628 Bartlett Avenue (off US 395)
760.246.8777
36 Units, pets OK Continental breakfast. Pool. Jacuzzi. Rooms come with phones, refrigerators and cable TV. Wheelchair accessible. Major credit cards.

ALTURAS
Frontier Motel
$35
1033 N. Main Street • 530.233.3383
11 Units, pets OK. Rooms come with phones and cable TV. Some rooms have microwaves and refrigerators. Major credit cards.

ANAHEIM — *see also Buena Park and Stanton*
Econo Lodge
$35-40
837 S. Beach Blvd. • 714.952.0898
45 Units, no pets. Continental breakfast. Pool. Laundry facility. Rooms come with phones and cable TV. AAA discount. Major credit cards.

Motel 6
$40-52
1440 N. State College • 714.956.9690
126 Units, pets OK. Restaurant on premises. Laundry facility. Rooms come with A/C, phones and cable TV. Wheelchair accessible. Credit cards: AE, CB, DC, DS, MC, V.

Red Roof Inn—Main Gate
$45
100 W. Freedman Way
I-5/Katella Ave. Exit • 714.520.9696
227 Units, pets OK. Restaurant on premises. Pool. Laundry facility. Rooms come with A/C, phones and cable TV. Wheelchair accessible. Credit cards: AE, CB, DC, DS, MC, V.

ARCADIA
Motel 6
$42-46 (52-56)*
225 Colorado Place, I-10/I-210, Santa Anita Exit • 626.446.2660
87 Units, pets OK. Pool. Rooms come with A/C, phones and cable TV. Wheelchair accessible. Credit cards: AE, CB, DC, DS, MC, V.
*Higher rates effective weekends.

ARCATA
Motel 6
$40-50
4755 Valley W. Blvd. • 707.822.7061
81 Units, pets OK. Pool. Laundry facility. Data ports. Rooms come with A/C, phones and cable TV. Wheelchair accessible. Credit cards: AE, CB, DC, DS, MC, V.

ARROYO GRANDE
Premier Inn
$45 (59)*
555 Camino Mercado • 805.481.4774
100 Units, no pets. Laundry facility. Rooms come with phones, A/C and cable TV. Credit cards: AE, MC, V.
*Higher rate effective weekends.

ATASCADERO
Motel 6
$38-45
9400 El Camino Real • 805.466.6701
117 Units, pets OK. Pool. Laundry facility. Rooms come with A/C, phones and cable TV. Wheelchair accessible. Credit cards: AE, CB, DC, DS, MC, V.

Super 8 Motel
$49*
6506 Morro Road • 805.466.0794
30 Units, pets OK. Rooms come with phones and cable TV. Wheelchair accessible. Senior discount. Credit cards: AE, CB, DC, DS, MC, V.
*Rates as high as $70/night.

AZUSA
Super 8 Motel
$50
117 N. Azusa Avenue, I-210, Azusa Exit
626.969.8871
44 Units, no pets. Continental breakfast. Jacuzzi. Meeting rooms. Laundry facility.

Rooms come with phones and cable TV. Senior discount. Wheelchair accessible. Credit cards: AE, DS, MC, V.

BAKER
Bun Boy Motel
$46-53*
At junction of I-15 & SR 127
760.733.4363
20 Units, pets OK. Restaurant on premises. Rooms come with phones and cable TV. AAA/Senior discount. Credit cards: AE, DS, MC, V.
*AAA discounted rates.

BAKERSFIELD
Best Inn
$44-49
200 Trask Street, I-5, Stockdale Hwy. Exit
661.764.5221
53 Units, pets OK ($5). Continental breakfast. Pool. Rooms come with phones and cable TV. AAA/Senior discount. Major credit cards.

Motel 6—East
$36-40
8223 E. Brundage Lane • 661.366.7231
109 Units, pets OK. Pool. Laundry facility. Data ports. Rooms come with A/C, phones and cable TV. Wheelchair accessible. Credit cards: AE, CB, DC, DS, MC, V.

Motel 6—Airport
$32-35
5241 Olive Tree Ct., Hwy 99, Olive Dr. Exit
661.392.9700
149 Units, pets OK. Pool. Laundry facility. Data ports. Rooms come with A/C, phones and cable TV. Wheelchair accessible. Credit cards: AE, CB, DC, DS, MC, V.

Motel 6—South
$36-42
2727 White Lane, Hwy 99, White Lane Exit
661.834.2828
102 Units, pets OK. Pool. Laundry facility. Data ports. Rooms come with A/C, phones and cable TV. Wheelchair accessible. Credit cards: AE, CB, DC, DS, MC, V.

Vagabond Inn
$35-39
6100 Knudsen Dr., Hwy 99, Exit Olive Dr.
661.392.1800
154 Units, pets OK. Pool. Rooms come with A/C, phones and cable TV. AAA/Senior discount. Major credit cards.

BALDWIN PARK
Motel 6
$36-46
14510 Garvey Ave., I-10, Puente Ave. Exit
626.960.5011
75 Units, pets OK. Pool. Laundry facility. Rooms come with A/C, phones and cable TV. Wheelchair accessible. Credit cards: AE, CB, DC, DS, MC, V.

BARSTOW
Econo Lodge
$29-50*
1230 E. Main Street • 760.256.2133
51 Units, pets OK ($5). Heated pool. Rooms come with phones, refrigerators and cable TV. Some rooms have kitchens and refrigerators. Credit cards: AE, DC, DS, MC, V.
*Rates as high as $79/night.

Good Nite Inn
$45-55
2551 Commerce Pkwy • 760.253.2121
110 Units, pets OK. Heated pool, jacuzzi and gym. Laundry facility. Rooms come with phones and cable TV. AAA discount. Credit cards: AE, CB, DC, DS, MC, V.

Motel 6
$35-36
150 N. Yucca Avenue • 760.256.1752
121 Units, pets OK. Pool. Rooms come with A/C, phones and cable TV. Wheelchair accessible. Credit cards: AE, CB, DC, DS, MC, V.

BEAUMONT
Budget Host Golden West Motel
$42-50
625 E. 5th Street • 909.845.2185
24 Units, pets OK. Pool. Laundry facility. Rooms come with color TVs and phones. Senior discount available ($3.00). Credit cards: AE, CB, DC, DS, MC, V.

Windsor Motel
$45
1265 E. 6th Street • 909.845.1436
16 Units, pets OK ($2). Pool. Rooms come with phones and cable TV. Some rooms have kitchenettes, microwaves, radios and refrigerators. Credit cards: AE, DC, DS, MC, V.

BELLFLOWER
Motel 6
$44-52
17220 Downey Avenue, From I-605, Hwy 90 westbound, Downey Avenue Exit
562.531.3933
154 Units, pets OK. Pool. Laundry facility. Rooms come with A/C, phones and cable TV. Wheelchair accessible. Credit cards: AE, CB, DC, DS, MC, V.

BERKELEY — *see Oakland/East Bay*

BIG BEAR
Motel 6
$38-44 (56)*
42899 Big Bear Blvd. • 909.585.6666
120 Units, pets OK. Pool. Laundry facility. Rooms come with A/C, phones and cable TV. Wheelchair accessible. Credit cards: AE, CB, DC, DS, MC, V.
*Higher rate effective winter weekends.

BIG PINE
Big Pine Motel
$34-50
370 S. Main • 760.938.2282
14 Units, pets OK ($4). Wood swings and barbecue. Rooms come with cable TV. Some rooms have refrigerators. Credit cards: AE, CB, DC, DS, JCB, MC, V.

Bristlecone Motel
$36-58
101 N. Main • 760.938.2067
17 Units, pets OK. Rooms come with phones and cable TV. Some rooms have kitchenettes and refrigerators. AAA discount. Credit cards: AE, DS, MC, V.

BISHOP
Bishop Elms Motel
$35-40
233 E. Elm Street • 760.873.8118
19 Units, no pets. Barbecues. Laundry facility. Rooms come with cable TV. No phones. Credit cards: DS, MC, V.

Super 8 Motel
$43-53*
535 S. Main Street • 760.872.1386
43 Units, pets OK. Continental breakfast. Laundry facility. Jacuzzi and sauna. Rooms come with phones and cable TV. Major credit cards.
*AAA discounted rates.

BLYTHE
Blythe Inn
$33
401 E. Hobson Way • 760.922.2184
62 Units, no pets. Pool. Playground. Laundry facility. Rooms come with A/C, phones and cable TV. Major credit cards.

Motel 6
$38-45
500 W. Donlon Street • 760.922.6666
92 Units, pets OK. Pool. Laundry facility. Rooms come with A/C, phones and cable TV. Wheelchair accessible. Credit cards: AE, CB, DC, DS, MC, V.

BUELLTON
Motel 6
$42-50 (48-68)*
333 McMurray Road • 805.688.7797
59 Units, pets OK. Restaurant on premises. Pool. Data ports. Rooms come with A/C, phones and cable TV. Wheelchair accessible. Credit cards: AE, CB, DC, DS, MC, V.
*Higher rates effective Memorial Day through September.

BUENA PARK
Days Inn
$40
8580 Stanton Avenue • 714.828.5211
62 Units, no pets. Continental breakfast. Heated pool. Laundry facility. Rooms come with phones and cable TV. Some rooms have refrigerators and microwaves. AAA discount. Credit cards: AE, CB, DC, DS, MC, V.

Motel 6
$36-47
7051 Valley View • 714.522.1200
187 Units, pets OK. Restaurant on premises. Pool. Laundry facility. Rooms come with A/C, phones and cable TV. Wheelchair accessible. Credit cards: AE, CB, DC, DS, MC, V.

Super 8 Motel
$45-55*
7930 Beach Blvd. • 714.994.6480
78 Units, no pets. Continental breakfast. Pool and jacuzzi. Laundry facility. Copy machine. Rooms come with phones and cable TV. Wheelchair accessible. AAA/ Senior discount. Credit cards: AE, CB, DC, DS, JCB, MC, V.
*AAA discounted rates.

BUTTONWILLOW
Motel 6
$30-34
20638 Tracy Avenue • 661.764.5153
123 Units, pets OK. Pool. Data ports. Rooms come with A/C, phones and cable TV. Wheelchair accessible. Credit cards: AE, CB, DC, DS, MC, V.

Super 8 Motel
$36-39
20681 Tracy Road • 805.764.5117
86 Units, pets OK. Pool, jacuzzi and game room. Laundry facility. Rooms come with phones and cable TV. Some rooms have microwaves and refrigerators. Credit cards: AE, CB, DC, DS, MC, V.

CALABASAS
Good Nite Inn
$45-55
26557 Agoura Road, US 101
Exit Lost Hills Road • 818.880.6000
169 Units, no pets. Pool. Laundry facility. Jacuzzi. Data ports. Rooms come with A/C, phones and cable TV. AAA/Senior discount. Major credit cards.

CALIMESA
Calimesa Inn Motel
$50-55*
1205 Calimesa Blvd. • 909.795.2536
36 Units, pets OK ($6). Pool. Rooms come with phones and cable TV. Senior discount. Major credit cards.
*AAA discounted rates.

CAMARILLO
Good Nite Inn
$38-50
1100 Ventura Blvd. • 805.388.5644
129 Units, pets OK. Pool. Laundry facility. Jacuzzi. Rooms come with phones and cable TV. Some rooms have microwaves and refrigerators. AAA discount. Major credit cards.

Motel 6
$42-52
1641 E. Daily Drive • 805.388.3467
82 Units, pets OK. Pool. Rooms come with A/C, phones and cable TV. Wheelchair accessible. Credit cards: AE, CB, DC, DS, MC, V.

CARLSBAD
Motel 6
$44-50 (56)*
1006 Carlsbad Vill. Dr. • 760.434.7135
109 Units, pets OK. Data ports. Rooms come with A/C, phones and cable TV. Wheelchair accessible. Credit cards: AE, CB, DC, DS, MC, V.
*Higher rate effective summer weekends.

Motel 6
$44-50 (56)*
6117 Paseo del Norte • 760.438.1242
142 Units, pets OK. Pool. Laundry facility. Data ports. Rooms come with A/C, phones and cable TV. Wheelchair accessible. Credit cards: AE, CB, DC, DS, MC, V.
*Higher rate effective summer weekends.

Motel 6
$44-50 (56)*
750 Raintree Drive • 760.431.0745
160 Units, pets OK. Pool. Laundry facility. Data ports. Rooms come with phones and cable TV. Wheelchair accessible. Credit cards: AE, CB, DC, DS, MC, V.
*Higher rate effective summer weekends.

CARPINTERIA
Motel 6
$45-50 (57)*
4200 Via Real • 805.684.6921
124 Units, pets OK. Pool. Laundry facility. Data ports. Rooms come with A/C, phones and cable TV. Wheelchair accessible. Credit cards: AE, CB, DC, DS, MC, V.
*Higher rate effective summer weekends.

Motel 6
$45-50 (57)*
5550 Carpinteria Ave. • 805.684.8602
138 Units, pets OK. Pool. Data ports. Rooms come with A/C, phones and cable TV. Wheelchair accessible. Credit cards: AE, CB, DC, DS, MC, V.
*Higher rate effective summer weekends.

CHATSWORTH
7-Star Suites Hotel
$49
21603 Devonshire Street • SR 118, Exit Topanga Canyon Blvd. • 818.998.8888
73 Units, no pets. Continental breakfast. Pool. Jacuzzi. Meeting rooms. Data ports. Rooms come with phones and cable TV. AAA/Senior discount. Major credit cards.

CHICO
Deluxe Inn
$40-59

2507 Esplanade • 530.342.8386
35 Units, pets OK ($5). Continental breakfast. Jacuzzi. Rooms come with phones and cable TV. Some rooms have microwaves and refrigerators. AAA discount. Major credit cards.

Motel 6
$38-46
665 Manzanita Court • 530.345.5500
78 Units, pets OK. Restaurant on premises. Pool. Data ports. Rooms come with A/C, phones and cable TV. Wheelchair accessible. Credit cards: AE, CB, DC, DS, MC, V.

CHINO
Chino Motel
$48-53
11885 Central Avenue • 909.591.9505
51 Units, no pets. Continental breakfast. Pool. Rooms come with phones and cable TV. AAA discount. Major credit cards.

Motel 6
$40-48
12266 Central Avenue • 909.591.3877
95 Units, pets OK. Pool. Laundry facility. Data ports. Rooms come with A/C, phones and cable TV. Wheelchair accessible. Credit cards: AE, CB, DC, DS, MC, V.

CHOWCHILLA
Days Inn
$48
220 E. Robertson Blvd. • 559.665.4821
30 Units, pets OK. Continental breakfast. Pool. Laundry facility. Rooms come with phones and cable TV. Major credit cards.

CHULA VISTA
Good Nite Inn—South Bay
$50
225 Bay Blvd. • 619.425.8200
118 Units, pets OK. Heated pool. Laundry facility. Rooms come with free and pay movies and cable TV. Some rooms have microwaves. AAA discount. Credit cards: AE, CB, DC, DS, MC, V.

Motel 6
$40-52
745 "E" Street • 619.422.4200
176 Units, pets OK. Pool. Laundry facility. Data ports. Rooms come with A/C, phones and cable TV. Wheelchair accessible. Credit cards: AE, CB, DC, DS, MC, V.

CLEARLAKE
Lamplighter Motel
$48
14165 Lakeshore Drive • 707.994.2129
20 Units, no pets. Pool. Spa. Barbecue and picnic area. Boat slip. Laundry facility. Rooms come with A/C, phones and cable TV. Some rooms have kitchenettes. Wheelchair accessible. Credit cards: AE, DS, MC, V.

COALINGA
Motel 6
$40
25008 W. Dorris Ave. • 559.935.1536
122 Units, pets OK. Pool. Data ports. Rooms come with A/C, phones and cable TV. Wheelchair accessible. Credit cards: AE, CB, DC, DS, MC, V.

Pleasant Valley Inn
$35
25278 W. Dorris Ave. • 559.935.2063
122 Units, pets OK. Pool. Laundry facility. Rooms come with A/C, phones and cable TV. Wheelchair accessible. Credit cards: AE, CB, DC, DS, MC, V.

CORNING
Days Inn
$45
3475 Hwy 99W • 916.824.2000
62 Units, pets OK ($5 and $25 dep. req.). Continental breakfast. Laundry facility. Rooms come with free and pay movies and cable TV. AAA/Senior discount. Credit cards: AE, CB, DC, DS, JCB, MC, V.

CORONA
Corona Travelodge
$47*
1701 W. 6th Street • 909.735.5500
46 Units, no pets. Continental breakfast. Pool. Laundry facility. Rooms come with phones and cable TV. Some rooms have microwaves and refrigerators. Credit cards: AE, CB, DC, DS, MC, V.
*AAA discounted rates.

Motel 6
$38
200 N. Lincoln Avenue • 909.735.6408
126 Units, pets OK. Pool. Laundry facility. Data ports. Rooms come with A/C, phones and cable TV. Wheelchair accessible. Credit cards: AE, CB, DC, DS, MC, V.

COSTA MESA
Motel 6
$44-52 (50-60)*
1441 Gisler Avenue • 949.957.3063
94 Units, pets OK. Pool. Laundry facility. Rooms come with A/C, phones and cable TV. Wheelchair accessible. Credit cards: AE, CB, DC, DS, MC, V.
*Higher rate effective weekends April through mid-May.

Sandpiper Motel
$46
1967 Newport Blvd. • 949.645.9137
43 Units, no pets. Continental breakfast. Laundry facility. Rooms come with phones and cable TV. Some rooms have kitchenettes, refrigerators and mini bars. AAA discount. Credit cards: AE, DS, MC, V.

CRESCENT CITY
Days Inn
$39-59
220 "M" St. (on US 101) • 707.464.9553
25 Units, no pets. Continental breakfast. Data ports. Rooms come with phones and cable TV. No A/C in rooms. AAA/Senior discount. Major credit cards.

Travelodge
$39-55 (49-69)*
353 "L" Street • 707.464.6124
27 Units, no pets. Continental breakfast. Sauna. Rooms come with phones and cable TV. No A/C in rooms. AAA discount. Major credit cards.
*Higher rates effective Memorial Day through August.

DALY CITY — *see San Francisco*

DAVIS
Motel 6
$40-50
4835 Chiles Road • 530.753.3777
103 Units, pets OK. Restaurant on premises. Pool. Laundry facility. Data ports. Rooms come with A/C, phones and cable TV. Wheelchair accessible. Credit cards: AE, CB, DC, DS, MC, V.

DESERT HOT SPRINGS
Stardust Motel
$50
66634 5th Street • 760.329.5443
16 Units, pets OK. Jacuzzi. Rooms come with cable TV. No phones in rooms. Some rooms have refrigerators. AAA discount. Credit cards: MC, V.

DUNNIGAN
Best Value Inn
$46-55
I-5, Dunnigan Exit • 530.724.3333
40 Units, pets OK. Continental breakfast. Laundry facility. Rooms come with phones, refrigerators and cable TV. AAA discount. Credit cards: AE, DS, MC, V.

DUNSMUIR
Best Choice Inn
$42
4221 Siskiyou Avenue • 530.235.0930
29 Units, pets OK. Restaurant on premises. Pool. Rooms come with A/C, phones and cable TV. Major credit cards.

EL CAJON
Motel 6
$40-50
550 Montrose Court • 619.588.6100
182 Units, pets OK. Pool. Laundry facility. Data ports. Rooms come with phones and cable TV. Wheelchair accessible. Credit cards: AE, CB, DC, DS, MC, V.

Plaza International Inn
$45
683 N. Mollison Avenue • 619.442.0973
60 Units, no pets. Pool, sauna and indoor jacuzzi. Rooms come with refrigerators and cable TV. Credit cards: AE, CB, DC, DS, MC, V.

EL CENTRO
Laguna Inn
$40-45
2030 Cottonwood Circle, I-8, Imperial Avenue Exit • 760.353.7750
27 Units, no pets. Continental breakfast. Pool. Laundry facility. Data ports. Rooms come with phones, A/C and cable TV. AAA/Senior discount. Major credit cards.

Motel 6
$38-42
395 Smoketree Drive • 760.353.6766
110 Units, pets OK. Pool. Laundry facility. Data ports. Rooms come with A/C, phones and cable TV. Wheelchair accessible. Credit cards: AE, CB, DC, DS, MC, V.

Value Inn & Suites
$37

455 Wake Avenue • 760.352.6620
50 Units, no pets. Laundry facility. Rooms come with phones, A/C and cable TV. AAA discount available ($2.00). Credit cards: AE, MC, V.

EL MONTE
Motel 6
$38-50
3429 Peck Road • 626.448.6660
68 Units, pets OK. Pool. Laundry facility. Rooms come with A/C, phones and cable TV. Wheelchair accessible. Credit cards: AE, CB, DC, DS, MC, V.

ESCONDIDO
Motel 6
$40-50
900 N. Quince Street • 760.745.9252
131 Units, pets OK. Pool. Laundry facility. Data ports. Rooms come with A/C, phones and cable TV. Wheelchair accessible. Credit cards: AE, CB, DC, DS, MC, V.

Palms Inn
$42-44
2650 S. Escondido Blvd. • 760.743.9733
44 Units, pets OK. Continental breakfast. Playground. Spa. Laundry facility. Rooms come with A/C, phones and cable TV. Senior discount. Wheelchair accessible. Credit cards: AE, DS, MC, V.

Palm Tree Lodge
$49 (59)*
425 W. Mission at Centre City Pkwy
760.745.7613
38 Units, pets OK ($20 dep. req.). Pool. Rooms come with cable TV. AAA discount. Credit cards: AE, DS, MC, V.
*Higher rate effective weekends.

EUREKA
Eureka Town House Motel
$38-55
933 4th Street • 707.443.4536 or 800.445.6888
20 Units, pets OK ($5). Laundry facility. Rooms come with phones and cable TV. No A/C in rooms. Some rooms have refrigerators and microwaves. AAA/Senior discounts available. Credit cards: AE, CB, DC, DS, MC, V.

Motel 6
$40-50
1934 Broadway • 707.445.9631
98 Units, pets OK. Data ports. Rooms come with A/C, phones and cable TV. Wheelchair accessible. Credit cards: AE, CB, DC, DS, MC, V.

Sunrise Inn & Suites
$35-49
129 4th Street • 707.443.9751 or 800.404.9751
25 Units, pets OK ($4). Rooms come with phones and cable TV. No A/C. Some rooms have jacuzzis. Credit cards: AE, CB, DC, DS, JCB, MC, V.

FAIRFIELD
Motel 6
$47-48 (55-58)*
1473 Holiday Lane • 707.425.4565
89 Units, pets OK. Data ports. Rooms come with A/C, phones and cable TV. Wheelchair accessible. Credit cards: AE, CB, DC, DS, MC, V.
*Higher rates effective weekends.

FONTANA
Motel 6
$40-50
10195 Sierra Avenue • 909.823.8686
101 Units, pets OK. Pool. Laundry facility. Rooms come with A/C, phones and cable TV. Wheelchair accessible. Credit cards: AE, CB, DC, DS, MC, V.

FORTUNA
Travel Inn
$45
275 12th Street • 707.725.6993
25 Units, pets OK. Rooms come with phones and cable TV. No A/C in rooms. Major credit cards.

FREMONT
Motel 6—North
$46-50 (56)*
34047 Fremont Blvd., I-880, Fremont/ Alvarado Exit • 510.793.4848
211 Units, pets OK. Pool. Laundry facility. Rooms come with A/C, phones and cable TV. Wheelchair accessible. Credit cards: AE, CB, DC, DS, MC, V.
*Higher rate effective weekends.

Motel 6—South
$46-50 (56)*
46101 Research Avenue, From I-680, Mission Springs Exit • 510.490.4528
159 Units, pets OK. Pool. Laundry facility.

2 Rooms come with A/C, phones and cable TV. Wheelchair accessible. Credit cards: AE, CB, DC, DS, MC, V.
*Higher rate effective weekends.

FRESNO
Days Inn
$45-55
4061 N. Blackstone • 559.222.5641
111 Units, no pets. Continental breakfast. Pool. Laundry facility. Rooms come with phones and cable TV. Wheelchair accessible. AAA/Senior discount. Credit cards: AE, CB, DC, DS, MC, V.

Motel 6
$35-44
4080 N. Blackstone • 559.222.2431
140 Units, pets OK. Restaurant on premises. Pool. Data ports. Rooms come with A/C, phones and cable TV. Wheelchair accessible. Credit cards: AE, CB, DC, DS, MC, V.

Motel 6
$35-37
1240 Crystal Avenue • 559.237.0855
98 Units, pets OK. Pool. Data ports. Rooms come with A/C, phones and cable TV. Wheelchair accessible. Credit cards: AE, CB, DC, DS, MC, V.

Super 8 Motel—Parkway
$43
1087 N. Parkway Dr.
Hwy 99, Exit Olive Ave. • 559.268.0741
48 Units, pets OK ($5). Continental breakfast. Pool. Rooms come with phones and cable TV. Some rooms have microwaves and refrigerators. AAA discount. Major credit cards.

GARDEN GROVE
Guest House International Inn
$44
7912 Garden Grove Blvd. • 714.894.7568
99 Units, no pets. Heated pool and saunas. Rooms come with phones and cable TV. Some rooms have refrigerators. AAA discount. Credit cards: AE, CB, DC, DS, JCB, MC, V.

GILROY
Motel 6
$50 (56-66)*
6110 Monterey Hwy. • 408.842.6061
127 Units, pets OK. Restaurant on premises. Pool. Laundry facility. Data ports. Rooms come with A/C, phones and cable TV. Wheelchair accessible. Credit cards: AE, CB, DC, DS, MC, V.
*Higher rates effective weekends and summers.

GRASS VALLEY
Stagecoach Motel
$39-60
405 S. Auburn Street • 530.272.3701
16 Units, no pets. Rooms come with phones and cable TV. Senior discount. Credit cards: AE, DS, MC, V.

HACIENDA HEIGHTS
Motel 6
$38-48
1154 S. Seventh Ave. • 626.968.9462
154 Units, pets OK. Restaurant on premises. Pool. Laundry facility. Rooms come with A/C, phones and cable TV. Wheelchair accessible. Credit cards: AE, CB, DC, DS, MC, V.

HAYWARD
Motel 6
$45 (56)*
30155 Industrial Pkwy SW • 510.489.8333
180 Units, pets OK. Restaurant on premises. Rooms come with A/C, phones and cable TV. Wheelchair accessible. Credit cards: AE, CB, DC, DS, MC, V.
*Higher rate effective during summer weekends.

Phoenix Lodge
$50*
500 West "A" Street • 510.786.0417
70 Units, no pets. Rooms come with phones and cable TV. AAA discount. Credit cards: AE, MC, V.
*AAA discounted rate.

HEMET
Hemet Inn
$46*
800 W. Florida Avenue • 909.929.6366
65 Units, pets OK ($5 dep. req.). Continental breakfast. Heated pool. Meeting rooms. Jacuzzi. Rooms come with A/C, phones, refrigerators and cable TV. Some rooms have microwaves. Major credit cards.
*AAA discounted rate.

Motel 6
$43-50
3885 W. Florida Avenue • 909.929.8900
99 Units, pets OK. Restaurant on premises. Pool. Laundry facility. Rooms come with A/C, phones and cable TV. Wheelchair accessible. Credit cards: AE, CB, DC, DS, MC, V.

Super 8 Motel
$44
3510 W. Florida Avenue • 909.658.2281
68 Units, pets OK. Heated pool, meeting rooms and jacuzzi. Rooms come with refrigerators and cable TV. Some rooms have microwaves. AAA discount. Credit cards: AE, CB, DC, DS, JCB, MC, V.

HIGHLAND
Super 8 Motel
$46-56
26667 E. Highland Ave. • 909.864.0100
39 Units, pets OK. Pool. Rooms come with phones and color TV. Some rooms have refrigerators. AAA discount. Major credit cards.

HOLLYWOOD — *see Los Angeles*

INDIO
Motel 6
$40-48
82195 Indio Blvd. • 760.342.6311
138 Units, pets OK. Pool. Laundry facility. Rooms come with A/C, phones and cable TV. Wheelchair accessible. Credit cards: AE, CB, DC, DS, MC, V.

Palm Tree Inn
$42
84115 Indio Blvd. • 760.342.4747
70 Units, pets OK. Pool. Laundry facility. Rooms come with A/C, phones and cable TV. Major credit cards.

INGLEWOOD/LAX — *see also Los Angeles*

Econo Lodge LAX
$50-55
4123 W. Century Blvd. • 310.672.7285
41 Units, no pets. Continental breakfast. Rooms come with phones and cable TV. AAA discount. Major credit cards.

Tourist Lodge
$50*
3649 W. Imperial Hwy. • 310.677.0112
40 Units, no pets. Continental breakfast. Rooms come with phones and cable TV. Major credit cards.
*AAA discounted rate.

JACKSON
Amador Motel
$40-57
12408 Kennedy Flat Rd. • 209.223.0970
10 Units, pets OK. Pool. Picnic area. Rooms come with phones and cable TV. Some rooms have refrigerators and microwaves. Major credit cards.

JAMESTOWN
Jamestown Railtown Motel
$40-60
10301 Willow Street • 209.984.3332
70 Units, pets OK ($5). Pool. Rooms come with phones and cable TV. Some rooms have refrigerators and microwaves. AAA/Senior discount. Major credit cards.

KETTLEMAN CITY
Super 8 Motel
$50*
33415 Powers Drive • 559.386.9530
60 Units, pets OK ($40 dep. req.). Pool. Rooms come with phones and cable TV. Major credit cards.
*AAA discounted rate.

KING CITY
Motel 6
$38-44
3 Broadway Circle • 831.385.5000
100 Units, pets OK. Pool. Laundry facility. Data ports. Rooms come with A/C, phones and cable TV. Wheelchair accessible. Credit cards: AE, CB, DC, DS, MC, V.

LAKE TAHOE — *see South Lake Tahoe*

LAKEPORT
Clear Lake Inn
$45
1010 N. Main Street • 707.263.3551
40 Units, no pets. Seasonal pool. Rooms come with phones and cable TV. AAA discount. Credit cards: AE, DS, MC, V.

LA MESA
Motel 6
$44-52
7621 Alvarado Road • 619.464.7151
51 Units, pets OK. Data ports. Rooms come

with A/C, phones and cable TV. Wheelchair accessible. Credit cards: AE, CB, DC, DS, MC, V.

LANCASTER
Motel 6
$37-42
43540 N. 17th Street W. • 661.948.0435
72 Units, pets OK. Pool. Data ports. Rooms come with A/C, phones and cable TV. Wheelchair accessible. Credit cards: AE, CB, DC, DS, MC, V.

LEMON GROVE
Value Inn
$45
7458 Broadway • 619.462.7022
39 Units, no pets. Laundry facility. Rooms come with phones, A/C and cable TV. Credit cards: AE, MC, V.

LIVERMORE
Motel 6
$50 (56)*
4673 Lassen Road, I-580, Springtown Blvd. Exit • 925.443.5300
102 Units, pets OK. Pool. Rooms come with A/C, phones and cable TV. Wheelchair accessible. Credit cards: AE, CB, DC, DS, MC, V.
*Higher rate effective summer weekends.

LOMPOC
Motel 6
$36
1521 N. "H" Street • 805.735.7631
134 Units, pets OK. Pool. Laundry facility. Data ports. Rooms come with A/C, phones and cable TV. Wheelchair accessible. Credit cards: AE, CB, DC, DS, MC, V.

Tally Ho Motor Inn
$50
1020 E. Ocean Avenue • 805.735.6444
53 Units, pets OK ($10). Continental breakfast. Sauna and indoor jacuzzi. Laundry facility. Rooms come with phones and cable TV. Some rooms have microwaves and refrigerators. AAA discount. Credit cards: AE, CB, DC, DS, MC, V.

LONG BEACH
Traveler Advisory: If your travels take you to Long Beach, accommodations will likely run you more than $50/night. Below are listed a few less expensive recommendations:

Days Inn—City Center ($60-75*)
1500 E. Pacific Coast Hwy.
562.591.0088

Inn of Long Beach ($65*)
185 Atlantic Avenue
(I-710, Broadway Exit)
562.435.3791

Motel 6 ($54-68)
5665 E. 7th Street
562.597.1311

Travelodge Convention Center
($49-99)
80 Atlantic Avenue
(I-710, Broadway Exit)
562.435.2471

***Additional AAA discount.**

LOS ALTOS HILLS
Hostelling International
$15
26870 Moody Road • 415.949.8648
35 Beds, Hours: 7:30-9:30 am & 4:30-9:30 pm (no curfew)
Facilities: heated cabins, equipment storage area, information desk, kitchen, linen rental, on-site parking. Private rooms available. Closed June through August. Reservations recommended for weekends. Credit cards.

LOS ANGELES — *see also Arcadia, Azusa, Baldwin Park, Bellflower, El Monte, Hacienda Heights, Norwalk, Pasadena, Pomona, Rosemead, Rowland Heights, San Dimas, Santa Fe Springs, Sun Valley, Sylmar, Van Nuys, Westminster and Whittier*

Traveler Advisory: If you are planning to spend the night in parts of Los Angeles, you will need to bring a bit more than $50 for your stay. With the exception of youth hostels, you would be very fortunate to find accommodations in Los Angeles for less than $50/night. Here are a few in-town recommendations to suit your budget:

Beverly Laurel Motor Hotel
($80-90*)
8018 Beverly Blvd.
323.651.2441

Days Inn ($55-75*)
457 S. Mariposa Avenue

213.380.6910
Dunes Motor Hotel ($67-96*)
4300 Wilshire Blvd.
323.938.3616

Econo Lodge ($49-59)
3400 W. 3rd Street
213.385.0061

Super 8 Motel ($55-67)
1341 Sunset Blvd.
213.250.2233

Travelodge — L.A. West ($69-109)
10740 Santa Monica Blvd.
310.474.4576

Hollywood
Dunes Motel ($67-96*)
5625 Sunset Blvd.
323.467.5171

Econo Lodge ($59-66)
777 N. Vine Street
323.463-5671

Travelodge ($70-80*)
7051 Sunset Blvd.
323.462.0905

Vagabond Inn ($69-89*)
1133 N. Vine Street
323.466.7501

Super 8 Motel ($49-79*)
4238 W. Century Blvd.
310.672.0740

Nearby Los Angeles Airport (Inglewood):
Days Inn ($59-89*)
901 W. Manchester Blvd.
310.649.0800

Howard Johnson Hotel Int'l at LAX ($65-95)
8620 Airport Blvd.
310.645.7700

***Additional AAA discounts available.**

LOS BANOS
Regency Inn
$47-50
349 W. Pacheco Blvd. • 209.826.3871
38 Units, pets OK ($3 and $20 dep. req.). Pool. Rooms come with phones and cable TV. AAA discount. Credit cards: AE, CB, DC, DS, MC, V.

LOST HILLS
Days Inn
$35-50
14684 Aloma Street • 661.797.2021
76 Units, pets OK. Pool. Laundry facility. Rooms come with phones and cable TV. Wheelchair accessible. Senior discount. Major credit cards.

Motel 6
$33-34
14685 Warren Street • 661.797.2346
105 Units, pets OK. Pool. Laundry facility. Data ports. Rooms come with phones and cable TV. Wheelchair accessible. Credit cards: AE, CB, DC, DS, MC, V.

MADERA
Days Inn
$50
25327 Avenue 16 • 559.674.8817
49 Units, pets OK. Continental breakfast. Pool. Laundry facility. Rooms come with phones and cable TV. Wheelchair accessible. Major credit cards.

Liberty Inn
$45-55
22683 Avenue 18+ • 559.675.8697
40 Units, no pets. Jacuzzi, sauna and game room. Laundry facility. Rooms come with phones and cable TV. AAA discount. Major credit cards.

MANTECA
Manteca Inn
$30-50
150 Northwoods Ave. • 209.239.1291
59 Units, no pets. Continental breakfast. Pool. Rooms come with phones and cable TV. Major credit cards.

MARINA
Motel 6
$42-46 (60)*
100 Reservation Road • 831.384.1000
126 Units, pets OK. Restaurant on premises. Laundry facility. Rooms come with A/C, phones and cable TV. Wheelchair accessible. Credit cards: AE, CB, DC, DS, MC, V. *Higher rate effective during summer months.

MARIPOSA
Miners Inn
$45-59
5181 Hwy. 49N • 209.742.7777
78 Units, pets OK ($5). Restaurant on premises. Pool. Jacuzzi. Rooms come with phones and cable TV. AAA/Senior discount. Credit cards: AE, DS, MC, V.

MARYSVILLE
Super 8 Motel
$45
1078 N. Beale Road • 530.742.8238
40 Units, no pets. Continental breakfast. Pool. Copy machine. Refrigerators available. Rooms come with phones and cable TV. Wheelchair accessible. AAA/Senior discount. Credit cards: AE, CB, DC, DS, MC, V.

Travelodge
$45-55
721 10th Street • 530.742.8586
43 Units, pets OK ($5). Continental breakfast. Pool. Rooms come with phones and cable TV. AAA discount. Major credit cards.

MERCED
Motel 6—North
$38-42
1410 "V" Street • 209.384.2181
77 Units, pets OK. Pool. Data ports. Rooms come with A/C, phones and cable TV. Wheelchair accessible. Credit cards: AE, CB, DC, DS, MC, V.

Super 8 Motel
$45-50*
1983 E. Childs Avenue, SR 99, Childs Avenue Exit • 209.384.1303
80 Units, pets OK ($5). Pool. Rooms come with phones, A/C and cable TV. Wheelchair accessible. Major credit cards.
*AAA discounted rates.

MODESTO
Chalet Motel
$50
115 Downey Avenue • 209.529.4370
40 Units, pets OK ($20 dep. req.). Continental breakfast. Pool. Rooms come with A/C, phones and cable TV. Some rooms have radios, jacuzzis and refrigerators. AAA discount. Major credit cards.

Econo Lodge
$49
500 Kansas Avenue • 209.578.5400
70 Units, no pets. Restaurant on premises. Pool. Laundry facility. Rooms come with phones and cable TV. Some rooms have refrigerators. AAA/Senior discount. Credit cards: AE, DC, DS, MC, V.

Motel 6—North
$40-44 (52)*
1920 W. Orangeburg Ave. • 209.522.7271
100 Units, pets OK. Pool. Rooms come with A/C, phones and cable TV. Wheelchair accessible. Credit cards: AE, CB, DC, DS, MC, V.
*Higher rate effective summer weekends.

MOJAVE
Econo Lodge
$35-49
2145 Hwy 58 • 661.824.2463
33 Units, pets OK. Continental breakfast. Pool. Laundry facility. Rooms come with phones and cable TV. Wheelchair accessible. AAA/Senior discount. Credit cards: AE, CB, DC, DS, MC, V.

Motel 6
$36-37
16958 Hwy 58 • 661.824.4571
121 Units, pets OK. Pool. Laundry facility. Data ports. Rooms come with A/C, phones and cable TV. Wheelchair accessible. Credit cards: AE, CB, DC, DS, MC, V.

MONTEREY — *see also Marina and Seaside*

Bayside Inn
$40-45
2055 N. Fremont St. • 831.372.8071
20 Units, pets OK. Continental breakfast. Rooms come with phones and cable TV. Major credit cards.

MORRO BAY
Best Value Inn
$45 (50-90)*
220 Beach Street • 805.772.3333
32 Units, pets OK ($6). Rooms come with phones and cable TV. No A/C. Some rooms have refrigerators. Credit cards: AE, DC, DS, MC, V.
*Higher rates effective during weekends.

Motel 6
$36-44 (56-66)*
298 Atascadero Road • 805.772.5641
70 Units, pets OK. Pool. Laundry facility. Rooms come with phones and cable TV. Wheelchair accessible. Credit cards: AE, CB, DC, DS, MC, V.
*Higher rates effective summer months.

MOUNT SHASTA
Mountain Air Lodge
$42-55
1121 S. Mt. Shasta Blvd. • 530.926.3411
38 Units, pets OK ($5 dep. req.). Continental breakfast. Jacuzzi and recreation room. Rooms come with phones and cable TV. Credit cards: AE, DC, DS, MC, V.

Swiss Holiday Lodge
$30-50
2400 S. Mt. Shasta Blvd.
I-5, McCloud Exit • 530.926.3446
21 Units, pets OK ($5). Continental breakfast. Heated pool. Jacuzzi. Rooms come with phones and cable TV. AAA/Senior discount. Credit cards: AE, DS, MC, V.

NATIONAL CITY
Value Inn
$50
1700 Plaza Blvd. • 619.474.6491
34 Units, no pets. Laundry facility. Rooms come with phones, A/C and cable TV. Credit cards: AE, MC, V.

Value Inn
$45
607 Roosevelt Avenue • 619.474.7502
40 Units, no pets. Laundry facility. Rooms come with phones, A/C and cable TV. Credit cards: AE, MC, V.

NEEDLES
Motel 6
$33-37
1420 "J" Street • 760.326.3399
81 Units, pets OK. Pool and jacuzzi. Laundry facility. Rooms come with phones and cable TV. Wheelchair accessible. Credit cards: AE, CB, DC, DS, MC, V.

Super 8 Motel
$40-50
1102 E. Broadway • 760.326.4501
30 Units, pets OK ($20 dep. req.). Continental breakfast. Laundry facility. Rooms come with phones and cable TV. Wheelchair accessible. Senior discount. Credit cards: AE, CB, DC, DS, MC, V.

Travelers Inn
$30-55
1195 3rd Street Hill • 760.326.4900
117 Units, no pets. Heated pool and jacuzzi. Laundry facility. Rooms come with phones and cable TV. Some rooms have refrigerators. AAA/Senior discount. Credit cards: AE, CB, DC, DS, MC, V.

NEWARK
Motel 6
$46-50 (56)*
5600 Cedar Court • 510.791.5900
217 Units, pets OK. Pool and jacuzzi. Laundry facility. Rooms come with phones and cable TV. Wheelchair accessible. Credit cards: AE, CB, DC, DS, MC, V.
*Higher rate effective summer weekends.

NEWBURY PARK
Best Value Inn
$44-45
2850 Camino Dos Rios • 805.499.2414
60 Units, pets OK. Pool. Rooms come with phones and cable TV. Wheelchair accessible. Major credit cards.

Premier Inn
$44
2434 W. Hillcrest Drive • 805.499.0755
130 Units, no pets. Laundry facility. Rooms come with phones, A/C and cable TV. Credit cards: AE, MC, V.

NORTH HIGHLANDS
Motel 6
$44-48 (56)*
4600 Watt Avenue, I-80, Watt Avenue Exit
916.973.8637
63 Units, pets OK. Rooms come with phones and cable TV. Wheelchair accessible. Credit cards: AE, CB, DC, DS, MC, V.
*Higher rate effective summer weekends.

NORWALK
Motel 6
$44-50
10646 E. Rosecrans Ave.
I-605, Rosecrans Exit • 562.864.2567
55 Units, pets OK. Restaurant on premises. Rooms come with A/C, phones and cable TV. Wheelchair accessible. Credit cards: AE, CB, DC, DS, MC, V.

OAKLAND/EAST BAY — *see also Hayward*
Travel Adcisory: Like the rest of the Bay Area, accommodations will be hard to find at less than $50/night in and around Oakland. Here are a few more affordable recommendations if you are headed in that direction:

Days Inn ($59-89)
8350 Edes Avenue
I-880, Hegenberger Road Exit
562.568.1880

Howard Johnson Express Inn ($69-89)
423 7th Street
I-880, Broadway/Alameda Exit
510.451.6316

Motel 6 ($60)
8480 Edes Avenue
I-880, Hegenberger Road Exit
510.638.1180

Ramada Inn ($70)
8471 Enterprise Way
I-880, Hegenberger Road Exit
510.562.4888

Berkeley
Golden Bear Inn ($70-90)
1620 San Pablo Avenue
I-80, Gilman Street Exit
510.525.6770

Ramada Inn ($65-80)
920 University Avenue
I-80, University Avenue Exit
510.849.1121

OCEANSIDE
Motel 6
$44-50 (56)*
3708 Plaza Drive • 760.941.1011
136 Units, pets OK. Pool. Rooms come with A/C, phones and cable TV. Wheelchair accessible. Credit cards: AE, CB, DC, DS, MC, V.
*Higher rate effective summer weekends.

ONTARIO
American Inn
$45
755 N. Euclid Avenue • 909.984.1775
33 Units, pets OK. Pool and jacuzzi. Rooms come with cable TV. Some rooms have, for a fee, refrigerators and microwaves. Credit cards: AE, DC, DS, MC, V.

Best Ontario Inn
$49
1045 W. Mission Blvd. • 909.391.6668
42 Units, no pets. Pool and jacuzzi. Laundry facility. Rooms come with cable TV. Some rooms have refrigerators and, for a fee, microwaves and jacuzzis. Senior discount. Credit cards: AE, CB, DC, DS, MC, V.

Motel 6
$40-48
1560 E. Fourth Street • 909.984.2424
69 Units, pets OK. Pool. Rooms come with A/C, phones and cable TV. Wheelchair accessible. Credit cards: AE, CB, DC, DS, MC, V.

ORANGE
Motel 6
$42-54
2920 W. Chapman Ave. • 714.634.2441
153 Units, pets OK. Restaurant on premises. Pool. Laundry facility. Rooms come with phones and cable TV. Wheelchair accessible. Credit cards: AE, CB, DC, DS, MC, V.

ORLAND
Amber Light Inn Motel
$40-45
828 Newville Road • 530.865.7655
40 Units, pets OK. Pool and jacuzzi. Rooms come with phones and cable TV. AAA/Senior discount. Credit cards: AE, DS, MC, V.

Orland Inn
$45-50
1052 South Street • 530.865.7632
40 Units, pets OK. Pool. Rooms come with phones and cable TV. Wheelchair accessible. AAA/Senior discount. Credit cards: AE, DS, MC, V.

OROVILLE
Motel 6
$36-38
505 Montgomery Street • 530.532.9400
102 Units, pets OK. Restaurant on premises. Pool. Laundry facility. Data ports. Rooms come with A/C, phones and cable TV. Wheelchair accessible. Credit cards: AE, CB, DC, DS, MC, V.

OXNARD
Vagabond Inn
$42-52*
1245 N. Oxnard Blvd. • 805.983.0251
69 Units, pets OK ($5). Continental

breakfast. Heated pool. Data ports. Rooms come with phones and cable TV. Senior discount. Major credit cards.
*AAA discounted rates.

PALMDALE
Motel 6
$36-40
407 W. Palmdale Blvd. • 661.272.0660
103 Units, pets OK. Pool. Laundry facility. Data ports. Rooms come with A/C, phones and cable TV. Wheelchair accessible. Credit cards: AE, CB, DC, DS, MC, V.

Super 8 Motel
$40
200 W. Palmdale Blvd. • 661.273.8000
94 Units, no pets. Continental breakfast. Heated pool and jacuzzi. Rooms come with phones and cable TV. Some rooms have refrigerators. Senior discount. Credit cards: AE, CB, DC, DS, MC, V.

PALM DESERT
Motel 6
$44-50 (52-60)*
78100 Varner Road • 760.345.0550
82 Units, pets OK. Pool. Rooms come with A/C, phones and cable TV. Wheelchair accessible. Credit cards: AE, CB, DC, DS, MC, V.
*Higher rate effective winter months.

PALM SPRINGS — *see also Desert Hot Springs, Indio, Palm Desert, Rancho Mirage and Thousand Palms*

Motel 6—Downtown
$38-50 (55)*
660 S. Palm Canyon Dr. • 760.327.4200
149 Units, pets OK. Pool. Laundry facility. Rooms come with A/C, phones and cable TV. Wheelchair accessible. Credit cards: AE, CB, DC, DS, MC, V.
*Higher rate effective winter weekends.

Motel 6—East
$40-46
595 E. Palm Canyon Dr. • 760.325.6129
125 Units, pets OK. Pool. Laundry facility. Rooms come with A/C, phones and cable TV. Wheelchair accessible. Credit cards: AE, CB, DC, DS, MC, V.

Motel 6—North
$42-48
63950 20th Avenue • 760.251.1425
96 Units, pets OK. Restaurant on premises. Pool. Laundry facility. Rooms come with A/C, phones and cable TV. Wheelchair accessible. Credit cards: AE, CB, DC, DS, MC, V.

PALO ALTO — *see San Jose*

PASADENA
Travelodge
$50-55*
2131 E. Colorado Blvd. • 626.796.3121
53 Units, no pets. Laundry facility. Jacuzzi. Rooms come with phones, microwaves, refrigerators and cable TV. AAA discount. Major credit cards.
*AAA discounted rates.

PASO ROBLES
Melody Ranch Motel
$45-54*
939 Spring Street • 805.238.3911
19 Units, no pets. Pool. Rooms come with A/C and TV. Wheelchair accessible. AAA discount. Major credit cards.
*Rates as high as $60/night.

Motel 6
$40-50
1134 Black Oak Drive • 805.239.9090
121 Units, pets OK. Laundry facility. Pool. Data ports. Rooms come with A/C, phones and cable TV. Wheelchair accessible. Credit cards: AE, CB, DC, DS, MC, V.

PETALUMA
Motel 6
$40-52
1368 N. McDowell Blvd. • 707.765.0333
121 Units, pets OK. Pool. Data ports. Rooms come with A/C, phones and cable TV. Wheelchair accessible. Credit cards: AE, CB, DC, DS, MC, V.

PISMO BEACH
Motel 6
$36-52
860 4th Street • 805.773.2665
136 Units, pets OK. Pool. Laundry facility. Rooms come with A/C, phones and cable TV. Wheelchair accessible. Credit cards: AE, CB, DC, DS, MC, V.

Ocean Palms Motel
$39-45*
390 Ocean View • 805.773.4669
22 Units, no pets. Heated pool. Rooms

come with phones and cable TV. No A/C. Some rooms have refrigerators. Credit cards: AE, DS, MC, V. Senior discount.
*Higher rates effective during weekends.

PITTSBURG
Motel 6
$45-50 (56)*
2101 Loveridge Road • 925.427.1600
176 Units, pets OK. Laundry facility. Pool. Data ports. Rooms come with A/C, phones and cable TV. Wheelchair accessible. Credit cards: AE, CB, DC, DS, MC, V.
*Higher rate effective summer weekends.

PLACERVILLE
Mother Lode Motel
$42-49*
1940 Broadway • 530.622.0895
21 Units, pets OK ($5). Pool. Rooms come with phones and cable TV. Some rooms have refrigerators. Senior discount. Major credit cards.
*AAA discounted rates.

National 9 Inn
$45-55
1500 Broadway • 530.622.3884
24 Units, no pets. Continental breakfast. Rooms come with phones and cable TV. AAA discount. Major credit cards.

POMONA
Motel 6
$40-50
1470 S. Garey Avenue • 909.591.1871
120 Units, pets OK. Pool. Laundry facility. Rooms come with A/C, phones and cable TV. Wheelchair accessible. Credit cards: AE, CB, DC, DS, MC, V.

PORTERVILLE
Motel 6
$34-40
935 W. Morton Avenue • 559.781.7600
107 Units, pets OK. Pool. Laundry facility. Data ports. Rooms come with A/C, phones and cable TV. Wheelchair accessible. Credit cards: AE, CB, DC, DS, MC, V.

RANCHO CORDOVA
Motel 6
$44-48 (54)*
10694 Olson Drive, From US 50, Zinfandel Drive Exit • 916.635.8784
68 Units, pets OK. Data ports. Rooms come with A/C, phones and cable TV. Wheelchair accessible. Credit cards: AE, CB, DC, DS, MC, V.
*Higher rate effective summer weekends.

RANCHO MIRAGE
Motel 6
$40-46 (56)*
69-570 Hwy 111 • 760.324.8475
104 Units, pets OK. Restaurant on premises. Pool. Rooms come with A/C, phones and cable TV. Wheelchair accessible. Credit cards: AE, CB, DC, DS, MC, V.
*Higher rate effective winter weekends.

RED BLUFF
Best Value Inn & Suites
$39-52
30 Gilmore Road • 530.529.2028
60 Units, pets OK ($20 dep. req.). Continental breakfast. Pool. Laundry facility. Rooms come with phones and cable TV. Some rooms have microwaves and refrigerators. AAA/Senior discount. Credit cards: AE, CB, DC, DS, MC, V.

Motel 6
$36-42
20 Williams Avenue • 530.527.9200
61 Units, pets OK. Pool. Laundry facility. Data ports. Rooms come with A/C, phones and cable TV. Wheelchair accessible. Credit cards: AE, CB, DC, DS, MC, V.

Travelodge
$43-50
38 Antelope Blvd. • 530.527.6020
41 Units, pets OK. Continental breakfast. Pool. Data ports. Rooms come with phones and cable TV. AAA/Senior discount. Credit cards: AE, CB, DC, DS, MC, V.

REDDING
Economy Inn
$40
525 N. Market Street • 530.246.9803
28 Units, pets OK. Pool. Rooms come with A/C, phones and cable TV. Some rooms have kitchenettes. Major credit cards.

Motel 6—North
$40-52
1250 Twin View Blvd. • 530.246.4470
97 Units, pets OK. Pool. Laundry facility. Data ports. Rooms come with A/C, phones and cable TV. Wheelchair accessible. Credit cards: AE, CB, DC, DS, MC, V.

Motel 6—South
$40-52
2385 Bechelli Lane • 530.221.0562
105 Units, pets OK. Pool. Laundry facility. Rooms come with A/C, phones and cable TV. Wheelchair accessible. Credit cards: AE, CB, DC, DS, MC, V.

REDLANDS
Good Nite Inn
$40-50
1675 Industrial Pk. Ave. • 909.793.3723
100 Units, pets OK. Heated pool. Rooms come with phones and cable TV. Credit cards: AE, DC, DS, MC, V.

Super 8 Motel
$50
1160 Arizona Street • 909.335.1612
80 Units, no pets. Laundry facility. Rooms come with phones and cable TV. Wheelchair accessible. AAA/Senior discount. Credit cards: AE, CB, DC, DS, MC, V.

RIDGECREST
Econo Lodge
$50
201 Inyokern Road • 760.446.2551
54 Units, pets OK. Continental breakfast. Pool. Rooms come with phones, refrigerators and cable TV. Some rooms have microwaves. Major credit cards.

Motel 6
$30-37
535 S. China Lake Blvd. • 760.375.6866
76 Units, pets OK. Pool. Laundry facility. Data ports. Rooms come with A/C, phones and cable TV. Wheelchair accessible. Credit cards: AE, CB, DC, DS, MC, V.

RIVERSIDE
Econo Lodge
$39-50
10705 Magnolia Avenue • 909.351.2424
52 Units, no pets. Continental breakfast. Pool. Rooms come with refrigerators and cable TV. Wheelchair accessible. Credit cards: AE, CB, DI, DS, MC, V.

Motel 6—East
$40-46
1260 University Avenue • 909.784.2131
60 Units, pets OK. Rooms come with A/C, phones and cable TV. Wheelchair accessible. Credit cards: AE, CB, DC, DS, MC, V.

Motel 6—South
$38-46
3663 La Sierra Avenue • 909.351.0764
121 Units, pets OK. Pool. Laundry facility. Rooms come with A/C, phones and cable TV. Wheelchair accessible. Credit cards: AE, CB, DC, DS, MC, V.

Super 8 Motel
$46
1350 University Avenue • 909.582.1144
82 Units, pets OK. Pool. Laundry facility. Copy machine. Rooms come with phones and cable TV. Senior discount. Credit cards: AE, CB, DC, DS, MC, V.

ROSEMEAD
Motel 6
$40-50 (56)*
1001 S. San Gabriel Blvd. • 626.572.6076
130 Units, pets OK. Restaurant on premises. Pool. Laundry facility. Rooms come with A/C, phones and cable TV. Wheelchair accessible. Credit cards: AE, CB, DC, DS, MC, V.
*Higher rate effective summer weekends.

Motel VIP
$45
2619 S. San Gabriel Blvd. • 626.571.6626
32 Units, no pets. Laundry facility. Rooms come with refrigerators and cable TV. Credit cards: MC, V.

ROWLAND HEIGHTS
Motel 6
$38-48
18970 E. Labin Court • 626.964.5333
125 Units, pets OK. Pool. Laundry facility. Rooms come with A/C, phones and cable TV. Wheelchair accessible. Credit cards: AE, CB, DC, DS, MC, V.

SACRAMENTO — *see also North Highlands and West Sacramento*
Capitol Inn
$49
228 Jibboom Street • 916.443.4811
69 Units, no pets. Pool. Laundry facility. Rooms come with phones and cable TV. Some rooms have refrigerators. AAA/Senior discount. Credit cards: AE, DC, DS, MC, V.

Morada Inn
$45
9646 Micron Way, US 50/
Bradshaw Rd. Exit • 916.361.3131

93 Units, no pets. Pool. Laundry facility. Rooms come with phones and cable TV. Wheelchair accessible. Senior discount. Credit cards: AE, CB, DC, DS, MC, V.

Motel 6—Downtown
$44-48 (54)*
1415 30th St., I 80/Hwy 99, "N" St. Exit
916.457.0777
94 Units, pets OK. Pool. Laundry facility. Data ports. Rooms come with A/C, phones and cable TV. Wheelchair accessible. Credit cards: AE, CB, DC, DS, MC, V.
*Higher rate effective summer weekends.

Motel 6—North
$44-48 (54)*
5110 Interstate Ave.
I-80, Madison Ave. Exit • 916.331.8100
82 Units, pets OK. Pool. Laundry facility. Rooms come with A/C, phones and cable TV. Wheelchair accessible. Credit cards: AE, CB, DC, DS, MC, V.
*Higher rate effective summer weekends.

Motel 6—Old Sacramento North
$44-48 (54)*
227 Jibboom Street • 916.441.0733
105 Units, pets OK. Rooms come with A/C, phones and cable TV. Wheelchair accessible. Credit cards: AE, CB, DC, DS, MC, V.
*Higher rate effective summer weekends.

Motel 6—Southwest
$44-48 (54)*
7780 Stockton Blvd. • 916.689.9141
59 Units, pets OK. Data ports. Rooms come with A/C, phones and cable TV. Wheelchair accessible. Credit cards: AE, CB, DC, DS, MC, V.
*Higher rate effective summer weekends.

Motel 6—South
$44-48 (54)*
7407 Elsie Avenue • 916.689.6555
118 Units, pets OK. Laundry facility. Pool. Data ports. Rooms come with A/C, phones and cable TV. Wheelchair accessible. Credit cards: AE, CB, DC, DS, MC, V.
*Higher rate effective summer weekends.

SALINAS
Motel 6—South
$40-52
1257 De La Torre Blvd. • 831.757.3077
128 Units, pets OK. Laundry facility. Pool. Data ports. Rooms come with A/C, phones and cable TV. Wheelchair accessible. Credit cards: AE, CB, DC, DS, MC, V.

Motel 6—North
$40-52
140 Kern Street • 831.753.1711
121 Units, pets OK. Pool. Rooms come with A/C, phones and cable TV. Wheelchair accessible. Credit cards: AE, CB, DC, DS, MC, V.

Super 8 Motel
$50*
1030 Fairview Avenue • 831.422.6486
44 Units, no pets. Continental breakfast. Refrigerators available. Rooms come with phones and cable TV. Wheelchair accessible. AAA/Senior discount. Credit cards: AE, CB, DC, DS, MC, V.
*Rates as high as $100/night.

SAN BERNARDINO
Leisure Inn
$42
777 W. 6th Street • 909.889.3561
58 Units, no pets. Continental breakfast. Sauna and jacuzzi. Laundry facility. Refrigerators and microwaves available. Rooms come with phones and cable TV. AAA/Senior discount. Credit cards: AE, CB, DC, DS, MC, V.

Motel 6—North
$38-44
1960 Ostrems Way • 909.887.8191
104 Units, pets OK. Pool. Laundry facility. Rooms come with A/C, phones and cable TV. Wheelchair accessible. Credit cards: AE, CB, DC, DS, MC, V.

Motel 6—South
$40-46
111 Redlands Blvd. • 909.825.6666
120 Units, pets OK. Laundry facility. Pool. Rooms come with A/C, phones and cable TV. Wheelchair accessible. Credit cards: AE, CB, DC, DS, MC, V.

SAN BRUNO — *see San Francisco*

SAN DIEGO — *see also Carlsbad, Chula Vista, El Cajon, La Mesa and San Ysidro*

E-Z 8 Motel—South Bay
$40
1010 Outer Road • 619.575.8808
89 Units, no pets. Laundry facility. Rooms

come with phones, A/C and cable TV. AAA discount. Credit cards: AE, MC, V.

Good Nite Inn—Seaworld Area
$45
3880 Greenwood Street • 619.543.9944
150 Units, pets OK. Laundry facility. Rooms come with phones and cable TV. Some rooms have refrigerators. AAA discount. Credit cards: AE, CB, DC, DS, MC, V.

Hostelling International
$19
521 Market Street • 619.525.1531
150 Beds, Hours: 7 am - midnight
Facilities: laundry facilities, lockers/storage, restaurant, 24-hour access, games room. Private rooms available. Open year-round. Reservations recommended. Credit cards: JCB, MC, V.

Hostelling Int'l—Point Loma
$16
3790 Udall Street • 619.223.4778
61 Beds, Hours: 8-10 a.m. & 4:30-10 p.m. (24-hour access)
Facilities: courtyard with ping pong and pool table, laundry, storage, kitchen, lockers, free parking. Private rooms available. Open year-round. Reservations recommended April through September. Credit cards: JCB, MC, V.

Premier Inn
$39-69
2484 Hotel Circle Place • 619.291.8252
89 Units, no pets. Laundry facility. Jacuzzi. Rooms come with phones, A/C and cable TV. AAA discount. Credit cards: AE, MC, V.

Premier Inn
$41-47
3333 Channel Way • 619.223.9500
119 Units, no pets. Laundry facility. Rooms come with phones, A/C and cable TV. AAA discount. Credit cards: AE, MC, V.

SAN DIMAS
Motel 6
$40-50
502 W. Arrow Hwy • 909.592.5631
118 Units, pets OK. Laundry facility. Rooms come with A/C, phones and cable TV. Wheelchair accessible. Credit cards: AE, CB, DC, DS, MC, V.

SAN FERNANDO VALLEY — *see Calabasas, Chatsworth, Sun Valley, Sylmar and Van Nuys*

SAN FRANCISCO
Traveler Advisory: If you are planning to spend the night in San Francisco, you will need to plan on spending a little more than $50/night. With the exception of youth hostels, you would be very fortunate to find accommodations in San Francisco, or in any other part of the Bay Area for that matter, for less than $50/night. Generally, you will find slightly cheaper accommodations in other Bay Area communities. There you will find a number of Motel 6s, Days Inns and Super 8 Motels whose rates range anywhere from $60 to $80 per night (see also **Berkeley, Fremont, Hayward, Oakland, Palo Alto, Santa Clara** and **San Jose**). For in-town travelers, here are a few recommendations to suit your budget:

Beck Motor Lodge ($99-109)
2222 Market Street
415.621.8212

Broadway Manor Inn ($73-101)
2201 Van Ness Avenue
415.776.7900

Days Inn ($79-135)
465 Grove Street
415.864.4040

Lombard Motor Inn ($86-125*)
1475 Lombard Street
415.441.6000

Mission Inn ($70-95*)
5630 Mission Street
415.584.5020

Redwood Inn ($75-90*)
1530 Lombard Street
415.776.3800

Roberts-at-the-Beach Motel ($75-95*)
2828 Sloat Blvd.
415.564.2610

Belmont
Motel 6 ($66-70)
1101 Shoreway Road
650.591.1471

Daly City
Royal Palace Inn ($80-90*)
2929 Geneva Avenue
415.468.4550

San Bruno—SFO Airport
Ritz Inn ($75-85*)
151 El Camino Real
US 101 to 1-380,
El Camino Real Exit
650.589.3553

Knights Inn ($79-159)
411 E. San Bruno Avenue
650.589.7535

San Rafael
San Rafael Inn ($60-85*)
865 Francisco Blvd. E.
415.454.9470

South San Francisco
Motel 6 ($70-95)
111 Mitchell Avenue
650.877.0770

***Additional AAA discount.**

Hostelling International
$22-25
Fort Mason, Building 240
415.771.7277; 415.771.3645 (for reservations only)
162 Beds, Hours: 24 hours
Facilities: equipment storage area, information desk, kitchen, laundry, free linen, lockers/baggage storage, on-site parking, wheelchair accessible. Open year-round. Reservations recommended for groups. Credit cards: MC, V.

Hostelling International
$22-25
312 Mason Street • 415.788.5604
230 Beds, Hours: 24 hours
Facilities: baggage storage area, kitchen, free linen, library, lockers, vending machines. Private rooms available. Open year-round. Reservations recommended June through September. Credit cards: MC, V.

SAN JACINTO
San Jacinto Inn
$45
1385 Ramona Blvd. • 909.654.7133
21 Units, pets OK. Pool. Jacuzzi. Laundry facility. Rooms come with A/C, phones and TV. Some rooms have microwaves and refrigerators. AAA/Senior discount. Major credit cards.

SAN JOSE
Traveler Advisory: Like San Francisco, the South Bay area offers very little in the way of budget accommodations. There are a few relatively inexpensive places, however, to be found in the San Jose area. Listed below are some recommendations which will hopefully help to keep a little money in your pocket:

Days Inn ($80)
4170 Monterey Road
408.224.4122

Motel 6 ($60-66)
2560 Fontaine Road
US 101, Tully Road E. Exit
408.270.3131

Motel 6 ($66-70)
2081 N. First Street
US 101 at First St./Brokaw Exit
408.436.8180

Ramada Limited ($65-95)
455 S. 2nd Street
408.298.3500

Palo Alto
Country Inn Motel ($70-105*)
4345 El Camino Real
650.948.9154

Motel 6 ($70-80)
4301 El Camino Real
650.949.0833

Santa Clara
Mariani's Inn ($99-139)
2500 El Camino Real
408.243.1431

Motel 6 ($60-66)
3208 El Camino Real
408.241.0200

Sunnyvale
Motel 6 ($60-66)
775 N. Mathilda Avenue
408.736.4595

Motel 6 ($60-66)
806 Ahwanee Avenue
408.720.1222

***Additional AAA discount.**

Hostelling International
$10
15808 Sanborn Road • 408.741.0166
39 Beds, Hours: 7-9 am & 5-11 pm
Facilities: equipment storage area, information desk, kitchen, laundry facilities, linen rental, lockers/baggage storage, on-site parking, wheelchair accessible. Private rooms available. Open year-round. Reservations recommended weekends and for groups. Credit cards not accepted.

SAN LUIS OBISPO
Motel 6
$38-48 (54)*
1625 Calle Joaquin • 805.541.6992
117 Units, pets OK. Pool. Data ports. Rooms come with A/C, phones and cable TV. Wheelchair accessible. Credit cards: AE, CB, DC, DS, MC, V.
*Higher rate effective summer weekends.

Motel 6
$38-48 (54)*
1433 Calle Joaquin • 805.549.9595
86 Units, pets OK. Pool. Laundry facility. Data ports. Rooms come with A/C, phones and cable TV. Wheelchair accessible. Credit cards: AE, CB, DC, DS, MC, V.
*Higher rate effective summer weekends.

SAN MIGUEL
Western States Inn
$45*
1099 "K" Street • 805.467.3674
17 Units, no pets. Rooms come with A/C, phones and TV. Some rooms have microwaves and refrigerators. AAA/Senior discount. Major credit cards.
*Rates as high as $89/night.

SAN PEDRO
Hostelling International
$13-15
3601 S. Gaffey Street #613
310.831.8109
42 Beds, Hours: 7-11 am & 4-midnight
Facilities: information desk, kitchen, linen rental, laundry, lockers, free parking, games, cable TV, VCR, barbecue, gardens. Private rooms available. Open year-round. Reservations recommended June through August. Credit cards: JCB, MC, V.

SAN RAFAEL — *see San Francisco*

SAN SIMEON
Motel 6 Premier
$39-51 (51-81)*
9070 Castillo Drive • 805.927.8691
100 Units, pets OK. Heated pool. Laundry facility. Rooms come with A/C, phones and TV. Wheelchair accessible. Major credit cards.
*Higher rates effective mid-June through September.

SANTA ANA
Best Western Civic Center Inn
$39-49
2720 N. Grand Avenue • 714.997.2330
44 Units, no pets. Continental breakfast. Pool. Data ports. Rooms come with A/C, phones and cable TV. AAA/Senior discount. Major credit cards.

Motel 6
$40-50 (54)*
1623 E. First Street • 714.558.0500
79 Units, pets OK. Laundry facility. Rooms come with A/C, phones and cable TV. Wheelchair accessible. Credit cards: AE, CB, DC, DS, MC, V.
*Higher rate effective summer weekends.

SANTA BARBARA — *see Carpinteria*

SANTA CLARA — *see San Jose*

SANTA CRUZ
Hostelling International
$17-19
321 Main Street • 831.423.8304
32 Beds, Hours: 8-10 am & 5-10 pm
Facilities: on-site cyclery, indoor/outdoor lockers, rose/herb garden, fireplace, barbecue, free evening snack, limited parking at additional charge, wheelchair accessible. Private rooms available. Open year-round. Reservations can be made with advance payment only. Credit cards not accepted.

Riverside Inn
$39-45
505 Riverside Avenue • 831.426.2899
25 Units, no pets. Continental breakfast. Copy and fax service. Rooms come with A/C, phones and TV. Kitchenettes available. Credit cards: AE, DS, MC, V.

SANTA FE SPRINGS
Motel 6
$38-48
13412 Excelsior Drive • 562.921.0596
79 Units, pets OK. Laundry facility. Rooms come with A/C, phones and cable TV. Wheelchair accessible. Credit cards: AE, CB, DC, DS, MC, V.

SANTA MARIA
Motel 6
$40-50
2040 N. Preisker Lane • 805.928.8111
126 Units, pets OK. Laundry facility. Pool. Data ports. Rooms come with A/C, phones and cable TV. Wheelchair accessible. Credit cards: AE, CB, DC, DS, MC, V.

SANTA ROSA
Motel 6—North
$45-50 (54-62)*
3145 Cleveland Avenue • 707.525.9010
119 Units, pets OK. Restaurant on premises. Pool. Rooms come with A/C, phones and cable TV. Wheelchair accessible. Major credit cards.
*Higher rates effective summer months.

Motel 6—South
$45-50 (54-62)*
2760 Cleveland Avenue • 707.546.1500
100 Units, pets OK. Restaurant on premises. Pool. Laundry facility. Rooms come with A/C, phones and cable TV. Wheelchair accessible. Credit cards: AE, CB, DC, DS, MC, V.
*Higher rates effective summer months.

SAN YSIDRO
Motel 6
$36-52
160 E. Calle Primera • 619.690.6663
103 Units, pets OK. Pool. Laundry facility. Data ports. Rooms come with A/C, phones and cable TV. Wheelchair accessible. Credit cards: AE, CB, DC, DS, MC, V.

SAUSALITO
Hostelling International
$15-17
Fort Barry, Building 941 • 415.331.2777
103 Beds, Hours: 7:30 am – 11:30 pm
Facilities: equipment storage area, information desk, kitchen, laundry facilities, linen rental, lockers/baggage storage, on-site parking, wheelchair accessible. Private rooms available. Open year-round. Reservations essential. Credit cards: MC, V.

SEASIDE
Bay Breeze Inn
$45-65
2049 Fremont Blvd. • 831.899.7111
50 Units, pets OK. Continental breakfast. Rooms come with phones and cable TV. No A/C. AAA/Senior discount. Major credit cards.

Thunderbird Motel
$39-50*
1933 Fremont Blvd. • 831.394.6797
33 Units, no pets. Continental breakfast. Small pool. Rooms come with phones and cable TV. No A/C. Some rooms have kitchenettes, microwaves and refrigerators. Senior discount. Major credit cards.
*Rates as high as $139/night.

SOLVANG
Viking Motel
$42*
1506 Mission Drive • 805.688.1337
12 Units, pets OK ($5). Continental breakfast. Rooms come with phones and cable TV. Some rooms have refrigerators. AAA discount. Credit cards: AE, DS, MC, V.
*Rates as high as $140/night.

SONORA
Miners Motel
$36-55
18740 SR 108 • 209.532.7850
18 Units, pets OK ($5). Continental breakfast. Pool. Rooms come with A/C, refrigerators, phones and cable TV. AAA/Senior discount. Major credit cards.

SOUTH LAKE TAHOE
Cedar Inn & Suites
$40-60
890 Stateline Avenue • 530.543.0159
39 Units, no pets. Continental breakfast. Heated pool. Jacuzzi. Rooms come with phones and cable TV. No A/C. AAA/Senior discount. Credit cards: AE, DS, MC, V.

Motel 6
$38-50 (70)*
2375 Lake Tahoe Blvd. • 530.542.1400
143 Units, pets OK. Pool. Data ports. Rooms come with phones and cable TV. Wheelchair accessible. Credit cards: AE, CB, DC, DS, MC, V.
*Higher rate effective summer weekends.

Tahoe Sunset Lodge
$30-50*
1171 Emerald Bay Road • 530.541.2940
15 Units, pets OK ($5). Rooms come with phones and cable TV. Some rooms have A/C. Senior discount. Credit cards: AE, DS, MC, V.
*AAA discounted rates. Higher rates effective weekends.

SPRING VALLEY
Crown Inn & Suites
$49
9603 Campo Road • 619.589.1111
44 Units, pets OK ($5 and $50 dep. req.). Pool. Laundry facility. Rooms come with phones and cable TV. Some rooms have mini bars, microwaves and refrigerators. AAA discount. Credit cards: AE, CB, DC, DS, MC, V.

STANTON
Knights Inn Anaheim-Buena Park
$35-50
10301 Beach Blvd. • 714.826.6060
28 Units, no pets. Continental breakfast. Airport transportation. Rooms come with phones and cable TV. Some rooms have microwaves and refrigerators. Wheelchair accessible. AAA discount. Credit cards: AE, CB, DC, DS, JCB, MC, V.

Motel 6
$36-44
7450 Katella Avenue • 714.891.0717
205 Units, pets OK. Pool. Laundry facility. Rooms come with A/C, phones and cable TV. Wheelchair accessible. Credit cards: AE, CB, DC, DS, MC, V.

STOCKTON
Motel 6—Southeast
$40-44
1625 French Camp Turnpike Road
209.467.3600
125 Units, pets OK. Pool. Laundry facility. Data ports. Rooms come with A/C, phones and cable TV. Wheelchair accessible. Credit cards: AE, CB, DC, DS, MC, V.

Motel 6—West
$40-46
817 Navy Drive, I-5, Charter Way Exit
209.946.0923
76 Units, pets OK. Restaurant on premises. Pool. Rooms come with A/C, phones and cable TV. Wheelchair accessible. Credit cards: AE, CB, DC, DS, MC, V.

Motel 6—North
$40-44
6717 Plymouth Rd.
I-5, Benjamin Holt Dr. Exit • 209.951.8120
76 Units, pets OK. Pool. Data ports. Rooms come with A/C, phones and cable TV. Wheelchair accessible. Credit cards: AE, CB, DC, DS, MC, V.

Sixpence Inn
$41
4100 E. Waterloo Road • 209.931.9511
59 Units, pets OK. Pool. Rooms come with phones and cable TV. Some rooms have A/C. Senior discount. Credit cards: MC, V, DC, DS.

SUNNYVALE — *see San Jose*

SUSANVILLE
Budget Host Frontier Inn Motel
$33-49
2685 Main Street • 530.257.4141
38 Units, pets OK. Continental breakfast. Laundry facility. Rooms come with phones and cable TV. Some rooms have microwaves and refrigerators. Senior discount. Major credit cards.

River Inn Motel
$46-50
1710 Main Street • 530.257.6051
49 Units, pets OK ($5). Continental breakfast. Pool. Rooms come with phones and cable TV. AAA/Senior discount. Major credit cards.

SYLMAR
Motel 6
$40-46 (52)*
12775 Encinitas Avenue, I-5/I-210, Roxford Street Exit • 818.362.9491
158 Units, pets OK. Pool. Laundry facility. Rooms come with A/C, phones and cable TV. Wheelchair accessible. Credit cards: AE, CB, DC, DS, MC, V.
*Higher rate effective summer weekends.

TEMECULA
Motel 6
$44-46 (60)*
41900 Moreno Drive • 909.676.7199
135 Units, pets OK. Laundry facility. Pool. Rooms come with A/C, phones and cable TV.

Wheelchair accessible. Credit cards: AE, CB, DC, DS, MC, V.
*Higher rate effective weekends.

THOUSAND OAKS — *see also Newbury Park*
Motel 6
$40-48
1516 Newbury Road • 805.499.0711
175 Units, pets OK. Pool. Rooms come with A/C, phones and cable TV. Wheelchair accessible. Major credit cards.

THOUSAND PALMS
Red Roof Inn
$45-55
72-215 Varner Road • 760.343.1381
114 Units, no pets. Continental breakfast. Heated pool and jacuzzi. Rooms come with phones and cable TV. AAA/Senior discount. Credit cards: AE, CB, DC, DS, MC, V.

TRACY
Motel 6
$40-50
3810 Tracy Blvd. • 209.836.4900
111 Units, pets OK. Restaurant on premises. Pool. Laundry facility. Rooms come with A/C, phones and cable TV. Wheelchair accessible. Credit cards: AE, CB, DC, DS, MC, V.

TULARE
Motel 6
$36-44
111 N. Blackstone Drive • 559.686.1611
111 Units, pets OK. Pool. Laundry facility. Data ports. Rooms come with A/C, phones and cable TV. Wheelchair accessible. Credit cards: AE, CB, DC, DS, MC, V.

TURLOCK
Turlock Inn
$45-55
701 20th Century Blvd. • 209.634.3111
30 Units, pets OK ($5). Rooms come with phones, AC and cable TV. Some rooms have microwaves and refrigerators. Major credit cards.

Motel 6
$37-42
250 S. Walnut Avenue • 209.667.4100
101 Units, pets OK. Pool. Laundry facility. Rooms come with A/C, phones and cable TV. Wheelchair accessible. Credit cards: AE, CB, DC, DS, MC, V.

TWENTYNINE PALMS
Motel 6
$38-40
72562 Twentynine Palms Hwy 760.367.2833
124 Units, pets OK. Restaurant on premises. Pool. Jacuzzi. Laundry facility. Rooms come with A/C, phones and cable TV. Wheelchair accessible. Credit cards: AE, CB, DC, DS, MC, V.

UKIAH
Motel 6
$40-50
1208 S. State Street • 707.468.5404
70 Units, pets OK. Pool. Laundry facility. Data ports. Rooms come with A/C, phones and cable TV. Wheelchair accessible. Credit cards: AE, CB, DC, DS, MC, V.

Sunrise Inn
$42-48
650 S. State Street • 707.462.6601
24 Units, no pets. Rooms come with phones and cable TV. AAA/Senior discount. Credit cards: AE, DS, MC, V.

UPLAND
Super 8 Motel
$47
1282 W. 7th Street • 909.985.8115
61 Units, no pets. Pool. Laundry facility. Rooms come with cable TV. Some rooms have refrigerators. Senior discount. Credit cards: AE, CB, DC, DS, JCB, MC, V.

VACAVILLE
Motel 6
$40-50
107 Lawrence Drive • 707.447.5550
97 Units, pets OK. Pool. Laundry facility. Data ports. Rooms come with A/C, phones and cable TV. Wheelchair accessible. Credit cards: AE, CB, DC, DS, MC, V.

VALLEJO
Best Value Inn
$46
4 Mariposa Street • 707.554.1840
85 Units, no pets. Laundry facility. Rooms come with phones, A/C and cable TV. AAA discount. Credit cards: AE, MC, V.

Motel 6
$38-48
597 Sandy Beach Road • 707.552.2912
149 Units, pets OK. Pool. Data ports. Rooms come with A/C, phones and cable TV.

Wheelchair accessible. Credit cards: AE, CB, DC, DS, MC, V.

Vallejo Inn
$35-43
101 Maritime Academy Drive 707.557.0746
101 Units, no pets. Continental breakfast. Pool. Rooms come with phones and cable TV. Wheelchair accessible. Major credit cards.

VAN NUYS
Motel 6
$44-54
15711 Roscoe Blvd. • 818.894.9341
114 Units, pets OK. Restaurant on premises. Laundry facility. Pool. Rooms come with A/C, phones and cable TV. Wheelchair accessible. Credit cards: AE, CB, DC, DS, MC, V.

VENTURA
Motel 6
$46-50 (58)*
2145 E. Harbor Blvd. • 805.643.5100
200 Units, pets OK. Pool. Laundry facility. Data ports. Rooms come with A/C, phones and cable TV. Wheelchair accessible. Credit cards: AE, CB, DC, DS, MC, V.
*Higher rate effective summer weekends.

Motel 6
$46-50 (58)*
3075 Johnson Drive • 805.650.0080
151 Units, no pets. Pool. Laundry facility. Jacuzzi. Data ports. Rooms come with phones and cable TV. Wheelchair accessible. Credit cards: AE, CB, DC, DS, MC, V.
*Higher rates effective summer weekends.

VICTORVILLE
American Inn
$42-52
12175 Mariposa Road
I-15, Bear Valley Road Exit • 760.241.7200
44 Units, no pets. Continental breakfast. Pool. Data ports. Rooms come with refrigerators, phones and cable TV. AAA/Senior discount. Major credit cards.

Motel 6
$36-42
16901 Stoddard Wells Rd. • 760.243.0666
63 Units, pets OK. Pool. Laundry facility. Rooms come with A/C, phones and cable TV. Wheelchair accessible. Credit cards: AE, CB, DC, DS, MC, V.

VISALIA
Marco Polo Motel
$45
4545 W. Mineral King • 559.732.4591
41 Units, no pets. Restaurant on premises. Pool. Rooms come with phones, AC and cable TV. Credit cards: AE, CB, DS, MC, V.

Mooney Motel
$45-49
2120 S. Mooney Blvd. • 559.733.2666
28 Units, no pets. Pool. Rooms come with phones, A/C and cable TV. Wheelchair accessible. Credit cards: AE, CB, DS, MC, V.

WATSONVILLE
Motel 6
$43-50 (52-64)*
125 Silver Leaf Drive • 831.728.4144
124 Units, pets OK. Pool. Laundry facility. Data ports. Rooms come with A/C, phones and cable TV. Wheelchair accessible. Credit cards: AE, CB, DC, DS, MC, V.
*Higher rates effective summer weekends.

WEAVERVILLE
49er Gold Country Inn
$30-50*
In town • 530.623.4937
13 Units, pets OK. Continental breakfast. Pool. Rooms come with phones and cable TV. AAA/Senior discount. Major credit cards.
*Rates as high as $90/night.

WEED
Motel 6
$36-43
466 N. Weed Blvd. • 530.938.4101
80 Units, pets OK. Pool. Laundry facility. Data ports. Rooms come with A/C, phones and cable TV. Wheelchair accessible. Credit cards: AE, CB, DC, DS, MC, V.

Sis-Q-Inn
$46-54
1825 Shastina Drive • 530.938.4194
22 Units, pets OK ($5). Continental breakfast. Rooms come with phones and cable TV. AAA/Senior discount. Major credit cards.

Summit Inn
$39
90 N. Weed Blvd. • 530.938.4481
22 Units, pets OK. Restaurant on premises.

Pool. Rooms come with A/C, phones and cable TV. Major credit cards.

WESTMINSTER
Days Inn
$44-55
5921 Westminster Ave. • 714.895.7099
30 Units, no pets. Airport transportation. Rooms come with phones and cable TV. Wheelchair accessible. Major credit cards.

Motel 6—North
$42-48
13100 Goldenwest • 714.895.0042
127 Units, pets OK. Pool. Rooms come with A/C, phones and cable TV. Wheelchair accessible. Credit cards: AE, CB, DC, DS, MC, V.

Motel 6—South
$42-48
6266 Westminster Ave. • 714.891.5366
98 Units, pets OK. Pool. Rooms come with A/C, phones and cable TV. Wheelchair accessible. Credit cards: AE, CB, DC, DS, MC, V.

WEST SACRAMENTO
Motel 6
$40-48
1254 Halyard Drive • 916.372.3624
116 Units, pets OK. Pool. Data ports. Rooms come with A/C, phones and cable TV. Wheelchair accessible. Credit cards: AE, CB, DC, DS, MC, V.

WHITTIER
Motel 6
$38-50
8221 S. Pioneer Blvd. • 562.692.9101
98 Units, pets OK. Pool. Laundry facility. Rooms come with A/C, phones and cable TV. Wheelchair accessible. Credit cards: AE, CB, DC, DS, MC, V.

WILLIAMS
Motel 6
$36-46
455 4th Street • 530.473.5337
121 Units, pets OK. Pool. Laundry facility. Data ports. Rooms come with A/C, phones and cable TV. Wheelchair accessible. Credit cards: AE, CB, DC, DS, MC, V.

Stage Stop Motel
$35-38
330 7th Street • 530.473.2281
25 Units, pets OK ($5). Small pool. Rooms come with refrigerators and cable TV. Senior discount. Credit cards: AE, CB, DC, DS, MC, V.

WILLOWS
Best Value Inn
$39-55
452 N. Humboldt Ave. • 530.934.7026
41 Units, pets OK. Small pool. Rooms come with phones and cable TV. AAA/Senior discount. Credit cards: AE, DS, MC, V.

Blue Gum Inn
$32-38
5 mi. north of town on I-5, exit via Bayliss-Blue Gum Road, 1.8 mi. north on business route • 530.934.5401
30 Units, pets OK ($6). Pool. Rooms come with cable TV. Some rooms have kitchens, microwaves and refrigerators. Credit cards: AE, MC, V.

WOODLAND
Motel 6
$42-48
1564 Main Street • 530.666.6777
79 Units, pets OK. Restaurant on premises. Pool. Laundry facility. Rooms come with A/C, phones and cable TV. Wheelchair accessible. Credit cards: AE, CB, DC, DS, MC, V.

Valley Oaks Inn
$47-55
600 N. East Street • 530.666.5511
62 Units, no pets. Continental breakfast. Pool. Jacuzzi. Laundry facility. Rooms come with A/C, phones and cable TV. AAA discount. Credit cards: AE, MC, V.

YREKA
Days Inn
$39-59
1806B Fort Jones Road • 530.842.1612
52 Units, pets OK ($5 and $20 dep. req.). Continental breakfast. Pool. Data ports. Rooms come with phones and cable TV. AAA/Senior discount. Credit cards: AE, DC, DS, MC, V. Senior discount.

Economy Inn
$36-45
526 S. Main Street • 530.842.4404
44 Units, pets OK in some rooms only ($4). Pool. Rooms come with phones and cable TV. Some rooms have microwaves and

refrigerators. Credit cards: AE, CB, DC, DS, MC, V.

Motel 6
$36-43
1785 S. Main Street • 530.842.4111
102 Units, pets OK. Pool. Laundry facility. Data ports. Rooms come with A/C, phones and cable TV. Wheelchair accessible. Credit cards: AE, CB, DC, DS, MC, V.

YUBA CITY — *see also Marysville*
Villager Lodge
$42-50
545 Colusa Avenue • 530.671.1151
40 Units, no pets. Continental breakfast. Rooms come with phones and cable TV. AAA/Senior discount. Credit cards: AE, DS, MC, V.

YUCCA VALLEY
Super 8 Motel
$44-54
57096 Twenty-Nine Palms Hwy.
760.228.1773
47 Units, pets OK ($25 dep. req.). Continental breakfast. Heated pool. Rooms come with phones and cable TV. AAA/Senior discount. Major credit cards.

colorado

Travel Advisory: If you are thinking about hunting down some budget accommodations in one of the Rocky Mountain resort towns (**Vail, Telluride, Snowmass Village, Breckenridge, Winter Park, Minturn, Steamboat Springs** or **Aspen**), be aware that they will be hard to come by at less than $50 per night, even during the off-season. The few exception are at the youth hostels, where you can spend the night for $12-35

ALAMOSA
Alamosa Lamplighter Motel
$43-48
425 Main Street • 719.589.6636
38 Units, no pets. Restaurant on premises. Meeting rooms. Airport transportation. Rooms come with phones and cable TV. Some rooms have microwaves and refrigerators. Senior discount. Major credit cards.

Days Inn
$33-48
224 O'Keefe Parkway • 719.589.9037
33 Units, pets OK ($10). Continental breakfast. Data ports. Rooms come with phones and cable TV. AAA/Senior discount. Major credit cards.

ANTONITO
Hostelling International
$12
3591 County Road E2 • 719.376.2518
10 Beds, Hours: 7-9 am & 5-10 pm
Facilities: wood stove, fireplace, kitchen, linen rental, on-site parking, croquet, gas grill, picnic tables, fishing poles, telescope. Private rooms available (reservations required). Closed October 6 through May 23. Reservations required. Credit cards not accepted.

Narrow Gauge Railroad Inn
$30-40
Junction of Hwys. 17 and 285 719.376.5441
33 Units, no pets. Rooms come with phones and cable TV. Credit cards: AE, DC, DS, MC, V.

AURORA
Motel 6
$40-50 (56)*
14031 E. Iliff Avenue • 303.873.0286
121 Units, pets OK. Pool. Laundry facility. Rooms come with phones, A/C and cable TV. Wheelchair accessible. Credit cards: AE, CB, DC, DS, MC, V.
*Higher rate effective during summer weekends.

Super 8 Motel
$45
14200 E. 6th Avenue • 303.366.7333
146 Units, no pets. Continental breakfast. Heated pool. Laundry facility. Rooms come with phones and cable TV. AAA/Senior discount. Major credit cards.

BRUSH
Budget Host Empire Motel
$30-35
1408 Edison Street • 970.842.2876
18 Units, pets OK ($2). Laundry facility. Picnic area. Rooms come with phones and cable TV. Senior discount. Credit cards: AE, DS, MC, V.

BURLINGTON
Burlington Inn
$46
450 S. Lincoln • 719.346.5555
112 Units, pets OK ($5). Restaurant on premises. Rooms come with phones and cable TV. AAA/Senior discount. Major credit cards.

Chaparral Motor Inn
$28-45
405 S. Lincoln • 719.346.5361
39 Units, pets OK. Continental breakfast. Heated pool. Rooms come with phones and cable TV. AAA/Senior discount. Credit cards: AE, CB, DC, DS, MC, V.

Sloan's Motel
$28-38
1901 Rose Avenue • 719.346.5333
29 Units, pets OK. Heated pool (open May through October). Data ports. Rooms come

with phones and cable TV. Some rooms have microwaves and refrigerators. Wheelchair accessible. AAA/Senior discount. Credit cards: AE, DS, MC, V.

CAÑON CITY
Holiday Motel
$36
1502 Main Street • 719.275.3317
15 Units, pets OK ($20 dep. req.). Heated pool. Rooms come with phones and cable TV. Some rooms have microwaves and refrigerators. Senior discount. Major credit cards.

COLORADO SPRINGS
Frontier Motel
$30-45
4300 N. Nevada Ave. • 719.598.1563
28 Units, no pets. Pool. Rooms come with microwaves, refrigerators, phones and cable TV. Some rooms have kitchenettes. Credit cards: AE, DC, DS, MC, V.

Motel 6
$32-50 (60-70)*
3228 N. Chestnut St. • 719.520.5400
83 Units, pets OK. Pool. Laundry facility. Data ports. Rooms come with phones, A/C and cable TV. Wheelchair accessible. Credit cards: AE, CB, DC, DS, MC, V.
*Higher rate effective during summer months.

Travel Inn
$28-60
512 S. Nevada Avenue • 719.636.3986
36 Units, no pets. Continental breakfast. Laundry facility. Rooms come with phones and cable TV. AAA discount. Credit cards: AE, DS, MC, V.

CORTEZ
Budget Host Inn
$32-69
2040 E. Main Street • 970.565.3738
40 Units, pets OK. Continental breakfast. Heated pool. Jacuzzi. Laundry facility. Playground. Rooms come with phones and cable TV. Wheelchair accessible. AAA/ Senior discount. Credit cards: AE, DS, MC, V.

Tomahawk Lodge
$31-53
728 S. Broadway • 970.565.8521
38 Units, pets OK ($25 dep. req.). Heated pool. Rooms come with phones and cable TV. AAA/Senior discount. Credit cards: AE, DS, MC, V.

Travelodge
$37-50
440 S. Broadway • 970.565.7778
42 Units, pets OK ($25 dep. req.). Heated pool. Jacuzzi. Laundry facility. Rooms come with phones and cable TV. AAA discount. Credit cards: AE, DS, MC, V.

CRAIG
Black Nugget Motel
$25-43
2855 W. Victory Way • 970.824.8161
20 Units, pets OK ($5). Continental breakfast. Basketball court, horseshoes and picnic area. Airport transportation. Laundry facility. Rooms come with phones and cable TV. Some rooms have refrigerators and microwaves. AAA/Senior discount. Credit cards: AE, DC, DS, MC, V.

Craig Motel
$34-40
894 Yampa Avenue • 970.824.4491
25 Units, pets OK ($2). Laundry facility. Rooms come with phones and cable TV. Some rooms have refrigerators and microwaves. AAA discount. Credit cards: AE, CB, DC, DS, MC, V.

DEL NORTE
Del Norte Motel & Cafe
$40
1050 Grand Avenue • 719.657.3581 or 800.372.2331
15 Units, pets OK. Restaurant on premises. Rooms come with phones and cable TV. Some rooms have refrigerators. Credit cards: AE, DS, MC, V.

DELTA
Riverwood Inn
$42-51
677 U.S. 50N • 970.874.5787
11 Units, no pets. Restaurant on premises. Airport transportation. Rooms come with phones and cable TV. AAA discount. Credit cards: AE, DS, MC, V.

Southgate Inn
$40-50
2124 S. Main Street • 970.874.9726
37 Units, pets OK ($5). Heated pool. Jacuzzi. Rooms come with phones and cable

TV. AAA/Senior discount. Major credit cards.

DENVER — *see also Aurora, Greenwood Village, Lakewood, Thornton and Wheat Ridge*

Budget Host Inn
$50
3015 E. Colfax • 303.388.4811
54 Units, no pets. Laundry facility. Rooms come with phones, A/C and cable TV. Senior discount available (10%). Major credit cards.

Budget Host—Downtown
$30-48
2747 Wyandot Street • 303.477.6229
36 Units, no pets. Laundry facility. Rooms come with phones, A/C and cable TV. Senior discount. Major credit cards.

Motel 6—Central
$38-50
3050 W. 49th Avenue, I-70, Exit 272 (Federal Blvd.) • 303.455.8888
191 Units, pets OK. Indoor pool. Laundry facility. Rooms come with phones, A/C and cable TV. Wheelchair accessible. Credit cards: AE, CB, DC, DS, MC, V.

Motel 6—Airport
$36-46
12020 E. 39th Avenue, I-70, Exit 281
303.371.1980
138 Units, pets OK. Pool. Laundry facility. Rooms come with phones, A/C and cable TV. Wheelchair accessible. Credit cards: AE, CB, DC, DS, MC, V.

Rockies Inn
$33-38
4760 E. Evans Avenue • 303.757.7601
77 Units, pets OK. Restaurant on premises. Rooms come with phones, A/C and cable TV. AAA/Senior discount. Major credit cards.

DURANGO
Budget Inn
$28-45
3077 Main Avenue • 970.257.5222 or 800.257.5222
35 Units, pets OK. Pool. Laundry facility. Rooms come with phones and cable TV. Major credit cards.

Days End
$29-39 (79-99)*
2202 Main Avenue • 970.259.3311 or 800.242.3297
46 Units, pets OK. Pool. Laundry facility. Rooms come with phones and cable TV. Some rooms have kitchenettes. Wheelchair accessible. Major credit cards.
*Higher rates effective summer months

Siesta Motel
$25-45 (45-65)*
3475 Main Avenue • 970.247.0741
22 Units, no pets. Jacuzzi. Picnic area. Rooms come with phones and cable TV. Some rooms have kitchenettes. AAA discount. Major credit cards.
*Higher rates effective Memorial Day through Labor Day.

ESTES PARK
Saddle & Surrey Motel
$44-50 (63)*
13415 St. Vrain Avenue • 970.586.3326
26 Units, no pets. Heated pool. Jacuzzi. Laundry facility. Airport transportation. Rooms come with phones and cable TV. Some rooms have A/C, microwaves and refrigerators. Senior discount. Credit cards: DS, MC, V.
*Higher rate effective summer months. AAA discounted rates.

Trappers Inn
$35-50 (40-75)*
553 W. Elkhorn • 970.586.2833 or 800.552.2833
20 Units, no pets. Jacuzzi. Playground. Rooms come with phones and cable TV. Some rooms have A/C, microwaves and refrigerators. AAA discount. Major credit cards.
*Higher rates effective April through September.

EVANS
Motel 6
$35-50
3015 8th Avenue • 970.351.6481
94 Units, pets OK. Pool. Laundry facility. Rooms come with phones, A/C and cable TV. Wheelchair accessible. Credit cards: AE, CB, DC, DS, MC, V.

FLORENCE
Super 8 Motel
$32-47*

45405 SR 67 • 719.784.4800
40 Units, no pets. Laundry facility. Rooms come with phones, A/C and cable TV. Senior discount. Major credit cards.
*AAA discounted rates.

FORT COLLINS
Budget Host Inn
$40-50
1513 N. College Avenue • 970.484.0870
30 Units, no pets. Jacuzzi. Picnic area. Rooms come with phones and cable TV. Some rooms have microwaves and refrigerators. AAA/Senior discount. Major credit cards.

Motel 6
$38-50
3900 E. Mulberry/State Hwy 14
970.482.6466
126 Units, pets OK. Pool. Laundry facility. Rooms come with phones, A/C and cable TV. Wheelchair accessible. Credit cards: AE, CB, DC, DS, MC, V.

FORT LUPTON
Motel 6
$38-42
65 S. Grand, Jct. Hwys. 52 & 85
303.857.1800
42 Units, pets OK. Data ports. Rooms come with phones, A/C and cable TV. Wheelchair accessible. Credit cards: AE, CB, DC, DS, MC, V.

FORT MORGAN
Super 8 Motel
$48-55
1220 N. Main • 970.867.9443
36 Units, no pets. Toast bar. Laundry facility. Data port. Rooms come with phones and cable TV. Wheelchair accessible. AAA/Senior discount. Credit cards: AE, CB, DC, DS, MC, V.

GEORGETOWN
Georgetown Mountain Inn
$40-51*
1100 Rose • 303.569.3201
33 Units, pets OK ($5-10 and $20 dep. req.). Continental breakfast. Heated pool. Jacuzzi. Laundry facility. Rooms come with phones and cable TV. No A/C in rooms. Credit cards: AE, DC, DS, MC, V.
*AAA discounted rates.

GLENWOOD SPRINGS
Budget Host of Glenwood
$33-57
51429 Hwy 6 & 24 • 970.945.5682
22 Units, pets OK. Restaurant on premises. Heated pool. Meeting rooms. Picnic area. Rooms come with phones and cable TV. Some rooms have microwaves and refrigerators. Senior discount. Credit cards: AE, DS, MC, V.

GRAND JUNCTION
Budget Host Inn
$40-54*
721 Horizon Drive • 970.243.6050
55 Units, pets OK. Continental breakfast. Heated pool. Laundry facility. Playground. Rooms come with phones, A/C and cable TV. Senior discount available (10%). Major credit cards.
*AAA discounted rates.

Motel 6
$30-48 (54-56)*
776 Horizon Drive • 970.243.2628
100 Units, pets OK. Pool. Laundry facility. Rooms come with phones, A/C and cable TV. Wheelchair accessible. Credit cards: AE, CB, DC, DS, MC, V.
*Higher rates effective summer weekends.

Value Lodge Grand Junction
$30-44
104 White Avenue • 970.242.0651
45 Units, no pets. Heated pool. Video rentals. Rooms come with phones and cable TV. AAA/Senior discount. Credit cards: AE, DS, MC, V.

GREELEY — *see also Evans*
Greeley Inn
$35
721 13th Street • 970.353.3216
38 Units, no pets. Pool. Rooms come with phones and cable TV. Major credit cards.

GREENWOOD VILLAGE
Motel 6
$38-50 (56)*
9201 E. Arapahoe Road, I-25, Exit 197
303.790.8220
139 Units, pets OK. Pool. Laundry facility. Rooms come with phones, A/C and cable TV. Wheelchair accessible. Credit cards: AE, CB, DC, DS, MC, V.
*Higher rate effective summer weekends.

GUNNISON
ABC Motel
$42-48 (56-62)*
212 E. Tomichi Avenue • 970.641.2400
24 Units, pets OK ($5). Airport transportation. Jacuzzi. Rooms come with phones and cable TV. AAA/Senior discount. Credit cards: AE, DC, DS, MC, V.
*Higher rate effective June through mid-September.

Western Motel
$30-52
405 E. Tomichi Avenue • 970.641.1722
20 Units, pets OK ($5). Jacuzzi. Rooms come with phones and cable TV. Major credit cards.

HOT SULPHUR SPRINGS
Canyon Motel
$45-49*
221 Byers Avenue • 970.725.3395
12 Units, pets OK ($8). Rooms come with refrigerators, phones and cable TV. No A/C in rooms. AAA/Senior discount. Credit cards: AE, DS, MC, V.
*Rates as high as $72/night.

IDAHO SPRINGS
Peoriana Motel
$38-43
2901 Colorado Blvd. • 303.567.2021
30 Units, pets OK. Jacuzzi. Rooms come with TV. No phones or A/C in rooms. AAA/Senior discount. Credit cards: AE, DS, MC, V.

6 & 40 Motel
$50
2920 Colorado Blvd. • 303.567.2692
31 Units, pets OK. Local transportation available. Picnic area. Rooms come with phones and cable TV. No A/C in rooms. Some rooms have refrigerators. AAA/Senior discount. Credit cards: AE, DS, MC, V.

JULESBURG
Platte Valley Inn
$41-46
15225 Hwy. 385 & I-76 • 970.474.3336
59 Units, pets OK. Restaurant on premises. Pool. Rooms come with phones and cable TV. AAA discount. Major credit cards.

LA JUNTA
Stagecoach Motel
$40-45
905 W. 3rd Street • 719.384.5476
31 Units, pets OK ($4 and $20 dep. req.). Pool. Local transportation available. Data ports. Rooms come with phones and cable TV. Some rooms have microwaves and refrigerators. AAA/Senior discount. Credit cards: AE, CB, DC, DS, MC, V.

Travel Inn
$29-32
110 E. First Street • 719.384.2504
28 Units, pets OK ($4). Rooms come with refrigerators, phones and cable TV. AAA/Senior discount. Major credit cards.

LAKEWOOD
Homestead Motel
$36
8837 W. Colfax • 303.232.8837
22 Units, no pets. Pool. Laundry facility. Rooms come with phones and cable TV. Some rooms have microwaves and refrigerators. AAA discount available (10%). Major credit cards.

Motel 6
$38-52
480 Wadsworth Blvd., US 6, Wadsworth Blvd Exit • 303.232.4924
119 Units, pets OK. Pool. Laundry facility. Rooms come with phones, A/C and cable TV. Wheelchair accessible. Credit cards: AE, CB, DC, DS, MC, V.

LAMAR
El Mar Budget Host Motel
$35-43
1210 S. Main Street • 719.336.4331
40 Units, no pets. Heated pool. Local transportation available. Rooms come with phones and cable TV. Some rooms have kitchens. AAA/Senior discount. Credit cards: AE, CB, DC, DS, MC, V.

Super 8 Motel
$40-55*
1202 N. Main Street • 719.336.3427
44 Units, no pets. Continental breakfast. Laundry facility. Rooms come with phones and cable TV. Wheelchair accessible. Senior discount. Credit cards: AE, CB, DC, DS, MC, V.
*Higher rate effective summer months.

LEADVILLE
Timberline Motel
$35-43 (55)*

216 Harrison Avenue • 719.486.1876
15 Units, no pets. Rooms come with phones and cable TV. No A/C in rooms. Some rooms have microwaves and refrigerators. Credit cards: AE, DC, DS, MC, V.
*Higher rate effective August through Labor Day.

LIMON
Preferred Motor Inn
$38-48
158 E. Main Street • 719.775.2385
57 Units, pets OK ($4). Continental breakfast. Laundry facility. Jacuzzi. Racquetball court. Meeting rooms. Rooms come with phones and cable TV. AAA/Senior discount. Major credit cards.

Safari Motel
$30-42
637 Main Street • 719.775.2363
28 Units, pets OK ($5). Laundry facility. Playground. Rooms come with phones and cable TV. AAA/Senior discount. Major credit cards.

LONGMONT
First Interstate Inn
$40-50
3940 Hwy. 119 • 303.772.6000
32 Units, pets OK. Rooms come with A/C, phones and cable TV. Credit cards: AE, DC, DS, MC, V.

Travelodge
$43-50*
3875 Hwy. 119 & I-25 (Exit 240)
303.776.8700
68 Units, pets OK. Restaurant on premises. Indoor heated pool. Wading pool. Laundry facility. Rooms come with A/C, cable TV and phones. Major credit cards.
*Higher rate effective summer months.

MANITOU SPRINGS
Red Wing Motel
$30-49
56 El Paso Blvd. • 719.685.5656
27 Units, pets OK ($10). Continental breakfast. Heated pool. Playground. Rooms come with phones and cable TV. Some rooms have microwaves and refrigerators. AAA/Senior discount. Credit cards: AE, DS, MC, V.

Ute Pass Motel
$35*
1132 Manitou Avenue • 719.685.5171 or 800.845.9762
17 Units, no pets. Rooms come with phones and cable TV. Hot tub. Major credit cards.
*Summer rates as high as $62/night.

MONTROSE
Canyon Trails Inn
$32-50
1225 Main Street • 970.249.3426
27 Units, pets OK. Continental breakfast. Rooms come with phones and cable TV. Some rooms have microwaves and refrigerators. AAA/Senior discount. Credit cards: AE, DS, MC, V.

Super 8 Motel
$39-55
1705 E. Main • 970.249.9294
42 Units, pets OK ($20 dep. req.). Toast bar. Hot tub. Rooms come with phones and cable TV. Wheelchair accessible. AAA/ Senior discount. Credit cards: AE, CB, DC, DS, MC, V.

Western Motel
$36-48
1200 E. Main Street • 970.249.3481
28 Units, pets OK ($5). Heated pool. Sauna. Jacuzzi. Rooms come with A/C, cable TV and phones. Some rooms have refrigerators. AAA/Senior discount. Major credit cards.

PUEBLO
Best Western Townhouse Motel
$45-50*
730 N. Santa Fe Ave. • 719.543.6530
88 Units, no pets. Restaurant on premises. Heated pool. Fitness facility. Laundry facility. Meeting rooms. Data ports. Rooms come with phones and cable TV. Some rooms have microwaves and refrigerators. Senior discount. Major credit cards.
*AAA discounted rates.

Motel 6
$32-50
960 Hwy 50 W., I-25, Exit 101
719.543.8900
86 Units, pets OK. Laundry facility. Data ports. Rooms come with phones, A/C and cable TV. Wheelchair accessible. Credit cards: AE, CB, DC, DS, MC, V.

Motel 6
$35-50

4103 N. Elizabeth Street, I-25, Exit 101
719.543.6221
108 Units, pets OK. Pool. Laundry facility. Data ports. Rooms come with phones, A/C and cable TV. Wheelchair accessible. Credit cards: AE, CB, DC, DS, MC, V.

Super 8 Motel
$35-50
1100 Hwy. 50. • 719.545.4104
60 Units, no pets. Rooms come with phones and cable TV. Wheelchair accessible. AAA/ Senior discount. Credit cards: AE, CB, DC, DS, MC, V.

RANGELY
Budget Host Inn
$36-40
117 S. Grand Street • 970.675.8461
25 Units, no pets. Laundry facility. Airport transportation. Rooms come with phones and cable TV. Some rooms have microwaves and refrigerators. Wheelchair accessible. Senior discount. Credit cards: AE, CB, DS, MC, V.

RIFLE
Red River Inn
$44
718 Taughenbaugh Blvd. • 970.625.3050
65 Units, pets OK ($25). Restaurant on premises. Continental breakfast. Rooms come with phones and cable TV. Some rooms have microwaves and refrigerators. Credit cards: AE, CB, DC, DS, MC, V.

Rusty Cannon Motel
$46-52
701 Taughenbaugh Blvd. • 970.625.4004
88 Units, pets OK. Heated pool. Sauna. Airport transportation. Laundry facility. Rooms come with phones and cable TV. Some rooms have refrigerators. AAA/Senior discount. Credit cards: AE, CB, DC, DS, MC, V.

SALIDA
Aspen Leaf Lodge
$29-49
7350 Hwy. 50W • 719.539.6733
18 Units, pets OK ($5). Jacuzzi. Data ports. Rooms come with phones and cable TV. Some rooms have microwaves and refrigerators. AAA/Senior discount. Major credit cards.

Silver Ridge Lodge
$33-50
545 W. Rainbow Blvd. • 719.539.2553
39 Units, pets OK ($5). Continental breakfast. Heated pool. Jacuzzi. Meeting rooms. Data ports. Rooms come with phones and cable TV. AAA/Senior discount. Major credit cards.

SILVERTON
Triangle Motel
$30-50*
864 Greene Street • 970.387.5780
16 Units, no pets. Rooms come with phones and cable TV. No A/C in rooms. Some rooms have kitchenettes. AAA discount. Credit cards: AE, DS, MC, V.
*Rates as high as $65/night.

SOUTH FORK
Budget Host/Ute Bluff Lodge
$37-50
27680 US 160W • 719.873.5595
29 Units, pets OK. Continental breakfast. Jacuzzi. Laundry facility. Rooms come with phones and TV. Some rooms have microwaves and refrigerators. No A/C in rooms. Wheelchair accessible. AAA discount. Credit cards: AE, DS, MC, V.

The Inn Motel
$35-40
30362 US 160W • 719.873.5514
19 Units, pets OK. Continental breakfast. Sauna. Rooms come with phones and cable TV. Some rooms have microwaves, kitchenettes and refrigerators. No A/C in rooms. AAA discount. Major credit cards.

STERLING
Colonial Motel
$31-37
915 S. Division • 970.522.3382
14 Units, pets OK ($5). Playground. Basketball hoop. Rooms come with phones and cable TV. Some rooms have refrigerators and microwaves. AAA discount. Credit cards: AE, DS, MC, V.

First Interstate Inn
$40
20930 Hwy. 6 • 970.522.7274
30 Units, pets OK ($5). Laundry facility. Rooms come with phones and cable TV. Credit cards: AE, DC, DS, MC, V.

THORNTON
Motel 6
**$38-50 (56)*
6 W. 83rd Place • 303.429.1550
121 Units, pets OK. Pool. Laundry facility. Rooms come with phones, A/C and cable TV. Wheelchair accessible. Credit cards: AE, CB, DC, DS, MC, V.
*Higher rate effective summer weekends.

TRINIDAD
Budget Host Trinidad
$30-50 (55-69)*
10301 Santa Fe Trail Dr. • 719.846.3307
26 Units, pets OK ($5). Continental breakfast. Picnic area. Laundry facility. Rooms come with phones and cable TV. Some rooms have refrigerators. AAA discount. Credit cards: AE, CB, DC, DS, MC, V.
*Higher rates effective April through September.

Super 8 Motel
$46-55 (57-66)*
1924 Freedom Road • 719.846.8280
42 Units, pets OK. Toast bar. Laundry facility. Rooms come with phones and cable TV. Wheelchair accessible. Senior discount. Credit cards: AE, CB, DC, DS, MC, V.
*Higher rate effective May through mid-September.

WALSENBURG
Budget Host Country Host Motel
$27-45
553 US 85/87 • 719.738.3800
17 Units, pets OK. Rooms come with phones and cable TV. AAA/Senior discount. Major credit cards.

WHEAT RIDGE
Motel 6—North
$37-50
9920 W. 49th Avenue • 303.424.0658
91 Units, pets OK. Laundry facility. Rooms come with phones, A/C and cable TV. Wheelchair accessible. Credit cards: AE, CB, DC, DS, MC, V.

Motel 6—South
$37-50
10300 S. I-70 Frontage Rd.
303.467.3172
113 Units, pets OK. Pool. Laundry facility. Rooms come with phones, A/C and cable TV. Wheelchair accessible. Credit cards: AE, CB, DC, DS, MC, V.

connecticut

ASHFORD
Ashford Motel
$45
26 Motel Road • 860.487.3900
43 Units, pets OK ($20 dep. req.). Rooms come with phones, A/C and TV. Credit cards: MC. V.

BERLIN
Kenilworth Motel
$50
176 Wilbur Cross Hwy. • 860.666.3306
25 Units, pets OK. Rooms come with phones, refrigerators and cable TV. Senior discount. Major credit cards.

BRANFORD
Branford Motel
$45
470 E. Main Street • 203.488.5442
80 Units, no pets. Sauna. Hot tub. Jacuzzi. Rooms come with phones and cable TV. Major credit cards.

Motel 6
$45-56
320 E. Main Street • 203.483.5828
100 Units, pets OK. Restaurant on premises. Data ports. Rooms come with phones, A/C and cable TV. Wheelchair accessible. Credit cards: AE, CB, DC, DS, MC, V.

ENFIELD
Motel 6
$40-52 (55)*
11 Hazard Avenue • 860.741.3685
121 Units, pets OK. Laundry facility. Data ports. Rooms come with phones, A/C and cable TV. Wheelchair accessible. Credit cards: AE, CB, DC, DS, MC, V.
*Higher rate effective summer weekends.

HARTFORD — *see also Wethersfield*
Hostelling International
$15-18
131 Tremont Street • 860.523.7255
42 Beds, Hours: 8-10 am; 5-10 pm
Facilities: common room, patio, kitchen, lockers, bike/baggage storage, laundry. Private rooms available. Open year-round. Reservations recommended. Credit cards: MC, V.

Super 8 Motel
$54
57 W. Service Road, I-91, Exit 33
860.246.8888
104 Units, no pets. Continental breakfast. Meeting rooms. Rooms come with phones and cable TV. Senior discount. Major credit cards.

MANCHESTER
Connecticut Motor Lodge
$45-55
400 Tolland Tpk., I-84, Exit 63
860.643.1555
31 Units, no pets. Rooms come with phones and cable TV. AAA/Senior discount. Credit cards: AE, CB, DI, DS, JCB, MC, V.

MERIDEN
Elwood Motel
$45
2055 N. Broad Street • 203.235.2256
16 Units, no pets. Rooms come with phones and cable TV. Wheelchair accessible. Senior discount. Major credit cards.

MILFORD
Devon Motel
$47
438 Bridgeport Avenue • 203.874.6634
35 Units, no pets. Rooms come with phones and cable TV. Wheelchair accessible. Major credit cards.

NEW HAVEN — *see also Branford*
Regal Inn
$50
1605 Whalley Avenue • 203.389.9504
80 Units, no pets. Jacuzzi. Rooms come with phones and cable TV. Senior discount. Major credit cards.

NIANTIC
Motel 6
$44-52 (60-80)*
269 Flanders Road • 860.739.6991
96 Units, pets OK. Pool. Laundry facility.

Data ports. Rooms come with phones, A/C and cable TV. Wheelchair accessible. Credit cards: AE, CB, DC, DS, MC, V.
*Higher rates effective summer months.

SOUTHINGTON
Howard Johnson Express
$41-53
462 Queen Street • 860.621.0181
148 Units, pets OK. Continental breakfast. Data ports. Rooms come with phones and cable TV. Wheelchair accessible. AAA discount. Major credit cards.

Motel 6
$40-50 (54)*
625 Queen Street • 860.621.7351
126 Units, pets OK. Restaurant on premises. Laundry facility. Data ports. Rooms come with phones, A/C and cable TV. Wheelchair accessible. Credit cards: AE, CB, DC, DS, MC, V.
*Higher rate effective summer weekends.

SOUTH WINDSOR
Nitey Nite Motel
$45
1519 John Fitch Blvd. • 860.289.2706
22 Units, no pets. Rooms come with cable TV. No phones in rooms. Wheelchair accessible. Major credit cards.

STONINGTON
Sea Breeze Motel
$50*
225 Lordship Blvd. • 860.535.2843
30 Units, no pets. Rooms come with cable TV. No phones in rooms. Some rooms have microwaves and refrigerators. Credit cards: MC, V.
*Summer rates as high as $89/night.

WATERBURY
Econo Lodge
$50*
2636 S. Main Street (I-84, Exit 19)
203.756.7961
80 Units, no pets. Restaurant on premises. Pool. Rooms come with phones and cable TV. Wheelchair accessible. Major credit cards.
*AAA discounted rate.

WETHERSFIELD
Motel 6
$40-50
1341 Silas Deane Hwy. • 860.563.5900
144 Units, pets OK. Laundry facility. Data ports. Rooms come with phones, A/C and cable TV. Wheelchair accessible. Credit cards: AE, CB, DC, DS, MC, V.

WINDSOR LOCKS
Motel 6
$40-52
3 National Drive • 860.292.6200
100 Units, pets OK. Pool. Laundry facility. Data ports. Rooms come with phones, A/C and cable TV. Wheelchair accessible. Credit cards: AE, CB, DC, DS, MC, V.

delaware

Note: If you are bound for Delaware either the first weekend after Memorial Day or the first weekend after Labor Day, please note that accommodations across the state are typically full due to the NASCAR races at Dover Downs.

CLAYMONT
Milan Motel
$42
3306 Philadelphia Pike • 302.798.6601
20 Units, no pets. Rooms come with phones and cable TV. Wheelchair accessible. Major credit cards.

Riverview Motel
$45-50
7811 Governor Printz Blvd. • 302.798.5601
42 Units, no pets. Laundry facility. Rooms come with phones and cable TV. Some rooms have refrigerators and microwaves. Credit cards: AE, MC, V.

DOVER
Dover Budget Inn
$45-50
1426 N. DuPont Hwy. • 302.734.4433
69 Units, pets OK. Laundry facility. Rooms come with phones and cable TV. Some rooms have refrigerators and kitchenettes. AAA/Senior discount. Major credit cards.

Haynie's Motel
$37-40
1760 N. DuPont Hwy. • 302.734.4042
16 Units, no pets. Restaurant on premises. Rooms come with phones and cable TV. Major credit cards.

Relax Inn
$45 (59)*
640 S. DuPont Hwy. • 302.734.8120
19 Units, no pets. Rooms come with A/C, phones and cable TV. Senior discount. Major credit cards.
*Higher rate effective weekends.

Super Lodge
$45-50
State Hwy. 13 • 302.678.0160
40 Units, no pets. Laundry facility. Rooms come with phones and cable TV. Major credit cards.

GEORGETOWN
Knights Inn
$50*
313 N. DuPont Hwy. • 302.856.7532
60 Units, no pets. Laundry facility. Rooms come with phones and cable TV. Wheelchair accessible. Major credit cards.
*Rates as high as $115/night.

LAUREL
Marathon Inn
$42
200 N. Dual Hwy. • 302.875.1554
20 Units, pets OK. Rooms come with phones and cable TV. Wheelchair accessible. Major credit cards.

LEWES
Vesuvio Motel
$45 (75)*
105 Savannah Road • 302.645.2224
16 Units, no pets. Rooms come with cable TV. No phones in rooms. Some rooms have refrigerators. AAA discount. Credit cards: AE, DS, MC, V.
*Higher rate effective mid-May through mid-September.

NEWARK
Red Roof Inn
$44-49
415 Stanton Christiana Rd. • I-95, Exit 4B
302.292.2870
119 Units, pets OK. Data ports. Rooms come with phones and cable TV. AAA discount. Major credit cards.

Travelodge
$42-50
268 E. Main Street, I-95, Exit 3
302.737.5050
47 Units, pets OK. Rooms come with phones and cable TV. Major credit cards.

NEW CASTLE
Budget Motor Lodge
$46
140 S. DuPont Hwy. • 302.322.1800
56 Units, no pets. Rooms come with phones, A/C and cable TV. Major credit cards.

Knights Inn
$35-50
133 S. DuPont Hwy. • 302.328.6691
49 Units, no pets. Rooms come with phones and cable TV. Major credit cards.

Motel 6
$36-46
1200 W. Avenue (S. Hwy. 9) • I-295, S. Hwy. 9N Exit • 302.571.1200
120 Units, pets OK. Pool. Laundry facility. Data ports. Rooms come with A/C, phones and cable TV. Wheelchair accessible. Credit cards: AE, CB, DC, DS, MC, V.

New Castle Travelodge
$49
1213 West Avenue • 302.654.5544
109 Units, pets OK. Pool. Meeting rooms. Rooms come with phones and cable TV. Some rooms have refrigerators and microwaves. AAA discount. Credit cards: AE, CB, DC, DS, JCB, MC, V.

Rodeway Inn
$45-55
On DuPont Hwy. • 302.328.6246
100 Units, no pets. Rooms come with A/C, phones and cable TV. AAA discount. Major credit cards.

ODESSA
Pleasant Hill Motel
$40
On US 13S • 302.378.2468
16 Units, pets OK. Picnic area. Rooms come with A/C, phones and cable TV. Major credit cards.

WILMINGTON — *see New Castle and Newark*

district of columbia

Traveler's Advisory: If you are looking for accommodations in the Washington, D.C. metro area, you will need to plan on spending a little more than $50/night for your room. Within the District of Columbia itself, there are very few inexpensive lodging options available. Below are listed some of the better bargains in and around Washington, D.C. If you are willing to drive out further away from the city, there are still better deals in **LAUREL (MD)**.

WASHINGTON
Hostelling International
$18-26
1009 11th Street N.W. • 202.737.2333
250 Beds, Office hours: 24 hours
Facilities: couples rooms, 24-hour access, information, kitchen, laundry facility, linen rental, lockers, meeting rooms, travel store, vending machines, wheelchair accessible. Private rooms available. Open year-round. Reservations essential. Credit cards: JCB, MC, V.

IN-TOWN

Gateway Travelodge ($60-110)
1917 Bladensburg Rd. N.E.
(on US 50)
202.529.7546

Super 8 Motel ($65-90)
501 New York Avenue N.E.
202.543.7400

NEARBY MARYLAND

Capitol Heights

Motel 6 ($50-66)
75 Hampton Park Blvd.
(I-95, Exit 15B)
301.499.0800

College Park

Econo Lodge ($49-85)
9624 Baltimore Ave. (I-495, Exit 25)
301.474.0003

Super 8 Motel ($56-66)
950 Baltimore Avenue
301.474.0894

Gaithersburg

Red Roof Inn ($49-74)
497 Quince Orchard Rd.
I-270, Exit 10 (northbound);
11B (southbound)
301.977.3311

Lanham

Days Inn ($69)
9023 Annapolis Road (Rte. 450)
I-95/495, Exit 20A
301.459.6600

Red Roof Inn ($49-79)
9050 Lanham Severn Road
I-95/495, Exit 20A
301.371.8830

Silver Spring

Days Inn ($49-89)
8040 13th Street
301.588.4400

NEARBY VIRGINIA

Alexandria

Days Inn ($41-89)
110 S. Bragg Street (I-395, Exit 3B)
703.354.4950

Econo Lodge ($60-74)
8849 Richmond Hwy.
703.780.0300

Red Roof Inn ($64-79)
5975 Richmond Hwy.
(I-95/495, Exit 1A)
703.960.5200

Travelodge ($55-99)
702 N. Washington Street
703.836.5100

Arlington

Travelodge ($59-84)
3030 Columbia Pike (on SR 244)
703.521.5570

Dumfries

Super 8 Motel ($50-75)

17416 Jefferson Davis Hwy.
(I-95, Exit 152)
703.221.8838

Fairfax
Econo Lodge ($60-79)
9700 Lee Hwy.
703.273.1160

Wellesley Inn ($69-79)
10327 Lee Hwy. (I-66, Exit 60)
703.359.2888

Springfield
Motel 6 ($56-60)
6868 Springfield Blvd.
(I-95, Exit 169B)
703.644.5311

Woodbridge
Quality Inn ($44-89)
1109 Horner Road (I-95, Exit 161)
703.494.0300

florida

Traveler Advisory: If you are planning to spend the night in the Florida Keys, be sure to bring extra cash for your room charge. Even during the off-season, rates in the Keys, as well as along the Atlantic and Gulf Coasts of Florida, are well above the $50/night yardstick. With the exception of youth hostels, you would be very fortunate to find accommodations in these parts of Florida for less than $50/night, particularly in the wintertime. In the Keys along US 1 (locally known as the Overseas Highway), there are a number of nice roadside motels whose rates for a single range from $50 to $70 per night. Peak season rates last generally from December through March. You might just try your luck at driving around and stopping in to check on rates and availability.

APALACHICOLA
Rancho Inn
$50 (55)*
240 Hwy. 98 • 850.653.9435
32 Units, pets OK ($5). Rooms come with phones and cable TV. AAA/Senior discount. Credit cards: AE, DS, MC, V.
*Higher rate effective weekends.

APOPKA
Days Inn
$46-56 (60)*
228 W. Main Street • 407.880.3800
60 Units, no pets. Continental breakfast. Pool. Rooms come with phones and cable TV. Wheelchair accessible. AAA/Senior discount. Major credit cards.
*Higher rate effective February through mid-April.

BELLE GLADE
Travelers Motor Lodge
$48-52 (52-58)*
1300 S. Main Street • 561.996.6761
26 Units, no pets. Rooms come with phones and cable TV. AAA/Senior discount. Credit cards: AE, DS, MC. V.
*Higher rates effective December through May.

BOYNTON BEACH
Atlantic Lodge
$40 (66)*
2607 S. Federal Hwy. • 561.732.4446
20 Units, no pets. Heated pool. Laundry facility. Rooms come with phones and cable TV. AAA/Senior discount. Major credit cards.
*Higher rate effective mid-December through mid-April.

BRADENTON
Econo Lodge
$45 (56-70)*
6727 14th Street W. • 941.758.7199
79 Units, pets OK ($5). Continental breakfast. Pool. Rooms come with phones and cable TV. Some rooms have microwaves and refrigerators. AAA/Senior discount. Credit cards: AE, CB, DC, DS, MC, V.
*Higher rates effective Christmas through mid-April.

Motel 6
$37-50*
660 67th Street Circle E. • 941.747.6005
121 Units, pets OK. Pool. Laundry facility. Data ports. Rooms come with phones, A/C and cable TV. Wheelchair accessible. Credit cards: AE, CB, DC, DS, MC, V.
*Higher rates during winter months.

Super 8 Motel
$43-45 (69-89)*
6516 14th Street W. • 941.756.6656
49 Units, pets OK ($10). Pool. Laundry facility. Rooms come with refrigerators, phones and cable TV. Some rooms have microwaves. Senior discount. Credit cards: AE, DS, MC, V.
*Higher rates effective February through mid-April.

BRANDON
Brandon Motor Lodge
$45-49 (55-69)*
906 E. Brandon Blvd. • 813.689.1261
35 Units, no pets. Pool. Laundry facility. Rooms come with phones and cable TV.

Some rooms have microwaves and refrigerators. AAA/Senior discount. Major credit cards.
*Higher rates effective December through late April.

BUSHNELL
Best Western Guest House Inn
$39-49*
2224 West SR 48 • 352.793.5010
48 Units, pets OK ($5). Continental breakfast. Pool. Playground. Rooms come with phones and cable TV. AAA/Senior discount. Major credit cards.
*Rates higher during special events.

CHATTAHOOCHEE
Admiral Benbow Inn
$41*
East US 90 • 850.663.4336
22 Units, pets OK. Rooms come with phones and cable TV. Some rooms have microwaves and refrigerators. Senior discount. Major credit cards.
*AAA discounted rates.

CHIPLEY
Super 8 Motel
$39-59
1700 Main Street • I-10, Exit 18
850.638.8530
40 Units, pets OK ($5). Rooms come with phones and cable TV. AAA/Senior discount. Major credit cards.

CLEARWATER — *see also Palm Harbor*
Bay Queen Motel
$45*
1925 Edgewater Drive • 727.441.3295
18 Units, no pets. Pool. Laundry facility. Rooms come with phones and cable TV. AAA/Senior discount. Credit cards: MC, V.
*Rates as high as $80/night.

Super 8 Motel
$49 (69)*
22950 US 19N • 727.799.2678
116 Units, no pets. Restaurant on premises. Continental breakfast. Pool. Meeting rooms. Laundry facility. Rooms come with phones and cable TV. Some rooms have microwaves and refrigerators. AAA/Senior discount. Credit cards: AE, CB, DC, DS, MC, V.
*Higher rate effective February and March.

CLEARWATER BEACH
Echo Sails Motel
$40-55 (60-80)*
216 Hamden Drive • 727.442.6962
15 Units, no pets. Heated pool. Laundry facility. Rooms come with phones and cable TV. AAA discount. Credit cards: MC, V.
*Higher rates effective February through late April.

COCOA BEACH
Motel 6
$43-48 (53-56)*
3701 N. Atlantic Avenue • 321.783.3103
151 Units, pets OK. Pool. Laundry facility. Data ports. Rooms come with phones, A/C and cable TV. Wheelchair accessible. Credit cards: AE, CB, DC, DS, MC, V.
*Higher rate effective late January through early April.

CRESTVIEW
Econo Lodge
$45
3101 S. Ferdon • 850.682.6255
84 Units, no pets. Rooms come with phones and cable TV. Some rooms have microwaves and refrigerators. Senior discount. Major credit cards.

Super 8 Motel
$38-58
3925 S. Ferdon Blvd. • 850.682.9649
63 Units, pets OK ($5). Continental breakfast. Rooms come with phones and cable TV. Some rooms have microwaves and refrigerators. AAA/Senior discount. Credit cards: AE, CB, DC, DS, MC, V.

CROSS CITY
Carriage Inn
$34-40
1.5 miles south of town on US 19, 27A & 98 • 352.498.0001
25 Units, pets OK ($4). Restaurant on premises. Pool. Rooms come with phones and cable TV. AAA/Senior discount. Credit cards: AE, DS, MC, V.

CRYSTAL RIVER
Econo Lodge
$40-55 (55-60)*
2575 US 19N • 352.795.9447
44 Units, pets OK. Continental breakfast. Pool. Rooms come with phones and cable TV. Major credit cards.
*Higher rates effective November through April.

DANIA BEACH
Motel 6
$40 (56)*
825 E. Dania Beach Blvd. • 954.921.5505
163 Units, pets OK. Pool. Laundry facility. Data ports. Rooms come with phones, A/C and cable TV. Wheelchair accessible. Credit cards: AE, CB, DC, DS, MC, V.
*Higher rate effective winter months.

DAVENPORT
Super 8 Motel
$30-60
5620 US 27N • 863.424.2521
155 Units, pets OK. Continental breakfast. Pool. Laundry facility. Rooms come with phones, A/C and cable TV. Wheelchair accessible. Credit cards: AE, CB, DC, DS, MC, V.

Tropicana Resorts
$39-49
4825 Hwy. 27 • 863.424.2211
256 Units, no pets. Continental breakfast. Pool. Laundry facility. Rooms come with phones, A/C and cable TV. AAA discount. Major credit cards.

DAYTONA BEACH — *see also South Daytona*
Aruba Inn
$30-45*
1254 N. Atlantic Avenue • 386.253.5643
22 Units, no pets. Pool. Laundry facility. Rooms come with phones and cable TV. AAA/Senior discount. Credit cards: AE, DS, MC, V.
*Rates as high as $75/night.

Budget Host Inn, The Candlelight
$32-38*
1305 S. Ridgewood Ave • 386.252.1142
25 Units, pets OK ($5). Laundry facility. Rooms come with phones and cable TV. Some rooms have refrigerators. AAA/Senior discount. Credit cards: AE, MC, V.
*Rates higher during special events.

Travelers Inn
$29-39*
735 N. Atlantic Avenue • 386.253.3501
20 Units, no pets. Heated pool. Laundry facility. Rooms come with refrigerators, phones and cable TV. Some rooms have kitchenettes. AAA/Senior discount. Credit cards: AE, DS, MC, V.
*Rates as high as $79/night.

DAYTONA BEACH SHORES
Super 8 Motel
$39-50*
2523 S. Atlantic Avenue • 386.767.2551
39 Units, no pets. Restaurant on premises. Pool. Rooms come with phones and cable TV. AAA/Senior discount. Major credit cards.
*Rates as high as $89/night.

EASTPOINT
Sportsman's Lodge Motel & Marina
$44
119 N. Bayshore Drive • 850.670.8423
30 Units, pets OK ($3). Boat dock. Boat ramp. Rooms come with cable TV. No phones in rooms. Some rooms have microwaves and refrigerators. AAA/Senior discount. Credit cards: AE, DS, MC, V.

FLORIDA CITY
Coral Roc Motel
$30-45*
1100 N. Krome Avenue • 305.247.4010
16 Units, pets OK ($50 dep. req.). Continental breakfast. Pool. Laundry facility. Data ports. Rooms come with refrigerators, phones and cable TV. AAA/Senior discount. Credit cards: AE, CB, DC, DS, MC, V.
*Rates as high as $78/night.

Knights Inn
$35-50 (110)*
1223 N.E. 1st Avenue • 305.247.6621
48 Units, no pets. Pool. Laundry facility. Airport transportation. Rooms come with phones and cable TV. Some rooms have microwaves. Credit cards: AE, DS, MC, V.
*Higher rate effective last week of December and all of February.

FORT LAUDERDALE — *see also Dania Beach, Hallandale Beach and Hollywood*
Motel 6
$45-48 (60)*
1801 SR 84 (I-95, Exit 27) • 954.760.7999
107 Units, pets OK. Pool. Laundry facility. Data ports. Rooms come with phones, A/C and cable TV. Wheelchair accessible. Credit cards: AE, CB, DC, DS, MC, V.
*Higher rate effective late January through early April.

Spindrift Motel
$36-46 (56-70)*
2501 N. Ocean Blvd. • 954.566.9866 or 800.447.7019

24 Units, no pets. Heated pool. Laundry facility. Rooms come with phones and cable TV. Some rooms have microwaves and refrigerators. Major credit cards.
*Higher rates effective mid-December through mid-April.

FORT MYERS
Motel 6
$38 (60)*
3350 Marinatown Lane • 941.656.5544
110 Units, pets OK. Pool. Laundry facility. Rooms come with phones, A/C and cable TV. Wheelchair accessible. Credit cards: AE, CB, DC, DS, MC, V.
*Higher rate effective winter months.

Ta Ki-Ki Motel
$44-56 (79-95)*
2631 1st Street • 941.334.2135
23 Units, pets OK. Heated pool. Rooms come with phones and cable TV. Some rooms have refrigerators. AAA discount. Credit cards: AE, CB, DC, DS, MC, V.
*Higher rates effective mid-December through mid-April.

FORT PIERCE
Motel 6
$36-46
2500 Peters Road • 772.461.9937
120 Units, pets OK. Pool. Laundry facility. Data ports. Rooms come with phones, A/C and cable TV. Wheelchair accessible. Credit cards: AE, CB, DC, DS, MC, V.

GAINESVILLE
Econo Lodge/University of Florida
$40-50
2649 S.W. 13th Street • 352.373.7816
53 Units, pets OK. Continental breakfast. Pool. Rooms come with phones and cable TV. Wheelchair accessible. AAA discount. Credit cards: AE, DC, DS, MC, V.

Motel 6
$36-40
4000 S.W. 40th Blvd. • 352.373.1604
121 Units, pets OK. Pool. Laundry facility. Data ports. Rooms come with phones, A/C and cable TV. Wheelchair accessible. Credit cards: AE, CB, DC, DS, MC, V.

Villager Lodge
$35-48
1900 S.W. 13th Street • 352.372.1880
92 Units, pets OK ($25). Restaurant on premises. Continental breakfast. Pool. Airport transportation provided. Laundry facility. Rooms come with phones and cable TV. Some rooms have microwaves and refrigerators. Major credit cards.

HALLANDALE BEACH
Hallandale Resort Motel
$35-55*
703 N.E. 7th Street • 954.456.3024
23 Units, no pets. Heated pool. Laundry facility. Jacuzzi. Data ports Rooms come with phones and cable TV. Credit cards: AE, MC, V.
*Rates as high as $85/night.

HOBE SOUND
Heritage Inn
$40-50
8605 S.E. Federal Hwy. • 772.546.3600
150 Units, pets OK. Restaurant on premises. Pool. Laundry facility. Rooms come with phones and cable TV. Senior discount. Major credit cards.
*AAA discounted rates.

HOLLYWOOD
Richards Motel
$34-49*
1219 S. Federal Hwy. • 954.921.6418 or 800.742.4431
24 Units, no pets. Pool. Laundry facility. Rooms come with refrigerators, phones and cable TV. Some rooms have microwaves. AAA/Senior discount. Credit cards: AE, CB, DC, DS, MC, V.
*Rates as high as $74/night.

Shell Motel
$35-49*
1201 S. Federal Hwy. • 954.923.8085 or 800.547.0044
35 Units, no pets. Heated pool. Laundry facility. Rooms come with refrigerators, phones and cable TV. AAA/Senior discount. Credit cards: AE, DS, MC, V.
*Rates as high as $75/night.

HOMESTEAD
Everglades Motel
$27-39
605 S. Krome Avenue • 305.247.4117
14 Units, pets OK ($5). Pool. Laundry facility. Rooms come with phones and cable TV. AAA/Senior discount. Credit cards: AE, DC, DS, MC, V.

JACKSONVILLE
Masters Inn
$34-45
14585 Duval Road, I-95, Exit 127B
904.741.1133
100 Units, no pets. Data ports. Rooms come with phones and cable TV. AAA/Senior discount. Major credit cards.

Motel 6—Airport
$36-40
10885 Harts Road, I-95, Exit 125
904.757.8600
125 Units, pets OK. Pool. Laundry facility. Data ports. Rooms come with phones, A/C and cable TV. Wheelchair accessible. Credit cards: AE, CB, DC, DS, MC, V.

Motel 6—Southeast
$36
8285 Dix Ellis Trail, I-95, Exit 100
904.731.8400
109 Units, pets OK. Pool. Laundry facility. Rooms come with phones, A/C and cable TV. Wheelchair accessible. Credit cards: AE, CB, DC, DS, MC, V.

Motel 6—Southwest
$36-40
6107 Youngerman Circle, I-295, Exit 4
904.777.6100
126 Units, pets OK. Pool. Laundry facility. Data ports. Rooms come with phones, A/C and cable TV. Wheelchair accessible. Credit cards: AE, CB, DC, DS, MC, V.

Super 8 Motel—North
$35-45
10901 Harts Road, I-95, Exit 125
904.751.3888
61 Units, no pets. Rooms come with phones and cable TV. Some rooms have microwaves and refrigerators. Senior discount. Major credit cards.

Super 8 Motel
$37-47*
5929 Ramona Blvd. • 904.781.3878
127 Units, pets OK. Pool. Laundry facility. Copy and fax service. Rooms come with phones and cable TV. Senior discount. Credit cards: AE, CB, DC, DS, MC, V.
*Rates may increase slightly during holidays, special events and weekends.

Villager Lodge—Airport
$32-40
14691 Duval Road, I-95, Exit 127
904.741.4254
119 Units, pets OK ($8). Pool. Meeting room. Airport transportation. Laundry facility. Rooms come with phones and cable TV. Some rooms have microwaves and refrigerators. Credit cards: AE, CB, DC, DS, MC, V.

JASPER
Days Inn
$35-50
I-75, Exit 86 • 904.792.1987
55 Units, pets OK ($5). Continental breakfast. Pool. Rooms come with phones and cable TV. Wheelchair accessible. AAA discount. Major credit cards.

KEY WEST
Hostelling International
$20
718 South Street • 305.296.5719
90 Beds, Office hours: 24 hours
Facilities: 24-hour access, kitchen, laundry, information, game room, library, TV, pool table, video games, scuba diving lessons, bicycle rentals. Open year-round. Reservations essential during winter months. Credit cards: DS, MC, V.

KISSIMMEE — *see also Davenport and Orlando*
Flamingo Inn
$29-39*
801 E. Vine Street • 407.846.1935
40 Units, pets OK ($8). Pool. Rooms come with microwaves, refrigerators, phones and cable TV. AAA/Senior discount. Credit cards: AE, DS, MC, V.
*Rates higher mid-December through early January.

Magic Castle Inn
$29-47
5055 W. Irlo Bronson Memorial Hwy.
407.396.2212
107 Units, pets OK ($6 and $25 dep. req.). Continental breakfast. Pool. Laundry facility. Rooms come with phones and cable TV. AAA/Senior discount. Major credit cards.

Motel 6
$34-40
5731 W. Irlo Bronson Memorial Hwy. (I-4, Exit 25A) • 407.396.6333
347 Units, pets OK. Pool. Laundry facility. Data ports. Rooms come with phones, A/C

and cable TV. Wheelchair accessible. Credit cards: AE, CB, DC, DS, MC, V.

Motel 6
$34-40
7455 W. Bronson Way, I-4, Exit 25B
407.396.6422
148 Units, pets OK. Pool. Laundry facility. Rooms come with phones, A/C and cable TV. Wheelchair accessible. Credit cards: AE, CB, DC, DS, MC, V.

Parkside Record Inn & Suites
$35-55
4651 W. Irlo Bronson Memorial Hwy.
407.396.8400
57 Units, no pets. Heated pool. Laundry facility. Rooms come with phones and cable TV. Some rooms have microwaves and refrigerators. AAA/Senior discount. Credit cards: AE, DS, MC, V.

Stadium Inn & Suites
$45
2039 E. Irlo Bronson Memorial Hwy.
407.846.7814
112 Units, no pets. Pool. Laundry facility. Jacuzzi. Rooms come with phones and cable TV. Some rooms have microwaves and refrigerators. AAA/Senior discount. Major credit cards.

LAKE CITY
Econo Lodge South
$38-43
Jct. I-75 & US 441 (Ex. 80) • 386.755.9311
59 Units, pets OK. Continental breakfast. Pool. Rooms come with phones and cable TV. AAA/Senior discount. Credit cards: AE, DS, MC, V.

Knights Inn
$30-45
On SR 47 (Exit 81 from I-75)
386.752.7720
100 Units, pets OK. Continental breakfast. Pool. Meeting rooms. Picnic area. Shuffleboard. Rooms come with phones and cable TV. Some rooms have jacuzzis. AAA/ Senior discount. Credit cards: AE, CB, DC, DS, MC, V.

Motel 6
$30
US 90W & Hall of Fame Drive
386.755.4664
98 Units, pets OK. Pool. Laundry facility. Rooms come with phones, A/C and cable TV. Wheelchair accessible. Credit cards: AE, CB, DC, DS, MC, V.

Super 8 Motel
$38-43
On SR 47, just west of Exit 81 from I-75
386.752.6450
87 Units, no pets. Pool. Rooms come with phones and cable TV. Wheelchair accessible. AAA/Senior discount. Credit cards: AE, CB, DC, DS, MC, V.

LAKELAND
Motel 6
$38-48*
3120 US Hwy. 98N • 863.682.0643
124 Units, pets OK. Pool. Laundry facility. Data ports. Rooms come with phones, A/C and cable TV. Wheelchair accessible. Credit cards: AE, CB, DC, DS, MC, V.
*Higher rate effective late January through early April.

Scottish Inns
$39-58
244 N. Florida Avenue • 863.687.2530
46 Units, no pets. Restaurant on premises. Pool. Laundry facility. Rooms come with phones and cable TV. AAA/Senior discount. Credit cards: AE, CB, DC, DS, MC, V.

LAKE WORTH
Martinique Motor Lodge
$45-55 (65-75)*
801 S. Dixie Hwy. • 561.585.2502
19 Units, pets OK ($7 and $20 dep. req.). Pool. Rooms come with refrigerators, phones and cable TV. AAA/Senior discount. Major credit cards.
*Higher rates effective December through April.

LANTANA
Motel 6
$40-50
1310 W. Lantana Road • 561.585.5833
154 Units, pets OK. Pool. Laundry facility. Data ports. Rooms come with phones, A/C and cable TV. Wheelchair accessible. Credit cards: AE, CB, DC, DS, MC, V.

Super 8 Motel
$49
1255 Hypoluxo Road, I-95, Exit 45
561.585.3970
129 Units, no pets. Continental breakfast.

Pool. Rooms come with phones, A/C and cable TV. Wheelchair accessible. Senior discount. Major credit cards.

LEESBURG
Days Inn
$39-49*
1115 W. North Blvd. • 352.787.3131
61 Units, no pets. Continental breakfast. Heated pool. Laundry facility. Rooms come with phones and cable TV. Some rooms have microwaves and refrigerators. AAA/Senior discount. Major credit cards.
*Rates as high as $65/night.

Super 8 Motel
$40-55
1392 North Blvd. W. • 352.787.6363
52 Units, pets OK. Continental breakfast. Heated pool. Rooms come with phones and cable TV. Some rooms have microwaves and refrigerators. Senior discount. Major credit cards.

LIVE OAK
Suwannee River Best Western Inn
$40*
Just south of town on US 129
(I-10, Exit 40) • 904.362.6000
64 Units, pets OK ($5). Continental breakfast. Pool. Laundry facility. Rooms come with phones and cable TV. Major credit cards.
*Rates as high as $110/night.

MADEIRA BEACH
Sea Dawn Motel
$35-50 (60-75)*
13733 Gulf Blvd. • 727.391.7500
14 Units, no pets. Laundry facility. Rooms come with phones and cable TV. AAA/Senior discount. Credit cards: MC, V.
*Higher rates effective January and April.

MADISON
Days Inn
$50
On SR 53 (half mile N of Exit 37 from I-10)
850.973.3330
62 Units, no pets. Pool. Playground. Laundry facility. Rooms come with phones and cable TV. AAA discount. Credit cards: AE, DC, DS, MC, V.

Super 8 Motel
$44
On SR 53 (I-10, Ex. 37) • 850.973.6267
44 Units, no pets. Pool. Rooms come with phones and cable TV. Wheelchair accessible. Senior discount. Major credit cards.

MARIANNA
Best Western Marianna Inn
$45-54
2086 Hwy. 71, I-10, Exit 21
850.526.5666
80 Units, pets OK. Continental breakfast. Pool. Laundry facility. Rooms come with phones and cable TV. AAA/Senior discount. Major Credit cards.

MELBOURNE
Super 8 Motel
$46-52 (52-60)*
1515 S. Harbor City Blvd • 321.723.4430
55 Units, pets OK. Continental breakfast. Laundry facility. Rooms come with phones and cable TV. Senior discount. Wheelchair accessible. AAA/Senior discount. Major credit cards.
*Higher rates effective January through March.

MIAMI
Traveler's Advisory: Accommodations in Miami and Miami Beach will run you more than $50/night. You can save a little money by traveling further south to **Homestead** or **Florida City**, or even north to **Hollywood** or **Ft. Lauderdale**. However, if your plans put you right in Miami, there are several relatively inexpensive places to stay which won't break the bank. Listed below are some recommendations:

Days Inn Medical Center ($59-79*)
1050 N.W. 14th Street
305.324.0200

Fairfield Inn — Miami West
($49-84*)
3959 N.W. 79th Avenue
305.599.5200

Homestead Studio Suites ($55-65)
(Miami Airport)
6605 N.W. 7th Street
305.260.0085

Knights Inn ($50-65)
3530 Biscayne Blvd.
305.572.9550

Red Roof Inn Airport ($55-85)
3401 LeJeune Road
305.871.4221

Super 8 Motel ($50-70)
3400 Biscayne Blvd. (US 1)
305.573.7700

ravelodge — Airport ($49-79)
1170 N.E. 11th Street
305.324.0800

***Additional discount offered with AAA membership.**

MIAMI BEACH
Hostelling International
$17-18
1438 Washington Ave • 305.534.2988
200 Beds, Office hours: 24 hours
Facilities: information, kitchen, laundry facilities, linen rental, lockers, restaurant. Private rooms available. Breakfast, lunch and dinner offered. Open year-round. Reservations essential mid-December through mid-April. Credit cards: JCB, MC, V.

MICANOPY
Knights Inn
$28-48*
17110 S.E. County Road 234, I-75, Exit 73 • 352.466.3163
60 Units, pets OK. Pool. Rooms come with phones and cable TV. AAA/Senior discount. Major credit cards.
*Rates as high as $75/night.

MONTICELLO
Super 8 Motel
$44-49
On US 19 (I-10, Exit 33) • 850.997.8888
52 Units, no pets. Pool. Rooms come with phones and cable TV. Wheelchair accessible. AAA/Senior discount. Major credit cards.

NAPLES
Knights Inn
$40*
6600 Dudley Drive • 941.434.0444
110 Units, no pets. Continental breakfast. Pool. Rooms come with phones and cable TV. Some rooms have refrigerators and microwaves. Major credit cards.
*Rates as high as $100/night in the winter.

Red Roof Inn
$44-54 (79-99)*
1925 Davis Blvd. • 941.774.3117
157 Units, pets OK. Heated pool. Jacuzzi. Picnic area. Laundry facility. Rooms come with phones and cable TV. AAA discount. Major credit cards.
*Higher rates effective late December through March.

NEW SMYRNA BEACH
Ocean Air Motel
$40
1161 N. Dixie Freeway • 386.428.5748
14 Units, no pets. Pool. Rooms come with phones and cable TV. Some rooms have refrigerators. Credit cards: AE, CB, DC, DS, MC, V.

Smyrna Motel
$40-55
1050 N. Dixie Freeway • 386.428.2495
10 Units, pets OK ($10 and $25 dep. req.). Rooms come with refrigerators, phones and cable TV. AAA discount. Credit cards: AE, DS, MC, V.

OCALA — *see also Silver Springs*
Budget Host Inn
$28-46
4013 N.W. Blitchton Rd. • 352.732.6940
21 Units, pets OK ($4). Continental breakfast. Rooms come with phones and cable TV. Some rooms have refrigerators. AAA/Senior discount. Credit cards: AE, DS, MC, V.

Super 8 Motel
$43-58
3924 W. Silver Springs Blvd.
I-75, Exit 69 • 352.629.8794
96 Units, pets OK. Pool. Laundry facility. Rooms come with phones and cable TV. Wheelchair accessible. Senior discount. Credit cards: AE, CB, DC, DS, MC, V.
*Rates may also increase slightly during special events and holidays.

OCOEE
Days Inn
$49
11100 W. Colonial Drive • 407.656.3333
273 Units, no pets. Restaurant on premises. Heated pool. Laundry facility. Playground. Miniature golf. Data ports. Rooms come with phones and cable TV. Some rooms

have refrigerators. AAA/Senior discount. Major credit cards.

OKEECHOBEE
Budget Inn
$39-59 (59-69)*
201 S. Parrott Avenue • 863.763.3185
24 Units, pets OK ($10). Continental breakfast. Pool. Rooms come with refrigerators, phones and cable TV. Some rooms have microwaves. AAA/Senior discount. Major credit cards.
*Higher rates effective January through mid-April.

Economy Inn
$35-50*
507 N. Parrott Avenue • 863.763.1148
24 Units, pets OK ($5). Rooms come with phones and cable TV. Some rooms have refrigerators. Senior discount. Credit cards: AE, DS, MC, V.
*Rates as high as $65/night.

ORANGE PARK
Econo Lodge
$40-50
141 Park Avenue • 904.264.5107
102 Units, no pets. Continental breakfast. Pool. Laundry facility. Rooms come with phones and cable TV. Some rooms have microwaves and refrigerators. Senior discount. Credit cards: AE, DC, DS, MC, V.

ORLANDO — *see also Davenport and Kissimmee*
Ambassador Hotel
$39-49
929 W. Colonial Drive • 407.843.1360
150 Units, no pets. Pool. Jacuzzi. Meeting rooms. Laundry facility. Rooms come with phones and cable TV. Some rooms have refrigerators. AAA discount. Credit cards: AE, CB, DC, DS, JCB, MC, V.

Econo Lodge — Central
$40-60
3300 Colonial Drive • 407.293.7221
102 Units, pets OK ($6). Pool. Laundry facility. Rooms come with phones and cable TV. AAA discount. Major credit cards.

Motel 6
$34-42
5909 American Way • 407.351.6500
112 Units, pets OK. Pool. Laundry facility. Data ports. Rooms come with phones, A/C and cable TV. Wheelchair accessible. Credit cards: AE, CB, DC, DS, MC, V.

Motel 6
$38-42
5300 Adanson Road • 407.647.1444
121 Units, pets OK. Pool. Laundry facility. Data ports. Rooms come with phones, A/C and cable TV. Wheelchair accessible. Credit cards: AE, CB, DC, DS, MC, V.

Travelers Inn & Suites
$40
606 Lee Road • 407.644.4100
132 Units, pets OK. Pool. Rooms come with phones and cable TV. AAA/Senior discount. Credit cards: AE, CB, DC, DS, MC, V.

PALM BAY
Motel 6
$37-47
1170 Malabar Road, I-95, Exit 70
321.951.8222
118 Units, pets OK ($5). Pool. Laundry facility. Data ports. Rooms come with phones and cable TV. Some rooms have microwaves and refrigerators. Wheelchair accessible. Senior discount. Credit cards: AE, DC, DS, MC, V.

PALM COAST
Palm Coast Villas
$50-60 (60-70)*
5454 N. Oceanshore Blvd. • 386.445.3525
14 Units, pets OK. Pool. Laundry facility. Rooms come with cable TV. No phones in rooms. AAA discount. Major credit cards.
*Higher rates effective weekends.

PALM HARBOR
Knights Inn
$30-50*
34106 US 19N • 727.789.2002
114 Units, no pets. Pool. Laundry facility. Meeting rooms. Rooms come with phones and cable TV. Wheelchair accessible. AAA/Senior discount. Major credit cards.
*Rates as high as $130/night.

PANAMA CITY
Scottish Inns
$25-40
4907 W. Hwy. 98 • 850.769.2432
32 Units, pets OK. Pool. Rooms come with phones and cable TV. Senior discount. Major credit cards.

Super 8 Motel
$38-48*
207 Hwy. 231N • 850.784.1988
63 Units, pets OK. Pool. Rooms come with phones and cable TV. Some rooms have microwaves and refrigerators. AAA/Senior discount. Major credit cards.
*Rates as high as $65/night.

PANAMA CITY BEACH
Sea Witch Motel
$40-55
21905 W. Front Beach • 850.234.5722
146 Units, no pets. Restaurant on premises. Pool. Meeting room. Rooms come with phones and cable TV. Major credit cards.

PENSACOLA
The Executive Inn
$35-43
6954 Pensacola Blvd. • 850.478.4015
36 Units, no pets. Pool. Rooms come with phones and cable TV. Some rooms have microwaves and refrigerators. Credit cards: AE, CB, DC, DS, MC, V.

Motel 6—East
$35-48
7226 Plantation Road • 850.474.1060
80 Units, pets OK. Pool. Laundry facility. Data ports. Rooms come with phones, A/C and cable TV. Wheelchair accessible. Credit cards: AE, CB, DC, DS, MC, V.

Motel 6—North
$35-44
7827 N. Davis Hwy. • I-10, Exit 5
850.476.5386
108 Units, pets OK. Pool. Data ports. Rooms come with phones, A/C and cable TV. Wheelchair accessible. Credit cards: AE, CB, DC, DS, MC, V.

Rodeway Inn
$41-51
8500 Pine Forest Road • 850.477.9150
100 Units, no pets. Continental breakfast. Pool. Laundry. Rooms come with phones and cable TV. Some rooms have microwaves and refrigerators. AAA discount. Major credit cards.

PERRY
Best Budget Inn
$38
2220 US 19S • 850.584.6231
61 Units, pets OK. Continental breakfast. Pool. Laundry facility. Rooms come with phones and cable TV. AAA/Senior discount. Credit cards: AE, CB, DC, DS, MC, V.

PINELLAS PARK
La Mark Charles Motel
$42-50
6200 34th Street N. • 727.527.7334
93 Units, pets OK ($10 and $25 dep. req.). Heated pool. Laundry facility. Jacuzzi. Rooms come with phones and cable TV. Credit cards: AE, DS, MC, V.

POMPANO BEACH
Motel 6
$40-48
1201 N.W. 31st Avenue • 954.977.8011
127 Units, pets OK. Pool. Laundry facility. Data ports. Rooms come with phones, A/C and cable TV. Wheelchair accessible. Credit cards: AE, CB, DC, DS, MC, V.

PUNTA GORDA
Motel 6
$36 (56)*
9300 Knights Drive • 941.639.9585
114 Units, pets OK. Pool. Laundry facility. Data ports. Rooms come with phones, A/C and cable TV. Wheelchair accessible. Credit cards: AE, CB, DC, DS, MC, V.
*Higher rate effective late January through early April.

ST. AUGUSTINE
Days Inn Historic
$44
2800 Ponce de Leon Bl. • 904.829.6581
124 Units, pets OK ($10). Restaurant on premises. Pool. Laundry facility. Playground. Fitness facility. Airport transportation. Picnic area. Rooms come with phones and cable TV. AAA/Senior discount. Major credit cards.

Super 8 Motel
$45-55
2550 SR 16 • 904.829.5686
64 Units. Pool. Laundry facility. Rooms come with phones and cable TV. AAA/Senior discount. Credit cards: AE, CB, DC, DS, JCB, MC, V.

ST. CLOUD
Budget Inn of St. Cloud
$35-45
602 13th Street • 407.892.2858
17 Units, no pets. Rooms come with

refrigerators, phones and cable TV. Some rooms have microwaves. AAA/Senior discount. Credit cards: AE, DS, MC, V.

SARASOTA
Knights Inn
$39-55 (49-75)*
5340 N. Tamiami Trail • 941.355.8867
48 Units, no pets. Pool. Laundry facility. Rooms come with phones and cable TV. AAA/Senior discount. Credit cards: AE, DS, MC, V.
*Higher rates effective Christmas through mid-April.

Super 8 Motel
$40*
4309 N. Tamiami Trail • 941.355.9326
50 Units, no pets. Continental breakfast. Pool. Rooms come with phones and cable TV. Some rooms have microwaves and refrigerators. Senior discount. Wheelchair accessible. Major credit cards.
*Rates as high as $90/night during winter.

SEFFNER
Masters Economy Inn
$31-50
6010 SR 579 • 813.821.4681
120 Units, pets OK ($5). Restaurant on premises. Laundry facility. Rooms come with phones and cable TV. Some rooms have microwaves and refrigerators. AAA/Senior discount. Credit cards: AE, CB, DC, DS, MC, V.

SILVER SPRINGS — *see also Ocala*
Econo Lodge
$45-60
5331 NE Silver Spgs. Bl. • 352.236.2383
48 Units, pets OK. Continental breakfast. Pool. Rooms come with phones and cable TV. Senior discount. Major credit cards.

Knights Inn
$35-65
5565 E Silver Spgs. Blvd. • 352.236.2616
40 Units, no pets. Continental breakfast. Pool. Rooms come with A/C, phones and cable TV. Some rooms have refrigerators and microwaves. Wheelchair accessible. Senior discount. Major credit cards.

Sun Plaza Motel
$40-55
5461 E Silver Spgs. Blvd. • 352.236.2343
38 Units, pets OK ($10). Pool. Playground. Rooms come with phones and cable TV. Some rooms have microwaves and refrigerators. AAA discount. Credit cards: AE, CB, DC, DS, MC, V.

SOUTH DAYTONA
Red Carpet Inn
$30-45
1855 S. Ridgewood Ave • 386.767.6681
30 Units, pets OK ($3). Pool. Rooms come with phones and cable TV. AAA/Senior discount. Major credit cards.

Sun Ranch Motor Lodge
$30-40*
2425 S. Ridgewood Ave • 386.767.0661
22 Units, no pets. Pool. Laundry facility. Airport transportation offered. Rooms come with refrigerators, phones and cable TV. AAA/Senior discount. Major credit cards.
*Higher rates effective early February through early March.

TALLAHASSEE
Days Inn
$39-49
2800 N. Monroe Street • I-10, Exit 29
850.385.0136
114 Units, no pets. Continental breakfast. Pool. Meeting rooms. Airport transportation. Rooms come with phones and cable TV. AAA discount. Major credit cards.

Motel 6—North
$36-37
1481 Timberlane Road • I-10, Exit 30
850.668.2600
153 Units, pets OK. Pool. Laundry facility. Data ports. Rooms come with phones, A/C and cable TV. Wheelchair accessible. Credit cards: AE, CB, DC, DS, MC, V.

Motel 6—West
$34
2738 N. Monroe Street • I-10, Exit 29
850.386.7878
101 Units, pets OK. Pool. Laundry facility. Data ports. Rooms come with phones, A/C and cable TV. Wheelchair accessible. Credit cards: AE, CB, DC, DS, MC, V.

TAMPA — *see also Brandon, Clearwater, Clearwater Beach, Madeira Beach, Tarpon Springs and Wesley Chapel*
Microtel Inn & Suites
$44-53
5405 N. Church Avenue • 813.739.2244

63 Units, no pets. Continental breakfast. Pool. Laundry facility. Meeting rooms. Rooms come with phones and cable TV. Wheelchair accessible. AAA/Senior discount. Credit cards: AE, DS, MC, V.

Motel 6—Downtown
$37-48
333 E. Fowler Avenue • 813.932.4948
150 Units, pets OK. Pool. Laundry facility. Data ports. Rooms come with phones, A/C and cable TV. Wheelchair accessible. Credit cards: AE, CB, DC, DS, MC, V.

Motel 6
$36-48
6510 N. Hwy. 301 • I-4, Exits 6 and 6B
813.628.0888
108 Units, pets OK. Pool. Laundry facility. Data ports. Rooms come with phones, A/C and cable TV. Wheelchair accessible. Credit cards: AE, CB, DC, DS, MC, V.

Villager Lodge
$39-45
3110 W. Hillsborough Ave.
I-275, Exit 30 • 813.876.8673
49 Units, no pets. Pool. Laundry facility. Rooms come with phones, A/C and cable TV. Major credit cards.

TARPON SPRINGS
Tarpon Shores Inn
$45-55
40346 US Hwy. 19N • 727.938.2483
51 Units, no pets. Heated pool. Sauna. Jacuzzi. Shuffleboard. Laundry facility. Rooms come with phones and cable TV. Some rooms have microwaves and refrigerators. Senior discount. Credit cards: AE, DS, MC, V.

TAVARES
Budget Inn
$40-44 (55-62)*
101 W. Burleigh Blvd. • 352.343.4666
40 Units, pets OK ($8). Pool. Rooms come with phones and cable TV. AAA/Senior discount. Credit cards: AE, DS, MC, V.
*Higher rates effective January through mid-April.

VENICE
Motel 6
$37-40 (60)*
281 US 41 Bypass N. • 941.485.8255
103 Units, pets OK. Pool. Laundry facility. Data ports. Rooms come with phones, A/C and cable TV. Wheelchair accessible. Credit cards: AE, CB, DC, DS, MC, V.
*Higher rate effective mid-January through early April.

VERO BEACH
Howard Johnson Express Inn
$45-55 (59-99)*
1985 90th Avenue • 561.778.1985
60 Units, no pets. Continental breakfast. Pool. Laundry facility. Rooms come with refrigerators, phones and cable TV. AAA discount. Major credit cards.
*Higher rates effective January through early April.

Vero Beach Resort
$44-49*
8800 20th St., I-95, Exit 68 • 561.562.9991
114 Units, pets OK ($5). Restaurant on premises. Pool. Laundry facility. Meeting rooms. Rooms come with refrigerators, phones and cable TV. AAA/Senior discount. Major credit cards.
*Higher rates effective January through early April.

WESLEY CHAPEL
Masters Inn Tampa North
$41-46
27807 SR 54W • 813.973.0155
119 Units, pets OK ($5). Restaurant on premises. Continental breakfast. Pool. Laundry facility. Rooms come with phones and cable TV. Some rooms have microwaves and refrigerators. AAA/Senior discount. Major credit cards.

WILDWOOD
Super 8 Motel
$40-50*
344 E. SR 44 • 352.748.3783
48 Units, pets OK. Continental breakfast. Fax service. Rooms come with phones and cable TV. Wheelchair accessible. Senior discount. Credit cards: AE, CB, DC, DS, MC, V.
*Rates may also increase slightly during special events and holidays.

WINTER HAVEN
Budget Host Driftwood Lodge
$38-52
970 Cypress Gardens Bl. • 863.294.4229
22 Units, pets OK. Restaurant on premises. Heated pool. Laundry facility. Rooms come

with phones and cable TV. Senior discount. Credit cards: AE, DS, MC, V.

YULEE
Days Inn
$35-45
3250 US 17N • 904.225.2011
100 Units, pets OK ($6). Continental breakfast. Pool. Airport transportation. Rooms come with phones and cable TV. Wheelchair accessible. AAA discount. Credit cards: AE, DC, DS, MC, V.

georgia

ACWORTH
Days Inn
$40
5035 Cowan Road • 770.974.1700
64 Units, pets OK. Continental breakfast. Rooms come with phones and cable TV. AAA/Senior discount. Credit cards: AE, DC, DS, MC, V.

Econo Lodge
$40
4980 Cowan Road • 770.974.1922
60 Units, pets OK. Continental breakfast. Pool. Meeting rooms. Rooms come with phones and cable TV. AAA/Senior discount. Major credit cards.

ADEL
Days Inn I-75
$36-44
1200 W. 4th Street • 229.896.4574
80 Units, pets OK ($5). Restaurant on premises. Continental breakfast. Pool. Wading Pool. Meeting room. Playground. Rooms come with phones and cable TV. AAA discount. Credit cards: AE, CB, DC, DS, JCB, MC, V.

Howard Johnson
$34-40
1103 W. 4th Street (I-75, Exit 10)
229.896.2244
70 Units, pets OK ($3). Continental breakfast. Wading pool. Rooms come with phones and cable TV. AAA discount. Credit cards: AE, CB, DC, DS, JCB, MC, V.

Super 8 Motel
$34-39
1103 W. 4th Street • 229.896.4523
50 Units, pets OK ($5). Continental breakfast. Wading pool. Rooms come with phones and cable TV. AAA/Senior discount. Credit cards: AE, CB, DC, DS, JCB, MC, V.

ALBANY
Motel 6
$30-32
201 S. Thornton Drive • 229.439.0078
102 Units, pets OK. Pool. Laundry facility. Data ports. Rooms come with phones, A/C and cable TV. Wheelchair accessible. Credit cards: AE, CB, DC, DS, MC, V.

Super 8 Motel
$40
2444 N. Slappey Blvd. • 229.888.8388
62 Units, pets OK. Continental breakfast. Rooms come with phones and cable TV. Wheelchair accessible. Senior discount. Major credit cards.

ASHBURN
Comfort Inn
$33-40
820 Shoneys Drive • 229.567.0080
56 Units, pets OK. Continental breakfast. Pool. Rooms come with phones and cable TV. Some rooms have microwaves and refrigerators. Major credit cards.

Super 8 Motel
$28-31
749 E. Washington Ave. • 229.567.4688
40 Units, pets OK. Continental breakfast. Copy and fax service. Rooms come with phones and cable TV. Some rooms have microwaves and refrigerators. Wheelchair accessible. Senior discount. Credit cards: AE, CB, DC, DS, MC, V.

ATHENS
Scottish Inns
$40 (65)*
410 Macon Hwy. • 706.546.8161 or 800.251.1962
48 Units, pets OK. Pool in summer. Rooms come with phones and cable TV. Senior discount. Major credit cards.
*Higher rate effective weekends.

Super 8 Motel
$38-40
3425 Atlanta Hwy. • 706.549.0251
40 Units, pets OK. Continental breakfast. Pool. Jacuzzi. Laundry facility. Rooms come with phones and cable TV. Wheelchair accessible. Senior discount. Credit cards: AE, CB, DC, DS, MC, V.

ATLANTA — *see also Austell, College Park, Decatur, Forest Park, Jonesboro, Marietta,*

Norcross, Stockbridge, Smyrna and Union City

Days Inn
$48
3585 Chamblee-Tucker Road
I-285, Exit 27 • 770.455.8000
107 Units, pets OK. Pool. Laundry facility. Meeting rooms. Rooms come with phones, A/C and cable TV. Wheelchair accessible. AAA discount. Credit cards: AE, CB, DC, DS, MC, V.

Econo Lodge
$42-56
4275 N.E. Expressway • 770.934.2770
90 Units, no pets. Continental breakfast. Rooms come with phones and cable TV. Major credit cards.

Masters Economy Inn
$44-52
4120 Fulton Industrial Blvd.
404.696.4690
169 Units, pets OK ($5-10). Restaurant on premises. Pool. Meeting rooms. Rooms come with phones and cable TV. AAA/Senior discount. Major credit cards.

Motel 6
$43-50
2820 Chamblee-Tucker Road
I-85, Exit 94 • 770.458.6626
98 Units, pets OK. Laundry facility. Rooms come with phones, A/C and cable TV. Wheelchair accessible. Credit cards: AE, CB, DC, DS, MC, V.

AUGUSTA — see also Martinez

Days Inn
$40-50
3320 Dean's Bridge Rd. • 706.793.9600
42 Units, no pets. Continental breakfast. Rooms come with phones and cable TV. Some rooms have microwaves and refrigerators. AAA/Senior discount. Credit cards: AE, CB, DC, DS, MC, V.

Super 8 Motel & Suites Riverwalk
$35
954 5th Street • 706.724.0757
62 Units, pets OK. Continental breakfast. Pool. Rooms come with refrigerators, phones and cable TV. Some rooms have microwaves. Credit cards: AE, CB, DC, DS, MC, V.

Travelodge
$35-50
3039 Washington Road • 706.868.6930
50 Units, no pets. Continental breakfast. Laundry facility. Rooms come with microwaves, refrigerators, phones and cable TV. Senior discount. Credit cards: AE, CB, DC, DS, MC, V.

West Bank Inn
$40-45
2904 Washington Road • 706.733.1724
47 Units, no pets. Continental breakfast. Laundry facility. Rooms come with phones and cable TV. Some rooms have microwaves and refrigerators. AAA/Senior discount. Major credit cards.

AUSTELL

Knights Inn
$33-65
1595 Blairs Bridge Road
I-20, Exit 44 • 770.944.0824
97 Units, no pets. Pool. Meeting rooms. Rooms come with phones and cable TV. Some rooms have microwaves and refrigerators. Wheelchair accessible. Major credit cards.

BAXLEY

Budget Host Inn
$36-40
713 E. Parker Street (US 341E)
912.367.2200
30 Units, pets OK. Pool. Laundry facility. Rooms come with phones, A/C and cable TV. Some rooms have microwaves and refrigerators. Senior discount. Major credit cards.

BRUNSWICK

Knights Inn
$40-43
5044 New Jesup Hwy. • 912.267.6500
105 Units, pets OK. Continental breakfast. Pool. Laundry facility. Rooms come with phones, A/C and cable TV. Wheelchair accessible. AAA/Senior discount. Major credit cards.

Motel 6
$36-40
403 Butler Drive • 912.264.8582
88 Units, pets OK. Pool. Laundry facility. Rooms come with phones, A/C and cable TV. Wheelchair accessible. Credit cards: AE, CB, DC, DS, MC, V.

BYRON
Days Inn
$35-50
246 N. Hwy. 49 • 478.956.5100
62 Units, pets OK ($5). Continental breakfast. Pool. Laundry facility. Rooms come with phones and cable TV. Some rooms have microwaves and refrigerators. Wheelchair accessible. AAA/Senior discount. Major credit cards.

Econo Lodge
$34-38
106 Old Macon Road • 478.956.5600
92 Units, pets OK ($5). Continental breakfast. Pool. Rooms come with phones and cable TV. Some rooms have microwaves, jacuzzis and refrigerators. Credit cards: AE, DS, MC, V.

CALHOUN
Budget Host Shepherd Motel
$37-39
3900 Fairmont Hwy. S.E. • 706.629.8644
31 Units, pets OK. Restaurant on premises. Pool. Laundry facility. Meeting rooms. Rooms come with phones and cable TV. Some rooms have microwaves and refrigerators. Major credit cards.

Knights Inn
$32-35
2261 US 41 N.E. • 706.629.4521
40 Units, pets OK. Continental breakfast. Pool. Laundry facility. Jacuzzi. Rooms come with phones and cable TV. Senior discount. Major credit cards.

Ramada Limited
$40-49
1204 Red Bud Rd. N.E. • 706.629.9207
49 Units, no pets. Continental breakfast. Pool. Rooms come with phones and cable TV. Some rooms have refrigerators. AAA/Senior discount. Credit cards: AE, DC, DS, MC, V.

CARROLLTON
Country Hearth Inn
$40-45
901 U.S. 27S • 770.834.2001
60 Units, no pets. Continental breakfast. Pool. Meeting rooms. Rooms come with phones and cable TV. AAA/Senior discount. Credit cards: AE, DS, MC, V.

CARTERSVILLE
Econo Lodge
$26-50
35 Carson Loop • 770.387.2696
68 Units, pets OK. Continental breakfast. Pool. Rooms come with phones and cable TV. Wheelchair accessible. Senior discount. Credit cards: AE, DC, DS, MC, V.

Motel 6
$36-40
5657 Hwy. 20 N.E.
I-75, Exit 125 • 770.386.1449
48 Units, pets OK ($5). Pool. Rooms come with phones and cable TV. Senior discount. Credit cards: AE, CB, DC, DS, JCB, MC, V.

Super 8 Motel
$37-40
I-75 & Hwy. 20 • 770.382.8881
62 Units, pets OK ($5). Rooms come with phones and cable TV. Wheelchair accessible. AAA/Senior discount. Credit cards: AE, CB, DC, DS, MC, V.
*Rates may increase slightly during holidays, special events and weekends.

CHATSWORTH
Key West Inn
$45
501 GI Maddox Pkwy. • 706.517.1155
43 Units, pets OK ($5). Laundry facility. Data ports. Rooms come with phones and cable TV. AAA discount. Credit cards: AE, DS, MC, V.

CLAXTON
American Inn
$35
On Duval Road • 912.739.2525
33 Units, no pets. Restaurant on premises. Continental breakfast. Rooms come with phones and cable TV. Wheelchair accessible. Major credit cards.

COLLEGE PARK
Red Roof Inn
$37-49
2471 Old National Pkwy.
I-85, Exit 69 • 404.761.9701
108 Units, pets OK. Data ports. Rooms come with phones and cable TV. AAA discount. Major credit cards.

COLUMBUS — *see also Phenix City (AL)*
Motel 6
$36-40

3050 Victory Drive • 706.687.7214
111 Units, pets OK. Pool. Laundry facility. Data ports. Rooms come with phones, A/C and cable TV. Wheelchair accessible. Credit cards: AE, CB, DC, DS, MC, V.

COMMERCE
Comfort Inn
$45-49
165 Eisenhower Drive • I-85, Exit 149
706.335.9001
62 Units, pets OK ($10-20). Continental breakfast. Pool. Jacuzzi. Rooms come with phones and cable TV. Senior discount. Major credit cards.

Days Inn
$43-55
On US 441 • I-85, Exit 149 • 706.335.2595
61 Units, no pets. Continental breakfast. Rooms come with phones and cable TV. AAA discount. Major credit cards.

CORDELE
Days Inn
$39-44
215 S. 7th Street • 229.273.1123
126 Units, pets OK. Pool. Laundry facility. Rooms come with phones and cable TV. Some rooms have microwaves and refrigerators. AAA discount. Major credit cards.

Ramada Inn
$45-48
2016 16th Avenue E.
I-75, Exit 101 • 229.273.5000
103 Units, pets OK. Restaurant on premises. Pool. Laundry facility. Meeting rooms. Fitness facility. Data ports. Rooms come with phones and cable TV. AAA/Senior discount. Major credit cards.

COVINGTON
Econo Lodge
$44-56
10101 Alcovy Jersey Rd • 770.786.4133
52 Units, no pets. Continental breakfast. Rooms come with phones and cable TV. Wheelchair accessible. Major credit cards.

DAHLONEGA
Econo Lodge
$40*
801 N. Grove Street • 706.864.6191
40 Units, no pets. Continental breakfast. Pool. Rooms come with phones and cable TV. Some rooms have microwaves, jacuzzis and refrigerators. Senior discount. Credit cards: AE, CB, DC, DS, MC, V.
*Rates higher during special events.

DALTON
Best Western Inn of Dalton
$45-50
2106 Chattanooga Rd. • 706.226.5022
99 Units, pets OK. Restaurant on premises. Pool. Laundry facility. Rooms come with phones and cable TV. AAA/Senior discount. Major credit cards.

Motel 6
$30-32
2200 Chattanooga Rd. • 706.278.5522
69 Units, pets OK. Laundry facility. Rooms come with phones, A/C and cable TV. Wheelchair accessible. Credit cards: AE, CB, DC, DS, MC, V.

Super 8 Motel
$39-47
236 Connector 3 S.W., I-75, Exit 135
706.278.9323
59 Units, no pets. Continental breakfast. Pool Rooms come with phones and cable TV. Wheelchair accessible. Senior discount. Major credit cards.

DECATUR
Econo Lodge
$45-50
2574 Candler Road • 404.243.4422
59 Units, no pets. Continental breakfast. Rooms come with phones and cable TV. AAA discount. Major credit cards.

Motel 6
$40-46
2565 Wesley Chapel Road
I-20, Exit 36N • 404.288.6911
99 Units, pets OK. Pool. Laundry facility. Rooms come with phones, A/C and cable TV. Wheelchair accessible. Credit cards: AE, CB, DC, DS, MC, V.

DONALDSVILLE
Days Inn
$40-50
On US 84 • 229.524.2185
31 Units, pets OK. Continental breakfast. Jacuzzi. Rooms come with phones and cable TV. Wheelchair accessible. AAA discount. Major credit cards.

DORAVILLE
Masters Inn
$39-49
3092 Presidential Pkwy. • 770.454.8373
88 Units, pets OK ($5-10). Pool. Rooms come with phones and cable TV. Some rooms have microwaves and refrigerators. AAA/Senior discount. Major credit cards.

DOUGLAS
Days Inn
$37-45
90 N. Peterson • 912.384.5190
70 Units, no pets. Continental breakfast. Pool. Jacuzzi. Rooms come with phones and cable TV. Wheelchair accessible. AAA discount. Major credit cards.

Super 8 Motel
$36-40*
1610 S. Peterson Ave. • 912.384.0886
49 Units, no pets. Rooms come with phones and cable TV. Wheelchair accessible. Senior discount. Credit cards: AE, CB, DC, DS, MC, V.
*Rates may increase slightly during holidays, special events and weekends.

DUBLIN
Days Inn
$50
2111 Hwy. 441S • 478.275.7637
49 Units, no pets. Pool. Laundry facility. Meeting rooms. Rooms come with phones and cable TV. AAA/Senior discount. Major credit cards.

Super 8 Motel
$46-49
2150 Hwy. 441S • 478.272.5141
52 Units, no pets. Pool. Laundry facility. Data ports. Rooms come with phones and cable TV. AAA discount. Major credit cards.

FOLKSTON
Days Inn
$38*
1201 S. 2nd Street • 912.496.2514
37 Units, pets OK. Restaurant on premises. Continental breakfast. Pool. Airport transportation. Rooms come with phones and cable TV. Credit cards: AE, CB, DC, DS, JCB, MC, V.
*Rates higher during special events, weekends and holidays.

FOREST PARK
Motel 6
$42-46
5060 Frontage Road (I-75, Exit 78)
404.363.6429
58 Units, pets OK. Rooms come with phones, A/C and cable TV. Wheelchair accessible. Credit cards: AE, CB, DC, DS, MC, V.

FORSYTH
Best Western Hilltop Inn
$38
951 Hwy. 42N (I-75, Exit 63)
478.994.9260
120 Units, pets OK ($25 dep. req.). Continental breakfast. Pool. Rooms come with phones and cable TV. Senior discount. AAA/Senior discount. Major credit cards.

GAINESVILLE
Masters Economy Inn
$34-40
I-985 & US 129 (Exit 6) • 770.532.7531
100 Units, pets OK. Pool. Meeting room. Fax service. Rooms come with phones and cable TV. Senior discount. Major credit cards.

GARDEN CITY
Masters Economy Inn
$40-50
4200 Hwy. 21N (Augusta Road)
912.964.4344
122 Units, pets OK ($4). Pool. Wading pool. Meeting rooms. Laundry facility. Airport transportation. Rooms come with phones and cable TV. Some rooms have kitchens, microwaves and refrigerators. AAA/Senior discount. Major credit cards.

GREENSBORO
Microtel Inn
$44-55
2470 Old Eatonton Hwy., I-20, Exit 53
706.453.7300
48 Units, no pets. Continental breakfast. Laundry facility. Data ports. Rooms come with phones and cable TV. Wheelchair accessible. Major credit cards.

HAZLEHURST
Days Inn
$38-42
312 Coffee Street • 912.375.4527
74 Units, pets OK. Restaurant on premises. Pool. Laundry facility. Rooms come with

phones and cable TV. Some rooms have microwaves and refrigerators. AAA discount. Credit cards: AE, CB, DC, DS, MC, V.

JACKSON
Days Inn
$42-52
625 E. Third Street • 770.504.8100
30 Units, no pets. Continental breakfast. Pool. Meeting rooms. Rooms come with phones and cable TV. Wheelchair accessible. AAA discount. Major credit cards.

JESUP
Days Inn
$32-39
384 US 301S • 912.427.3751
100 Units, pets OK. Continental breakfast. Pool. Rooms come with phones and cable TV. Wheelchair accessible. AAA discount. Major credit cards.

JONESBORO
Shoneys Inn—Atlanta South
$44-48
6358 Old Dixie Road, I-75, Exit 235
770.968.5018
135 Units, pets OK. Continental breakfast. Pool. Laundry facility. Meeting rooms. Data ports. Rooms come with phones and cable TV. AAA/Senior discount. Major credit cards.

KENNESAW
Red Roof Inn
$39-49
520 Roberts Ct. N.W. • 770.429.0323
136 Units, pets OK. Rooms come with phones and cable TV. Wheelchair accessible. AAA discount. Major credit cards.

Windsor Inn
$40-45
2655 Cobb Pkwy. • 770.424.6330
32 Units, no pets. Continental breakfast. Pool. Airport transportation. Rooms come with phones and cable TV. Some rooms have jacuzzis and refrigerators. AAA/Senior discount. Credit cards: AE, DS, MC, V.

KINGSLAND
Econo Lodge
$40-45
1135 E. King Avenue • I-95, Exit 3
912.673.7336
52 Units, pets OK ($5). Continental breakfast. Pool. Rooms come with phones and cable TV. Some rooms have microwaves and refrigerators. Wheelchair accessible. Credit cards: AE, DS, MC, V.

Super 8 Motel
$30-50
120 Edenfield Drive • 912.729.6888
60 Units, pets OK ($5). Rooms come with phones and cable TV. Some rooms have microwaves and refrigerators. AAA discount. Major credit cards.

LAKE PARK
Days Inn
$38-44
4913 Timber Drive • 229.559.0229
94 Units, pets OK. Continental breakfast. Pool. Rooms come with phones and cable TV. AAA/Senior discount. Credit cards: AE, CB, DC, DS, MC, V.

Travelodge
$38-45
4912 Timber Drive • 229.559.0110
80 Units, pets OK. Continental breakfast. Laundry facility. Rooms come with phones and cable TV. Some rooms have microwaves and refrigerators. AAA/Senior discount. Credit cards: AE, DC, DS, MC, V.

LITHIA SPRINGS
Motel 6
$40-52
920 Bob Arnold Blvd. • I-20, Exit 44
678.445.0606
74 Units, pets OK. Pool. Laundry facility. Data ports. Rooms come with phones, A/C and cable TV. Wheelchair accessible. Credit cards: AE, CB, DC, DS, MC, V.

LOCUST GROVE
Super 8 Motel
$45
4605 Bill Gardner Pkwy. • 770.957.2936
56 Units, pets OK. Continental breakfast. Pool. Laundry facility. Rooms come with phones and cable TV. Wheelchair accessible. AAA/Senior discount. Credit cards: AE, CB, DC, DS, MC, V.

LOUISVILLE
Louisville Motor Lodge
$43-51
308 Hwy. 1 Bypass, 1 mile NE on US 1 Bypass • 478.625.7168
40 Units, pets OK ($5). Picnic area. Rooms

come with phones and cable TV. AAA/Senior discount. Credit cards: AE, DS, MC, V.

MACON
Econo Lodge
$32-45
4951 Romeiser Drive • 478.474.1661
60 Units, pets OK ($4 daily and $10 dep. req.). Continental breakfast. Pool. Rooms come with phones and cable TV. Some rooms have microwaves and refrigerators. AAA discount. Credit cards: AE, DC, DS, JCB, MC, V.

Motel 6
$30-32
4991 Harrison Road • 478.474.2870
103 Units, pets OK. Pool. Laundry facility. Data ports. Rooms come with phones, A/C and cable TV. Wheelchair accessible. Credit cards: AE, CB, DC, DS, MC, V.

Super 8 Motel
$40-50
6007 Harrison Road • I-475, Exit 1
478.788.8800
60 Units, no pets. Pool. Laundry facility. Rooms come with phones and cable TV. Some rooms have microwaves and refrigerators. Wheelchair accessible. AAA/Senior discount. Major credit cards.

MADISON
Super 8 Motel
$42-50
2091 Eatonton Road • 706.342.7800
60 Units, pets OK. Continental breakfast. Laundry facility. Rooms come with phones and cable TV. Wheelchair accessible. AAA/Senior discount. Credit cards: AE, DS, MC, V.

MARIETTA
Masters Economy Inn
$39-49
2682 Windy Hill Road • 770.951.2005
87 Units, pets OK ($10). Laundry facility. Rooms come with phones and cable TV. Wheelchair accessible. AAA/Senior discount. Major credit cards.

Motel 6
$34-46
2360 Delk Road • I-75, Exit 111
770.952.8161
217 Units, pets OK. Pool. Laundry facility. Rooms come with phones, A/C and cable TV. Wheelchair accessible. Credit cards: *AE, CB, DC, DS, MC, V.

McDONOUGH
Masters Economy Inn
$32-42
1331 Hampton Road • 770.957.5818
120 Units, pets OK ($5). Pool. Laundry facility. Rooms come with phones and cable TV. AAA/Senior discount. Major credit cards.

Microtel Inn & Suites
$40
610 Hwy. 155S • I-85, Exit 216
678.432.6363
51 Units, no pets. Continental breakfast. Laundry facility. Meeting rooms. Rooms come with phones and cable TV. Wheelchair accessible. AAA/Senior discount. Major credit cards.

MILLEDGEVILLE
Scottish Inns
$28-30
2474 N. Columbia St. • 478.453.9491
50 Units, pets OK. Rooms come with phones and cable TV. Senior discount. Major credit cards.

MORROW
Red Roof Inn
$39-59
1348 S. Lake Plaza Dr. • 770.968.1483
109 Units, pets OK. Rooms come with phones and cable TV. AAA discount. Major credit cards.

NEWNAN
Motel 6
$40-46
40 Parkway North • I-85, Exit 47
770.251.4580
107 Units, pets OK. Pool. Laundry facility. Rooms come with phones, A/C and cable TV. Wheelchair accessible. Credit cards: AE, CB, DC, DS, MC, V.

Super 8 Motel
$46-48
1334 South Hwy. 29 (Exit 8 from I-85)
770.683.0089
52 Units, no pets. Pool. Laundry facility. Rooms come with phones and cable TV. AAA/Senior discount. Credit cards: AE, CB, DC, DS, MC, V.

NORCROSS
Motel 6
$35-37
6015 Oakbrook Pkwy., I-85, Exit 37
770.446.2311
145 Units, pets OK. Pool. Laundry facility. Rooms come with phones, A/C and cable TV. Wheelchair accessible. Credit cards: AE, CB, DC, DS, MC, V.

Red Roof Inn
$36-45
5171 Brook Hollow Pkwy. • 770.448.8944
115 Units, pets OK. Rooms come with phones and cable TV. AAA discount. Major credit cards.

PERRY
Super 8 Motel
$40-45
1410 Sam Nunn Blvd. • 478.987.0999
56 Units, pets OK. Continental breakfast. Pool. Spa. Copy and fax service. Laundry facility. Rooms come with phones and cable TV. Wheelchair accessible. AAA/Senior discount. Credit cards: AE, CB, DC, DS, MC, V.

Travelodge
$44-49
100 Westview Lane • 478.987.7355
62 Units, no pets. Continental breakfast. Pool. Jacuzzi. Laundry. Rooms come with phones and cable TV. Some rooms have microwaves and refrigerators. AAA discount. Major credit cards.

POOLER
Microtel Inns
$45-55
125 Continental Blvd. • 912.748.1112
71 Units, no pets. Continental breakfast. Pool. Rooms come with phones and cable TV. Some rooms have microwaves and refrigerators. Wheelchair accessible. AAA/ Senior discount. Major credit cards.

RICHLAND
Days Inn
$40-50
46 Nicholson Street • 229.887.9000
31 Units, no pets. Continental breakfast. Pool. Jacuzzi. Rooms come with phones and cable TV. Wheelchair accessible. AAA discount. Major credit cards.

RICHMOND HILL
Econo Lodge
$45
I-95 & US 17 (Exit 14) • 912.756.3312
48 Units, pets OK. Continental breakfast. Pool. Fax service. Rooms come with phones and cable TV. Some rooms have microwaves and refrigerators. Wheelchair accessible. AAA discount. Credit cards: AE, DS, MC, V.

Motel 6
$30-36
I-95 & US 17 (Exit 14) • 912.756.3543
122 Units, pets OK. Pool. Laundry facility. Rooms come with phones, A/C and cable TV. Wheelchair accessible. Credit cards: AE, CB, DC, DS, MC, V.

RINGGOLD
Knights Inn
$28-33
584 Pine Grove Access Road (From I-75, Exit 142) • 706.891.1824
108 Units, no pets. Continental breakfast. Pool. Rooms come with phones and cable TV. Wheelchair accessible. Major credit cards.

Super 8 Motel
$40-50
5400 Alabama Hwy. • 706.965.7080
40 Units, pets OK ($3). Continental breakfast. Pool. Rooms come with phones and cable TV. Wheelchair accessible. Senior discount. Major credit cards.

ROME
Ramada Inn
$40
707 Turner McCall Blvd. • 706.232.0444
155 Units, no pets. Restaurant on premises. Continental breakfast. Pool. Laundry facility. Fitness facility. Meeting rooms. Rooms come with phones and cable TV. Major credit cards.

Super 8 Motel
$40-50*
1590 Dodd Blvd. S.E. • 706.234.8182
62 Units, pets OK. Rooms come with phones and cable TV. Wheelchair accessible. Senior discount. Credit cards: AE, CB, DC, DS, MC, V.
*Rates may increase slightly during special events, holidays and weekends.

SAVANNAH — *see also Garden City, Pooler and Richmond Hill*
Days Inn
$49
4 Gateway Blvd. • I-95, Exit 94
912.925.3680
82 Units, pets OK. Pool. Laundry facility. Meeting rooms. Data ports. Rooms come with phones and cable TV. AAA discount. Major credit cards.

Super 8 Motel
$35-42*
15 Ft. Argyle Road • 912.927.8550
61 Units, pets OK ($10). Continental breakfast. Pool. Rooms come with phones and cable TV. Wheelchair accessible. Senior discount. Major credit cards.
*Rates may increase slightly during special events, holidays and weekends.

Travelodge
$36-41
1 Ft. Argyle Road • 912.925.2640
100 Units, pets OK. Rooms come with phones and cable TV. AAA/AARP discount available. Major credit cards.

SMYRNA
Red Roof Inn
$38-49
2200 Corporate Plaza • 770.952.6966
136 Units, pets OK. Laundry facility. Rooms come with phones and cable TV. AAA discount. Major credit cards.

STOCKBRIDGE
Motel 6
$36-46
7233 Davidson Pkwy. • 770.389.1142
107 Units, pets OK. Pool. Rooms come with phones, A/C and cable TV. Wheelchair accessible. Credit cards: AE, CB, DC, DS, MC, V.

SWAINSBORO
Days Inn
$40-50
654 Main Street • 912.237.9333
32 Units, pets OK. Continental breakfast. Rooms come with phones and cable TV. Wheelchair accessible. AAA discount. Major credit cards.

THOMASVILLE
Days Inn of Thomasville
$38-55
102 US 19S • 229.226.6025
120 Units, pets OK ($5). Restaurant on premises. Pool. Laundry facility. Rooms come with phones and cable TV. Some rooms have refrigerators. Wheelchair accessible. AAA discount. Credit cards: AE, DC, DS, MC, V.

Super 8 Motel
$45
15211 US 19S • 229.226.9585
48 Units, no pets. Continental breakfast. Rooms come with phones and cable TV. Some rooms have microwaves and refrigerators. AAA/Senior discount. Major credit cards.

THOMSON
Econo Lodge
$42-45
130 N. Seymoor Dr. NW • 706.595.7144
47 Units, no pets. Rooms come with phones and cable TV. Some rooms have microwaves and refrigerators. AAA/Senior discount. Credit cards: AE, CB, DC, DS, MC, V.

TIFTON — *see also Lenox*
Masters Economy Inn
$32-37
Jct. I-75, US 82 & 319 • 229.382.8100
120 Units, pets OK ($5). Pool. Laundry facility. Rooms come with phones and cable TV. AAA discount. Credit cards: AE, CB, DC, DS, MC, V.

Super 8 Motel
$36*
I-75 & W. 2nd Street • 229.382.9500
70 Units, pets OK ($5). Pool. Copy and fax service. Rooms come with phones and cable TV. Wheelchair accessible. Senior discount. Major credit cards.
*Rates may increase slightly during special events and holidays.

TOWNSEND
Days Inn
$48-53
I-95, Exit 11 • 912.832.4411
117 Units, pets OK. Restaurant on premises. Pool. Rooms come with phones and cable TV. Wheelchair accessible. AAA discount. Major credit cards.

TUCKER
Knights Inn
$35-60
2942 Lawrenceville Hwy. • 770.934.5060
94 Units, pets OK Pool. Rooms come with phones and cable TV. Wheelchair accessible. AAA/Senior discount. Major credit cards.

Masters Inn
$39-49
1435 Montreal Road • 770.938.3552
107 Units, pets OK ($5). Pool. Laundry facility. Rooms come with phones and cable TV. AAA/Senior discount. Major credit cards.

UNADILLA
Scottish Inn
$32
I-75 (Exit 39) • 478.627.3228
60 Units, pets OK ($2). Pool. Playground. Rooms come with phones and cable TV. AAA/Senior discount. Credit cards: AE, DS, MC, V.

UNION CITY
Motel 6
$40-46
3860 Flat Shoals Road, I-85, Exit 66
770.969.0110
99 Units, pets OK. Pool. Laundry facility. Data ports. Airport transportation. Rooms come with phones, A/C and cable TV. Wheelchair accessible. Credit cards: AE, CB, DC, DS, MC, V.

VALDOSTA
Days Inn I-75
$35-42
4598 N. Valdosta Road • 229.244.4460
100 Units, pets OK ($5). Pool. Rooms come with phones and cable TV. AAA/Senior discount. Credit cards: AE, CB, DC, DS, JCB, MC, V.

Motel 6
$30
2003 W. Hill Avenue • 229.333.0047
96 Units, pets OK. Pool. Laundry facility. Data ports. Rooms come with phones, A/C and cable TV. Wheelchair accessible. Credit cards: AE, CB, DC, DS, MC, V.

Super 8 Motel
$35-45
1825 W. Hill Avenue • I-75, Exit 16
229.249.8000
80 Units, no pets. Pool. Rooms come with phones and cable TV. Wheelchair accessible. Senior discount. Credit cards: AE, CB, DC, DS, MC, V.

VIDALIA
Days Inn
$40-55
1503 Lyons Hwy. • 912.537.9251
65 Units, pets OK ($10). Continental breakfast. Pool. Laundry facility. Rooms come with phones and cable TV. AAA/Senior discount. Major credit cards.

WARNER ROBINS
Super 8 Motel
$40
105 Woodcrest Blvd., I-75, Exit 146
478.923.8600
62 Units, pets OK. Laundry facility. Rooms come with phones and cable TV. Wheelchair accessible. AAA/Senior discount. Credit cards: AE, CB, DC, DS, MC, V.

WAYCROSS
Super 8 Motel
$34-36
132 Havanna Avenue • 912.285.8885
62 Units, no pets. Continental breakfast. Rooms come with phones and cable TV. Wheelchair accessible. Senior discount. Credit cards: AE, CB, DC, DS, MC, V.

WAYNESBORO
Days Inn
$45-50
On US 25S • 706.554.9941
41 Units, pets OK. Continental breakfast. Rooms come with phones and cable TV. Wheelchair accessible. AAA discount. Major credit cards.

hawaii

Traveler's Advisory: As you might expect, accommodations in the Hawaiian Islands go for a little more than they do on the mainland. That does not mean that you can't get a nice room for $50 or less per night. How is this possible? **Travel packages.** Take a look in your Sunday newspaper's travel section or go online and check out travel packages offered on sites like **travelzoo.com**, **orbitz.com** or **expedia.com**. You will notice only a very slight difference in the price for a package with round-trip airfare plus car rental, and a package which includes round-trip airfare, car rental and accommodations. The amount charged for the accommodations portion of the package is typically very small. Some package deals offer 2 or 3 nights lodgings while others offer a full week. When you break down the cost of the accommodations into a nightly rate, it usually comes out to a figure at or under $50/night. Package deals also fluctuate in price according to high and low season, but even during high season (generally wintertime), you are bound to find good deals on packages with hotel included. Since you're going to have to fly to Hawaii anyway, you might as well pick up a travel package deal. It's a great value for the money. Otherwise, there are a number of very nice, inexpensive youth hostels scattered throughout the islands.

KAUAI
Kauai International Hostel
$20
4532 Lehua Street (Kapaa) • 808.823.6142
Single rooms $50. Facility: Kitchen, laundry facility, volleyball and picnic areas. Credit cards: MC, V.

HAWAII (BIG ISLAND)
Arnott's Lodge
$17
98 Apapane Road (Hilo) • 808.969.7097
36 Beds. Single rooms available ($37). Double rooms are $42. Check-in time: 10:00. Laundry facility, kitchens, bike rentals, snorkel gear rental, hiking adventures, airport shuttle available, barbecue on Wednesday and Saturday. Across the street from the beaches. Credit cards: MC, V.

Hostelling Int'l —Volcano
$15
17-4036 Kalani Honua Road (Volcano)
808.967.7950
10 Beds, Hours: 7-9 am; 4:30-9:30 pm
Facilities: kitchen, laundry facilities, sauna. Private rooms available. Open year-round. Reservations required. Cash only.

MAUI
Banana Bungalow
$20
310 N. Market Street (Wailuku)
808.244.5090
27 Beds. Private rooms available ($35). Check-in times: 7 am - 11 pm Newly renovated. Outdoor cooking facilities, barbecues, picnic tables, jacuzzi, TV room, reading lounge, laundry facility, five bathrooms. Tours offered, snorkeling, sailing, volleyball court. Credit cards: AE, MC, V (small fee charged).

OAHU
Hostelling International
$14
2323A Seaview Avenue (Honolulu)
808.946.0591
43 Beds. Hours: 8 am - noon & 4 pm - midnight
Facilities: patio under coconut trees, day use, TV room, tours and activities, kitchen, laundry facilities, linen rental, on-site parking, lockers/baggage storage. Private rooms available. Open year-round. Reservations recommended. Credit cards: AE, JCB, MC, V.

Hostelling Int'l —Waikiki
$17
2417 Prince Edward Street (Waikiki)
808.926.8313
60 Beds, Open 24 hours
Facilities: kitchen, patio, TV room, laundry facilities, linen rental, on-site parking, tours and activities. Private rooms available. Open year-round. Reservations recommended. Credit cards: AE, JCB, MC, V.

idaho

AMERICAN FALLS
Hillview Motel
$34-48
2799 Lakeview Road • 208.226.5151
34 Units, pets OK ($5). Pool. Laundry facility. Winter plug-ins. Some rooms have refrigerators. Credit cards: MC, V, DC, DS, JCB, AE.

ARCO
Arco Inn
$38-50
540 Grand Avenue W. • 208.527.3100
12 Units, pets OK. Rooms come with phones and cable TV. Some rooms have microwaves and refrigerators. Wheelchair accessible. AAA/Senior discount. Credit cards: AE, DS, MC, V.

Lost River Motel
$30-60
Jct. E. Hwy 20 and 26 • 208.527.3600
14 Units, pets OK. Continental breakfast. Hot tub. Laundry facility. Rooms come with phones, kitchens and cable TV. Senior discount available (10%). Major credit cards.

BELLEVUE
High Country Motel
$50
365 Main Street • 208.788.2050 or 800.692.2050
13 Units, pets OK. Rooms come with phones and cable TV. Wheelchair accessible. Major credit cards.

BLACKFOOT
Y-Motel
$35-55
1375 S. Broadway • I-15, Exit 89
208.785.1550
20 Units, no pets. Continental breakfast. Rooms come with kitchens and cable TV. Major credit cards.

BLISS
Amber Inn
$33
At I-84 Interchange (I-84, Exit 141)
208.352.4441
30 Units, pets OK ($4). Restaurant on premises. Rooms comes with phones and cable TV. AAA/Senior discount. Credit cards: AE, DS, MC, V.

BOISE
Best Rest Inn
$40-50
8002 Overland Road, I-84, Exit 50A
208.322.4404
87 Units, pets OK ($10). Continental breakfast. Heated pool. Jacuzzi. Laundry facility. Rooms come with phones, kitchens and cable TV. AAA/Senior discount. Major credit cards.

Boise Center Guest Lodge
$43
1314 Grove Street • 208.342.9351
48 Units, no pets. Small heated pool. Laundry facility. Airport transportation. Rooms come with phones and cable TV. Some rooms have refrigerators. Credit cards: AE, CB, DC, DS, MC, V.

Econo Lodge
$45-50
4060 Fairview Avenue • 208.344.4030
52 Units, pets OK. Continental breakfast. Airport transportation. Rooms come with phones and cable TV. Some rooms have microwaves, radios and refrigerators. AAA/Senior discount. Major credit cards.

Motel 6
$42-52 (58)*
2323 Airport Way (I-84, Exit 53)
208.344.3506
90 Units, pets OK. Pool. Laundry facility. Data ports. Rooms come with A/C, phones and cable TV. Wheelchair accessible. Credit cards: AE, CB, DC, DS, MC, V.
*Higher rate effective summer weekends.

BONNERS FERRY
Bonners Ferry Resort
$20-60
6438 Main Street • 208.267.2422
Just south of town on US 95 near Co-op.
24 Units, pets OK. Pool and hot tub.

Laundry facility. Rooms come with phones, kitchens and cable TV. Major credit cards.

BURLEY
Budget Motel of Burley
$45-50
900 N. Overland Ave. • 208.678.2200
139 Units, pets OK. Pool. Laundry facility. Jacuzzi. Rooms comes with phones and cable TV. AAA/Senior discount. Major credit cards.

CALDWELL
Sundowner Motel
$42-52
1002 Arthur Street • 208.459.1585
66 Units, pets OK. Continental breakfast. Pool. Rooms come with phones and cable TV. Wheelchair accessible. Major credit cards.

CASCADE
Mountain View Motel
$40-60
762 S. Hwy 55 • 208.382.4238 or 800.265.7666
26 Units, pets OK. Continental breakfast. Rooms come with phones and cable TV. Major credit cards.

CHALLIS
Challis Motor Lodge & Lounge
$34-54
Hwy 93 and Main Street • 208.879.2251
19 Units, pets OK. Restaurant on premises. Rooms come with phones, kitchens and cable TV. Major credit cards.

Northgate Inn
$40-55
On US 93N • 208.879.2490
56 Units, pets OK ($4). Airport transportation. Rooms comes with phones and cable TV. Wheelchair accessible. Credit cards: AE, DS, MC, V.

CHUBBUCK
Northgate Inn
$40
On SR 93 in town • 208.879.2490
56 Units, pets OK ($4/$25 dep. req.). Rooms come with phones and cable TV. Some rooms have microwaves and refrigerators. Major credit cards.

Pine Ridge Inn
$40-45
4333 Yellowstone Avenue • I-86, Exit 61
208.237.3100
105 Units, pets OK ($5). Restaurant on premises. Jacuzzi. Sauna. Laundry facility. Rooms come with phones and cable TV. Some rooms have kitchenettes. Major credit cards.

COEUR D'ALENE
Budget Host Inn
$26-43
330 W. Appleway Avenue • I-90, Exit 12
208.765.3011
59 Units, pets OK. Continental breakfast. Laundry facility. Rooms come with phones and cable TV. Senior discount. Major credit cards.

Budget Saver Motel
$22-50
1519 E. Sherman Ave. • 208.667.9505
44 Units, pets OK. Continental breakfast. Laundry facility. Rooms come with phones and cable TV. Major credit cards.

State Motel
$45
1314 E. Sherman Ave. • 208.664.8239
15 Units, pets OK. Rooms come with phones and cable TV. Wheelchair accessible. Major credit cards.

DRIGGS
Pines Motel—Guest Haus
$35-45*
105 S. Main • 208.354.2774 or 800.354.2778
8 Units, pets OK. Continental breakfast. Hot tub. Rooms come with cable TV. Major credit cards.
*Economy rooms with shared bath available.

Super 8 Motel
$40 (68-88)*
133 State Hwy. 33 • 208.354.8888
22 Units, no pets. Continental breakfast. Jacuzzi. Laundry facility. Airport transportation. Rooms come with phones and cable TV. Wheelchair accessible. AAA/Senior discount. Credit cards: AE, CB, DC, DS, MC, V.
*Higher rates effective June through August.

GOODING
Skyler Inn
$33-48
1331 S. Main Street • 208.934.9987 or 800.979.4055
16 Units, pets OK. Continental breakfast. Rooms come with kitchens and cable TV.

Major credit cards.

GRANGEVILLE
Monty's Motel
$40-48
W. 700 Main Street • 208.983.2500
24 Units, pets OK. Pool. Rooms come with phones and cable TV. Major credit cards.

HAGERMAN
Hagerman Valley Inn
$45-50
661 Frog's Landing (on US 30)
208.837.6196
16 Units, pets OK ($5). Meeting rooms. Rooms come with phones and cable TV. AAA discount. Credit cards: AE, MC, V.

HAILEY
Hitchrack Motel
$39-60
619 S. Main Street • 208.788.1696
8 Units, pets OK. Rooms come with phones and cable TV. Major credit cards.

IDAHO CITY
Idaho City Hotel/Prospector Motel
$25-49
215 Montgomery Street • 208.392.4290
12 Units, pets OK. Laundry facility. Rooms come with phones and cable TV. Some rooms have microwaves and refrigerators. Wheelchair accessible. Major credit cards.

IDAHO FALLS
Motel 6
$38-50 (55)*
1448 W. Broadway • 208.522.0112
79 Units, pets OK. Pool. Laundry facility. Data ports. Rooms come with A/C, phones and cable TV. Wheelchair accessible. Credit cards: AE, CB, DC, DS, MC, V.
*Higher rate effective summer weekends.

Motel West
$36-55
1540 W. Broadway • 208.522.1112 or 800.582.1063
80 Units, pets OK. Restaurant on premises. Pool and hot tub. Meeting room. Rooms come with phones and cable TV. Major credit cards.

Towne Lodge
$39-47
255 "E" Street • 208.523.2960
40 Units, no pets. Laundry facility. Rooms come with phones and cable TV. AAA/Senior discount. Some rooms have refrigerators. Credit cards: AE, MC, V.

JEROME
Crest Motel
$42-60
2983 S. Lincoln • 208.324.2670
18 Units, pets OK ($4). Winter plug-ins. Rooms come with cable TV. Some rooms have, for a fee, microwaves and refrigerators. Wheelchair accessible. AAA/Senior discount. Credit cards: AE, DC, DS, MC, V.

KAMIAH
Lewis-Clark Motel
$37-41
Rt. 1, Box 17 (1.5 miles E on US 12)
208.935.2556
21 Units, pets OK ($5). Restaurant on premises. Heated pool and jacuzzi. Laundry facility. Rooms come with free movies and refrigerators. Credit cards: AE, DS, MC, V.

Sundown Motel
$24-39
1004 Third Street • 208.835.2568
14 Units, pets OK. Laundry facility. Rooms come with phones and cable TV. Some rooms have microwaves and refrigerators. Wheelchair accessible. Senior discount. Major credit cards.

KELLOGG
Super 8 Motel
$45-50 (53-59)*
601 Bunker Avenue, I-90, Exit 49
208.783-1234
61 Units, pets OK ($20 dep. req.). Heated indoor pool. Jacuzzi. Laundry facility. Airport transportation. Rooms come with phones and cable TV. AAA discount. Major credit cards.
*Higher rates effective June-September and December-February.

KETCHUM/SUN VALLEY
Traveler Advisory: Ketchum, Idaho, final resting place of Ernest Hemingway and gateway to the Sawtooth National Recreational Area, is located about 80 miles north of Twin Falls on State Highway 75. Sun Valley, a popular ski resort area, is just a few miles from Ketchum. Because of Ketchum/Sun Valley's popularity as a winter recreational destination and resort area, it is very difficult to find any single accommodation at

any time of year for $50/night or less. Room rates are cheaper 17 miles south of town in **Bellevue**.

LAVA HOT SPRINGS
Home Hotel and Motel
$30*
306 E. Main • 208.776.5507
26 Units, no pets. Hot tub. Rooms come with kitchens and cable TV. Major credit cards.
*Summer rates may jump to $90/night.

LEWISTON
Riverview Inn
$38-50
1325 Main Street • 208.746.3311 or 800.806.ROOM
75 Units, pets OK. Restaurant on premises. Continental breakfast. Heated pool. Fitness facility. Rooms come with phones and cable TV. Senior discount. Major credit cards.

Sacajawea Select Inn
$45-50*
1824 Main Street • 208.746.1393
90 Units, pets OK ($2). Restaurant on premises. Continental breakfast. Airport transportation. Jacuzzi. Laundry facility. Rooms come with phones, cable TV and refrigerators. Some rooms have microwaves. Major credit cards.
*AAA discounted rates.

Travel Motor Inn
$30-49
1021 Main Street • 208.843.4501
62 Units, pets OK. Continental breakfast. Pool and hot tub. Rooms come with phones, kitchens and cable TV. Major credit cards.

MACKAY
Wagon Wheel Motel
$36
809 W. Custer • 208.588.3331
15 Units, pets OK ($20 dep. req.). Playground, single basketball court and volleyball. Laundry facility. Rooms come with phones and cable TV. Some rooms have refrigerators, microwaves and kitchenettes. No A/C. AAA discount. Credit cards: DS, MC, V.

White Knob Motel & RV Park
$22-42
4243 US 93 • 208.588.2622
Two miles south of town on Hwy 93.
6 Units, pets OK. Pool. Laundry facility. Rooms come with kitchens and televisions. Major credit cards.

McCALL
Scandia Inn Motel
$49-54 (58-68)*
401 N. 3rd Street • 208.674.7394
17 Units, no pets. Rooms come with phones and cable TV. No A/C in rooms. Major credit cards.
*Higher rates effect June-September and mid-December through February.

Woodsman Motel
$32-58
402 N. 3rd Street • 208.634.7671
60 Units, pets OK. Restaurant on premises. Rooms come with phones and cable TV. Major credit cards.

MONTPELIER
The Fisher Inn
$26-44
601 N. 4th Street • 208.847.1772
10 Units, pets OK ($5). Heated pool. Laundry facility. Rooms come with phones and cable TV. No A/C. AAA discount. Credit cards: AE, DS, MC, V.

Park Motel
$35-50
745 Washington • 208.847.1911
25 Units, pets OK. Winter plug-ins. Rooms come with cable TV. No A/C. Some rooms have A/C, microwaves and refrigerators. Credit cards: AE, DS, MC, V.

MOSCOW
The Mark IV Motor Inn
$49*
414 N. Main • 208.882.7557 or 800.833.4240
86 Units, pets OK. Restaurant on premises. Pool, hot tub and meeting room. Rooms come with phones and cable TV. Some rooms have microwaves and refrigerators. AAA discount. Major credit cards.
*Rates as high as $99 during U of Idaho home games.

Palouse Inn
$26-38
101 Baker Street • 208.882.5511
110 Units, pets OK. Continental breakfast. Laundry facility. Pool. Rooms come with A/C, phones and cable TV. Wheelchair accessible. Major credit cards.

Royal Motor Inn
$32-50*
120 W. 6th Street • 208.882.2581
38 Units, pets OK. Restaurant on premises. Pool. Sauna. Rooms come with phones, kitchens and cable TV. Wheelchair accessible. Major credit cards.
*Rates higher during U of Idaho home games.

Super 8 Motel
$40*
175 Peterson Drive • 208.883.1503
60 Units, no pets. Meeting room. Sauna. Copy machine. Rooms come with phones and cable TV. Wheelchair accessible. Senior discount. Credit cards: AE, CB, DC, DS, MC, V.
*Rates higher during special events.

MOUNTAIN HOME
Hi Lander Motel & Steak House
$35-49
615 S. 3rd W. dot • 208.587.3311
34 Units, pets OK. Restaurant on premises. Pool. Rooms come with phones, kitchens and cable TV. Senior discount. Major credit cards.

Towne Center Motel
$24-40
410 N. 2nd E. • 208.587.3373
31 Units, pets OK. Small pool. Rooms come with cable TV. Some rooms have refrigerators. Wheelchair accessible. Senior discount. Credit cards: AE, DC, DS, MC, V.

NAMPA
Desert Inn
$42-52
115 Ninth Avenue S. • 208.467.1161
40 Units, pets OK. Continental breakfast. Pool. Rooms come with phones and cable TV. Major credit cards.

Inn America
$44-56
130 Shannon Drive • I-85, Exit 35
208.442.0800
61 Units, no pets. Heated pool. Laundry facility. Rooms come with phones and cable TV. Wheelchair accessible. Major credit cards.

NEW MEADOWS
Hartland Inn and Motel
$44
211 Nora St. (on US 95) • 208.347.2114
14 Units, no pets. Jacuzzi. No A/C. Fitness facility. Some rooms have kitchens, refrigerators, microwaves, phones and cable TV. AAA discount. Credit cards: AE, DS, MC, V.

Meadows Motel
$35-49
302 N. Norris (US 95) • 208.347.2175
16 Units, no pets. Laundry facility. Rooms come with phones, kitchens and cable TV. Wheelchair accessible. Major credit cards.

OROFINO
Konkolville Motel
$50
2000 Konkolville Road • 208.476.5584
40 Units, pets OK ($5). Continental breakfast. Heated pool and whirlpool. Laundry facility. Rooms come with cable TV. Some rooms have refrigerators and radios. Credit cards: AE, DS, MC, V.

POCATELLO — *see also Chubbuck*
Econo Lodge
$46-50
835 S. 5th Avenue • I-15, Exit 67
208.233.0451
54 Units, pets OK ($20 dep. req.). Restaurant on premises. Laundry facility. Fitness facility. Meeting rooms. Rooms come with phones and cable TV. AAA/Senior discount. Credit cards: AE, DS, MC, V.

Motel 6
$35-38
291 W. Burnside Ave. • 208.237.7880
108 Units, pets OK. Pool. Laundry facility. Data ports. Rooms come with A/C, phones and cable TV. Wheelchair accessible. Credit cards: AE, CB, DC, DS, MC, V.

Pine Ridge Inn
$35-60
4333 Yellowstone • 208.237.3100
102 Units, pets OK. Pool. Jacuzzi. Laundry facility. Meeting rooms. Rooms come with cable TV. Some rooms have refrigerators and microwaves. Wheelchair accessible. Major credit cards.

Thunderbird Motel
$40-45
1415 S. 5th Avenue • I-15, Exit 67
208.232.6330
45 Units, pets OK. Heated pool. Laundry

facility. Rooms come with cable TV. Some rooms have refrigerators and microwaves. Senior discount. Credit cards: AE, DC, DS, MC, V.

PRESTON
Plaza Motel
$45-55
427 S. Hwy 91 • 208.852.2020
31 Units, pets OK. Laundry facility. Rooms come with phones and cable TV. Wheelchair accessible. Major credit cards.

REXBURG
Days Inn
$47-57
271 S. 2nd W. • 208.356-9222
43 Units, pets OK. Heated pool. Rooms come with phones and cable TV. Some rooms have microwaves and refrigerators. AAA discount. Major credit cards.

RIGGINS
Bruce Motel
$30-50
515 N. Main Street (north end of town on Hwy 95) • 208.628.3005
20 Units, pets OK. Picnic area and deck. Rooms come with A/C, cable TV, phones and coffee packets. Some rooms have kitchenettes and coffee pots. One large room available with 4 double beds. Credit cards: MC, V.

Riggins Motel
$38
615 S. Main Street • 208.669.6739
19 Units, pets OK. Hot tub. Wheelchair accessible. Rooms come with kitchens and cable TV. Major credit cards.

Salmon River Motel
$38
1203 S. Hwy 95 • 208.628.3231 or 888.628.3025
16 Units, pets OK. Laundry facility. Wheelchair accessible. Rooms come with phones and cable TV. Senior discount. Major credit cards.

ST. ANTHONY
Best Western Inn
$45-47 (55)*
115 S. Bridge Street • 208.624.3711
30 Units, pets OK ($20 dep. req.). Restaurant on premises. Rooms come with phones and cable TV. AAA/Senior discount. Major credit cards.
*Higher rate effective June through August.

SALMON
Motel De Luxe
$35-50
112 S. Church Street • 208.756.2231
24 Units, pets OK. Airport transportation. Rooms come with microwaves, refrigerators and cable TV. Some rooms have kitchenettes. Credit cards: AE, CB, DC, DS, MC, V.

Suncrest Motel
$33-65
705 Challis Street • 208.756.2294
20 Units, pets OK ($3). Continental breakfast. Airport transportation. Rooms come with cable TV. Some rooms have refrigerators. Credit cards: DS, MC, V.

Wagon's West Motel
$40-50
503 Hwy 93N • 208.756.4281
52 Units, pets OK. Continental breakfast. Laundry facility. Jacuzzi. Sauna. Rooms come with phones and cable TV. Some rooms have microwaves and refrigerators. Wheelchair accessible. AAA/Senior discount. Major credit cards.

SANDPOINT
Monarch Mountain Lodge
$37-54
363 Bonner Mall Way • 208.263.1222
49 Units, pets OK ($5). Continental breakfast. Laundry facility. Jacuzzi. Sauna. Rooms come with phones, kitchens and cable TV. AAA/Senior discount. Major credit cards.

Motel 6
$35-45
4650 US 95N • 208.263.5363
70 Units, pets OK. Laundry facility. Data ports. Rooms come with A/C, phones and cable TV. Wheelchair accessible. Credit cards: AE, CB, DC, DS, MC, V.

SODA SPRINGS
Caribou Lodge & Motel
$28-55
110 W. 2nd S. • 208.547.3377 or 800.270.9178
30 Units, pets OK. Continental breakfast. Rooms come with phones, kitchens and cable TV. Major credit cards.

Trail Motel & Restaurant
$35-39
213 E. 200 S. • 208.547.3909
50 Units, no pets. Restaurant on premises. Laundry facility. Meeting rooms. Rooms comes with phones and TV. Wheelchair accessible. Major credit cards.

SUN VALLEY — *see Ketchum*

TWIN FALLS

Days Inn
$47
1200 Centennial Spur • 208.324.6400
I-84, Exit 173
73 Units, pets OK ($100 dep. req.). Continental breakfast. Jacuzzi. Laundry facility. Meeting rooms. Data ports. Rooms come with A/C, phones and cable TV. AAA/Senior discount. Major credit cards.

Monterey Motor Inn
$30-50
433 Addison Avenue W. • 208.733.5151
28 Units, pets OK ($5). Heated pool and whirlpool. Laundry facility. Rooms come with phones and cable TV. Some rooms have radios, refrigerators and microwaves. Credit cards: AE, DS, MC, V.

Motel 6
$36-50
1472 Blue Lakes Blvd. N. • 208.734.3993
132 Units, pets OK. Pool. Laundry facility. Data ports. Rooms come with A/C, phones and cable TV. Wheelchair accessible. Credit cards: AE, CB, DC, DS, MC, V.

Super 7 Motel
$30-50
320 Main Avenue S. • 208.733.8770 or 800.530.0138
40 Units, pets OK. Continental breakfast. Pool. Laundry facility. Rooms come with phones and cable TV. Wheelchair accessible. Major credit cards.

WALLACE

Ryan Hotel
$33-55
608 Cedar • 208.753.6001
14 Units, pets OK. Continental breakfast. Rooms come with phones, kitchens and cable TV. Major credit cards.

illinois

ADDISON
Days Inn
$50
600 E. Lake Street • 630.834.8600
145 Units, no pets. Continental breakfast. Rooms come with phones and cable TV. AAA discount. Major credit cards.

ALTAMONT
Knights Inn
$30-55
1304 S. Main Street • I-70, Exit 82
618.483.6101
44 Units, pets OK. Continental breakfast. Pool. Rooms come with phones and cable TV. Some rooms have kitchens. Wheelchair accessible. AAA discount. Major credit cards.

Super 8 Motel
$36-48*
RR 2, Box 296 • 618.483.6300
25 Units, pets OK. Continental breakfast. Fax service. Laundry facility. Rooms come with phones and cable TV. AAA/Senior discount. Credit cards: AE, CB, DC, DS, MC, V.
*Rates may increase slightly during special events and weekends.

ALTON
Lewis & Clark Motor Lodge
$29*
530 Lewis & Clark Blvd. • 618.254.3831
30 Units, no pets. Rooms come with phones and cable TV. Major credit cards.
*Key deposit of $5 extra.

ARCOLA
Arcola Inn
$30-45
236 S. Jacques Street • 217.268.4971
73 Units, pets OK ($5). Continental breakfast. Rooms come with phones and cable TV. AAA/senior discount available (10%). Credit cards: AE, CB, DC, DS, MC, V.

Knights Inn
$29-46
640 E. Springfield Road • I-57, Exit 203
217.268.3031
74 Units, pets OK ($7). Continental breakfast. Pool. Laundry facility. Rooms come with phones and cable TV. Wheelchair accessible. AAA/senior discount available (10%). Major credit cards.

ARLINGTON HEIGHTS
Motel 6
$42-52
441 W. Algonquin Road, I-90 at N. Arlington Hts. Rd. Exit • 847.806.1230
144 Units, pets OK. Laundry facility. Rooms come with phones, A/C and cable TV. Wheelchair accessible. Credit cards: AE, CB, DC, DS, MC, V.

Red Roof Inn
$50-56*
22 W. Algonquin Road • 847.228.6650
136 Units, pets OK. Rooms come with phones and cable TV. Major credit cards.
*Higher rate effective mid-June through September.

AURORA
Motel 6
$40-50*
2380 N. Farnsworth Ave.
I-88 & Farnsworth Ave. • 630.851.3600
119 Units, pets OK. Restaurant on premises. Laundry facility. Rooms come with phones, A/C and cable TV. Wheelchair accessible. Credit cards: AE, CB, DC, DS, MC, V.
*Higher rates effective weekends during spring and summer.

BEARDSTOWN
Super 8 Motel
$35-45
Hwys. 67 & 100 • 217.323.5858
40 Units, pets OK ($25 dep. req.). Continental breakfast. Pool. Meeting rooms. Rooms come with phones and cable TV. AAA/Senior discount. Major credit cards.

BELLEVILLE
Super 8 Motel
$43
600 E. Main Street • 618.234.9670
42 Units, pets OK ($5). Continental

breakfast. Laundry facility. Rooms come with phones and cable TV. AAA/Senior discount. Major credit cards.

BENTON
Days Inn
$45-50
711 W. Main Street • 618.439.3183
57 Units, pets OK ($5). Restaurant on premises. Laundry facility. Rooms come with phones and cable TV. Some rooms have microwaves and refrigerators. AAA/ Senior discount. Major credit cards.

Super 8 Motel
$40-50
711+ W. Main Street • 618.438.8205
54 Units, pets OK. Continental breakfast. Meeting rooms. Rooms come with phones and cable TV. AAA/Senior discount. Major credit cards.

BLOOMINGTON — *see also Normal*
Best Inns of America
$40-46
1905 W. Market Street • 309.827.5333
107 Units, pets OK. Continental breakfast. Pool. Rooms come with phones and cable TV. Some rooms have refrigerators. AAA discount. Major credit cards.

The Parkway Inn
$35-45
2419 Springfield Road
I-74 & Veterans Parkway • 309.828.1505
100 Units, pets OK. Restaurant on premises. Pool. Meeting rooms. Rooms come with phones and cable TV. Wheelchair accessible. AAA discount. Major credit cards.

Super 8 Motel
$39-46
818 IAA Drive • Veterans Parkway Exit
309-663-2388
60 Units, pets OK ($10). Continental breakfast. Laundry facility. Meeting rooms. Rooms come with phones and cable TV. Wheelchair accessible. AAA discount. Major credit cards.

BOURBONNAIS
Motel 6
$37-46
SR 50 and Armour Road • I-57, Exit 315
815.933.2300
96 Units, pets OK. Pool. Rooms come with phones, A/C and cable TV. Wheelchair accessible. Credit cards: AE, CB, DC, DS, MC, V.

BROOKFIELD
Colony Motel
$45
9232 W. Ogden Avenue • 708.485.0300
37 Units, no pets. Continental breakfast. Rooms come with phones and cable TV. Credit cards: AE, CB, DC, DS, MC, V.

CANTON
Super 8 Motel
$46*
2110 Main Street • 309.647.1888
32 Units, no pets. Continental breakfast. Rooms come with phones and cable TV. Senior discount. Wheelchair accessible. Major credit cards.
*Rates as high as $70/night.

CARBONDALE
Best Inns of America
$42-55
1345 E. Main Street • 618.529.4801
86 Units, no pets. Continental breakfast. Pool. Rooms come with phones and cable TV. Some rooms have refrigerators. AAA/ Senior discount. Credit cards: AE, CB, DC, DS, MC, V.

Sun Motel
$45 (56)*
3000 W. Main Street • 618.529.2424
58 Units, pets OK. Pool. Rooms come with phones and cable TV. Wheelchair accessible. AAA/Senior discount. Major credit cards.
*Higher rate effective weekends.

CARLINVILLE
Carlin Villa Motel
$36-50
Half mile from Jct. of SR 108 & SR 4
217.854.3201
35 Units, pets OK ($3). Continental breakfast. Pool. Sauna. Jacuzzi. Meeting rooms. Rooms come with phones and cable TV. Some rooms have microwaves, refrigerators and jacuzzis. Credit cards: AE, DC, DS, MC, V.

CASEYVILLE
Motel 6
$38-50
2431 Old Country Inn Rd. • I-64, Exit 9
618.397.8867

121 Units, pets OK. Pool. Laundry facility. Data ports. Rooms come with phones, A/C and cable TV. Wheelchair accessible. Credit cards: AE, CB, DC, DS, MC, V.

CENTRALIA
Bell Tower Inn
$44
200 E. Noleman Street • 618.533.1300
57 Units, pets OK. Continental breakfast. Heated Pool. Laundry facility. Playground. Meeting rooms. Rooms come with phones and cable TV. Major credit cards.

Motel Centralia
$38
215 S. Poplar • 618.532.7357
56 Units, pets OK. Rooms come with phones and cable TV. Wheelchair accessible. Major credit cards.

CHAMPAIGN
Red Roof Inn
$35-56
212 W. Anthony Drive • 217.352.0101
112 Units, pets OK. Rooms come with phones and cable TV. AAA discount. Credit cards: AE, CB, DC, DS, MC, V.

CHARLESTON
Days Inn
$46-49
810 W. Lincoln Hwy. • 217.345.7689
52 Units, pets OK. Rooms come with phones and cable TV. Some rooms have microwaves and refrigerators. AAA/Senior discount. Major credit cards.

CHENOA
Super 8 Motel
$45
I-55, Exit 187 • 815.945.5900
38 Units, pets OK. Continental breakfast. Rooms come with phones and cable TV. Senior discount. Wheelchair accessible. Major credit cards.

CHICAGO — *see also Addison, Arlington Heights, Aurora, Downers Grove, East Hazelcrest, Elk Grove Village (O'Hare), Glenview, Harvey, Hoffman Estates, Lansing, Lyons, Palatine, Prospect Heights, Rolling Meadows and Villa Park*
Traveler Advisory: If you are planning to spend the night in the heart of Chicago, you will need to plan on spending a little more than $50/night. The following are a few recommendations to suit your budget in-town:

Comfort Inn ($80)
601 W. Diversey Parkway
773.348.2810

Days Inn ($101-131)
644 W. Diversey Parkway
773.525.7010

Heart O' Chicago Motel ($75-85*)
5990 N. Ridge Avenue
773.271.9181

Majestic Hotel ($99)
528 W. Brompton Place
773.404.3499

Quality Inn Downtown ($89-99)
1 S. Halsted (Madison St. & Kennedy Expressway)
312.829.5000

Red Roof Inn ($90-110)
162 E. Ontario Street
312.787.3580

Travelodge ($89-99)
65 E. Harrison Street
312.427.8000

In addition, there are a number of reasonably priced motels in the Chicago metropolitan area (see listings under surrounding communities).

***Additional AAA discount.**

Hostelling International
$20-25
731 S. Plymouth Court • 312.327.5350
165 Beds, Office hours: 7-midnight
Facilities: 24-hour access, kitchen, laundry facilities, linen rental, TV lounge, wheelchair accessible, game room, exercise facility. Private rooms available. Closed September 3 through June 7. Reservations essential late August. Credit cards: MC, V.

CHILLICOTHE
Super 8 Motel
$45-55
615 S. Fourth Street • 309.274.2568
36 Units, pets OK ($10 and $50 dep. req.). Continental breakfast. Laundry facility. Rooms come with phones and cable TV. Wheelchair accessible. AAA/Senior discount. Major credit cards.

COLLINSVILLE
Motel 6
$33-55
295-A N. Bluff Road • 618.345.2100
86 Units, pets OK. Pool. Data ports. Rooms come with phones, A/C and cable TV. Wheelchair accessible. Credit cards: AE, CB, DC, DS, MC, V.

DANVILLE
Knights Inn
$35-50
411 Lynch Road • 217.443.3690
80 Units, pets OK. Continental breakfast. Heated pool. Meeting rooms. Rooms come with phones and cable TV. Some rooms have kitchens, microwaves and jacuzzis. Senior discount. Credit cards: AE, CB, DC, DS, MC, V.

DECATUR
Days Inn
$40-47
333 N. Wyckles Road • 217.422.5900
60 Units, pets OK ($5 dep. req.). Continental breakfast. Rooms come with phones and cable TV. AAA/Senior discount. Major credit cards.

Red Carpet Inn
$35*
3035 N. Water Street • 217.877.3380
45 Units, pets OK ($20 dep. req.). Meeting rooms. Laundry facility. Rooms come with phones and cable TV. Some rooms have refrigerators. Senior discount. Credit cards: AE, CB, DC, DS, MC, V.
*AAA discounted rates.

DE KALB
Super 8 Motel
$45-55
800 Fairview Drive • 815.748.4688
44 Units, no pets. Continental breakfast. Laundry facility. Rooms come with phones and cable TV. Wheelchair accessible. Senior discount. Major credit cards.

Travelodge
$36
1116 W. Lincoln Hwy. • 815.756.3398
111 Units, pets OK. Pool. Rooms come with phones, A/C and cable TV. Wheelchair accessible. Credit cards: AE, CB, DC, DS, MC, V.

DOWNERS GROVE
Red Roof Inn
$39-63
1113 Butterfield Road • 630.963.4205
135 Units, pets OK. Data ports. Rooms come with phones and cable TV. AAA/Senior discount. Major credit cards.

DU QUOIN
Super 8 Motel
$50
1010 S. Jefferson Street • 618.542.4335
38 Units, no pets. Continental breakfast. Laundry facility. Meeting room. Rooms come with phones and cable TV. Senior discount. Wheelchair accessible. Major credit cards.

DWIGHT
Super 8 Motel
$42-47
14 E. Northbrook Drive • I-55, Exit 220 • 815.584.1888
40 Units, pets OK ($25 dep. req.). Rooms come with phones and cable TV. Senior discount. Major credit cards.

EAST HAZELCREST
Rodeway Inn
$45
17214 Halsted Street, I-80/294 at SR 1S, Exit Halsted St. • 708.957.9233
121 Units, pets OK. Pool. Laundry facility. Rooms come with phones, A/C and cable TV. Wheelchair accessible. Credit cards: AE, CB, DC, DS, MC, V.

EAST PEORIA
Motel 6
$36-40
104 W. Camp Street • 309.699.7281
78 Units, pets OK. Pool. Data ports. Rooms come with phones, A/C and cable TV. Wheelchair accessible. Credit cards: AE, CB, DC, DS, MC, V.

EFFINGHAM
Best Inns of America
$46
1209 N. Keller Drive • 217.347.5141
83 Units, pets OK. Continental breakfast. Pool. Rooms come with phones and cable TV. AAA discount. Credit cards: AE, CB, DC, DS, MC, V.

Econo Lodge
$30-49
1205 N. Keller Drive • 217.347.7131
74 Units, pets OK. Heated pool. Sauna. Jacuzzi. Fitness facility. Playground. Volleyball court. Laundry facility. Rooms come with phones and cable TV. Some rooms have microwaves, refrigerators and jacuzzis. AAA discount. Credit cards: AE, CB, DC, DS, MC, V.

ELK GROVE VILLAGE
Motel 6
$40-46
1601 Oakton Street, I-90 at SR 83/Oakton Street • 847.981.9766
222 Units, pets OK. Laundry facility. Rooms come with phones, A/C and cable TV. Wheelchair accessible. Credit cards: AE, CB, DC, DS, MC, V.

EL PASO
Super 8 Motel
$46
25 Linco Road • 309.527.4949
27 Units, pets OK. Continental breakfast. Laundry facility. Rooms come with phones and cable TV. Senior discount. Wheelchair accessible. Major credit cards.

FAIRVIEW HEIGHTS
Trailway Motel
$35
10039 Lincoln Trail • 618.397.5757
30 Units, pets OK. Rooms come with phones and cable TV. Major credit cards.

FREEPORT
Knights Inn
$43-45
1156 W. Galena Avenue • 815.232.2191
30 Units, pets OK. Complimentary coffee. Rooms come with phones and cable TV. Major credit cards.

Super 8 Motel
$48
1649 Willard Drive • Hwy. 26 & South Street • 815.232.8880
52 Units, no pets. Continental breakfast. Rooms come with phones and cable TV. Senior discount. Major credit cards.

GALESBURG
Econo Inn
$40
1475 N. Henderson St. • 309.344.2401
75 Units, pets OK. Indoor pool. Rooms come with phones, A/C and cable TV. Wheelchair accessible. Credit cards: AE, CB, DC, DS, MC, V.

Super 8 Motel
$45*
260 W. Main Street • 309.342.5174
48 Units, no pets. Rooms come with phones and cable TV. Wheelchair accessible. Senior discount. Credit cards: AE, CB, DC, DS, MC, V.
*Rates may increase slightly during special events, holidays and weekends.

GENESEO
Deck Plaza Motel
$38
2181 S. Oakwood Ave. • 309.944.4651
120 Units, pets OK. Restaurant on premises. Heated pool. Wading pool. Meeting rooms. Laundry facility. Rooms come with phones and cable TV. Credit cards: AE, CB, DC, DS, MC, V.

GILMAN
Budget Host Inn
$35-50
723 S. Crescent Street • 815.265.7261
22 Units, pets OK. Laundry facility. Jacuzzi. Rooms come with phones and cable TV. Some rooms have microwaves and refrigerators. Senior discount. Credit cards: AE, DS, MC, V.

Travel Inn
$45
834 Hwy. 24W • 815.265.7283
38 Units, pets OK ($4). Continental breakfast. Heated pool. Laundry facility. Jacuzzi. Rooms come with phones and cable TV. AAA/Senior discount. Credit cards: AE, DC, DS, MC, V.

GLENVIEW
Motel 6
$44-50
1535 Milwaukee Avenue • I-294 at Willow Road Exit • 847.390.7200
111 Units, pets OK. Laundry facility. Rooms come with phones, A/C and cable TV. Wheelchair accessible. Credit cards: AE, CB, DC, DS, MC, V.

GODFREY
Hiway House Motel
$40-45
3023 Godfrey Road • 618.466.6676
62 Units, no pets. Restaurant on premises. Pool. Rooms come with phones and cable TV. Wheelchair accessible. Major credit cards.

GRANITE CITY
Chain of Rocks Motel
$35
3228 W. Chain of Rocks Rd.
618.931.6600
37 Units, pets OK. Pool. Rooms come with phones and cable TV. Major credit cards.

Relax Inn
$40
1100 Niedringhaus Ave. • 618.877.7100
40 Units, pets OK. Rooms come with phones and cable TV. Major credit cards.

GREENUP
Budget Host Inn
$33-39
I-70 & Rte. 130 (Exit 119)
716 E. Elizabeth Street • 217.923.3176
29 Units, pets OK. Restaurant adjacent. Rooms come with phones and cable TV. Senior discount. Credit cards: AE, DS, MC, V.

GREENVILLE
Budget Host Inn
$28-36
1525 S. SR 127, I-70, Exit 45
618.664.1950
46 Units, pets ($5). Continental breakfast. Heated pool. Laundry facility. Rooms come with phones and cable TV. Some rooms have jacuzzis. Senior discount. Credit cards: AE, DS, MC, V.

Super 8 Motel
$39-48
221 W. College Avenue • I-70, Exit 45
618.664.0800
43 Units, no pets. Continental breakfast. Laundry facility. Rooms come with phones and cable TV. AAA/Senior discount. Credit cards: AE, DS, MC, V.

HARRISBURG
Budget Host Inn
$36
411 E. Poplar Street • 618.253.7651
46 Units, pets OK. Laundry facility. Picnic area. Rooms come with phones and cable TV. Credit cards: AE, DS, MC, V.

Super 8 Motel
$47
100 E. Seright Street • 618.253.8081
38 Units, pets OK. Continental breakfast. Rooms come with phones and cable TV. Senior discount. Wheelchair accessible. Major credit cards.

HARVEY
Knights Inn
$30-36
17003 S. Halsted Street • 708.596.7470
150 Units, no pets. Airport transportation. Rooms come with phones and cable TV. Wheelchair accessible. Major credit cards.

HOFFMAN ESTATES
Red Roof Inn
$45-55
2500 Hossell Rd.
I-90, Barrington Rd., Exit • 847.885.7877
118 Units, pets OK. Laundry facility. Data ports. Rooms come with phones and cable TV. AAA discount. Major credit cards.

JACKSONVILLE
Knights Inn
$36-59
1716 W. Morton Drive • 217.243.7157
77 Units, pets OK. Continental breakfast. Pool. Laundry facility. Rooms come with phones, A/C and cable TV. Wheelchair accessible. Credit cards: AE, CB, DC, DS, MC, V.

Star Lite Motel
$38-42
1910 W. Morton Ave. • 217.245.7184
32 Units, pets OK ($5). Playground. Rooms come with phones and cable TV. Some rooms have microwaves and refrigerators. AAA/Senior discount. Credit cards: AE, DS, MC, V.

JERSEYVILLE
Super 8 Motel
$46
1281 McClusky Road • 618.498.7888
40 Units, no pets. Continental breakfast. Laundry facility. Rooms come with phones and cable TV. Some rooms have refrigerators. AAA discount. Major credit cards.

JOLIET
Motel 6
$33-44
1850 McDonough Road • I-80, Exit 130B
815.729.2800
129 Units, pets OK. Laundry facility. Rooms come with phones, A/C and cable TV. Wheelchair accessible. Credit cards: AE, CB, DC, DS, MC, V.

Motel 6
$36-44
3551 Mall Loop Drive • I-55, Exit 257
815.439.1332
121 Units, pets OK. Laundry facility. Rooms come with phones, A/C and cable TV. Wheelchair accessible. Credit cards: AE, CB, DC, DS, MC, V.

KANKAKEE — *see also Bourbonnais*
Knights Inn
$40-50
1786 South Rte. 45/52 • 815.939.4551
60 Units, pets OK. Meeting rooms. Rooms come with phones and cable TV. AAA/Senior discount. Major credit cards.

KEWANEE
Kewanee Motor Lodge
$40
400 S. Main Street • 309.853.4000
29 Units, pets OK. Rooms come with phones and cable TV. Some rooms have microwaves and refrigerators. AAA discount. Major credit cards.

LANSING
Starway Inn
$41-50
2505 Bernice Road • I-80/I-94, Exit 161B
708.895.7810
101 Units, pets OK ($25 dep. req.). Continental breakfast. Laundry facility. Rooms come with phones and cable TV. AAA discount. Major credit cards.

LA SALLE — *see also Peru*
Tiki Motel
$26-29
206 La Salle Road • 815.224.1109
111 Units, no pets. Rooms come with phones and cable TV. Wheelchair accessible. Major credit cards.

LE ROY
Super 8 Motel
$48
1 Demma Drive, I-74, Exit 149
309.962.4700
41 Units, pets OK. Continental breakfast. Laundry facility. Rooms come with phones and cable TV. Senior discount. Wheelchair accessible. Major credit cards.

LINCOLN
Lincoln Country Inn
$27-37
1750 Fifth Street • 217.732.9641
62 Units, pets OK. Meeting rooms. Fitness facility. Rooms come with phones and cable TV. Major credit cards.

LITCHFIELD
Super 8 Motel
$45
I-55, SR 16 (Exit 52) • 217.324.7788
61 Units, pets OK. Rooms come with phones and cable TV. Senior discount. Wheelchair accessible. Major credit cards.

LYONS
Budget Host Chalet Motel
$47
8640 W. Ogden Avenue • 708.447.6363
41 Units, no pets. Indoor heated pool. Laundry facility. Rooms come with phones and cable TV. Some rooms have jacuzzis and kitchenettes. Senior discount available (10%). Major credit cards.

MARION
Best Inns of America
$40-55
2700 W. De Young • 618.997.9421
104 Units, pets OK. Continental breakfast. Pool. Laundry facility. Rooms come with phones and cable TV. AAA/Senior discount. Credit cards: AE, CB, DC, DS, MC, V.

Motel 6
$33-37
1008 Halfway Road • 618.993.2631
79 Units, pets OK. Pool. Data ports. Rooms come with phones, A/C and cable TV. Wheelchair accessible. Credit cards: AE, CB, DC, DS, MC, V.

MARSHALL
Super 8 Motel
$44-56
I-70 & Hwy. 1 • 217.826.8043

41 Units, no pets. Continental breakfast. Indoor pool. Rooms come with phones and cable TV. Wheelchair accessible. Senior discount. Credit cards: AE, CB, DC, DS, MC, V.

MATTOON
Budget Inn
$31-40
I-5 & SR 45 (Exit 184) • 217.235.4011
120 Units, pets OK. Pool. Rooms come with phones and cable TV. Wheelchair accessible. Major credit cards.

Knights Inn
$35-45
4922 Paradise Road • 217.235.4161
95 Units, pets OK. Restaurant on premises. Continental breakfast. Pool. Laundry facility. Sauna. Meeting rooms. Rooms come with phones and cable TV. Wheelchair accessible. Major credit cards.

MENDOTA
Super 8 Motel
$46
508 Hwy. 34E • I-39 & Hwy. 34
815.539.7429
43 Units, pets OK. Continental breakfast. Rooms come with phones and cable TV. Senior discount. Wheelchair accessible. Major credit cards.

METROPOLIS
Days Inn
$35-50
1415 E. 5th Street • 618.524.9341
46 Units, no pets. Restaurant on premises. Pool. Rooms come with phones and cable TV. AAA/Senior discount. Major credit cards.

MINONK
Motel 6
$37-40
1312 Caroly Drive • I-39, Exit 27
309.432.3663
41 Units, pets OK. Data ports. Rooms come with phones, A/C and cable TV. Wheelchair accessible. Credit cards: AE, CB, DC, DS, MC, V.

MOLINE
Exel Inn of Moline
$37-49
2501 52nd Avenue • I-280/74, Exit 5B
309.797.5580
102 Units, pets OK. Continental breakfast. Laundry facility. Rooms come with phones and cable TV. Senior discount. Major credit cards.

Motel 6
$36-47
Quad City Airport Road • I-74, Exit 58/I-280, Exit 18A • 309.764.8711
98 Units, pets OK. Pool. Data ports. Rooms come with phones, A/C and cable TV. Wheelchair accessible. Credit cards: AE, CB, DC, DS, MC, V.

MONMOUTH
Meling's Motel & Restaurant
$37
1129 N. Main Street • 309.734.2196
55 Units, pets OK. Restaurant on premises. Meeting rooms. Rooms come with phones and cable TV. Major credit cards.

Super 8 Motel
$49
1122 N. 6th Street • 309.734.8558
38 Units, no pets. Laundry facility. Data ports. Rooms come with phones and cable TV. Wheelchair accessible. Senior discount. Major credit cards.

MORRIS
Morris Motel
$36
1801 N. Division Street • 815.942.4991
35 Units, no pets. Rooms come with phones and cable TV. Major credit cards.

Park Motel
$36
1923 N. Division Street • 815.942.1321
24 Units, no pets. Rooms come with phones and cable TV. Major credit cards.

MORTON
Relax Inn
$45
128 W. Queenswood Rd • 309.263.2511
50 Units, pets OK. Laundry facility. Rooms come with phones and cable TV. Major credit cards.

MORTON GROVE
Grove Motel
$50*
9110 Waukegan Road • 847.966.0960
40 Units, no pets. Pool. Rooms come with phones and cable TV. Credit cards: AE, DS,

MC, V.
*AAA discounted rates.

MOUNT VERNON
Best Inns of America
$30-45
222 S. 44th Street • 618.244.4343
152 Units, pets OK ($10). Continental breakfast. Pool. Rooms come with phones and cable TV. Some rooms have refrigerators. AAA/Senior discount. Credit cards: AE, CB, DC, DS, MC, V.

Motel 6
$30-40
333 S. 44th Street • 618.244.2383
78 Units, pets OK. Pool. Laundry facility. Data ports. Rooms come with phones, A/C and cable TV. Wheelchair accessible. Credit cards: AE, CB, DC, DS, MC, V.

Super 8 Motel
$46
401 S. 44th Street • 618.242.8800
63 Units, pets OK. Rooms come with phones and cable TV. AAA/Senior discount. Major credit cards.

MURPHYSBORO
Super 8 Motel
$45-55
128 E. Walnut Street • 618.687.2244
38 Units, no pets. Continental breakfast. Fax service. Rooms come with phones and cable TV. Wheelchair accessible. Senior discount. Credit cards: AE, CB, DC, DS, MC, V.

NASHVILLE
Best Western U.S. Inn
$40-50
11640 S.R. 127, I-64, Exit 50
618.478.5341
50 Units, pets OK ($20 dep. req.). Continental breakfast. Laundry facility. Rooms comes with A/C, phones and cable TV. Wheelchair accessible. AAA/Senior discount. Major credit cards.

NAUVOO
Motel Nauvoo
$43-55
1610 Mulholland Street • 217.453.2219
12 Units, no pets. Continental breakfast. Rooms come with A/C, phones and cable TV. Credit cards: AE, DS, MC, V.
*Closed mid-November through March.

Nauvoo Family Inn & Suites
$50
150 N. Warsaw • 217.453.6527
67 Units, pets OK. Indoor pool. Laundry facility. Rooms come with phones and cable TV. Wheelchair accessible. Major credit cards.

NORMAL
Motel 6
$34-42
1600 N. Main Street • 309.452.0422
98 Units, pets OK. Pool. Data ports. Rooms come with phones, A/C and cable TV. Wheelchair accessible. Credit cards: AE, CB, DC, DS, MC, V.

Super 8 Motel
$44-55
Two Traders Circle • I-55 at Business 51S
309.454.5858
52 Units, pets OK. Continental breakfast. Rooms come with phones and cable TV. Senior discount. Major credit cards.

O'HARE AIRPORT — *see Elk Grove Village*

OKAWVILLE
Super 8 Motel
$46
812 N. Henhouse Road • I-64, Exit 41
618.243.6525
40 Units, pets OK. Rooms come with phones and cable TV. Senior discount. Wheelchair accessible. Major credit cards.

OLNEY
Super 8 Motel
$41
Rte. 130 & North Avenue • 618.392.7888
41 Units, pets OK. Continental breakfast. Rooms come with phones and cable TV. Senior discount. Major credit cards.

PALATINE
Motel 6
$40-48
1450 E. Dundee Road • Hwy. 53 at Dundee Road Exit • 847.359.0046
123 Units, pets OK. Laundry facility. Rooms come with phones, A/C and cable TV. Wheelchair accessible. Credit cards: AE, CB, DC, DS, MC, V.

PEKIN
Mineral Springs Motel
$31-36*
1901 Court Street • 309.346.2147
32 Units, no pets. Rooms come with phones and cable TV. Some rooms have jacuzzis and refrigerators. Credit cards: AE, DS, MC, V.
*AAA discounted rates.

Super 8 Motel
$50
3830 Kelly Avenue • 309.347.8888
43 Units, no pets. Continental breakfast. Laundry facility. Jacuzzi. Laundry facility. Rooms come with phones and cable TV. AAA/Senior discount. Major credit cards.

PEORIA — *see also East Peoria*
Peoria Inn
$45-60
2726 Westlake Avenue • 309.688.7000
117 Units, pets OK. Continental breakfast. Pool. Rooms come with phones and cable TV. AAA/Senior discount. Major credit cards.

Red Roof Inn
$39-55
4031 N. War Memorial Dr. • 309.685.3911
108 Units, pets OK. Laundry facility. Data ports. Rooms come with phones and cable TV. AAA discount. Major credit cards.

PERU
Super 8 Motel
$45*
1851 May Road • 815.223.1848
62 Units, pets OK. Rooms come with phones and cable TV. Wheelchair accessible. Senior discount. Credit cards: AE, CB, DC, DS, MC, V.
*Rates may increase slightly during special events, holidays and weekends.

PRINCETON
Days Inn
$45-49
2238 N. Main Street • I-80, Exit 56
815.875.3371
87 Units, pets OK ($6). Pool. Meeting rooms. Rooms come with phones and cable TV. Wheelchair accessible. Senior discount. Major credit cards.

Super 8 Motel
$48
2929 N. Main Street • I-80, Exit 56
815.872.8888
35 Units, no pets. Pool. Rooms come with phones and cable TV. Wheelchair accessible. Senior discount. Major credit cards.

PROSPECT HEIGHTS
Exel Inn of Prospect Heights
$40-52
540 Milwaukee Avenue • 847.459.0545
123 Units, pets OK. Continental breakfast. Laundry facility. Fitness facility. Data ports. Rooms come with phones and cable TV. AAA/Senior discount. Major credit cards.

QUAD CITIES — *see Moline or Davenport (IA)*

QUINCY
Super 8 Motel
$43
224 N. 36th Street • 217.228.8808
59 Units, pets OK. Meeting rooms. Fitness facility. Rooms come with phones and cable TV. Some rooms have microwaves and refrigerators. Wheelchair accessible. AAA/Senior discount. Major credit cards.

Travelodge
$46-52
200 S. 3rd Street • 217.222.5620
68 Units, pets OK. Continental breakfast. Laundry facility. Pool. Rooms come with phones and cable TV. Some rooms have microwaves and refrigerators. Major credit cards.

RANTOUL
Best Western Heritage Inn
$45-50
420 S. Murray Road • I-57, Exit 250
217.892.9292
47 Units, pets OK. Continental breakfast. Heated pool. Sauna. Jacuzzi. Laundry facility. Rooms come with phones and cable TV. AAA/Senior discount. Major credit cards.

Super 8 Motel
$46-56
207 S. Murray Road • I-57, Exit 250
217.893.8888
57 Units, pets OK ($5). Toast bar. Laundry facility. Rooms come with phones and cable

TV. Senior discount. Wheelchair accessible. Major credit cards.

ROCHELLE
Super 8 Motel
$47
601 E. Hwy. 38 • I-35, Exit 99
815.562.2468
63 Units, no pets. Laundry facility. Rooms come with phones and cable TV. Senior discount. Wheelchair accessible. Major credit cards.

ROCK FALLS
Super 8 Motel
$46-48
2100 First Avenue, I-88, Exit 41
815.626.8800
63 Units, pets OK. Rooms come with phones and cable TV. AAA/Senior discount. Major credit cards.

ROCKFORD
Exel Inn of Rockford
$38-55
280 S. Lyford Road • 815.332.4915
101 Units, pets OK. Continental breakfast. Fitness facility. Laundry facility. Data ports. Rooms come with phones and cable TV. AAA/Senior discount. Major credit cards.

Knights Inn
$29-54
733 E. State Street • 815.961.9300
67 Units, no pets. Laundry facility. Jacuzzi. Airport transportation. Meeting rooms. Rooms come with phones, A/C and cable TV. Wheelchair accessible. Credit cards: AE, CB, DC, DS, MC, V.

ROLLING MEADOWS
Motel 6
$36-50
1800 Winnetka Circle, I-90 at SR 53/Euclid Avenue • 847.818.8088
128 Units, pets OK. Pool. Rooms come with phones, A/C and cable TV. Wheelchair accessible. Credit cards: AE, CB, DC, DS, MC, V.

SALEM
Continental Motel
$29
1600 E. Main Street • 618.548.3090
25 Units, pets OK. Continental breakfast. Rooms come with phones and cable TV. AAA discount. Credit cards: AE, CB, DC, DS, MC, V.

SAVOY
Best Western Paradise Inn
$50 (65)*
1001 N. Dunlap • 217.356.1824
62 Units, pets OK ($2). Continental breakfast. Playground. Pool. Laundry facility. Rooms come with phones and cable TV. Major credit cards.
*Higher rate effective weekends.

SOUTH BELOIT
Knights Inn
$30-50
1710 Gardner Street • 815.389.2281
50 Units, no pets. Rooms come with phones and cable TV. Major credit cards.

SOUTH HOLLAND
Cherry Lane Motel
$45 (55)*
1122 E. 162nd Street • 708.331.7799
66 Units, no pets. Rooms come with phones and cable TV. Major credit cards.
*Higher rate effective weekends.

Motel 6
$36-40
17301 S. Halsted St. • 708.331.1621
136 Units, pets OK. Rooms come with phones, A/C and cable TV. Wheelchair accessible. Credit cards: AE, CB, DC, DS, MC, V.

SPRINGFIELD
Knights Inn
$33-49
3125 Wide Track Drive • I-55, Exit 96B
217.789.9471
119 Units, no pets. Rooms come with phones and cable TV. Major credit cards.

Motel 6
$34-48
6011 S. 6th Street • 217.529.1633
104 Units, pets OK. Restaurant on premises. Pool. Data ports. Rooms come with phones, A/C and cable TV. Wheelchair accessible. Credit cards: AE, CB, DC, DS, MC, V.

Red Roof Inn
$40-54
3200 Singer Avenue • 217.753.4302
108 Units, pets OK. Fitness facility. Laundry facility. Rooms come with phones and cable

TV. AAA discount. Credit cards: AE, CB, DC, DS, MC, V.

Super 8 Motel
$35-50
1330 S. Dirksen Pkwy. • 217.528.8889
66 Units, pets OK. Rooms come with phones and cable TV. Wheelchair accessible. Senior discount. Credit cards: AE, CB, DC, DS, MC, V.
*Rates may increase slightly during special events, holidays and weekends.

STAUNTON
Super 8 Motel
$50
832 E. Main Street • 618.635.5353
52 Units, pets OK. Continental breakfast. Meeting rooms. Rooms come with phones and cable TV. Wheelchair accessible. AAA/Senior discount. Credit cards: AE, CB, DC, DS, MC, V.

STREATOR
Town & Country Inn
$44
2110 N. Bloomington St. • 815.672.3183
99 Units, no pets. Restaurant on premises. Pool. Sauna. Meeting rooms. Rooms come with phones and cable TV. Major credit cards.

TAYLORVILLE
Super 8 Motel
$50*
400 Abe's Way • 217.287.7211
32 Units, pets OK. Continental breakfast. Rooms come with phones, A/C and cable TV. Senior discount. Major credit cards.
*Rates higher during special events and weekends.

29 West Motel
$40
709 Springfield Road • 217.824.2216
22 Units, pets OK ($5). Fitness facility. Rooms come with phones and cable TV. Some rooms have refrigerators. AAA discount. Credit cards: AE, CB, DC, DS, MC, V.

URBANA
Motel 6
$30
1906 N. Cunningham Ave. • 217.344.1082
103 Units, pets OK. Pool. Data ports. Rooms come with phones, A/C and cable TV. Wheelchair accessible. Credit cards: AE, CB, DC, DS, MC, V.

VANDALIA
Ramada Limited
$50
2707 Veterans Avenue • I-70, Exit 61
618.283.1400
60 Units, pets OK ($10 dep. req.). Continental breakfast. Pool. Fitness facility. Laundry facility. Meeting rooms. Data ports. Rooms come with phones and cable TV. Some rooms have microwaves and refrigerators. AAA/Senior discount. Major credit cards.

Travelodge
$36-45
1500 N. 6th Street • 618.283.2363
45 Units, pets OK ($3). Continental breakfast. Pool. Playground. Rooms come with phones, A/C and cable TV. AAA/Senior discount. Major credit cards.

VILLA PARK
Motel 6
$43-48 (56-58)*
10 W. Roosevelt Rd., 1.5 miles W of SR 83 on Roosevelt Rd. • 630.941.9100
110 Units, pets OK. Pool. Laundry facility. Rooms come with phones, A/C and cable TV. Wheelchair accessible. Credit cards: AE, CB, DC, DS, MC, V.
*Higher rates effective summer weekends.

WASHINGTON
Super 8 Motel
$46-53
1884 Washington Road • 309.444.8881
48 Units, pets OK. Rooms come with phones and cable TV. Wheelchair accessible. AAA/Senior discount. Credit cards: AE, CB, DC, DS, MC, V.

WAUKEGAN
Slumberland Motel
$50
3030 Belvidere Road • 847.623.6830
35 Units, pets OK. Rooms come with phones and cable TV. Wheelchair accessible. Major credit cards.

WENONA
Super 8 Motel
$45-55
I-39 & SR 17 (Exit 35) • 815.853.4371
36 Units, pets OK. Continental breakfast. Laundry facility. Rooms come with phones

and cable TV. Wheelchair accessible. Senior discount. Major credit cards.

WEST CHICAGO
Du Wayne Motel
$45-51
27 W. 641st North Ave. • 630.231.1040
34 Units, no pets. Pool. Rooms come with phones and cable TV. Credit cards: AE, MC, V.

YORKVILLE
Super 8 Motel
$50*
1510A N. Bridge Street • 630.553.1634
42 Units, no pets. Continental breakfast. Laundry facility. Rooms come with phones and cable TV. Wheelchair accessible. Major credit cards.
*Rates higher during special events and weekends.

indiana

ANDERSON — *see also Daleville*
Best Inns
$34-58
5706 Scatterfield Road • I-69, Exit 26
765.644.2000
93 Units, pets OK. Continental breakfast. Rooms come with phones and cable TV. AAA/Senior discount. Major credit cards.

Motel 6
$32-35
5810 Scatterfield Road • I-69, Exit 26
765.642.9023
125 Units, pets OK. Pool. Laundry facility. Data ports. Rooms come with phones, A/C and cable TV. Wheelchair accessible. Credit cards: AE, CB, DC, DS, MC, V.

BEDFORD
Mark III Motel
$30-35
1709 "M" Street • 812.275.5935
21 Units, no pets. Rooms come with phones and cable TV. AAA discount. Credit cards: AE, DC, DS, MC, V.

Rosemount Motel
$35
1923 "M" Street • 812.275.5953
24 Units, pets OK ($5). Rooms come with phones and cable TV. Some rooms have refrigerators. AAA discount. Credit cards: AE, CB, DC, DS, MC, V.

BERNE
Black Bear Inn & Suites
$45-50*
1335 US 27N • 260.589.8955
45 Units, no pets. Continental breakfast. Heated pool. Jacuzzi. Meeting rooms. Data ports. Rooms come with phones and cable TV. AAA/Senior discount. Major credit cards.
*AAA discounted rates.

BLOOMINGTON
Motel 6
$33-36
1800 N. Walnut Street • 812.332.0820
109 Units, pets OK. Pool. Laundry facility. Data ports. Rooms come with phones, A/C and cable TV. Wheelchair accessible. Credit cards: AE, CB, DC, DS, MC, V.

Travelodge
$42-46
2615 E. 3rd Street • 812.339.6191
58 Units, pets OK. Rooms come with phones and cable TV. Wheelchair accessible. AAA discount. Major credit cards.

BLUFFTON
Budget Inn
$35-38
1420 N. Main Street • 260.834.0820
20 Units, pets OK ($5). Rooms come with phones and cable TV. Some rooms have microwaves, kitchens and refrigerators. Senior discount. Credit cards: AE, DS, MC, V.

CARLISLE
Carlisle Super 8
$45
On US 41 & 150 • 812.398.2500
Half mile south of junction SR 58.
37 Units, pets OK. Laundry facility. Rooms come with phones and cable TV. AAA discount. Credit cards: AE, CB, DC, DS, MC, V.

CENTERVILLE — *see also Richmond*
Super 8 Motel
$38*
2407 N. Centerville Road
I-70, Centerville Exit • 765.855.5461
41 Units, pets OK. Rooms come with phones and cable TV. Wheelchair accessible. Senior discount. Credit cards: AE, CB, DC, DS, MC, V.
*Rates may increase slightly during holidays, special events and weekends.

CLINTON
Renatto Inn
$35*
Junction SR 63 & 163 • 765.832.3557
34 Units, pets OK. Restaurant on premises. Continental breakfast. Meeting rooms. Rooms come with phones and cable TV. AAA discount. Credit cards: AE, DC, DS, MC, V.
*Rates as high as $77/night.

CLOVERDALE
Days Inn
$40-55
1031 N. Main Street • 765.795.6400
60 Units, no pets. Continental breakfast. Rooms come with phones and cable TV. AAA/Senior discount. Major credit cards.

COLUMBIA CITY
Super 8 Motel
$50*
351 W. Plaza Drive (US 30) • 260.244.2655
52 Units, pets OK. Data ports. Rooms come with phones and cable TV. Some rooms have refrigerators. Senior discount. Major credit cards.
*AAA discounted rates.

COLUMBUS
Knights Inn
$47*
101 Carrie Lane • 812.378.3100
90 Units, pets OK. Pool. Meeting rooms. Rooms come with phones and cable TV. Wheelchair accessible. AAA/Senior discount. Major credit cards.
*Rates as high as $89/night.

Super 8 Motel
$49
110 Brexpark Drive • I-65, Exit 68
812.372.8828
62 Units, no pets. Rooms come with phones and cable TV. Senior discount. Major credit cards.

CORYDON
Old Capitol Inn
$49
115 Skypark Lane • 812.738.4192
77 Units, pets OK. Restaurant on premises. Continental breakfast. Pool. Laundry facility. Playground. Rooms come with phones and cable TV. Wheelchair accessible. Major credit cards.

CRAWFORDSVILLE
Super 8 Motel
$49*
1025 Corey Blvd • 765.364.9999
58 Units, pets OK ($10 dep. req.). Continental breakfast. Rooms come with phones and cable TV. Senior discount. Major credit cards.
*Rates as high as $59/night.

DALE
Stone's Budget Host Motel
$35
410 S. Washington St. • 812.937.4448
23 Units, no pets. Restaurant on premises. Rooms come with phones and cable TV. AAA/Senior discount. Credit cards: AE, CB, DC, DS, MC, V.

DALEVILLE
Budget Inn
$30
I-69 & SR 67 • 765.378.1215
39 Units, pets OK ($5 dep. req.). Rooms come with phones and cable TV. Major credit cards.

Super 8 Motel
$43-53
I-69, Exit 34 • 765.378.0888
43 Units, pets OK ($25 dep. req.). Laundry facility. Rooms come with phones and cable TV. Senior discount. Wheelchair accessible. Major credit cards.

DECATUR
Days Inn
$46-49
1033 N. 13th Street • 260.728.2196
42 Units, pets OK ($5). Continental breakfast. Heated pool. Laundry facility. Data ports. Rooms come with phones and cable TV. AAA/Senior discount. Major credit cards.

ELKHART
Diplomat Motel
$25-38
3300 Cassopolis Street • 574.264.4118
20 Units, pets OK ($4). Continental breakfast. Rooms come with phones and cable TV. Some rooms have refrigerators. AAA discount. Credit cards: AE, DS, MC, V.

Econo Lodge
$25-42
3440 Cassopolis Street • 574.262.0540
35 Units, pets OK. Laundry facility. Rooms come with phones and cable TV. AAA/Senior discount. Credit cards: AE, CB, DC, DS, MC, V.

Knights Inn
$33-46
3252 Cassopolis Street • 574.264.4262
118 Units, no pets. Pool. Meeting rooms. Rooms come with phones and cable TV.

Wheelchair accessible. AAA/Senior discount. Major credit cards.

EVANSVILLE

Economy Inn

$35-40

701 First Avenue • 812.424.3886

56 Units, no pets. Continental breakfast. Pool. Rooms come with phones and cable TV. Senior discount. Major credit cards.

Motel 6

$32-34

4321 US 41N. • 812.424.6431

102 Units, pets OK. Restaurant on premises. Laundry facility. Data ports. Rooms come with phones, A/C and cable TV. Credit cards: AE, CB, DC, DS, MC, V.

Super 8 Motel

$40-45

4600 Morgan Avenue • 812.476.4008

62 Units, pets OK. Laundry facility. Rooms come with phones and cable TV. Senior discount. Wheelchair accessible. Major credit cards.

FORT WAYNE

Best Inns of America

$43-53

3017 W. Coliseum Blvd. • 260.483.0091

105 Units, pets OK. Continental breakfast. Rooms come with phones and cable TV. Some rooms have refrigerators. AAA/Senior discount. Major credit cards.

Hometown Inn

$32

6910 US 30E • 260.749.5058

79 Units, pets OK. Meeting rooms. Laundry facility. Rooms come with phones and cable TV. Some rooms have microwaves and refrigerators. AAA discount. Credit cards: AE, CB, DC, DS, MC, V.

Knights Inn

$39-53

2901 Goshen Road, I-69, Exit 109A

260.484.2669

96 Units, pets OK ($5). Pool. Meeting rooms. Laundry facility. Rooms come with phones and cable TV. Wheelchair accessible. AAA/Senior discount. Credit cards: AE, DS, MC, V.

Motel 6

$28-30

3003 Coliseum Blvd. W. • 260.482.3972

105 Units, pets OK. Restaurant on premises. Pool. Laundry facility. Data ports. Rooms come with phones, A/C and cable TV. Wheelchair accessible. Credit cards: AE, CB, DC, DS, MC, V.

Travelodge

$40

4606 US 30E • 260.422.9511

96 Units, no pets. Pool. Meeting rooms. Rooms come with phones and cable TV. AAA/Senior discount. Major credit cards.

FRANKFORT

Super 8 Motel

$39

1875 W. State Road • I-65, Exit 158, E on SR 28 for 6 miles • 765.654.0088

41 Units, no pets. Continental breakfast. Indoor pool. Jacuzzi. Rooms come with phones and cable TV. Senior discount. Wheelchair accessible. Major credit cards.

GEORGETOWN

Motel 6

$46-50

1079 N. Luther Road • 812.923.0441

61 Units, pets OK. Pool. Data ports. Rooms come with phones, A/C and cable TV. Wheelchair accessible. Credit cards: AE, CB, DC, DS, MC, V.

GREENFIELD

Super 8 Motel

$45-55*

2100 N. State Street • 317.462.8899

80 Units, no pets. Rooms come with phones and cable TV. Senior discount. Major credit cards.

*Rates as high as $65/night.

HAMMOND

American Inn

$40

I-90 & US 41 • 219.931.0900 or 800.90.LODGE

168 Units, no pets. Continental breakfast. Meeting rooms. Rooms come with phones and cable TV. Major credit cards.

Motel 6

$40-44 (54)*

3840 179th Street • I-80/94 at Exit 5A

219.845.0330

133 Units, pets OK. Laundry facility. Rooms come with phones, A/C and cable TV.

Wheelchair accessible. Credit cards: AE, CB, DC, DS, MC, V.
*Higher rate effective spring and summer weekends.

HOWE
Travel Inn Motel
$38-50
50 W. 815N • 260.562.3481
38 Units, no pets. Restaurant on premises. Rooms come with phones and cable TV. Wheelchair accessible. Credit cards: AE, MC, V.

HUNTINGTON
Days Inn
$44-55
2996 W. Park Drive • 219.359.8989
62 Units, pets OK ($7). Pool. Meeting rooms. Rooms come with phones and cable TV. AAA discount. Major credit cards.

INDIANAPOLIS
Best Inns
$45-55
450 Bixler Road • I-465/I-74, Exit 2B, on US 31 • 317.788.0811
100 Units, pets OK ($10). Pool. Laundry facility. Meeting rooms. Rooms come with phones and cable TV. AAA/Senior discount. Major credit cards.

Knights Inn—South
$37-49
4909 Knights Way • 317.788.0125
105 Units, pets OK ($5). Pool. Meeting rooms. Laundry facility. Airport transportation. Rooms come with phones and cable TV. Wheelchair accessible. AAA/Senior discount. Credit cards: AE, CB, DC, DS, MC, V.

Knights Inn—East
$32-39
7101 E. 21st Street • I-70, Exit 89
317.353.8484
97 Units, no pets. Pool. Meeting rooms. Rooms come with phones and cable TV. Wheelchair accessible. Major credit cards.

Motel 6—Airport
$36-40
5241 W. Bradbury Avenue
I-465, Exit 11A • 317.248.1231
133 Units, pets OK. Pool. Laundry facility. Data ports. Rooms come with phones, A/C and cable TV. Wheelchair accessible. Credit cards: AE, CB, DC, DS, MC, V.

Motel 6
$36-40
2851 Shadeland Avenue • 317.546.5864
116 Units, pets OK. Laundry facility. Data ports. Rooms come with phones, A/C and cable TV. Wheelchair accessible. Credit cards: AE, CB, DC, DS, MC, V.

Super 8 Motel
$44
4530 S. Emerson Avenue, I-465, Exit 52
317.788.0955
61 Units, no pets. Continental breakfast. Rooms come with phones and cable TV. AAA discount. Credit cards: AE, CB, DC, DS, MC, V.

Super 8 Motel
$42
4502 S. Harding Street • 317.788.4774
69 Units, pets OK ($5). Laundry facility. Rooms come with phones and cable TV. Credit cards: AE, CB, DC, DS, MC, V.

JEFFERSONVILLE
Motel 6
$34-40
2016 Old Hwy. 31E • 812.283.7703
98 Units, pets OK. Pool. Laundry facility. Data ports. Rooms come with phones, A/C and cable TV. Wheelchair accessible. Credit cards: AE, CB, DC, DS, MC, V.

Super 8 Motel
$40*
2102 Hwy. 31E. • 812.282.8000
64 Units, no pets. Laundry facility. Rooms come with phones and cable TV. Wheelchair accessible. Senior discount. Credit cards: AE, CB, DC, DS, MC, V.
*Rates may increase slightly during special events, holidays and weekends.

KOKOMO
Days Inn
$48
268 S. US 31 • 765.453.7100
119 Units, pets OK. Restaurant on premises. Pool. Rooms come with phones and cable TV. AAA/Senior discount. Credit cards: AE, DC, DS, MC, V.

Motel 6
$36-38
2808 S. Reed Road • 765.457.8211
93 Units, pets OK. Laundry facility. Rooms come with phones, A/C and cable TV.

Wheelchair accessible. Credit cards: AE, CB, DC, DS, MC, V.

LAFAYETTE
Budget Inn of America
$45
I-65 & SR 26E • 765.447.7566
144 Units, pets OK. Continental breakfast. Laundry facility. Rooms come with phones and cable TV. AAA/Senior discount. Major credit cards.

Knights Inn
$37-50*
4110 SR 26E (at I-65) • 765.447.5611
112 Units, no pets. Pool. Rooms come with phones and cable TV. Some rooms have kitchenettes. Wheelchair accessible. Senior discount. Major credit cards.
*Rates as high as $95/night.

Super 8 Motel
$43-49
4301 SR 26E (at I-65) • 765.447.5551
62 Units, pets OK. Continental breakfast. Rooms come with phones and cable TV. Senior discount. Major credit cards.

LA PORTE
Super 8 Motel
$50*
438 Pine Lake Avenue • 219.325.3808
51 Units, pets OK. Rooms come with phones and cable TV. Wheelchair accessible. Senior discount. Credit cards: AE, CB, DC, DS, MC, V.
*Rates as high as $70/night.

LAWRENCEBURG
Riverside Inn
$49
515 Eads Pkwy. E. • 812.537.4041
109 Units, no pets. Laundry facility. Meeting rooms. Data ports. Rooms come with phones and cable TV. Credit cards: AE, MC, V.

LEBANON
Super 8 Motel
$45-55*
405 Mt. Zion Road • 765.482.9999
55 Units, no pets. Continental breakfast. Indoor pool. Rooms come with phones and cable TV. Senior discount. Major credit cards.
*Rates as high as $63/night.

MADISON
President Madison Motel
$35-60
906 E. First (Off Hwy. 421) • 812.265.2361 or 800.456.6835
28 Units, pets OK. Pool (summer only). Rooms come with phones and cable TV and have view of Ohio River. Major credit cards.
*Higher rate effective summer months.

Super 8 Motel
$40-50
Jct. SR 56, 62 & 256 • 812.273.4443
25 Units, no pets. Pool. Rooms come with phones and cable TV. Credit cards: AE, DS, MC, V.

MARION
Super 8 Motel
$45-55
5172 S Kaybee Drive • I-69, Exit 59
765.998.6800
45 Units, pets OK ($15). Laundry facility. Data ports. Rooms come with refrigerators, phones and cable TV. AAA/Senior discount. Major credit cards.

MARKLE
Super 8 Motel
$47
610 Annette Drive • I-69, Exit 86
260.758.8888
30 Units, pets OK ($7). Continental breakfast. Rooms come with refrigerators, phones and cable TV. AAA/Senior discount. Credit cards: AE, DS, MC, V.

MARTINSVILLE
Super 8 Motel
$45
Ohio St. & Bill's Blvd. • 765.349.2222
49 Units, no pets. Continental breakfast. Indoor pool. Laundry facility. Rooms come with phones and cable TV. Senior discount. Major credit cards.

MERRILLVILLE
Knights Inn
$39-50
8250 Louisiana • 219.736.5100
129 Units, pets OK ($10). Continental breakfast. Pool. Laundry facility. Meeting room. Rooms come with phones and cable TV. AAA/Senior discount. Major credit cards.

Motel 6
$30-38
8290 Louisiana Street • I-65 at US 30
219.738.2701
125 Units, pets OK. Pool. Laundry facility. Rooms come with phones, A/C and cable TV. Wheelchair accessible. Credit cards: AE, CB, DC, DS, MC, V.

Super 8 Motel
$37-55
8300 Louisiana Street • 219.736.8383
59 Units, pets OK. Continental breakfast. Laundry facility. Meeting room. Rooms come with phones and cable TV. Wheelchair accessible. AAA/Senior discount. Major credit cards.

MICHIGAN CITY
Al & Sally's Motel
$40-55
3221 W. Dunes Hwy. • 219.872.9131
16 Units, no pets. Heated pool. Playground. Tennis court. Rooms come with refrigerators, phones and cable TV. AAA/Senior discount. Credit cards: AE, DS, MC, V.

Knights Inn
$35-45*
201 W. Kieffer Road • 219.874.9500
103 Units, pets OK ($10). Pool. Meeting rooms. Rooms come with phones and cable TV. Wheelchair accessible. AAA/Senior discount. Major credit cards.
*Summer rates as high as $150/night.

Super 8 Motel
$40-50
5724 S. Franklin • 219.879.0411
51 Units, no pets. Rooms come with phones and cable TV. Wheelchair accessible. Senior discount. Credit cards: AE, CB, DC, DS, MC, V.

MISHAWAKA
Super 8 Motel
$50*
535 W. University Drive • 574.247.0888
66 Units, pets OK. Laundry facility. Meeting rooms. Rooms come with phones and cable TV. Senior discount. Wheelchair accessible. Major credit cards.
*Rates as high as $60/night.

MUNCIE
Bestway Inn
$30
4000 N. Broadway Ave. • 765.288.3671
48 Units, no pets. Rooms come with phones and cable TV. Major credit cards.

Super 8 Motel
$46-55
3601 W. Fox Ridge Ln. • 765.286.4333
63 Units, pets OK ($10). Rooms come with phones and cable TV. AAA/Senior discount. Major credit cards.

NEW CASTLE
Days Inn
$39-44
5243 S. SR 3, I-70, Exit 123
765.987.8205
83 Units, pets OK ($5). Continental breakfast. Pool. Rooms come with phones and cable TV. AAA discount. Major credit cards.

New Castle Inn
$30-44
2005 S. Memorial Drive • 765.529.1670
52 Units, pets OK. Continental breakfast. Pool. Rooms come with phones and cable TV. Major credit cards.

PERU
Knights Inn
$45-50
2661 S. Bus. Rte. 31 • 765.472.3971
30 Units, no pets. Restaurant on premises. Laundry facility. Rooms come with phones and cable TV. Major credit cards.

PLYMOUTH
Days Inn
$31-55 (62-78)*
2229 N. Michigan Street • 574.935.4276
40 Units, pets OK ($5). Restaurant on premises. Laundry facility. Meeting rooms. Rooms come with phones and cable TV. AAA discount. Major credit cards.
*Higher rates effective Labor Day through Thanksgiving.

Villager Lodge
$40
2535 N. Michigan Ave. • 574.935.5911
103 Units, pets OK. Pool. Laundry facility. Rooms come with phones, A/C and cable TV. Wheelchair accessible. Credit cards: AE, CB, DC, DS, MC, V.

PORTAGE
Knights Inn
$43-50

6101 Melton Rd. (Rte. 20) • 219.763.3121
150 Units, pets OK. Pool. Laundry facility. Airport transportation. Rooms come with phones, A/C and cable TV. Wheelchair accessible. AAA/Senior discount. Credit cards: AE, CB, DC, DS, MC, V.

PORTLAND
Hoosier Inn
$38-45
1620 Meridian Street • 260.726.7113
25 Units, pets OK ($4). Laundry facility. Rooms come with phones and cable TV. AAA discount. Major credit cards.

RENSSELAER
Knights Inn
$45-50
8530 W. SR 114 • 219.866.4164
30 Units, pets OK ($15 dep. req.). Rooms come with phones and cable TV. Senior discount. Credit cards: AE, DC, DS, MC, V.

RICHMOND — *see also Centerville*
Best Western
$38-55
3020 E. Main Street • 765.966.1505
44 Units, pets OK ($10 dep. req.). Continental breakfast. Heated pool. Rooms come with phones and cable TV. Some rooms have kitchens, microwaves and refrigerators. AAA/Senior discount. Credit cards: AE, CB, DC, DS, MC, V.

Motel 6
$37-46
419 Commerce Drive • 765.966.6682
103 Units, pets OK. Pool. Laundry facility. Rooms come with A/C, phones and cable TV. Wheelchair accessible. Major credit cards.

Super 8 Motel
$45
2525 Chester Blvd. • Jct. US 27 & I-70
765.962.7576
74 Units, pets OK. Pool. Rooms come with phones and cable TV. Wheelchair accessible. Senior discount. Major credit cards.

ROCKVILLE
Motel Forrest
$30-50
On US 40 • 765.569.5250
17 Units, no pets. Rooms come with phones and cable TV. Credit cards: DS, MC, V.

Parke Bridge Motel
$30-51
304 E. Ohio Street • 765.569.3525
10 Units, no pets. Rooms come with phones and cable TV. Some rooms have microwaves and refrigerators. Credit cards: AE, DS, MC, V.

SALEM
Salem Motel
$30-47*
1209 W. Mulberry • 812.883.2491
28 Units, no pets. Rooms come with refrigerators, phones and cable TV. Credit cards: AE, MC, V.
*AAA discounted rates.

SCOTTSBURG
Mariann Travel Inn
$44-47
I-65 (Exit 29A) • 812.752.3398
96 Units, pets OK. Restaurant on premises. Pool and wading pool. Playground. Rooms come with phones and cable TV. Some rooms have microwaves and refrigerators. AAA/Senior discount. Credit cards: AE, CB, DC, DS, MC, V.

SEYMOUR
Days Inn
$39-48
302 S. Commerce Drive • 812.522.3678
120 Units, pets OK. Continental breakfast. Pool. Jacuzzi. Rooms come with phones and cable TV. Wheelchair accessible. AAA discount. Major credit cards.

Econo Lodge
$30-50*
220 Commerce Drive • 812.522.8000
50 Units, pets OK. Restaurant on premises. Continental breakfast. Rooms come with phones and cable TV. Wheelchair accessible. Major credit cards.
*Rates as high as $70/night.

Knights Inn
$40-55
207 N. Sandy Ck. Dr. • 812.522.3523
117 Units, pets OK. Pool. Meeting rooms. Rooms come with phones and cable TV. Some rooms have microwaves, jacuzzis and refrigerators. AAA/Senior discount. Credit cards: AE, CB, DC, DS, MC, V.

SHELBYVILLE
Super 8 Motel
$46
20 Rampart Drive • I-74, Exit 113
317.392.6239
61 Units, pets OK. Continental breakfast. Sauna. Laundry and fitness facilities. Meeting rooms. Continental breakfast. Senior discount. Wheelchair accessible. Major credit cards.

SOUTH BEND — *see also Mishawaka*
Knights Inn
$45*
236 N. Dixie Way • 574.277.2960
108 Units, no pets. Continental breakfast. Pool. Rooms come with phones and cable TV. Wheelchair accessible. AAA/Senior discount. Major credit cards.
*Rates as high as $79/night.

Motel 6
$30-44
52624 US 31N
I-80/90 at Exit 77 • 574.272.7072
146 Units, pets OK. Pool. Laundry facility. Rooms come with phones, A/C and cable TV. Wheelchair accessible. Credit cards: AE, CB, DC, DS, MC, V.

Super 8 Motel
$45*
52825 US 31/33N, I-80/90, Exit 77, one mile north • 574.272.9000
111 Units, no pets. Continental breakfast. Laundry facility. Rooms come with phones and cable TV. Some rooms have kitchenettes. Senior discount. Major credit cards.
*Rates as high as $60/night.

SPEEDWAY
Motel 6
$30-36
6330 Debonair Lane • I-465, Exit 16A
317.293.3220
164 Units, pets OK. Pool. Laundry facility. Data ports. Rooms come with phones, A/C and cable TV. Wheelchair accessible. Credit cards: AE, CB, DC, DS, MC, V.

Red Roof Inn
$34-56
6415 Debonair Lane • I-465, Exit 16A
317.293.6881
108 Units, pets OK. Fitness facility. Data ports. Rooms come with phones and cable TV. AAA discount. Major credit cards.

TELL CITY
Daystop
$40-44
Hwy. 66 & 14th Street • 812.547.3474
67 Units, pets OK. Restaurant on premises. Continental breakfast. Pool. Meeting room. Rooms come with phones and cable TV. Major credit cards.

TERRE HAUTE
Knights Inn
$44-57
401 E. Margaret Drive, I-70, Exit 7
812.234.9931
125 Units, pets OK. Continental breakfast. Laundry facility. Data ports. Rooms come with phones and cable TV. AAA/Senior discount. Major credit cards.

Motel 6
$30-38
1 W. Honey Creek Drive, I-70, US 41 Exit
812.238.1586
116 Units, pets OK. Indoor pool. Data ports. Rooms come with phones, A/C and cable TV. Wheelchair accessible. Credit cards: AE, CB, DC, DS, MC, V.

Travelodge
$40
530 S. 3rd Street • 812.232.7075
57 Units, pets OK. Pool. Laundry facility. Rooms come with phones and cable TV. Senior discount. Credit cards: AE, CB, DC, DS, JCB, MC, V.

VINCENNES
Relax Inn
$29-35
1411 Willow Street • 812.882.1282
39 Units, pets OK. Pool. Rooms come with phones and cable TV. Wheelchair accessible. Major credit cards.

Super 8 Motel
$44
609 Shirlee Street • 812.882.5101
39 Units, pets OK ($3 and $25 dep. req.). Continental breakfast. Pool. Rooms come with phones and cable TV. Senior discount. Wheelchair accessible. Major credit cards.

WARREN
Super 8 Motel
$40-44
7281 S. 75th E. • I-69, Exit 78
219.375.4688

47 Units, no pets. Rooms come with phones and cable TV. AAA/Senior discount. Credit cards: AE, DS, MC, V.

WARSAW
Days Inn
$47*
2575 E. Center Street • 574.267.3344
50 Units, pets OK ($5). Continental breakfast. Rooms come with phones and cable TV. Major credit cards.
*AAA discounted rate.

iowa

ADAIR
Adair Budget Inn
$29-39
From I-80, Exit 76 • 641.742.5553
34 Units, pets OK. Rooms come with phones and cable TV. Some rooms have phones. AAA/Senior discount. Major credit cards.

ALGONA
Super 8 Motel
$38
210 Norwood Drive • 515.295.7225
30 Units, no pets. Rooms come with phones and cable TV. Wheelchair accessible. Senior discount. Credit cards: AE, CB, DC, DS, MC, V.

ALTOONA
Motel 6
$36-44 (56)*
3225 Adventureland Dr. • 515.967.5252
116 Units, pets OK. Indoor pool. Laundry facility. Data ports. Rooms come with phones, A/C and cable TV. Wheelchair accessible. Major credit cards.
*Higher rate effective summer weekends.

AMANA
Days Inn
$39-49
2214 "U" Avenue • 319.668.2097
119 Units, pets OK ($8). Continental breakfast. Sauna. Putting green. Jacuzzi. Laundry facility. Rooms come with phones and cable TV. AAA discount. Major credit cards.

AMES — *see also Boone and Nevada*
Howard Johnson Express Inn
$50*
1709 S. Duff • 515.232.8363
73 Units, pets OK ($100 dep. req.). Continental breakfast. Heated pool. Laundry and fitness facility. Airport transportation. Rooms come with phones and cable TV. Senior discount. Major credit cards.
*AAA discounted rates.

Super 8 Motel
$43
1418 S. Dayton Road • 515.232.6510
60 Units, no pets. Continental breakfast. Rooms come with phones and cable TV. Senior discount. Wheelchair accessible. Major credit cards.

ANAMOSA
Super 8 Motel
$45-55
100 Grant Wood Drive • 319.462.3888
33 Units, no pets. Continental breakfast. Sauna. Rooms come with phones and cable TV. Wheelchair accessible. Senior discount. Major credit cards.

ATLANTIC
Econo Lodge
$44
64968 Baston Road • 712.243.4067
I-80, Exit 60, one half mile south.
51 Units, pets OK. Heated pool. Meeting room. Rooms come with phones and cable TV. Senior discount. Credit cards: AE, DC, DS, MC, V.

Super 8 Motel
$45-50
1902 E. 7th Street • 712.243.4723
54 Units, pets OK. Continental breakfast. Jacuzzi and sauna. Fitness facility. Airport transportation. Data ports. Rooms come with phones and cable TV. AAA/Senior discount. Major credit cards.

AVOCA
Capri Motel
$37
110 E. Pershing Street • 712.343.6301
27 Units, pets OK ($4). Rooms come with phones and cable TV. Credit cards: AE, DC, DS, MC, V.

BETTENDORF — *see also Davenport*
Twin Bridges Motor Inn
$39-48
221 15th Street • 563.355.6451
69 Units, pets OK ($25 dep. req.). Restaurant on premises. Jacuzzi. Laundry facility.

Rooms come with phones and cable TV. Some rooms have refrigerators. AAA discount. Major credit cards.

BLOOMFIELD
Southfork Inn
$42-56
Junction Hwys. 2 & 63 • 641.664.1063 or 800.926.2860
23 Units, pets OK. Restaurant on premises. Rooms come with phones and cable TV. Wheelchair accessible. Major credit cards.

BOONE
Super 8 Motel
$43
1715 S. Story Street • 515.432.8890
56 Units, pets OK. Continental breakfast. Rooms come with phones and cable TV. Wheelchair accessible. Senior discount. Major credit cards.

BURLINGTON
Lincolnville Motel
$25-39
1701 Mt. Pleasant St. • 319.752.2748
33 Units, pets OK. Rooms come with phones and cable TV. Wheelchair accessible. Major credit cards.

Midtown Motel
$27-45
2731 Mt. Pleasant St. • 319.752.7777
38 Units, no pets. Rooms come with phones and cable TV. Some rooms have microwaves and refrigerators. AAA/Senior discount. Credit cards: AE, CB, DC, DS, JCB, MC, V.

CARROLL
Burke Inn
$34-42
1225 Plaza Drive • 712.792-5156 or 800.348.5156
41 Units, pets OK. Continental breakfast. Rooms come with phones and cable TV. Wheelchair accessible. Major credit cards.

Super 8 Motel
$47-54
1757 Hwy. 71N • 712.792.4753
30 Units, no pets. Continental breakfast. Rooms come with phones and cable TV. AAA/Senior discount. Credit cards: AE, DS, MC, V.

CEDAR FALLS
Blackhawk Motor Inn
$36-39
122 Washington • 319.277.1161
15 Units, pets OK. Rooms come with phones and cable TV. Some rooms have refrigerators. Credit cards: AE, CB, DC, DS, MC, V.

University Inn
$40-50
4711 University Avenue • 319.277.1412
50 Units, pets OK ($30 dep. req.). Continental breakfast. Sauna. Jacuzzi. Video arcade. Laundry facility. Rooms come with phones and cable TV. Some rooms have refrigerators. Senior discount. Credit cards: AE, CB, DC, DS, MC, V.

CEDAR RAPIDS
Exel Inn of Cedar Rapids
$35-45
616 33rd Avenue S.W. • 319.366.2475
103 Units, pets OK. Continental breakfast. Game room. Laundry facility. Fitness facility. Data ports. Rooms come with phones and cable TV. Some rooms have microwaves and refrigerators. AAA/Senior discount. Credit cards: AE, CB, DC, DS, MC, V.

Motel 6
$34-37
3325 Southgate Ct. S.W. • 319.366.7523
108 Units, pets OK. Rooms come with A/C, phones and cable TV. Wheelchair accessible. Major credit cards.

Super 8 Motel
$50
400 33rd Avenue S.W. • I-380 & 33rd Avenue S. • 319.363.1755
62 Units, pets OK ($10). Continental breakfast. Rooms come with phones and cable TV. Major credit cards.

CHARITON
Royal Rest Motel
$39-47
Chariton, IA 50049 • 641.774.5961
On US 34, 0.5 mile east of jct. with SR 14. 27 Units, pets OK. Continental breakfast. Meeting rooms. Rooms come with phones and cable TV. Some rooms have refrigerators. Senior discount. Credit cards: DS, MC, V.

CHARLES CITY
Hartwood Inn
$40-49
1312 Gilbert Street • 641.288.4352 or 800.972.2335
35 Units, no pets. Pool. Data ports. Rooms come with phones and cable TV. Wheelchair accessible. AAA/Senior discount. Major credit cards.

Lamplighter Motel
$38-50
1416 Gilbert Street • 641.228.6711
47 Units, no pets. Heated indoor pool. Wading pool. Jacuzzi. Meeting rooms. Rooms come with phones and cable TV. Some rooms have refrigerators. Senior discount. Credit cards: AE, CB, DC, DS, MC, V.

CLARINDA
Celebrity Inn
$40-50
S. Jct. Hwys. 2 & 71 • 712.542.5178
36 Units, no pets. Rooms come with phones and cable TV. Major credit cards.

CLEAR LAKE
Budget Inn Motel
$35-55
Hwy. 18 and I-35 • 641.357.8700 or 800.341.8000
60 Units, pets OK. Continental breakfast. Heated pool. Playground and picnic tables. Rooms come with cable TV. Wheelchair accessible. AAA/Senior discount. Credit cards: AE, DS, MC, V.

Lake County Inn
$30
518 Hwy. 18W • 641.357.2184
28 Units, pets OK. Continental breakfast. Rooms come with phones and cable TV. AAA/Senior discount. Credit cards: AE, DS, MC, V.

Super 8 Motel
$41*
From I-35, Exit 193 • 641.357.7521
60 Units, pets OK. Toast bar. Rooms come with phones and cable TV. Wheelchair accessible. Senior discount. Credit cards: AE, CB, DC, DS, MC, V.
*Rates may increase during special events.

CLINTON
Travel Inn
$38
302 6th Avenue S. • 563.243.4730
50 Units, pets OK. Restaurant on premises. Rooms come with phones and cable TV. Major credit cards.

COLUMBUS JUNCTION
Columbus Motel
$39
On SR 82 (one half mile east of town) 319.728.8080
27 Units, pets OK ($3). Laundry facility. Meeting room. Rooms come with phones and cable TV. Some rooms have refrigerators. Senior discount. Credit cards: DS, MC, V.

CORALVILLE
Econo Lodge
$30-50
815 1st Avenue • 319.354.6000 or 800.842.4424
90 Units, pets OK. Pool. Rooms come with phones and cable TV. Wheelchair accessible. Major credit cards.

Expressway Motel
$30-50
I-80 at Hwy. 965 • 319.645.2466
100 Units, pets OK. Restaurant on premises. Rooms come with phones and cable TV. Wheelchair accessible. Major credit cards.

Motel 6
$33-43
810 1st Avenue • I-80, Exit 242
319.354.0030
103 Units, pets OK. Pool. Laundry facility. Data ports. Rooms come with phones, A/C and cable TV. Wheelchair accessible. Credit cards: AE, CB, DC, DS, MC, V.

COUNCIL BLUFFS
Interstate Inn
$39-50
2717 S. 24th Street, I-80, Exit 1B
712.328.8899
166 Units. Breakfast vouchers offered at check-in for local casino. Laundry facility. Rooms come with phones, A/C and cable TV. Major credit cards.

Motel 6
$40-53
3032 S. Expressway • 712.366.2405

84 Units, pets OK. Restaurant on premises. Indoor pool. Laundry facility. Data ports. Rooms come with phones, A/C and cable TV. Wheelchair accessible. Credit cards: AE, CB, DC, DS, MC, V.

Super 8 Motel
$48
2712 S. 24th Street • 712.322.2888
87 Units, pets OK. Continental breakfast. Rooms come with phones and cable TV. Wheelchair accessible. Senior discount. Credit cards: AE, CB, DC, DS, MC, V.

CRESTON
Berning Motor Inn
$35
301 W. Adams • 641.782.7001
48 Units. Restaurant on premises. Rooms come with phones and cable TV. Major credit cards.

Super 8 Motel
$45
900 S. Sumner • 641.782.6541
123 Units, no pets. Jacuzzi. Fitness facility. Continental breakfast. Rooms come with phones and cable TV. Major credit cards.

DAVENPORT — *see also Bettendorf and Moline (IL)*
Exel Inn
$36-56
6310 N. Brady Street • 563.386.6350
103 Units, pets OK. Continental breakfast. Laundry facility. Rooms come with phones and cable TV. Some rooms have microwaves, jacuzzis and refrigerators. Senior discount. Credit cards: AE, CB, DC, DS, MC, V.

Motel 6
$30-46
6111 N. Brady Street • 563.391.8997
98 Units, pets OK. Pool. Laundry facility. Data ports. Rooms come with phones, A/C and cable TV. Wheelchair accessible. Credit cards: AE, CB, DC, DS, MC, V.

DECORAH
Villager Lodge Motel
$28-54
Junction Hwys. 9 & 52 • 563.382.4241 or 800.632.5980
100 Units, pets OK. Restaurant on premises. Continental breakfast. Pool. Rooms come with phones and cable TV. Major credit cards.

DENISON
Super 8 Motel
$38-54
502 Boyer Valley Road • 712.263.5081
40 Units, pets OK. Continental breakfast. Airport transportation. Rooms come with phones and cable TV. Some rooms have microwaves and refrigerators. Credit cards: AE, CB, DC, DS, MC, V.

Days Inn
$44-55
Jct. Hwys. 30 & 59S • 712.263.2500
43 Units, pets OK. Continental breakfast. Rooms come with phones and cable TV. AAA discount. Major credit cards.

DES MOINES — *see also Altoona, Ankeny, Urbandale and West Des Moines*
Bavarian Inn
$40
5220 N.E. 14th Street, I-80, Exit 136
515.265.5611
106 Units, pets OK ($50 dep. req.). Continental breakfast. Heated pool. Jacuzzi. Laundry facility. Meeting rooms. Data ports. Rooms come with phones and cable TV. AAA/Senior discount. Major credit cards.

Best Western Colonial
$43-53
5020 N.E. 14th Street • 515.265.7511
62 Units, pets OK. Fitness facility. Rooms come with phones and cable TV. AAA/Senior discount. Major credit cards.

Hickman Motor Lodge
$44-48
6500 Hickman Road • 515.276.8591
38 Units, pets OK. Meeting rooms. Rooms come with phones and cable TV. Some rooms have kitchens. AAA/Senior discount. Credit cards: AE, DS, MC, V.

Motel 6
$36-40
4817 Fleur Drive, I-80/35, Exit 136
515.287.6364
98 Units, pets OK. Laundry facility. Rooms come with phones, A/C and cable TV. Wheelchair accessible. Credit cards: AE, CB, DC, DS, MC, V.

Motel 6
$35-39
4940 N.E. 14th Street • 515.266.5456
120 Units, pets OK. Pool. Laundry facility. Data ports. Rooms come with phones, A/C and cable TV. Wheelchair accessible. Credit cards: AE, CB, DC, DS, MC, V.

Villager Lodge
$35-50
7625 Hickman Road • I-80/35, Exit 125
515.276.5401
52 Units, pets OK. Rooms come with phones and cable TV. Senior discount available (10%) Credit cards: AE, CB, DC, DS, MC, V.

DUBUQUE
The Julien Inn
$39-55
200 Main Street • 563.556.4200
145 Units, no pets. Restaurant on premises. Airport transportation. Fitness facility. Meeting rooms. Laundry facility. Rooms come with phones and cable TV. Some rooms have refrigerators and jacuzzis. AAA/ Senior discount. Credit cards: AE, CB, DC, DS, MC, V.

North Country Inn
$33
2670 Dodge Street • On US 20, west of town • 563.556.0880
98 Units, pets OK. Rooms come with phones, A/C and cable TV. Wheelchair accessible. Credit cards: AE, CB, DC, DS, MC, V.

DYERSVILLE
Super 8 Motel
$46
925 15th Avenue S.E. • 563.875.8885
45 Units, no pets. Continental breakfast. Sauna. Meeting room. Rooms come with phones and cable TV. Senior discount. Wheelchair accessible. Major credit cards.

EMMETSBURG
Best Value Suburban Motel
$44-49
3635 450th Avenue • 712.852.2626
40 Units, no pets. Pool. Laundry facility. Rooms come with phones and cable TV. Some rooms have jacuzzis. AAA discount. Credit cards: AE, DS, MC, V.

ESTHERVILLE
Super 8 Motel
$43-49
1919 Central Avenue • 712.362.2400
34 Units, no pets. Jacuzzi. Fitness facility. Sauna. Rooms come with phones and cable TV. Wheelchair accessible. Senior discount. Credit cards: AE, CB, DC, DS, MC, V.

FOREST CITY
Super 8 Motel
$43-49
11215 Hwy. 69S. • 641.585.1300
34 Units, no pets. Continental breakfast. Pool. Rooms come with phones and cable TV. Senior discount. Major credit cards.

Village Chateau Motor Inn
$29-45
1115 Hwy. 69N. • 641.582.4351
40 Units, pets OK. Pool. Rooms come with phones and cable TV. Major credit cards.

FORT DODGE
Budget Host Inn
$44
116 Kenyon Road • 515.955.8501
110 Units, pets OK. Restaurant on premises. Indoor heated pool. Meeting rooms. Jacuzzi. Game room. Laundry. Airport transportation. Rooms come with phones and cable TV. Major credit cards.

Super 8 Motel
$41-54
3040 E. 5th Avenue • 515.576.8000
81 Units, pets OK ($6). Continental breakfast. Heated indoor pool. Copy and fax service. Laundry facility. Rooms come with phones and cable TV. Wheelchair accessible. AAA/Senior discount. Credit cards: AE, DS, MC, V.

FORT MADISON
The Madison Inn Motel
$42-49
3440 Avenue "L" • 319.372.7740
20 Units, pets OK ($5). Continental breakfast. Rooms come with phones and cable TV. Some rooms have refrigerators. AAA/Senior discount. Credit cards: AE, DC, DS, V.

Santa Fe Motel
$21-42
2639 Avenue "L" • 319.372.1310 or 800.472.4657

31 Units, no pets. Rooms come with phones and cable TV. Wheelchair accessible. Major credit cards.

HARLAN
Harlan 59-er Motel
$40
1148 Hwy. 59N. • 712.755.5999 or 800.960.5999
32 Units, no pets. Restaurant on premises. Continental breakfast. Rooms come with phones and cable TV. Major credit cards.

HUMBOLDT
Broadway Inn
$29-44
812 N. 13th Street • 515.332.3545
38 Units, no pets. Continental breakfast. Rooms come with phones, A/C and cable TV. Wheelchair accessible. Major credit cards.

Super 8 Motel
$44*
Humboldt, IA 50548 • 515.332.1131
Two blocks west of Jct. Hwys. 3 & 169.
34 Units, pets OK. Sauna. Fitness facility. Rooms come with phones and cable TV. Wheelchair accessible. Senior discount. Credit cards: AE, CB, DC, DS, MC, V.
*Rates may increase special events, weekends and holidays.

IDA GROVE
Delux Motel
$35-50
5981 Hwy. 175 • 712.364.3317
53 Units, pets OK. Data ports. Rooms come with phones and cable TV. Some rooms have microwaves and refrigerators. Senior discount. Credit cards: AE, DS, MC, V.

INDEPENDENCE
Super 8 Motel
$50
2000 1st Street W. • 319.334.7041
39 Units, pets OK ($5-10). Continental breakfast. Rooms come with phones and cable TV. Some rooms have microwaves and refrigerator. Wheelchair accessible. AAA/Senior discount. Credit cards: AE, CB, DC, DS, MC, V.

INDIANOLA
Super 8 Motel
$49*
1701 N. Jefferson • 515.961.0058
44 Units, no pets. Continental breakfast. Pool. Rooms come with phones and cable TV. Senior discount. Wheelchair accessible. Major credit cards.
*Rates higher weekends, special events and holidays.

IOWA CITY — *see Coralville*

IOWA FALLS
Super 8 Motel
$48
839 S. Oak (Hwy 65S) • 641.648.4618
47 Units, no pets. Continental breakfast. Meeting rooms. Rooms come with phones and TV. No cable in rooms. Wheelchair accessible. Senior discount. Major credit cards.

JEFFERSON
Budget Host Inn
$33
209 E. Hwy. 30 • 515.386.3116
26 Units, pets OK ($25 dep. req.). Laundry facility. Picnic tables. Rooms come with phones and TV. AAA/Senior discount. Credit cards: AE, DS, MC. V.

Super 8 Motel
$42-49
Jct. of Hwys. 30 and 4 • 515.386.2464
34 Units, pets OK. Sauna. Fitness facility. Copy and fax service. Rooms come with phones and cable TV. Wheelchair accessible. Senior discount. Credit cards: AE, CB, DC, DS, MC, V.

KALONA
Pull'r Inn Motel
$49
110 "E" Avenue • 319.656.3611
29 Units, no pets. Continental breakfast. Data ports. Rooms come with phones and cable TV. Wheelchair accessible. Credit cards: AE, MC, V.

KEOKUK
Chief Motel
$30-50
2701 Main Street Road • 319.524.2565
17 Units, pets OK. Rooms come with phones and cable TV. Some rooms have refrigerators. AAA discount. Credit cards: AE, CB, DC, DS, MC, V.

Econo Lodge
$40-45
3764 Main Street • 319.524.3252 or

800.252.2256
45 Units, pets OK ($5). Continental breakfast. Pool. Rooms come with phones and cable TV. AAA/Senior discount. Wheelchair accessible. Credit cards: AE, DS, MC. V.

KNOXVILLE
Red Carpet Motel
$40
1702 N. Lincoln • 641.842.3191
40 Units, pets OK. Continental breakfast. Rooms come with phones and cable TV. Major credit cards.

Super 8 Motel
$50
2205 N. Lincoln Street • 641.828.8808
40 Units, no pets. Continental breakfast. Laundry facility. Rooms come with phones and cable TV. AAA/Senior discount. Major credit cards.

LAMONI
Super 8 Motel
$47
I-35 & US 69, Exit 4 • 641.784.7500
30 Units, no pets. Meeting rooms. Rooms come with phones and cable TV. Wheelchair accessible. Senior discount. Credit cards: AE, CB, DC, DS, MC, V.

LE MARS
Amber Inn Motel
$30-50
635 8th Avenue • 712.546.7066 or 800.338.0298
73 Units, pets OK. Continental breakfast. Meeting rooms. Rooms come with phones and cable TV. Some rooms have refrigerators. Credit cards: AE, DS, MC, V.

Super 8 Motel
$47-50*
1201 Hawkeye Ave. SW • 712.546.8800
61 Units, pets OK ($5). Continental breakfast. Heated pool. Laundry facility. Rooms come with phones and cable TV. Wheelchair accessible. AAA/Senior discount. Major credit cards.
*Rates may increase during special events, weekends and holidays.

MAQUOKETA
Super 8 Motel
$47-60*
1019 W. Platt Street • 563.652.6888
50 Units, no pets. Laundry facility. Rooms come with phones and cable TV. AAA/Senior discount. Major credit cards.
*Higher rate effective weekends.

MARQUETTE
The Frontier Motel
$45
Hwys. 18 & 76 • 563.873.3497
20 Units, pets OK ($10). Heated pool. Data ports. Rooms come with phones and cable TV. Credit cards: AE, DS, MC, V.

MARSHALLTOWN
Super 8 Motel
$41
Jct. of US 30 & Hwy. 14 • 641.753.8181
61 Units, no pets. Rooms come with phones and cable TV. Wheelchair accessible. AAA/Senior discount. Credit cards: AE, CB, DC, DS, MC, V.

MASON CITY
Thriftlodge
$45-49
24 5th Street S.W. • 641.424.2910
47 Units, pets OK. Continental breakfast. Heated pool. Rooms come with phones and cable TV. Some rooms have refrigerators. AAA/Senior discount. Major credit cards.

MILFORD
Okoboji Avenue Inn
$36-52
1511 Okoboji Avenue • 712.338.4701 or 888.422.3887
24 Units, pets OK. Continental breakfast. Rooms come with phones and cable TV. Major credit cards.

MISSOURI VALLEY
Rath Inn
$35-50
I-29 & Hwy. 30 • 712.642.2723
44 Units, no pets. Rooms come with phones and cable TV. Major credit cards.

Super 8 Motel
$47
I-29 & Hwy. 30 • 712.642.4788
71 Units, no pets. Continental breakfast. Laundry and fitness facility. Meeting room. Rooms come with phones and cable TV. Senior discount. Wheelchair accessible. Major credit cards.

MONTICELLO
The Blue Inn
$40-50
250 N. Main Street • 319.465.6116
12 Units, pets OK ($4 and $20 dep. req.). Continental breakfast. Restaurant on premises. Meeting rooms. Rooms come with phones and cable TV. Some rooms have kitchens. AAA/Senior discount. Credit cards: AE, DS, MC, V.

MOUNT PLEASANT
Iris Motel
$30-45
905 W. Washington St. • 319.385.2248
63 Units, pets OK. Restaurant on premises. Rooms come with phones and cable TV. Wheelchair accessible. Major credit cards.

MUSCATINE
The Lamplight Inn of Muscatine
$31-49
2107 Grandview Ave. • 563.263.7191
38 Units. Rooms come with phones and cable TV. Wheelchair accessible. Major credit cards.

NEVADA
Super 8 Motel
$42*
I-35, Exit 158, then 6 miles east on US 30
515.382.5588
35 Units, no pets. Rooms come with phones and cable TV. Senior discount. Major credit cards.
*Rates higher during weekends.

NEW HAMPTON
Howard Johnson Express Inn
$45-55
2199 McCloud Avenue • 641.394.4145
56 Units, pets OK. Continental breakfast. Laundry facility. Rooms come with phones and cable TV. Some rooms have microwaves and refrigerators. AAA/Senior discount. Credit cards: AE, DC, DS, MC, V.

NEWTON
Ramada Limited
$41-45
1405 W. 19th Street • 641.792.8100
78 Units, pets OK. Continental breakfast. Meeting rooms. Rooms come with phones and cable TV. AAA/Senior discount. Major credit cards.

OKOBOJI — *see Milford and Spirit Lake*

ONAWA
Super 8 Motel
$48*
I-29, Exit 112 • 712.423.2102
80 Units, pets OK. Continental breakfast. Rooms come with phones and cable TV. Wheelchair accessible. Senior discount. Major credit cards.
*Rates higher during weekends.

ORANGE CITY
Dutch Colony Inn
$42-55
712.737.3490 • Three miles W of jct. with Hwy. 60 on Hwy. 10
38 Units, no pets. Continental breakfast. Laundry facility. Meeting rooms. Rooms come with phones and cable TV. Credit cards: AE, DC, DS, MC, V.

Super 8 Motel
$42-49
Hwy 10 & Lincoln Place • 712.737.2600
34 Units, no pets. Continental breakfast. Fitness facility. Rooms come with phones and cable TV. Wheelchair accessible. Senior discount. Credit cards: AE, DC, DS, MC, V.

OSCEOLA
Best Western Regal Inn
$40-55
1520 Jeffrey's Drive • 641.342.2123
35 Units, pets OK. Rooms come with phones and cable TV. Senior discount. Major credit cards.

OSKALOOSA
Red Carpet Inn
$40-50
2278 Hwy. 63N. • 641.673.8641 or 800.251.1962
40 Units, pets OK. Continental breakfast. Pool. Rooms come with phones and cable TV. Major credit cards.

Rodeway Inn
$40-50
1315 "A" Avenue E. • 641.673.8351
41 Units, pets OK. Continental breakfast. Laundry facility. Meeting rooms. Rooms come with phones and cable TV. Some rooms have microwaves and refrigerators. Senior discount. Credit cards: AE, DC, DS, JCB, MC, V.

OTTUMWA
Colonial Motor Inn
$35-40
1534 Albia Road • 641.683.1661
25 Units, pets OK ($10). Rooms come with phones and cable TV. Senior discount. Credit cards: AE, DS, MC, V.

Stardust Motel
$29-45
Hwy. 34E. • 641.684.6535 or 800.246.6535
24 Units, pets OK. Restaurant on premises. Continental breakfast. Rooms come with phones and cable TV. Major credit cards.

PACIFIC JUNCTION
Bluff View Motel
$38-50
From I-29, Exit 35, west on US 34
712.622.8191
28 Units, pets OK. Restaurant on premises. Meeting rooms. Rooms come with phones and cable TV. AAA discount. Credit cards: AE, CB, DC, DS, JCB, MC, V.

PELLA
Pella Motor Inn
$36-47
703 E. Oskaloosa Street • 641.628.9500 or 800.292.2956
24 Units, pets OK. Continental breakfast. Rooms come with phones and cable TV. Major credit cards.

QUAD CITIES — *see Bettendorf, Davenport or Moline (IL)*

RED OAK
Red Coach Inn
$35-47
On Hwy. 34 (in town) • 712.523.4864
72 Units, no pets. Restaurant on premises. Pool. Rooms come with phones and cable TV. Wheelchair accessible. Major credit cards.

Super 8 Motel
$45-50
800 Senate Avenue • 712.623.6919
40 Units, pets OK ($15). Continental breakfast. Pool. Laundry facility. Rooms come with phones and cable TV. Senior discount. Wheelchair accessible. Major credit cards.

SHELDON
Iron Horse Inn
$37-50
1111 2nd Avenue • 712.324.5353
33 Units. Restaurant on premises. Continental breakfast. Rooms come with phones and cable TV. Wheelchair accessible. Major credit cards.

SHENANDOAH
Country Inn Restaurant & Motel
$35-45
Sheridan Ave. at US 59 • 712.246.1550
92 Units, pets OK. Restaurant on premises. Pool. Rooms come with phones and cable TV. Major credit cards.

Days Inn
$45-55
108 N. Fremont • 712.246.5733
54 Units, no pets. Continental breakfast. Data ports. Rooms come with phones, refrigerators and cable TV. AAA/Senior discount. Major credit cards.

SIBLEY
Super 8 Motel
$40-50
1108 2nd Avenue • 712.754.3603
32 Units, pets OK ($8). Continental breakfast. Laundry facility. Meeting room. Rooms come with phones and cable TV. AAA/Senior discount. Wheelchair accessible. Major credit cards.

SIOUX CENTER
Econo Lodge
$41-50
86 9th Street Cir. N.E. • 712.722.4000
56 Units, pets OK ($5). Continental breakfast. Laundry facility. Game room. jacuzzi. Rooms come with phones and cable TV. Some rooms have microwaves and refrigerators. AAA/Senior discount. Credit cards: AE, DS, MC. V.

SIOUX CITY
Motel 6
$30-40
6166 Harbor Drive, I-29, Exit 141
712.277.3131
71 Units, pets OK. Pool. Data ports. Rooms come with phones, A/C and cable TV. Wheelchair accessible. Credit cards: AE, CB, DC, DS, MC, V.

Rath Inn—Sergeant Bluff
$28-53
I-29 Airport Exit • 712.943.5079 or 800.972.4651
52 Units, no pets. Rooms come with phones and cable TV. Major credit cards.

Super 8 Motel
$45-55*
4307 Stone Avenue • 712.274.1520
60 Units, pets OK ($10-20). Continental breakfast. Rooms come with phones and cable TV. Wheelchair accessible. AAA/ Senior discount. Credit cards: AE, CB, DC, DS, MC, V.
*Rates may increase during special events and weekends.

SLOAN
Winna Vegas Inn
$43
1862 Hwy 141, I-29, Exit 127
712.428.4280
53 Units, pets OK ($5). Meeting rooms. Data ports. Rooms come with phones and cable TV. Wheelchair accessible. AAA/ Senior discount. Major credit cards.

SPENCER
Iron Horse Motel & Suites
$31-40
Jct. Hwys. 71 & 185 • 712.262.9123
66 Units, no pets. Continental breakfast. Rooms come with phones and cable TV. Wheelchair accessible. Major credit cards.

SPIRIT LAKE
Northland Inn
$30-47
Junction Hwys. 9 & 86 • 712.336.1450
18 Units, pets OK. Continental breakfast. Rooms come with phones and cable TV. Major credit cards.

STORM LAKE
The Budget Inn
$30-44
1504 N. Lake Avenue • 712.732.2505 or 800.383.7666
49 Units, pets OK. Pool. Rooms come with phones and cable TV. Wheelchair accessible. Major credit cards.

Vista Economy Inn
$28-44
1316 N. Lake • 712.732.2342
37 Units, pets OK in smoking rooms only ($3). Rooms come with phones and cable TV. Senior discount. Credit cards: AE, DC, DS, MC, V.

STORY CITY
Super 8 Motel
$42
515 Factory Outlet Dr. • 515.733.5281
42 Units, pets OK ($25 dep. req.). Continental breakfast. Rooms come with phones and cable TV. Major credit cards.

Viking Motor Inn
$38
1520 Broad Street • 515.733.4306
32 Units, pets OK. Laundry facility. Playground. Rooms come with phones and cable TV. Some rooms have refrigerators. AAA discount. Credit cards: AE, DS, MC. V.

STUART
Super 8 Motel
$50
I-80 (Exit 93) • 515.523.2888
49 Units, pets OK ($25 dep. req.). Continental breakfast. Rooms come with phones and cable TV. Wheelchair accessible. AAA/ Senior discount. Credit cards: AE, CB, DC, DS, MC, V.

TOLEDO
Days Inn
$40-50
403 US 30W • 641.484.5678
43 Units, no pets. Continental breakfast. Rooms come with phones and cable TV. AAA discount. Major credit cards.

Super 8 Motel
$42-46*
641.484.5888 • On US 30W, one block west of the jct. of Hwys. 63 and 30.
49 Units, pets OK. Toast bar. Spa. Game room. Meeting rooms. Laundry facility. Rooms come with phones and cable TV. Wheelchair accessible. AAA/Senior discount. Credit cards: AE, CB, DC, DS, MC, V.
*Higher rates effective weekends.

URBANDALE
Microtel Inn & Suites
$50
8711 Plum Drive, I-35/80, Exit 129
515.727.5424
76 Units, pets OK ($25 dep. req.). Continental breakfast. Laundry facility. Fitness facility. Meeting rooms. Rooms come with phones

and cable TV. Wheelchair accessible. AAA/ Senior discount. Major credit cards.

WALCOTT
Super 8 Motel
$44
I-80 Industrial Park • 319.284.5083
60 Units, pets OK. Continental breakfast. Rooms come with phones and cable TV. Wheelchair accessible. Senior discount. Major credit cards.

WALNUT
Super 8 Motel
$50
I-80 (Exit 46) • 712.784.2221
51 Units, pets OK. Continental breakfast. Indoor pool. Meeting rooms. Rooms come with phones and cable TV. AAA/Senior discount. Credit cards: AE, CB, DC, DS, MC, V.

WATERLOO
Motel 6
$46-50
2343 Logan Avenue • 319.236.3238
50 Units, pets OK. Indoor pool. Laundry facility. Data ports. Rooms come with A/C, phones and cable TV. Wheelchair accessible. Credit cards: AE, CB, DC, DS, MC, V.

Travel Inn
$36-55
3350 University Avenue • 319.235.2165
104 Units, pets OK. Continental breakfast. Game room. Laundry facility. Rooms come with phones and cable TV. Some rooms have microwaves, refrigerators and jacuzzis. Senior discount. Credit cards: AE, CB, DC, DS, MC, V.

WAVERLY
Super 8 Motel
$43-44*
301 13th Avenue • 319.352.0888
43 Units, no pets. Fitness facility. Jacuzzi and sauna. Meeting room. Rooms come with phones and cable TV. AAA/Senior discount. Wheelchair accessible. Major credit cards.
*Rates higher weekends, special events and holidays.

WEBSTER CITY
The Executive Inn
$49-54
1700 Superior Street • 515.832.3631
39 Units, pets OK. Continental breakfast. Meeting rooms. Rooms come with phones and cable TV. AAA/Senior discount. Major credit cards.

Super 8 Motel
$46
305 Closz Drive, US 20 & Hwy. 17
515.832.2000
44 Units, pets OK. Continental breakfast. Indoor heated pool. Game room. Rooms come with phones and cable TV. Senior discount. Major credit cards.

WEST BRANCH
Presidential Motor Inn
$40
711 S. Doney Street • 319.643.2526
38 Units, pets OK. Rooms come with phones and cable TV. Major credit cards.

WEST DES MOINES
Motel 6
$36-40
7655 Office Plaza Drive N., I-80, Exit 121
515.267.8885
121 Units, pets OK. Pool. Laundry facility. Data ports. Rooms come with A/C, phones and cable TV. Wheelchair accessible. Credit cards: AE, CB, DC, DS, MC, V.

WEST LIBERTY
Econo Lodge
$47-49
1943 Garfield Avenue • 319.627.2171 or 800.424.4777
37 Units, pets OK ($3). Restaurant on premises. Pool. Rooms come with phones and cable TV. Senior discount. Major credit cards.

WILLIAMS
Best Western Norseman Inn
$42-54
I-35, Exit 144 • 515.854.2281 or 800.528.1234
33 Units, pets OK. Data ports. Rooms come with phones and cable TV. Wheelchair accessible. Senior discount. Major credit cards.

WILLIAMSBURG
Super 8 Motel
$38-39
2228 "U" Avenue • 319.668.2800
67 Units, pets OK. Toast bar. Rooms come with phones and cable TV. Senior discount. Wheelchair accessible. Major credit cards.

kansas

ABILENE
Best Western
$36-48
2210 N. Buckeye • I-70, Exit 275
785.263.2050
64 Units, pets OK. Restaurant on premises. Pool. Jacuzzi. Meeting rooms. Data ports. Rooms come with phones, refrigerators and cable TV. AAA/Senior discount. Credit cards: AE, CB, DC, DS, MC, V.

White House Motel
$22-37
101 N.W. 14th • 785.263.3600
60 Units, pets OK. Continental breakfast. Rooms come with phones and cable TV. Wheelchair accessible. Major credit cards.

ARKANSAS CITY
Scottish Hallmark Motor Inn
$44-49
1617 N. Summit Street • 620.442.1400
47 Units, pets OK ($5). Pool. Data ports. Rooms come with phones and cable TV. Some rooms have microwaves and refrigerators. Senior discount. Major credit cards.

ATCHISON
Atchison Motor Inn
$36-40
401 S. 10th Street • 913.367.7000
45 Units, pets OK ($10 dep. req.). Continental breakfast. Pool. Rooms come with phones and cable TV. Some rooms have refrigerators. Credit cards: AE, CB, DC, DS, JCB, MC, V.

Comfort Inn
$47-55
509 S. 9th Street • 913.367.7666
45 Units, no pets. Continental breakfast. Jacuzzi. Meeting rooms. Rooms come with phones and cable TV. Major credit cards.

BAXTER SPRINGS
Baxter Inn-4-Less
$38-45
2451 Military Avenue • 620.856.2106
32 Units, pets OK. Pool. Rooms come with phones and cable TV. Some rooms have microwaves and refrigerators. AAA/Senior discount. Credit cards: AE, DS, MC, V.

BELLEVILLE
Super 8 Motel
$46-51
1410 28th Street • 785.527.2112
35 Units, pets OK. Continental breakfast. Spa. Laundry facility. Data ports. Rooms come with phones and cable TV. Wheelchair accessible. Senior discount. Major credit cards.

BELOIT
Super 8 Motel
$42-46
205 West Hwy. 24 • 785.738.4300
40 Units, pets OK. Continental breakfast. Meeting rooms. Laundry facility. Fitness facility. Data ports. Rooms come with phones and cable TV. AAA/Senior discount. Wheelchair accessible. Major credit cards.

CHANUTE
Chanute Safari Inn
$42
3500 S. Santa Fe • 620.431.9460
41 Units, pets OK ($10). Continental breakfast. Rooms come with phones and cable TV. Some rooms have microwaves and refrigerators. AAA/Senior discount. Credit cards: AE, CB, DC, DS, MC, V.

Guest House Motor Inn
$27-37
1814 S. Santa Fe • 620.431.0600
29 Units, pets OK. Pool. Rooms come with phones and cable TV. AAA discount. Credit cards: AE, DC, DS, MC, V.

CLAY CENTER
Cedar Court Motel
$35-50
905 Crawford • 785.632.2148
44 Units, pets OK. Restaurant on premises. Heated pool. Meeting rooms. Data ports. Rooms come with phones and cable TV. AAA discount. Credit cards: AE, DS, MC, V.

COLBY
Super 8 Motel
$45
1040 Zelfer Avenue • 785.462.8248
63 Units, pets OK. Continental breakfast. Spa. Rooms come with phones and cable TV. Senior discount. Wheelchair accessible. Major credit cards.

CONCORDIA
Econo Lodge
$49-53
89 Lincoln Street • 785.243.4545
48 Units, pets OK. Restaurant on premises. Continental breakfast. Pool. Rooms come with phones and cable TV. Major credit cards.

COUNCIL GROVE
The Cottage House Hotel & Motel
$50*
25 N. Neosho • 620.767.6828
40 Units, pets OK ($8). Continental breakfast. Sauna. Jacuzzi. Meeting rooms. Rooms come with phones and cable TV. Some rooms have refrigerators and jacuzzis. Wheelchair accessible. Credit cards: AE, CB, DC, DS, MC, V.
*Ask for economy rooms.

DODGE CITY
Astro Motel
$30-52
2200 W. Wyatt Earp Bl. • 620.227.8146
34 Units, pets OK. Continental breakfast. Pool. Rooms come with phones and cable TV. Credit cards: AE, CB, DC, MC, V.

Budget Lodge
$30-45
2110 E. Wyatt Earp Bl. • 620.225.2654
32 Units, no pets. Continental breakfast. Pool. Fax service. Rooms come with phones and cable TV. Senior discount. Major credit cards.

EL DORADO
Heritage Inn
$40-45
2515 W. Central • 316.321.6800
32 Units, pets OK ($20 dep. req.). Continental breakfast. Rooms come with phones and cable TV. Some rooms have jacuzzis and refrigerators. AAA/Senior discount. Credit cards: AE, CB, DC, DS, MC, V.

Sunset Inn
$36-61
1901 W. Central • 316.321.9172
36 Units, pets OK. Restaurant on premises. Continental breakfast. Rooms come with phones and cable TV. Major credit cards.

ELKHART
El Rancho Motel
$45
E. Hwy. 65 • 620.697.2117
41 Units, pets OK. Restaurant on premises. Pool. Laundry facility nearby. Rooms come with phones and cable TV. Major credit cards.

EMPORIA
Budget Host Inn
$29-34
1830 E. Hwy. 50 • 620.343.6922
26 Units, pets OK. Laundry facility. Playground. Picnic tables. Airport transportation. Rooms come with phones and cable TV. AAA/Senior discount. Credit cards: AE, DS, MC, V.

Econo Lodge
$40-55
2511 W. 18th • 620.343.7750
48 Units, pets OK. Continental breakfast. Rooms come with phones and cable TV. Some rooms have microwaves and refrigerators. Wheelchair accessible. AAA discount. Credit cards: AE, DC, DS, MC, V.

Motel 6
$36-40
2630 W. 18th Avenue • 620.343.1240
58 Units, pets OK. Laundry facility. Data ports. Rooms come with phones, A/C and cable TV. Wheelchair accessible. Credit cards: AE, CB, DC, DS, MC, V.

FORT SCOTT
Microtel
$39-59
2505 S. Hwy 69 • 620.768.7000
53 Units, no pets. Restaurant on premises. Continental breakfast. Pool. Rooms come with phones and cable TV. Wheelchair accessible. Major credit cards.

GARDEN CITY
Continental Inn
$36
1408 Jones Avenue • 620.276.7691 or 800.621.0318

54 Units, pets OK. Restaurant on premises. Continental breakfast. Pool. Rooms come with phones and cable TV. Major credit cards.

National 9 Inn
$44-49
123 Honey Bee Court • 620.275.0677 or 800.333.2387
34 Units, pets OK. Pool. Laundry facility. Rooms come with phones and cable TV. AAA/Senior discount. Major credit cards.

GOODLAND
Economy 9 Motel
$35-50
2420 Commerce Road • 785.899.5672
84 Units, pets OK. Pool. Laundry facility. Rooms come with phones, A/C and cable TV. Wheelchair accessible. Credit cards: AE, CB, DC, DS, MC, V.

Super 8 Motel
$39-50
2520 S. Hwy 27 (I-70, Exit 17)
785.899.7566
48 Units, pets OK ($25 dep. req.). Continental breakfast. Meeting rooms. Rooms come with phones and cable TV. Senior discount. Wheelchair accessible. Major credit cards.

GREAT BEND
Super 8 Motel
$42-52*
3500 10th Street • 620.793.8486
42 Units, pets OK. Continental breakfast. Heated indoor pool. Jacuzzi. Spa. Laundry facility. Rooms come with phones and cable TV. Wheelchair accessible. Senior discount. Major credit cards.
*Rates may increase slightly during specials, weekends and holidays.

Travelers Budget Inn
$36-46
4200 W. 10th Street • 620.793.5448
28 Units, pets OK. Airport transportation. Rooms come with refrigerators, microwaves, phones and cable TV. AAA/Senior discount. Credit cards: AE, DC, DS, MC, V.

GREENSBURG
Best Western J-Hawk Motel
$49
515 W. Kansas Avenue • 620.723.2121
30 Units, pets OK. Continental breakfast. Pool. Jacuzzi. Laundry facility. Fitness facility. Meeting rooms. Data ports. Rooms come with refrigerators, microwaves, phones and cable TV. AAA/Senior discount. Credit cards: AE, CB, DC, DS, MC, V.

HAYS
Budget Host Villa
$29-51
810 E. 8th Street • 785.625.2563
49 Units, pets OK. Heated pool. Laundry facility. Airport transportation. Rooms come with phones and cable TV. Some rooms have refrigerators and microwaves. AAA/Senior discount. Credit cards: AE, CB, DC, DS, MC, V.

Motel 6
$40-46 (52-54)*
3404 Vine Street • 785.625.4282
87 Units, pets OK. Pool. Laundry facility. Data pots. Rooms come with phones, A/C and cable TV. Wheelchair accessible. Credit cards: AE, CB, DC, DS, MC, V.
*Higher rates effective summer weekends.

HAYSVILLE
Haysville Inn
$38
301 E. 71st Street • I-35, Exit 39
316.522.1000
25 Units, pets OK. Continental breakfast. Data ports. Rooms come with phones and cable TV. AAA/Senior discount. Credit cards: AE, DS, MC, V.

HESSTON
Hesston Heritage Inn
$35-46
606 E. Lincoln Blvd. • 620.327.4231
37 Units, pets OK. Restaurant on premises. Continental breakfast. Pool. Rooms come with phones and cable TV. Wheelchair accessible. Major credit cards.

HUTCHINSON
Scotsman Inn
$30-40
322 E. 4th Street • 620.669.8281
47 Units, no pets. Laundry facility. Airport transportation. Rooms come with phones and cable TV. Senior discount. Major credit cards.

Super 8 Motel
$46*
1315 E. 11th Avenue • 620.662.6394
46 Units, pets OK ($10). Continental

breakfast. Rooms come with phones and cable TV. Wheelchair accessible. Senior discount. Credit cards: AE, CB, DC, DS, MC, V.
*Rates may increase slightly during weekends, holidays and special events.

INDEPENDENCE
Best Western Prairie Inn
$46-50
3222 W. Main • 620.331.3300
41 Units, pets OK ($3 dep. req.). Continental breakfast. Pool. Jacuzzi. Airport transportation. Data ports. Rooms come with phones and cable TV. AAA/Senior discount. Major credit cards.

Super 8 Motel
$46
2800 W. Main Street • 620.331.8288
52 Units, no pets. Continental breakfast. Pool. Laundry facility. Data ports. Rooms come with phones and cable TV. Senior discount. Wheelchair accessible. Major credit cards.

IOLA
Best Western Inn
$45-50
1315 N. State • 620.365.5161
59 Units, pets OK. Restaurant on premises. Laundry facility. Airport transportation. Pool. Data ports. Rooms come with refrigerators, phones and cable TV. AAA/Senior discount. Credit cards: AE, CB, DC, DS, MC, V.

JUNCTION CITY
Econo Lodge
$30-60
211 Flint Hills Blvd. • I-70, Exit 299
785.238.8181
58 Units, pets OK ($10 dep. req.). Continental breakfast. Rooms come with phones and cable TV. Some rooms have microwaves and refrigerators. AAA/Senior discount. Credit cards: AE, CB, DC, DS, JCB, MC, V.

Golden Wheat Budget Host Inn
$25-40
820 S. Washington • 785.238.5106
20 Units, pets OK ($5). Data ports. Rooms come with phones and cable TV. AAA/Senior discount. Credit cards: AE, DS, MC, V.

KANSAS CITY — *see also Lenexa, Olathe, Overland Park and Kansas City (MO)*
American Motel
$35-50
7949 Splitlog Avenue • 78th Street & I-70
913.299.2999 or 800.905.6343
158 Units, no pets. Pool. Rooms come with phones and cable TV. Wheelchair accessible. Major credit cards.

KINGMAN
Budget Host Copa Motel
$35-39
1113 E. Hwy. 54 • 620.532.3118
30 Units, pets OK. Pool. Laundry facility. Playground. Rooms come with phones and cable TV. Senior discount available ($2.00). Credit cards: AE, CB, DC, DS, MC, V.

LANSING
Econo Lodge
$44-52
504 N. Main Street • 913.727.2777
39 Units, pets OK ($25 dep. req.). Rooms come with phones and cable TV. Some rooms have microwaves and refrigerators. AAA/Senior discount. Credit cards: AE, DC, DS, MC, V.

LARNED
Best Western Townsman Inn
$45-54*
123 E. 14th Street • 620.285.3114
44 Units, pets OK. Pool. Airport transportation. Meeting rooms. Data ports. Rooms come with phones and cable TV. Senior discount. Major credit cards.
*AAA discounted rates.

LAWRENCE
Virginia Inn
$45-50
2907 W. 6th Street • 785.843.6611 or 800.468.8979
58 Units, no pets. Restaurant on premises. Pool. Rooms come with phones and cable TV. Wheelchair accessible. Major credit cards.

Westminster Inn & Suites
$49-63*
2525 W. 6th Street • 785.841.8410
60 Units, pets OK ($20 dep. req.). Continental breakfast. Pool. Data ports. Rooms come with phones and cable TV. Senior discount. Major credit cards.
*AAA discounted rates.

LEAVENWORTH
Village Lodge
$47-51*
3211 S. 4th Street • 913.651.6000
52 Units, pets OK. Continental breakfast. Laundry facility. Data ports. Rooms come with phones and cable TV. Senior discount. Major credit cards.
*AAA discounted rates.

Super 8 Motel
$50*
303 Montana Court • 913.682.0744
60 Units, pets OK. Continental breakfast. Rooms come with phones and cable TV. Wheelchair accessible. Senior discount. Credit cards: AE, CB, DC, DS, MC, V.
*Rates may increase slightly during weekends, holidays and special events.

LENEXA
Motel 6
$38-48
9725 Lenexa Drive • 913.541.8558
121 Units, guide dogs only due to local ordinance. Pool. Laundry facility. Data ports. Rooms come with phones, A/C and cable TV. Wheelchair accessible. Credit cards: AE, CB, DC, DS, MC, V.

LIBERAL
Cimarron Inn
$33-36
564 E. Pancake Blvd. • 620.624.6203
31 Units, pets OK ($5). Pool. Laundry facility. Data ports. Rooms come with phones and cable TV. Some rooms have microwaves and refrigerators. AAA/Senior discount. Credit cards: AE, DS, MC, V.

Gateway Inn Motel
$44
720 E. Hwy. 54 • 620.624.0242
100 Units, pets OK. Restaurant on premises. Local transportation available. Pool. Tennis and volley courts. Laundry facility. Rooms come with phones and cable TV. Senior discount. Major credit cards.

LINDSBORG
Coronado Motel
$36
305 Harrison • 785.227.3943 or 800.747.2793
29 Units, pets OK. Continental breakfast. Pool. Rooms come with phones and cable TV. Wheelchair accessible. Major credit cards.

Viking Motel
$39-46
446 Harrison • 785.227.3336
24 Units, pets OK. Continental breakfast. Pool. Data ports. Rooms come with phones and cable TV. Credit cards: AE, CB, DC, DS, MC, V.

MANHATTAN
Motel 6
$35-46
510 Tuttle Creek Blvd. (I-70, Exit 373) 785.537.1022
87 Units, pets OK. Pool. Laundry facility. Rooms come with phones, A/C and cable TV. Wheelchair accessible. Credit cards: AE, CB, DC, DS, MC, V.

MARYSVILLE
Super 8 Motel
$43
1155 Pony Express Rd. • 785.562.5588
42 Units, pets OK ($10). Restaurant on premises. Continental breakfast. Fitness facility. Meeting room. Laundry facility. Rooms come with phones and cable TV. Wheelchair accessible. AAA/Senior discount. Credit cards: AE, CB, DC, DS, MC, V.

Thunderbird Motel
$33
819 Pony Express Hwy. • 785.562.2373
21 Units, pets OK. Continental breakfast. Laundry facility. Playground. Fax service. Rooms come with A/C, refrigerators, phones and cable TV. Some rooms have microwaves. Major credit cards.

McPHERSON
Super 8 Motel
$46
2100 E. Kansas • 620.241.8881
42 Units, pets OK ($10). Continental breakfast. Rooms come with phones and cable TV. Wheelchair accessible. Senior discount. Credit cards: AE, CB, DC, DS, MC, V.

Wheat State Motel
$30-43
1137 W. Kansas Ave. • 620.241.6981
64 Units, pets OK. Pool. Rooms come with phones and cable TV. Wheelchair accessible. Major credit cards.

MEADE
Budget Host Moon Mist Motel
$27
804 W. Carthage • 620.873.2121
23 Units, pets OK. Laundry facility. Jacuzzi. Airport transportation. Playground. Picnic tables. Rooms come with phones and cable TV. Senior discount. Major credit cards.

MEDICINE LODGE
Copa Motel
$38-47
401 W. Fowler • 620.886.5673
54 Units, no pets. Pool. Rooms come with phones and cable TV. AAA/Senior discount. Credit cards: AE, CB, DS, MC, V.

NEWTON
1st Interstate Inn
$32-50
1515 E. 1st Street • 316.283.8850
43 Units, pets OK. Restaurant on premises. Rooms come with phones and cable TV. Wheelchair accessible. Major credit cards.

Super 8 Motel
$40-51
1620 E. 2nd Street • 316.283.7611
38 Units, pets OK. Continental breakfast. Rooms come with phones and cable TV. Wheelchair accessible. Senior discount. Credit cards: AE, CB, DC, DS, MC, V.

NORTON
Brooks Motel
$44-50
900 N. State Street • 785.877.3381
35 Units, pets OK. Pool. Rooms come with phones and cable TV. Senior discount. Major credit cards.

Hillcrest Motel
$35
785.877.3343 • On US 36 & 383, 0.3 miles west of US 283 Jct.
26 Units, no pets. Pool. Playground. Rooms come with phones and cable TV. Senior discount. Credit cards: AE, DC, DS, MC, V.

OAKLEY
First Interstate Inn
$35-50
I-70 & Hwy. 40 • 785.672.3203 or 800.462.4667
29 Units, pets OK. Rooms come with phones and cable TV. Wheelchair accessible. Major credit cards.

First Travel Inn
$37-40
708 Center Avenue • 785.672.3226
25 Units, pets OK ($4). Restaurant on premises. Pool. Rooms come with phones and cable TV. AAA/Senior discount. Credit cards: AE, DS, MC, V.

OLATHE
Econo Lodge
$40-50
209 E. Flaming Road • 913.829.1312
58 Units, no pets. Rooms come with phones and cable TV. Major credit cards.

Microtel
$45-54
1501 S. Hamilton Circle • 913.397.9455
67 Units, no pets. Continental breakfast. Rooms come with phones and cable TV. Wheelchair accessible. Major credit cards.

OSAWATOMIE
Landmark Inn
$45-50
304 Eastgate Drive • 913.755.3051
39 Units, pets OK. Restaurant on premises. Meeting rooms. Rooms come with phones and cable TV. Senior discount. Credit cards: AE, DS, MC, V.

OTTAWA
Econo Lodge
$40-63*
2331 S. Cedar Road • 785.242.3400
56 Units, pets OK. Continental breakfast. Rooms come with phones and cable TV. Some rooms have refrigerators. AAA discount. Major credit cards.
*AAA discounted rates.

OVERLAND PARK
Super 8 Motel
$50
10750 Berkley Street • I-435, Exit 79
913.341.4440
95 Units, no pets. Continental breakfast. Laundry facility. Fitness facility. Data ports. Rooms come with phones, refrigerators and cable TV. Wheelchair accessible. AAA/Senior discount. Major credit cards.

White Haven Motor Lodge
$41-43*
8039 Metcalf Avenue • 913.649.8200
79 Units, pets OK. Pool. Laundry facility. Rooms come with phones, refrigerators and

cable TV. Major credit cards.
*AAA discounted rates.

PITTSBURG
The Extra Inn
$39*
4023 Parkview Drive • 620.232.2800
61 Units, no pets. Continental breakfast. Meeting rooms. Rooms come with phones and cable TV. Major credit cards.
*Rates increase during special events.

University Park Inn
$34-40
2408 S. Broadway • 620.231.8300
69 Units, pets OK. Pool. Rooms come with phones and cable TV. Senior discount. Major credit cards.

PRATT
Best Western Hillcrest Motel
$40-46
1336 E. 1st Street • 620.672.6407
40 Units, pets OK. Continental breakfast. Heated pool. Laundry facility. Meeting rooms. Rooms come with phones and cable TV. Some rooms have refrigerators. AAA/Senior discount. Credit cards: AE, CB, DC, DS, MC, V.

Super 8 Motel
$45-52
1906 E. 1st Street • 620.672.5945
45 Units, pets OK. Continental breakfast. Jacuzzi. Data ports. Rooms come with phones and cable TV. AAA/Senior discount. Credit cards: AE, CB, DC, DS, MC, V.

QUINTER
Budget Host "Q" Motel
$40-50
1202 Castle Rock Street • 785.754.3337
From I-70, Exit 107, on SR 212.
50 Units, pets OK ($5). Restaurant on premises. Meeting rooms. Data ports. Rooms come with phones and cable TV. AAA/Senior discount. Credit cards: AE, DS, MC, V.

RUSSELL
Days Inn
$42-50
1225 S. Fossil Street • 785.483.6660
49 Units, no pets. Restaurant on premises. Pool. Laundry facility. Rooms come with phones and cable TV. Wheelchair accessible. AAA/senior discount available (10%). Major credit cards.

Russell's Inn
$44
Junction I-70 & Hwy. 281 • 785.483.2107 or 800.736.4598
65 Units, pets OK. Restaurant on premises. Pool. Game room. Meeting room. Rooms come with phones and cable TV. Senior discount. Wheelchair accessible. Major credit cards.

Super 8 Motel
$49
1405 S. Fossil • 785.483.2488
45 Units, no pets. Continental breakfast. Jacuzzi. Rooms come with phones and cable TV. Wheelchair accessible. Senior discount. Credit cards: AE, CB, DC, DS, MC, V.

SALINA
First Inn Gold
$40-50
2403 S. 9th Street • 785.827.5511
70 Units, pets OK. Continental breakfast. Heated pool. Wading pool. Meeting rooms. Airport transportation. Laundry facility. Data ports. Rooms come with phones and cable TV. Some rooms have refrigerators. AAA/Senior discount. Credit cards: AE, DC, DS, MC, V.

Motel 6
$37-48
638 W. Diamond Drive • 785.827.8397
81 Units, pets OK. Pool. Laundry facility. Data ports. Rooms come with phones, A/C and cable TV. Wheelchair accessible. Credit cards: AE, CB, DC, DS, MC, V.

Super 8 Motel
$40-49
1640 W. Crawford Street • I-135, Exit 92 • 785.823.8808
61 Units, pets OK. Data ports. Rooms come with phones and cable TV. AAA/Senior discount. Credit cards: AE, CB, DC, DS, MC, V.

SCOTT CITY
Chaparral Inn
$35-40
102 Main Street • 620.872.2181 or 800.242.6319
26 Units, pets OK. Restaurant on premises. Pool. Rooms come with phones and cable TV. Major credit cards.

SMITH CENTER
U.S. Center Motel
$36-42
116 Hwy. 36E • 785.282.6611 or 800.875.6613
21 Units, pets OK. Heated pool. Airport transportation. Playground. Rooms come with phones and cable TV. AAA/Senior discount. Credit cards: AE, DS, MC, V.

SYRACUSE
Syracuse Inn
$33
W. Hwy. 50 • 620.384.7411
29 Units, no pets. Restaurant on premises. Rooms come with phones and cable TV. Major credit cards.

TOPEKA
Country Inn
$32-45
601 N.W. Hwy. 24 • 785.233.7704
82 Units, pets OK. Restaurant on premises. Pool. Meeting rooms. Rooms come with phones and cable TV. Wheelchair accessible. Senior discount. Major credit cards.

Motel 6—Northwest
$38-44
709 Fairlawn Road • I-70, Exit 357
785.272.8283
102 Units, pets OK. Pool. Laundry facility. Rooms come with phones, A/C and cable TV. Wheelchair accessible. Credit cards: AE, CB, DC, DS, MC, V.

Motel 6—West
$38-46 (54)*
1224 Wanamaker Road S.W.
I-470, Exit 1 • 785.273.9888
91 Units, pets OK. Pool. Laundry facility. Rooms come with phones, A/C and cable TV. Wheelchair accessible. Credit cards: AE, CB, DC, DS, MC, V.
*Higher rate effective summer weekends.

Travelodge
$35-45
3846 S. Topeka Avenue • 785.267.1222
70 Units, pets OK. Continental breakfast. Pool. Fax service. Rooms come with phones and cable TV. Wheelchair accessible. Major credit cards.

ULYSSES
Wagon Bed Inn
$33-44
1101 E. Oklahoma • 620.356.3111
48 Units, pets OK. Pool. Rooms come with phones and cable TV. Wheelchair accessible. Major credit cards.

WAKEENEY
Budget Host Travel Inn
$30-35
668 S. 13th Street • I-70 & US 283
785.743.2121
27 Units, pets OK. Restaurant on premises. Heated pool. Meeting rooms. Laundry facility. Rooms come with phones and cable TV. Senior discount. Credit cards: AE, DS, MC, V.

WICHITA — *see also Haysville*
Mark 8 Inn
$28
1130 N. Broadway • 316.265.4679
70 Units, no pets. Laundry facility. Data ports. Rooms come with phones and cable TV. AAA/Senior discount. Credit cards: AE, CB, DC, DS, MC, V.

Motel 6—Airport
$29-41
5736 W. Kellogg • 316.945.8440
146 Units, pets OK. Pool. Laundry facility. Data ports. Rooms come with phones, A/C and cable TV. Wheelchair accessible. Credit cards: AE, CB, DC, DS, MC, V.

Scotsman Inn East
$35
465 S. Webb Road • 316.684.6363
121 Units, no pets. Laundry facility. Rooms come with phones and cable TV. Some rooms have microwaves and refrigerators. AAA discount. Credit cards: AE, CB, DC, DS, MC, V.

Scotsman Inn West
$34
5922 W. Kellogg • 316.943.3800
71 Units, no pets. Laundry facility. Rooms come with phones and cable TV. Some rooms have kitchens. AAA/Senior discount. Credit cards: AE, CB, DC, DS, MC, V.

Wichita Inn—East
$40
8220 E. Kellogg • 316.685.8291
96 Units, no pets. Laundry facility. No A/C in rooms. VCRs and movie rentals. Rooms come with phones and cable TV. Some rooms have kitchens. Credit cards: AE, CB, DC, DS, JCB, MC, V.

WINFIELD
Sonner Motor Inn
$40
1812 Main Street • 620.221.4400
28 Units, no pets. Rooms come with phones and cable TV. AAA/Senior discount. Credit cards: AE, CB, DC, DS, MC, V.

YATES CENTER
Townsman Motel
$28
609 W. Mary • 620.625.2131
32 Units, pets OK. Rooms come with phones and cable TV. Senior discount. Credit cards: AE, DC, DS, MC, V.

kentucky

ASHLAND
Knights Inn
$38-43
7216 US 60 • 606.928.9501
122 Units, pets OK ($5). Pool. Laundry facility. Meeting rooms. Fitness facility. Rooms come with phones and cable TV. Some rooms have microwaves and refrigerators. AAA/Senior discount. Credit cards: AE, CB, DC, DS, MC, V.

Western Hills Motor Lodge
$36
346 13th Street • 606.325.8461
34 Units, pets OK. Restaurant on premises. Pool. Rooms come with phones and cable TV. Wheelchair accessible. Major credit cards.

BARDSTOWN
Old Kentucky Home Motel
$35-47
414 W. Stephen Foster Avenue
502.348.5979 or 800.772.1174
36 Units, pets OK ($10 dep. req.). Pool. Rooms come with phones and cable TV. AAA/Senior discount. Credit cards: AE, DS, MC, V.

Red Carpet Inn
$42-46
1714 New Havens Road (Bluegrass Pkwy, Exit 21) • 502.348.1112
24 Units, pets OK. Restaurant on premises. Rooms come with phones and cable TV. AAA discount. Major credit cards.

BEREA
Knights Inn
$40-50
715 Chestnut Street • 859.986.2384
63 Units, pets OK. Continental breakfast. Pool. Rooms come with phones and cable TV. Some rooms have microwaves and refrigerators. Credit cards: AE, MC, V.

Super 8 Motel
$35-55
196 Prince Royal Drive • 859.986.8426
60 Units, pets OK. Continental breakfast. Rooms come with phones and cable TV. Wheelchair accessible. AAA/Senior discount. Credit cards: AE, CB, DC, DS, MC, V.

BOWLING GREEN
Days Inn
$42-58
4617 Scottsville Rd. (I-65, Exit 22)
270.781.6470
77 Units, no pets. Pool. Rooms come with phones and cable TV. AAA/Senior discount. Major credit cards.

Motel 6
$32-38
3139 Scottsville Road • I-65, Exit 22
270.843.0140
91 Units, pets OK. Pool. Laundry facility. Rooms come with phones, A/C and cable TV. Wheelchair accessible. Credit cards: AE, CB, DC, DS, MC, V.

Super 8 Motel
$39-50
250 Cumberland Trace Road
I-65, Exit 22 • 270.781.9594
89 Units, pets OK ($5). Pool. Data ports. Rooms come with phones and cable TV. Wheelchair accessible. AAA/Senior discount. Major credit cards.

BURKESVILLE
Riverfront Lodge
$45-55
305 Keen Street • 270.864.3300
40 Units, pets OK. Pool. Rooms come with phones and cable TV. Senior discount. Major credit cards.

CADIZ
Knights Inn
$42-45
5698 Hopkinsville Road • I-24, Exit 65
270.522.9395
17 Units, pets OK. Continental breakfast. Rooms come with phones and TV. Wheelchair accessible. Major credit cards.

Super 8 Motel
$45-55
154 Hospitality Lane • I-24, Exit 65
270.522.7007

47 Units, pets OK. Continental breakfast. Pool. Meeting rooms. Rooms come with phones and cable TV. Senior discount. Major credit cards.

CAMPBELLSVILLE
Lakeview Motel
$40
1291 Old Lebanon Road • 270.465.8139
17 Units, no pets. Laundry facility. Rooms come with phones and cable TV. Some rooms have refrigerators. AAA/Senior discount. Credit cards: AE, DS, MC, V.

CAVE CITY
Days Inn
$25-51*
822 Mammoth Cave Road
I-65, Exit 53 • 270.773.2151
110 Units, pets OK ($5). Heated pool. Game room. Laundry facility. Meeting rooms. Rooms come with phones and cable TV. Senior discount. Major credit cards.
*AAA discounted rates.

Scottish Inns
$40-45
414 N. Dixie Hwy. • 270.773.3118
25 Units, no pets. Pool. Playground. Rooms come with phones and cable TV. Some rooms have refrigerators. Senior discount. Credit cards: AE, DS, MC, V.

CORBIN
Knights Inn
$30-50
37 Hwy. 770 • 606.523.1500
109 Units, pets OK. Pool. Laundry facility. Rooms come with phones and cable TV. Some rooms have microwaves and refrigerators. Major credit cards.

Super 8 Motel
$38
171 W. Cumberland Gap Pkwy.
606.528.8888
62 Units, pets OK ($25 dep. req.). Continental breakfast. Laundry facility. Rooms come with phones and cable TV. AAA discount. Major credit cards.

DRY RIDGE
Super 8 Motel
$42*
88 Blackburn Lane • 859.824.3700
50 Units, pets OK. Rooms come with phones and cable TV. Wheelchair accessible. Senior discount. Credit cards: AE, CB, DC, DS, MC, V.
*Rates may increase slightly during holidays, special events and weekends.

ELIZABETHTOWN
Motel 6
$34-40
Hwy. 62 & I-65 • 270.769.3102
98 Units, pets OK. Pool. Laundry facility. Data ports. Rooms come with phones, A/C and cable TV. Wheelchair accessible. Credit cards: AE, CB, DC, DS, MC, V.

Red Roof Inn
$50
2009 N. Mulberry Street • 270.765.4166
106 Units, pets OK ($10). Pool. Meeting rooms. Laundry facility. Rooms come with phones and cable TV. Senior discount. Credit cards: AE, CB, DC, DS, MC, V.

Super 8 Motel
$40-55*
2028 N. Mulberry Street • 270.737.1088
59 Units, pets OK ($5). Continental breakfast. Pool. Laundry facility. Rooms come with phones and cable TV. Wheelchair accessible. Senior discount. Credit cards: AE, CB, DC, DS, MC, V.
*Rates higher during weekends and special events.

ERLANGER
Econo Lodge
$30-45*
633 Donaldson Road • 859.342.5500
71 Units, pets OK. Fax service. Rooms come with phones and cable TV. Wheelchair accessible. Major credit cards.
*Rates as high as $85/night.

FLORENCE
Cross Country Inn
$40-47
7810 Commerce Drive (Jct. 1-71/I-75, Exit 181) • 859.283.2030
112 Units, no pets. Heated pool. Rooms come with phones and cable TV. AAA/Senior discount. Credit cards: AE, DC, DS, MC, V.

Knights Inn
$30-50
8049 Dream Street (I-71/I-75, Exit 180)
859.371.9711
116 Units, pets OK ($10). Pool. Laundry facility. Meeting rooms. Rooms come with

phones and cable TV. Some rooms have refrigerators. AAA/Senior discount. Credit cards: AE, DS, MC, V.

Motel 6
$30-48
7937 Dream Street • I-75, Exit 180
859.283.0909
78 Units, pets OK. Pool. Laundry facility. Data ports. Rooms come with phones, A/C and cable TV. Wheelchair accessible. Credit cards: AE, CB, DC, DS, MC, V.

Travelodge
$34-42
8075 Steilen Drive • 859.371.0277
103 Units, pets OK. Rooms come with phones and cable TV. Some rooms have refrigerators. AAA/Senior discount. Credit cards: AE, CB, DC, DS, JCB, MC, V.

FORT KNOX — *see Muldraugh*

FORT MITCHELL
Cross Country Inn
$40-47
2350 Royal Drive • 859.341.2090
106 Units, no pets. Heated pool. Rooms come with phones and cable TV. AAA/Senior discount. Credit cards: AE, DC, DS, MC, V.

FORT WRIGHT
Days Inn
$40-60
1945 Dixie Hwy. • 859.341.8801
115 Units, pets OK. Pool. Rooms come with phones and cable TV. AAA discount. Credit cards: AE, CB, DC, DS, JCB, MC, V.

FRANKFORT
Bluegrass Inn
$42-58
635 Versailles Road • 502.695.1800
62 Units, pets OK. Pool. Rooms come with phones and cable TV. Some rooms have kitchenettes and refrigerators. AAA discount. Major credit cards.

Super 8 Motel
$45-55
1225 US 127S • I-64, Exit 53B
502.875.3220
46 Units, pets OK ($10). Continental breakfast. Rooms come with phones and cable TV. AAA/Senior discount. Major credit cards.

FRANKLIN
Days Inn
$40-45
103 Trotter Ln. • I-6, Exit 6 • 270.598.0163
60 Units, pets OK ($5). Continental breakfast. Pool. Rooms come with phones and cable TV. Wheelchair accessible. AAA discount. Credit cards: AE, CB, DC, DS, MC, V.

Super 8 Motel
$35
2805 Scottsville Road • 270.586.8885
40 Units, pets OK. Continental breakfast. Meeting room. Rooms come with phones and cable TV. Wheelchair accessible. Senior discount. Credit cards: AE, CB, DC, DS, MC, V.

GEORGETOWN
Motel 6
$36-39
401 Delaplain Road • 502.863.1166
98 Units, pets OK. Pool. Laundry facility. Data ports. Rooms come with phones, A/C and cable TV. Wheelchair accessible. Credit cards: AE, CB, DC, DS, MC, V.

Super 8 Motel
$44-49
250 Shoney Drive • 502.863.4888
62 Units, pets OK ($6). Pool. Meeting rooms. Laundry facility. Rooms come with phones and cable TV. Some rooms have kitchenettes, microwaves and refrigerators. Senior discount. Major credit cards.

GLASGOW
Houston Inn
$35
1003 W. Main Street • 270.651.5191
80 Units, pets OK. Pool. Rooms come with phones and cable TV. Some rooms have microwaves and refrigerators. Senior discount. Major credit cards.

GRAYSON
Knights Inn
$32-46
370 SR 1947 • I-64, Exit 172
606.474.6605
57 Units, no pets. Meeting rooms. Rooms come with phones and cable TV. Some rooms have microwaves and refrigerators. Wheelchair accessible. Major credit cards.

Travelodge
$43*
Jct. I-64 & SR 1 (Exit 172) • 606.474.7854
60 Units, no pets. Continental breakfast. Pool. Meeting rooms. Rooms come with phones and cable TV. Some rooms have microwaves and refrigerators. AAA discount. Major credit cards.
*Higher rates effective June through November.

HARRODSBURG
Harrodsburg Motel
$38
213 S. College Street • 859.734.7782
21 Units, pets OK. Restaurant on premises. Rooms come with phones and cable TV. Wheelchair accessible. Major credit cards.

HAZARD
Daniel Boone Motor Inn
$42
On Highway 15N • 606.439.5896
70 Units, pets OK. Rooms come with phones and cable TV. Major credit cards.

HENDERSON
Henderson Downtown Motel
$33
425 N. Green Street • 270.827.2577
38 Units, no pets. Continental breakfast. Rooms come with phones and cable TV. Major credit cards.

Sugar Creek Inn
$36-39
2077 US 41N • 270.827.0127
65 Units, no pets. Meeting rooms. Rooms come with phones and cable TV. Some rooms have refrigerators. Credit cards: AE, DC, DS, MC, V.

HOPKINSVILLE
Econo Lodge
$40-49
2916 Ft. Campbell Blvd. • 270.886.5242
90 Units, no pets. Continental breakfast. Pool. Sauna. Jacuzzi. Rooms come with phones and cable TV. Wheelchair accessible. Major credit cards.

Rodeway Inn
$35-46
2923 Ft. Campbell Blvd. • 270.885.1126
55 Units, pets OK. Continental breakfast. Fitness facility. Rooms come with phones and cable TV. Wheelchair accessible. Major credit cards.

HORSE CAVE
Budget Host Inn
$30-38
I-65 (Exit 58) • 270.786.2165
80 Units, no pets. Restaurant on premises. Pool. Laundry facility. Playground. Rooms come with phones and cable TV. Some rooms have kitchens and refrigerators. AAA discount. Major credit cards.

INEZ
Super 8 Motel
$46
On Rte. 40 (Blacklog Rd.) • 606.298.7800
32 Units, pets OK. Continental breakfast. Jacuzzi. Laundry facility. Rooms come with phones and cable TV. Major credit cards.

IRVINE
Oak Tree Inn
$47
1075 Richmond Road • 606.723.2600
28 Units, pets OK. Fitness facility. Rooms come with phones and cable TV. Senior discount. Major credit cards.

JEFFERSONTOWN
Microtel Inn
$50
1221 Kentucky Mills (I-64, Exit 17)
502.266.6590
99 Units, no pets. Continental breakfast. Rooms come with phones and cable TV. Wheelchair accessible. AAA discount. Major credit cards.

LA GRANGE
Super 8 Motel
$49
1420 E. Crystal Drive • I-71, Exit 22
502.225.9778
60 Units, no pets. Continental breakfast. Pool. Laundry facility. Rooms come with phones and cable TV. Major credit cards.

LEBANON
Country Hearth Inn
$49
720 W. Main Street • 270.692.4445
40 Units, pets OK. Pool. Laundry facility. Rooms come with phones and cable TV. Some rooms have microwaves and refrigerators. Senior discount. Major credit cards.

LEITCHFIELD
Countryside Inn
$35
315 Commerce Drive • 270.259.4021
46 Units, pets OK. Rooms come with phones and cable TV. Major credit cards.

LEXINGTON
Econo Lodge
$35-55
5527 Athens-Boonesboro Rd.
859.263.5101
67 Units, pets OK ($10 dep. req.). Continental breakfast. Rooms come with phones and cable TV. Some rooms have refrigerators. Wheelchair accessible. Credit cards: AE, DC, DS, MC, V.

Microtel
$40-50
I-75 (Exit 110) • 859.299.9600 or 800.844.8608
99 Units, pets OK. Continental breakfast. Rooms come with phones and TV. Wheelchair accessible. Major credit cards.

Motel 6
$36-46
2260 Elkhorn Road • 859.293.1431
98 Units, pets OK. Pool. Laundry facility. Data ports. Rooms come with phones, A/C and cable TV. Wheelchair accessible. Credit cards: AE, CB, DC, DS, MC, V.

New Circle Inn
$30
588 New Circle Rd. N.E. • 859.233.3538
56 Units, pets OK. Restaurant on premises. Meeting rooms. Laundry facility. Rooms come with phones and cable TV. Some rooms have refrigerators. Credit cards: AE, DC, DS, MC, V.

Super 8 Motel
$43-60
2351 Buena Vista Road • 859.299.6241
62 Units, pets OK. Rooms come with phones and cable TV. Senior discount. Major credit cards.

LIBERTY
The Brown Motel
$46-50
1 mile north of town on US 127 Bypass
606.787.6224
23 Units, no pets. Pool. Playground. Rooms come with phones and cable TV. Some rooms have kitchenettes, microwaves and refrigerators. AAA/Senior discount. Major credit cards.

LONDON
Budget Host Westgate Inn
$39
254 W. Daniel Boone Pkwy.
606.878.7330
46 Units, pets OK (with permission). Continental breakfast. Heated pool. Laundry facility. Playground. Rooms come with phones and cable TV. Some rooms have refrigerators. Wheelchair accessible. AAA/senior discount available (10%). Credit cards: AE, CB, DC, DS, MC, V.

LOUISA
Best Western Village Inn
$36-45
117 E. Madison Street • 606.638.9417
28 Units, pets OK ($5). Rooms come with phones and cable TV. Some rooms have refrigerators. Credit cards: AE, DC, DS, MC, V.

LOUISVILLE — *see also Jeffersontown, Shepherdsville, Georgetown (IN) and Jeffersonville (IN)*
Motel 6
$38-50
3200 Kemmons Drive • I-264, Exit 15
502.473.0000
110 Units, pets OK. Laundry facility. Data ports. Rooms come with phones, A/C and cable TV. Wheelchair accessible. Credit cards: AE, CB, DC, DS, MC, V.

Red Carpet Inn
$36-44
1640 S. Hurstbourne Pkwy.
I-64, Exit 15 • 502.491.7320
174 Units, no pets. Continental breakfast. Rooms come with phones and cable TV. Senior discount. Major credit cards.

Red Roof Inn
$40-46
4704 Preston Hwy. • 502.968.0151
110 Units, pets OK. Restaurant on premises. Laundry facility. Rooms come with phones and cable TV. Major credit cards.

Thrifty Dutchman Motel
$50
3357 Fern Valley Road • 502.968.8124
110 Units, pets OK ($35 dep. req.). Airport

transportation. Laundry facility. Rooms come with phones and cable TV. Some rooms have microwaves and refrigerators. AAA discount. Credit cards: AE, DC, DS, MC, V.

MADISONVILLE
Red Cardinal Inn
$30
4765 US 41N • 270.821.0009
44 Units, pets OK. Restaurant on premises. Pool. Jacuzzi. Game room. Rooms come with phones and cable TV. Wheelchair accessible. Major credit cards.

MAYFIELD
Super 8 Motel
$43
On Purchase Pkwy. • 270.247.8899
47 Units, pets OK. Continental breakfast. Meeting rooms. Rooms come with phones and cable TV. Wheelchair accessible. Major credit cards.

MAYSVILLE — *see also Aberdeen (OH)*
Super 8 Motel
$50
550 Tucker Drive • 606.759.8888
46 Units, no pets. Continental breakfast. Meeting rooms. Laundry facility. Rooms come with phones and TV. Wheelchair accessible. Senior discount. Major credit cards.

MIDDLESBORO
Best Western Inn
$41-45
1623 E. Cumberland Ave. • 606.248.5630
100 Units, pets OK. Restaurant on premises. Pool. Rooms come with phones and cable TV. Some rooms have refrigerators. AAA/ Senior discount. Credit cards: AE, CB, DC, DS, MC, V.

MOREHEAD
Super 8 Motel
$44-51*
602 Fraley Drive • 606.784.8882
56 Units, no pets. Laundry facility. Rooms come with phones and cable TV. Wheelchair accessible. Senior discount. Major credit cards.
*Rates may increase slightly during special events and weekends.

MORGANTOWN
Motel 6
$43-46
1460 S. Main Street • 270.526.9481
46 Units, pets OK. Pool. Data ports. Rooms come with phones, A/C and cable TV. Wheelchair accessible. Credit cards: AE, CB, DC, DS, MC, V.

MORTONS GAP
Best Western Pennyrile Inn
$45-54
On US 41 (Exit 37) • 270.258.5201
60 Units, pets OK ($15 dep. req.). Pool. Meeting rooms. Rooms come with phones and cable TV. Some rooms have refrigerators. AAA discount. Credit cards: AE, CB, DC, DS, MC, V.

MOUNT STERLING
Days Inn
$32-54
705 Maysville Road • 859.498.4680
94 Units, pets OK. Pool. Rooms come with phones and cable TV. Some rooms have microwaves and refrigerators. AAA discount. Major credit cards.

MOUNT VERNON
Econo Lodge
$41 (60-70)*
I-75 & US 25 (Exit 62) • 606.256.4621
35 Units, pets OK ($10 dep. req.). Pool. Rooms come with phones and cable TV. Credit cards: AE, CB, DC, DS, JCB, MC, V.
*Higher rates effective weekends March through October.

Kastle Inn Motel
$34-54
Junction US 25 & I-75 (Exit 59)
606.256.5156
50 Units, pets OK. Heated pool. Rooms come with phones and cable TV. Credit cards: AE, CB, DC, DS, JCB, MC, V.

Super 8 Motel
$33
I-75 (Exit 59) • 606.256.5313
46 Units, pets OK. Rooms come with phones and TV. Wheelchair accessible. Senior discount. Major credit cards.

MULDRAUGH
Golden Manor Motel
$50
346 Dixie Hwy. • 502.942.2800
40 Units, pets OK ($10 and $10 dep. req.). Continental breakfast. Pool. Laundry facility. Rooms come with phones and cable

TV. Some rooms have kitchenettes, microwaves and refrigerators. AAA/Senior discount. Major credit cards.

MUNFORDVILLE
Super 8 Motel
$47
88 Stock Pen Road • I-65, Exit 65
270.524.4888
50 Units, no pets. Continental breakfast. Rooms come with phones and cable TV. Some rooms have microwaves and refrigerators. Wheelchair accessible. Senior discount. Major credit cards.

NICHOLASVILLE
Super 8 Motel
$40
181 Imperial Way • 859.885.9889
50 Units, no pets. Continental breakfast. Rooms come with phones and cable TV. Some rooms have kitchenettes. Wheelchair accessible. Senior discount. Credit cards: AE, CB, DC, DS, MC, V.

OWENSBORO
Motel 6
$35-36
4585 Frederica Street • 270.686.8606
89 Units, pets OK. Pool. Laundry facility. Data ports. Rooms come with phones, A/C and cable TV. Wheelchair accessible. Credit cards: AE, CB, DC, DS, MC, V.

Super 8 Motel
$45-50
1027 Goetz Drive • 270.685.3388
52 Units, pets OK. Continental breakfast. Rooms come with phones and cable TV. Senior discount. Major credit cards.

PADUCAH
Best Inns of America
$41
5001 Hinkleville Road • I-24, Exit 4
270.442.3334
90 Units, pets OK. Continental breakfast. Pool. Laundry facility. Rooms come with phones and cable TV. AAA/Senior discount. Major credit cards.

Motel 6
$37-48
5120 Hinkleville Road • I-24, Exit 4
270.443.3672
80 Units, pets OK. Pool. Laundry facility. Data ports. Rooms come with phones, A/C and cable TV. Wheelchair accessible. Credit cards: AE, CB, DC, DS, MC, V.

Pear Tree Inn
$40-43
4910 Hinkleville Road • 270.444.7200
125 Units, pets OK. Continental breakfast. Pool. Laundry facility. Rooms come with phones and cable TV. Some rooms have microwaves and refrigerators. Senior discount. Major credit cards.

Super 8 Motel
$47-52
5125 Old Cairo Road • I-24, Exit 3
270.575.9605
42 Units, no pets. Rooms come with phones and TV. Some rooms have microwaves and refrigerators. AAA/Senior discount. Major credit cards.

PIKEVILLE
Daniel Boone Motor Inn
$40
US 23 (north of town) • 606.432.0365 or 800.435.4564
120 Units, pets OK. Rooms come with phones and cable TV. Wheelchair accessible. Major credit cards.

PRINCETON
Stratton Inn
$44-50
534 Marion Road • 270.365.2828
42 Units, no pets. Laundry facility. Rooms come with phones, A/C and cable TV. Some rooms have microwaves and refrigerators. Major credit cards.

RADCLIFF
Econo Lodge
$48*
261 N. Dixie Hwy. • 270.351.4488
49 Units, pets OK. Pool. Laundry facility. Rooms come with refrigerators, phones and cable TV. Some rooms have microwaves. AAA discount. Credit cards: AE, CB, DC, DS, MC, V.
*Rates as high as $90/night.

RICHMOND
Econo Lodge
$34-46
230 Eastern Bypass • 859.623.8813
98 Units. Pool. Rooms come with phones and cable TV. Some rooms have micro-

waves and refrigerators. AAA discount. Credit cards: AE, CB, DC, DS, JCB, MC, V.

Knights Inn
$32-48
1688 Northgate Drive • 859.624.2612
111 Units, pets OK ($25). Continental breakfast. Pool. Laundry facility. Rooms come with phones and cable TV. AAA/Senior discount. Credit cards: AE, CB, DC, DS, MC, V.

Super 8 Motel
$35-55
107 N. Keeneland • 859.624.1550
63 Units, pets OK. Continental breakfast. Meeting room. Rooms come with phones and cable TV. Wheelchair accessible. Senior discount. Credit cards: AE, CB, DC, DS, MC, V.

RICHWOOD
Econo Lodge
$33-44
11165 Frontage Road (I-75/I-71, Exit 175)
859.485.4123
56 Units, no pets. Continental breakfast. Pool. Rooms come with phones and cable TV. Senior discount. Major credit cards.

SHELBYVILLE
Country Hearth Inn
$40-45
100 Howard Drive • I-64, Exit 32
502.633.5771
40 Units, no pets. Continental breakfast. Laundry facility. Data ports. Rooms come with phones and cable TV. AAA/Senior discount. Major credit cards.

SHEPHERDSVILLE
Motel 6
$36-44
144 Paroquest Springs Dr.
I-65, Exit 117 • 502.543.4400
97 Units, pets OK. Pool. Laundry facility. Rooms come with phones, A/C and cable TV. Wheelchair accessible. Credit cards: AE, CB, DC, DS, MC, V.

Super 8 Motel
$46*
275 Keystone Crossroads • 502.543.8870
59 Units, no pets. Continental breakfast. Pool. Meeting room. Fitness facility. Rooms come with phones and cable TV. Wheelchair accessible. Senior discount. Credit cards: AE, CB, DC, DS, MC, V.
*Rates may increase during special events.

SOMERSET
Super 8 Motel
$40*
601 S. Hwy. 27 • 606.679.9279
63 Units, no pets. Continental breakfast. Rooms come with phones and cable TV. Wheelchair accessible. Senior discount. Credit cards: AE, CB, DC, DS, MC, V.
*Rates may increase slightly during special events and weekends.

WALTON
Days Inn
$41-59
11177 Frontage Road • 859.485.4151
137 Units, pets OK. Continental breakfast. Pool. Playground. Rooms come with phones and cable TV. AAA discount. Credit cards: AE, CB, DC, DS, MC, V.

WILLIAMSBURG
Days Inn
$39-55
I-75 (Exit 11) • 606.549.1500
83 Units, pets OK. Continental breakfast. Pool. Laundry facility. Rooms come with phones and cable TV. Wheelchair accessible. AAA discount. Credit cards: AE, CB, DC, DS, MC, V.

WILLIAMSTOWN
Days Inn
$45-55
211 SR 36W • 859.824.5025
50 Units, pets OK ($3). Continental breakfast. Pool. Rooms come with phones and cable TV. Some rooms have microwaves and refrigerators. AAA/Senior discount. Credit cards: AE, CB, DC, DS, JCB, MC, V.

Knights Inn
$32-49
401 S. Main Street
I-75, Exit 154 • 859.824.4305
40 Units, no pets. Restaurant on premises. Rooms come with phones and cable TV. Some rooms have microwaves and refrigerators. Major credit cards.

louisiana

ALEXANDRIA
Days Inn
$42-45
1146 MacArthur Drive • 318.443.1841
66 Units, pets OK ($10). Pool. Rooms come with phones and cable TV. AAA/Senior discount. Major credit cards.

Motel 6
$35-40
546 MacArthur Drive • 318.445.2336
113 Units, pets OK. Pool. Laundry facility. Data ports. Rooms come with phones, A/C and cable TV. Wheelchair accessible. Credit cards: AE, CB, DC, DS, MC, V.

Ramada Limited
$36-41
742 MacArthur Drive • 318.448.1611
121 Units, pets OK ($25 dep. req.). Pool. Laundry facility. Rooms come with phones and cable TV. Some rooms have microwaves and refrigerators. AAA/Senior discount. Major credit cards.

AMITE
Colonial Inn of Amite
$36
11255 Hwy. 16 & I-55 • 985.748.3202
40 Units, pets OK ($10 dep. req.). Restaurant on premises. Rooms come with phones and cable TV. Major credit cards.

BASTROP
Country Inn
$42
1815 E. Madison Ave. • 318.281.8100
30 Units, pets OK. Continental breakfast. Rooms come with phones and cable TV. Some rooms have microwaves and refrigerators. AAA discount. Major credit cards.

Preferred Inn
$27-44
1053 E. Madison Ave. • 318.281.3621
109 Units, pets OK. Rooms come with phones and cable TV. Major credit cards.
BATON ROUGE — see also Port Allen

Motel 6—East
$36-40
9901 Gwen Adele Ave. • 225.924.2130
177 Units, pets OK. Pool. Laundry facility. Data ports. Rooms come with phones, A/C and cable TV. Wheelchair accessible. Credit cards: AE, CB, DC, DS, MC, V.

Motel 6—Southeast
$38-44
10445 Rieger Road • 225.291.4912
110 Units, pets OK. Pool. Laundry facility. Data ports. Rooms come with phones, A/C and cable TV. Wheelchair accessible. Credit cards: AE, CB, DC, DS, MC, V.

Red Roof Inn
$37-49
11314 Boardwalk Drive • I-12, Exit 4
225.275.6600
109 Units, pets OK. Rooms come with phones and cable TV. AAA discount. Major credit cards.

BOSSIER CITY — *see also Shreveport*
Motel 6
$30-50
210 John Wesley Blvd. • 318.742.3472
98 Units, guide dogs only. Pool. Laundry facility. Data ports. Rooms come with phones, A/C and cable TV. Wheelchair accessible. Credit cards: AE, CB, DC, DS, MC, V.

Red Carpet Inn
$33-40
1968 Airline Drive • 318.746.9400
85 Units, no pets. Pool. Rooms come with phones and cable TV. Major credit cards.

CARENCRO
Economy Inn
$32-38
3525 N.W. Evangeline Thruway
337.896.0093
28 Units, pets OK (dep. req.). Rooms come with phones and cable TV. Wheelchair accessible. Credit cards: AE, MC, V.

DELHI
Best Western Delhi Inn
$46-51
35 Snider Road (I-20 • 318.878.5126
46 Units, pets OK ($5). Pool. Airport transportation offered. Rooms come with phones and cable TV. AAA/Senior discount. Major credit cards.

Days Inn
$40
113 Snider Road • I-20, Exit 153
318.878.9000
48 Units, pets OK ($10). Pool. Laundry facility. Rooms come with phones and cable TV. AAA/Senior discount. Major credit cards.

DE RIDDER
Red Carpet Inn
$41
806 N. Pine Street • 337.463.8605
65 Units, pets OK. Pool. Laundry facility. Rooms come with phones and cable TV. Some rooms have refrigerators and microwaves. Credit cards: AE, CB, DC, DS, MC, V.

HAMMOND
Budget Inn
$39-49
2000 S. Morrison Blvd. • 985.542.9425
104 Units, no pets. Restaurant on premises. Continental breakfast. Pool. Rooms come with phones and cable TV. Major credit cards.

Friendly Inn
$42
43106 S. Airport Road • 985.542.9939
17 Units, no pets. Rooms come with phones and cable TV. Major credit cards.

HOUMA
Holiday Motel
$34
744 US 90E • 985.879.2737
77 Units, no pets. Restaurant on premises. Pool. Rooms come with phones and cable TV. Major credit cards.

Lake Houma Inn
$35-37
US 90E • 985.868.9021
64 Units, no pets. Restaurant on premises. Laundry facility. Rooms come with phones and cable TV. Major credit cards.

Sugar Bowl Motel
$40
625 E. Park Avenue • 985.872.4521
55 Units, no pets. Restaurant on premises. Laundry facility. Rooms come with phones and cable TV. Major credit cards.

JENNINGS
Budget Inn
$30
15368 Hwy. 26 • 337.824.7041
28 Units, pets OK ($10). Rooms come with phones and cable TV. Major credit cards.

KENNER
Park Plaza Inn Hotel
$40-42
2125 Veteran's Blvd. (I-10, Exit 223A)
504.464.6464
129 Units, no pets. Pool. Laundry facility. Rooms come with phones and cable TV. Major credit cards.

LAFAYETTE
Motel 6
$30-40
2724 N.E. Evangeline Throughway
337.233.2055
101 Units, pets OK. Pool. Laundry facility. Data ports. Rooms come with phones, A/C and cable TV. Wheelchair accessible. Credit cards: AE, CB, DC, DS, MC, V.

Red Roof Inn
$35-47
1718 N. University Ave. • 337.233.3339
108 Units, pets OK. Rooms come with phones and cable TV. AAA discount. Credit cards: AE, CB, DC, DS, MC, V.

Travel Host Inn South
$37
1314 N.E. Evangeline Throughway
337.233.2090
166 Units, no pets. Restaurant on premises. Pool. Laundry facility. Rooms come with phones and cable TV. Credit cards: AE, DC, DS, MC, V.

LAKE CHARLES
Motel 6
$34-50
335 Hwy. 171 • 337.433.1773
129 Units, guide dogs only. Pool. Laundry facility. Data ports. Rooms come with phones, A/C and cable TV. Wheelchair accessible. Credit cards: AE, CB, DC, DS, MC, V.

Sunrise Inn
$33-45
5390 US 90E (I-10, Exit 31B)
337.437.8339
108 Units, no pets. Pool. Rooms come with phones and cable TV. Major credit cards.

Travel Inn
$48-54*
1212 N. Lakeshore Dr. • 337.433.9461
80 Units, no pets. Restaurant on premises. Pool. Rooms come with phones and cable TV. Major credit cards.
*AAA discounted rates.

LEESVILLE
Sandman Travel Inn
$34
3093 Lake Charles Hwy • 337.239.0950
50 Units, no pets. Rooms come with phones and cable TV. Major credit cards.

LIVONIA
Oak Tree Inn
$50
7875 Airline Hwy. • 225.637.2590
42 Units, pets OK ($10). Laundry facility. Rooms come with phones and cable TV. Senior discount. Major credit cards.

MANSFIELD
Mansfield Inn
$46
1055 Washington Ave. • 318.872.5034
68 Units, pets OK. Restaurant on premises. Pool. Laundry facility. Rooms come with phones and cable TV. AAA/Senior discount. Major credit cards.

MANY
Starlite Motel
$32
160 Fisher Rd (US 171) • 318.256.0515
20 Units, no pets. Restaurant on premises. Continental breakfast. Data ports. Rooms come with refrigerators, microwaves, phones and cable TV. Major credit cards.

MINDEN
Exacta Inn
$45-55
1404 Sibley Road • 318.377.3200
62 Units, no pets. Restaurant on premises. Pool. Meeting rooms. Airport transportation. Rooms come with phones and cable TV. AAA discount. Credit cards: AE, CB, DC, DS, MC, V.

Southern Inn
$36
1318 Lee St. • I-20, Exit 47 • 318.371.2880
28 Units, no pets. Pool. Rooms come with phones and cable TV. AAA/Senior discount. Major credit cards.

MONROE — *see also West Monroe*
Civic Center Inn
$30-42
610 Lea Joyner • 318.323.4451
91 Units, no pets. Restaurant on premises. Pool. Meeting rooms. Rooms come with refrigerators, phones and cable TV. Some rooms have microwaves. Credit cards: AE, CB, DC, DS, MC, V.

Motel 6
$32-40
1501 US 165 Bypass • 318.322.5430
105 Units, pets OK. Pool. Laundry facility. Data ports. Rooms come with phones, A/C and cable TV. Wheelchair accessible. Credit cards: AE, CB, DC, DS, MC, V.

MORGAN CITY
Morgan City Motel
$28-30
505 Brashear Avenue • 985.384.6640
36 Units, no pets. Rooms come with phones, A/C and cable TV. Some rooms have kitchenettes. Major credit cards.

Twin City Motel
$34
7405 Hwy. 90E • 985.384.1530
45 Units, no pets. Pool. Rooms come with refrigerators, phones, A/C and cable TV. Major credit cards.

NATCHITOCHES
Lakeview Inn
$42
1316 Washington St. • 318.352.9561
30 Units, pets OK. Rooms come with phones and cable TV. Major credit cards.

Super 8 Motel
$39-50
801 Hwy. 1N Bypass • 318.352.1700
43 Units, pets OK ($25 dep. req.). Rooms come with phones and cable TV. Some rooms have refrigerators. AAA discount. Credit cards: AE, DC, DS, MC, V.

NEW IBERIA
Inn of New Iberia
$45
924 Admiral Doyle Dr. • 337.367.3211
130 Units, no pets. Continental breakfast. Pool. Meeting rooms. Rooms come with phones and cable TV. Major credit cards.

Kajun Inn
$35
1506 Center Street • 337.367.3608
36 Units, no pets. Pool. Rooms come with phones and cable TV. Major credit cards.

Southland Inn
$32-36
503 E. Hwy. 90 • 337.365.6711
80 Units, no pets. Pool. Rooms come with phones and cable TV. Major credit cards.

NEW ORLEANS — *see also Kenner and Slidell*
Traveler Advisory: If you are planning to spend the night in New Orleans, you will need to plan on spending more than $50/night, particularly during Mardi Gras which usually runs through most of February. With the exception of a few places listed here, it will be difficult to find accommodations in New Orleans or in the surrounding communities for less than $50/night. The following are a few recommendations to suit your budget:

New Orleans
Econo Lodge ($55-95)
4940 Chef Menteur Pkwy
504.940.5550

La Quinta Inn—Bullard Rd. ($60-89)
From I-10, Exit 245
504.246.3003

La Quinta Inn—Crowder ($60-89)
From I-10, Exit 242
504.246.5800

Chalmette
Quality Inn Marina ($54-119)
5353 Paris Road
504.277.5353 or 800.221.2222

Gretna
Econo Lodge ($49-69)
1411 Claire Avenue
504.366.4311

La Quinta Inn West Bank ($60-89)
50 Terry Pkwy.
504.368.5600

Harvey
Travelodge ($55-75)
2200 Westbank Expwy.
504.366.5311

Kenner
Days Inn ($39-95)
1300 Veterans Blvd.
504.469.2531

Rodeway Inn ($58-78)
851 Airline Hwy.
504.467.1391

Metairie
Orleans Courtyard Inn ($80)
3800 Hessmer Avenue
504.455.6110

Travelodge ($48-78)
5733 Airline Hwy.
504.733.1550

Hostelling International
$17-28
2253 Carondelet Street • 504.523.3014
176 Beds, Hours: 7 am – midnight
Facilities: equipment storage area, information desk, kitchen, laundry facilities, linen rental, lockers, parking. Private rooms available. Open year-round. Reservations essential during Mardi Gras (last few weeks of February). Credit cards: JCB, MC, V.

Knights Inn
$36-56*
4180 Old Gentilly Road • 504.944.0151
65 Units, no pets. Pool. Laundry facility. Rooms come with phones and cable TV. Wheelchair accessible. Major credit cards.
*Rates may climb as high as $95/night.

Motel 6
$40-50
12330 I-10 Service Road • I-10, Exit 245
504.240.2867
124 Units, pets OK. Pool. Laundry facility. Data ports. Rooms come with phones, A/C and cable TV. Wheelchair accessible. Credit cards: AE, CB, DC, DS, MC, V.

Super 8 Motel
$48-53
6322 Chef Menteur Hwy. • 504.241.5650
106 Units, no pets. Pool. Laundry facility. Rooms come with phones and cable TV. Senior discount. Major credit cards.

OPELOUSAS
Sunset Motor Inn
$35
8451 Hwy. 167S • 337.662.3726
28 Units, pets OK ($5). Rooms come with phones and cable TV. Major credit cards.

PORT ALLEN — *see also Baton Rouge*
Motel 6
$32-40
2800 I-10 Frontage Rd. • 225.343.5945
121 Units, pets OK. Pool. Laundry facility. Data ports. Rooms come with phones, A/C and cable TV. Wheelchair accessible. Credit cards: AE, CB, DC, DS, MC, V.

Super 8 Motel
$44
I-10, Exit 151 • 225.381.9134
148 Units, pets OK. Continental breakfast. Pool. Rooms come with phones and cable TV. Senior discount. Major credit cards.

RAYVILLE
Cottonland Inn
$39-49
I-20 & Hwy. 137 • 318.728.5985
78 Units, pets OK. Restaurant on premises. Pool. Picnic area. Laundry facility. Rooms come with phones and cable TV. Credit cards: AE, DS, MC, V.

RUSTON
Econo Lodge
$49
1301 Goodwin Road • I-20, Exit 86
318.255.0354
81 Units, pets OK. Pool. Playground. Fitness facility. Laundry facility. Rooms come with phones and cable TV. Senior discount. Major credit cards.

Super 8 Motel
$45-55
1101 Cooktown Road (I-20, Exit 84)
318.255.0588
42 Units, no pets. Continental breakfast. Pool. Laundry facility. Rooms come with phones and cable TV. Some rooms have microwaves and refrigerators. AAA discount. Major credit cards.

SHREVEPORT — *see also Bossier City*
Econo Lodge
$45-56
4911 Monkhouse Drive • 318.636.0771
65 Units, no pets. Pool. Rooms come with phones and cable TV. Senior discount. Credit cards: AE, DS, MC, V.

Red Roof Inn
$34-54
7296 Greenwood Road • 318.938.5342
108 Units, pets OK. Rooms come with phones and cable TV. AAA discount. Major credit cards.

Super 8 Motel
$40-50
5204 Monkhouse Drive • 318.255.0588
42 Units, no pets. Continental breakfast. Pool. Laundry facility. Rooms come with phones, refrigerators, microwaves and cable TV. Senior discount. Wheelchair accessible. Major credit cards.

Travelodge
$40
2134 Greenwood Road, (I-20, Exit 16B)
318.425.7467
100 Units, no pets. Restaurant on premises. Pool. Rooms come with phones and cable TV. Major credit cards.

SLIDELL
Motel 6
$33-40
136 Taos Street • 985.649.7925
153 Units, pets OK. Pool. Laundry facility. Rooms come with phones, A/C and cable TV. Wheelchair accessible. Credit cards: AE, CB, DC, DS, MC, V.

Super 8 Motel
$39-50
1662 Gause Blvd. (I-10, Exit 266)
985.641.8800
100 Units, pets OK. Restaurant on premises. Pool. Laundry facility. Rooms come with phones and cable TV. AAA/Senior discount. Major credit cards.

SULPHUR
Chateau Inn & Suites
$40
2022 Ruth Street • 337.527.8146
61 Units, no pets. Rooms come with phones and cable TV. Major credit cards.

TALLULAH
Super 8 Motel
$45-57
1604 New Hwy. 65S (I-20, Exit 171)
318.574.2000
53 Units, pets OK ($10). Continental breakfast. Pool. Rooms come with phones and cable TV. Senior discount. Wheelchair accessible. Major credit cards.

WEST MONROE — *see also Monroe*
Red Roof Inn
$35-49
102 Constitution Drive • 318.388.2420
97 Units, pets OK. Rooms come with phones and cable TV. Some rooms have refrigerators. AAA discount. Credit cards: AE, CB, DC, DS, MC, V.

Super 8 Motel
$45
1101 Glenwood Drive • 318.325.6361
99 Units, no pets. Continental breakfast. Pool. Rooms come with phones and cable TV. Senior discount. Wheelchair accessible. Major credit cards.

WINNFIELD
Economy Inn
$37
US 84E • 318.628.4691
50 Units, pets OK. Rooms come with phones and cable TV. Major credit cards.

maine

AUGUSTA
Motel 6
$38-50
18 Edison Drive • I-95, Exit 30
207.622.0000
69 Units, pets OK. Laundry facility. Rooms come with phones, A/C and cable TV. Wheelchair accessible. Credit cards: AE, CB, DC, DS, MC, V.

Super 8 Motel
$48
395 Western Avenue • 207.626.2888
50 Units, no pets. Rooms come with phones, A/C and cable TV. Wheelchair accessible. Senior discount. Major credit cards.

BANGOR
Econo Lodge
$29-55*
327 Odlin Road • 207.945.0111
127 Units, pets OK ($6 dep. req.). Laundry facility. Rooms come with phones and cable TV. Senior discount. Credit cards: AE, DS, MC, V.
*Rates as high as $75 from July through mid-October.

Main Street Inn
$45-49
480 Main Street • I-95, Exit 45A to I-395, Exit 3B • 207.942.5282
64 Units, pets OK. Continental breakfast. Rooms come with phones and cable TV. Major credit cards.

Motel 6
$30-50
1100 Hammond Street • 207.947.6921
60 Units, pets OK. Laundry facility. Rooms come with phones, A/C and cable TV. Wheelchair accessible. Credit cards: AE, CB, DC, DS, MC, V.

Super 8 Motel
$40-55
462 Odlin Road • 207.945.5681
77 Units, no pets. Continental breakfast. Rooms come with phones, A/C and cable TV. Major credit cards.

BAR HARBOR
Sunnyside Motel
$35-45*
9 miles west on SR 3 • 207.288.3602
20 Units, no pets. Pool. Laundry facility. Rooms come with phones and cable TV. AAA discount. Credit cards: MC, V.
*Open May through mid-October. Rates higher during July and August ($60-70).

BETHEL
The Inn at the Rostay
$40-45*
186 Mayville Road • 207.824.3111
18 Units, no pets. Rooms come with cable TV. No A/C or phones in rooms. Some rooms have microwaves and refrigerators. Credit cards: AE, DS, MC, V.
*Rates as high as $120/night.

BOOTHBAY
White Anchor Motel
$45-50 (65-79)*
7.5 miles south on SR 27 from US 1
207.633.3788
31 Units, pets OK (credit card dep. req.). Continental breakfast. Rooms come with phones and cable TV. Some rooms have A/C and refrigerators. Credit cards: AE, DS, MC, V.
*AAA discounted rates. Higher rates effective late June through Labor Day.

BREWER
The Brewer Motor Inn
$45-49
359 Wilson Street • 207.989.4476
30 Units, pets OK. Continental breakfast. Rooms come with phones and cable TV. AAA/Senior discount. Major credit cards.

BRUNSWICK
Maineland Motel
$35-54
133 Pleasant Street • I-95, Exit 22
207.725.8761
53 Units, pets OK ($10). Pool. Laundry facility. Rooms come with phones and cable TV. Some rooms have refrigerators. AAA/ Senior discount. Credit cards: AE, DS, MC. V.

Travelers Inn
$35-55
130 Pleasant Street • I-95, Exit 22
207.729.3364
37 Units, no pets. Continental breakfast. Laundry facility. Rooms come with phones and cable TV. Some rooms have refrigerators. Senior discount. Credit cards: AE, DS, MC. V.

CALAIS
Heslin's Motel
$50*
5.5 miles south on US 1 • 207.454.3762
25 Units, no pets. Restaurant on premises. Rooms come with phones and cable TV. Credit cards: MC, V.
*AAA discounted rates. Closed November through May.

International Motel
$45-50
276 Main Street • 207.454.7515
61 Units, pets OK. Rooms come with phones and cable TV. AAA/Senior discount. Major credit cards.

ELLSWORTH
Ellsworth Motel
$38-44 (52-56)*
24 High Street • 207.667.4424
16 Units, no pets. Pool. Rooms come with phones and cable TV. No A/C in rooms. Credit cards: MC, V.
*Motel closed November through mid-May. Higher rates effective July through Labor Day.

The White Birches
$49*
1.5 miles north from junction of Rte. 3 on US 1 • 207.667.3621
67 Units, pets OK. Meeting rooms. 9-hole golf course. Rooms come with phones and cable TV. No A/C in rooms. Some rooms have jacuzzis. Credit cards: AE, DC, DS, MC, V.
*Rates as high as $99/night.

FARMINGTON
Farmington Motel
$50
On US 2, two miles east of town
207.778.4680
39 Units, no pets. Rooms come with phones and cable TV. Credit cards: AE, DC, DS, MC, V.

Mount Blue Motel
$44-50
On Wilton Rd. (2 mi. west on US 2 & SR 4)
207.778.6004
18 Units, pets OK ($7). Rooms come with phones, A/C and cable TV. AAA/Senior discount. Major credit cards.

HOULTON
Scottish Inns
$40-50
Rt. 2A Bangor Road • 207.532.2236
43 Units, pets OK ($6). Rooms come with phones and cable TV. Some rooms have refrigerators. AAA discount. Credit cards: AE, DS, MC, V.

LEWISTON
Chalet Motel
$50
1243 Lisbon Street • 207.784.0600
74 Units, no pets. Restaurant on premises. Heated indoor pool. Sauna. Jacuzzi. Laundry facility. Rooms come with phones and cable TV. Some rooms have refrigerators and jacuzzis. AAA discount. Credit cards: AE, CB, DC, DS, MC, V.

Motel 6
$40-52
516 Pleasant Street • 207.782.6558
66 Units, pets OK. Rooms come with phones, A/C and cable TV. Wheelchair accessible. Credit cards: AE, CB, DC, DS, MC, V.

LUBEC
Eastland Motel
$38-55
On Rte. 189 (8 miles from US 1 junction)
207.733.5501
19 Units, pets OK. Rooms come with phones and cable TV. No A/C in rooms. AAA discount. Major credit cards.

MACHIAS
Bluebird Motel
$48-54
One mile south on US 1 • 207.255.3332
40 Units, pets OK. Rooms come with phones and cable TV. Wheelchair accessible. AAA/ Senior discount. Credit cards: AE, MC, V.

MILLINOCKET
Pamola Motor Lodge
$45*
973 Central Street • 207.723.9746

29 Units, pets OK. Continental breakfast. Pool. Jacuzzis. Rooms come with phones and cable TV. Credit cards: AE, DC, DS, MC, V.
*AAA discounted rates.

NEWPORT
Lovely's Motel
$30-50
From I-95, Exit 39 • 207.368.4311
63 Units, pets OK. Heated pool. Jacuzzi. Playground. Laundry facility. AAA discount. Rooms come with phones and cable TV. Credit cards: AE, DS, MC, V.

NORWAY
Inn Town Motel
$45-52
43 Paris Street • 207.743.7706
29 Units, pets OK. Continental breakfast. Rooms come with phones and cable TV. AAA discount. Credit cards: AE, DS, MC, V.

PORTLAND
Motel 6
$37-48 (58-66)*
One Riverside Street • I-95, Exit 8
207.775.0111
126 Units, pets OK. Laundry facility. Rooms come with phones, A/C and cable TV. Wheelchair accessible. Credit cards: AE, CB, DC, DS, MC, V.
*Higher rates effective summer months.

PRESQUE ISLE
The Budget Traveler Motor Lodge
$37-42
71 Main Street • 207.769.0111
53 Units, no pets. Continental breakfast. Meeting rooms. Laundry facility. Rooms come with phones and cable TV. Some rooms have microwaves and refrigerators. Senior discount. Major credit cards.

Northern Lights Motel
$39-46
72 Houlton Road • 207.764.4441
13 Units, pets OK. Continental breakfast. Data ports. Rooms come with phones and cable TV. Some rooms have microwaves and refrigerators. AAA discount. Credit cards: AE, DS, MC, V.

SACO
Saco Motel
$35-50*
473 Main Street • 207.284.6952
26 Units, pets OK. Pool. Rooms come with cable TV. No phones in rooms. Senior discount. Credit cards: AE, DS, MC, V.
*Closed mid-November through April.

Wagon Wheel Motel
$40-50 (65-95)*
726 Portland Road • 207.284.6387
11 Units, pets OK. Pool. VCRs and movie rentals. Rooms come with phones and cable TV. Some rooms have refrigerators and microwaves. Credit cards: AE, DS, MC, V.
*Higher rates effective July and August.

WATERVILLE
Budget Host Airport Inn
$32-60 (50-70)*
400 Kennedy Mem. Dr. • 207.873.3366
45 Units, pets OK ($10). Continental breakfast. Airport transportation. Picnic area. Playground. Laundry facility. Rooms come with phones and cable TV. AAA/Senior discount. Credit cards: AE, DS, MC, V.
*Higher rate effective July through October.

WESTBROOK
Super 8 Motel
$41-56 (70-103)*
208 Larrabee Road • 207.854.1881
104 Units, pets OK ($50 dep. req.). Rooms come with phones and cable TV. AAA/Senior discount. Major credit cards.
*Higher rates effective July through September.

maryland

ABERDEEN

Knights Inn
$45
744 S. Philadelphia Blvd. • 410.272.3600
40 Units, no pets. Pool. Laundry facility. Rooms come with phones and cable TV. Wheelchair accessible. AAA discount. Major credit cards.

Red Roof Inn
$39-55
988 Hospitality Way • I-95, Exit 85
410.273.7800
109 Units, pets OK. Data ports. Rooms come with phones and cable TV. AAA discount. Major credit cards.

BALTIMORE

Traveler Advisory: An overnight in Baltimore will likely cost you more than $50. If you are willing to drive away from the city center a bit (**Ellicott City, Linthicum Heights** or **Jessup**), you can find accommodations at a reasonable price. However, if you have made up your mind to stay in town, here are a few recommendations to suit your budget:

Best Inn Moravia ($53-62)
6510 Frankford Avenue
(I-95 at Exit 60)
410.485.7900

Comfort Inn West ($70-85*)
6700 Security Blvd.
(I-695 at Exit 17)
410.281.1800

Days Inn ($44-99)
1660 Whitehead Court
(I-695 at Exit 17)
410.944.7400

Executive Inn ($65)
3600 Pulaski Hwy.
410.327.7801

Quality Inn Inner Harbor ($65-83)
1701 Russell Street
410.727.3400

Super 8 Motel ($55-65)
98 Stemmers Rum Rd.
410.780.0030

***Additional AAA discount.**

Knights Inn
$50
6422 Baltimore National Pike
I-695 at Rte. 40W • 410.788.3900
125 Units, pets OK. Pool. Rooms come with phones, A/C and cable TV. Wheelchair accessible. AAA/Senior discount. Major credit cards.

Motel 6—Airport
$50 (54-64)*
5179 Raynor Avenue (I-695, Exit 8)
410.636.9070
136 Units, pets OK. Pool. Laundry facility. Data ports. Rooms come with phones, A/C and cable TV. Wheelchair accessible. Credit cards: AE, CB, DC, DS, MC, V.
*Higher rates effective summers and weekends.

Motel 6
$44-50 (60)*
1654 Whitehead Court (I-695, Exit 17)
410.265.7660
133 Units, pets OK. Rooms come with phones, A/C and cable TV. Wheelchair accessible. Major credit cards.
*Higher rate effective during summer weekends.

CAMBRIDGE

Best Value Inn
$50-60*
2831 Ocean Gateway • 410.221.0800
98 Units, pets OK. Rooms come with phones and cable TV. Major credit cards.
*Summer rates may be higher.

CAMP SPRINGS

Motel 6
$48 (56-60)*
5701 Allentown Road (I-95, Exit 7A)
301.702.1061

145 Units, pets OK. Rooms come with phones, A/C and cable TV. Wheelchair accessible. Credit cards: AE, CB, DC, DS, MC, V.
*Higher rates effective weekends.

CAPITOL HEIGHTS — *see District of Columbia*

COLLEGE PARK — *see District of Columbia*

CUMBERLAND — *see also La Vale*
Continental Motor Inn
$35-40
15001 National Hwy. S.W. • 301.729.2201
51 Units, no pets. Rooms come with phones and cable TV. Major credit cards.

Diplomat Motel
$44
17012 McMullen Hwy. • 301.729.2311
16 Units, pets OK ($5). Rooms come with phones and cable TV. Some rooms have microwaves and refrigerators. Senior discount. Credit cards: AE, CB, DC, DS, MC, V.

DELMAR
Delmarva Inn
$45 (65)*
9544 Ocean Hwy. • 410.896.3434
90 Units, pets OK. Rooms come with phones and cable TV. Major credit cards.
*Higher rate effective during summer.

ELKTON
Econo Lodge
$45
311 Belle Hill Road • 410.392.5010
59 Units, pets OK. Laundry facility. Rooms come with phones and cable TV. Some rooms have microwaves and refrigerators. Credit cards: AE, CB, DC, DS, MC, V.

Knights Inn
$40
262 Belle Hill Road • 410.392.6680
119 Units, pets OK. Pool. Meeting rooms. Rooms come with phones, A/C and cable TV. Wheelchair accessible. AAA/Senior discount. Major credit cards.

Motel 6
$36-44
223 Belle Hill Road • 410.392.5020
127 Units, pets OK. Data ports. Rooms come with phones, A/C and cable TV. Wheelchair accessible. Credit cards: AE, CB, DC, DS, MC, V.

ELLICOTT CITY
Forest Motel
$50*
10021 Baltimore National Pike
410.465.2090
25 Units, pets OK. Rooms come with phones and cable TV. Major credit cards.
*AAA discounted rate.

ESSEX
Christlen Motel
$48
8733 Pulaski Hwy. • 410.687.1740
28 Units, no pets. Rooms come with phones and cable TV. Some rooms have refrigerators. Credit cards: AE, DC, DS, MC, V.

FREDERICK
Travelodge
$48
200 E. Walser Drive • 301.663.0500
130 Units, pets OK. Laundry facility. Rooms come with phones and cable TV. Some rooms have microwaves and refrigerators. AAA/Senior discount. Major credit cards.

GAITHERSBURG — *see District of Columbia*

HAGERSTOWN — *see also Williamsport*
Econo Lodge
$40-55*
18221 Mason Dixon Road
I-70, Exit 54 • 301.733.8262
22 Units, pets OK ($3). Pool. Rooms come with phones and cable TV. Wheelchair accessible. Credit cards: AE, DS, MC, V.
*AAA discounted rates.

Motel 6
$39-52
11321 Massey Blvd. • 301.582.4445
103 Units, pets OK. Pool. Laundry facility. Rooms come with phones, A/C and cable TV. Wheelchair accessible. Credit cards: AE, CB, DC, DS, MC, V.

Super 8 Motel
$39-50*
1220 Dual Hwy. • 301.739.5800
62 Units, pets OK. Continental breakfast. Rooms come with phones and cable TV. Wheelchair accessible. Senior discount. Credit cards: AE, CB, DC, DS, MC, V.

*Rates may increase slightly during special events, holidays and weekends.

HANCOCK
Hancock Budget Motel
$40-48
210 E. Main Street • 301.678.7351
22 Units, no pets. Rooms come with phones and cable TV. AAA discount. Major credit cards.

Hancock Motel
$46*
2 Blue Hill Road • I-70, Exit 1B
301.678.6108
22 Units, no pets. Rooms come with phones and cable TV. AAA/Senior discount. Credit cards: AE, MC, V.
*AAA discounted rate.

HAVRE DE GRACE
Super 8 Motel
$46-58
929 Pulaski Hwy. • 410.939.1880
63 Units, no pets. Rooms come with phones and cable TV. Some rooms have microwaves and refrigerators. Wheelchair accessible. AAA/Senior discount. Major credit cards.

INDIAN HEAD
Super 8 Motel
$50
4694 Indian Head Hwy. • 301.753.8100
44 Units, pets OK ($5). Continental breakfast. Laundry facility. Rooms come with phones and cable TV. Wheelchair accessible. AAA/Senior discount. Major credit cards.

JESSUP
Knights Inn
$38-45
7451 Assateague Drive • 410.799.3837
50 Units, no pets. Restaurant on premises. Laundry facility. Rooms come with phones and cable TV. Wheelchair accessible. Major credit cards.

Super 8 Motel
$50-60
8094 Washington Blvd. • 410.796.0400
35 Units, no pets. Rooms come with phones and cable TV. AAA/Senior discount. Major credit cards.

LANHAM — *see District of Columbia*

LAUREL
Knights Inn
$50-60*
3380 Ft. Meade Road • 301.498.5553
119 Units, no pets. Pool. Laundry facility. Rooms come with phones and cable TV. Some rooms have refrigerators. Major credit cards.
*AAA discounted rates.

Motel 6
$40-52 (60)*
3510 Old Annapolis Rd.
I-295 at Rte. 198 • 301.497.1544
126 Units, pets OK. Pool. Laundry facility. Data ports. Rooms come with phones, A/C and cable TV. Wheelchair accessible. Credit cards: AE, CB, DC, DS, MC, V.
*Higher rate effective summer weekends.

Red Roof Inn
$44-54
12525 Laurel-Bowie Rd. • 301.498.8811
120 Units, pets OK. Rooms come with phones and cable TV. AAA discount. Credit cards: AE, CB, DC, DS, MC, V.

LA VALE
Super 8 Motel
$46-56*
1301 National Hwy. • 301.729.6265
63 Units, no pets. Rooms come with phones and cable TV. Senior discount. Wheelchair accessible. Major credit cards.
*Rates higher during weekends, special events and holidays.

LINTHICUM HEIGHTS — *see Baltimore*

PRINCESS ANNE
Travelers Budget Inn
$44*
30359 Mt. Vernon Road • 410.651.4075
28 Units, no pets. Data ports. Rooms come with phones and cable TV. AAA/Senior discount. Major credit cards.
*Rates as high as $84/night.

SALISBURY
Econo Lodge
$34-59
712 N. Salisbury Blvd. • 410.749.7155
92 Units, pets OK. Continental breakfast. Pool. Rooms come with phones and cable TV. Major credit cards.

Lord Salisbury Inn
$45-55
2637 N. Salisbury Blvd. (US 13)
410.742.3251 or 800.299.3232
40 Units, pets OK. Seasonal pool. Rooms come with phones and cable TV. AAA discount. Major credit cards.
*Higher rate effective during summer months.

Temple Hill Motel
$36-45
1510 S. Salisbury Blvd. • 410.742.3284
62 Units, pets OK. Continental breakfast. Pool. Laundry facility. Rooms come with A/C, phones and cable TV. AAA/senior discounts available. Major credit cards.

SILVER SPRING — *see District of Columbia*

THURMONT
Cozy Inn Motel
$50*
103 Frederick Road • 301.271.4301
21 Units, pets OK. Restaurant on premises. Continental breakfast. Meeting rooms. Data ports. Rooms come with phones and cable TV. AAA/Senior discount. Major credit cards.
*Rates as high as $150/night.

WALDORF
Days Inn of Waldorf
$49*
11370 Days Court • 301.932.9200
100 Units, pets OK ($10). Continental breakfast. Rooms come with phones and cable TV. AAA/Senior discount. Major credit cards.
*Rates as high as $89/night.

Waldorf Motel
$44
2125 Crain Hwy. • 301.645.5555
100 Units, no pets. Laundry facility. Rooms come with phones and cable TV. Senior discount. Major credit cards.

WESTMINSTER
The Boston Inn
$38-52
533 Baltimore Blvd. • 410.848.9095
115 Units, pets OK. Pool. Meeting room. Rooms come with phones and cable TV. Some rooms have kitchens and refrigerators. Senior discount. Credit cards: AE, DC, DS, MC, V.

WILLIAMSPORT
Red Roof Inn
$39-49
310 E. Potomac Street • I-81, Exit 2
301.582.3500
116 Units, pets OK. Continental breakfast. Pool. Picnic tables. Rooms come with phones and cable TV. AAA/Senior discount. Major credit cards.

massachusetts

Traveler Advisory: Finding a room for $50 or less in the Boston metro area or on Cape Cod will be next to impossible. Room rates are incredibly high in and around Boston, Cape Cod, and most of New England, for that matter. Your best bets are going to be national franchises, such as Motel 6s and Super 8 Motels, whose rates range anywhere from $56 to $80 per night (a few of these places are listed below). Otherwise, there are a few suggested places listed below which offer relatively inexpensive lodgings. Winter and spring are good times to find inexpensive rooms on Cape Cod, but be aware that many motels close for the season.

AYER
Ayer Motor Inn
$48*
18 Fitchburg Road • 978.772.0797
50 Units, no pets. Rooms come with phones and cable TV. Major credit cards.
*Summer rates higher.

BOSTON METRO AREA

Bedford
Travelodge ($79-99)
285 Great Road
781.275.6120

Braintree
Motel 6 ($66-86)
125 Union Street (Rte. 3, Exit 17)
781.848.7890

Danvers
Motel 6 ($56-75)
65 Newbury Street (I-95 at US 1)
978.774.8045

Super 8 Motel ($69-77)
225 Newbury Street (I-95 at US 1)
978.774.6500

Foxboro
End-Zone Motor Inn ($70-85)
105 Washington St.
508.543.4000

Framingham
Econo Lodge ($70-100*)
1186 Worcester Road
I-90 (Mass Pike) Exit 12, Rte. 9E
508.879.1510

Motel 6 ($56-66)
1668 Worcester Road
I-90 (Mass Pike), Exit 12
508.620.0500

Red Roof Inn ($59-99)
650 Cochituate Road
508.872.4499

Mansfield
Red Roof Inn ($64-70)
60 Forbes Blvd.
I-95 & I-495 at SR 140
508.339.2323

Sharon
Super 8 Motel ($90)
395 Old Post Road
I-95, Exit 9, then Rte. 1 south
781.784.1000

Tewksbury
Motel 6 ($60-70)
I-495, Exit 38
978.851.8677

***AAA discount.**

Hostelling International
$27-29
12 Hemenway Street • 617.536.9455
One block west of Massachusetts Avenue at Boylston & Hemenway Sts.
196 Beds, Office hours: 24 hours
Facilities: equipment storage, information, laundry facilities, kitchen, linen rental, lockers, wheelchair accessible. Private rooms available. Open year-round. Reservations recommended. Credit cards: JCB, MC, V.

Hostelling International
$27-29
512 Beacon Street • 617.731.5430

100 Beds, Hours: 7a-10a & 5p-2a
Facilities: storage area, laundry facilities, linen rental, vending machines, microwaves and refrigerators. Private rooms available. Closed August 27 through June 13. Reservations recommended. Credit cards: MC, V.

BUZZARDS BAY
Silver Lake Motel
$45
3026 Cranberry Hwy. (Rtes. 6 & 28)
508.295.1266
23 Units, pets OK. Rooms come with phones and cable TV. Major credit cards.

CAPE COD — *see Buzzards Bay, Eastham, Hyannis, South Wellfleet, South Yarmouth and Truro*

CHICOPEE
Motel 6
$40-50
On Burnett Rd. (I-90, Exit 6)
413.592.5141
88 Units, pets OK. Pool. Laundry facility. Rooms come with A/C, phones and cable TV. Wheelchair accessible. Credit cards: AE, CB, DC, DS, MC, V.

DARTMOUTH
Capri Motel
$50
741 State Road • 508.997.7877
72 Units, no pets. Rooms come with phones and cable TV. Wheelchair accessible. Major credit cards.

EASTHAM
Hostelling International
$19
75 Goody Hallet Drive • 508.255.2785
50 Beds, Hours: 7:30-10a & 5-10p
Facilities: outdoor showers, information, kitchen, linen rental, parking, barbecue and volleyball. Private rooms available (2 cabins). Closed September 15 through May 9. Reservations essential. Credit cards: MC, V.

FAIRHAVEN
The Huttleston Motel
$50 (60)*
128 Huttleston Avenue • 508.997.7655
29 Units, pets OK. Rooms come with phones and cable TV. Wheelchair accessible. Major credit cards.
*Higher rate effective weekends.

HOLYOKE
Super 8 Motel
$55*
1515 Northampton St. • 413.536.1980
52 Units, no pets. Continental breakfast. Pool. Rooms come with phones and cable TV. Major credit cards.
*Rates as high as $105/night.

HYANNIS
Budget Host Hyannis Motel
$45-59 (65-95)*
On Rte. 132 • 508.775.8910 or 800.322.3354
41 Units, no pets. Continental breakfast. Laundry facility. Rooms come with phones and cable TV. Some rooms have kitchenettes. Major credit cards.
*Higher rate effective Memorial Day through Labor Day.

LANESBOROUGH
The Weathervane Motel
$35-65 (35-110)*
475 S. Main Street • 413.443.3230
16 Units, pets OK ($5). Pool. Rooms come with phones, refrigerators and cable TV. AAA discount. Major credit cards.
*Higher rates effective weekends July through August and all of September and October.

LEOMINSTER
Motel 6
$46-50 (56)*
Commercial Street • 978.537.8161
115 Units, pets OK. Restaurant on premises. Pool. Laundry facility. Data ports. Rooms come with A/C, phones and cable TV. Wheelchair accessible. Credit cards: AE, CB, DC, DS, MC, V.
*Higher rate effective spring and summer weekends.

MARTHA'S VINYARD
Hostelling International
$19-22
Edgartown-West Tisbury Rd.
508.693.2665
From ferry terminal, left on Water St., right on State Rd., left on Old County Rd., left on Edgartown-West Tisbury Rd.
78 Beds, Hours: 7:30-10a & 5-10p
Facilities: Information, kitchen, parking, bike storage, wheelchair accessible. Closed November 7 through March. Reservations essential. Credit cards: MC, V.

NANTUCKET
Hostelling International
$19
508.228.5672
From ferry wharf, go up Main Street, left at Orange St., right at E. York St, left at Atlantic Ave. which becomes Surfside. Go another 2 miles. At beach, right onto Western Avenue.
49 Beds, Hours: 7:30-10a & 5-10p
Facilities: Kitchen, picnic area with barbecue, volleyball. Private rooms available. Closed October 17 through April 22. Reservations essential. Credit cards: MC, V.

ORANGE
Executive Inn
$45*
110 Daniel Shays Hwy. • 978.544.8864
27 Units, pets OK ($7 and $7 dep. req.). Continental breakfast. Rooms come with phones and cable TV. Some rooms have microwaves and refrigerators. AAA/Senior discount. Major credit cards.
*Rates as high as $75/night.

SOMERSET
Super 8 Motel
$50-55
537 Riverside Avenue • 508.678.7665
48 Units, no pets. Continental breakfast. Pool. Rooms come with A/C, phones and cable TV. Major credit cards.

SOUTH DEERFIELD
Red Roof Inn
$47*
I-91, Exit 24 • 413.665.7161
123 Units, pets OK. Pool. Laundry facility. Rooms come with A/C, phones and cable TV. Wheelchair accessible. Credit cards: AE, CB, DC, DS, MC, V.
*AAA discounted rate. Rates as high as $69/night.

SOUTH YARMOUTH
Beach 'N Towne Motel
$38-54 (63-70)*
1261 Main Street • 508.398.2311
21 Units, no pets. Playground. Rooms come with phones and cable TV. AAA discount. Credit cards: AE, DS, MC, V.
*Higher rates effective July and August.

Motel 6
$39-41*
1314 Rte. 28 • 508.394.4000
89 Units, pets OK. Restaurant on premises. Pool. Rooms come with A/C, phones and cable TV. Wheelchair accessible. Major credit cards.
*Off-season weekend rates $47-56 nightly. Higher rates from late June through Labor Day ($74/night).

Red Mill Motel
$38-55 (75)*
793 Main Street • 508.398.5583
18 Units, no pets. Continental breakfast. Pool. Picnic area. Rooms come with phones and cable TV. AAA discount. Credit cards: AE, DS, MC, V.
*Higher rates effective late-June through Labor Day.

SPRINGFIELD — *see also Chicopee and West Springfield*

Rodeway Inn
$50-60
1356 Boston Road • 413.783.2111
110 Units, no pets. Continental breakfast. Pool. Meeting rooms. Rooms come with phones and cable TV. Major credit cards.

UXBRIDGE
Quaker Inn & Conference Center
$55*
442 Quaker Hwy. • 508.278.2445
22 Units, pets OK ($10). Continental breakfast. Pool. Fitness facility. Rooms come with phones and cable TV. Senior discount. Credit cards: AE, MC, V.
*AAA discounted rate. Rates as high as $90/night.

WEST SPRINGFIELD
Rodeway Inn
$45-50
572 Riverdale Street • 413.788.9648
38 Units, no pets. Rooms come with phones and cable TV. Major credit cards.

WILLIAMSTOWN
Northside Motel
$49-70 (57-88)*
45 North Street (Rte. 7) • 413.458.8107
34 Units, no pets. Pool. Rooms come with phones and cable TV. Wheelchair accessible. Credit cards: AE, DS, MC, V.
*Higher rate effective May through October.

WRENTHAM
Arbor Inn Motor Lodge
$50*
900 Washington Street • 508.384.2122
40 Units, no pets. Rooms come with phones and cable TV. Wheelchair accessible. AAA discount available (10%). Major credit cards.
*Summer rates may be higher.

michigan

ADRIAN
Days Inn
$50*
1575 W. Maumee St. • 517.263.5741
80 Units, no pets. Continental breakfast. Pool. Game room. Rooms come with phones, A/C and cable TV. Wheelchair accessible. Senior discount. Major credit cards.
*AAA discounted rate.

ALBION
Knights Inn
$40-60
400 "R" Drive N. • 517.629.3966
30 Units, pets OK. Continental breakfast. Pool. Meeting rooms. Rooms come with phones and cable TV. Major credit cards.

ALMA
Days Inn
$45-59*
7996 N. Alger Rd. (US 27) • 989.463.6131
49 Units, no pets. Continental breakfast. Indoor pool. Sauna. Rooms come with phones and cable TV. Wheelchair accessible. AAA/Senior discount. Major credit cards.
*Rates as high as $89/night.

Triangle Motel
$35
1313 W. Lincoln Road • 989.463.2296
10 Units, pets OK. Rooms come with phones, A/C and cable TV. Senior discount. Wheelchair accessible. Major credit cards.

ALPENA
Alpena Motel
$29-35
3011 US 23 S. • 989.356.2178
19 Units, pets OK. Continental breakfast. Game room. Meeting room. Rooms come with A/C, phones and cable TV. Credit cards: MC, V.

Dew Drop Inn
$38-46
2469 French Road • 989.356.4414
14 Units, no pets. Rooms come with A/C, phones and cable TV. Some rooms have microwaves and refrigerators. AAA/Senior discount. Credit cards: AE, DS, MC, V.

ANN ARBOR
Motel 6
$40-46 (56)*
3764 S. State Street • I-94, Exit 177
734.665.9900
107 Units, pets OK. Pool. Data ports. Rooms come with phones, A/C and cable TV. Wheelchair accessible. Credit cards: AE, CB, DC, DS, MC, V.
*Higher rate effective summer weekends.

AUBURN HILLS
Motel 6
$44
1471 Opdyke Road • 248.373.8440
114 Units, pets OK. Pool. Data ports. Rooms come with phones, A/C and cable TV. Wheelchair accessible. Credit cards: AE, CB, DC, DS, MC, V.

BATTLE CREEK
Knights Inn
$37-50
2595 Capital Avenue S.W. • I-94, Exit 97
616.964.2600
95 Units, pets OK. Continental breakfast. Pool. Meeting rooms. Laundry facility. Rooms come with phones and cable TV. Some rooms have microwaves and refrigerators. Wheelchair accessible. AAA discount. Credit cards: AE, DC, DS, MC, V.

Motel 6
$30-42
4775 Beckley Road • 616.979.1141
77 Units, pets OK. Pool. Laundry facility. Data ports. Rooms come with phones, A/C and cable TV. Wheelchair accessible. Credit cards: AE, CB, DC, DS, MC, V.

Super 8 Motel
$40-50
5395 Beckley Road • 616.979.1828
62 Units, pets OK. Rooms come with phones and cable TV. Wheelchair accessible. Senior discount. Credit cards: AE, CB, DC, DS, MC, V.

BAY CITY
Euclid Motel
$36-40
809 N. Euclid Avenue • 989.684.9455
36 Units, no pets. Heated pool. Playground. Rooms come with phones and cable TV. Some rooms have refrigerators. AAA discount. Credit cards: AE, CB, DC, DS, MC, V.

BELLEVILLE
Red Roof Inn
$44-56*
45501 N. I-94 Expwy. Service Dr.
I-94, Exit 190 • 734.697.2244
112 Units, pets OK. Rooms come with phones and cable TV. Major credit cards.
*AAA discounted rates.

BENTON HARBOR
Motel 6
$30-50
2063 Pipestone Road • 616.925.5100
88 Units, pets OK. Pool. Laundry facility. Data ports. Rooms come with phones, A/C and cable TV. Wheelchair accessible. Credit cards: AE, CB, DC, DS, MC, V.

Red Roof Inn
$34-51*
1630 Mall Drive • 616.927.2484
108 Units, pets OK. Rooms come with phones and cable TV. Credit cards: AE, CB, DC, DS, MC, V.
*Summer rates as high as $76/night.

BOYNE CITY
Fieldcrest Inn
$30-50 (60)*
01165 M-75S • 231.582.7502
14 Units, no pets. Continental breakfast. Rooms come with phones and cable TV. Major credit cards.
*Higher rate effective summer weekends.

BOYNE FALLS
Brown Trout Motel
$50
2150 Nelson Avenue • 231.549.2791
15 Units, pets OK. Heated pool. Jacuzzi. Rooms come with phones and cable TV. Senior discount. Credit cards: MC, V.

BREVORT
Chapel Hill Motel
$44-59
4422 W. US 2 • 906.292.5534
26 Units, pets OK ($5). Heated pool. Playground. Rooms come with phones and cable TV. Some rooms have A/C and refrigerators. Credit cards: DS, MC, V.

BRIDGEPORT
Villager Lodge
$34-50
6361 Dixie Hwy. • 989.777.2582
111 Units, pets OK. Rooms come with phones, A/C and cable TV. Wheelchair accessible. AAA/Senior discount. Credit cards: AE, CB, DC, DS, MC, V.

BRIDGMAN
Bridgman Inn
$35-45
9999 Red Arrow Hwy. • 616.465.3187
33 Units, pets OK. Pool. Playground. Rooms come with phones and cable TV. Wheelchair accessible. Major credit cards.

BURTON
Super 8 Motel
$45-50
1343 S. Center Road • I-69, Exit 139
810.743.8850
69 Units, no pets. Restaurant on premises. Continental breakfast. Rooms come with phones and cable TV. Wheelchair accessible. Senior discount. Credit cards: AE, CB, DC, DS, MC, V.

CADILLAC
Super 8 Motel
$43-52 (60-66)*
211 W. M-55 • 231.775.8561
27 Units, no pets. Continental breakfast. Indoor heated pool and jacuzzi. Rooms come with phones and cable TV. Senior discount. Credit cards: AE, CB, DC, DS, MC, V.
*Higher rates effective July and August.

CANTON
Motel 6
$40-52
41216 Ford Road • 734.981.5000
107 Units, pets OK. Pool. Data ports. Rooms come with phones, A/C and cable TV. Wheelchair accessible. Credit cards: AE, CB, DC, DS, MC, V.

CASCADE
Exel Inn of Grand Rapids
$40-60
4855 28th Street S.E. • I-96, Exit 43A

616.957.3000
109 Units, pets OK. Continental breakfast. Laundry facility. Fitness facility. Rooms come with phones and cable TV. AAA/Senior discount. Major credit cards.

CHARLEVOIX
Courtside Motel
$50 (70)*
1580 US 31 • 616.547.0505
11 Units, no pets. Rooms come with A/C and cable TV. No phones in rooms. Credit cards: DS, MC, V.
*Higher rate effective weekends.

CHEBOYGAN
Birch Haus Motel
$30-45
1301 Mackinaw Avenue • 231.627.5862
13 Units, pets OK ($5). Continental breakfast. Rooms come with phones and cable TV. AAA/Senior discount. Credit cards: AE, DS, MC, V.

Pine River Motel
$30-50
102 Lafayette • 231.627.5119
15 Units, pets OK ($5). Rooms come with phones and cable TV. AAA/Senior discount. Credit cards: AE, DS, MC, V.

CLARE
Budget Inn
$38-40
1110 N. McEwan • 989.386.7201
34 Units, pets OK. Pool and jacuzzi in season. Rooms come with phones and cable TV. Senior discount. Credit cards: AE, CB, DC, DS, MC, V.

COLDWATER
Econo Lodge
$40-53
884 W. Chicago Road • 517.278.4501
46 Units, pets OK. Continental breakfast. Rooms come with phones and cable TV. Major credit cards.

Super 8 Motel
$45-55*
600 Orleans Blvd. • I-69, Exit 13
517.278.8833
58 Units, pets OK ($50 dep. req.). Continental breakfast. Laundry facility. Rooms come with phones and cable TV. Some rooms have microwaves and refrigerators. Major credit cards.
*AAA discounted rates.

COPPER HARBOR
Nordland Motel
$48-53*
906.289.4815
On US 41, 2 miles east of town.
9 Units, pets OK ($5). Pool. Meeting rooms. Laundry facility. Rooms come with refrigerators and cable TV. No phones or A/C in rooms. AAA discount. Some rooms have microwaves.
*Open mid-May through mid-October.

CRYSTAL FALLS
Cedar Inn Motel
$50-55*
600 S. Fifth Street • 906.875.6655
26 Units, no pets. Continental breakfast. Rooms come with phones and cable TV. Wheelchair accessible. Major credit cards.
*AAA discounted rates.

DEARBORN
Mercury Motor Inn
$48
22361 Michigan Avenue • 313.274.1900
40 Units, no pets. Meeting rooms. Laundry facility. Rooms come with phones and cable TV. Some rooms have microwaves, kitchens and refrigerators. AAA discount. Credit cards: AE, CB, DC, DS, MC, V.

DETROIT — *see also Auburn Hills, Belleville, Canton, Farmington Hills, Inkster, Madison Heights, Romulus (Airport), Roseville, Royal Oak, St. Clair Shores, Southfield, Sterling Heights, Warren and Woodhaven*
Traveler Advisory: If you are planning to spend the night in the heart of Detroit, you will need to plan on spending a little more than $45/night. You would be very fortunate to find accommodations in downtown Detroit for less than $50/night. The following are a few recommendations to suit your budget in-town:

Econo Lodge ($50-70)
17729 Telegraph Road
313.531.2550

Shorecrest Motor Inn ($69)
1316 E. Jefferson Avenue
313.568.3000

Metro Lodge
$49
10501 E. Jefferson • 313.822.3501
37 Units, no pets. Rooms come with phones

and cable TV. Senior discount. Wheelchair accessible. Major credit cards.

Suburban Motel
$40
16920 Telegraph • 313.535.9646
50 Units, pets OK. Pool. Meeting room. Rooms come with phones and cable TV. Some rooms have kitchenettes. Major credit cards.

EAST LANSING
Super 8 Motel
$43-50
2736 E. Grand River • 517.337.1621
75 Units, no pets. Jacuzzi. Meeting rooms. Rooms come with phones and cable TV. Senior discount. Major credit cards.

ERIE
Bedford Inn
$39-51
6444 Telegraph Road • I-75, Exit 210 (from Ohio side) • 734.847.6768
47 Units, no pets. Jacuzzi. Data ports. Rooms come with phones and cable TV. AAA/Senior discount. Credit cards: AE, DS, MC, V.

ESCANABA — *see also Gladstone*
Bay View Motel
$35-60
7110 Hwy. 2/41 & M-35 • 4.5 miles north of town • 906.786.2843
22 Units, pets OK ($8). Heated pool. Playground. Sauna. Rooms come with phones and cable TV. Some rooms have microwaves and refrigerators. Credit cards: AE, DS, MC, V.

Budget Host Inn & Resort
$42-44 (54)*
7146 "P" Rd (US 2/41) • 906.786.7554
71 Units, no pets. Restaurant on premises. Continental breakfast. Indoor heated pool. Movie rentals. Sauna. Game room. Laundry facility. Rooms come with phones and cable TV. Senior discount available (except in July and August). Major credit cards.
*Higher rate effective mid-June through August.

Hiawatha Motel
$34-38
2400 Ludington Street • 906.786.1341
27 Units, pets OK ($2). Rooms come with phones and cable TV. Some rooms have refrigerators and jacuzzis. AAA/Senior discount. Credit cards: AE, DS, MC, V.

FARMINGTON HILLS
Knights Inn
$40-50
37527 Grand River Ave. • 248.477.3200
110 Units, no pets. Continental breakfast. Pool. Laundry facility. Rooms come with phones and cable TV. Some rooms have microwaves, kitchenettes and refrigerators. Wheelchair accessible. Major credit cards.

Motel 6
$40-45
38300 Grand River Ave. • 248.471.0590
106 Units, pets OK. Data ports. Rooms come with phones, A/C and cable TV. Wheelchair accessible. Credit cards: AE, CB, DC, DS, MC, V.

FLINT — *see also Burton*
Motel 6
$36-50
2324 Austin Parkway • 810.767.7100
108 Units, pets OK. Pool. Laundry facility. Data ports. Rooms come with phones, A/C and cable TV. Wheelchair accessible. Credit cards: AE, CB, DC, DS, MC, V.

Red Roof Inn
$39-60
G-3219 Miller Road • I-75, Exit 117B
810.733.1660
107 Units, pets OK. Laundry facility. Rooms come with phones and cable TV. AAA discount. Major credit cards.

Super 8 Motel
$45-50
4184 W. Pierson Road • I-75, Exit 122
810.789.0400
67 Units, no pets. Continental breakfast. Laundry facility. Rooms come with phones and cable TV. Wheelchair accessible. Senior discount. Major credit cards.

FRANKENMUTH — *see Bridgeport*

GLADSTONE
Norway Pines Motel
$48
7111 US 2, 41 & SR 35 • 906.786.5119
11 Units, pets OK ($5). Rooms come with phones and cable TV. Some rooms have refrigerators. AAA discount. Credit cards: AE, DC, DS, MC, V.

GRAND RAPIDS — *see also Cascade, Comstock Park, Walker and Wyoming*
Knights Inn
$35-60
35 28th Street S.W. • 616.452.5141
104 Units, no pets. Restaurant on premises. Pool. Meeting rooms. Rooms come with phones and cable TV. Wheelchair accessible. AAA/Senior discount. Major credit cards.

Motel 6
$37-38
3524 28th Street S.E. • 616.957.3511
118 Units, pets OK. Pool. Data ports. Rooms come with phones, A/C and cable TV. Wheelchair accessible. Credit cards: AE, CB, DC, DS, MC, V.

GRAYLING
Fay's Motel
$38-42
78 N. I-75 Bus. Loop • 989.348.7031
17 Units, no pets. Rooms come with A/C, phones, refrigerators and cable TV. Some rooms have kitchenettes and jacuzzis. Senior discount. Major credit cards.

River Country Motor Lodge
$40
I-75 Business Loop • 989.348.8619 or 800.733.7396
16 Units, pets OK. Cookies and coffee offered in the morning. Playground. Picnic area. Rooms come with phones, refrigerators, microwaves, A/C and cable TV. Major credit cards.

HANCOCK
Best Western Crown Motel
$52
235 Hancock Avenue • 906.482.6111
47 Units, pets OK. Continental breakfast. Pool. Spa. Sauna. Rooms come with phones and cable TV. Senior discount. Major credit cards.

HOLLAND
Budget Host Wooden Shoe Motel
$25-35 (48-53)*
465 US 31 & 16th St. • 616.392.8521
29 Units, no pets. Continental breakfast. Heated pool. Game room. Tanning salon. Rooms come with phones and cable TV. Senior discount. Major credit cards.
*Higher rates May thru September.

HOUGHTON — *see also Hancock*
Vacationland Motel
$35-40*
On US 41 (2 miles south of town)
906.482.5351 or 800.822.3279
24 Units, no pets. Restaurant on premises. Continental breakfast. Pool. Laundry facility. Rooms come with A/C, phones and cable TV. AAA/Senior discount. Major credit cards.
*Summer rates as high as $58/night.

HOUGHTON LAKE
Mazur's Skytop Resort
$46
5620 W. Houghton Lake Drive
989.366.9107
19 Units, no pets. Lakefront beach, heated pool, playground, horseshoes, basketball and volleyball courts. Rooms come with phones and cable TV. Some rooms have microwaves, refrigerators and A/C. Credit cards: AE, DS, MC, V.

INDIAN RIVER
Nor Gate Motel
$32-36
4846 S. Straits Hwy. • 231.238.7788
14 Units, no pets. Picnic area. Playground. Rooms come with cable TV. Some rooms have microwaves, refrigerators and phones. AAA discount. Credit cards: DS, MC, V.

Star Gate Motel
$36-46
4646 S. Straits Hwy. • 231.238.7371
15 Units, pets OK. Playground. Rooms come with phones and cable TV. Some rooms have kitchens and refrigerators. AAA discount. Credit cards: DC, DS, MC, V.

INKSTER
Esquire Motel
$40
25911 Michigan Avenue • 313.277.0760
50 Units, no pets. Pool. Rooms come with phones and cable TV. Some rooms have kitchenettes. Major credit cards.

IONIA
Super 8 Motel
$45-55
7254 S. State Road • 616.527.2828
73 Units, pets OK. Continental breakfast. Rooms come with phones and cable TV. Some rooms have microwaves and

refrigerators. Wheelchair accessible. AAA discount. Major credit cards.

IRON MOUNTAIN
Budget Host Inn
$35-39
1663 N. Stephenson Ave. • 906.774.6797
21 Units, pets OK. Continental breakfast. Heated pool. Laundry facility. Airport transportation. Rooms come with phones and cable TV. Some rooms have refrigerators. AAA/Senior discount. Credit cards: AE, DS, MC, V.

Timbers Motor Lodge
$40
200 S. Stephenson • 906.774.7600 or 800.433.8533
53 Units, no pets. Continental breakfast. Pool. Sauna. Hot tub. Game room. Meeting room. Rooms come with phones, A/C and cable TV. Wheelchair accessible. Senior discount. Major credit cards.

IRONWOOD
Budget Host Cloverland Motel
$30-40
447 W. Cloverland Dr. • 906.932.1260
16 Units, no pets. Laundry facility. Airport transportation. Picnic table. Rooms come with phones and cable TV. Some rooms have refrigerators. AAA/Senior discount. Credit cards: AE, CB, DC, DS, MC, V.

Crestview Cozy Inn
$40-60
424 Cloverland Drive • 906.932.4845
12 Units, pets OK ($3). Sauna. Rooms come with refrigerators, phones and cable TV. Some rooms have microwaves. AAA/Senior discount. Credit cards: AE, DS, MC, V.

ISHPEMING
Triangle Motel
$32-36
105 N. Rose St. (US 41W) • 906.485.5537
29 Units, pets OK. Continental breakfast. Picnic area. Rooms come with phones, refrigerators, A/C and cable TV. Major credit cards.

JACKSON
Motel 6
$40-50
830 Royal Drive • 517.789.7186
96 Units, pets OK. Pool. Laundry facility. Data ports. Rooms come with phones, A/C and cable TV. Wheelchair accessible. Credit cards: AE, CB, DC, DS, MC, V.

Super 8 Motel
$48-50*
2001 Shirley Drive, I-94, Exit 138
517.788.8780
54 Units, pets OK. Continental breakfast. Rooms come with phones and cable TV. Major credit cards.
*Rates as high as $60/night.

KALAMAZOO
Knights Inn
$36-41
1211 S. Westhedge Ave • 616.381.5000
55 Units, pets OK ($25 dep. req.). Laundry facility. Meeting rooms. Airport transportation. Rooms come with phones and cable TV. Some rooms have microwaves and refrigerators. Wheelchair accessible. AAA/Senior discount. Major credit cards.

Motel 6
$36-48
3704 Van Rick Road • 616.344.9255
104 Units, pets OK. Pool. Laundry facility. Data ports. Rooms come with phones, A/C and cable TV. Wheelchair accessible. Credit cards: AE, CB, DC, DS, MC, V.

Red Roof Inn—West
$46-51
5425 W. Michigan Ave. • 616.375.7400
108 Units, pets OK. Rooms come with phones and cable TV. AAA discount. Credit cards: AE, CB, DC, DS, MC, V.

LANSING — *see also East Lansing*
Motel 6—West
$40-48
7326 W. Saginaw Hwy. • 517.321.1444
109 Units, pets OK. Pool. Laundry facility. Rooms come with phones, A/C and cable TV. Wheelchair accessible. Credit cards: AE, CB, DC, DS, MC, V.

Regent Inn
$35-40
6501 S. Cedar Street • 517.393.2030
99 Units, pets OK. Laundry facility. Rooms come with phones and cable TV. Major credit cards.

Super 8 Motel
$48*
910 American Road • 517.393.8008
42 Units, no pets. Rooms come with phones and cable TV. Wheelchair accessible. Senior discount. Credit cards: AE, CB, DC, DS, MC, V.
*Rates may increase slightly during weekends, holidays and special events.

LUDINGTON
Greiner Motel
$30-55
4616 W. US 10 • 231.843.3927
22 Units, no pets. Continental breakfast. Picnic area. Rooms come with phones and cable TV. Wheelchair accessible. Credit cards: DS, MC, V.

Stearns Motor Inn
$45 (75)*
212 E. Ludington Avenue • 231.843.3407 or 800.365.1904
35 Units, no pets. Rooms come with phones and cable TV. Major credit cards.
*Higher rates effective during summer months.

MACKINAW CITY
Chief Motel
$32-59 (49-99)*
231.436.7981 or 800.968.1511
On US 23, one mile south of town.
15 Units, no pets. Heated pool. Picnic area available. Rooms come with A/C, phones and cable TV. Credit cards: MC, V.
*Closed late October through April. Higher rates late June through mid-August.

Val-Ru Motel
$30-60*
223 W. Central Avenue • 231.436.7691
25 Units, pets OK. Heated pool. Playground. Rooms come with cable TV. No phones in rooms. Credit cards: AE, CB, DC, DS, MC, V.
*Closed late October through March.

Vin-Del Motel
$35-60
223 W. Central Avenue • 231.436.5273
16 Units, pets OK ($10). Heated pool. Rooms come with phones and cable TV. Senior discount. Credit cards: AE, DS, MC, V.

MADISON HEIGHTS
Knights Inn
$39-45
26091 Dequindre Road, I-696, Exit 20
248.545.9930
125 Units, pets OK. Continental breakfast. Pool. Laundry facility. Meeting rooms. Rooms come with phones, A/C and cable TV. Wheelchair accessible. AAA/Senior discount. Credit cards: AE, CB, DC, DS, MC, V.

Motel 6
$40-45
32700 Barrington Road • 248.583.0500
100 Units, pets OK. Data ports. Rooms come with phones, A/C and cable TV. Wheelchair accessible. Credit cards: AE, CB, DC, DS, MC, V.

Red Roof Inn
$45-57
32511 Concord Drive • 248.583.4700
109 Units, pets OK. Rooms come with phones and cable TV. AAA discount. Credit cards: AE, CB, DC, DS, MC, V.

MANISTEE
Moonlite Motel & Marina
$40-55
111 US 31 • 231.723.3587
25 Units, no pets. Playground. Beach. Rooms come with phones and cable TV. Some rooms have kitchens. Credit cards: AE, DS, MC, V.

MANISTIQUE
Budget Host Manistique Motor Inn
$48-55
US 2E (3 miles east of town)
906.341.2552
26 Units, no pets. Airport transportation. Heated pool (in season). Picnic area. Laundry facility. Rooms come with phones and cable TV. Senior discount. Credit cards: AE, CB, DC, DS, MC, V.

Holiday Motel
$38-52
906.341.2710 • On US 2, 4.5 miles east from town, opposite Schoolcraft County Airport.
20 Units, pets OK ($5). Continental breakfast. Heated pool. Playground. Rooms come with phones and cable TV. No A/C in rooms. Credit cards: AE, DS, MC, V.

MARQUETTE
Birchmont Motel
$38-52
2090 US 41S • 906.228.7538
35 Units, pets OK ($6). Continental breakfast. Heated pool. Rooms come with refrigerators, phones and cable TV. No A/C in rooms. Some rooms have microwaves. AAA discount. Credit cards: AE, DS, MC, V.

Budget Host Inn
$38-46
2603 US 41W. • 906.228.7494
41 Units, no pets. Continental breakfast. Laundry facility. Rooms come with phones and cable TV. Some rooms have refrigerators. AAA discount. Credit cards: AE, DS, MC, V.

Imperial Motel
$45-50
2493 US 41W. • 906.228.7430
43 Units, no pets. Heated indoor pool. Sauna. Rooms come with phones and cable TV. Some rooms have refrigerators. AAA/Senior discount. Credit cards: AE, CB, DC, DS, MC, V.

MENOMINEE
Howard Johnson Express
$40-50*
2516 10th Street • 906.863.4431
50 Units, pets OK. Continental breakfast. Jacuzzi. Meeting room. Rooms come with refrigerators, microwaves, phones and cable TV. AAA/Senior discount. Major credit cards.
*Rates increase substantially during special events.

MICHIGAMME
Philomena on the Lake Resort
$50*
906.323.6318 • Just south of US 41 & SR 28 on Brook St.
12 Units, no pets. Boat dock. Playground. Rooms come with cable TV. No phones or A/C in rooms. Some rooms have refrigerators. Credit cards: MC, V.
*Closed mid-October through early May.

MONROE
Cross Country Inn
$41-48
1900 Welcome Way • 734.289.2330
120 Units, no pets. Heated pool. Rooms come with phones and cable TV. AAA/Senior discount. Credit cards: AE, DC, DS, MC, V.

Hometown Inn
$46
1885 Welcome Way • 734.289.1080
89 Units, pets OK. Meeting rooms. Laundry facility. Rooms come with phones and cable TV. Some rooms have microwaves, kitchens, jacuzzis and refrigerators. AAA discount. Credit cards: AE, DC, DS, MC, V.

MOUNT PLEASANT
Chippewa Inn
$48 (60)*
5662 E. Pickard Avenue • 989.772.1751
29 Units, no pets. Rooms come with phones and cable TV. Credit cards: AE, DC, DS, MC, V.
*Higher rate effective weekends.

MUNISING
Terrace Motel
$36-48
420 Prospect • 906.387.2735
18 Units, pets OK. Recreation room. Sauna. Rooms come with cable TV. No A/C or phones in rooms. Some rooms have refrigerators. Credit cards: AE, MC, V.

MUSKEGON
Seaway Motel
$35-45*
631 W. Norton Avenue • 231.733.1220
29 Units, pets OK ($50 dep. req.). Pool. Rooms come with phones and cable TV. Some rooms have microwaves and refrigerators. Credit cards: AE, DC, DS, MC, V.
*Summer rates higher.

NEGAUNEE
Quartz Mountain Inn Motel
$40
791 US 41E • 906.475.7165 or 800.330.5807
26 Units, pets OK. Continental breakfast. Rooms come with phones, A/C and cable TV. Some rooms have kitchenettes. Wheelchair accessible. Major credit cards.

NEWBERRY
Park-A-Way Motel
$49*
On M123 (half mile south of town)
906.293.5771 or 800.292.5771
26 Units, pets OK. Continental breakfast. Indoor heated pool. Rooms come with A/C, phones and cable TV. Wheelchair accessible. Major credit cards.
*Summer rates higher.

NEW BUFFALO
Grand Beach Motel
$35-55*
19189 US 12 • 616.469.1555
14 Units, pets OK. Heated pool. Rooms come with cable TV. No phones in rooms. Some rooms have refrigerators. AAA discount. Credit cards: DS, MC, V.
*Closed mid-October through April.

ONTONAGON
Scott's Superior Inn & Cabins
$45
277 Lakeshore Road • 906.884.4866
14 Units, pets OK ($5). Beach. Sauna. Jacuzzi. Playground. Rooms come with phones and cable TV. Some rooms have A/C, kitchens and refrigerators. AAA discount. Credit cards: AE, DC, DS, MC, V.

PORT HURON — *see also Marysville*
Knights Inn
$40*
2160 Water Street • 810.982.1022
104 Units, no pets. Pool. Meeting room. Rooms come with phones and cable TV. Wheelchair accessible. Major credit cards.
*Rates as high as $70/night.

PRUDENVILLE
Shea's Lake Front Lodge
$39-55
517.366.5910 • I-75, Exit 227, 8 miles west on SR 55
39 Units, no pets. Beach. Boat dock. Playground. Rooms come with cable TV. No phones or A/C in rooms. Some rooms have microwaves and refrigerators. AAA discount. Credit cards: AE, DC, DS, MC, V.

QUINNESEC
Hillcrest Motel
$30-35*
On US 2 • 906.774.6866
15 Units, pets OK. Continental breakfast. Rooms come with phones, A/C and cable TV. Some rooms have kitchenettes. Wheelchair accessible. Senior discount. Major credit cards.
*Closed in winter.

ROMULUS
Motel 6
$48
9095 Wickham • I-94, Exit 198
734.595.7400
78 Units, pets OK. Laundry facility. Airport transportation. Data ports. Rooms come with phones, A/C and cable TV. Credit cards: AE, CB, DC, DS, MC, V.

ROSEVILLE
Red Roof Inn
$40-55
31800 Little Mack Road • 586.296.0316
109 Units, pets OK. Rooms come with phones and cable TV. AAA discount. Major credit cards.

ROYAL OAK
Sagamore Motor Lodge
$35-45
3220 N. Woodward Ave • 248.549.1600
79 Units, no pets. Continental breakfast. Rooms come with phones and cable TV. Some rooms have microwaves and refrigerators. AAA/Senior discount. Credit cards: AE, CB, DC, DS, MC, V.

SAGINAW
Econo Lodge
$40-50
2225 Tittabawasee Rd. • 989.791.1411
101 Units, pets OK. Continental breakfast. Laundry facility. Rooms come with phones and cable TV. AAA discount. Major credit cards.

Knights Inn—South
$35-45
1415 S. Outer Drive • I-75, Exit 149B
989.754.9200
108 Units, pets OK. Pool. Rooms come with phones and cable TV. Wheelchair accessible. AAA/Senior discount. Major credit cards.

ST. CLAIRE SHORES
Shore Pointe Motor Lodge
$45
20000 E. Nine Mile Rd. • 586.773.3700
56 Units, no pets. Rooms come with phones and cable TV. Credit cards: AE, DS, MC, V.

ST. IGNACE
Four Star Motel
$34-42*
1064 US 2W • 906.643.9360
20 Units, no pets. Playground. Rooms come with cable TV. No phones or A/C in rooms. AAA discount. Credit cards: MC, V.
*Closed early October through mid-May.

K-Royale Motor Inn
$42-58*
1037 N. State Street • 906.643.7737
95 Units, no pets. Continental breakfast. Playground. Jacuzzi. Laundry facility. Rooms come with phones, refrigerators and cable TV. AAA discount. Credit cards: DS, MC, V.
*Closed November through mid-April.

ST. JOSEPH
Econo Lodge
$35-50*
2723 Niles Avenue • 616.983.6321
36 Units, no pets. Continental breakfast. Heated pool. Laundry facility. Rooms come with phones and cable TV. Some rooms have microwaves, jacuzzis and refrigerators. Credit cards: AE, CB, DC, DS, MC, V.
*Rates as high as $70/night.

SAULT STE. MARIE
Mid-City Motel
$36-54
204 E. Portage Avenue • 906.632.6832
26 Units, pets OK. Rooms come with phones and cable TV. AAA/Senior discount. Credit cards: AE, DC, DS, MC, V.

Royal Motel
$38-42*
1707 Ashmun Street • 906.632.6323
22 Units, pets OK. Rooms come with phones and cable TV. Senior discount. Credit cards: DS, MC, V.
*Closed mid-October through late May.

SOUTHFIELD
Marvin's Garden Inn
$50
27650 Northwestern Hwy. • 248.353.6777
110 Units, no pets. Continental breakfast. Game room. Laundry facility. Rooms come with phones, microwaves, refrigerators and cable TV. AAA discount. Major credit cards.

SOUTHGATE
Cross Country Inn
$47-54
18777 Northline Road • 734.287.8340
136 Units, no pets. Heated pool. Meeting rooms. Rooms come with phones and cable TV. AAA/Senior discount. Credit cards: AE, CB, DC, DS, MC, V.

STERLING HEIGHTS
Knights Inn
$45-55
7887 17 Mile Road • 810.268.0600
103 Units, pets OK. Continental breakfast. Laundry facility. Meeting rooms. Rooms come with phones and cable TV. Some rooms have microwaves, jacuzzis and refrigerators. Wheelchair accessible. AAA/Senior discount. Major credit cards.

STURGIS
Knights Inn
$30-52
70045 S. Centerville Rd. • 616.651.8505
64 Units, no pets. Heated pool. Meeting rooms. Rooms come with phones and cable TV. Some rooms have refrigerators. AAA discount. Credit cards: AE, DC, DS, MC, V.

TAWAS CITY/EAST TAWAS
Crow's Nest Motel
$38-50
1028 W. Lake Street • 989.362.4455
24 Units, no pets. Heated pool. Playground. Rooms come with A/C, refrigerators, phones and cable TV. Major credit cards.

Dale Motel
$35-55 (49-69)*
1086 US 23S • 989.362.6153
16 Units, no pets. Rooms come with phones and cable TV. Some rooms have refrigerators. Credit cards: AE, CB, DC, DS, MC, V.
*Higher rates May through October.

TRAVERSE CITY
Traveler's Advisory: Please note that accommodations are hard to come by at $50 or less during the summertime in communities along Grand Traverse Bay and Little Traverse Bay (Traverse City, Charlevoix, Petoskey and Harbor Springs).

Motel 6
$34-44 (70-80)*
1582 US 31N • 231.938.3002
43 Units, pets OK. Indoor pool. Laundry facility. Rooms come with phones, A/C and cable TV. Wheelchair accessible. Credit cards: AE, CB, DC, DS, MC, V.
*Higher rates effective during summer months.

Waterland Motel
$35 (60-80)*
834 E. Front Street • 231.947.8349
20 Units, no pets. Casino passbooks available. Rooms come with phones and cable TV. Some rooms have microwaves and refrigerators. Major credit cards.
*Higher rates effective during summer months.

WALKER
Motel 6
$38-46
777 Three Mile Road • 616.784.9375
102 Units, pets OK. Pool. Laundry facility. Data ports. Rooms come with phones, A/C and cable TV. Wheelchair accessible. Credit cards: AE, CB, DC, DS, MC, V.

WARREN
Knights Inn
$29-45
7500 Miller Road • 586.978.7500
116 Units, pets OK. Meeting rooms. Rooms come with phones and cable TV. Wheelchair accessible. AAA/Senior discount. Major credit cards.

Motel 6
$38-50
8300 Chicago Road • 586.826.9300
117 Units, pets OK. Airport transportation. Data ports. Rooms come with phones, A/C and cable TV. Wheelchair accessible. Credit cards: AE, CB, DC, DS, MC, V.

Red Roof Inn
$47-51
26300 Dequindre Road • 586.573.4300
136 Units, pets OK. Rooms come with phones and cable TV. Credit cards: AE, CB, DC, DS, MC, V.

WEST BRANCH
La Hacienda Motel
$36-58
969 W. Houghton Ave. • 586.345.2345
13 Units, pets OK. Rooms come with phones and cable TV. Some rooms have refrigerators. AAA/Senior discount. Credit cards: AE, DS, MC, V.

WHITEHALL
Lake Land Motel
$33-50 (65-70)*
1002 E. Colby Street • 231.894.5644
12 Units, pets OK ($5). Rooms come with phones and cable TV. Credit cards: AE, DS, MC, V.
*AAA discounted rates. Higher rates effective weekends Memorial Day through Labor Day.

WOODHAVEN
Knights Inn—Detroit South
$35-50
21880 West Road • 734.676.8550
100 Units, pets OK. Pool. Meeting rooms. Game room. Laundry facility. Rooms come with phones and cable TV. Some rooms have microwaves, kitchens, refrigerators and jacuzzis. AAA/Senior discount. Credit cards: AE, CB, DC, DS, MC, V.

WYOMING
Super 8 Motel
$48
727 44th Street S.W. • Hwy. 131, Exit 79
616.530.8588
62 Units, pets OK. Rooms come with phones and cable TV. Senior discount. Major credit cards.

minnesota

AITKIN
Ripple River Motel
$45-55
701 Minnesota Avenue • 218.927.3734
30 Units, pets OK ($5). Rooms come with phones, A/C and cable TV. Some rooms have microwaves and refrigerators. Credit cards: DS, MC, V.

ALBERT LEA
Bel Aire Motor Inn
$35-45
700 Hwy. 69S • 507.373.3983 or 800.373.4073
46 Units, pets OK ($3-5). Laundry facility. Rooms come with phones, A/C and cable TV. Some rooms have microwaves and refrigerators. AAA/Senior discount. Major credit cards.

Super 8 Motel
$40-49*
2019 E. Main Street • 507.377.0591
60 Units, pets OK ($10). Continental breakfast. Meeting room. Rooms come with phones and cable TV. Wheelchair accessible. Senior discount. Credit cards: AE, CB, DC, DS, MC, V.
*Rates as high as $58/night.

AUSTIN
Country Side Inn
$39-50
3303 Oakland Avenue W. • I-90, Exit 175
507.437.7774
53 Units, pets OK ($5). Continental breakfast. Jacuzzi. Meeting rooms. Rooms come with refrigerators, phones and cable TV. AAA/Senior discount. Major credit cards.

Super 8 Motel
$43-53*
1401 14th Street N.W. (I-90, Exit 177)
507.433.1801
34 Units, pets OK ($10 dep. req.). Pastries offered Monday through Friday. Rooms come with phones and cable TV. Wheelchair accessible. Senior discount. Credit cards: AE, CB, DC, DS, MC, V.
*Rates as high as $65/night.

BAUDETTE
Walleye Inn Motel
$32-42
On Hwy. 11W • 218.634.1550 or 800.634.8944
39 Units, no pets. Continental breakfast. Rooms come with phones and cable TV. Wheelchair accessible. Major credit cards.

BAXTER — *see Brainerd*

BECKER
Super 8 Motel
$45-55
13804 1st Street • 763.261.4440
32 Units, pets OK with deposit. Continental breakfast. Jacuzzi and sauna. Rooms come with phones and cable TV. Wheelchair accessible. Senior discount. Major credit cards.

BEMIDJI
Best Western
$35-55
2420 Paul Bunyan Drive • 218.751.0390
60 Units, pets OK. Indoor pool. Jacuzzi. Sauna. Laundry facility. Rooms come with phones and cable TV. Major credit cards.

Edgewater Motel
$34-50
1015 Paul Bunyan Drive N.E.
218.751.3600 or 800.776.3343
71 Units, pets OK ($50 dep. req.). Beach, boat dock and ramp. Sauna, jacuzzi and playground. Laundry facility. Rooms come with phones and cable TV. Some rooms have refrigerators and microwaves. AAA discount. Major credit cards.

BRAINERD
Downtown Motel
$45-50
507 S. 6th Street • 218.829.4789
12 Units, pets OK. Rooms come with A/C, kitchens, microwaves, phones and cable TV. Credit cards: AE, DS, MC, V.

BRECKENRIDGE
Select Inn
$39-52

821 Hwy 75 N • 218.643.9201
27 Units, pets OK. Continental breakfast. Indoor pool. Jacuzzi. Laundry facility. Meeting rooms. Rooms come with phones and cable TV. Wheelchair accessible. Senior discount. Major credit cards.

BUFFALO
Super 8 Motel
$50
303 10th Avenue S. • 763.682.5930
32 Units, pets OK. Indoor pool. Jacuzzi. Rooms come with A/C, phones and cable TV. Senior discount. Major credit cards.

BURNSVILLE
Red Roof Inn
$34-59
12920 Aldrich Ave. S. • 952.890.1420
84 Units, pets OK. Rooms come with phones and cable TV. Credit cards: AE, CB, DC, DS, MC, V.

CAMBRIDGE
Imperial Motel
$32-50
643 N. Main • 612.689.2200
39 Units, no pets. Continental breakfast. Indoor heated pool, hot tub and sauna. Laundry facility. Airport transportation. Rooms come with phones and cable TV. Senior discount. Major credit cards.

CHISAGO CITY
Super 8 Motel
$44-46
11650 Lake Blvd. • 651.257.8088
24 Units, pets OK ($6). Laundry facility. Rooms come with phones and cable TV. Microwaves and refrigerators available. Senior discount. Credit cards: AE, CB, DC, DS, MC, V.

CLOQUET
Golden Gate Motel
$35-55
3202 River Gate Ave. • 218.879.6752
25 Units, pets OK. Rooms come with phones, A/C and cable TV. Some rooms have microwaves and refrigerators. Credit cards: AE, DS, MC, V.

CROOKSTON
Country Club Motel
$30
W. 6th & University Ave • 218.281.1607
20 Units, pets OK. Picnic area and playground. Rooms come with A/C, phones and cable TV. Senior discount. Major credit cards.

Golf Terrace Motel
$30
Jct. Hwys. 2 & 75 N. • 218.281.2626
17 Units, no pets. Laundry facility. Rooms come with phones and cable TV. Senior discount. Credit cards: AE, DC, DS, MC, V.

CROSBY
Lakeview Motel/Resort
$35-42*
426 Lakeshore Drive • 218.546.5924
12 Units, no pets. Boat dock. Rooms come with phones and cable TV. Some rooms have microwaves and refrigerators. Credit cards: DS, MC, V.
*Rates as high as $84/night.

CRYSTAL
Super 8 Motel
$46
6000 Lakeland Ave. N. • 763.537.8888
36 Units, no pets. Continental breakfast. Laundry facility. Rooms come with phones and cable TV. Major credit cards.

DETROIT LAKES
Budget Host Inn
$38-46*
895 Hwy 10E • 218.847.4454
24 Units, pets OK. Rooms come with phones and cable TV. Some rooms have microwaves and refrigerators. AAA/Senior discount. Credit cards: AE, DS, MC, V.
*Summer rates as high as $75/night, depending on availability.

Castaway Inn & Resort
$39
Hwy. 10E • 218.847.4449 or 800.640.3395
24 Units, pets OK. Playground. Laundry facility. Rooms come with phones and cable TV. Some rooms have microwaves. Senior discount. Major credit cards.

Super 8 Motel
$43-53*
400 Morrow Avenue • 218.847.1651
39 Units, pets OK. Rooms come with phones and cable TV. Wheelchair accessible. Senior discount. Credit cards: AE, CB, DC, DS, MC, V.
*Rates may increase slightly on weekends.

DULUTH — *see also Superior (WI)*
Allyndale Motel
$48
510 N. 66th Avenue W. • 218.628.1061 or 800.341.8000
21 Units, pets OK. Picnic area. Rooms come with A/C, phones and cable TV. Senior discount. Major credit cards.

Motel 6
$34-46 (56)*
200 S. 27th Avenue W. • 218.723.1123
100 Units, pets OK. Laundry facility. Data ports. Rooms come with phones, A/C and cable TV. Wheelchair accessible. Credit cards: AE, CB, DC, DS, MC, V.
*Higher rate effective summer weekends.

Willard Munger Inn
$29-49
7408 Grand Avenue • 218.624.4814 or 800.982.2453
23 Units, no pets. Continental breakfast. Rooms come with phones and cable TV. Senior discount. Major credit cards.

EAGAN
Budget Host Inn
$40-45
2745 Hwy 55 • 651.454.1211
17 Units, no pets. Picnic area. Laundry facility. Rooms come with phones and cable TV. Microwaves and refrigerators available. Senior discount available (5%). Credit cards: AE, CB, DC, DS, MC, V.

EAST GRAND FORKS — *see also Grand Forks (ND)*
East Gate Motel
$33
Hwy 2 E. • 218.773.9822
60 Units, pets OK. Rooms come with phones, A/C and cable TV. Major credit cards.

ELY
Budget Host Inn
$45-55
1047 E. Sheridan Street • 218.365.3237
17 Units, pets OK. Free coffee and muffins in a.m. Playground. Rooms come with phones and cable TV. Senior discount. Credit cards: DS, MC, V.

West Gate Motel
$45-50
110 N. 2nd Avenue W. • 218.365.4513 or 800.806.4979
16 Units, pets OK. Continental breakfast. Rooms come with phones and cable TV. Major credit cards.

FAIRMONT
Budget Inn
$30
1122 N. State Street • 507.235.3373
40 Units, pets OK. Indoor heated pool, sauna, hot tub, game room. Fax service. Rooms come with A/C, phones and cable TV. Senior discount. Credit cards: MC, V.

FARIBAULT
Budget Inn
$39
841 Faribault Road • 507.334.1841
52 Units, pets OK. Continental breakfast. Rooms come with A/C, phones and cable TV. AAA/Senior discount. Major credit cards.

Select Inn
$40-53
4040 Hwy. 60W • 507.334.2051
67 Units, pets OK ($25 dep. req.). Continental breakfast. Heated pool. Meeting rooms. Rooms come with phones and cable TV. AAA/Senior discount. Credit cards: AE, DC, DS, MC, V.

Super 8 Motel
$45-52*
2509 N. Lyndale Ave. • 507.334.1634
34 Units, no pets. Game room. Rooms come with phones and cable TV. Wheelchair accessible. Senior discount. Credit cards: AE, CB, DC, DS, MC, V.
*Rates may increase slightly on weekends.

FARMINGTON
Rest Well Motel
$37-45
20991 Chippendale Ave. W.
651.463.7101 or 800.241.WELL
24 Units, no pets. Outdoor pool. Laundry facility. Rooms come with A/C, phones and cable TV. Major credit cards.

FERGUS FALLS
Days Inn
$46-55
610 Western Avenue • 218.739.3311
57 Units, no pets. Continental breakfast. Heated pool. Rooms come with phones and cable TV. AAA/Senior discount. Major credit cards.

Super 8 Motel
$43-52
2454 College Way • 218.739.3261
32 Units, pets OK with permission. Continental breakfast. Copy and fax service. Rooms come with phones and cable TV. Wheelchair accessible. Senior discount. Credit cards: AE, CB, DC, DS, MC, V.

FOSSTON
Super 8 Motel
$44-49*
Hwy 2 E. • 218.435.1088
29 Units, pets OK ($10). Continental breakfast. Copy and fax service. Rooms come with phones and cable TV. Wheelchair accessible. AAA/Senior discount. Major credit cards.
*Rates may increase slightly on weekends.

GLENCOE
Super 8 Motel
$46
717 Morningside Drive • 320.864.6191
33 Units, pets OK ($5). Rooms come with phones and cable TV. Meeting rooms. Some rooms have microwaves and refrigerators. AAA/Senior discount. Major credit cards.

GLENWOOD
Scot Wood Motel
$46
Hwy. 28 & 55 • 320.634.5105
55 Units, pets OK. Continental breakfast. Indoor pool. Jacuzzi. Game room. Rooms come with phones and cable TV. Senior discount. Wheelchair accessible. Major credit cards.

GRAND MARAIS
Gunflint Motel
$39-50*
One block north of Hwy. 61 on Gunflint Trail • 218.387.1454
5 Units, pets OK. Rooms come with phones and cable TV. Kitchenettes available. Senior discount. Credit cards: DS, MC, V.
*Rates as high as $79/night.

Wedgewood Motel
$32-35*
218.387.2944 • On SR 61, 2.5 miles northeast of town.
10 Units, pets OK (dogs only). No A/C or phones. AAA discount. Credit cards: DS, MC, V.
*Closed November through April.

GRAND RAPIDS
Itascan Motel
$42
610 S. Pokegama Avenue • 218.326.3489 or 800.842.7733
27 Units, pets OK. Rooms come with kitchenettes, phones and cable TV. Senior discount. Major credit cards.

Pine Grove Motel
$39
1420 4th Street N.W. • 218.326.9674
20 Units, pets OK. Rooms come with A/C, phones and cable TV. Senior discount. Major credit cards.

GRANITE FALLS
Super 8 Motel
$50
845 W. SR 212 • 320.564.4075
63 Units, pets OK ($10 dep. req.). Heated pool. Jacuzzi. Sauna. Laundry facility. Rooms come with phones and cable TV. Wheelchair accessible. AAA/Senior discount. Major credit cards.

HAMEL
Medina Inn
$45 (60)*
400 Hwy. 55 (4 miles west of I-494)
612.478.9770 or 800.643.9211
66 Units, no pets. Restaurant on premises. Continental breakfast. Fitness facility. Laundry facility. Rooms come with phones and cable TV. Senior discount. Wheelchair accessible. Major credit cards.
*Higher rate effective weekends.

HARMONY
Country Lodge Motel
$45
525 Main Avenue N. • 507.886.2515
24 Units, no pets. Continental breakfast. Meeting rooms. Rooms come with phones and cable TV. Some rooms have microwaves, jacuzzis, radios and refrigerators. Credit cards: DS, MC, V.

HASTINGS
Hastings Inn
$40-50
1520 Vermillion Street • 651.437.3153
43 Units, no pets. Indoor pool. Jacuzzi and sauna. Game room. Laundry facility. Rooms come with phones and cable TV. Senior discount. Major credit cards.

HINCKLEY
Hinckley Gold Pine Inn
$39-54*
325 Fire Monument, I-35, Exit 183
320.384.6112
50 Units, pets OK. Laundry facility. Meeting rooms. Rooms come with phones and cable TV. AAA/Senior discount. Major credit cards.
*Rates as high as $64/night.

INTERNATIONAL FALLS
Budget Host Inn
$33-50
10 Riverview Blvd. • 218.283.2577
27 Units, pets OK. Laundry facility. Picnic area. Playground. Meeting rooms. Rooms come with phones and cable TV. Senior discount. Credit cards: AE, DS, MC, V.

Super 8 Motel
$46-53*
2326 Hwy. 53 Frontage Rd • 218.283.8811
53 Units, no pets. Toast offered. Laundry facility. Rooms come with phones and cable TV. Wheelchair accessible. Senior discount. Credit cards: AE, CB, DC, DS, MC, V.
*Rates may increase slightly on weekends.

JACKSON
Budget Host Inn
$36-40
1/3 mile south of I-90 on Hwys 16 & 71
507.847.2020
24 Units, pets OK with permission. Continental breakfast. Picnic area. Playground. Laundry facility. Meeting rooms. Rooms come with phones and cable TV. Wheelchair accessible. AAA/Senior discount. Major credit cards.

LA CRESCENT
Ranch Motel
$30
Junction of Hwys. 14, 16 & 61 (1.5 miles south of I-90) • 507.895.4422
24 Units, pets OK. Outdoor heated pool. Rooms come with phones and cable TV. Senior discount. Major credit cards.

LAKE CITY
Lake City Country Inn
$32-50
1401 N. Lakeshore Dr. • 651.345.5351
22 Units, no pets. Outdoor pool. Sauna. Jacuzzi. Game room. Rooms come with A/C, phones and TV. Major credit cards.

LAKEVILLE
Motel 6
$34-50
11274 210th Street • 952.469.1900
86 Units, pets OK. Laundry facility. Data ports. Rooms come with phones, A/C and cable TV. Wheelchair accessible. Credit cards: AE, CB, DC, DS, MC, V.

LE SUEUR
Le Sueur Downtown Motel
$36
510 N. Main Street • 507.665.6246
37 Units, no pets. Meeting room. Rooms come with A/C, phones and cable TV. Senior discount. Wheelchair accessible. Major credit cards.

LITTLE FALLS
Super 8 Motel
$45-55
300 12th Street N.E. • 320.632.2351
51 Units, no pets. Morning coffee. Rooms come with phones and cable TV. Wheelchair accessible. AAA/Senior discount. Credit cards: AE, CB, DC, DS, MC, V.

LONG PRAIRIE
Budget Host Inn
$38-42
417 Lake Street S. • 320.732.6118
17 Units, pets OK with permission. Laundry facility nearby. Airport transportation. Fax service. Rooms come with phones and cable TV. Microwaves and refrigerators available. AAA/Senior discount. Credit cards: AE, DC, DS, MC, V.

Super 8 Motel
$47
646 Lake Street S. • 320.732.4188
24 Units, no pets. Continental breakfast. Rooms come with phones and cable TV. Some rooms have jacuzzis and refrigerators. AAA discount. Major credit cards.

LUVERNE
Comfort Inn
$45
801 S. Kniss • 507.283.9488
44 Units, no pets. Continental breakfast. Rooms come with phones and cable TV. Senior discount. Major credit cards.

MAHNOMEN
Stardust Suites
$50
791 US 59S • 218.935.2761

60 Units, no pets. Continental breakfast. Rooms come with phones and cable TV. Senior discount. Major credit cards.

MANKATO
Budget Host Inn
$40-45
1255 Range St. (Hwy. 169) • 507.388.1644
52 Units, no pets. Laundry facility. Rooms come with phones and cable TV. AAA/Senior discount. Major credit cards.

Riverfront Inn
$37*
1727 N. Riverfront Dr. • 507.388.1638
19 Units, no pets. Rooms come with phones and cable TV. Microwaves and refrigerators available. AAA and Senior discount. Credit cards: AE, CB, DC, DS, MC, V.
*Higher rates effective during weekends.

MARSHALL
Traveler's Lodge Motel
$38-43
1425 E. College Drive • 507.532.5721 or 800.532.5721
90 Units, no pets. Continental breakfast. Transportation available. Rooms come with phones and cable TV. Senior discount. Senior discount. Major credit cards.

MELROSE
Super 8 Motel
$41*
231 E. County Rd. 173 • 612.256.4261
26 Units, pets OK with permission. Toast offered. Rooms come with phones and cable TV. Wheelchair accessible. Senior discount. Credit cards: AE, CB, DC, DS, MC, V.
*Rates may increase slightly on weekends.

MINNEAPOLIS — *see also Burnsville, Clearwater, Eagan, Hamel, Hastings, Lakeville, Richfield (Mall of America), Roseville, Shakopee, St. Paul and Woodbury*
Hotel Amsterdam
$39
828 Hennepin Avenue • 612.288.0459
30 Units, no pets. Euro-style hotel. Rooms come with phones and TV. Major credit cards.

Metro Inn
$50
5637 Lyndale Avenue S. • 612.861.6011
37 Units, pets OK. Rooms come with phones and cable TV. Senior discount. Credit cards: AE, DS, MC, V.

MINNESOTA CITY — *see Winona*

MONTEVIDEO
Fiesta City Motel
$30
Junction of Hwys. 59, 212 and 7 W.
320.269.8896 or 800.472.6478
24 Units, pets OK. Rooms come with phones and cable TV. Senior discount. Major credit cards.

Viking Motel
$23-28
1428 E. Hwy. 7 • 320.269.9545 or 800.670.0777
21 Units, pets OK. Rooms come with phones and cable TV. Some rooms have microwaves and refrigerators. Senior discount. Major credit cards.

MOORHEAD — *see also Fargo (ND)*
Guest House Motel
$33-38
2107 Main Avenue S.E. • 218.233.2471
20 Units, pets OK ($3). Rooms come with phones and cable TV. Some rooms have refrigerators and microwaves. Senior discount. Credit cards: AE, DS, MC, V.

Motel 75
$37-40
I-94 & Hwy. 75 S. • 218.233.7501 or 800.628.4171
68 Units, pets OK. Continental breakfast. Rooms come with cable TV. AAA/Senior discount. Credit cards: AE, DS, MC, V.

Super 8 Motel
$38*
3621 S. 8th Street • 218.233.8880
61 Units, no pets. Pastries offered. Laundry facility. Rooms come with phones and cable TV. Wheelchair accessible. Senior discount. Credit cards: AE, CB, DC, DS, MC, V.
*Rates may increase slightly on weekends.

MORRIS
Best Western Prairie Inn
$46-47
200 Hwy. 28E • 320.589.3030
89 Units, no pets. Restaurant on premises. Indoor pool and jacuzzi. Fax and Data ports. Rooms come with A/C, phones and cable TV. AAA/Senior discount. Major credit cards.

NEW ULM
Colonial Inn Motel
$33-50
1315 N. Broadway • 507.354.3128
24 Units, no pets. Rooms come with phones and cable TV. AAA/Senior discount. Credit cards: AE, DS, MC, V.

Microtel Inns & Suites
$45-50
424 20th South Street • 507.354.9800
63 Units, pets OK. Continental breakfast. Pool. spa. Meeting rooms. Rooms come with phones and cable TV. Wheelchair accessible. Senior discount. Major credit cards.

NISSWA
Nisswa Motel
$40-58 (51-67)*
Located in town • 218.963.7611
17 Units, pets OK ($3). Rooms come with A/C, phones and cable TV. Credit cards: AE, DS, MC, V.
*Higher rates effective weekends Memorial Day through Labor Day.

ORR
North Country Inn
$46-48
4483 Hwy. 53 • 218.757.3778
12 Units, pets OK ($11). Data ports. Rooms come with phones, A/C and cable TV. Wheelchair accessible. Credit cards: AE, DS, MC, V.

ORTONVILLE
Econo Lodge
$45-55
320.839.2414 • From Jct. US 12 & 75, 0.3 miles north.
32 Units, no pets. Continental breakfast. Rooms come with phones and cable TV. No A/C. Some rooms have microwaves, refrigerators and jacuzzis. AAA/Senior discount. Credit cards: AE, DS, MC, V.

OWATONNA
Budget Host Inn
$35-45
745 State Avenue • 507.451.8712
27 Units, pets OK. Continental breakfast. Meeting rooms. Rooms come with phones and cable TV. Some rooms have microwaves and refrigerators. Senior discount. Credit cards: AE, DS, MC, V.

Oakdale Motel
$30-50
1418 S. Oak Avenue • 507.451.5480
25 Units, pets OK ($7, in smoking rooms only). Rooms come with phones and cable TV. Some rooms have microwaves and refrigerators. AAA/Senior discount. Credit cards: AE, DS, MC, V.

PARK RAPIDS
Terrace View Motor Lodge
$33
716 N. Park (Hwy. 71N) • 218.732.1213 or 800.731.1213
20 Units, pets OK. Restaurant on premises. Meeting room. Playground. Rooms come with A/C, phones and cable TV. Senior discount. Major credit cards.

PERHAM
Budget Host Oasis Inn
$33
Jct. Hwys. 78 and 10 • 218.346.7810
20 Units, pets OK. Continental breakfast. Laundry facility nearby. Rooms come with phones and cable TV. Credit cards: AE, DS, MC, V.

PIPESTONE
Super 8 Motel
$48-54
605 8th Avenue S.E. • 507.825.4217
39 Units, no pets. Continental breakfast. Laundry facility. Rooms come with A/C, phones and cable TV. Senior discount. Major credit cards.

PRINCETON
Rum River Motel
$40-45
510 19th Avenue N. • 763.389.3120
28 Units, pets OK. Continental breakfast. Rooms come with phones and cable TV. Some rooms have refrigerators and jacuzzis. Major credit cards.

RED WING
Parkway Motel
$35-39
3425 Hwy. 61 N. • 651.388.8231 or 800.762.0934
27 Units, pets OK. Rooms come with A/C, phones and cable TV. Major credit cards.

REDWOOD FALLS
Motel #71
$25-29

1020 E. Bridge Street • 507.637.2981 or 800.437.4789
24 Units, no pets. Continental breakfast. Heated seasonal pool. Rooms come with phones and cable TV. Senior discount. Major credit cards.

RICHFIELD
Motel 6
$42-52
7640 Cedar Avenue S., I-494, Exit 3
612.861.4491
103 Units, pets OK. Data ports. Rooms come with phones, A/C and cable TV. Wheelchair accessible. Credit cards: AE, CB, DC, DS, MC, V.

ROCHESTER
Courtesy Inn
$39-45
510 17th Avenue N.W. • 507.289.1801
46 Units, pets OK in smoking rooms only. Transportation available to Mayo Clinic. Rooms come with phones and cable TV. AAA/Senior discount. Credit cards: AE, DC, DS, MC, V.

Motel 6
$37-43
2107 W. Frontage Road • 507.282.6625
66 Units, pets OK. Laundry facility. Data ports. Transportation available to Mayo Clinic and area hospitals. Rooms come with phones, A/C and cable TV. Wheelchair accessible. Credit cards: AE, CB, DC, DS, MC, V.

ROSEAU
Super 8 Motel
$45-50*
318 Westside • 218.463.2196
36 Units, pets OK with permission. Laundry facility. Rooms come with phones and cable TV. Senior discount. Credit cards: AE, CB, DC, DS, MC, V.
*Rates may increase slightly on weekends, holidays and special events.

ROSEVILLE
Motel 6
$40-50 (60)*
2300 Cleveland Ave. N. • 651.639.3988
113 Units, guide dogs only. Laundry facility. Data ports. Rooms come with phones, A/C and cable TV. Wheelchair accessible. Credit cards: AE, CB, DC, DS, MC, V.
*Higher rate summer weekends.

ST. CLOUD
Motel 6
$30-40
815 1st Street S. • 320.253.7070
93 Units, pets OK. Data ports. Rooms come with phones, A/C and cable TV. Wheelchair accessible. Credit cards: AE, CB, DC, DS, MC, V.

Super 8 Motel
$41*
50 Park Avenue S. • 320.253.5530
68 Units, pets OK. Continental breakfast. Copy and fax service. Meeting room. Rooms come with phones and cable TV. Senior discount. Credit cards: AE, CB, DC, DS, MC, V.
*Rates may increase slightly on weekends and special events.

Travelodge
$45
3820 Roosevelt Road • 320.253.3338
28 Units, pets OK ($3). Continental breakfast. Meeting rooms. Rooms come with refrigerators, A/C, phones and cable TV. Wheelchair accessible. AAA/Senior discount. Credit cards: AE, DC, DS, MC, V.

ST. JOSEPH
Super 8 Motel
$49*
612.363.7711 • From I-94E, Exit 158, follow SR 75. From I-94W, Exit 160 and follow Hwy. 2 into town.
27 Units, pets OK in smoking rooms only. Continental breakfast. Rooms come with phones and cable TV. Senior discount. Wheelchair accessible. Major credit cards.
*Rates may increase slightly on weekends and special events.

ST. PAUL — ***see also Anoka, Burnsville, Clearwater, Eagan, Hamel, Hastings, Lakeville, Minneapolis, Richfield, Roseville, Shakopee and Woodbury***
Economy Inn
$45
149 E. University Inn • 651.227.8801
50 Units, no pets. Rooms come with phones and cable TV. Major credit cards.

SAUK CENTRE
Gopher Prairie Motel
$32-36
1222 S. Getty • 320.352.2275
23 Units, pets OK. Picnic area. Meeting

room. Fax service. Rooms come with phones and cable TV. Senior discount. Wheelchair accessible. Credit cards: AE, DS, MC, V.

Hillcrest Motel
$31-37
965 S. Main Street • 320.352.2215
21 Units, pets OK ($5). Laundry facility. Rooms come with phones and cable TV. AAA discount. Major credit cards.

SHAKOPEE
Hillview Motel
$39-55
12826 Johnson Mem. Dr • 612.445.7111
41 Units. Laundry facility. Rooms come with A/C, phones and cable TV. Some rooms have microwaves and refrigerators. Major credit cards.

SILVER BAY
Mariner Motel
$40-50
46 Outer Drive • 218.226.4488
28 Units, pets OK in smoking rooms only ($5). Rooms come with phones and cable TV. No A/C. Some rooms have microwaves, refrigerators and jacuzzis. Senior discount. Credit cards: DS, MC, V.

SLEEPY EYE
Orchid Inn and Motor Lodge
$20-30
500 Burnside Street • 507.794.3211
20 Units, pets OK. Restaurant on premises. Rooms come with A/C, phones and cable TV. Wheelchair accessible. Major credit cards.

STAPLES
Super 8 Motel
$43-48
109 2nd Avenue W. • 218.894.3585
36 Units, pets OK with permission ($2.50 daily). Rooms come with phones and cable TV. Senior discount. Wheelchair accessible. Credit cards: AE, CB, DC, DS, MC, V.

TAYLORS FALLS
The Springs Country Inn
$45-55
361 Government Street • 651.465.6565
29 Units, pets OK ($7). Jacuzzi. Laundry facility. Rooms come with phones and cable TV. Some rooms have refrigerators. AAA discount. Credit cards: AE, DS.

THIEF RIVER FALLS
Super 8 Motel
$42-44
1915 US 59 S.E. • 218.681.6205
46 Units, pets OK. Rooms come with phones and cable TV. AAA discount. Major credit cards.

VIRGINIA
Lakeshore Motor Inn
$39-52
404 N. 6th Avenue • 218.741.3360
15 Units, pets OK. Data ports. Rooms come with phones and cable TV. Senior discount. Credit cards: AE, CB, DC, DS, MC, V.

WACONIA
Super 8 Motel
$50-55
301 E. Frontage Road • 612.442.5147
26 Units, pets OK ($5 and $25 dep. req.). Complimentary doughnuts and coffee. Rooms come with phones and cable TV. Major credit cards.

WARROAD
Best Western Can-Am Inn
$40
406 Main Avenue N.E. • 218.386.3807
40 Units, pets OK in smoking rooms only. Continental breakfast. Laundry facility. Rooms come with phones and cable TV. AAA/Senior discount. Credit cards: AE, DC, DS, MC, V.

The Patch Motel
$41
218.386.2723 • On SR 11, one mile west of town.
80 Units, pets OK. Meeting rooms. Heated indoor pool. Jacuzzi. Fitness facility. Laundry facility. Rooms come with phones and cable TV. Wheelchair accessible. AAA/ Senior discount. Credit cards: AE, MC, V.

Super 8 Motel
$39
909 N. State Street • 218.386.3723
41 Units, no pets. Continental breakfast. Meeting rooms. Laundry facility. Rooms come with phones and cable TV. Some rooms have microwaves, refrigerators and jacuzzis. Credit cards: AE, CB, DC, DS, MC, V.

WILLMAR
Colonial Inn
$40
1102 S. 1st Street • 320.235.4444 or 800.396.4445
24 Units, pets OK. Rooms come with refrigerators, phones and cable TV. Some rooms have microwaves. Major credit cards.

Lakeview Inn
$34-42
N. Business 71 & 23 • 320.253.3424
36 Units, pets OK. Continental breakfast. Rooms come with phones and cable TV. Senior discount. Major credit cards.

WINONA
Sterling Motel
$30-50
1450 Gilmore Avenue • 507.454.1120 or 800.452.1235
32 Units, pets OK. Rooms come with AC, phones and cable TV. Senior discount. Major credit cards.

Super 8 Motel
$49
1025 Sugar Loaf Road • 507.454.6066
61 Units, pets OK ($10 dep. req.). Continental breakfast. Rooms come with phones and cable TV. Senior discount. Major credit cards.

WOODBURY
Red Roof Inn
$40-45 (63)*
1806 Wooddale Drive • I-494, Exit 60
651.738.7160
108 Units, pets OK. Rooms come with AC, phones and cable TV. Major credit cards. *Higher rate effective June through August.

WORTHINGTON
Budget Inn
$28
1231 Oxford Street • I-90, Exit 43
507.376.6136
31 Units, no pets. Fax and Rooms come with phones, A/C and cable TV. Senior discount. Credit cards: AE, DS, MC, V.

ZUMBROTA
Super 8 Motel
$43-55*
507.732.7852 • On US 52, 1 mile north of jct. of SR 60 & US 52
30 Units, pets OK. Toast bar offered. Rooms come with phones and cable TV. Senior discount. Wheelchair accessible. Credit cards: AE, CB, DC, DS, MC, V. *Rates may increase slightly on weekends, holidays and special events.

mississippi

BATESVILLE
Skyline Motel
$33
311 Hwy. 51S • 662.563.7671
33 Units, pets OK. Laundry facility. Rooms come with refrigerators, phones and cable TV. Some rooms have microwaves. AAA/ Senior discount. Credit cards: AE, DC, DS, MC, V.

BILOXI
Diamond Inn
$35 (55)*
100 Brady Drive • 228.388.7321
40 Units, no pets. Continental breakfast. Pool. Rooms come with phones and cable TV. Major credit cards.
*Higher rate effective weekends.

Motel 6
$36-40 (60)*
2476 Beach Blvd. • 228.388.5130
100 Units, pets OK. Pool. Laundry facility. Data ports. Rooms come with phones, A/C and cable TV. Wheelchair accessible. Credit cards: AE, CB, DC, DS, MC, V.
*Higher rate effective summer weekends.

Sand Dollar Inn
$30-40 (59)*
1884 Beach Blvd. • 228.388.3202
30 Units, no pets. Pool. Rooms come with phones and cable TV. Wheelchair accessible. Senior discount. Major credit cards.
*Higher rate effective summer weekends.

BROOKHAVEN
Best Value Inn & Suites
$50
1210 Brookway Blvd. • 601.833.1341
120 Units, pets OK. Restaurant on premises. Pool. Meeting rooms. Laundry facility. Rooms come with phones and TV. Some rooms have microwaves and refrigerators. AAA discount. Major credit cards.

Best Western
$43
749 Magee Drive • I-55, Exit 40
601.835.1053
63 Units, no pets. Continental breakfast. Pool. Laundry facility. Rooms come with phones and cable TV. AAA/Senior discount. Major credit cards.

Days Inn
$38-45
811 Magee Drive • 601.833.6954
49 Units, no pets. Pool. Laundry facility. Rooms come with phones and cable TV. Some rooms have microwaves and refrigerators. AAA discount. Major credit cards.

CANTON
Days Inn
$48
123 Sidney Runnels Drive (I-55, Exit 119)
601.859.0760
32 Units, no pets. Continental breakfast. Rooms come with phones and cable TV. Some rooms have microwaves and refrigerators. AAA discount. Major credit cards.

Econo Lodge
$40-50
I-55 & Frontage Road (Exit 119)
601.859.2643
40 Units, pets OK ($5). Continental breakfast. Pool. Rooms come with phones and TV. Some rooms have microwaves and refrigerators. Senior discount. Major credit cards.

CARTHAGE
Econo Lodge
$46-54
211 Hwy. 25N • 601.267.7900
26 Units, no pets. Pool. Rooms come with phones and cable TV. Some rooms have microwaves and refrigerators. Major credit cards.

CLARKSDALE
Econo Lodge
$42-53
350 S. State Street • 662.621.1110
50 Units, pets OK. Continental breakfast. Rooms come with phones and cable TV. Some rooms have microwaves and

refrigerators. Wheelchair accessible. AAA discount. Major credit cards.

CLEVELAND
Colonial Inn Motel
$30-35
Jct. Hwys. 61 and 8 • 662.843.3641
53 Units, no pets. Restaurant on premises. Pool. Rooms come with phones and cable TV. Senior discount. Major credit cards.

COLLINS
Days Inn
$42
Hwy. 49N • 601.765.6531
45 Units, no pets. Restaurant on premises. Pool. Rooms come with phones and cable TV. AAA/Senior discount. Credit cards: AE, DC, DS, JCB, MC, V.

COLUMBUS
Motel 6
$32
1203 US 45N (US 45/82 Junction)
662.327.4450
57 Units, pets OK. Restaurant on premises. Airport transportation. Data ports. Rooms come with phones, A/C and cable TV. Wheelchair accessible. Credit cards: AE, CB, DC, DS, MC, V.

Super 8 Motel
$48
510 Hwy. 45N • 662.329.8788
46 Units, no pets. Continental breakfast. Rooms come with phones and cable TV. Senior discount. Major credit cards.

CORINTH
Crossroads Inn
$38
1500 Hwy. 72W • 662.287.8051
100 Units, pets OK. Restaurant on premises. Pool. Game room. Rooms come with phones and cable TV. Wheelchair accessible. Senior discount. Major credit cards.

DURANT
Super 8 Motel
$45-50*
31201 Hwy. 12 • 662.653.3881
50 Units, pets OK. Continental breakfast. Rooms come with phones and cable TV. Senior discount. Wheelchair accessible. Major credit cards.
*Rates higher during weekends and special events.

GREENVILLE
Days Inn
$35-40
2500 Hwy. 82E • 662.335.1999
152 Units, pets OK ($5). Continental breakfast. Pool. Laundry facility. Meeting rooms. Rooms come with phones and cable TV. Wheelchair accessible. AAA discount. Major credit cards.

Relax Inn
$24
2630 Hwy. 82E • 662.332.1527
30 Units, no pets. Rooms come with phones and cable TV. Senior discount. Major credit cards.

GREENWOOD
Executive Inn
$35
621 Hwy. 82W • 662.453.0030
50 Units, no pets. Pool. Sauna. Fax service. Rooms come with phones and cable TV. Wheelchair accessible. Credit cards: AE, CB, DC, DS, MC, V.

GRENADA
Best Western
$42-49
1750 Sunset Drive • I-55, Exit 206
662.226.7816
61 Units, pets OK. Restaurant on premises. Continental breakfast. Pool. Playground. Laundry facility. Meeting rooms. Rooms come with phones and cable TV. AAA/Senior discount. Major credit cards.

GULFPORT
Coast Motel
$32-44*
130 Tegarden Road (at US 90)
228.896.7881
20 Units, pets OK ($30). Pool. Rooms come with phones and cable TV. Senior discount. Major credit cards.
*Higher rate effective during weekends.

Motel 6
$30-46 (58)*
9355 US 49 (I-10, Exit 34A)
228.863.1890
98 Units, pets OK. Pool. Laundry facility. Data ports. Rooms come with phones, A/C and cable TV. Wheelchair accessible. Credit cards: AE, CB, DC, DS, MC, V.
*Higher rate effective summer weekends.

Super 8 Motel
$49*
826 E. Beach Drive • 228.896.7515
52 Units, no pets. Continental breakfast. Pool. Jacuzzi. Rooms come with phones and cable TV. Senior discount. Wheelchair accessible. Major credit cards.
*Rates higher during weekends and special events.

HATTIESBURG
Econo Lodge
$36-49
3501 Hardy Street • 601.264.7221
47 Units, no pets. Continental breakfast. Rooms come with phones and cable TV. Some rooms have refrigerators. Credit cards: AE, CB, DC, DS, MC, V.

Motel 6
$32-40
6508 US 49 • 601.544.6096
117 Units, pets OK. Pool. Laundry facility. Data ports. Rooms come with phones, A/C and cable TV. Wheelchair accessible. Credit cards: AE, CB, DC, DS, MC, V.

HAZLEHURST
Western Inn Express
$45
28077 Hwy. 28 • 601.894.1111
42 Units, no pets. Pool. Rooms come with phones and cable TV. Senior discount. Major credit cards.

HERNANDO
The Hernando Inn
$46
900 E. Commerce St. • 662.429.7811
55 Units, no pets. Restaurant on premises. Rooms come with phones and cable TV. Senior discount. Major credit cards.

Super 8 Motel
$47-55
2425 Sloane's Way • I-55, Exit 280
662.429.5334
48 Units, no pets. Continental breakfast. Pool. Laundry facility. Rooms come with phones and cable TV. Major credit cards.

HORN LAKE
Motel 6
$45-48
701 Southwest Drive (I-55, Exit 289)
662.544.6096
59 Units, pets OK. Pool. Laundry facility. Data ports. Rooms come with phones, A/C and cable TV. Wheelchair accessible. Credit cards: AE, CB, DC, DS, MC, V.

INDIANOLA
Days Inn
$38-42
1015 Hwy. 82E • 601.887.4242
38 Units, no pets. Continental breakfast. Rooms come with phones and cable TV. Some rooms have microwaves and refrigerators. AAA discount. Major credit cards.

IUKA
Victorian Inn
$32-40
199 County Road 180 • 662.423.9221
59 Units, pets OK. Continental breakfast. Pool. Laundry facility. Rooms come with phones and cable TV. Some rooms have microwaves and refrigerators. AAA/Senior discount. Major credit cards.

JACKSON — *see also Pearl and Ridgeland*
Classic Inn
$39
3880 I-55S • I-55, Exit 90A • 601.373.1244
80 Units, no pets. Continental breakfast. Pool. Playground. Laundry facility. Rooms come with phones and cable TV. Wheelchair accessible. Major credit cards.

Days Inn
$44-51
2616 Hwy. 80W • I-20 & Hwy. 80
601.969.5511
50 Units, pets OK ($5). Continental breakfast. Laundry facility. Jacuzzi. Airport transportation. Rooms come with phones and cable TV. Wheelchair accessible. AAA discount. Major credit cards.

Knights Inn
$39-43
4641 I-55 N (Exit 100) • 601.981.3320
78 Units, no pets. Pool. Laundry facility. Rooms come with phones and cable TV. Wheelchair accessible. Major credit cards.

Motel 6
$36-40
6145 I-55N (Exit 103) • 601.956.8848
100 Units, pets OK. Pool. Laundry facility. Data ports. Rooms come with phones, A/C and cable TV. Wheelchair accessible. Credit cards: AE, CB, DC, DS, MC, V.

Super 8 Motel
$43-50
2655 I-55S • 601.372.1006
80 Units, pets OK. Restaurant on premises. Pool. Rooms come with phones and cable TV. Senior discount. Wheelchair accessible. Major credit cards.

KOSCIUSKO
Super 8 Motel
$45-50
718 Veterans Mem. Dr. • 662.289.7880
40 Units, pets OK ($5). Continental breakfast. Pool. Rooms come with phones and cable TV. Senior discount. Major credit cards.

LAUREL
Executive Inn & Suites
$44-48
123 16th Avenue N. • 601.426.6585
52 Units, no pets. Laundry facility. Rooms come with refrigerators and cable TV. Some rooms have phones. Senior discount. Credit cards: AE, CB, DC, DS, JCB, MC, V.

Super 8 Motel
$50
1107 Sawmill Road • 601.649.8885
57 Units, pets OK. Continental breakfast. Rooms come with phones and cable TV. Senior discount. Wheelchair accessible. Major credit cards.

LUCEDALE
Western Motel
$40-45
31 Ventura Drive, Hwy 63S • 601.766.3400
27 Units, pets OK. Rooms come with phones and cable TV. Senior discount. Major credit cards.

MAGEE
Super 8 Motel
$45-53
1471 Simpson Hwy. 49 • 601.849.2049
40 Units, no pets. Continental breakfast. Pool. Rooms come with phones, refrigerators, microwaves and cable TV. Senior discount. Wheelchair accessible. Major credit cards.

McCOMB
Super 8 Motel
$40-55
100 Commerce Street • 601.684.7654
41 Units, pets OK. Continental breakfast. Rooms come with phones and cable TV. Senior discount. Major credit cards.

MERIDIAN
Econo Lodge
$40
2405 S. Frontage Road • 601.693.9393
32 Units, pets OK ($25 dep. req.). Continental breakfast. Rooms come with phones and cable TV. Senior discount. Credit cards: AE, CB, DC, DS, JCB, MC, V.

Motel 6
$33-38
2309 S. Frontage Road • 601.482.1182
88 Units, pets OK. Pool. Laundry facility. Data ports. Rooms come with phones, A/C and cable TV. Wheelchair accessible. Credit cards: AE, CB, DC, DS, MC, V.

MOSS POINT
Shular Inn
$40-45
6623 Hwy. 63 • 228.475.8444
49 Units, pets OK. Continental breakfast. Laundry facility. Rooms come with phones and cable TV. Some rooms have microwaves and refrigerators. Major credit cards.

Super 8 Motel
$45-50
6824 Hwy. 613 • I-10, Exit 68
228.474.1855
57 Units, pets OK. Continental breakfast. Pool. Laundry facility. Rooms come with phones and cable TV. Some rooms have microwaves and refrigerators. Senior discount. Major credit cards.

NATCHEZ
Scottish Inns
$30-35
40 Sgt. Prentis Drive • 601.442.9141
50 Units, pets OK. Continental breakfast. Pool. Laundry facility. Rooms come with phones and cable TV. Senior discount. Major credit cards.

Travel Inn
$35
271-E D'Evereaux Drive • 601.446.8796
37 Units, no pets. Rooms come with phones and cable TV. Major credit cards.

NEWTON
Days Inn
$45-55
I-20 & Hwy. 15 • 601.683.3361

40 Units, pets ($8). Continental breakfast. Pool. Meeting rooms. Rooms come with phones and cable TV. Wheelchair accessible. AAA discount. Credit cards: AE, CB, DC, DS, JCB, MC, V.

OLIVE BRANCH
Super 8 Motel
$50
11064 Business Center Dr.
Hwy. 78, Exit 6 • 662.893.8930
65 Units, no pets. Continental breakfast. Pool. Jacuzzi. Rooms come with phones and cable TV. Senior discount. Major credit cards.

OXFORD
Johnson's Motor Inn
$35
2305 Jackson Ave. W. • 662.234.3611
32 Units, no pets. Rooms come with phones and cable TV. Major credit cards.

Ole Miss Motel
$32-40
1517 University Avenue • 662.234.2424
35 Units, pets OK. Fitness facility. Rooms come with phones and cable TV. Major credit cards.

PASCAGOULA
Travel Motor Inn
$35-45
2102 Denny Avenue • 228.762.8210
77 Units, no pets. Restaurant on premises. Pool. Meeting room. Rooms come with phones and cable TV. Wheelchair accessible. Senior discount. Major credit cards.

PEARL
Motel 6
$40-43
216 N. Pearson Road (I-20, Exit 48)
601.936.9988
79 Units, pets OK. Pool. Laundry facility. Data ports. Rooms come with phones, A/C and cable TV. Wheelchair accessible. Credit cards: AE, CB, DC, DS, MC, V.

Super 8 Motel
$40
111 Airport Road • I-20, Exit 52
601.718.1860
52 Units, no pets. Continental breakfast. Airport transportation. Rooms come with phones, A/C and cable TV. Senior discount. Major credit cards.

PICAYUNE
Budget Host Majestic Inn
$32-38
999 Cooper Road • 601.798.3859
50 Units, pets OK ($20). Pool. Picnic area. Laundry facility. Rooms come with phones and cable TV. Senior discount. Major credit cards.

PONTOTOC
Days Inn
$45-55
217 Hwy. 15N • 662.489.5200
61 Units, pets OK ($5). Restaurant on premises. Pool. Rooms come with phones and cable TV. Wheelchair accessible. AAA/Senior discount. Major credit cards.

RIDGELAND
Red Roof Inn
$37-47
810 Adcock Drive • I-55, Exit 103
601.956.7707
103 Units, pets OK. Data ports. Rooms come with phones and cable TV. AAA discount. Major credit cards.

SARDIS
Super 8 Motel
$40-49
601 E. Lee Street • 662.487.2311
41 Units, no pets. Continental breakfast. Pool. Rooms come with phones and cable TV. Wheelchair accessible. AAA discount. Credit cards: AE, CB, DC, DS, MC, V.

SENATOBIA
Motel 6
$36-42
501 E. Main Street (I-55, Exit 265)
662.562.5241
80 Units, pets OK. Pool. Data ports. Rooms come with phones, A/C and cable TV. Wheelchair accessible. Credit cards: AE, CB, DC, DS, MC, V.

TUPELO
Red Roof Inn
$36-53
1500 McCullough Blvd. • 662.844.1904
100 Units, pets OK. Pool. Laundry facility. Rooms come with phones and cable TV. AAA discount. Major credit cards.

Super 8 Motel
$43-55
3898 McCullough Blvd. • 662.842.0448

41 Units, no pets. Continental breakfast. Laundry facility. Rooms come with phones and cable TV. Wheelchair accessible. Senior discount. Major credit cards.

VICKSBURG
Deluxe Inn
$28-30
2751 N. I-20 (Exit 3) • 601.636.5121
20 Units, no pets. Rooms come with phones and cable TV. Some rooms have refrigerators and microwaves. Credit cards: AE, CB, DC, DS, MC, V.

Motel 6
$40-45
4127 I-20 Frontage Rd. • 601.638.5077
58 Units, pets OK. Pool. Data ports. Rooms come with phones, A/C and cable TV. Wheelchair accessible. Credit cards: AE, CB, DC, DS, MC, V.

Travel Inn
$40-45
1675 N. Frontage Road • 601.630.0100
30 Units, no pets. Continental breakfast. Pool. Rooms come with phones and cable TV. Some rooms have microwaves and refrigerators. Credit cards: AE, DS, MC, V.

WEST POINT
Days Inn
$39-54
1025 Hwy. 45N Alt. • 662.494.1995
37 Units, no pets. Continental breakfast. Pool. Jacuzzi. Rooms come with phones and cable TV. AAA/Senior discount. Major credit cards.

YAZOO CITY
Days Inn
$42-55
1801 Jerry Clower Blvd. • 662.746.4119
30 Units, no pets. Continental breakfast. Pool. Rooms come with phones and cable TV. Some rooms have microwaves and refrigerators. AAA discount. Major credit cards.

missouri

BELTON
Belton Inn
$34
107 County Line Road • 816.331.6300
131 Units, no pets. Pool. Laundry facility. Rooms come with phones and cable TV. Wheelchair accessible. Major credit cards.

Econo Lodge
$43-49*
222 Peculiar Drive • 816.322.1222
52 Units, pets OK. Restaurant on premises. Continental breakfast. Pool. Laundry facility. Rooms come with phones and cable TV. Wheelchair accessible. Senior discount. Major credit cards.
*AAA discounted rates.

BETHANY
Family Budget Inn
$35-40
4014 Miller Street • I-35, Exit 92
660.425.7915
78 Units, pets OK ($5). Pool. Meeting rooms. Rooms come with phones and cable TV. Senior discount. Credit cards: AE, DC, DS, MC, V.

Super 8 Motel
$50*
811 S. 37th Street • I-35, Exit 92
660.425.8881
49 Units, no pets. Toast bar. Rooms come with phones and cable TV. Senior discount. Wheelchair accessible. Major credit cards.
*Rates higher weekends, special events and holidays.

BLUE SPRINGS
American Inn
$39-55
3300 W. Jefferson • 816.228.1080 or 800.90.LODGE
170 Units. Pool. Laundry facility. Rooms come with phones and cable TV. Wheelchair accessible. Major credit cards.

Motel 6
$30-40
901 W. Jefferson • I-70, Exit 20
816.228.9133
123 Units, pets OK. Pool. Laundry facility. Data ports. Rooms come with phones, A/C and cable TV. Wheelchair accessible. Credit cards: AE, CB, DC, DS, MC, V.

BOLIVAR
Country Inn
$38-50
1817 S. Killingsworth Ave. • 417.326.8004
35 Units, no pets. Pool. Rooms come with phones and cable TV. Senior discount. Credit cards: AE, DS, MC. V.

Super 8 Motel
$48-58
1919 S. Killingsworth Ave. • 417.777.8888
63 Units, pets OK. Continental breakfast. Meeting room. Rooms come with phones and cable TV. Wheelchair accessible. Senior discount. Credit cards: AE, CB, DC, DS, MC, V.

BONNE TERRE
Red Cedar Lodge
$27-40
7036 S. Hwy. 67 • 573.358.8900
43 Units, no pets. Laundry facility. Rooms come with phones and cable TV. Wheelchair accessible. Major credit cards.

Super 8 Motel
$45-52
8 Northwood Drive
Hwy. 67, Exit 47 & K • 573.358.5888
40 Units, no pets. Continental breakfast. Indoor pool. Laundry facility. Meeting rooms. Rooms come with phones and cable TV. Senior discount. Major credit cards.

BOONVILLE
Super 8 Motel
$48-53 (65-75)*
420 Americana Road • I-70, Exit 103
660.882.2900
39 Units, no pets. Laundry facility. Rooms come with phones and cable TV. Senior discount. Wheelchair accessible. Major credit cards.
*Higher rates effective August.

BOWLING GREEN
Super 8 Motel
$48
1216 E. Champ Clark Dr. • 573.324.6000
64 Units, no pets. Continental breakfast. Laundry facility. Rooms come with phones and cable TV. Senior discount. Wheelchair accessible. Major credit cards.

BRANSON — *see also Branson West*
Country Hearth Inn
$33-42*
1360 W. Hwy. 76 • 417.334.0040
89 Units, pets OK ($10). Continental breakfast. Pool. Jacuzzi. Laundry facility. Meeting rooms. Rooms come with phones and cable TV. AAA discount. Credit cards: AE, DC, DS, JCB, MC, V.
*Closed mid-December through March.

Motel 6
$40-46
2825 Green Mtn. Dr. • 417.335.8990
51 Units, pets OK. Rooms come with phones, A/C and cable TV. Wheelchair accessible. Credit cards: AE, CB, DC, DS, MC, V.

Shady Acre Motel
$34
On US 76 (1.5 mi. west of Silver Dollar City) • 417.338.2316
14 Units, pets OK ($10). Pool. Rooms come with phones and cable TV. Some rooms have microwaves and refrigerators. Senior discount. Major credit cards.

Taney Motel
$29-35
311 Hwy. 65N. • 417.334.3143 or 800.334.3193
28 Units, pets OK ($5). Continental breakfast. Pool. Rooms come with refrigerators, phones and cable TV. Some rooms have microwaves and jacuzzis. AAA/Senior discount. Major credit cards.

BRANSON WEST
Colonial Mountain Inn
$35-45
10770 SR 76 • 417.272.8414
52 Units, pets OK ($5). Pool. Laundry facility. Playground. Rooms come with phones and cable TV. Credit cards: DC, DS, MC, V.

White Oak Inn
$25-30
On Hwy. 76 (2.5 miles west of Silver Dollar City) • 417.272.8300
30 Units, no pets. Pool. Laundry facility. Rooms come with phones and cable TV. Senior discount. Credit cards: CB, DC, DS, MC, V.

BRIDGETON
Knights Inn
$35-44
12433 St. Charles Rock Rd. • 314.291.8545
103 Units, pets OK ($25 dep. req.). Pool. Meeting rooms. Rooms come with phones and cable TV. AAA/Senior discount. Credit cards: AE, DC, DS, MC, V.

Motel 6
$34-46
3655 Pennridge Drive • 314.291.6100
243 Units, pets OK. Pool. Laundry facility. Data ports. Rooms come with phones, A/C and cable TV. Wheelchair accessible. Credit cards: AE, CB, DC, DS, MC, V.

Super 8 Motel
$40-45
12705 St. Charles Rock Rd. • 314.291.8845
100 Units, pets OK. Airport transportation. Laundry facility. Rooms come with phones and cable TV. Wheelchair accessible. Senior discount. Credit cards: AE, CB, DC, DS, MC, V.

BROOKFIELD
Brookfield Country Inn
$27-43
800 S. Main Street • 660.258.7262
30 Units, pets OK. Continental breakfast. Pool. Rooms come with phones and cable TV. Major credit cards.

BUTLER
Super 8 Motel
$41-61
Junction of Hwys. 71 & 52 • 1114 W. Fort Scott St. • 660.679.6183
48 Units, pets OK. Continental breakfast. Rooms come with phones and cable TV. Wheelchair accessible. Senior discount. Credit cards: AE, CB, DC, DS, MC, V.

CABOOL
Super 8 Motel
$42
US 60 (Exit 181S) • 417.962.5888

27 Units, no pets. Continental breakfast. Fax service. Rooms come with phones and cable TV. Wheelchair accessible. Senior discount. Credit cards: AE, CB, DC, DS, MC, V.

CAMERON
Days Inn
$35-50
501 Northland Drive • 816.632.6623
39 Units, pets OK. Continental breakfast. Pool. Rooms come with phones and cable TV. Some rooms have microwaves and refrigerators. AAA/senior discount available (10%). Credit cards: AE, DS, MC, V.

Econo Lodge
$35-48
On US 69 (half mile west I-35, Exit 54)
816.632.6571
36 Units, pets OK. Continental breakfast. Pool. Rooms come with phones and cable TV. AAA/Senior discount. Credit cards: AE, DC, DS, MC, V.

CAPE GIRARDEAU
Budget Inn
$35
1448 N. Kingshighway • 573.334.2828
37 Units, pets OK. Rooms come with phones and cable TV. Major credit cards.

CARTHAGE
Capri Motel
$36
I-44 & Alt. 71 Hwy. • 417.623.0391
48 Units, pets OK ($10 dep. req.). Restaurant on premises. Rooms come with phones and cable TV. Wheelchair accessible. Major credit cards.

Days Inn
$40-54
2244 Grand Avenue • 417.358.2499
40 Units, pets OK ($10). Continental breakfast. Data ports. Rooms come with phones and cable TV. Some rooms have microwaves and refrigerators. AAA/Senior discount. Credit cards: AE, CB, DC, DS, JCB, MC, V.

CASSVILLE
Super 8 Motel
$47
Jct. Hwys. 37 & 76/86 • 417.847.4888
46 Units, pets OK. Continental breakfast. Pool. Data ports. Rooms come with phones and cable TV. Some rooms have microwaves and refrigerators. Wheelchair accessible. AAA/Senior discount. Credit cards: AE, CB, DC, DS, MC, V.

CHILLICOTHE
Super 8 Motel
$50*
580 Old Hwy. 36E • 660.646.7888
55 Units, pets OK. Continental breakfast. Laundry facility. Rooms come with phones and cable TV. Senior discount. Major credit cards.
*AAA discounted rates.

CLARKSVILLE
Clarksville Inn
$38-48
2nd & Lewis Streets • 573.242.3324
23 Units, pets OK ($10). Continental breakfast. Laundry facility. Rooms come with phones and cable TV. Some rooms have kitchens and refrigerators. Senior discount. Credit cards: AE, CB, DC, DS, MC, V.

CLINTON
Best Western Colonial Motel
$45-55
13 Bypass, E. Franklin • 660.885.2206
32 Units, pets OK ($3). Continental breakfast. Rooms come with phones and cable TV. Some rooms have microwaves and refrigerators. AAA/Senior discount. Credit cards: AE, DC, DS, MC, V.

Knights Inn
$27-40
1508 N. 2nd Street • 660.885.2267
25 Units, pets OK ($5). Continental breakfast. Playground. Picnic area. Rooms come with phones and cable TV. AAA/Senior discount. Credit cards: AE, DC, DS, MC, V.

COLUMBIA
Eastwood Motel
$35-55
2518 Bus. Loop 70E. • 573.343.8793
36 Units, no pets. Heated pool. Sauna. Jacuzzi. Fitness facility. Playground. Rooms come with phones and cable TV. Some rooms have jacuzzis. AAA discount. Credit cards: AE, CB, DC, DS, MC, V.

Motel 6
$33-49
1800 I-70 Drive S.W. • 573.445.8433

87 Units, pets OK. Laundry facility. Data ports. Rooms come with phones, A/C and cable TV. Wheelchair accessible. Credit cards: AE, CB, DC, DS, MC, V.

Red Roof Inn
$39-61
201 E. Texas Avenue • 573.442.0145
108 Units, pets OK. Data ports. Rooms come with phones and cable TV. AAA discount. Credit cards: AE, CB, DC, DS, MC, V.

CONCORDIA
Days Inn
$39-60
200 N. West Street • 660.463.7987
44 Units, pets OK ($5). Continental breakfast. Heated pool. Game room. Meeting rooms. Laundry facility. Rooms come with phones and cable TV. AAA/Senior discount. Credit cards: AE, DS, MC, V.

CONWAY
Budget Inn
$40-50
101 Martindale Drive • I-44, Exit 113
417.589.2503
20 Units, pets OK ($10). Data ports. Rooms come with phones and cable TV. Some rooms have microwaves and refrigerators. Senior discount. Credit cards: AE, DS, MC, V.

CUBA
Best Western Cuba Inn
$45-60
I-44, Exit 208 • 573.885.7421
50 Units, pets OK ($5). Continental breakfast. Pool. Meeting rooms. Rooms come with phones and cable TV. Some rooms have refrigerators. AAA discount. Major credit cards.

Super 8 Motel
$47
28 Hwy P • I-44, Exit 208 • 573.885.2087
58 Units, pets OK. Laundry facility. Rooms come with phones and cable TV. Senior discount. Wheelchair accessible. Major credit cards.

DEXTER
Country Hearth Inn
$40-55
913 Outer Road • 573.624.7400
40 Units, no pets. Continental breakfast. Rooms come with phones and cable TV. AAA/Senior discount. Credit cards: AE, DC, DS, MC, V.

Super 8 Motel
$43
1807 Business 60W • 573.624.7465
51 Units, pets OK. Continental breakfast. Pool. Rooms come with phones and cable TV. Senior discount. Wheelchair accessible. Major credit cards.

DONIPHAN
Econo Lodge
$38-55
109 Smith Drive • 573.996.2101
31 Units, no pets. Continental breakfast. Pool. Jacuzzi. Rooms come with phones and cable TV. Wheelchair accessible. Major credit cards.

EUREKA
Super 8 Motel
$38-50 (66-76)*
1733 W. 5th Street • 636.938.4368
60 Units, pets OK ($10). Pool. Rooms come with phones and cable TV. Senior discount. Major credit cards.
*Higher rates effective late-May through August.

Red Carpet Inn
$30-50 (60-65)*
1725 W. 5th Street • 636.938.5348
62 Units, pets OK ($20 dep. req.). Pool. Miniature golf. Rooms come with phones and cable TV. Some rooms have refrigerators. AAA discount. Credit cards: AE, CB, DC, DS, MC, V.
*Higher rates effective Memorial Day through mid-September.

FARMINGTON
Days Inn
$48-52
1400 W. Liberty Street • 573.756.8951
50 Units, no pets. Continental breakfast. Rooms come with phones and cable TV. AAA discount. Major credit cards.

FENTON
Motel 6
$36-52
1860 Bowles Avenue • I-44, Exit 274
636.349.1800
110 Units, pets OK. Pool. Laundry facility. Data ports. Rooms come with phones, A/C

and cable TV. Wheelchair accessible. Credit cards: AE, CB, DC, DS, MC, V.

FERGUSON
Super 8 Motel
$47-52
2790 Target Drive • I-27, Exit 30
314.355.7808
55 Units, no pets. Continental breakfast. Rooms come with phones and cable TV. Some rooms have microwaves and refrigerators. Major credit cards.

FLORISSANT
Red Roof Inn
$37-45
307 Dunn Road • I-270, Exit 26B
314.831.7900
108 Units, pets OK. Rooms come with phones and cable TV. Some rooms have microwaves and refrigerators. AAA discount. Major credit cards.

GRAIN VALLEY
Travelodge
$45-50
105 Sunny Lane Drive • 816.224.3420
42 Units, pets OK ($5). Continental breakfast. Pool. Airport transportation. Rooms come with phones and cable TV. Some rooms have kitchens and refrigerators. AAA/Senior discount. Credit cards: AE, CB, DC, DS, MC, V.

GRANDVIEW
Super 8 Motel
$47-49*
15201 S. 71 Hwy. • 816.331.0300
100 Units, no pets. Heated indoor pool. Meeting rooms. Laundry facility. Rooms come with phones and cable TV. Senior discount. Credit cards: AE, CB, DC, DS, MC, V.
*Rates may increase slightly during weekends, holidays and special events.

HANNIBAL
Econo Lodge
$40-54*
3604 McMasters Ave. • 573.221.0422
31 Units, no pets. Continental breakfast. Rooms come with phones and cable TV. Some rooms have microwaves and refrigerators. Senior discount. Credit cards: AE, DS, MC, V.
*AAA discounted rates.

Super 7 Motel
$30-55
612 Mark Twain Ave. • 573.221.1666
49 Units, no pets. Pool. Rooms come with phones and cable TV. AAA discount. Credit cards: AE, DC, DS, MC, V.

HARRISONVILLE
Budget Host Caravan Motel
$31-36
1705 Hwy. 291N. • 816.884.4100
24 Units, pets OK. Picnic area. Rooms come with phones and cable TV. AAA/senior discount available ($2.00). Credit cards: AE, DC, DS, MC, V.

Slumber Inn Motel
$32-35
21400 E. 275th Street
Jct. Hwys. 71 & 7 S. • 816.884.3100
28 Units, pets OK. Continental breakfast. Pool. Picnic area. Rooms come with phones and cable TV. Some rooms have microwaves and refrigerators. AAA/Senior discount. Credit cards: AE, DS, MC, V.

Super 8 Motel
$49
2400 Rockhaven Road • 816.887.2999
39 Units, no pets. Laundry facility. Rooms come with phones and cable TV. Wheelchair accessible. Senior discount. Credit cards: AE, CB, DC, DS, MC, V.

HIGGINSVILLE
Super 8 Motel
$48-55
6471 Oakview Lane • I-70, Exit 49
660.584.7781
44 Units, pets OK ($5 and $10 dep. req.). Toast bar. Laundry facility. Rooms come with phones and cable TV. Senior discount. Wheelchair accessible. Major credit cards.

HOUSTON
Southern Inn Motel
$38-43
1493 Hwy. 63S. • 417.967.4591
32 Units, pets OK ($5). Airport transportation. Rooms come with phones and cable TV. AAA discount. Credit cards: AE, DC, DS, MC, V.

INDEPENDENCE
Budget Host Inn
$40-50
15014 E. Hwy. 40, I-70, Exit 14

816.373.7500
50 Units, no pets. Laundry facility. Rooms come with phones and cable TV. AAA/senior discount available ($2.00). Credit cards: AE, DS, MC, V.

Red Roof Inn
$39-65
13712 E. 43rd Terrace • 816.373.2800
108 Units, pets OK. Fitness facility. Data ports. Rooms come with phones and cable TV. Wheelchair accessible. AAA discount. Credit cards: AE, CB, DC, DS, MC, V.

Super 8 Motel
$49
4032 S. Lynn Court Drive • I-70, Exit 12
816.833.1888
77 Units, pets OK. Laundry facility. Rooms come with phones and cable TV. Senior discount. Wheelchair accessible. Major credit cards.

JEFFERSON CITY
Motel 6
$34-44
1624 Jefferson Street • 573.634.4220
99 Units, pets OK. Data ports. Rooms come with phones, A/C and cable TV. Wheelchair accessible. Credit cards: AE, CB, DC, DS, MC, V.

JOPLIN
Motel 6
$33-38
3031 S. Range Line Rd. • 417.781.6400
122 Units, pets OK. Pool. Laundry facility. Rooms come with phones, A/C and cable TV. Wheelchair accessible. Credit cards: AE, CB, DC, DS, MC, V.

Solar Inn & Suites
$35-49
3508 S. Range Line Rd. • 417.781.6776
111 Units, no pets. Continental breakfast. Pool. Rooms come with cable TV. Some rooms have phones and jacuzzis. AAA/ Senior discount. Major credit cards.

Westwood Motel
$33-40
1700 W. 30th Street • 417.782.7212
27 Units, pets OK ($5 and $25 dep. req.). Pool. Laundry facility. Rooms come with phones and cable TV. Some rooms have microwaves and refrigerators. AAA/Senior discount. Credit cards: AE, DS, MC, V.

KANSAS CITY — *see also Belton, Blue Springs, Independence, Kansas City (KS), Kearney, Lenexa (KS), Olathe (KS) and Overland Park (KS)*

Budget Host Inn
$36-50
15014 E. 40 Hwy. • 816.373.7500 or 800.BUDHOST
50 Units, no pets. Laundry facility. Rooms come with phones and cable TV. AAA/Senior discount. Credit cards: AE, DS, MC, V.

Motel 6—Airport
$38-50
8230 N.W. Prairie View Rd
I-29/US 71, Exit 8 • 816.741.6400
86 Units, pets OK. Pool. Laundry facility. Data ports. Rooms come with phones, A/C and cable TV. Wheelchair accessible. Credit cards: AE, CB, DC, DS, MC, V.

Motel 6—Southeast
$38-46
6400 E. 87th Street • 816.333.4468
112 Units, pets OK. Indoor pool. Rooms come with phones, A/C and cable TV. Wheelchair accessible. Credit cards: AE, CB, DC, DS, MC, V.

Red Roof Inn
$47
3636 N.E. Randolph Rd. • 816.452.8585
108 Units, pets OK. Rooms come with phones and cable TV. Credit cards: AE, CB, DC, DS, MC, V.

Travelers Inn
$35-44
6006 E. 31st Street • 816.861.4100
100 Units, pets OK. Pool. Game room. Meeting rooms. Rooms come with phones and cable TV. AAA/Senior discount. Major credit cards.

KEARNEY
Econo Lodge
$38-50*
505 Shanks Avenue • I-35, Exit 26
816.628.5111
40 Units, pets OK ($7). Continental breakfast. Pool. Rooms come with phones and cable TV. Senior discount. Major credit cards.
*AAA discounted rates.

KIMBERLING CITY
Kimberling Heights Resort Motel
$39-49*
1.5 mile south on SR 13 • 417.779.4158
14 Units, pets OK. Playground. Picnic area. Rooms some with cable TV. No phones in rooms. Some rooms have refrigerators. AAA/Senior discount. Major credit cards. *Closed December through February.

KIRKSVILLE
Budget Host Village Inn
$40-42
1304 S. Baltimore • 660.665.3722
30 Units, pets OK ($5). Rooms come with phones and cable TV. Some rooms have microwaves and refrigerators. AAA/Senior discount. Credit cards: AE, CB, DC, DS.

KNOB NOSTER
Whiteman Inn
$38-58
2340 W. Irish Lane • 660.563.3000
87 Units, pets OK ($3 and $20 dep. req.). Continental breakfast. Pool. Laundry facility. Meeting rooms. Data ports. Rooms come with phones and cable TV. Some rooms have microwaves and refrigerators. AAA/Senior discount. Major credit cards.

LAKE OZARK
Shoreland Motel
$40-45
1172 Bagnell Dam Blvd. (on US 54)
573.365.2354
25 Units, pets OK. Heated pool. Playground. Rooms come with cable TV. No phones in rooms. Senior discount. Credit cards: MC, V.

LAMAR
Super 8 Motel
$43-53
45 S.E. 1st Lane
Jct. Hwys. 71 & 180 • 417.682.6888
57 Units, no pets. Continental breakfast. Pool. Meeting room. Laundry facility. Rooms come with phones and cable TV. Wheelchair accessible. Senior discount. Credit cards: AE, CB, DC, DS, MC, V.

LEBANON
Econo Lodge
$33-45
2125 W. Elm Street • I-44, Exit 127
417.588.3226
40 Units, pets OK ($25 dep. req.). Continental breakfast. Rooms come with phones and cable TV. AAA/Senior discount. Credit cards: AE, CB, DC, DS, JCB, MC, V.

Super 8 Motel
$46
1831 W. Elm • 417.588.2574
83 Units, no pets. Continental breakfast. Pool. Laundry facility. Rooms come with phones and cable TV. Wheelchair accessible. Senior discount. Credit cards: AE, CB, DC, DS, MC, V.

LEXINGTON
Lexington Inn
$39-55
Junction Hwys. 24 & 13 • 660.259.4641
60 Units, pets OK ($100 dep. req.). Restaurant on premises. Laundry facility. Rooms come with phones and cable TV. AAA discount. Credit cards: AE, CB, DC, DS, MC, V.

LIBERTY
Super 8 Motel
$50
115 N. Stewart Road • 816.781.9400
60 Units, pets OK. Rooms come with phones and cable TV. Senior discount. Major credit cards.

MACON
Best Western Inn
$46-50
28933 Sunset Dr. (US 36W)
660.385.2125
46 Units, pets OK ($20 dep. req.). Continental breakfast. Pool. Meeting rooms. Airport transportation. Rooms come with phones and cable TV. Some rooms have microwaves and refrigerators. AAA/Senior discount. Credit cards: AE, CB, DC, DS, MC, V.

Welcome Travelier Motel
$26-50
Jct. of Hwys. 36 & 63 • 660.385.2102 or 888.279.9605
38 Units. Playground. Rooms come with phones and cable TV. Major credit cards.

MARSTON
Super 8 Motel
$44-51
501 S.E. Outer Road • I-55 at Hwy. EE (Exit 40) • 573.643.9888
63 Units, pets OK ($25 dep. req.). Continen-

tal breakfast. Laundry facility. Rooms come with phones and cable TV. AAA/Senior discount. Wheelchair accessible. Major credit cards.

MARYVILLE
Super 8 Motel
$43
222 Summit Drive, on US 71 (2 miles south from town) • 660.582.8088
32 Units, pets OK ($10 dep. req.). Data ports. Rooms come with phones and cable TV. Some rooms have refrigerators. Wheelchair accessible. AAA/Senior discount. Credit cards: AE, DC, DS, MC, V.

MEXICO
Villager Lodge
$38-56
1010 E. Liberty Street • 573.581.1440
60 Units, pets OK ($5). Continental breakfast. Pool. Meeting rooms. Laundry facility. Fitness facility. Data ports. Rooms come with refrigerators, phones and cable TV. Some rooms have microwaves. AAA/ Senior discount. Credit cards: AE, CB, DC, DS, MC, V.

MOBERLY
Super 8 Motel
$50
300 Hwy. 24E • 660.263.8862
60 Units, no pets. Continental breakfast. Data ports. Rooms come with phones and cable TV. AAA/Senior discount. Major credit cards.

MONETT
Cambridge Inn
$38-48
868 Hwy. 60 • 417.235.8039
41 Units, pets OK ($10). Pool. Laundry facility. Playground. Meeting rooms. Rooms come with phones and cable TV. AAA/Senior discount. Major credit cards.

MONROE CITY
Monroe City Inn
$30-55
3 Gateway Square • 573.735.4200
47 Units, pets OK ($5 surcharge, in smoking rooms only). Heated indoor pool (closed mid-October through March). Meeting rooms. Jacuzzi. Rooms come with phones and cable TV. Wheelchair accessible. Senior discount. Credit cards: AE, CB, DC, DS, MC, V.

Rainbow Motel
$28-32
308 5th Street • 573.735.4526
20 Units, pets OK ($5). Pool. Rooms come with phones and cable TV. Some rooms have microwaves and refrigerators. Credit cards: AE, DS, MC, V.

MOUNTAIN GROVE
Best Western House Inn
$38-46
111 E. 17th Street • 417.926.3152
51 Units, pets OK ($5). Continental breakfast. Pool. Rooms come with phones and cable TV. AAA/Senior discount. Major credit cards.

Days Inn of Mountain Grove
$36-48
300 E. 19th Street • 417.926.5555
37 Units, pets OK ($6). Continental breakfast. Pool. Meeting rooms. Rooms come with phones and cable TV. AAA/Senior discount. Major credit cards.

MOUNTAIN VIEW
Honeysuckle Inn
$45
1207 E. Hwy. 60 • 417.934.1144
24 Units, no pets. Continental breakfast. Rooms come with phones and cable TV. Credit cards: AE, DS, MC, V.

MOUNT VERNON
Budget Host Ranch Motel
$40-42
Jct. Hwy. 39 & I-44 • 417.466.2125
21 Units, pets OK. Pool. Picnic area. Rooms come with phones and cable TV. AAA discount. Major credit cards.

NEOSHO
Super 8 Motel
$48
3085 Gardner/Edgewood Drive
417.455.1888
South end of town on US 71
58 Units, pets OK ($10 dep. req.). Continental breakfast. Laundry facility. Rooms come with phones and cable TV. AAA/Senior discount. Wheelchair accessible. Major credit cards.

NEVADA
Rambler Motel
$36-59
1401 E. Austin Street • 417.667.3351

53 Units, pets OK ($10). Continental breakfast. Pool. Rooms come with phones and cable TV. Some rooms have refrigerators. AAA/Senior discount. Major credit cards.

Super 8 Motel
$46
2301 E. Austin Street • 417.667.8888
59 Units, pets OK. Meeting rooms. Laundry facility. Rooms come with phones and cable TV. Some rooms have refrigerators. Senior discount. Credit cards: AE, CB, DC, DS, MC, V.

NEW MADRID — *see Marston*

NIXA
Super 8 Motel
$44-54
418 Massey Blvd. • 417.725.0880
44 Units, pets OK. Continental breakfast. Rooms come with phones and cable TV. Wheelchair accessible. AAA/Senior discount. Major credit cards.

OAK GROVE
Econo Lodge
$40-50 (50-60)*
410 S.E. 1st Street • 816.625.3681
39 Units, pets OK ($25 dep. req.). Continental breakfast. Rooms come with phones and cable TV. Senior discount. Credit cards: AE, DS, MC, V.
*Higher rates effective May through August.

ODESSA
Parkside Inn
$40-50
400 W. 40 Hwy. • 816.230.7588
40 Units, pets OK. Continental breakfast. Meeting rooms. Data ports. Rooms come with phones and cable TV. AAA/Senior discount. Credit cards: AE, DS, MC, V.

O'FALLON
Super 8 Motel
$43-47*
987 W. Terra Lane • 636.272.7272
45 Units, pets OK. Continental breakfast. Pool. Jacuzzi. Laundry facility. Copy machine. Rooms come with phones and cable TV. Wheelchair accessible. Senior discount. Major credit cards.
*Rates may increase slightly during weekends, holidays and special events.

OSAGE BEACH
Scottish Inns
$30-55
5404 Hwy. 54 • 573.348.3123
23 Units, pets OK ($5). Picnic area. Rooms come with phones and cable TV. AAA/Senior discount. Major credit cards.

OZARK
Super 8 Motel
$39-52
299 N. 20th Street • 417.581.8800
60 Units, pets OK. Pool. Laundry facility. Playground. Rooms come with phones and cable TV. Wheelchair accessible. AAA/Senior discount. Major credit cards.

POTOSI
Super 8 Motel
$45-57
820 E. High Street • 573.438.8888
49 Units, pets OK. Laundry facility. Meeting rooms. Rooms come with phones and cable TV. Senior discount. Wheelchair accessible. Major credit cards.

ROCK PORT
Rock Port Inn
$40
Junction I-29 and US 136 (Exit 110)
660.744.6282
36 Units, pets OK. Pool. Laundry facility. Rooms come with phones and cable TV. Some rooms have refrigerators and jacuzzis. Senior discount. Credit cards: AE, CB, DC, DS, MC, V.

Super 8 Motel
$40-45
1301 Hwy. 136W • 660.744.5357
40 Units, pets OK. Continental breakfast. Laundry facility. Rooms come with phones and cable TV. Wheelchair accessible. Senior discount. Major credit cards.

ROLLA
Econo Lodge
$40-50
1417 Martin Springs Dr. • 573.341.3130
60 Units, pets OK. Continental breakfast. Pool. Laundry facility. Rooms come with phones and cable TV. AAA/Senior discount. Credit cards: AE, CB, DC, DS, MC, V.

Super 8 Motel
$40*
1201 Kingshighway • 573.386.4156
44 Units, no pets. Continental breakfast.

Rooms come with phones and cable TV. Wheelchair accessible. Senior discount. Credit cards: AE, CB, DC, DS, MC, V.
*Rates may increase slightly during weekends and special events.

Zeno's Motel
$50
1621 Martin Springs Dr. • 573.364.1301
50 Units, pets OK. Heated and indoor pools. Saunas. Jacuzzi. Tennis court. Fitness facility. Playground. Meeting rooms. Laundry facility. Rooms come with phones and cable TV. AAA/Senior discount. Credit cards: AE, CB, DC, DS, MC, V.

ST. ANN
Best Way Inn of St. Louis
$40
3679 N. Lindbergh • 314.291.3994
23 Units, pets OK. Restaurant on premises. Rooms come with phones and cable TV. Wheelchair accessible. Major credit cards.

ST. CHARLES
Motel 6
$40-42
3800 Harry Truman Blvd. • 636.925.2020
109 Units, pets OK. Pool. Laundry facility. Data ports. Rooms come with phones, A/C and cable TV. Wheelchair accessible. Credit cards: AE, CB, DC, DS, MC, V.

STE. GENEVIEVE
Family Budget Inns
$40-50
17030 New Bremen • 573.543.2272
65 Units, pets OK ($3 and $20 dep. req.). Pool. Meeting rooms. Laundry facility. Rooms come with phones and cable TV. AAA discount. Major credit cards.

ST. JOSEPH
Motel 6
$38-48
4021 Frederick Blvd. • I-29. Exit 47
816.232.2311
117 Units, pets OK. Restaurant on premises. Pool. Data ports. Rooms come with phones, A/C and cable TV. Wheelchair accessible. Credit cards: AE, CB, DC, DS, MC, V.

Super 8 Motel
$46-55
4024 Frederick Avenue • I-29, Exit 47
816.364.3031
54 Units, pets OK. Laundry facility. Rooms come with phones and cable TV. Senior discount. Major credit cards.

ST. LOUIS — *see also Belleville (IL), Bridgeton, Caseyville (IL), Fenton, Ferguson, Florissant, Hazelwood and St. Charles*
Econo Lodge
$40-55
1351 Dunn Road • I-270, Exit 32
314.388.1500
78 Units, no pets. Restaurant on premises. Continental breakfast. Pool. Rooms come with phones and cable TV. Major credit cards.

Motel 6—Airport
$40-54
4576 Woodson Road
I-70, Exit 236 • 314.427.1313
104 Units, pets OK. Pool. Data ports. Rooms come with phones, A/C and cable TV. Wheelchair accessible. Credit cards: AE, CB, DC, DS, MC, V.

Motel 6—North
$40-48
1405 Dunn Road • 314.869.9400
81 Units, pets OK. Pool. Laundry facility. Data ports. Rooms come with phones, A/C and cable TV. Wheelchair accessible. Credit cards: AE, CB, DC, DS, MC, V.

Motel 6—South
$40-50 (53-55)*
6500 S. Lindbergh Blvd. • 314.892.3664
117 Units, pets OK. Pool. Data ports. Rooms come with phones, A/C and cable TV. Wheelchair accessible. Credit cards: AE, CB, DC, DS, MC, V.
*Higher rates effective summer weekends.

Super 8 Motel
$47*
2790 Target Drive • I-270, Exit 30N
314.355.7808
53 Units, pets OK. Rooms come with phones and cable TV. Senior discount. Wheelchair accessible. Major credit cards.
*Rates higher during special events and weekends.

ST. ROBERT
Days Inn
$31-54*
I-44, Exit 164 • 573.336.5556
35 Units, pets OK ($5). Continental breakfast. Pool. Laundry facility. Rooms

come with phones, microwaves, refrigerators and cable TV. Major credit cards.
*AAA discounted rates.

Villager Lodge
$43-50*
I-44, Exit 163 • 573.336.3036
50 Units, pets OK. Pool. Laundry facility. Rooms come with phones and cable TV. Senior discount. Wheelchair accessible. Major credit cards.
*Higher rates weekends, special events and holidays.

SEDALIA
Budget Host Super 7 Motel
$34-49
5650 S. Limit Avenue • On US 65S
660.827.0215
24 Units, no pets. Rooms come with microwaves, refrigerators, phones and cable TV. Senior discount. Credit cards: AE, DS, MC, V.

SPRINGFIELD — *see also Nixa, Ozark and Strafford*
Motel 6
$31-38
3114 N. Kentwood • 417.833.0880
102 Units, pets OK. Pool. Rooms come with phones, A/C and cable TV. Wheelchair accessible. Credit cards: AE, CB, DC, DS, MC, V.

Ozark Inn
$25-50
2601 N. Glenstone • 417.865.6565
52 Units, pets OK. Rooms come with phones and cable TV. AAA/Senior discount. Wheelchair accessible. Credit cards: AE, CB, DC, DS, MC, V.

Scottish Inn
$35-40
2933 N Glenstone • 417.862.4301
28 Units, pets OK ($10). Continental breakfast. Pool. Rooms come with phones and cable TV. Some rooms have microwaves and refrigerators. AAA/Senior discount. Credit cards: AE, CB, DC, DS, MC, V.

Solar Inn
$40-50
2355 N. Glenstone • 417.866.6776
132 Units, pets OK. Continental breakfast. Pool. Rooms come with phones and cable TV. AAA discount. Major credit cards.

STRAFFORD
Super 8 Motel
$45-50
315 E. Chestnut Street • 417.736.3883
42 Units, pets OK. Continental breakfast. Laundry facility. Rooms come with phones and cable TV. AAA discount. Credit cards: AE, CB, DC, DS, MC, V.

SULLIVAN
Family Motor Inn
$30-44
209 N. Service Road • 573.468.4119
63 Units, pets OK ($5). Pool. Playground. Game room. Jacuzzi. Laundry facility. Rooms come with phones and cable TV. Wheelchair accessible. AAA/Senior discount. Major credit cards.

Super 8 Motel
$42-48
601 N. Service Road • 573.468.8076
60 Units, pets OK ($5). Continental breakfast. Laundry facility. Rooms come with phones and cable TV. Senior discount. Wheelchair accessible. Major credit cards.

WARRENSBURG
Super 8 Motel
$42-52*
439 E. Russell Avenue • 660.429.2183
40 Units, no pets. Continental breakfast. Rooms come with phones and cable TV. AAA/Senior discount. Major credit cards.
*AAA discounted rates.

WARRENTON
Budget Host Inn
$30-36
804 N. Hwy. 47 • I-70, Exit 193
636.456.2522
55 Units, no pets. Pool. Laundry facility adjacent. Rooms come with phones, A/C and cable TV. Wheelchair accessible. Credit cards: AE, CB, DC, DS, MC, V.

Super 8 Motel
$42-46*
1429 N. Service Road • 636.456.5157
46 Units, no pets. Laundry facility. Rooms come with phones and cable TV. Wheelchair accessible. AAA/Senior discount. Credit cards: AE, CB, DC, DS, MC, V.
*Rates may increase slightly during weekends and special events.

WAYNESVILLE
DeVille Motor Inn
$41-45
461 Old Rte. 66 • 573.336.3113
40 Units, no pets. Pool. Rooms come with phones and cable TV. Major credit cards.

WENTZVILLE
Econo Lodge
$34-40
1400 Continental Drive • 636.327.5515
80 Units, pets OK ($10). Continental breakfast. Laundry facility. Rooms come with phones and cable TV. Some rooms have refrigerators. AAA discount. Major credit cards.

Super 8 Motel
$45
4 Pantera Drive • I-70, Exit 208
636.327.5300
62 Units, no pets. Continental breakfast. Pool. Game room. Rooms come with phones and cable TV. AAA/Senior discount. Credit cards: AE, DC, DS, MC, V.

montana

BAKER
Roy's Motel & Campground
$30
327 W. Montana Avenue • 406.778.3321 or 800.552.3321
22 Units, pets OK. Rooms come with cable TV. Wheelchair accessible. Major credit cards.

BIGFORK
Timbers Motel
$42 (84)*
8540 SR 35 • 406.837.6200 or 800.821.4546
40 Units, pets OK ($5 and $50 dep. req.). Pool. Rooms come with phones and cable TV. Wheelchair accessible. Credit cards: AE, DS, MC. V.
*Higher rates effective June through Labor Day.

BIG TIMBER
Big Timber Budget Host
$44-54
600 W. 2nd • I-90, Exit 367
406.932.4943
22 Units, no pets. Continental breakfast. Rooms come with phones and cable TV. Wheelchair accessible. Major credit cards.
*AAA discounted rates.

Lazy J Motel
$34-40
On Hwy. 10 • 406.932.5533
25 Units, pets OK. Rooms come with phones and cable TV. Wheelchair accessible. Major credit cards.

BILLINGS
Cherry Tree Inn
$37
923 N. Broadway • I-90, Exit 450
406.252.5603
65 Units, pets OK. Continental breakfast. Laundry facility. Rooms come with phones and cable TV. Some rooms have kitchens and refrigerators. AAA discount. Credit cards: AE, CB, DC, DS, JCB, MC, V.

Motel 6
$35-50
5400 Midland Road • 406.252.0093
99 Units, pets OK. Pool. Laundry facility. Data ports. Rooms come with A/C, phones and cable TV. Wheelchair accessible. Credit cards: AE, CB, DC, DS, MC, V.

Red Roof Inn
$35-53
5353 Midland Road • 406.248.7551
118 Units, pets OK. Indoor pool. Laundry facility. Rooms come with A/C, phones and cable TV. Wheelchair accessible. Credit cards: AE, CB, DC, DS, MC, V.

Rimview Inn
$47
1025 N. 27th Street • 406.248.2622 or 800.551.1418
54 Units, pets OK. Continental breakfast. Jacuzzi. Laundry facility. Rooms come with phones and cable TV. Some rooms have microwaves and kitchenettes. Wheelchair accessible. AAA discount. Major credit cards.

BOZEMAN
Blue Sky Motel
$37-40
1010 E. Main Street • 406.578.2311 or 800.845.9032
27 Units, pets OK. Restaurant on premises. Rooms come with phones and cable TV. Major credit cards.

Rainbow Motel
$39
510 N. 7th Street • 406.587.4201
42 Units, pets OK ($10). Pool. Rooms come with phones and cable TV. Some rooms have microwaves, refrigerators and kitchenettes. Major credit cards.

Royal "7" Budget Inn
$37-46
310 N. 7th Avenue • I-90, Exit 306
406.587.3103
47 Units, pets OK. Rooms come with phones and cable TV. Credit cards: DS, MC. V.

BROADUS
Broadus Motels*
$37-44
101 N. Park • 406.436.2626

54 Units, pets OK. Jacuzzi. Laundry facility. Rooms comes with phones and cable TV. Wheelchair accessible. Major credit cards.
*Business operates 3 motels in town.

BROWNING
Western Motel
$50
On US 2 • 406.338.7572
15 Units, pets OK. Rooms come with phones and cable TV. Wheelchair accessible. Major credit cards.

BUTTE
Capri Motel
$34-40
220 N. Wyoming St. • 406.723.4391
68 Units, pets OK ($5). Continental breakfast. Laundry and fitness facility. Rooms come with phones and cable TV. Some rooms have microwaves and refrigerators. AAA discount. Credit cards: AE, DS, MC, V.

Finlen Hotel
$37-42*
100 E. Broadway • 406.723.5461
52 Units, no pets. Rooms come with phones and cable TV. Some rooms have A/C. Senior discount. Credit cards: AE, DS, MC. V.
*AAA discounted rates.

Rocker Inn
$40-45
122001 W. Brown's Gulch Road
I-15, Exit 12 • 406.723.5464
49 Units, no pets. Laundry facility. Rooms come with phones and cable TV. Some rooms have refrigerators. Wheelchair accessible. AAA discount. Major credit cards.

CHINOOK
Chinook Motor Inn
$47
100 Indiana Street • 406.357.2248
38 Units, pets OK. Restaurant on premises. Rooms come with free movies and cable TV. Some rooms have kitchens and refrigerators. AAA discount. Credit cards: AE, DS, MC, V.

CIRCLE
Travelers Inn
$29-35*
On SR 200 • 406.485.3323
14 Units, pets OK. Rooms come with phones and cable TV. Wheelchair accessible. Major credit cards.
*Discount if paid in cash.

COLSTRIP
Fort Union Inn
$35-45
5 Dogwood • 406.748.2553
20 Units, no pets. Rooms come with phones and cable TV. Wheelchair accessible. Senior discount. Major credit cards.

COLUMBIA FALLS
Glacier Inn Motel
$38-45*
1401 2nd Avenue E. • 406.892.4341
19 Units, pets OK. Rooms come with phones and cable TV. Wheelchair accessible. Major credit cards.
*Summer rates higher.

CULBERTSON
The Kings Inn
$35
408 E. 6th • 406.787.6277
20 Units, no pets. Airport transportation. Rooms come with phones and cable TV. Credit cards: AE, DC, DS, MC, V.

CUT BANK
Glacier Gateway Inn
$46
1121 E. Railroad Street • 406.873.5588 or 800.851.5541
19 Units, pets OK. Continental breakfast. Rooms come with phones and cable TV. Some rooms have microwaves and refrigerators. Wheelchair accessible. AAA discount. Major credit cards.

Super 8 Motel
$49
609 W. Main • 406.873.5662
61 Units, no pets. Heated indoor pool and jacuzzi. Rooms come with coffeemakers and cable TV. Some rooms have refrigerators. AAA/Senior discount. Credit cards: AE, DC, DS, MC, V.

DEER LODGE
Scharf's Motor Inn
$30-35
819 Main Street • 406.846.2810
42 Units, pets OK. Laundry facility. Rooms come with phones and cable TV. Some rooms have kitchens, microwaves and refrigerators. AAA/Senior discount. Credit cards: AE, CB, DC, DS, MC, V.

DILLON
Sundowner Motel
$29-34
500 N. Montana Street • 406.683.2375
32 Units, pets OK. Playground. Airport transportation. Rooms come with phones and cable TV. Some rooms have refrigerators. AAA discount. Credit cards: AE, CB, DC, DS, MC, V.

Super 8 Motel
$41-56*
550 N. Montana • 406.683.4288
48 Units, pets OK ($25 dep. req.). Copy machine. Rooms come with phones and cable TV. Wheelchair accessible. Senior discount. Credit cards: AE, CB, DC, DS, MC, V.
*Higher rates effective June through Sept.

EAST GLACIER PARK
Hostelling International
$12
1020 SR 49 • 406.226.4426
25 Beds, Hours: 7:30 am - 10 pm
Facilities: equipment storage area, information desk, kitchen, laundry facilities, linens, baggage storage, on-site parking, bike rentals. Private rooms available. Closed October 15 through May 1. Reservations recommended July 4 through August 15. Credit cards: DS, MC, V.

Dancing Bears Inn
$45-55
147 Montana Street • 406.226.4402
14 Units, pets OK. Rooms come with cable TV. Some rooms have refrigerators, kitchenettes and phones. AAA discount. Major credit cards.

ENNIS
Fan Mountain Inn
$41
204 N. Main • 406.682.5200
28 Units, pets OK ($5). Rooms come with A/C and cable TV. Some rooms have microwaves and refrigerators. Wheelchair accessible. Credit cards: AE, CB, DC, DS, MC, V.

FORSYTH
Restwel Motel
$34
810 Front Street • 406.356.2771
18 Units, pets OK. Continental breakfast. Rooms come with refrigerators and cable TV. Some rooms have microwaves and radios. AAA discount. Credit cards: AE, CB, DC, DS, MC, V.

Westwind Motor Inn
$50*
I-94, Exit 93 • 406.356.2038 or 888.356.2038
33 Units, pets OK ($2). Continental breakfast. Airport transportation. Rooms come with phones and cable TV. Some rooms have refrigerators. Credit cards: AE, CB, DC, DS, MC, V.
*AAA discounted rates.

GARDINER
Motel 6
$42-50 (60-80)*
109 Hell Roaring Road • 406.848.7520
40 Units, pets OK. Laundry facility. Rooms come with A/C, phones and cable TV. Wheelchair accessible. Credit cards: AE, CB, DC, DS, MC, V.
*Higher rates effective summer months.

GLACIER NATIONAL PARK — *see Browning, Columbia Falls, East Glacier Park, and Whitefish*

GLASGOW
Campbell Lodge
$29-35
534 3rd Avenue S. • 406.228.9328
31 Units, pets OK. Rooms come with phones and cable TV. Major credit cards.

Star Lodge Motel
$26-30
On US 2 W. • 406.228.2494
30 Units, pets OK. Rooms come with phones and cable TV. Wheelchair accessible. Major credit cards.

GLENDIVE
Budget Host Riverside Inn
$28-37
Hwy 16 • 406.377.2349
36 Units, pets OK. Continental breakfast. Rooms come with phones and cable TV. Some rooms have kitchenettes. AAA/Senior discount. Credit cards: AE, CB, DC, DS, MC, V.

Super 8 Motel
$46-51
1904 N. Merrill Avenue • 406.365.5671
51 Units, pets OK. Complementary breakfast offered. Meeting rooms. Copy machine. Rooms come with phones and cable TV. Wheelchair accessible. Senior discount. Credit cards: AE, CB, DC, DS, MC, V.

GREAT FALLS
Central Motel
$36-46
715 Central Avenue W. • 406.453.0161
28 Units, pets OK. Jacuzzi. Rooms come with cable TV. Some rooms have kitchens and refrigerators. AAA/Senior discount. Credit cards: AE, DS, MC, V.

Imperial Inn
$35
601 2nd Avenue N. • 406.452.9581 or 800.735.7173
30 Units, pets OK. Rooms come with phones and cable TV. Major credit cards.

Ski's Western Motel
$35-45
2420 10th Avenue S. • 406.453.3281
25 Units, pets OK ($5 dep. req.). Rooms come with phones and cable TV. Major credit cards.

HAMILTON
Bitterroot Motel
$33
408 S. 1st Street • 406.363.1142
10 Units, pets OK. Rooms come with phones and cable TV. Major credit cards.

City Center Motel
$33
W. 415 Main Street • 406.363.1651
14 Units, pets OK. Rooms come with phones and cable TV. Wheelchair accessible. Major credit cards.

HARDIN
American Inn
$45
1324 N. Crawford • 406.665.1870
42 Units, no pets. Restaurant on premises. Pool. Playground. Fitness facility. Laundry facility. Rooms come with A/C, phones and cable TV. Wheelchair accessible. Major credit cards.

Western Motel
$45
830 W. 3rd Street • 406.665.2296
28 Units, pets OK ($3). Rooms come with phones and cable TV. Major credit cards.

HARLOWTON
Corral Motel
$35
Jct. US 12 & 191 (east of town)
406.632.4331 or 800.392.4723
18 Units, pets OK. Rooms come with phones and cable TV. Some rooms have refrigerators. Credit cards: AE, DS, MC. V.

HAVRE
El Toro Inn
$38
521 First Street • 406.265.5414
41 Units, no pets. Laundry facility. Rooms come with cable TV. Some rooms have microwaves and refrigerators. Senior discount. Credit cards: AE, DC, DS, MC, V.

Super 8 Motel
$42-46
1901 Hwy. 2 W. • 406.265.1411
64 Units, pets OK with permission. Pastries offered. Rooms come with phones and cable TV. Wheelchair accessible. Senior discount. Credit cards: AE, CB, DC, DS, MC, V.

HELENA
Budget Inn Express
$34
524 N. Last Chance Gulch • 406.442.0600
46 Units, no pets. Rooms come with phones and cable TV. Laundry and fitness facility. Game room. Some rooms have refrigerators. Senior discount. Credit cards: AE, CB, DC, DS, MC, V.

Lamplighter Motel
$36-39
1006 Madison • 406.442.9200
16 Units, no pets. Rooms come with refrigerators, phones and cable TV. Some rooms have kitchenettes. AAA discount. Credit cards: AE, DC, DS, MC, V.

Motel 6
$37-50
800 N. Oregon Street • 406.442.9990
80 Units, pets OK. Pool. Laundry facility. Data ports. Rooms come with A/C, phones and cable TV. Wheelchair accessible. Credit cards: AE, CB, DC, DS, MC, V.

JORDAN
Fellman's Motel
$25-30
On SR 200 in town • 406.557.2209
16 Units, no pets. Rooms come with phones, cable TV and A/C. Major credit cards.

KALISPELL
Aero Inn
$34*
1830 US 93S • 406.755.3798 or

800.843.6114
62 Units, pets OK ($10 dep. req.). Pool. Sauna and jacuzzi. Rooms come with phones and cable TV. Wheelchair accessible. AAA discount. Major credit cards.
*Higher rate effective mid-June through mid-September.

Blue & White Motel
$33 (58)*
640 E. Idaho • 406.755.4311 or 800.382.3577
107 Units, pets OK. Restaurant on premises. Pool. Rooms come with phones and cable TV. Wheelchair accessible. Major credit cards.
*Higher rate effective summer months.

Motel 6
$35-50 (60-66)*
1540 Hwy 93 S. • 406.752.6355
114 Units, pets OK. Pool. Laundry facility. Data ports. Rooms come with A/C, phones and cable TV. Wheelchair accessible. Credit cards: AE, CB, DC, DS, MC, V.
*Higher rates effective mid-June through August.

LEWISTOWN
B&B Motel
$35-40
520 E. Main Street • 406.538.5496
36 Units, pets OK ($3). Rooms come with phones and cable TV. Some rooms have kitchens and refrigerators. Credit cards: AE, CB, DC, DS, MC, V.

Super 8 Motel
$47-50
102 Wendell Avenue • 406.538.2581
44 Units, no pets. Laundry facility. Rooms come with phones and cable TV. Wheelchair accessible. Senior discount. Credit cards: AE, CB, DC, DS, MC, V.

LIBBY
Caboose Motel
$33-40
Hwy. 2W (2 blocks west of downtown) 406.293.6201
29 Units, pets OK. Laundry facility. Picnic area. Rooms come with phones and cable TV. Credit cards: AE, CB, DC, DS, MC, V.

LINCOLN
Leeper's Motel
$35
406.362.4333 • West of town on SR 200
15 Units, pets OK ($5). Continental breakfast. Sauna and jacuzzi. Rooms come with cable TV. No A/C. Some rooms have refrigerators and microwaves. Credit cards: AE, DS, MC, V.

LIVINGSTON
Budget Host Parkway Motel
$32-40 (52-56)*
1124 W. Park • 406.222.3840
28 Units, pets OK. Heated pool. Rooms come with phones and cable TV. Some rooms have refrigerators. AAA discount. Major credit cards.
*Higher rates effective June through August.

Rainbow Motel
$32-38
5574 E. Park Street • 406.222.3780 or 800.788.2301
24 Units, pets OK. Rooms come with phones and cable TV. Major credit cards.

Super 8 Motel
$44-52 (56-61)*
105 Centennial Drive • 406.222.7711
36 Units, no pets. Laundry facility. Rooms come with phones and cable TV. Wheelchair accessible. Senior discount. Credit cards: AE, CB, DC, DS, MC, V.
*Higher rates effective mid-June through September.

MALTA
Maltana Motel
$39
138 S. 1st Avenue W. • 406.654.2610
19 Units, no pets. Airport transportation. Rooms come with phones and cable TV. AAA discount. Credit cards: AE, CB, DC, DS, MC, V.

MILES CITY
Budget Inn
$34
1006 S. Haynes Avenue • 406.232.3550
57 Units, pets OK. Continental breakfast. Heated pool and jacuzzi. Airport transportation. Rooms come with phones and cable TV. AAA/Senior discount. Credit cards: AE, CB, DC, DS, MC, V.

Motel 6
$34-37
1314 Haynes Avenue • 406.232.7040
88 Units, pets OK. Pool. Laundry facility.

Data ports. Rooms come with A/C, phones and cable TV. Wheelchair accessible. Credit cards: AE, CB, DC, DS, MC, V.

Super 8 Motel
$46-50
406.232.5261 • I-94, Exit 138, turn south on SR 59 toward Broadus.
58 Units, pets OK. Meeting rooms. Toast bar. Rooms come with phones and cable TV. Wheelchair accessible. Senior discount. Major credit cards.

MISSOULA
Bel Aire Motel
$44-55
300 E. Broadway • 406.543.3183 or 800.543.3184
52 Units, pets OK ($5). Continental breakfast. Pool and jacuzzi. Rooms come with phones and cable TV. AAA discount. Major credit cards.

Downtown Motel
$28-37
502 E. Broadway • 406.549.5191
22 Units, pets OK ($6). Rooms come with phones and cable TV. AAA discount. Credit cards: MC, V.

Sleepy Inn Motel
$37
1427 W. Broadway • 406.549.6484
35 Units, pets OK. Rooms come with phones and cable TV. Major credit cards.

Super 7 Motel
$35
1135 W. Broadway • 406.549.2358
50 Units, pets OK. Rooms come with cable TV. Some rooms have phones. Major credit cards.

RED LODGE
Eagle's Nest Motel
$36-42
702 S. Broadway • 406.446.2312
16 Units, pets OK. Rooms come with phones and cable TV. Wheelchair accessible. Major credit cards.

Yodeler Motel
$35-43
601 S. Broadway • 406.446.1435
22 Units, pets OK. Jacuzzi. Rooms come with phones and cable TV. Some rooms have microwaves, A/C and refrigerators. Wheelchair accessible. AAA discount. Major credit cards.

ROUNDUP
Best Inn
$24-30
630 Main Street • 406.323.1000
20 Units, no pets. Rooms come with phones and cable TV. Major credit cards.

Big Sky Motel
$35
740 Main Street • 406.323.2303
22 Units, pets OK. Rooms come with phones and cable TV. Wheelchair accessible. Major credit cards.

ST. REGIS
Super 8 Motel
$47-51 (55-65)*
Old Hwy. 10 (I-90, Exit 33) • 406.549.2422
53 Units, pets OK. Laundry facility. Rooms come with phones and cable TV. Senior discount. Major credit cards.
*Higher rates effective July and August.

SEELEY LAKE
Wilderness Gateway Inn
$44-50
On SR 83, south end of town
406.677.2095
19 Units, pets OK ($5). Jacuzzi. Rooms come with phones and cable TV. No A/C in rooms. AAA discount. Credit cards: AE, DS, MC. V.

SHELBY
O'Haire Manor Motel
$35
204 2nd Street S. • 406.434.5555
40 Units, pets OK ($5). Jacuzzi. Airport transportation. Laundry facility. Rooms come with phones and cable TV. Some rooms have A/C and refrigerators. Credit cards: AE, DC, DS, MC, V.

SIDNEY
Angus Ranchouse Motel
$26
2300 S. Central • 406.482.3826
48 Units, no pets. Restaurant on premises. Rooms come with cable TV. Wheelchair accessible. Major credit cards.

SUPERIOR
Budget Host Big Sky Motel
$40-48
103 4th Avenue E. (I-90, Exit 47)
406.822.4831
24 Units, pets OK. Continental breakfast.

Laundry facility. Rooms come with phones and cable TV. AAA/Senior discount. Major credit cards.

THREE FORKS
Broken Spur Motel
$34-44
124 West Elm • 406.285.3237
21 Units, pets OK ($5). Continental breakfast. Rooms come with phones and cable TV. Credit cards: AE, DS, MC, V.

Fort Three Forks Motel
$42
10776 Hwy 287 • 406.285.3233
24 Units, pets OK ($5). Continental breakfast. Laundry facility. Credit cards: AE, CB, DC, DS, MC, V.

WEST YELLOWSTONE
Alpine Motel
$30-45*
120 Madison • 406.646.7544
12 Units, no pets. Airport transportation. Rooms come with cable TV. No A/C or phones in rooms. Credit cards: MC, V.
*Motel closed November through April.

Al's Westward Ho Motel
$30-48*
16 Boundary Street • 406.646.7331
33 Units, no pets. Rooms come with phones and cable TV. No A/C in rooms. Credit cards: DS, MC. V.
*Open May through October.

Lazy G Motel
$32-43
123 Hayden Street • 406.646.7586
15 Units, no pets. Airport transportation. Rooms come with cable TV. No A/C in rooms. AAA discount. Credit cards: DS, MC, V.
*Motel closed April.

WHITEFISH
Allen's Motel
$30-55
6540 US 93S • 406.862.3995
17 Units, pets OK. Rooms come with phones and cable TV. Major credit cards.

Whitefish Motel
$48 (68)*
620 8th Street • 406.862.3507
18 Units, pets OK. Rooms come with phones and cable TV. Wheelchair accessible. Major credit cards.
*Higher rates effective mid-June through mid-August.

WHITEHALL
Super 8 Motel
$40-50
515 N. Whitehall Street • 406.287.5588
33 Units, pets OK with deposit in smoking rooms. Jacuzzi. Rooms come with phones and cable TV. Wheelchair accessible. Senior discount. Credit cards: AE, CB, DC, DS, MC, V.

WHITE SULPHUR SPRINGS
Gordon's Highland Motel
$30-40
410 E. Main Street • 406.547.3880
10 Units, pets OK. Rooms come with phones and cable TV. Wheelchair accessible. Major credit cards.

Tenderfoot/Hiland Motel
$30
301 W. Main Street • 406.547.3303 or 800.898.3303
21 Units, pets OK. Rooms come with phones and cable TV. Wheelchair accessible. Major credit cards.

WIBAUX
Super 8 Motel
$42
400 W. 2nd Avenue N. • 406.795.2666
35 Units, no pets. Continental breakfast. Copy machine. Rooms come with phones and cable TV. Wheelchair accessible. Senior discount. Credit cards: AE, CB, DC, DS, MC, V.

WOLF POINT
Homestead Inn
$35
101 US 2 E. • 406.653.1300 or 800.231.0986
47 Units, pets OK. Rooms come with phones and cable TV. Wheelchair accessible. Major credit cards.

Sherman Motor Inn
$39
200 E. Main • 406.653.1100 or 800.952.1100
46 Units, pets OK. Airport transportation. Meeting rooms. Rooms come with cable TV. Credit cards: AE, DC, DS, MC, V.

nebraska

AINSWORTH
Super 8 Motel
$35-45
1025 E. 4th • 402.387.0700
35 Units, pets OK. Meeting rooms. Rooms come with phones and cable TV. Wheelchair accessible. Senior discount. Credit cards: AE, CB, DC, DS, MC, V.

ALLIANCE
Sunset Motel
$45-55
1210 E. Hwy. 2 • 308.762.8660
20 Units, pets OK ($5). Jacuzzi. Laundry facility. Rooms come with phones, refrigerators and cable TV. Some rooms have microwaves and jacuzzis. AAA/Senior discount. Major credit cards.

ARAPAHOE
Shady Rest Camp Motel
$40
309 Chestnut • 308.962.5461
26 Units, pets OK. Rooms come with phones and cable TV. Wheelchair accessible. Senior discount. Major credit cards.

AUBURN
Arbor Manor
$41
1617 Central Avenue • 402.274.3663
25 Units, no pets. Restaurant on premises. Rooms come with phones and cable TV. Wheelchair accessible. Senior discount. Major credit cards.

Auburn Inn Motel
$30
517 "J" Street • 402.274.3143
36 Units, pets OK. Continental breakfast. Fax service. Laundry facility. Rooms come with A/C, phones and cable TV. Major credit cards.

AURORA
Budget Host Ken's Motel
$32
1515 11th Street • 402.694.3141
40 Units, pets OK. Rooms come with refrigerators, phones and cable TV. Credit cards: AE, DS, MC, V.

BEATRICE
Holiday Villa Motel
$31
1820 N. 6th Street • 402.223.4036
50 Units, pets OK. Rooms come with phones and cable TV. Some rooms have kitchenettes. Wheelchair accessible. Senior discount. Major credit cards.

BELLEVUE
American Family Inn
$43-48
1110 S Fort Cook Road • 402.291.0804
105 Units, pets OK ($7). Heated pool. Laundry facility. Playground. Game room. Data ports. Rooms come with phones, refrigerators, microwaves and cable TV. Wheelchair accessible. AAA/Senior discount. Major credit cards.

Super 8 Motel
$47-51
303 S. Fort Crook Road • 402.291.1518
40 Units, no pets. Rooms come with phones and cable TV. Wheelchair accessible. Senior discount. Credit cards: AE, CB, DC, DS, MC, V.

BIG SPRINGS
Budget 8 Panhandle Inn
$37
I-80 at Exit 107 • 308.889.3671
62 Units, pets OK. Indoor pool. Rooms come with phones and cable TV. Major credit cards.

BLAIR
Econo Lodge
$47
On Hwy. 30 • 402.426.2340
32 Units, pets OK. Restaurant on premises. Continental breakfast. Pool. Rooms come with phones and cable TV. Major credit cards.

BRIDGEPORT
Bell Motor Inn & Restaurant
$35
N. Hwy. 385 • 308.262.0557
22 Units, pets OK. Restaurant on premises. Rooms come with phones and cable TV. Wheelchair accessible. Major credit cards.

BROKEN BOW
Arrow Hotel
$40
509 S. 9th Avenue • 308.872.6662
24 Units, no pets. Meeting room. Restaurant on premises. Laundry facility. Rooms come with phones and cable TV. Some rooms have kitchens and refrigerators. Credit cards: AE, DS, MC, V.

Super 8 Motel
$46
215 E. "E" Street • 308.872.6428
33 Units, no pets. Continental breakfast. Game room and jacuzzi. Laundry facility. Rooms come with phones and cable TV. Wheelchair accessible. AAA/Senior discount. Credit cards: AE, CB, DC, DS, MC, V.

CENTRAL CITY
Super 8 Motel
$45-50
308.946.5055 • On Hwy 14, one mile south of US 30.
33 Units, no pets. Continental breakfast. Meeting room available. Rooms come with phones and cable TV. Wheelchair accessible. Senior discount. Credit cards: AE, CB, DC, DS, MC, V.

CHADRON
Pine View Motel
$29
901 E. 3rd Street • 308.432.5591
23 Units, no pets. Rooms come with phones and cable TV. Wheelchair accessible. Major credit cards.

Westerner Motel
$29-35
300 Oak Street • 308.432.5577
25 Units, pets OK ($5). Rooms come with phones and cable TV. AAA/Senior discount. Credit cards: AE, DS, MC, V.

COLUMBUS
Eco-Lux Inn
$37-43
3803 23rd Street • 402.564.9955
39 Units, no pets. Continental breakfast. Rooms come with phones and cable TV. AAA discount. Major credit cards.

Seven Knights Motel
$23-39
2222 23rd Street • 402.563.3533
35 Units, pets OK. Sauna and jacuzzi. Rooms come with A/C, phones and cable TV. Major credit cards.

COZAD
Budget Host Circle S Motel
$32-36
440 S. Meridian • I-80, Exit 222
308.784.2290
49 Units, pets OK. Restaurant on premises. Laundry facility. Heated pool. Rooms come with phones and cable TV. Some rooms have refrigerators. Credit cards: AE, DS, MC, V.

Motel 6
$37-44
809 S. Meridian • I-80, Exit 222
308.784.4900
50 Units, pets OK. Laundry facility. Data ports. Rooms come with phones, A/C and cable TV. Wheelchair accessible. Credit cards: AE, CB, DC, DS, MC, V.

ELM CREEK
First Interstate Inn
$40
I-80 & Hwy. 183 • 308.856.4652
50 Units, pets OK. Restaurant on premises. Rooms come with phones and cable TV. Wheelchair accessible. Senior discount. Major credit cards.

FAIRBURY
Capri Motel
$32-35
1100 14th Street • 402.729.3317
44 Units, pets OK ($2 and $10 dep. req.). Rooms come with phones and cable TV. AAA discount. Major credit cards.

FALLS CITY
Stephenson Motor Hotel
$30
1800 Stone Street • 402.245.2448
50 Units, no pets. Restaurant on premises. Rooms come with phones and cable TV. Wheelchair accessible. Major credit cards.

FREMONT
Budget Host Relax Inn
$40
1435 E. 23rd Street • 402.721.5656
35 Units, no pets. Rooms come with phones and cable TV. AAA/Senior discount. Credit cards: AE, DS, MC, V.

GERING
Cavalier Motel
$38-40
Hwy. 71 (between Gering & Scottsbluff)
308.635.3176
39 Units, no pets. Rooms come with phones and cable TV. Major credit cards.

GORDON
Jefco Inn
$38-44
308 S. Cornell • 308.282.2935
22 Units, no pets. Continental breakfast. Jacuzzi. Meeting rooms. Rooms come with phones and cable TV. Some rooms have microwaves and refrigerators. Senior discount. Credit cards: AE, DC, DS, MC, V.

GOTHENBURG
Travel Inn
$36
I-80 & Hwy. 47 (Exit 211) • 308.537.3638
32 Units, pets OK. Restaurant on premises. Rooms come with phones and cable TV. Senior discount. Major credit cards.

Western Motor Inn
$35*
I-80, Exit 211 • 308.537.3622
26 Units, pets OK. Rooms come with phones and cable TV. AAA discount. Wheelchair accessible. Major credit cards.
*Rates as high as $65/night during summer.

GRAND ISLAND
Budget Host Island Inn
$36-60
2311 S. Locust Street • 308.382.1815
44 Units, pets OK. Rooms come with phones and cable TV. Some rooms have refrigerators. AAA/Senior discount. Credit cards: AE, CB, DS, MC, V.

Days Inn
$40-45
2620 N. Diers Avenue • 308.384.8624
63 Units, pets OK ($7.50). Continental breakfast. Sauna and jacuzzi. Data ports. Rooms come with phones and cable TV. AAA/Senior discount. Credit cards: AE, DC, DS, MC, V.

Oak Grove Inn
$32
3205 S. Locust Street • 308.384.1333
59 Units, pets OK ($10 dep. req.). Rooms come with phones and cable TV. AAA discount. Credit cards: AE, DC, DS, MC, V.

Resident Suites
$30-40
2114 W. 2nd Street • 308.384.2240
95 Units, no pets. Restaurant on premises. Indoor pool. Rooms come with phones and cable TV. Senior discount. Major credit cards.

HASTINGS
Best Value Inn X-L Motel
$33-46
1400 West "J" Street • 402.463.3148
41 Units, no pets. Continental breakfast. Heated pool, wading pool and jacuzzi. Laundry facility. Rooms come with refrigerators, phones and cable TV. AAA discount. Credit cards: AE, CB, DC, DS, MC, V.

Midlands Lodge
$33-48
910 West "J" Street • 402.463.2428
47 Units, pets OK. Heated pool. Rooms come with refrigerators, phones and cable TV. AAA/Senior discount. Credit cards: AE, DC, DS, MC, V.

Rainbow Motel
$34-40
1000 West "J" Street • 402.463.2989
21 Units, pets OK ($2). Laundry facility. Airport transportation. Rooms come with refrigerators, phones and cable TV. AAA discount. Credit cards: AE, DS, MC, V.

HENDERSON
First Interstate Inn
$36
I-80, Exit 342 • 402.723.5856
34 Units, pets OK. Restaurant on premises. Pool. Rooms come with phones and cable TV. Major credit cards.

HOLDREGE
Best Value Plains Motel
$40
619 W. Highway 6 • 308.995.8646
22 Units, pets OK. Playground. Rooms come with A/C, phones and cable TV. Wheelchair accessible. Major credit cards.

Tower Motel
$34
413 W. 4th Avenue • 308.995.4488 or 800.750.1158
34 Units, no pets. Restaurant on premises. Pool. Rooms come with phones and cable TV. Major credit cards.

KEARNEY
Motel 6
$37-44
101 Talmadge Road • I-80, Exit 272 • 308.338.0705
59 Units, pets OK. Data ports. Rooms come with phones, A/C and cable TV. Wheelchair accessible. Credit cards: AE, CB, DC, DS, MC, V.

Western Inn South
$37-42
510 Third Avenue • 308.234.1876
45 Units, pets OK ($20 dep. req.). Continental breakfast offered October 15 through May 15. Heated indoor pool, sauna, jacuzzi. Rooms come with phones and cable TV. Credit cards: AE, DC, DS, MC, V.

KIMBALL
First Interstate Inn
$35-47
I-80 & Hwy. 71 • 308.235.4601
29 Units, pets OK ($5). Restaurant on premises. Rooms come with phones and cable TV. Senior discount. Credit cards: AE, DS, MC, V.

Super 8 Motel
$49-51
I-80 and Hwy. 71 Interchange
308.235.4888
42 Units, pets OK with permission. Toast bar. Rooms come with phones and cable TV. Wheelchair accessible. Senior discount. Credit cards: AE, CB, DC, DS, MC, V.

LEXINGTON
Budget Host Minute Man Motel
$34-40
801 Plum Creek Pkwy. • I-80, Exit 237
308.324.5544
36 Units, pets OK (no cats). Pool. Meeting rooms. Rooms come with phones and cable TV. AAA/Senior discount. Credit cards: AE, CB, DC, DS, MC, V.

First Interstate Inn
$38
308.324.5601 • I-80, Exit 237, 0.3 miles north on US 283.
50 Units, pets OK. Heated pool. Rooms come with phones and cable TV. Credit cards: AE, DC, DS, MC, V.

Super 8 Motel
$45-48*
104 E. River Road • 308.324.7434
47 Units, no pets. Continental breakfast. Jacuzzi and hot tub. Rooms come with phones and cable TV. Wheelchair accessible. Senior discount. Credit cards: AE, CB, DC, DS, MC, V.
*Higher rate effective June through September.

LINCOLN
Econo Lodge
$35-50
2410 N.W. 12th Street • 402.474.1311
141 Units, pets OK. Pool. Meeting rooms. Fitness facility. Rooms come with phones and cable TV. Senior discount. Major credit cards.

Great Plains Budget Host Inn
$35-45
2732 "O" Street • 402.476.3253
42 Units, no pets. Rooms come with refrigerators, phones and cable TV. Senior discount. Major credit cards.

Motel 6
$34-46
3001 N.W. 12th Street • 402.475.3211
98 Units, pets OK. Pool. Laundry facility. Data ports. Rooms come with phones, A/C and cable TV. Wheelchair accessible. Credit cards: AE, CB, DC, DS, MC, V.

Travelodge
$40
2801 West "O" Street • 402.475.4921
53 Units, pets OK. Continental breakfast. Pool. Rooms come with phones and cable TV. Some rooms have microwaves and refrigerators. Senior discount. Major credit cards.

McCOOK
Cedar Inn
$35
1400 East "C" Street • 308.345.7091 or 800.352.4489
22 Units, pets OK. Restaurant on premises. Rooms come with phones and cable TV. Wheelchair accessible. Major credit cards.

Super 8 Motel
$41
1103 E. "B" Street • 308.345.1141
40 Units, pets OK. Rooms come with phones and cable TV. Wheelchair accessible. AAA/senior discounts available. Credit cards: AE, CB, DC, DS, MC, V.

MINDEN
Pioneer Village Motel
$43
224 E. Hwy. 6 • 308.832.2750 or 800.445.4447
90 Units, pets OK. Restaurant on premises. Rooms come with phones and cable TV. Wheelchair accessible. Major credit cards.

NEBRASKA CITY
Apple Inn
$45-55
502 S. 11th Street • 402.873.5959
65 Units, pets OK ($5). Continental breakfast. Pool. Laundry facility. Data ports. Rooms come with phones and cable TV. Some rooms have refrigerators and jacuzzis. AAA/Senior discount. Credit cards: AE, CB, DC, DS, MC, V.

Days Inn
$40-55
1715 S. 11th Street • 402.873.6656
29 Units, no pets. Continental breakfast. Laundry facility. Data ports. Rooms come with phones and cable TV. Some rooms have refrigerators. AAA/Senior discount. Major credit cards.

NORFOLK
Eco-Lux Inn
$42-55
1909 Krenzien • 402.371.7157
43 Units, no pets. Continental breakfast. Laundry facility. Rooms come with phones and cable TV. Some rooms have refrigerators. AAA/Senior discount. Credit cards: AE, CB, DC, DS, MC, V.

NORTH PLATTE
Country Inn Motel
$27-42
321 S. Dewey Street • 308.532.8130 or 800.532.8130
40 Units, pets OK. Pool. Jacuzzi. Rooms come with phones and cable TV. Wheelchair accessible. Senior discount. Major credit cards.

First Interstate Inn
$35-47
I-80 & Hwy. 83 (Exit 177) • 308.532.6980
29 Units, pets OK. Restaurant on premises. Rooms come with phones and cable TV. Wheelchair accessible. AAA/Senior discount. Major credit cards.

Motel 6
$35-50 (56)*
1520 S. Jeffers Street • 308.534.6200
61 Units, pets OK. Pool. Laundry facility. Data ports. Rooms come with phones, A/C and cable TV. Wheelchair accessible. Major credit cards.
*Higher rate effective summer weekends.

OGALLALA
Econo Lodge
$36-50
108 Prospector • 308.284.2056
40 Units, pets OK. Heated pool. Rooms come with phones and cable TV. AAA discount. Credit cards: AE, DS, MC, V.

Super 8 Motel
$45 (55)*
500 E. "A" South • 308.284.2076
90 Units, pets OK (with deposit). Continental breakfast. Fitness facility. Hot tub. Meeting room available. Rooms come with phones and cable TV. Wheelchair accessible. Senior discount. Credit cards: AE, CB, DC, DS, MC, V.
*Higher rate effective Memorial Day through September.

OMAHA — *see also Council Bluffs (IA)*
Ben Franklin Motel
$46*
I-80 & 144th Street (Exit 440)
402.895.2200
96 Units, pets OK ($5). Pool. Laundry facility. Rooms come with phones, A/C and cable TV. Some rooms have microwaves, jacuzzis and refrigerators. Wheelchair accessible. AAA/Senior discount. Major credit cards.
*Rates as high as $62/night.

Days Inn
$45-55
10560 Sapp Bros. Drive, I-80, Exit 439 • 402.896.6868
66 Units, no pets. Heated pool. Jacuzzi. Laundry facility. Rooms come with phones, A/C and cable TV. Wheelchair accessible. AAA/Senior discount. Credit cards: AE, DS, MC, V.

Motel 6
$37-46
10708 "M" Street, I-80, Exit 445
402.331.3161
103 Units, pets OK. Pool. Laundry facility.

Data ports. Rooms come with phones, A/C and cable TV. Wheelchair accessible. Credit cards: AE, CB, DC, DS, MC, V.

Suburban Inn
$40
11023 Sapp Brothers Dr. • 402.332.3911 or 800.599.3911
71 Units, pets OK. Pool. Fitness facility. Game room. Rooms come with phones and cable TV. Wheelchair accessible. Major credit cards.

O'NEILL
Budget Host Carriage House Motel
$33-37
929 E. Douglas Street • 402.336.3403 or 800.345.7989
14 Units, pets OK. Restaurant on premises. Laundry facility nearby. Rooms come with phones and cable TV. Senior discount. Major credit cards.

PAXTON
Days Inn
$40-50
P.O. Box 098 • I-80, Exit 145
308.239.4510
35 Units, pets OK ($10 dep. req.). Continental breakfast. Putting green. Driving range. Laundry facility. Data ports. Rooms come with phones and cable TV. AAA/Senior discount. Credit cards: AE, DS, MC, V.

ST. PAUL
Best Value Inn
$32
1158 Hwy. 281 • 308.754.4466
20 Units, no pets. Playground. Rooms come with A/C, phones and cable TV. Some rooms have microwaves and refrigerators. Wheelchair accessible. Major credit cards.

Super 8 Motel
$46
116 Howard Avenue • 308.754.4554
37 Units, pets OK with permission (dep. req.). Continental breakfast. Meeting room available. Rooms come with phones and cable TV. Wheelchair accessible. Senior discount. Major credit cards.

SCOTTSBLUFF
Capri Motel
$31-35
2424 Avenue "I" • 308.635.2057
30 Units, pets OK ($5). Continental breakfast. Laundry facility. Rooms come with phones and cable TV. Some rooms have refrigerators. AAA/Senior discount. Credit cards: AE, CB, DC, DS, MC, V.

Lamplighter American Inn
$30*
606 E. 27th Street • 308.632.7108
39 Units, pets OK ($3). Continental breakfast. Heated pool. Rooms come with phones and cable TV. Credit cards: AE, DS, MC, V.
*AAA discounted rate.

Super 8 Motel
$45-48
2202 Delta Drive • 308.635.1800
55 Units, no pets. Continental breakfast. Jacuzzi. Rooms come with phones and cable TV. Wheelchair accessible. Senior discount. Credit cards: AE, CB, DC, DS, MC, V.

SEWARD
Super 8 Motel
$45-50*
1329 Progressive Rd. • 402.643.3388
I-80, Exit 379, 3 mi. north on Hwy. 15.
45 Units, pets OK ($3). Toast bar. Rooms come with phones and cable TV. Wheelchair accessible. AAA/Senior discount. Credit cards: AE, CB, DC, DS, MC, V.
*Rates may increase during weekends and special events.

SIDNEY
Best Value Sidney Motor Lodge
$40-50
2031 Illinois Street (on US 30)
308.254.4581
16 Units, pets OK. Rooms come with phones and cable TV. Some rooms have kitchens and refrigerators. AAA/Senior discount. Major credit cards.

Super 8 Motel
$49-51
2115 W. Illinois St. • 308.254.2081
60 Units, pets OK with permission. Toast bar. Meeting room. Rooms come with phones and cable TV. Wheelchair accessible. Senior discount. Credit cards: AE, CB, DC, DS, MC, V.

SOUTH SIOUX CITY
Econo Lodge
$44-46
4402 Dakota Avenue • 402.494.4114

60 Units, no pets. Continental breakfast. Meeting rooms. Laundry facility. Rooms come with phones and cable TV. AAA/Senior discount. Credit cards: AE, CB, DC, DS, MC, V.

Regency Inn
$36
400 Dakota Avenue • 402.494.3046
61 Units, pets OK ($25 dep. req.). Continental breakfast. Meeting rooms. Laundry facility. Rooms come with phones and cable TV. AAA discount. Credit cards: AE, CB, DC, DS, MC, V.

THEDFORD
Rodeway Inn
$42-50
1 mile east on SR 2 • 308.645.2284
42 Units, pets OK ($5 and $25-30 dep. req.). Continental breakfast. Jacuzzi. Laundry facility. Data ports. Rooms come with phones and cable TV. AAA/Senior discount. Major credit cards.

VALENTINE
Trade Winds Lodge
$37-55
HC 37, Box 2 • 402.376.1600
32 Units, pets OK. Heated pool. Airport transportation. Rooms come with phones and cable TV. Some rooms have refrigerators. AAA/Senior discount. Credit cards: AE, CB, DC, DS, MC, V.

WAHOO
Super 8 Motel
$48
950 N. Chestnut Street • 402.443.1288
40 Units, pets OK. Continental breakfast. Meeting rooms. Rooms come with phones and cable TV. Senior discount. Major credit cards.

WEST POINT
Super 8 Motel
$48
1211 N. Lincoln • 402.372.3998
39 Units, pets OK. Continental breakfast. Meeting rooms. Laundry and fitness facilities. Game room. Rooms come with phones and cable TV. Senior discount. Wheelchair accessible. Major credit cards.

YORK
Quality Inn
$40-45
3724 S. Lincoln Avenue • I-80, Exit 353
402.362.1686
50 Units, no pets. Continental breakfast. Heated pool. Jacuzzi. Laundry facility. Rooms come with phones and cable TV. Senior discount. Major credit cards.

Super 8 Motel
$44-47
I-80 & US 81 • 402.362.3388
95 Units, pets OK. Continental breakfast. Pool. Jacuzzi. Laundry facility. Game room. Rooms come with phones and cable TV. Wheelchair accessible. Senior discount. Major credit cards.

nevada

Traveler Advisory: A number of hotels and motels in Nevada offer significant discounts on room rates in order to attract visitors to their casinos. One way to take advantage of these discounts is to call the Nevada Commission on Tourism at 1-800-NEVADA8 and request a free copy of the Discover Nevada Bonus Book to be mailed to your address. The Discover Nevada Bonus Book contains a number of coupons valid at hotels and motels throughout the State of Nevada. Many of the coupons found in this book bring the cost of accommodations well below the $50/night mark.

AUSTIN
Lincoln Motel
$30
28 Main Street • 775.864.2698
17 Units, no pets. Restaurant. Rooms come with kitchenettes and cable TV. Major credit cards.

Pony Canyon Motel
$34
775.864.2605 • On US 50 in town.
10 Units, pets OK. Rooms come with phones and cable TV. Major credit cards.

BAKER
Border Inn
$31-41
Jct. US 50 & 6 • 775.234.7300
29 Units, pets OK. Casino and restaurant on premises. Jacuzzi and spa. Rooms come with phones and cable TV. Major credit cards.

BATTLE MOUNTAIN
Big Chief Motel
$35-39
434 W. Front Street • 775.635.2416
58 Units, pets OK ($5). Continental breakfast. Heated pool. Jacuzzi. Laundry facility. Rooms come with phones and cable TV. AAA/Senior discount. Major credit cards.

BEATTY
Phoenix Inn
$25-45
At Hwy. 95 & First Street • 775.553.2250 or 800.845.7401
54 Units, no pets. Rooms come with phones and cable TV. Major credit cards.

Stagecoach Hotel & Casino
$32-41
On Hwy. 95 in town • 775.553.2419 or 800.4BIGWIN
32 Units, pets OK. Casino and restaurant on premises. Playground. Jacuzzi and pool. Rooms come with phones and cable TV. Major credit cards.

BOULDER CITY
Nevada Inn
$25-50
1009 Nevada Hwy. • 702.293.2044 or 800.638.8890
55 Units, pets OK. Airport transportation. Pool. Rooms come with kitchenettes, phones and cable TV. Major credit cards.

Sands Motel
$47
809 Nevada Hwy (on US 93)
702.293.2589
25 Units, no pets. Rooms come with refrigerators and cable TV. AAA discount. Credit cards: AE, DC, DS, MC, V.

CALIENTE
Caliente Hot Springs Motel
$36
On Hwy. 93 north of town • 775.726.3777 or 800.748.4785
18 Units, pets OK. Jacuzzi. Rooms come with kitchenettes, phones and cable TV. Major credit cards.

Shady Motel
$39-48
450 Front Street • 775.726.3106
28 Units, pets OK. Rooms come with kitchenettes, phones and TV. Major credit cards.

CARSON CITY
Best Value Inn
$29-53
2731 S. Carson Street • 775.882.2007 or

800.626.1900
58 Units, pets OK ($25 and $100 dep. req.). Jacuzzi and pool. Laundry facility. Rooms come with phones and cable TV. Some rooms have microwaves. AAA discount. Major credit cards.

Carson City Inn
$30-55
1930 N. Carson Street • 775.882.1785
60 Units, no pets. Restaurant on premises. Rooms come with kitchenettes, phones and TV. Major credit cards.

City Center Motel
$28-54
507 N. Carson Street • 775.882.5535 or 800.338.7760
79 Units, no pets. Casino on premises. Rooms come with phones and cable TV. Major credit cards.

Motel 6
$30-48
2749 S. Carson Street • 775.885.7710
82 Units, pets OK. Pool. Laundry facility. Data ports. Rooms come with A/C, phones and cable TV. Wheelchair accessible. Credit cards: AE, CB, DC, DS, MC, V.

ELKO
Centre Motel
$35*
475 Third Street • 775.738.3226
22 Units, pets OK. Airport transportation. Pool. Rooms come with phones and TV. Major credit cards.
*Rates higher during weekends.

Esquire Motor Lodge
$28*
505 Idaho Street • 775.738.3157 or 800.822.7473
21 Units, pets OK. Airport transportation. Rooms come with phones and TV. Major credit cards.
*Rates higher during weekends.

Motel 6
$30-36
3021 Idaho Street • 775.738.4337
123 Units, pets OK. Pool. Laundry facility. Data ports. Rooms come with A/C, phones and cable TV. Wheelchair accessible. Credit cards: AE, CB, DC, DS, MC, V.

National 9 El Neva Motel
$35-38*
736 Idaho Street • 775.738.7152 or 800.348.0850
28 Units, no pets. Airport transportation. Rooms come with phones and TV. Major credit cards.
*Rates higher during weekends.

ELY
Bristlecone Motel
$42-44
700 Avenue "I" • 775.289.8838
31 Units, no pets. Rooms come with refrigerators. Some rooms have cable TV. Credit cards: AE, DC, DS, MC, V.

Fireside Inn
$39-45
3 miles north on US 93 • 775.289.3765
14 Units, pets OK ($5). Rooms come with coffeemakers, refrigerators and cable TV. AAA/Senior discount. Credit cards: AE, DS, MC, V.

Motel 6
$34-42
7th Street and Avenue "O" • 775.289.6671
99 Units, pets OK. Pool. Laundry facility. Data ports. Rooms come with A/C, phones and cable TV. Wheelchair accessible. Credit cards: AE, CB, DC, DS, MC, V.

EUREKA
Sundown Lodge
$34-44
On Main Street • 775.237.5334
27 Units, pets OK. Rooms come with phones and cable TV. Major credit cards.

FALLON
Western Motel
$37
125 S. Carson Street • 775.423.5118
22 Units, pets OK ($3). Two heated pools. Rooms come with cable TV. Some rooms have refrigerators. AAA/Senior discount. Credit cards: AE, DC, DS, MC, V.

FERNLEY
Lazy Inn
$30-50
325 Main Street • 775.575.4452 or 800.682.6445
46 Units, pets OK. Casino and restaurant on premises. Pool. Rooms come with phones and TV. Major credit cards.

Truck Inn
$27-43
485 Truck Inn Way • 775.351.1000
53 Units, no pets. Casino and restaurant on premises. Jacuzzi. Playground. Rooms come with phones and TV. Major credit cards.

GARDNERVILLE
Westerner Motel
$32-45
1353 US 395 S. (south end of town)
775.782.3602
25 Units, pets OK. Pool. Rooms come with phones and cable TV. AAA discount. Credit cards: AE, DS, MC, V.

HAWTHORNE
El Capitan Motor Lodge
$32-41
540 "F" Street • 775.945.3321
103 Units, pets OK ($10 dep. req.). Casino, meeting rooms and pool. Rooms come with refrigerators and cable TV. Credit cards: AE, CB, DC, DS, MC, V.

Sand N Sage Lodge
$30-45
1301 E. Fifth Street • 775.945.3352
37 Units, no pets. Pool. Rooms come with kitchenettes, phones and TV. Major credit cards.

HENDERSON
Boby Motel
$30*
2100 S. Boulder Hwy. • 702.565.9711
21 Units, pets OK. Restaurant on premises. Rooms come with kitchenettes, phones and TV. Major credit cards.
*Rates higher during weekends.

Railroad Pass Hotel & Casino
$29-40*
2800 S. Boulder Hwy. • 702.294.5000 or 800.654.0877
120 Units, no pets. Casino and restaurant on premises. Pool. Playground. Rooms come with phones and TV. Major credit cards.
*Rates higher during weekends.

INDIAN SPRINGS
Indian Springs Motor Hotel
$33-39
320 E. Tonopah Hwy. • 702.879.3700
45 Units, pets OK ($5). Casino and restaurant on premises. Rooms come with phones and TV. AAA discount. Major credit cards.

JACKPOT
Local time in Jackpot is set to Mountain Time
Barton's Club 93
$35-55*
On Hwy. 93 in town • 775.755.2341 or 800.258.2937
100 Units, pets OK. Casino and restaurant on premises. Airport transportation. Rooms come with phones and cable TV. Major credit cards.
*Rates higher during weekends.

Covered Wagon Motel
$20-50
1602 US 93 • 775.755.2241 or 877.838.1214
92 Units, pets OK. Rooms come with phones and cable TV. Major credit cards.

JEAN
Buffalo Bills Resort & Casino
$22-55*
East of and adjacent to I-15, State Line exit
702.382.1111
1246 Units, no pets. Pool, waterslide, jacuzzi, 18-hole golf, motion simulator, roller coaster, video arcade, casino. Rooms come with cable TV and pay movies. Credit cards: AE, DC, DS, MC, V.
*Two-night minimum stay weekends.

Whiskey Pete's Hotel & Casino
$25-55*
West of and adjacent to I-15, State Line exit • 702.382.4388
777 Units, no pets. Pool, waterslide, jacuzzi, 18-hole golf. Rooms come with coffeemakers and pay movies. Some rooms have pay jacuzzis. AAA discount. Credit cards: AE, CB, DC, DS, MC, V.
*Two-night minimum stay during weekends.

LAS VEGAS — *see also North Las Vegas*
Barcelona Motel
$45 (60-65)*
5011 E. Craig Road • 702.644.6300
178 Units, no pets. Pool and jacuzzi. Laundry facility. Rooms come with phones and pay movies. Some rooms have kitchens and refrigerators. Credit cards: AE, DC, DS, MC, V.
*Higher rate effective during weekends.

Crest Budget Inn
$25-55
207 N. Sixth Street • 702.382.5642 or 800.777.1817
200 Units, no pets. Pool. Rooms come with kitchenettes, phones and cable TV. Major credit cards.

Downtowner Motel
$25-50
129 N. Eighth Street • 702.384.1441 or 800.777.2566
200 Units, no pets. Pool. Rooms come with kitchenettes, phones and cable TV. Major credit cards.

El Cortez Hotel
$23-40
600 E. Fremont Street • 702.385.5200 or 800.634.6703
308 Units, no pets. Casino and restaurant on premises. Airport transportation. Play area for children. Rooms come with phones and cable TV. Major credit cards.

Motel 6
$30-46
4125 Boulder Hwy • 702.457.8051
161 Units, pets OK. Pool. Laundry facility. Rooms come with A/C, phones and cable TV. Wheelchair accessible. Credit cards: AE, CB, DC, DS, MC, V.

Motel 6
$30-46 (54)*
5085 S. Industrial Road • 702.739.6747
139 Units, pets OK. Pool. Laundry facility. Rooms come with A/C, phones and cable TV. Wheelchair accessible. Credit cards: AE, CB, DC, DS, MC, V.
*Higher rate effective during weekends.

Motel 6
$34-50 (56)*
195 E. Tropicana Ave. • 702.798.0728
608 Units, pets OK. Restaurant on premises. Pool. Laundry facility. Rooms come with A/C, phones and cable TV. Wheelchair accessible. Credit cards: AE, CB, DC, DS, MC, V.
*Higher rate effective during weekends.

Parkway Inn
$29-55
5201 S. Industrial Road • 702.739.9513 or 800.326.6835
127 Units, no pets. Laundry facility. Rooms come with phones, A/C and cable TV. Credit cards: AE, MC, V.

Somerset House Motel
$35-55
294 Convention Ctr. Dr. • 702.735.4411
104 Units, no pets. Pool. Laundry facility. Rooms come with refrigerators. Some rooms have kitchens. Senior discount. Credit cards: AE, DC, DS, JCB, MC, V.

LAUGHLIN — *see also Bullhead City (AZ)*
Bayshore Inn
$25-55
1955 W. Casino Drive • 702.299.9010
87 Units, pets OK ($10). Pool and jacuzzi. Rooms come with cable TV. Credit cards: DS, MC, V.

McDERMITT
McDermitt Motel
$40-50
On US 95 in town • 775.532.8588
23 Units, no pets. Rooms come with phones and TV. Major credit cards.

MESQUITE
Desert Palms Motel
$15-45
On Mesquite Blvd. • 702.346.5756
22 Units, pets OK. Rooms come with kitchenettes, phones and TV. Major credit cards.

Virgin River Hotel & Casino
$18-55
West of and adjacent to I-15
702.346.7777
723 Units, pets OK ($25 dep. req.). Pools, jacuzzi, casino, video arcade and two movie theaters. Laundry facility. Rooms come with coffeemakers, cable TV and pay movies. Some rooms have A/C. AAA discount. Credit cards: AE, DS, MC, V.

MILL CITY
Super 8 Motel
$36-50
6000 E. Frontage Road • 775.538.7311
50 Units, pets OK ($5 and $20 dep. req.). Rooms come with cable TV. Credit cards: AE, DS, MC, V. Senior discount.

MINDEN
Holiday Lodge
$32-45
1591 Hwy. 395 • 775.782.2288

20 Units, pets OK ($4 and $20 dep. req.). Restaurant on premises. Pool. Rooms come with kitchenettes, phones and cable TV. Major credit cards.

NORTH LAS VEGAS
Vegas Chalet Motel
$35-45
2401 Las Vegas Blvd. N • 702.642.2115
50 Units, pets OK. Pool. Rooms come with kitchenettes, phones and cable TV. Major credit cards.

PAHRUMP
Saddle West Hotel & Casino
$42-55
On Hwy. 160 (in town) • 775.727.1111 or 800.GEDDYUP
110 Units, no pets. Casino and restaurant on premises. Jacuzzi. Pool. Rooms come with phones and cable TV. Major credit cards.

RACHEL
Little A'Le'Inn
$30
HCR Box 45, Hwy 375 • 775.729.2515
7 Units, pets OK. Restaurant on premises. Rooms come with kitchenettes, phones and TV. Major credit cards.

RENO
Gold Key Motel
$25-50
445 Lake Street • 775.323.0731 or 800.648.3744
31 Units, no pets. Pool. Rooms come with kitchenettes, phones and TV. Major credit cards.

Motel 6—South
$30-50
1901 S. Virginia Street • 775.827.0255
115 Units, pets OK. Restaurant on premises. Pool. Laundry facility. Data ports. Rooms come with A/C, phones and cable TV. Wheelchair accessible. Credit cards: AE, CB, DC, DS, MC, V.

Motel 6
$30-50
866 N. Wells Avenue • 775.786.9852
142 Units, pets OK. Pool. laundry facility. Data ports. Rooms come with A/C, phones and cable TV. Wheelchair accessible. Credit cards: AE, CB, DC, DS, MC, V.

Motel 6—West
$30-50
1400 Stardust Street • 775.747.7390
123 Units, pets OK. Pool. Laundry facility. Data ports. Rooms come with A/C, phones and cable TV. Wheelchair accessible. Credit cards: AE, CB, DC, DS, MC, V.

Super 8 Motel
$50
1651 N. Virginia Street • 775.329.3464
20 Units, pets OK ($10). Heated pool. Rooms come with phones and TV. Senior discount. Major credit cards.

SPARKS
Motel 6
$30-50
2405 Victorian Avenue • I-80, Exit 16
775.358.1080
95 Units, pets OK. Laundry. Data ports. Rooms come with A/C, phones and cable TV. Wheelchair accessible. Credit cards: AE, CB, DC, DS, MC, V.

Western Village Inn
$39-55
815 E. Nichols Blvd. • 775.331.1069 or 800.648.1170
280 Units, pets OK. Casino and restaurant on premises. Airport transportation. Pool. Play area for children. Rooms come with phones and cable TV. Major credit cards.

TONOPAH
Golden Hills Motel
$28-48
826 Erie Main • 775.482.6238
40 Units, pets OK. Restaurant on premises. Rooms come with phones and cable TV. Major credit cards.

Silver Queen Motel
$31-45
255 Erie Main • 775.482.6291
85 Units, pets OK. Restaurant on premises. Pool. Rooms come with kitchenettes, phones and cable TV. Major credit cards.

WELLS
Motel 6
$32-36
I-80/US Hwy 40 & US 93 • 775.752.2116
99 Units, pets OK. Pool. Laundry facility. Data ports. Rooms come with A/C, phones and cable TV. Wheelchair accessible. Credit cards: AE, CB, DC, DS, MC, V.

Old West Inn
$20-24
456 Sixth Street • 775.752.3888
20 Units, no pets. Restaurant on premises. Rooms come with phones and TV. Major credit cards.

WEST WENDOVER — *see also Wendover (UT). Local time in West Wendover is set to Mountain Time*

Red Garter Hotel & Casino
$24-59
P.O. Box 2399 (in town) • 775.664.2111 or 800.982.2111
46 Units, no pets. Casino and restaurant on premises. Airport transportation. Rooms come with phones and cable TV. Major credit cards.

WINNEMUCCA

Bull Head Motel
$28-44
500 E. Winnemucca Blvd. • 775.623.3636
46 Units, pets OK. Rooms come with phones and cable TV. Major credit cards.

Motel 6
$34-46
1600 Winnemucca Blvd. • 775.623.1180
103 Units, pets OK. Pool. Laundry facility. Data ports. Rooms come with phones and cable TV. Wheelchair accessible. Credit cards: AE, CB, DC, DS, MC, V.

Scottish Inn
$32-35*
333 W. Winnemucca Blvd. • 775.623.3703
23 Units, no pets. Rooms come with phones and cable TV. Major credit cards.
*Rates higher during weekends.

Scott's Shady Court Motel
$35*
400 West 1st Street • 775.623.3646
70 Units, pets OK. Pool and sauna. Playground. Complimentary vouchers for coupons at local casinos are presented at check-in. Rooms come with phones, A/C, coffee service and cable TV. Major credit cards.
*Rates higher during weekends.

new hampshire

BEDFORD
Hill-Brook Motel
$45-55
250 Rte. 101 • 603.472.3788
18 Units, no pets. Rooms come with phones and cable TV. Some rooms have kitchenettes. Wheelchair accessible. Major credit cards.

BERLIN
Budget Inn
$49*
25 Pleasant Street • 603.752.2500
30 Units, pets OK ($25 dep. req.). Rooms come with phones and cable TV. Some rooms have microwaves and refrigerators. Senior discount. Credit cards: AE, CB, DC, DS, JCB, MC, V.
*Summer rates higher.

BETHLEHEM
Pinewood Motel
$35-43*
Rte. 302 • 603.444.2075 or 800.328.9307
Pets OK. Pool. Picnic area and barbecues. Rooms come with phones and cable TV. Major credit cards.
*Rooms without kitchenettes. Summer rates higher.

CLAREMONT
Best Budget Inn
$38-50
24 Sullivan Street • 603.542.9567
21 Units, pets OK ($5-10). Rooms come with phones and cable TV. Some rooms have refrigerators. AAA/Senior discount. Credit cards: AE, CB, DC, DS, JCB, MC, V.

Claremont Motor Lodge
$39-45
On Beauregard Street • 603.542.2540 • I-91, Exit 8, one mile north on SR 103.
19 Units, pets OK. Continental breakfast. Rooms come with phones and cable TV. Some rooms have refrigerators. AAA discount. Credit cards: AE, DS, MC, V.

GORHAM
Mt. Madison Motel
$38-48 (45-69)*
365 Main Street • 603.466.3622
33 Units, pets OK. Heated pool. Rooms come with phones and cable TV. Senior discount. Credit cards: AE, DS, MC, V.
*Higher rates effective July through mid-October.

KEENE
Valley Green Motel
$45-55
379 West Street • 603.352.7350
60 Units, pets OK ($6 and $25 dep. req.). Continental breakfast. Heated pool. Rooms come with phones and cable TV. Some rooms have microwaves and refrigerators. Credit cards: AE, CB, DC, DS, MC, V.

LANCASTER
Lancaster Motor Inn
$39-45
112 Main Street • 603.788.4921
36 Units, pets OK. Continental breakfast. Meeting room. Rooms come with phones and cable TV. Some rooms have microwaves, A/C and refrigerators. AAA discount. Credit cards: AE, CB, DC, DS, MC, V.

LINCOLN
Mt. Coolidge Motel
$32-59*
On US 3 • I-93, Exit 33 • 603.745.8052
20 Units, no pets. Heated pool. Rooms come with phones and cable TV. Some rooms have refrigerators. AAA/Senior discount. Credit cards: DS, MC, V.
*Open May through October.

Parker's Motel
$36-59*
603.745.8341 • From I-93, Exit 33, 2 miles NE from exit on US 3.
27 Units, pets OK ($25 dep. req.). Heated pool. Sauna. Jacuzzi. Rooms come with phones and cable TV. Some rooms have refrigerators. AAA discount. Credit cards: AE, DS, MC, V.
*Higher rate effective during summer and winter weekends.

Profile Motel & Cottages
$32-49
On US 3 • I-93, Exit 33 • 603.745.2759
18 Units, no pets. Heated pool. Playground. Rooms come with phones and cable TV. AAA/ Senior discount. Credit cards: DS, MC, V.

LITTLETON – *see also Woodstock*
Littleton Motel
$44-52*
166 Main Street • 603.444.5780
19 Units, no pets. Pool. Rooms come with phones and cable TV. Credit cards: AE, MC, V.
*Closed November through April.

Maple Leaf Motel
$39-52 (54-59)*
150 W. Main Street • 603.444.5105
13 Units, no pets. Heated pool. Playground. Rooms come with phones, A/C and cable TV. Major credit cards.
*Higher rates effective mid-September through mid-October. Closed April.

NASHUA
Motel 6
$48-52 (56)*
2 Progress Avenue • Rt. 3N, Exit 5W
603.889.4151
80 Units, pets OK. Pool. Rooms come with phones, A/C and cable TV. Wheelchair accessible. Credit cards: AE, CB, DC, DS, MC, V.
*Higher rate effective summer and autumn months.

Red Roof Inn
$50-52 (63)*
77 Spitbrook Road • 603.888.1893
116 Units, pets OK. Laundry facility. Rooms come with phones and cable TV. Credit cards: AE, CB, DC, DS, MC, V.
*Higher rate effective Memorial Day through August.

NORTH CONWAY
Eastern Inns
$50-55
0.5 miles north on US 302/SR 16
603.356.5447
56 Units, no pets. Restaurant on premises. Sauna, jacuzzi, playground and basketball court. Laundry facility. Rooms come with phones and cable TV. Some rooms have microwaves and refrigerators. AAA/Senior discount. Major credit cards.

White Trellis Motel
$40-45
3245 White Mtn. Hwy. • 603.356.2492
22 Units, no pets. Rooms come with phones and cable TV. Some rooms have microwaves and refrigerators. Credit cards: DS, MC, V.

OSSIPEE VALLEY
Mount Whittier Motel
$49*
1695 SR 16 • 603.539.4951
22 Units, no pets. Continental breakfast offered in summer and fall. Pool. Rooms come with phones and cable TV. Major credit cards.
*Summer rates higher.

THORNTON
Shamrock Motel
$34-53*
I-93 • 2.3 miles north on US 3
603.726.3534
87 Units, pets OK. Pool. Rooms come with phones and cable TV. No A/C in rooms. AAA/Senior discount. Credit cards: AE, DS, MC, V.
*Rates as high as $73/night.

TWIN MOUNTAIN
Seven Dwarfs Motel
$48-56*
528 Little River Road • 603.846.5535
14 Units, no pets. Playground. Rooms come with phones, VCRs and cable TV. AAA discount. Credit cards: DS, MC, V.
*Closed November through April.

Shakespeare's Inn
$50-60
675 Profile Road • 603.846.5562
33 Units, no pets. Pool. Rooms come with phones and cable TV. Senior discount. Credit cards: AE, MC, V.

WEST LEBANON
Airport Economy Inn
$45-50*
45 Airport Rd. • I-89, Exit 20
603.298.8888
56 Units, pets OK. Continental breakfast. Pool. Game room. Laundry facility. Data ports. Rooms come with phones and cable TV. Wheelchair accessible. Senior discount. Major credit cards.
*AAA discounted rates. Rates higher during weekends and fall foliage.

WEST OSSIPEE
Wind Song Motor Inn
$49 (60)*
Jct. SR 16 & SR 25W • 603.539.4536
34 Units, pets OK. Restaurant on premises. Pool. Sauna. Picnic tables. Game room. Meeting room. Laundry and fitness facility. Rooms come with phones and cable TV. Some rooms have kitchenettes. AAA discount. Credit cards: AE, DS, MC, V.
*Higher rate effective mid-June through mid-October.

WINNISQUAM
Lynnmere Motel & Cottages
$45-55*
850 Laconia Road • 603.524.0912
12 Units, pets OK ($100 dep. req.). Rooms come with cable TV. No phones or A/C in rooms. Some rooms have kitchens and refrigerators. AAA discount. Credit cards: DS, MC, V.
*Rates as high as $85/night.

WOODSTOCK — *see also Lincoln*
Riverbank Motel & Cottages
$35-44*
Box 314 • 603.745.3374 or 800.633.5624
11 Units, no pets. Rooms come with cable TV. No phones in rooms. Major credit cards.
*Motel rooms without kitchenettes. Summer rates higher.

WOODSVILLE
All Seasons Motel
$40-55*
36 Smith Street • 603.747.2157
14 Units, pets OK. Playground. Pool. Rooms come with phones and cable TV. Some rooms have kitchenettes and refrigerators. AAA discount. Major credit cards.
*Higher rates effective mid-September through mid-October.

new jersey

Travel Advisory: Rates for accommodations along the New Jersey shore in the summertime are very high, well above the $50/night target of this guide. These rates come down substantially during the off-season, but if you want to visit the shore during the summer, you will find more affordable rooms in communities a few miles inland from the beach. A few such towns featured here in this section are **Absecon, Belmar, Eatontown** and **North Wildwood**.

ABSECON
Budget Inn 4-U
$40 (50-75)*
930 White Horse Pike • 609.641.2279
32 Units, no pets. Rooms come with phones and cable TV. Major credit cards.
*Higher rates effective weekends.

Economy Motel
$35 (55-65)*
547 E. Absecon Blvd. • 609.646.3867
32 Units, no pets. Rooms come with phones and cable TV. Major credit cards.
*Higher rates effective weekends.

Red Carpet Inn
$39 (60-80)*
206 E. White Horse Pike • 609.652.3322
22 Units, no pets. Continental breakfast. Rooms come with phones and cable TV. Some rooms have microwaves and refrigerators. Senior discount. Credit cards: AE, CB, DC, DS, MC, V.
*Higher rates effective weekends.

Super 8 Motel
$29-55*
229 E. Rte. 30 • 609.652.2477
58 Units, no pets. Rooms come with phones and cable TV. Wheelchair accessible. Senior discount. AAA discount. Credit cards: AE, CB, DC, DS, MC, V.
*Rates as high as $120/night.

Travelodge
$35 (55-75)*
316 White Horse Pike • 609.652.0904
27 Units, no pets. Restaurant on premises. Pool. Rooms come with phones and cable TV. Wheelchair accessible. Major credit cards.
*Higher rates effective weekends.

ATLANTIC CITY — ***see also Absecon and Pleasantville***
Sunset Inn
$35-50 (50-120)*
1400 Absecon Blvd. • 609.345.3555
14 Units, no pets. Rooms come with phones and cable TV. AAA/Senior discount. Major credit cards.
*Higher rates effective weekends.

Super 8 Motel
$39-69
175 S. Tennessee Ave. • 609.344.8956
71 Units, no pets. Continental breakfast. Pool. Data ports. Rooms come with phones and cable TV. Senior discount. Major credit cards.

BELLMAWR
Bellmawr Motor Inn
$41-52
312 S. Black Horse Pike • 609.931.6300
28 Units, no pets. Rooms come with phones and cable TV. AAA/Senior discount. Major credit cards.

BERLIN
Red Carpet Inn
$50-55*
1036 Hwy. 73 • 856.768.5353
20 Units, pets OK. Continental breakfast. Rooms come with phones and cable TV. Some rooms have jacuzzis. Senior discount. Major credit cards.
*AAA discounted rates.

BORDENTOWN
Imperial Inn
$45-60
3312 Rte. 206 South • NJ Tpke., Exit 7
609.298.3355
28 Units, pets OK. Rooms come with phones and cable TV. AAA/Senior discount. Major credit cards.

BRIDGETON — *see Millville and Vineland*

BROOKLAWN — *see Philadelphia (PA)*

BUENA
Econo Lodge
$50-60 (60-80)*
146 Old Tuckahoe Road • 856.697.9000
45 Units, no pets. Continental breakfast. Rooms come with phones and cable TV. Some rooms have microwaves, jacuzzis and refrigerators. AAA discount. Major credit cards.
*Higher rates effective mid-May through September.

CAPE MAY — *see Wildwood*

CHERRY HILL — *see Philadelphia (PA)*

EATONTOWN
Crystal Motor Lodge
$50 (60)*
170 Hwy. 35 • 732.542.4900
77 Units, pets OK. Rooms come with phones and cable TV. AARP discount available. Major credit cards.
*AAA discounted rates. Higher rate effective weekends.

HIGHTSTOWN
Town House Motor Inn
$50-55*
351 Franklin Street • 609.448.2400
105 Units, pets OK. Restaurant on premises. Rooms come with phones and cable TV. Senior discount available (10%). Major credit cards.
*AAA discounted rates.

MANASQUAN
Twin Oaks Motel
$47 (55-65)*
2300 Rte. 35 • 732.223.1247
18 Units, no pets. Pool. Rooms come with phones, A/C and cable TV. Some rooms have microwaves and refrigerators. Major credit cards.
*Higher rates effective weekends.

MAPLE SHADE
Motel 6
$40-50 (56)*
Rte. 73N • I-295, Exit 36B • 856.235.3550
91 Units, pets OK. Pool. Laundry facility. Rooms come with A/C, phones and cable TV. Wheelchair accessible. Credit cards: AE, CB, DC, DS, MC, V.
*Higher rate effective summer weekends.

Rodeway Inn
$45-50*
2840 SR 73N • 856.235.3200
50 Units, no pets. Continental breakfast. Rooms come with phones and cable TV. Some rooms have refrigerators. Wheelchair accessible. Major credit cards.
*AAA discounted rates. Rates as high as $65/night.

MILLVILLE
Best Western Inn
$50 (60)*
1701 N. 2nd Street • 856.327.3300
100 Units, no pets. Restaurant on premises. Rooms come with phones and cable TV. AAA discount. Major credit cards.
*Higher rate effective weekends.

MONMOUTH JUNCTION
Days Inn
$45-54 (100-110)*
South on US 1, 0.5 mile north of Raymond Rd. • 732.329.4555
73 Units, no pets. Continental breakfast. Rooms come with phones and cable TV. Some rooms have microwaves and refrigerators. Major credit cards.
*AAA discounted rates. Higher rate effective May through mid-June.

Red Roof Inn/North Princeton
$49 (59)*
208 New Road • 723.821.8800
119 Units, pets OK. Rooms come with phones and cable TV. Credit cards: AE, CB, DC, DS, MC, V.
*Higher rate effective May through mid-November.

MOUNT EPHRAIM
Budget Inn & Suites
$38-44
310 N. Black Horse • 856.931.4730
72 Units, pets OK. Rooms come with phones and cable TV. Major credit cards.

MOUNT LAUREL — *see also Philadelphia (PA)*
Track & Turf Motel
$33-40
809 SR 73 • 609.235.6500
30 Units, pets OK. Rooms come with phones and cable TV. AAA/Senior discount. Credit cards: AE, CB, DC, DS, MC, V.

NORTH WILDWOOD
European Motel
$42-95*
300 Ocean Avenue • Garden St. Pkwy., Exit 6 (on SR 147) • 609.729.4622
20 Units, no pets. Pool. Rooms come with phones and cable TV. AAA discount. Credit cards: AE, DS, MC, V.
*Closed October through April.

Mediterranean Motel
$38-85*
405 Ocean Avenue • Garden St. Pkwy., Exit 6 (on SR 147) • 609.522.0112
33 Units, no pets. Pool. Laundry facility. Rooms come with phones and cable TV. AAA discount. Credit cards: AE, DS, MC, V.
*Closed October through April.

NEW JERSEY METRO

East Brunswick
McIntosh Inn ($68-82)
764 Rte. 18N
732.238.4900

Motel 6 ($58-72)
244 Rte. 18 (I-95, Exit 9)
732.390.4545

Jersey City
Holland Motor Lodge ($61-66)
737 Newark Avenue
201.963.6200

North Bergen
Super 8 Motel ($70-90)
1-495, JFK Exit,
2800 Columbia Ave.
201.864.4500

Parsippany
Howard Johnson Express Inn ($70-90)
Red Roof Inn ($62-87)
855 US 46E (I-80, Exit 47)
973.334.3737

Phillipsburg
Phillipsburg Inn ($70-80)
1311 US 22W (I-78, Exit 3)
908.454.6461

Piscataway
Motel 6 ($58-68)
1012 Stelton Road
(I-287 at CR 529)
732.981.9200

Somerset
Quality Inn ($65)
1850 Easton Avenue
(I-287, Exit 10)
732.469.5050

Ramada Inn ($65)
60 Cottontail Lane (I-287, Exit 12)
732.560.9880

PLEASANTVILLE
Days Inn
$49
6708 Tilton Road • 609.641.4500
117 Units, no pets. Continental breakfast. Pool. Playground. Laundry facility. Fitness facility. Area transportation available. Meeting rooms. Data ports. Rooms come with A/C, phones and cable TV. Wheelchair accessible. AAA/Senior discount. Major credit cards.

TRENTON* — *see Bordentown*
*There are no hotels or motels within the city limits of Trenton, NJ.

VINELAND
Economy Lodge
$50*
911 E. Landis Avenue • 856.691.3400
60 Units, no pets. Continental breakfast. Rooms come with phones and cable TV. Major credit cards.
*Rates as high as $60/night.

WILLIAMSTOWN
Red Carpet Inn
$45-55*
105 N. Black Horse Pike • I-295, Exit 28 to Hwy. 42 South • 856.728.8000
25 Units, no pets. Restaurant on premises. Rooms come with phones and cable TV. Senior discount. Major credit cards.
*AAA discounted rates.

WINSLOW
Winslow Inn & Suites
$40-55 (60-95)*
530 Rte. 73 • 609.561.6200
49 Units, pets OK. Continental breakfast. Rooms come with phones and cable TV. Wheelchair accessible. Senior discount. Major credit cards.
*Higher rates effective July through October.

new mexico

ALAMAGORDO
All American Inn
$34
508 S. White Sands Blvd. • 505.437.1850
28 Units, pets OK. Pool. Laundry facility. Rooms come with phones and cable TV. Some rooms have refrigerators. AAA discount. Credit cards: AE, CB, DC, DS, MC, V.

Motel 6
$32-35
251 Panorama Blvd. • 505.434.5970
97 Units, pets OK. Pool. Laundry facility. Rooms come with phones, A/C and cable TV. Wheelchair accessible. Credit cards: AE, CB, DC, DS, MC, V.

Super 8 Motel
$39-54
3204 N. White Sands • 505.434.4205
57 Units, pets OK. Continental breakfast. Laundry facility. Rooms come with phones and cable TV. Wheelchair accessible. Senior discount. Credit cards: AE, CB, DC, DS, MC, V.

ALBUQUERQUE
Luxury Inn
$30-45
6718 Central Avenue • 505.255.5900
58 Units, no pets. Continental breakfast. Heated indoor pool. Jacuzzi. Rooms come with phones and cable TV. Wheelchair accessible. AAA/Senior discount. Credit cards: AE, CB, DC, DS, JCB, MC, V.

Motel 6—Midtown
$30-33
1701 University Blvd. N.E. • 505.843.9228
118 Units, pets OK. Pool. Data ports. Rooms come with phones, A/C and cable TV. Wheelchair accessible. Credit cards: AE, CB, DC, DS, MC, V.

Motel 6
$35-40
5701 Iliff Road N.W. • 505.831.8888
109 Units, pets OK. Pool. Laundry facility. Data ports. Rooms come with phones, A/C and cable TV. Wheelchair accessible. Credit cards: AE, CB, DC, DS, MC, V.

Motel 6
$36-43*
1000 Avenida Cesar Chavez S.E.
505.243.8017
97 Units, pets OK. Pool. Laundry facility. Data ports. Rooms come with phones, A/C and cable TV. Wheelchair accessible. Credit cards: AE, CB, DC, DS, MC, V.
*Higher rate effective October 1-11.

Travelodge
$35-50
13139 Central Avenue N.E., I-40, Exit 167
505.292.4878
41 Units, pets OK ($5). Continental breakfast. Data ports. Rooms come with phones and cable TV. AAA/Senior discount. Major credit cards.

University Lodge
$30-33
3711 Central Ave. N.E. • 505.266.7663
55 Units, pets OK. Continental breakfast. Pool. Rooms come with phones and cable TV. Wheelchair accessible. Major credit cards.

ARTESIA
Artesia Inn
$38-48
1820 S. 1st Street • 505.746.9801
34 Units, pets OK. Pool. Rooms come with refrigerators, phones and cable TV. AAA/ Senior discount. Credit cards: AE, DC, DS, MC, V.

AZTEC
Enchantment Lodge
$33-45
1800 W. Aztec Blvd. • 505.334.6143
20 Units, no pets. Heated pool. Playground and picnic area. Laundry facility. Rooms come with phones and cable TV. Some rooms have refrigerators and microwaves. Credit cards: DS, MC, V.

BELEN
Super 8 Motel
$43-54
428 S. Main Street • I-25, Exit 191
505.864.8188

43 Units, no pets. Continental breakfast. Laundry facility. Rooms come with phones and cable TV. Wheelchair accessible. Major credit cards.

BERNALILLO
Super 8 Motel
$42*
265 Hwy. 44E • 505.867.0766
68 Units, pets OK. Continental breakfast. Laundry facility. Rooms come with phones and cable TV. Wheelchair accessible. Senior discount. Major credit cards.
*Rates climb to $65/night during first two weeks of October.

BLOOMFIELD
Super 8 Motel
$46-48
525 W. Broadway • 505.632.8886
42 Units, pets OK ($20 dep. req.). Continental breakfast. Laundry facility. Rooms come with phones and cable TV. AAA/Senior discount. Credit cards: AE, DS, MC, V.

CARLSBAD
Carlsbad Inn
$30-45
2019 S. Canal Street • 505.887.1171
30 Units, pets OK ($20 dep. req.). Continental breakfast. Heated pool. Playground. Airport transportation. Rooms come with phones and cable TV. Some rooms have microwaves and refrigerators. AAA discount. Credit cards: AE, CB, DC, DS, MC, V.

Continental Inn
$32-45
3820 National Parks Hwy. • 505.887.0341
60 Units, pets OK ($10 dep. req.). Heated pool. Rooms come with phones and cable TV. Some rooms have refrigerators. AAA/Senior discount. Credit cards: AE, CB, DC, DS, MC, V.

Motel 6
$30-36
3824 National Parks Hwy. • 505.885.0011
80 Units, pets OK. Pool. Laundry facility. Rooms come with phones, A/C and cable TV. Wheelchair accessible. Credit cards: AE, CB, DC, DS, MC, V.

Stagecoach Inn
$34-40
1819 S. Canal Street • 505.887.1148
55 Units, pets OK ($5). Pool. Wading pool. Jacuzzi. Playground. Laundry facility. Rooms come with phones and cable TV. Some rooms have refrigerators. AAA/Senior discount. Credit cards: AE, CB, DC, DS, MC, V.

CARRIZOZO
Four Winds Motel
$36
P.O. Box 366 (in town) • 505.648.2356
23 Units, pets OK ($15). Rooms come with phones and cable TV. Major credit cards.

CLAYTON
Super 8 Motel
$45
1425 Hwy. 89 • 505.374.8127
31 Units, pets OK. Continental breakfast. Rooms come with phones and TV. Senior discount. Major credit cards.

CLOVIS
Comfort Inn
$47-52*
1616 Mabry Drive • 505.762.4591
49 Units, pets OK. Continental breakfast. Heated pool. Laundry facility. Rooms come with phones and cable TV. Some rooms have refrigerators. Senior discount. Major credit cards.
*AAA discounted rates.

Motel 6
$30
2620 Mabry Drive • 505.762.2995
81 Units, pets OK. Pool. Laundry facility. Data ports. Rooms come with phones, A/C and cable TV. Wheelchair accessible. Credit cards: AE, CB, DC, DS, MC, V.

CUBA
Frontier Motel
$30-40
6474 Main Street • 505.289.3474
34 Units, pets OK. Rooms come with phones and cable TV. Major credit cards.

DEMING
Days Inn
$38-46
1709 E. Spruce Street • 505.546.8813
57 Units, pets OK ($5). Continental breakfast. Heated pool. Meeting rooms. Laundry facility. Rooms come with phones and cable TV. AAA discount. Credit cards: AE, CB, DC, DS, MC, V.

Grand Motor Inn
$40
1721 E. Spruce Street • 505.546.2632
60 Units, pets OK. Restaurant on premises. Heated pool. Laundry facility. Rooms come with phones and cable TV. AAA/Senior discount. Major credit cards.

Motel 6
$34
I-10 and Motel Drive (Exit 85)
505.546.2623
80 Units, pets OK. Pool. Laundry facility. Rooms come with phones, A/C and cable TV. Wheelchair accessible. Credit cards: AE, CB, DC, DS, MC, V.

ESPANOLA
Super 8 Motel
$45-55
811 S. Riverside Drive • 505.753.5374
48 Units, no pets. Rooms come with phones and cable TV. Rooms come with phones and cable TV. AAA/Senior discount. Major credit cards.

FARMINGTON
Motel 6
$32-34
1600 Bloomfield Hwy. • 505.326.4501
134 Units, pets OK. Pool. Laundry facility. Data ports. Rooms come with phones, A/C and cable TV. Wheelchair accessible. Credit cards: AE, CB, DC, DS, MC, V.

Super 8 Motel
$36-51
1601 Bloomfield Hwy. • 505.325.1813
60 Units, no pets. Continental breakfast. Laundry facility. Game room. Fitness facility. Rooms come with phones and cable TV. Wheelchair accessible. AAA/Senior discount. Credit cards: AE, DC, DS, MC, V.

Travelodge
$39
510 Scott Avenue • 505.327.0242 or 888.697.4680
98 Units, pets OK. Continental breakfast. Pool. Laundry facility. Rooms come with phones, A/C and cable TV. Wheelchair accessible. Credit cards: AE, CB, DC, DS, MC, V.

FORT SUMNER
Super 8 Motel
$43-58*
1707 E. Sumner Ave. • 505.355.7888
44 Units, no pets. Laundry facility. Rooms come with phones and cable TV. Wheelchair accessible. Senior discount. Credit cards: AE, CB, DC, DS, MC, V.
*Rates may increase slightly during weekends, holidays and special events.

GALLUP
Economy Inn
$19-29
1709 US 66W • 505.863.9301
50 Units, pets OK. Airport transportation. Laundry facility. Sauna. Jacuzzi. Rooms come with phones and cable TV. Some rooms have microwaves and refrigerators. AAA discount. Credit cards: AE, DS, MC, V.

Motel 6
$30-40
3306 US 66W • 505.863.4492
80 Units, pets OK. Pool. Laundry facility. Data ports. Rooms come with phones, A/C and cable TV. Wheelchair accessible. Credit cards: AE, CB, DC, DS, MC, V.

Roadrunner Motel
$29-42
3012 US 66E • 505.863.3804
31 Units, pets OK ($20 dep. req.). Restaurant on premises. Continental breakfast. Heated pool. Rooms come with phones and cable TV. AAA/Senior discount. Credit cards: AE, CB, DC, DS, MC, V.

GRANTS
Leisure Lodge
$28
1204 E. Santa Fe Ave. • 505.287.2991
32 Units, pets OK. Heated pool. Rooms come with phones and cable TV. AAA/Senior discount. Credit cards: AE, DS, MC, V.

Motel 6
$28-30
1505 E. Santa Fe Ave. • 505.285.4607
103 Units, pets OK. Pool. Laundry facility. Data ports. Rooms come with phones, A/C and cable TV. Wheelchair accessible. Credit cards: AE, CB, DC, DS, MC, V.

Super 8 Motel
$38*
1604 E. Santa Fe Ave. • 505.287.8811
69 Units, no pets. Toast bar. Jacuzzi. Laundry facility. Rooms come with phones and cable TV. Wheelchair accessible. Senior

discount. Credit cards: AE, CB, DC, DS, MC, V.
*Rates may increase slightly during weekends, holidays and special events.

HOBBS
Days Inn
$40-50
211 N. Marland Blvd. • 505.397.6541
57 Units, pets OK ($10 dep. req.). Continental breakfast. Pool. Rooms come with phones and cable TV. Some rooms have microwaves and refrigerators. AAA/Senior discount. Credit cards: AE, CB, DC, DS, MC, V.

Econo Lodge
$33-39
619 N. Marland Blvd. • 505.397.3591
38 Units, pets OK. Heated pool. Laundry facility. Rooms come with phones and cable TV. Some rooms have refrigerators. AAA/Senior discount. Credit cards: AE, CB, DC, DS, MC, V.

LAS CRUCES
Days End Lodge
$27-31
755 N. Valley Drive • 505.524.7753
32 Units, no pets. Heated pool. Rooms come with phones and cable TV. Some rooms have refrigerators. AAA/Senior discount. Credit cards: AE, CB, DC, DS, MC, V.

Motel 6
$35-38
235 La Posada Lane • 505.525.1010
106 Units, pets OK. Pool. Laundry facility. Rooms come with phones, A/C and cable TV. Wheelchair accessible. Credit cards: AE, CB, DC, DS, MC, V.

Royal Host Motel
$30-34
2146 W. Picacho Street • 505.524.8536
26 Units, pets OK ($7). Heated pool. Rooms come with phones and cable TV. AAA/Senior discount. Credit cards: AE, DS, MC, V.

LAS VEGAS
El Camino Motel
$35-50
1152 N. Grand Avenue • 505.425.5994
23 Units, pets OK ($6 and $20 dep. req.). Restaurant on premises. Rooms come with phones and cable TV. AAA/Senior discount. Credit cards: AE, CB, DC, DS, MC, V.

LORDSBURG
Best Western American Motor Inn
$40-50
944 E. Motel Drive • 505.542.3591
88 Units, pets OK. Restaurant on premises. Playground. Pool. Rooms come with phones and cable TV. AAA/Senior discount. Major credit cards.

Super 8 Motel
$37
110 E. Maple • 505.542.8882
41 Units, no pets. Continental breakfast. Rooms come with phones and cable TV. AAA discount. Credit cards: AE, CB, DC, DS, MC, V.

MORIARTY
Luxury Inn
$35-40
1316 Central Avenue • I-40, Exit 194
505.832.4457
29 Units, pets OK ($3). Continental breakfast. Rooms come with phones and cable TV. Some rooms have microwaves and refrigerators. AAA/Senior discount. Major credit cards.

Motel 6
$38-44
109 Rte. 66E • I-40, Exit 196
505.832.6666
69 Units, pets OK. Indoor pool. Laundry facility. Rooms come with phones, A/C and cable TV. Wheelchair accessible. Credit cards: AE, CB, DC, DS, MC, V.

PORTALES
Classic American Economy Inn
$50
1613 W. Second Street • 505.356.6668
40 Units, pets OK. Continental breakfast. Pool. Playground. Rooms come with phones and cable TV. AAA/Senior discount. Credit cards: AE, MC, V.

RATON
Budget Host Motel
$38-48
136 Canyon Drive • 505.445.3655 or 800.421.5210
27 Units, pets OK ($1). Continental breakfast. Rooms come with phones and

cable TV. Wheelchair accessible. AAA/ Senior discount. Major credit cards.

Motel 6
$35-52 (56)*
1600 Cedar Street • 505.445.2777
103 Units, pets OK. Pool. Laundry facility. Data ports. Rooms come with phones, A/C and cable TV. Wheelchair accessible. Credit cards: AE, CB, DC, DS, MC, V.
*Higher rate effective summer weekends.

Super 8 Motel
$38-40 (50)*
1610 Cedar • 505.445.2355
48 Units, pets OK. Rooms come with phones and cable TV. Wheelchair accessible. Senior discount. Credit cards: AE, CB, DC, DS, MC, V.
*Higher rate effective June through September.

RIO RANCHO
Days Inn
$42-55
4200 Crestview Drive • I-25, Exit 232
505.892.8800
46 Units, pets OK. Continental breakfast. Heated pool. Jacuzzi. Laundry facility. Rooms come with phones and cable TV. AAA/Senior discount. Major credit cards.

ROSWELL
Budget Inn-North
$30-35
2101 N. Main Street • 505.623.6050
42 Units, pets OK ($2). Continental breakfast. Pool. Jacuzzi. Rooms come with phones and cable TV. Some rooms have refrigerators. AAA/Senior discount. Credit cards: AE, CB, DC, DS, MC, V.

Budget Inn-West
$27-37
2200 W. 2nd Street • 505.623.3811
28 Units, pets OK ($2). Pool. Jacuzzi. Rooms come with phones and cable TV. Some rooms have kitchens and refrigerators. AAA/Senior discount. Credit cards: AE, DS, MC, V.

Leisure Inn
$38-55
2700 W. 2nd Street • 505.622.2575
102 Units, pets OK. Continental breakfast. Heated pool. Meeting rooms. Rooms come with phones and cable TV. Some rooms have kitchens, microwaves and refrigerators. AAA/Senior discount. Credit cards: AE, DS, MC, V.

RUIDOSO
Super 8 Motel
$41-45
100 Cliff Drive • 505.378.8180
63 Units, no pets. Continental breakfast. Laundry facility. Sauna. Rooms come with phones and cable TV. Senior discount. Wheelchair accessible. Major credit cards.

Town Lodge
$36-45*
W. Hwy. 70 at the "Y" • 505.378.4471
60 Units, pets OK. Rooms come with phones and cable TV. Major credit cards.
*Summer rates as high as $110/night.

SANTA FE
Motel 6
$40-52 (56-66)*
3007 Cerrillos Road • 505.473.1380
104 Units, pets OK. Pool. Rooms come with phones, A/C and cable TV. Wheelchair accessible. Credit cards: AE, CB, DC, DS, MC, V.
*Higher rates effective summer months.

Red Roof Inn
$40-50
3695 Cerrillos Road • I-25, Exit 278
505.471.4140
121 Units, pets OK. Pool. Rooms come with phones, A/C and cable TV. Wheelchair accessible. Credit cards: AE, CB, DC, DS, MC, V.

SANTA ROSA
Motel 6
$34-46
3400 Will Rogers Drive • 505.472.3045
90 Units, pets OK. Pool. Laundry facility. Data ports. Rooms come with phones, A/C and cable TV. Wheelchair accessible. Credit cards: AE, CB, DC, DS, MC, V.

Super 8 Motel
$44
1201 Will Rogers Drive • 505.472.5388
88 Units, no pets. Laundry facility. Rooms come with phones and cable TV. Wheelchair accessible. Senior discount. Credit cards: AE, CB, DC, DS, MC, V.

SILVER CITY
The Drifter Motel
$41-47
711 Silver Heights Blvd. • 505.538.2916
69 Units, pets OK. Restaurant on premises. Continental breakfast. Heated pool. Laundry facility. Rooms come with phones and cable TV. AAA/Senior discount. Major credit cards.

Super 8 Motel
$39-55
1040 E. Hwy. 180 • 505.388.1983
69 Units, pets OK ($20 dep. req.). Laundry facility. Rooms come with phones and cable TV. Senior discount. Credit cards: AE, CB, DC, DS, MC, V.

SOCORRO
Econo Lodge
$32-50
713 California Ave. N.E. • 505.835.1500
44 Units, pets OK ($5). Restaurant on premises. Continental breakfast. Pool. Rooms come with phones and cable TV. Wheelchair accessible. AAA/Senior discount. Major credit cards.

Motel 6
$34-35
807 S. US Hwy. 85 • 505.835.4300
96 Units, pets OK. Pool. Laundry facility. Data ports. Rooms come with phones, A/C and cable TV. Wheelchair accessible. Credit cards: AE, CB, DC, DS, MC, V.

TAOS
Budget Host Inn
$39-49
1798 Paseo del Pueblo Sur (Hwy 68)
505.758.2524
28 Units, pets OK. Continental breakfast. Airport transportation. Rooms come with phones, A/C and cable TV. AAA/Senior discount. Credit cards: AE, DS, MC, V.

TRUTH OR CONSEQUENCES — *see also Williamsburg*
Super 8 Motel
$39-57
2151 N. Date Street • 505.894.7888
40 Units, pets OK ($15 dep. req.). Rooms come with phones and cable TV. AAA/Senior discount. Major credit cards.

TUCUMCARI
Motel 6
$34-42
2900 E. Tucumcari Blvd. • 505.461.4791
90 Units, pets OK. Pool. Laundry facility. Data ports. Rooms come with phones, A/C and cable TV. Wheelchair accessible. Credit cards: AE, CB, DC, DS, MC, V.

Tucumcari Travelodge
$27-37
1214 E. Tucumcari Blvd. • 505.461.1401
38 Units, pets OK ($5). Continental breakfast. Restaurant on premises. Pool. Rooms come with phones and cable TV. AAA/Senior discount. Credit cards: AE, DC, DS, MC, V.

WILLIAMSBURG
Rio Grande Motel
$33
720 Broadway • 505.894.9769
50 Units, pets OK. Pool. Rooms come with phones and cable TV. Major credit cards.

new york

ADIRONDACKS — *see Elizabethtown, Lake George, Schroon Lake and Tupper Lake*

ALBANY — *see also Latham and Schenectady*
Motel 6
$46-50 (52-60)*
100 Watervliet Avenue • I-90, Exit 5
518.438.7447
98 Units, pets OK. Laundry facility. Rooms come with phones and cable TV. Wheelchair accessible. Major credit cards.
*Higher rates effective summer months.

Red Carpet Inn
$50
500 Northern Blvd. • 518.462.5562
103 Units, no pets. Laundry facility. Rooms come with phones and cable TV. Senior discount. Major credit cards.

ALEXANDRIA BAY
Fitz Inn
$44-55*
On Rte. 26 • 315.482.2641
10 Units, no pets. Rooms come with phones, A/C and cable TV. Major credit cards.
*Closed October through mid-May.

Pinehurst on the St. Lawrence
$35-45*
20683 Pinehurst Road • 315.482.9452
23 Units, no pets. Pool. Playground. Rooms come with phones, A/C and cable TV. Major credit cards.
*Closed October through April.

AMSTERDAM
Valley View Motor Inn
$45 (65-70)*
On SR 5S (half mile north of junction I-80, Exit 27), 518.842.5637
60 Units, pets OK. Laundry facility. Rooms come with phones and cable TV. Some rooms have microwaves and refrigerators. Senior discount. Major credit cards.
*Higher rates effective July and August.

AUBURN
Microtel
$45
12 Seminary Avenue • I-90, Exit 40
315.253.5000
79 Units, pets OK ($40 dep. req.). Continental breakfast. Fitness and laundry facility. Rooms come with phones and cable TV. Wheelchair accessible. AAA/Senior discount. Major credit cards.

AVOCA
Caboose Motel
$33-38*
On SR 415 (From I-390, Exit 1)
607.566.2216
23 Units, pets OK. Pool. Rooms come with phones and cable TV. Some rooms have refrigerators. Credit cards: MC, V.
*Closed January and February.

BALLSTON LAKE — *see Saratoga Springs*

BATAVIA
Park Oak Motel
$40-45 (60-70)*
310 Oak Street • 585.343.7921
20 Units, pets OK. Continental breakfast. Rooms come with phones and cable TV. AAA discount. Major credit cards.
*Higher rates effective May through August.

Red Carpet Inn
$50 (56)*
8212 Park Road • 585.343.2311
20 Units, pets OK. Laundry facility. Data ports. Rooms come with phones and cable TV. Some rooms have microwaves and refrigerators. Senior discount. Major credit cards.
*AAA discounted rates. Higher rate effective weekends.

BATH
Super 8 Motel
$50
333 W. Morris Street • 607.776.2187
50 Units, pets OK. Continental breakfast. Laundry facility. Rooms come with phones and cable TV. Major credit cards.

BINGHAMTON — *see also Johnson City*

Motel 6
$34-45
1012 Front Street • 607.771.0400
98 Units, pets OK. Laundry facility. Rooms come with phones and cable TV. Wheelchair accessible. Major credit cards.

Super 8 Motel
$36-60
650 Old Front Street • I-81, Exit 5
607.773.8111
63 Units, pets OK ($35 dep. req.). Laundry facility. Rooms come with phones and cable TV. AAA/Senior discount. Major credit cards.

BOONVILLE
Headwaters Motor Lodge
$45-49
13524 Rte. 12, Jct. US 12 and 120
315.942.4993
37 Units, pets OK. Continental breakfast. Rooms come with phones and cable TV. AAA/Senior discount. Credit cards: AE, DS, MC, V.

BRIGHTON
Towpath Motel
$45-55
2323 Monroe Avenue • 585.271.2147
20 Units, no pets. Continental breakfast. Rooms come with phones and cable TV. Some rooms have refrigerators. AAA/Senior discount. Major credit cards.

BUFFALO — *see also Clarence, Grand Island, Kenmore, Springville, Tonawanda, West Seneca and Williamsville*
Buffalo Exit 53 Motor Lodge
$45-50*
475 Dingens Street • 716.896.2800
80 Units, pets OK. Restaurant on premises. Pool. Meeting rooms. Rooms come with phones and cable TV. Major credit cards.
*Summer rates may be higher.

Motel 6
$30-46 (54)*
4400 Maple Road • I-290, Exit 5B
716.834.2231
94 Units, pets OK. Rooms come with phones and cable TV. Wheelchair accessible. Major credit cards.
*Higher rate effective summer weekends.

CALCIUM
Microtel
$44
8000 Virginia Smith Drive • 315.629.5000 or 800.447.9660
100 Units, pets OK. Continental breakfast. Rooms come with phones, A/C and cable TV. Wheelchair accessible. Major credit cards.

CANANDAIGUA
Finger Lakes Inn
$44
4343 Rtes. 5 & 20E • 585.394.2800 or 800.727.2775
124 Units, pets OK ($20 dep. req.). Continental breakfast. Heated pool. Rooms come with phones, A/C and cable TV. Wheelchair accessible. Major credit cards.

CATSKILL
Red Ranch Motel
$45-55*
4555 Rte. 32 • 518.678.3380
39 Units, no pets. Pool. Playground. Rooms come with phones and cable TV. AAA/Senior discount. Major credit cards.
*Rates as high as $75/night.

CLARENCE
Judy Ann Motel
$30
9079 Main Street • 716.633.6490
14 Units, no pets. Indoor pool. Rooms come with phones and cable TV. Some rooms have refrigerators and microwaves. Major credit cards.

Three Crowns Motel
$32
10220 Main Street • 716.759.8381
34 Units, no pets. Indoor pool. Rooms come with phones and cable TV. Major credit cards.

CLAYTON
West Winds Motel & Cottages
$40-50*
38267 SR 12E • 315.686.3352
22 Units, pets OK. Pool. Rooms come with cable TV. No phones in rooms. Some rooms have microwaves and refrigerators. AAA discount. Credit cards: MC, V.
*Closed mid-October through April.

COOPERS PLAINS
Stiles Motel
$42-52
9239 Victory Hwy. • 607.962.5221
15 Units, pets OK ($3). Playground. Rooms come with phones and cable TV. Some rooms have refrigerators. AAA/Senior discount. Credit cards: DS, MC, V.

CORNING
Gate House Motel
$33-46
145 E. Corning • 607.936.4131
20 Units, no pets. Restaurant on premises. Laundry facility. Rooms come with phones and cable TV. AAA discount. Credit cards: AE, MC, V.

CORTLAND
Downes Motel
$38-59
10 Church Street • I-81, Exit 11
607.756.2856
42 Units, no pets. Rooms come with phones and cable TV. AAA/Senior discount. Major credit cards.

Imperial Motel
$38-42
28 Port Watson Street • 607.753.3383
20 Units, no pets. Rooms come with phones and cable TV. Major credit cards.

CUBA
Cuba Coachlight Motel
$42-47
1 N. Branch Road • 585.968.1992
27 Units, pets OK ($5). Continental breakfast. Rooms come with phones and cable TV. AAA/Senior discount. Major credit cards.

DANSVILLE
Daystop
$46-51
I-390, Exit 5 • 585.335.6023
20 Units, no pets. Restaurant on premises. Rooms come with phones and cable TV. AAA discount. Credit cards: AE, DS, MC.

DELHI
Buena Vista Motel
$50*
On SR 28 • 607.746.2135
32 Units, pets OK. Breakfast served on premises. Rooms come with phones and cable TV. Major credit cards.
*AAA discounted rate.

DUNKIRK
Dunkirk Inn
$43-50
310 Lake Shore Drive • 716.366.2200
48 Units, pets OK. Continental breakfast. Rooms come with phones and cable TV. Major credit cards.

EAST GREENBUSH
Mt. Vernon Motel
$50
576 Columbia Turnpike • I-90, Exit 11
518.477.9352
49 Units, pets OK. Pool. Rooms come with phones and cable TV. Some rooms have refrigerators. Major credit cards.

EAST SYRACUSE
Microtel
$30-50
6608 Old Collamer Road • I-90, Exit 35 to SR 298E • 315.437.3500
100 Units, pets OK. Continental breakfast. Laundry facility. Rooms come with phones and cable TV. Wheelchair accessible. AAA/ Senior discount. Major credit cards.

ELIZABETHTOWN
Park Motor Inn
$42 (59)*
On Court Street • 518.873.2233
8 Units, no pets. Rooms come with A/C and cable TV. No phones in rooms. Credit cards: MC, V.
*Higher rate effective late June through mid-October.

ELMIRA
Mark Twain Motor Inn
$40
1996 Lake Street • 607.733.9144
64 Units, no pets. Continental breakfast. Rooms come with phones and cable TV. Major credit cards.

Red Jacket Motel
$38*
On Rte. 17 • 607.734.1616
48 Units, pets OK. Restaurant on premises. Pool. Rooms come with phones and cable TV. AAA discount. Major credit cards.
*Rates as high as $55/night.

FAIRPORT
Budget Inn
$40
7340 Pittsford-Palmyra Rd. • 585.223.1710
32 Units, pets OK ($2). Rooms come with phones, refrigerators and cable TV. AAA discount. Major credit cards.

FALCONER
Red Roof Inn
$48
1980 E. Main Street • 716.665.3670
79 Units, pets OK. Rooms come with phones and cable TV. Wheelchair accessible. Major credit cards.

FARMINGTON
Budget Inn
$36-54
6001 SR 96 • 585.924.5020
20 Units, pets OK ($5). Rooms come with phones and cable TV. Some rooms have refrigerators. AAA/Senior discount. Credit cards: AE, DS, MC, V.

Economy Inn
$32-35
6037 Rte. 96 • 585.924.2300
40 Units. Restaurant on premises. Rooms come with phones, A/C and cable TV. Major credit cards.

FORT COVINGTON
Great View Motel
$40
Rte. 37, Box 116 • 518.358.9971
26 Units, pets OK. Restaurant on premises. Playground. Rooms come with A/C and color TV. Wheelchair accessible. Major credit cards.

GATES
Motel 6
$40-52
155 Buell Road • I-90, Exit 46 or I-390, Exit 18B • 716.436.2170
96 Units, pets OK. Laundry facility. Airport transportation. Rooms come with phones, A/C and cable TV. Wheelchair accessible. Credit cards: AE, CB, DC, DS, MC, V.

GENEVA
Chanticleer Motor Inn
$32-45
473 Hamilton Street • 315.789.7600 or 800.441.5227
79 Units. Continental breakfast. Pool. Meeting rooms. Rooms come with phones, A/C and cable TV. Wheelchair accessible. Major credit cards.

Motel 6
$38-52 (60)*
485 Hamilton Street • 315.789.4050
61 Units, pets OK. Rooms come with phones, A/C and cable TV. Wheelchair accessible. Credit cards: AE, CB, DC, DS, MC, V.
*Higher rate effective summer weekends.

GRAND ISLAND
Budget Motel of Grand Island
$35-55
3080 Grand Island Blvd • 716.773.3902
21 Units, no pets. Restaurant on premises. Indoor pool. Rooms come with phones and cable TV. Wheelchair accessible. AAA/Senior discount. Credit cards: AE, DS, MC, V.

Chateau Motor Lodge
$30-45*
1810 Grand Island Blvd • 716.773.2868
17 Units, pets OK ($8). Rooms come with phones and cable TV. AAA/Senior discount. Credit cards: AE, DS, MC, V.
*Rates as high as $69/night during summer.

HAMBURG
Tallyho-Tel
$32-50*
5245 Camp Road • 716.648.2000
117 Units, pets OK. Pool. Airport transportation provided. Laundry facility. Rooms come with phones and cable TV. Wheelchair accessible. AAA/Senior discount. Major credit cards.
*Rates as high as $85/night.

HENRIETTA
Microtel
$36-50
905 Lehigh Station Rd. • 585.334.3400
99 Units, pets OK. Continental breakfast. Laundry facility. Data ports. Rooms come with phones and cable TV. Wheelchair accessible. AAA/Senior discount. Major credit cards.

Red Roof Inn
$41-61
4820 W. Henrietta Rd. • 585.359.1100
108 Units, pets OK. Rooms come with phones and cable TV. AAA discount. Credit cards: AE, CB, DC, DS, MC, V.

Super 8 Motel
$46-53
1000 Lehigh Station Rd. • 585.359.1630
121 Units, pets OK. Continental breakfast. Laundry facility. Meeting rooms. Data ports. Rooms come with phones and cable TV. AAA/Senior discount. Major credit cards.

HERKIMER
Inn Towne Motel
$29-55
227 N. Washington St. • 315.866.1101
33 Units, pets OK. Rooms come with phones and cable TV. Some rooms have microwaves and refrigerators. AAA/Senior discount. Credit cards: AE, DS, MC, V.

HORSEHEADS
Motel 6
$38-46 (54)*
4133 Rte. 17 • 607.739.2525
81 Units, pets OK. Rooms come with phones, A/C and cable TV. Wheelchair accessible. Major credit cards.
*Higher rate effective summer weekends.

Red Carpet Inn
$32-35 (70)*
325 S. Main Street • 607.739.3831
60 Units, no pets. Restaurant on premises. Continental breakfast. Pool. Rooms come with phones and cable TV. Major credit cards.
*Higher rate effective during special events and holidays.

HYDE PARK
Golden Manor Motel
$40-55
On US 9 (1.5 miles south of Jct. C.R. 41)
845.229.2157
38 Units, no pets. Continental breakfast. Pool. Rooms come with phones and cable TV. Some rooms have microwaves and refrigerators. AAA/Senior discount. Credit cards: AE, DC, DS, MC, V.

ITHACA
Economy Inn
$35 (65)*
658 Elmira Road • 607.277.0370
13 Units, pets OK. Rooms come with phones and cable TV. Some rooms have refrigerators. Senior discount. Credit cards: AE, DS, MC, V.
*Higher rate effective weekends.

Hillside Inn
$45-55
518 Stewart Avenue • 607.272.9507
41 Units, pets OK. Continental breakfast. Rooms come with phones and cable TV. Cheaper rooms are without A/C. Major credit cards.

Spring Water Motel
$45 (75)*
1083 Dryden Road (Rte. 366)
607.272.3721
25 Units, pets OK. Continental breakfast. Rooms come with phones, A/C and cable TV. Some rooms have kitchenettes. Major credit cards.
*Higher rate effective weekends.

JOHNSON CITY
Red Roof Inn
$34-55
590 Fairview Street • SR 17, Exit 70N
607.729.8940
107 Units, pets OK. Laundry facility. Rooms come with phones and cable TV. AAA discount. Major credit cards.

KEESEVILLE
Villa Motel
$40*
1875 Rte. 9 • 518.834.7579
60 Units, pets OK. Pool. Rooms come with A/C, phones and cable TV. Major credit cards.
*Rates higher during summer months.

KENMORE
Super 8 Motel
$40-57
1288 Sheridan Drive • I-190, Exit 15
716.876.4020
59 Units, pets OK. Continental breakfast. Meeting rooms. Data ports. Rooms come with phones and cable TV. AAA/Senior discount. Major credit cards.

LAKE GEORGE
Green Haven Resort Motel
$44-59*
3136 Lake Shore Drive • 518.668.2489
20 Units, pets OK during off season. Pool. Playground. Jacuzzi. Rooms come with phones and cable TV. Some rooms have kitchenettes. Senior discount. Credit cards: AE, DC, DS, MC. V.
*Rates as high as $79/night.

LATHAM
Microtel
$44-49*
7 Rensselaer Avenue • 518.782.9161
100 Units, pets OK. Continental breakfast. Rooms come with phones and cable TV. Some rooms have microwaves and refrigerators. Wheelchair accessible. AAA/ Senior discount. Credit cards: AE, CB, DC, DS, JCB, MC, V.
*Rates as high as $89/night.

LIVERPOOL
Knights Inn
$40*
430 Electronics Pkwy. • 315.453.6330
79 Units, pets OK ($3). Rooms come with phones and cable TV. Some rooms have refrigerators. AAA/Senior discount. Credit cards: AE, CB, DC, DS, MC, V.
*Rates as high as $89/night.

LONG ISLAND
Traveler Advisory: A popular getaway destination, Long Island offers a number of accommodations options. Unfortunately, most options are well above the $50/night yardstick, particularly during the summertime. Listed below are a few of Long Island's less expensive places to stay:

Commack
Courtesy Inn ($54-69)
1126 Jericho Tpk.
631.864.3500

Hauppauge
Olympic Motor Lodge ($70)
650 Vanderbilt Motor Pkwy.
631.231.5050

Holbrook
MacArthur Red Carpet Inn ($75)
4444 Veterans Mem'l Hwy.
631.588.7700

Huntington
Abbey Motor Inn
($60-70)
317 W. Jericho Tpke.
631.423.0800

Jericho
Jericho Motel ($65-80)
32 W. Jericho Tpke.
631.997.2800

Meadowbrook Motor Inn ($57-67)
440 Jericho Tpke.
631.681.4200

Massapequa
Budget Inn ($59-110)
400 Carman Mill Road
631.795.4800

Montauk
Blue Haven Motel
($65-75)
W. Lake Drive
631.668.5943

North Babylon
Brook Motel ($65-85)
915 W. Sunrise Hwy.
631.661.1272

North Lindenhurst
Pines Motel Lodge ($69-89)
636 Rte. 109
631.957.3330

Patchogue
Shore Motor Inn ($65-70)
576 W. Sunrise Hwy.
631.363.2500

Shirley
Shirley Motel ($50-85)
681 Montauk Hwy.
631.281.9418

Smith Point Motel ($65-75)
165 Wm. Floyd Pkwy.
631.281.8887

Smithtown
Towne House Motor Inn ($50-65)
880 Jericho Tpke.
631.543.4040

Westbury
Pines Motor Lodge ($69-89)
101 Taylor Avenue
516.832.8330

LOWMAN
Red Jacket Motor Inn
$30-60
On SR 17, east of CR 8 • 607.734.1616
48 Units, pets OK ($10). Continental breakfast. Pool. Playground. Laundry facility. Data ports. Rooms come with

phones and cable TV. AAA/Senior discount. Major credit cards.

MALONE — *see also Moira*
Clark's Motel
$28-45
East Main Street • 518.483.0900
19 Units, no pets. Continental breakfast. Rooms come with phones, A/C and color TV. Some rooms have kitchenettes. Wheelchair accessible. Major credit cards.

Gateway Motel
$36-42
On Finney Blvd. (Rte. 30) • 518.483.4200 or 800.551.0611
19 Units, pets OK. Heated pool. Playground. Rooms come with phones and cable TV. Some rooms have kitchenettes. Wheelchair accessible. Major credit cards.

MARATHON
Three Bear Inn
$32
3 Broome Street • 607.849.3258
22 Units, no pets. Restaurant on premises. Rooms come with phones and cable TV. Credit cards: AE, DC, DS, MC, V.

MOIRA
Crossroads Inn
$45
On Main Street (US 11) • 518.529.7372
41 Units, pets OK. Restaurant on premises. Pool. Meeting rooms. Rooms come with phones and cable TV. Major credit cards.

NEW WINDSOR
Windsor Motel
$39-49*
2976 Route 9W • 845.562.7777
32 Units, pets OK. Continental breakfast. Pool. Airport transportation. Rooms come with phones and cable TV. Major credit cards.
*Rates as high as $140/night.

NEW YORK CITY
Traveler Advisory: If you are planning to spend the night in New York City, you will need to plan on spending more than $50/night. With the exception of youth hostels, you would be very fortunate to find accommodations in New York for less than $90/night. If you have made up your mind that you are going to spend the night in the Big Apple, here are a few recommendations to suit your budget:

Arlington Hotel ($118)
18 W. 25th Street
212.645.3990 or 800.488.0920

Herald Square Hotel ($60-120)
19 W. 31st Street
212.279.4017 or 800.727.1888

Hotel Deauville ($100)
103 E. 29th Street
212.683.0990 or 800.333.8843

The Hotel Newton ($99-160*)
2528 Broadway
(Between 94th and 95th Sts.)
212.678.8500

New York Inn ($100)
765 8th Avenue
212.247.5400

Park Savoy Hotel ($89-140)
158 W. 58th Street
212.245.5755

Pickwick Arms Hotel ($80-109)
230 E. 51st Street
212.355.0300 or 800.PICKWIK

Stanford Hotel ($99-130)
43 W. 32nd Street
212.563.1500 or 800.365.1114

Washington-Jefferson Hotel
($109-149)
318 W. 51st Street
212.246.7550 or 888.567.7550

***AAA discount.**

Hostelling International
$27-31
891 Amsterdam Avenue • 212.932.2300
480 Beds, Office hours: 24 hours
Facilities: 24-hour access, A/C, game and TV room, meeting rooms, information desk, laundry facility, linen rental, lockers. Private rooms available. Sells Hostelling International membership cards. Open year-round. Reservations essential June through October and week of Christmas. Credit cards: JCB, MC, V.

NIAGARA FALLS
Thriftlodge
$36-59*
9401 Niagara Falls Blvd • 716.297.2660
43 Units, pets OK ($10). Heated pool. Picnic area. Laundry facility. Rooms come with phones and cable TV. Some rooms have jacuzzis. Major credit cards.
*Rates as high as $139/night.

Niagara Rainbow Motel
$30-40*
7900 Niagara Falls Blvd • 716.283.1760
26 Units, pets OK. Pool. Rooms come with phones and cable TV. Some rooms have refrigerators. Senior discount. Credit cards: AE, MC, V.
*Rates can climb as high as $89/night depending upon availability.

Travelers Budget Inn
$29-39*
9001 Niagara Falls Blvd • 716.297.3228
24 Units, pets OK. Rooms come with phones and cable TV. Some rooms have kitchens, jacuzzis and refrigerators. Senior discount. Credit cards: AE, MC, V.
*Rates as high as $99/night in summer.

NORTH HORNELL
Econo Lodge
$39-55
7462 Seneca Road • 607.324.0800
67 Units, pets OK ($7). Restaurant on premises. Continental breakfast. Meeting rooms. Airport transportation. Rooms come with phones and cable TV. AAA/Senior discount. Major credit cards.

OLEAN
Motel DeSoto
$40
3139 West State Road • 716.373.1400 or 800.325.0043
76 Units, no pets. Pool. Rooms come with phones and cable TV. Major credit cards.

OWEGO
Sunrise Motel
$45-49
3778 Waverly Road • 607.687.5666
20 Units, pets OK ($5). Continental breakfast. Rooms come with phones and cable TV. AAA/Senior discount. Credit cards: AE, CB, DC, DS, MC, V.

PAINTED POST
Erwin Motel
$34-49
806 Addison Road • SR 17, Exit 44, south on US 15 3 miles • 607.962.7411
25 Units, pets OK. Pool. Laundry facility. Rooms come with phones and cable TV. AAA discount. Major credit cards.

PEMBROKE
Darien Lakes Econo Lodge
$44-65 (79-119)*
8493 SR 77 • I-90, Exit 48A
716.599.4681
73 Units, pets OK. Laundry facility. Game room. Rooms come with phones and cable TV. Some rooms have microwaves and refrigerators. Wheelchair accessible. AAA discount. Major credit cards.
*Higher rates effective late June through Labor Day.

PLATTSBURGH
Golden Gate Beach Motel
$48
432 Margaret Street • 518.561.2040
50 Units, no pets. Rooms come with phones and cable TV. Wheelchair accessible. Major credit cards.

Super 8 Motel
$45-55 (55-65)*
7129 Rte. 9 • I-87, Exit 39 • 518.562.8888
61 Units, pets OK ($5). Continental breakfast. Laundry facility. Picnic area. Rooms come with phones and cable TV. Some rooms have microwaves and refrigerators. AAA discount. Major credit cards.
*Higher rates effective July through September.

POUGHKEEPSIE — *see Hyde Park*

POTSDAM
The Smalling Motel
$47
6775 SR 56 • 315.265.4640
15 Units, no pets. Pool. Rooms come with phones and cable TV. AAA/Senior discount. Credit cards: AE, DS, MC, V.

ROCHESTER — *see also Gates and Henrietta*
Cadillac Hotel
$40
45 Chestnut Street • 585.454.4340

92 Units, no pets. Laundry facility. Rooms come with A/C, phones and cable TV. Major credit cards.

ROME
American Heritage Motor Inn
$40
799 Lawrence Street • 315.339.3610
27 Units, pets OK ($5). Continental breakfast. Rooms come with phones and cable TV. Senior discount. Major credit cards.

ROSCOE
Roscoe Motel
$45
Exit 94 to town center, left at blinker, then half mile • 607.498.5220
18 Units, pets OK ($10). Rooms come with phones and cable TV. AAA discount. Major credit cards.

SARATOGA SPRINGS
Gateway Motel
$50*
260 Maple Avenue • 518.584.2611
20 Units, pets OK ($10). Pool. Rooms come with A/C, phones and cable TV. Major credit cards.
*Rates increase during racing season (August).

Saratoga Lake Motel
$48*
On Rte. 9P (on Saratoga Lake)
518.584.7438
12 Units. Rooms come with A/C, phones, refrigerators, microwaves and cable TV. Major credit cards.
*Rates increase for racing season to $70-75/ night in August.

SAUGERTIES
Wenton Motel
$38-45
3127 Rte. 9W • 845.246.1071
19 Units, no pets. Rooms come with phones and cable TV. Wheelchair accessible. Major credit cards.

SCHENECTADY
Scottish Chalet Motor Lodge
$46
1616 State Street • 518.370.3000
52 Units, no pets. Rooms come with phones and cable TV. Major credit cards.

SCHROON LAKE
Blue Ridge Motel
$50-60*
I-87, Exit 28, 4 miles north on US 9
518.532.7521
17 Units, pets OK ($5). Rooms come with color TV. No phones in rooms. Credit cards: MC, V.
*Closed October through mid-May.

SENECA FALLS
Microtel
$46-56
1966 Rte. 5/20 • 315.539.8438
50 Units, pets OK. Continental breakfast. Continental breakfast. Fitness facility. Rooms come with phones and cable TV. Wheelchair accessible. Major credit cards.

SKANEATELES
Bird's Nest Motel
$45
1601 E. Genessee St. • 315.685.5641
28 Units, pets OK (dep. req.). Rooms come with phones and cable TV. Major credit cards.

SPRINGVILLE
Microtel Inn & Suites
$44-55
I-90, Exit 55 • 716.592.3141
60 Units, pets OK. Continental breakfast. Meeting rooms. Rooms come with phones and cable TV. Wheelchair accessible. Major credit cards.

SYRACUSE — *see also East Syracuse*
Budget Inn
$45 (55-65)*
901 S. Bay Road • 315.458.3510
36 Units, pets OK. Continental breakfast. Rooms come with phones and cable TV. Wheelchair accessible. Major credit cards.
*Higher rates effective weekends.

Days Inn
$45-50
6609 Thompson Road • I-90, Exit 35
315.437.5998
97 Units, pets OK ($10). Continental breakfast. Rooms come with phones and cable TV. AAA/Senior discount. Major credit cards.

Motel 6
$30-50
6577 Baptist Way • I-90, Exit 35

315.433.1300
88 Units, pets OK. Rooms come with phones, A/C and cable TV. Wheelchair accessible. Credit cards: AE, CB, DC, DS, MC, V.

TONAWANDA
Microtel
$34-59
One Hospitality Centre Way • 716.693.8100 or 800.227.6346
100 Units, no pets. Continental breakfast. Rooms come with phones and cable TV. Wheelchair accessible. AAA/Senior discount. Major credit cards.

TUPPER LAKE
Red Top Inn
$46-55
1562 SR 30 • 3 miles south on SR 30
518.359.9209
17 Units, no pets. Restaurant on premises. Rooms come with phones and cable TV. Some rooms have microwaves and refrigerators. AAA/Senior discount. Major credit cards.

Tupper Lake Motel
$40-55
259 Park Street • 518.359.3381
18 Units, no pets. Pool. Rooms come with phones and cable TV. AAA/Senior discount. Credit cards: AE, DS, MC. V.

UTICA
Country Motel
$35-55
1477 Herkimer Road • 315.732.4628
25 Units, no pets. Rooms come with phones and cable TV. Some rooms have refrigerators. AAA discount. Credit cards: AE, DS, MC, V.

Motel 6
$38-50 (54-62)*
150 N. Genesee Street • I-90, Exit 31
315.797.8743
59 Units, pets OK. Rooms come with phones, A/C and cable TV. Wheelchair accessible. Credit cards: AE, CB, DC, DS, MC, V.
*Higher rates effective summer months.

VESTAL
Parkway Motel
$39-49
900 Vestal Parkway E. • 607.785.3311
58 Units, no pets. Laundry facility. Rooms come with phones and cable TV. Some rooms have refrigerators. AAA/Senior discount. Major credit cards.

Vestal Motel
$45
1016 Vestal Pkwy. • 607.754.8090
23 Units, pets OK. Continental breakfast. Rooms come with phones and cable TV. Major credit cards.

VICTOR
Exit 45 Motel
$38-48*
On SR 96 (0.8 miles south of I-90, Exit 45)
585.924.2121
34 Units, no pets. Rooms come with phones and cable TV. AAA discount. Credit cards: AE, DC, DS, MC, V.
*Rates as high as $62/night.

Microtel Inn & Suites
$38-55
7498 Main Street • 585.924.9240
99 Units, pets OK. Continental breakfast. Rooms come with phones and cable TV. Wheelchair accessible. AAA discount. Major credit cards.

WATERLOO
Waterloo Motel
$40 (65-70)*
989 Waterloo Geneva Rd. • 315.539.8042
16 Units, no pets. Rooms come with phones and cable TV. Major credit cards.
*Higher rates effective during summer months.

WATERTOWN
Allen's Budget Motel
$40
24019 SR 342 • 315.782.5319 or 800.545.4184
21 Units, no pets. Rooms come with phones, A/C and cable TV. Some rooms have kitchenettes. Wheelchair accessible. Major credit cards.

Davidson's Motel
$35-45
26177 SR 3 • 315.782.3861
20 Units, pets OK. Rooms come with phones and cable TV. Some rooms have microwaves and refrigerators. Senior discount. Credit cards: AE, DS, MC, V.

New Parrot Motel
$30-45
19325 Outer Washington St.
315.788.5080
26 Units, pets OK. Pool. Rooms come with phones and cable TV. AAA discount. Credit cards: AE, CB, DC, DS, MC, V.

WATKINS GLEN
Queen Catherine Motel
$40-55
436 S. Franklin Street • 607.535.2441
15 Units, no pets. Continental breakfast. Rooms come with phones, A/C and cable TV. AAA/Senior discount. Credit cards: AE, DS, MC, V.

WELLSVILLE
Microtel Inn & Suites
$39-44
30 W. Dyke Street • 716.593.3449
60 Units, no pets. Continental breakfast. Rooms come with phones, A/C and cable TV. Wheelchair accessible. Major credit cards.

WESTMORELAND
Carriage Motor Inn
$35-50
On SR 233 (From I-90, Exit 32)
315.853.3561
24 Units, pets OK. Restaurant on premises. Continental breakfast. Laundry facility. Rooms come with phones and cable TV. AAA/Senior discount. Credit cards: AE, DC, DS, MC, V.

WEST SENECA
Orchard Park Inn
$45
2268 Southwestern Blvd. • 716.674.6000
64 Units, no pets. Pool. Rooms come with phones and cable TV. Major credit cards.

WHITNEY POINT
Point Motel
$35-42
2961 SR 11 • 607.692.4451
14 Units, no pets. Laundry facility. Rooms come with phones and cable TV. AAA/Senior discount. Credit cards: AE, DS, MC, V.

WILLIAMSVILLE
Microtel-Lancaster
$35-50
50 Freeman Road • 716.633.6200
100 Units, pets OK ($5). Continental breakfast. Laundry facility. Rooms come with phones and cable TV. Wheelchair accessible. AAA/Senior discount. Credit cards: AE, CB, DC, DS, MC, V.

north carolina

Traveler Advisory: If you are headed out to the Outer Banks of North Carolina to find lodging during the summertime, you should know that it will be very difficult to find a room for $50 or less. Be prepared to pay anywhere from $50 to $90 per night at some of the smaller, independently owned and operated motels along the Outer Banks. On the other hand, the Outer Banks are a terrific bargain if you travel there during the off season when rates fall substantially, many below the $50 or less target.

ABERDEEN
Motel 6
$36-40
1408 N. Sandhills Blvd. • 910.944.5633
80 Units, pets OK. Restaurant on premises. Pool. Laundry facility. Data ports. Rooms come with phones, A/C and cable TV. Wheelchair accessible. Credit cards: AE, CB, DC, DS, MC, V.

ASHEVILLE — *see also Black Mountain*
Log Cabin Motor Court
$34-36*
330 Weaverville Hwy. • 828.645.6546
18 Units, no pets. Pool. Laundry facility. Rooms come with cable TV. No phones or A/C in rooms. Some rooms have kitchens. AAA discount. Credit cards: DS, MC, V.
*Rates as high as $75-85/night.

Motel 6
$30-45
1415 Tunnel Road • 828.299.3040
105 Units, pets OK. Pool. Laundry facility. Data ports. Rooms come with phones, A/C and cable TV. Wheelchair accessible. Credit cards: AE, CB, DC, DS, MC, V.

Thunderbird Motel
$42
835 Tunnel Road • 828.298.4061
32 Units, pets OK (dep. req.). Pool. Rooms come with phones and cable TV. Wheelchair accessible. Major credit cards.

BATTLEBORO
Days Inn
$40-50*
From I-95, Exit 145 • 252.446.0621
120 Units, pets OK ($6). Pool. Playground. Rooms come with phones and cable TV. AAA discount. Credit cards: AE, CB, DC, DS, JCB, MC, V.
*Rates as high as $67/night.

Super 8 Motel
$39-45
I-95, Exit 145 • 252.442.8075
135 Units, pets OK. Continental breakfast. Pool. Laundry facility. Rooms come with phones and cable TV. Wheelchair accessible. Senior discount. Major credit cards.

Travelodge
$35-55
I-95, Exit 145 • 252.977.3505
100 Units, pets OK. Pool. Rooms come with phones, A/C and cable TV. Wheelchair accessible. Credit cards: AE, CB, DC, DS, MC, V.

BENSON
Days Inn
$30-50
I-95, Exit 795 • 919.894.2031
120 Units, pets OK ($5). Continental breakfast. Pool. Rooms come with phones and cable TV. AAA discount. Major credit cards.

BLACK MOUNTAIN
Acorn Motel
$32*
600 W. State Street • 828.669.7232
22 Units, no pets. Restaurant on premises. Rooms come with phones and TV. Some rooms have kitchens. Wheelchair accessible. Major credit cards.
*Summer rates may be higher.

Apple Blossom Motel
$40
602 W. State Street • 828.669.7922
20 Units, no pets. Heated pool. Rooms come with phones and cable TV. Some

rooms have microwaves and refrigerators. Senior discount. Credit cards: AE, DS, MC, V.

BOONE
Scottish Inns
$48 (68)*
782 Blowing Rock Road • 828.264.2483
42 Units, pets OK. Restaurant on premises. Pool. Jacuzzi. Picnic area. Fitness facility. Rooms come with phones and cable TV. Major credit cards.
*Higher rate effective fall weekends.

BURLINGTON
Days Inn
$30-50
978 Plantation Drive • 336.227.3681
111 Units, pets OK ($10). Continental breakfast. Laundry facility. Meeting rooms. Rooms come with phones and cable TV. AAA discount. Major credit cards.

Motel 6
$35-40
2155 Hanford Road • 336.226.1325
111 Units, pets OK. Pool. Laundry facility. Data ports. Rooms come with phones, A/C and cable TV. Wheelchair accessible. Credit cards: AE, CB, DC, DS, MC, V.

CARY
Red Roof Inn
$44-54
1800 Walnut Street • I-40, Exit 293
919.469.3400
129 Units, pets OK. Data ports. Rooms come with phones and cable TV. Wheelchair accessible. AAA discount. Major credit cards.

CHAPEL HILL — *see Durham*

CHARLOTTE — *see also Matthews*

Days Inn
$34-55
1408 W. Sugar Creek Road (I-85, Exit 41)
704.597.8110
150 Units, pets OK. Restaurant on premises. Pool. Laundry facility. Rooms come with phones and cable TV. Wheelchair accessible. AAA discount. Major credit cards.

Microtel
$37-49
1111 W. Sugar Creek Road (I-85, Exit 41)
704.598.2882
61 Units, no pets. Continental breakfast. Rooms come with phones and cable TV. Wheelchair accessible. AAA/Senior discount. Major credit cards.

Motel 6
$35-37
3430 St. Vardell Lane (I-77, Exit 7)
704.527.0144
121 Units, pets OK. Pool. Laundry facility. Data ports. Rooms come with phones, A/C and cable TV. Wheelchair accessible. Credit cards: AE, CB, DC, DS, MC, V.

Motel 6
$35-37
5116 I-85N • 704.596.8222
105 Units, pets OK. Data ports. Rooms come with phones, A/C and cable TV. Wheelchair accessible. Credit cards: AE, CB, DC, DS, MC, V.

Red Roof Inn
$34-49
131 Red Roof Drive • I-77, Exit 4
704.529.1020
115 Units, pets OK. Data ports. Rooms come with phones, A/C and cable TV. Wheelchair accessible. AAA discount. Major credit cards.

Super 8 Motel
$44
5125 N. I-85 Service Rd • 704.598.8820
81 Units, no pets. Continental breakfast. Pool. Meeting room. Rooms come with phones and cable TV. Wheelchair accessible. Senior discount. Credit cards: AE, CB, DC, DS, MC, V.

CHEROKEE
Budget Host Inn
$32-55*
5280 Ela Road • 828.488.2284
21 Units, no pets. Pool. Playground. Rooms come with phones and cable TV. AAA discount. Credit cards: DS, MC, V.
*Rates as high as $80/night.

CONCORD
Colonial Inn
$45
1325 Hwy. 29N • 704.782.2146
65 Units, no pets. Pool. Meeting rooms. Rooms come with phones and cable TV. Credit cards: AE, DC, DS, MC, V.

CREEDMOOR
Econo Lodge
$35-43
2574 Lyon Station Road • 919.575.6451
62 Units, no pets. Rooms come with phones and cable TV. Wheelchair accessible. Major credit cards.

Ramada Limited
$45-50
2575 Lyon Station Road • 919.575.6565
70 Units, no pets. Continental breakfast. Rooms come with phones and cable TV. Some rooms have refrigerators. AAA/Senior discount. Credit cards: AE, CB, DC, DS, MC, V.

DUNN
Express Inn
$30
510 Spring Branch Rd. • 910.892.8711
120 Units, pets OK. Pool. Rooms come with phones and cable TV. Senior discount. Credit cards: AE, CB, DC, DS, MC, V.

DURHAM
Carolina Duke Motor Inn
$45-50
2517 Guess Road • 919.286.0771
169 Units, pets OK (dogs only, $3). Restaurant on premises. Continental breakfast. Pool. Area transportation available. Meeting rooms. Laundry facility. Rooms come with phones and cable TV. Some rooms have refrigerators. AAA/Senior discount. Credit cards: AE, DC, DS, MC, V.

Days Inn
$30-50
5139 Redwood (I-85, Exit 183)
919.688.4338
119 Units, pets OK ($10). Restaurant on premises. Pool. Rooms come with phones and cable TV. Rooms come with phones and cable TV. AAA/Senior discount. Major credit cards.

Super 8 Motel
$46-52
2337 Guess Road • I-85, Exit 175
919.286.7746
48 Units, pets OK. Continental breakfast. Rooms come with phones and cable TV. Senior discount. Credit cards: AE, CB, DC, DS, MC, V.

EDENTON
Travel Host Inn
$47-55
501 Virginia Road • 252.482.2017
66 Units, no pets. Continental breakfast. Pool. Laundry facility. Rooms come with phones and cable TV. Wheelchair accessible. Senior discount. Credit cards: AE, MC, V.

ELIZABETH CITY
Queen Elizabeth Motel
$35-40 (55)*
1160 US 17S • 252.338.3961
40 Units, pets OK. Pool. Rooms come with phones and cable TV. Major credit cards.
*Higher rate effective special weekends.

Days Inn
$45-55
308 S. Hughes Blvd. (Hwy. 17 Bypass)
252.335.4316
48 Units, pets OK. Continental breakfast. Rooms come with phones and cable TV. Wheelchair accessible. AAA/Senior discount. Major credit cards.

ELIZABETHTOWN
Days Inn
$44-55
605 E. Broad Street • 910.867.7444
30 Units, no pets. Laundry facility. Data ports. Rooms come with phones and cable TV. AAA/Senior discount. Major credit cards.

ELKIN
Elk Inn
$30-50
1101 N. Bridge Street • 336.835.7780
32 Units, no pets. Rooms come with phones and cable TV. AAA/Senior discount. Credit cards: AE, DS, MC, V.

FAYETTEVILLE — *see also Spring Lake*
Innkeeper Fayetteville
$42-48
1725 Jim Johnson Road • I-95, Exit 49
910.485.6866
88 Units, no pets. Continental breakfast. Laundry facility. Data ports. Rooms come with phones and cable TV. Wheelchair accessible. AAA/Senior discount. Major credit cards.

Motel 6
$34-38
2076 Cedar Creek Road • 910.485.8122
113 Units, pets OK. Pool. Laundry facility. Data ports. Rooms come with phones, A/C and cable TV. Wheelchair accessible. Credit cards: AE, CB, DC, DS, MC, V.

FRANKLIN
Colonial Inn
$45-50
3157 Georgia Road • 828.524.6600
42 Units, pets OK. Pool. Laundry facility. Rooms come with phones and cable TV. Credit cards: AE, DS, MC, V.

Country Inn Town Motel
$30-37
277 E. Main Street • 828.524.4451
46 Units, no pets. Pool. Rooms come with phones and cable TV. AAA discount. Credit cards: AE, DS, MC, V.

GASTONIA — *see also Bessemer City*
Days Inn Gastonia-Charlotte
$45-50
1700 N. Chester Street • 704.864.9981
69 Units, pets OK ($5). Pool. Laundry facility. Rooms come with phones and cable TV. Some rooms have microwaves and refrigerators. AAA discount. Credit cards: AE, CB, DC, DS, MC, V.

Motel 6
$34-36
1721 Broadcast Street • 704.868.4900
109 Units, pets OK. Pool. Laundry facility. Data ports. Rooms come with phones, A/C and cable TV. Wheelchair accessible. Credit cards: AE, CB, DC, DS, MC, V.

Super 8 Motel
$45
502 Cox Road • 704.867.3846
45 Units, pets OK. Pool. Rooms come with phones and cable TV. Wheelchair accessible. Senior discount. Major credit cards.

GERTON
Mountain Meadows Motel
$40-60*
On Hwy 74E, 12.5 miles S.E. of Asheville
828.625.1025
10 Units, no pets. Volleyball. Basketball. Rooms come with phones and cable TV. Some rooms have microwaves and refrigerators. Credit cards: DS, MC, V.
*Two-night minimum stay.

GOLD ROCK — *see Battleboro*

GOLDSBORO
Motel 6
$30-37
701 Bypass 70E • 919.734.4542
86 Units, pets OK. Pool. Rooms come with phones, A/C and cable TV. Wheelchair accessible. Credit cards: AE, CB, DC, DS, MC, V.

GREENSBORO — *see also Whitsett*
Motel 6—Airport
$34-40
605 S. Regional Road • I-40, Exit 210
336.668.2085
125 Units, pets OK. Pool. Laundry facility. Data ports. Rooms come with phones, A/C and cable TV. Wheelchair accessible. Credit cards: AE, CB, DC, DS, MC, V.

Motel 6—South
$33-38
831 Greenhaven Drive • I-85, Exit 122C
336.854.0995
148 Units, pets OK. Pool. Laundry facility. Data ports. Rooms come with phones, A/C and cable TV. Wheelchair accessible. Credit cards: AE, CB, DC, DS, MC, V.

Red Roof Inn
$35-54
615 Regional Road S. • I-40, Exit 210
336.271.2636
112 Units, pets OK. Rooms come with phones and cable TV. AAA/Senior discount. Major credit cards.

GREENVILLE
Fairfield Inn
$49-52
821 S. Memorial Drive • 252.758.5544
114 Units, no pets. Continental breakfast. Pool. Fitness facility. Area transportation available. Meeting rooms. Laundry facility. Data ports. Rooms come with phones and cable TV. Wheelchair accessible. AAA/ Senior discount. Major credit cards.

Super 8 Motel
$43-50*
1004 S. Memorial Drive • 252.758.8888
52 Units, no pets. Continental breakfast. Rooms come with phones and cable TV. Wheelchair accessible. Senior discount. Credit cards: AE, CB, DC, DS, MC, V.
*Rates may increase slightly during holidays, special events and weekends.

Travelodge
$36-40
3435 S. Memorial Drive • 252.355.5699
59 Units, guide dogs only. Rooms come with phones, A/C and cable TV. Wheelchair accessible. Credit cards: AE, CB, DC, DS, MC, V.

HAMPTONVILLE
Yadkin Inn
$32-45
US 421 & I-77 (Exit 73A) • 336.468.2801
40 Units, pets OK ($10). Pool. Rooms come with phones and cable TV. Senior discount. AAA discount. Credit cards: AE, DS, MC, V.

HAVELOCK
Sherwood Motel
$30-35
318 W. Main Street • 252.447.3184
89 Units, pets OK ($5). Pool. Rooms come with phones and cable TV. Wheelchair accessible. Major credit cards.

HENDERSON
Budget Host Inn
$36-42
1727 N. Garnett Street • 252.492.2013
25 Units, pets OK. Rooms come with phones and cable TV. Some rooms have refrigerators. Wheelchair accessible. AAA/Senior discount. Credit cards: AE, CB, DC, DS, MC, V.

HICKORY
Red Roof Inn Hickory
$38-58
1184 Lenoir Rhyne Blvd • 828.323.1500
108 Units, pets OK. Rooms come with phones and cable TV. AAA discount. Credit cards: AE, CB, DC, DS, MC, V.

HIGH POINT
Travelodge
$45
200 Ardale Drive • 336.841.7717
83 Units, pets OK. Pool. Rooms come with phones, A/C and cable TV. Wheelchair accessible. Credit cards: AE, CB, DC, DS, MC, V.

JACKSONVILLE
Days Inn
$49
505 Marine Blvd. • 910.347.5131
73 Units, no pets. Restaurant on premises. Continental breakfast. Pool. Rooms come with phones and cable TV. AAA discount. Major credit cards.

KANNAPOLIS
Microtel
$47-49
3113 Cloverleaf Pkwy. • I-85, Exit 58
704.782.2300
59 Units, no pets. Continental breakfast. Rooms come with phones and cable TV. Wheelchair accessible. AAA/Senior discount. Major credit cards.

KENLY
Days Inn
$50*
1139 Johnston Pkwy. • I-95, Exit 106
919.284.3400
79 Units, no pets. Pool. Rooms come with phones and cable TV. Wheelchair accessible. AAA/Senior discount. Major credit cards.
*AAA discounted rate.

Econo Lodge
$35-55
405 S. Church Street • 919.284.1000
60 Units, pets OK. Continental breakfast. Pool. Rooms come with phones and cable TV. AAA/Senior discount. Major credit cards.

KILL DEVIL HILLS
Budget Host Inn
$35-50 (75-90)*
In town on SR 12 • 252.441.2503
40 Units, pets OK. Indoor heated pool. Laundry facility. Rooms come with phones and cable TV. Some rooms have microwaves and refrigerators. Wheelchair accessible. Senior discount available (10%), except weekends and holidays. Major credit cards.
*Higher rates effective June through August.

KINSTON
Days Inn
$48*
410 E. New Bern Road • 919.527.6064
60 Units, no pets. Continental breakfast. Meeting rooms. Rooms come with phones and cable TV. Some rooms have microwaves and refrigerators. Wheelchair accessible. Credit cards: AE, DS, MC, V.
*AAA discounted rates.

Super 8 Motel
$45
212 E. New Bern Road • 252.523.8146
48 Units, no pets. Continental breakfast. Rooms come with phones and cable TV. Major credit cards.

KITTY HAWK
Hostelling International
$15-18
1004 W. Kitty Hawk Rd. • 252.261.2294
40 Beds, Hours: 8-10 am & 4-9 pm
Facilities: Lounge, kitchen, information desk, lockers, bike and luggage storage, A/C, picnic area, volleyball and badminton area, parking. Private rooms available. Open year-round. Reservations advisable. Credit card accepted: MC, V.

LEXINGTON
Best Western Lexington Triad Inn
$48
418 Piedmont Drive • I-85, Exit 96
336.249.0111
100 Units, pets OK ($25). Continental breakfast. Pool. Meeting rooms. Data ports. Rooms come with phones and cable TV. AAA/Senior discount. Major credit cards.

Super 8 Motel
$48
1631 Cotton Grove Road (I-85, Exit 91)
336.357.6444
42 Units, no pets. Continental breakfast. Pool. Rooms come with phones and cable TV. Wheelchair accessible. Senior discount. Major credit cards.

LINCOLNTON
Days Inn
$45-50
614 Clark Drive (SR 150 & 155 Bypass)
704.735.8271
62 Units, pets OK ($10). Continental breakfast. Pool. Meeting rooms. Rooms come with phones and cable TV. AAA/Senior discount. Major credit cards.

LUMBERTON
Econo Lodge
$35-40
3591 Lackey Street • 910.738.7121
103 Units, no pets. Continental breakfast. Pool. Rooms come with phones and cable TV. Some rooms have microwaves and refrigerators. Credit cards: AE, CB, DC, DS, MC, V.

Motel 6
$28-30
2361 Lackey Road • 910.738.2410
83 Units, pets OK. Pool. Laundry facility. Data ports. Rooms come with phones, A/C and cable TV. Wheelchair accessible. Credit cards: AE, CB, DC, DS, MC, V.

MANTEO
Duke of Dare Motor Lodge
$40
100 S. Virginia Dare Rd. • 252.473.2175
57 Units, no pets. Pool. Rooms come with phones and cable TV. Credit cards: MC, V.

MARION
Super 8 Motel
$40-45*
2035 US 221S • 828.659.7940
60 Units, no pets. Continental breakfast. Rooms come with phones and cable TV. Wheelchair accessible. AAA/Senior discount. Major credit cards.
*Rates higher weekends, special events and holidays.

MATTHEWS
Microtel
$40-50
1603 Matthews-Minthill Rd. • 704.814.9131
81 Units, no pets. Continental breakfast. Rooms come with phones and cable TV. Wheelchair accessible. Major credit cards.

MONROE
Knights Inn
$35-39
350 Venus Street • 704.289.9111
109 Units, pets OK. Pool. Fitness facility. Rooms come with phones and cable TV. AAA discount. Wheelchair accessible. Major credit cards.

MOORESVILLE
Days Inn
$46-55
140 Days Inn Drive • I-77 & Hwy. 150 (Exit 36) • 704.664.6100
101 Units, no pets. Continental breakfast. Pool. Meeting rooms. Rooms come with phones and cable TV. Wheelchair accessible. AAA discount. Major credit cards.

MORGANTON
Days Inn
$40-60
2402 S. Sterling Street • 828.433.0011
115 Units, pets OK. Continental breakfast. Pool. Rooms come with phones and cable TV. AAA discount. Major credit cards.

NAGS HEAD
Tar Heel Motel
$40-58*
7010 S. Virginia Dare Tr • 252.441.6150
33 Units, no pets. Pool. Rooms come with phones and cable TV. Credit cards: AE, MC, V.
*Open mid-March through October.

NEW BERN
Days Inn
$39-50
925 Broad Street • 252.636.0150
110 Units, no pets. Continental breakfast. Pool Meeting rooms. Fitness facility. Rooms come with phones and cable TV. AAA/Senior discount. Major credit cards.

Travelodge
$50
3409 Clarendon Blvd. • 252.638.8166
41 Units, no pets. Rooms come with phones and cable TV. AAA discount. Major credit cards.

OUTER BANKS — *see Kill Devil Hills, Kitty Hawk, Manteo and Nags Head*

RAEFORD
Days Inn
$46-50
115 N. US 401 Bypass • 910.904.1050
44 Units, pets OK. Continental breakfast. Rooms come with phones and cable TV. Some rooms have microwaves and refrigerators. AAA/Senior discount. Wheelchair accessible. Major credit cards.

RALEIGH — *see also Cary*
Econo Lodge
$38-60
5110 Holly Ridge Dr. • 919.782.3201
84 Units, no pets. Rooms come with phones and cable TV. Wheelchair accessible. Major credit cards.

Motel 6
$36-38
3921 Arrow Drive • 919.782.7071
63 Units, pets OK. Laundry facility. Data ports. Rooms come with phones, A/C and cable TV. Wheelchair accessible. Credit cards: AE, CB, DC, DS, MC, V.

Motel 6
$36-38
1401 Buck Jones Road (I-40, Exit 293)
919.467.6171
116 Units, pets OK. Restaurant on premises. Pool. Laundry facility. Data ports. Rooms come with phones, A/C and cable TV. Wheelchair accessible. Credit cards: AE, CB, DC, DS, MC, V.

Red Roof Inn
$38-54
5320 Maitland Drive • I-440, Exit 13B
919.231.0200
115 Units, pets OK. Laundry facility. Rooms come with phones and cable TV. Some rooms have microwaves and refrigerators. AAA/Senior discount. Major credit cards.

ROANOKE RAPIDS
Motel 6
$30-46
1911 Weldon Road • 252.537.5252
96 Units. pets OK. Restaurant on premises. Pool. Laundry facility. Data ports. Rooms come with phones, A/C and cable TV. Wheelchair accessible. Credit cards: AE, CB, DC, DS, MC, V.

ROCKINGHAM
Regal Inn Motel
$35-50*
130 W. Broad Street • 910.997.3336
38 Units, no pets. Laundry facility. Rooms come with phones and cable TV. Wheelchair accessible. Major credit cards.
*Rates higher during special events.

ROCKY MOUNT — *see also Battleboro*
Red Roof Inn
$35-45
1370 N. Weslyan Blvd. • 252.984.0907
124 Units, pets OK. Pool. Rooms come with phones and cable TV. AAA discount. Major credit cards.

Super 8 Motel
$43-46
307 Mosley Court • 252.977.2858
62 Units, no pets. Toast bar. Rooms come with phones and cable TV. Wheelchair accessible. Senior discount. Major credit cards.

SALISBURY
Happy Travelers Inn
$30
1420 E. Innes Street • 704.636.6640
52 Units, no pets. Pool. Rooms come with phones and cable TV. Wheelchair accessible. Major credit cards.

SANFORD
Palomino Motel
$42
2.5 miles south on US 1, 15 and 501 Bypass • 919.776.7531
92 Units, pets OK. Pool. Sauna and jacuzzi. Fitness facility. Playground. Meeting rooms. Indoor golf simulator. Rooms come with phones and cable TV. Some rooms have microwaves and refrigerators. AAA discount. Credit cards: AE, DC, DS, MC, V.

SELMA
Masters Inn
$33
US 70E & I-95 (Exit 97) • 919.965.3771
117 Units, no pets. Rooms come with phones and cable TV. Wheelchair accessible. Major credit cards.

SHELBY
Super 8 Motel
$35-50
1716 E. Dixon Blvd. • 704.484.2101
59 Units, no pets. Continental breakfast. Fax and Rooms come with phones and cable TV. Wheelchair accessible. AAA/Senior discount. Credit cards: AE, CB, DC, DS, MC, V.

SOUTHERN PINES
Microtel Inn
$39-52
205 Windstar Place • 910.693.3737
78 Units, no pets. Continental breakfast. Laundry facility. Data ports. Rooms come with phones and cable TV. Wheelchair accessible. AAA/Senior discount. Major credit cards.

SPINDALE
Super 8 Spindale
$40
210 Reservation Drive • 704.286.3681
62 Units, pets OK. Continental breakfast. Pool. Rooms come with phones and cable TV. Some rooms have microwaves and refrigerators. AAA discount. Credit cards: AE, DC, DS, MC, V.

SPRING LAKE
Super 8 Motel
$39-54
256 S. Main Street • 910.436.8588
62 Units, pets OK. Continental breakfast. Rooms come with phones and cable TV. Some rooms have microwaves and refrigerators. Wheelchair accessible. Major credit cards.

STATESVILLE
Masters Inn
$33-38
702 Sullivan Road • 704.873.5252
119 Units, no pets. Continental breakfast. Pool Rooms come with phones and cable TV. Some rooms have microwaves and refrigerators. Senior discount. Major credit cards.

Motel 6
$30-46
1137 Moreland Drive • 704.871.1115
96 Units, pets OK. Restaurant on premises. Pool. Laundry facility. Data ports. Rooms come with phones, A/C and cable TV. Wheelchair accessible. Credit cards: AE, CB, DC, DS, MC, V.

Red Roof Inn
$37-49
1508 E. Broad Street • I-77, Exit 50
704.878.2051
115 Units. pets OK. Rooms come with phones, A/C and cable TV. AAA discount. Major credit cards.

WADESBORO
Days Inn
$40-50
209 E. Caswell Street • 704.694.7070
48 Units, pets OK. Rooms come with phones and cable TV. Some rooms have microwaves and refrigerators. AAA discount. Major credit cards.

WASHINGTON
Econo Lodge
$38-45
1220 W. 15th Street • 252.946.7781
45 Units, pets OK ($5). Rooms come with phones and cable TV. Some rooms have microwaves and refrigerators. AAA/Senior discount. Major credit cards.

WAYNESVILLE
Parkway Inn
$36-48*
2093 Dellwood Road • 828.926.1841
30 Units, no pets. Rooms come with phones and cable TV. Credit cards: DS, MC, V.
*Rates as high as $95/night.

WELDON
Days Inn
$50
1611 Roanoke Rapids Road (I-95, Exit 173)
252.536.4867
97 Units, pets OK. Continental breakfast. Pool. Jacuzzi. Meeting rooms. Rooms come with phones and cable TV. Wheelchair accessible. AAA/Senior discount. Major credit cards.

Interstate Inn
$36
Jct. US 158 & I-95 (Exit 173)
252.536.4111
116 Units, pets OK. Pool. Rooms come with phones and cable TV. Senior discount. Credit cards: AE, CB, DC, DS, MC, V.

WHITEVILLE
Holiday Motel
$45
US 701N • 910.642.5162
99 Units, no pets. Restaurant on premises. Pool. Picnic area. Meeting room. Rooms come with phones and cable TV. Wheelchair accessible. Major credit cards.

WHITSETT
Daystop
$39-50
I-85 (Exit 138) • 336.449.6060
33 Units, no pets. Restaurant on premises. Meeting room. Laundry facility. Rooms come with phones and cable TV. Wheelchair accessible. AAA discount. Major credit cards.

WILLIAMSTON
Economy Lodge
$32
317 E. Boulevard • 252.792.4106
40 Units, no pets. Restaurant on premises. Pool. Rooms come with phones and TV. Wheelchair accessible. Major credit cards.

WILMINGTON
Motel 6
$30-50
2828 Market on US 17/74 Business
910.762.0120
113 Units, pets OK. Pool. Laundry facility. Data ports. Rooms come with phones, A/C and cable TV. Wheelchair accessible. Credit cards: AE, CB, DC, DS, MC, V.

Super 8 Motel
$45-57
3604 Market Street • 910.343.9778
62 Units, pets OK. Continental breakfast. Rooms come with phones and cable TV. Wheelchair accessible. Major credit cards.

WILSON
Microtel Inn
$40-55
5013 Hayes Place • 252.234.0444
60 Units, no pets. Continental breakfast. Rooms come with phones and cable TV. Wheelchair accessible. Major credit cards.

WINSTON-SALEM
Days Inn North
$43-53*
5218 Germanton Road • 336.744.5755
60 Units, no pets. Rooms come with phones and TV. Some rooms have refrigerators. Senior discount. Major credit cards.
*AAA discounted rates.

Kings Inn
$40
5906 University Pkwy. • 336.377.9131
40 Units, no pets. Restaurant on premises. Rooms come with phones and cable TV. Some rooms have kitchens. Wheelchair accessible. Major credit cards.

Motel 6
$34-40
3810 Patterson Avenue • 336.661.1588
102 Units, pets OK. Pool. Laundry facility. Data ports. Rooms come with phones, A/C and cable TV. Wheelchair accessible. Credit cards: AE, CB, DC, DS, MC, V.

north dakota

BEACH
Buckboard Inn
$31
701.872.4794 • I-94, Exit 1, south on SR 16 for 0.3 miles.
36 Units, pets OK. Continental breakfast. Rooms come with phones and cable TV. Credit cards: AE, DS, MC, V.

BEULAH
Super 8 Motel
$35
720 Hwy. 49 N. • 701.873.2850
39 Units, no pets. Rooms come with cable TV. Wheelchair accessible. Senior discount. Credit cards: AE, CB, DC, DS, MC, V.

BISMARCK — see also Mandan
Budget Inn Express
$45
122 E. Thayer Avenue • 701.255.1450
58 Units, pets OK. Continental breakfast. Heated pool. Laundry facility. Rooms come with phones and cable TV. Some rooms have refrigerators. AAA discount. Major credit cards.

Days Inn
$44
1300 E. Capitol Avenue • 701.223.9151
110 Units, no pets. Continental breakfast. Indoor pool, sauna and jacuzzi. Rooms come with cable TV and A/C. AAA discount. Major credit cards.

Expressway Inn
$45
200 Bismarck Expwy. • 701.222.2900
162 Units, pets OK ($5). Continental breakfast. Heated pool, jacuzzi and playground. Airport transportation. Laundry facility. Rooms come with phones and cable TV. Senior discount. Wheelchair accessible. Credit cards: AE, DC, DS, MC, V.

Motel 6
$31-42
2433 State Street • 701.255.6878
101 Units, pets OK. Pool. Laundry facility. Data ports. Rooms come with phones and cable TV. Wheelchair accessible. Credit cards: AE, CB, DC, DS, MC, V.

Select Inn
$38-55
1505 Interchange Ave. • 701.223.8060
101 Units, pets OK ($25 dep. req.). Continental breakfast. Laundry facility. Rooms come with phones and cable TV. Some rooms have microwaves, radios and refrigerators. AAA/Senior discount. Credit cards: AE, CB, DC, DS, MC, V.

BOTTINEAU
Super 8 Motel
$41
1007 E. 11th Street • 701.228.2125
31 Units, no pets. Continental breakfast. Jacuzzi. Rooms come with phones and cable TV. Senior discount. Major credit cards.

BOWMAN
Budget Host 4U Motel
$28
704 Hwy 12W • 701.523.3243
40 Units, pets OK. Sauna. Laundry facility nearby. Rooms come with phones and cable TV. Credit cards: AE, CB, DC, DS, MC, V.

Super 8 Motel
$46-50
614 Third Avenue S.W. • 701.523.5613
31 Units, pets OK ($20 dep. req.). Continental breakfast. Sauna and jacuzzi. Rooms come with phones and cable TV. Credit cards: AE, DC, DS, MC, V. Senior discount.

CARRINGTON
Super 8 Motel
$41-48
701.652.3982 • Half mile east on US 52/281 from town, just south of junction of SR 200 on Hwy 281.
40 Units, pets OK ($5). Laundry facility. Rooms come with phones and cable TV. AAA/Senior discount. Credit cards: AE, DC, DS, MC, V.

CAVALIER
Cedar Inn
$35

On Hwy 18S • 701.265.8341 or 800.338.7440
40 Units, pets OK. Restaurant on premises. Rooms come with phones, A/C and cable TV. Major credit cards.

DEVILS LAKE
Great American Inn & Suites
$29-50
Hwy 2E • 701.662.4001
80 Units, pets OK ($25 dep. req.). Continental breakfast. Indoor pool. Rooms come with A/C, phones and cable TV. Wheelchair accessible. Major credit cards.

Trails West Motel
$35
701.662.5011 • 0.8 miles SW on US 2.
74 Units, pets OK ($5). Continental breakfast. Meeting rooms. Rooms come with phones and cable TV. AAA/Senior discount. Credit cards: AE, CB, DC, DS, MC, V.

DICKINSON
Budget Inn
$36-40
529 12th Street W. • 701.225.9123
54 Units, pets OK. Laundry facility. Rooms come with phones and cable TV. Some rooms have jacuzzis. AAA/Senior discount. Credit cards: AE, DC, DS, MC, V.

Nodak Motel
$32
600 E. Villard Street • 701.225.5119
26 Units, pets OK ($25 and $25 dep. req.). Heated pool and playground. Rooms come with phones and cable TV. Some rooms have microwaves and refrigerators. Credit cards: AE, DS, MC, V.

Super 8 Motel
$46-51
637 12th Street W. • 701.227.1215
59 Units, pets OK. Rooms come with phones and cable TV. Wheelchair accessible. Senior discount. Credit cards: AE, CB, DC, DS, MC, V.

EDGELEY
Edgeley Super 8 Motel
$41-49
Jct. US 281 & SR 13 • 701.493.2075
24 Units, no pets. Continental breakfast. Laundry facility. Rooms come with phones and cable TV. AAA/Senior discount. Credit cards: AE, CB, DC, DS, MC, V.

FARGO — *see also West Fargo and Moorhead (MN)*
Econo Lodge of Fargo
$34-54
1401 35th Street S. • 701.232.3412
40 Units, pets OK. Laundry facility. Rooms come with phones and cable TV. Senior discount. Credit cards: AE, CB, DC, DS, JCB, MC, V.

Flying J Inn
$35
3150 39th Street S.W. • 701.282.8473
41 Units, pets OK ($10 plus $25 dep. req.). Continental breakfast. Laundry facility. Rooms come with phones and cable TV. Some rooms have kitchens, microwaves and refrigerators. AAA/Senior discount. Credit cards: AE, DS, MC, V.

Microtel Inn & Suites
$44
1101 38th Street N.W. • I-29, Exit 66
701.281.2109
82 Units, no pets. Continental breakfast. Heated pool. Laundry facility. Jacuzzi. Meeting rooms. Data ports. Rooms come with A/C, phones and cable TV. Wheelchair accessible. AAA/Senior discount. Major credit cards.

Motel 6
$31-40
1202 36th Street S. • I-29, Exit 64
701.232.9251
97 Units, pets OK. Indoor Pool. Laundry facility. Data ports. Rooms come with phones and cable TV. Wheelchair accessible. Credit cards: AE, CB, DC, DS, MC, V.

Select Inn
$36-47
1025 38th Street S.W. • 701.282.6300
127 Units, pets OK ($25 dep. req.). Continental breakfast. Laundry facility. Rooms come with phones and cable TV. Some rooms have kitchenettes, microwaves, refrigerators and radios. AAA/Senior discount. Credit cards: AE, CB, DC, DS, MC, V.

GRAFTON
Super 8 Motel
$39-55
948 W. 12th Street • 701.352.0888
32 Units, no pets. Rooms come with phones and cable TV. Wheelchair accessible. Senior discount. Credit cards: AE, CB, DC, DS, MC, V.

GRAND FORKS — *see also East Grand Forks (MN)*

Happy Host Inn
$33-35
3101 S. 17th Street • 701.746.4411 or 800.489.4411
62 Units, no pets. Continental breakfast. Rooms come with phones, A/C and cable TV. Credit cards: DC, DS, MC, V.

Plainsman Motel
$33-44
2201 Gateway Drive • 701.792.0435
50 Units, pets OK ($5). Continental breakfast. Rooms come with phones, A/C and cable TV. Wheelchair accessible. Credit cards: AE, DS, MC, V.

Roadking Inn
$38-43
1015 N. 43rd Street • 701.775.0691
85 Units, no pets. Pool. Jacuzzi. Continental breakfast. Laundry facility. Rooms come with phones and cable TV. Wheelchair accessible. Credit cards: AE, DS, MC, V.

Select Inn
$32-42
1000 N. 42nd Street • 701.775.0555
120 Units, pets OK ($5 plus $25 deposit). Continental breakfast. Laundry facility. Rooms come with phones and cable TV. AAA/Senior discount. Credit cards: AE, DC, DS, MC, V.

JAMESTOWN

Days Inn
$44-51
824 S.W. 20th Street • I-94, Ex. 258
701.251.9085
40 Units, pets OK ($5). Continental breakfast. Fitness facility. Laundry facility. Rooms come with A/C, phones and cable TV. Wheelchair accessible. AAA discount. Major credit cards.

Gladstone Inn & Suites
$40
111 2nd Street S.E. • 701.252.0700
100 Units, pets OK. Restaurant on premises. Indoor Pool. Jacuzzi. Rooms come with A/C, phones and cable TV. Major credit cards.

Ranch House Motel
$30-35
408 Business Loop W. • 701.252.0222
38 Units, pets OK ($3). Heated pool. Laundry facility. Rooms come with phones and cable TV. Some rooms have kitchenettes. AAA discount. Credit cards: AE, DC, DS, MC, V.

LAKOTA

Sunlac Inn
$39
701.247.2487 • Half mile east on US 2 from town.
40 Units, pets OK ($5). Restaurant on premises. Meeting rooms and a tanning bed (fee). Rooms come with cable TV. Credit cards: AE, DC, DS, MC, V.

LANGDON

Langdon Motor Inn
$33
210 9th Avenue • 701.256.3600
26 Units, pets OK. Continental breakfast. Rooms come with A/C, phones and cable TV. Wheelchair accessible. Major credit cards.

LISBON

Super 8 Motel
$43
724 Main Street • 701.683.9076
20 Units, no pets. Continental breakfast. Laundry facility. Rooms come with cable TV. Wheelchair accessible. Senior discount. Credit cards: AE, CB, DC, DS, MC, V.

MANDAN — *see also Bismarck*

Rivertree Inn
$38-48
4524 Memorial Hwy. • 701.663.9856 or 800.927.5661
50 Units, no pets. Rooms come with phones, cable TV and A/C. Major credit cards.

MAYVILLE

Super 8 Motel
$40
34 Center Avenue S. • 701.786.9081
20 Units, no pets. Continental breakfast. Laundry facility. Rooms come with cable TV. Wheelchair accessible. Senior discount. Credit cards: AE, CB, DC, DS, MC, V.

MINOT

Dakota Inn
$33
US 2 & 52 Bypass • 701.838.2700
120 Units, pets OK. Continental breakfast. Two pools (one heated and one indoor), jacuzzi, solarium, wading pool. Laundry

facility. Rooms come with phones and cable TV. AAA/Senior discount. Credit cards: AE, CB, DC, DS, MC, V.

Select Inn
$33-44
225 22nd Avenue N.W. • 701.852.3411
100 Units, pets OK ($25 dep. req.). Continental breakfast. Laundry facility. Data ports. Rooms come with phones and cable TV. Some rooms have kitchenettes and radios. AAA/Senior discount. Credit cards: AE, DC, DS, MC, V.

Super 8 Motel
$40-49
1315 N. Broadway • 701.852.1817
60 Units, pets OK. Laundry facility. Rooms come with phones and cable TV. Wheelchair accessible. Senior discount. Credit cards: AE, CB, DC, DS, MC, V.

ROLLA
Bilmar Motel
$35
Hwy 5 • 701.477.3157 or 800.521.0443
36 Units, pets OK. Restaurant on premises. Sauna and jacuzzi. Rooms come with A/C, phones and cable TV. Major credit cards.

RUGBY
Econo Lodge
$40-46
On US 2 East • 701.776.5776
60 Units, pets OK. Restaurant on premises. Continental breakfast. Two pools and wading pool. Rooms come with cable TV. Some rooms have jacuzzis. Credit cards: AE, DC, DS, JCB, MC, V.

VALLEY CITY
Super 8 Motel
$46
822 11th Street S.W. • 701.845.1140
30 Units, no pets. Rooms come with phones and cable TV. Senior discount. Credit cards: AE, CB, DC, DS, MC, V.

Wagon Wheel Inn & Suites
$40-50
455 Winter Show Drive • 701.845.5333
88 Units, pets OK. Continental breakfast. Laundry facility. Meeting rooms, heated indoor pool and jacuzzi. Rooms come with phones and cable TV. Some rooms have microwaves, refrigerators and radios. AAA discount. Credit cards: AE, CB, DC, DS, MC, V.

WAHPETON
Super 8 Motel
$40-43
995 21st Avenue N. • 701.642.8731
58 Units, pets OK. Heated pool. Jacuzzi. Restaurant on premises. Continental breakfast. Rooms come with phones and cable TV. AAA/Senior discount. Major credit cards.

WATFORD CITY
Roosevelt Inn & Suites
$40-45
600 Second Avenue S.W. • 701.842.3686 or 800.887.9170
41 Units, no pets. Continental breakfast. Indoor pool. Spa. Sauna. Rooms come with phones, A/C and cable TV. Major credit cards.

WEST FARGO — *see also Fargo*
Super 8 Motel
$35-46
825 E. Main Avenue • 701.282.7121
41 Units, pets OK. Rooms come with cable TV. Wheelchair accessible. Senior discount. Credit cards: AE, CB, DC, DS, MC, V.

WILLISTON
Airport International Inn
$43
Hwys. 2 and 85N • 701.774.0241
143 Units, pets OK. Restaurant on premises. Indoor pool and jacuzzi. Meeting rooms. Rooms come with A/C, phones and cable TV. Major credit cards.

El Rancho Motor Hotel
$43-49
1623 2nd Avenue W. • 701.572.6321
91 Units, pets OK. Restaurant on premises. Fitness facility. Meeting rooms. Airport transportation. Laundry facility. Rooms come with refrigerators and cable TV. AAA/Senior discount. Credit cards: AE, DC, DS, MC, V.

ohio

ABERDEEN
Brown's Motel
$28-30
On US 52 • Half mile west of Maysville Bridge
937.795.2231 or 937.795.2232
36 Units, pets OK ($3 plus dep. req.). Rooms come with phones, A/C and cable TV. Credit cards: AE, MC, V.

Daniel Boone Motor Inn
$34-40
On US 52 (west of town) • 937.795.2203 or 800.521.8570
97 Units, pets OK. Restaurant on premises. Rooms come with phones and cable TV. Major credit cards.

AKRON — *see also Barberton, Kent and Macedonia*
Econo Lodge
$40-50
3237+ S. Arlington Road • I-77, Exit 120
330.644.1847
39 Units, pets OK ($5). Pool. Rooms come with phones and cable TV. Senior discount. Credit cards: AE, CB, DC, DS, MC, V.

Red Roof Inn
$35-59
2939 S. Arlington Road • I-77, Exit 120
330.644.7748
121 Units, pets OK. Rooms come with phones and cable TV. AAA discount. Major credit cards.

Super 8 Motel
$44-55*
79 Rothrock Road • 330.666.8887
59 Units, pets OK. Rooms come with phones and cable TV. Wheelchair accessible. Senior discount. Credit cards: AE, CB, DC, DS, MC, V.
*Rates may increase slightly during weekends, special events and holidays.

ALLIANCE
Super 8 Motel
$44-55
2330 W. State Street • 330.821.5688
46 Units, no pets. Continental breakfast. Pool. Rooms come with phones and cable TV. AAA/Senior discount. Wheelchair accessible. Major credit cards.

AMHERST
Motel 6
$37-50*
704 N. Leavitt Road • SR 2 & SR 58
440.988.3266
126 Units, pets OK. Pool. Data ports. Rooms come with phones, A/C and cable TV. Wheelchair accessible. Credit cards: AE, CB, DC, DS, MC, V.
*Prices higher during weekends and special events.

ASHLAND
Days Inn
$39-58
1423 County Road 1575 (I-75, Exit 186)
419.289.0101
61 Units, pets OK. Continental breakfast. Pool. Rooms come with phones and cable TV. Wheelchair accessible. AAA/Senior discount. Major credit cards.

ASHTABULA
Cedars Motel
$50
2015 W. Prospect Road • 440.992.5406
15 Units, pets OK ($5). Laundry facility. Rooms come with phones and cable TV. AAA discount. Credit cards: AE, DS, MC, V.

Edge-O-Town Motel
$40-45
2328 N. Ridge • 440.992.8527
14 Units, no pets. Rooms come with phones and cable TV. Some rooms have kitchenettes. Senior discount. Major credit cards.

ATHENS
Budget Host Inn
$37-50
100 Albany Road • 740.594.2294
29 Units, no pets. Continental breakfast. Rooms come with phones and cable TV. AAA/Senior discount. Major credit cards.

Budget Inn Express
$40
997 E. State Street • 740.593.5565
52 Units, no pets. Continental breakfast. Rooms come with phones and cable TV. Wheelchair accessible. Major credit cards.

AUSTINTOWN
Motel 6
$40-55*
5431 Seventy-Six Drive • I-80, Exit 223A
330.793.9305
97 Units, pets OK. Pool. Laundry facility. Rooms come with phones, A/C and cable TV. Wheelchair accessible. Credit cards: AE, CB, DC, DS, MC, V.
*Prices higher during weekends and special events.

BLUFFTON
Knights Inn
$35-40
855 SR 103 • 419.358.7000
32 Units, no pets. Rooms come with A/C, phones and cable TV. Wheelchair accessible. Major credit cards.

BOARDMAN
Microtel Inn
$30-50
7393 South Avenue • 330.758.1816
92 Units, pets OK ($25). Continental breakfast. Laundry facility. Meeting rooms. Data ports. Rooms come with phones and cable TV. Wheelchair accessible. Major credit cards.

Wagon Wheel Motel
$35
7015 Market Street • 330.758.4551
20 Units, no pets. Rooms come with phones and cable TV. Some rooms have microwaves, refrigerators and jacuzzis. AAA discount. Credit cards: AE, DC, DS, MC, V.

BOTKINS
Budget Host Inn
$32-38
I-75 & SR 219 • 937.693.6911
50 Units, no pets. Restaurant on premises. Continental breakfast. Pool. Meeting rooms. Tennis court. Playground. Laundry facility. Rooms come with phones and cable TV. Major credit cards.

BOWLING GREEN
Buckeye Budget Motor Inn
$46-50
1740 E. Wooster Street • 419.352.1520
70 Units, pets OK. Pool. Laundry facility. Rooms come with phones and cable TV. Some rooms have kitchenettes. Wheelchair accessible. AAA discount. Major credit cards.

BROOKVILLE
Days Inn
$50
100 Parkview Drive • I-70, Exit 21
937.833.4003
62 Units, pets OK ($5). Continental breakfast. Pool. Rooms come with phones and cable TV. AAA discount. Major credit cards.

BRYAN
Colonial Manor Motel
$50
924 E. High Street • 419.636.3123
52 Units, no pets. Restaurant on premises. Meeting room. Rooms come with phones and cable TV. Wheelchair accessible. Major credit cards.

CAMBRIDGE
Budget Host Deer Creek Motel
$33-50
2321 Southgate Pkwy. • 740.432.6391 or 800.637.2917
90 Units, pets OK ($5). Restaurant on premises. Continental breakfast. Indoor pool. Picnic area. Rooms come with A/C and color TV. Senior discount. Major credit cards.

CANTON/NORTH CANTON
Motel 6
$34-46
6880 Sunset Strip Ave NW • 330.494.7611
89 Units, pets OK. Pool. Laundry facility. Data ports. Rooms come with phones, A/C and cable TV. Wheelchair accessible. Credit cards: AE, CB, DC, DS, MC, V.

Red Roof Inn
$37-59
5353 Inn Circle Court NW • 330.499.1970
108 Units, pets OK. Data ports. Rooms come with phones and cable TV. AAA discount. Major credit cards.

CHILLICOTHE
Chillicothe Inn
$33-47
24 N. Bridge Street • 740.774.2512
40 Units, no pets. Rooms come with phones

and cable TV. AAA discount. Credit cards: AE, DS, MC, V.

CINCINNATI — *see also Norwood, Sharonville, Springdale, Erlanger (KY), Ft. Mitchell (KY), Ft. Wright (KY) and Florence (KY)*

Budget Host Town Center Motel
$43-58
3356 Central Pkwy. • I-75, Exit 3
513.559.1600
56 Units, no pets. Pool. Rooms come with phones and cable TV. Some rooms have microwaves, refrigerators and jacuzzis. Senior discount. Major credit cards.

Cross Country Inn
$43*
4004 Williams Drive • I-275, Exit 65
513.528.7702
128 Units, no pets. Heated pool. Rooms come with phones and cable TV. Senior discount. Credit cards: AE, DC, DS, MC, V. *Prices higher during weekends and special events.

Motel 6
$35-50
3960 Nine Mile Road, I-275, Exit 65
513.752.2262
108 Units, pets OK. Pool. Laundry facility. Data ports. Rooms come with phones, A/C and cable TV. Wheelchair accessible. Credit cards: AE, CB, DC, DS, MC, V.

Super 8 Motel
$40-50
11335 Chester Road • 513.772.3140
144 Units, pets OK. Continental breakfast. Pool. Laundry facility. Rooms come with phones and cable TV. Senior discount. Wheelchair accessible. Major credit cards.

CIRCLEVILLE

Knights Inn
$40
23897 US 23S • 740.474.6006
70 Units, pets OK ($5). Meeting rooms. Rooms come with phones and cable TV. Some rooms have microwaves, refrigerators and jacuzzis. AAA/Senior discount. Credit cards: AE, CB, DC, DS, MC, V.

CLEVELAND — *see Amherst, Fairview Park, Independence, Macedonia, Mentor, Middleburg Heights, North Olmstead, Strongsville, Twinsburg, Westlake, Wickliffe and Willoughby*

COLUMBUS — *see also Circleville, Dublin, Grove City, Heath, Hilliard, Lancaster, Marysville, Reynoldsburg, Westerville and Worthington*

Cross Country Inn
$37-44
6225 Zumstein Drive • I-17, Exit 117
614.848.3819
142 Units, no pets. Heated pool. Meeting rooms. Rooms come with phones and cable TV. AAA/Senior discount. Credit cards: AE, DC, DS, MC, V.

Cross Country Inn
$37-44
4875 Sinclair Road • I-17, Exit 116
614.431.3670
136 Units, no pets. Pool. Rooms come with phones and cable TV. AAA/Senior discount. Credit cards: AE, DC, DS, MC, V.

Cross Country Inn—OSU North
$43-50
3246 Olentangy River Rd. • 614.267.4646
96 Units, no pets. Heated pool. Data ports. Rooms come with phones and cable TV. AAA/Senior discount. Major credit cards.

Cross Country Inn
$42-49
1313 W. St. James Lutheran Ln. • I-70, Exit 91 (eastbound) or Exit 91B (westbound)
614.870.7090
120 Units, no pets. Heated pool. Rooms come with phones and cable TV. AAA/Senior discount. Major credit cards.

Days Inn
$36-50
3160 Olentangy River Road • 614.261.0523
99 Units, pets OK. Rooms come with phones and cable TV. Some rooms have refrigerators. AAA discount. Credit cards: AE, CB, DC, DS, MC, V.

Microtel Inn
$37-59
7500 Vantage Drive • I-270, Exit 23
614.436.0556
100 Units, pets OK ($5). Continental breakfast. Rooms come with phones and cable TV. Wheelchair accessible. AAA/Senior discount. Credit cards: AE, DC, DS, MC, V.

Motel 6—East
$35-48
5910 Scarborough Blvd. • 614.755.2250

100 Units, pets OK. Pool. Laundry facility. Data ports. Rooms come with phones, A/C and cable TV. Wheelchair accessible. Credit cards: AE, CB, DC, DS, MC, V.

Motel 6—West
$36-46
5500 Renner Road • 614.870.0993
116 Units, pets OK. Pool. Laundry facility. Data ports. Rooms come with phones, A/C and cable TV. Wheelchair accessible. Credit cards: AE, CB, DC, DS, MC, V.

DAYTON — *see also Brookville, Englewood, Huber Heights, Riverside and Vandalia*
Days Inn
$50-55
7470 Miller Lane • 937.898.4946
188 Units, pets OK. Continental breakfast. Laundry facility. Pool. Rooms come with phones and cable TV. Wheelchair accessible. AAA discount. Credit cards: AE, DC, DS, MC, V.

Knights Inn
$35-60
3663 Maxton Road • I-75, Exit 60
937.898.1212
73 Units, no pets. Continental breakfast. Rooms come with phones and cable TV. Pool. Rooms come with phones and cable TV. Some rooms have kitchenettes. Major credit cards.

Motel 6
$30-40
7130 Miller Lane • 937.898.3606
96 Units, pets OK. Pool. Laundry facility. Data ports. Rooms come with phones, A/C and cable TV. Wheelchair accessible. Credit cards: AE, CB, DC, DS, MC, V.

DEFIANCE
Ranchland Village Motor Inn
$36
1983 S. Jefferson Street • 419.782.9946
42 Units, no pets. Rooms come with phones and cable TV. Some rooms have kitchenettes. Major credit cards.

DOVER
Hospitality Inn
$35-50
889 Commercial Pkwy. • 330.364.7724
100 Units, pets OK ($10). Pool. Laundry facility. Rooms come with phones and cable TV. Wheelchair accessible. AAA/Senior discount. Major credit cards.

DUBLIN
Cross Country Inn
$39-46
6364 Frantz Road • 614.764.4545
112 Units, no pets. Heated pool. Meeting rooms. Rooms come with phones and cable TV. AAA/Senior discount. Major credit cards.

EATON
Econo Lodge
$40-45
6161 Rte. 127N • 937.456.5959
51 Units, pets OK ($10). Meeting rooms. Rooms come with phones and cable TV. AAA/Senior discount. Credit cards: AE, DS, MC, V.

ENGLEWOOD
Cross Country Inn
$38-45
9325 N. Main Street • 937.836.8339
120 Units, no pets. Heated pool. Rooms come with phones and cable TV. AAA/Senior discount. Credit cards: AE, CB, DC, DS, MC, V.

Motel 6
$34-40
1212 S. Main Street • 937.832.3770
106 Units, pets OK. Pool. Laundry facility. Data ports. Rooms come with phones, A/C and cable TV. Wheelchair accessible. Credit cards: AE, CB, DC, DS, MC, V.

FAIRVIEW PARK
Knights Inn
$38-50*
22115 Brookpark Road • 440.734.4500
78 Units, pets OK. Restaurant on premises. Airport transportation. Rooms come with phones and cable TV. Wheelchair accessible. Major credit cards.
*Rates as high as $65/night.

FINDLAY
Cross Country Inn
$40-47
1951 Broad Avenue • 419.424.0466
120 Units, no pets. Heated pool. Rooms come with phones and cable TV. AAA/Senior discount. Major credit cards.

Rodeway Inn
$33-49
1901 Broad Avenue • 419.424.1133
100 Units, pets OK ($10). Continental breakfast. Meeting room. Pool. Rooms come with phones and cable TV. AAA/Senior discount. Credit cards: AE, CB, DC, DS, MC, V.

Super 8 Motel
$43-45
1600 Fox Street • 419.422.8863
62 Units, no pets. Rooms come with phones and cable TV. Wheelchair accessible. AAA/Senior discount. Credit cards: AE, CB, DC, DS, MC, V.

FOSTORIA
Days Inn
$42-50
601 Findlay Street • 419.435.6511
42 Units, pets OK. Rooms come with phones and cable TV. Some rooms have jacuzzis and refrigerators. Wheelchair accessible. AAA discount. Major credit cards.

FRANKLIN
Knights Inn
$40-45
8500 Claude-Thomas Road • I-75, Exit 38
937.746.2841
66 Units, no pets. Continental breakfast. Rooms come with phones and cable TV. Wheelchair accessible. Major credit cards.

Super 8 Motel
$40-55 (55-65)*
3553 Commerce Drive • 937.422.4888
49 Units, pets OK. Laundry facility. Rooms come with phones and cable TV. Senior discount. Major credit cards.
*Higher rates effective June through September.

FREMONT
Double A Motel
$37-45
919 E. State Street • 419.332.6457
35 Units, pets OK. Restaurant on premises. Pool. Rooms come with phones and cable TV. Some rooms have microwaves and refrigerators. Wheelchair accessible. Major credit cards.

GALLIPOLIS
William Ann Motel
$40-45
918 2nd Avenue • 740.446.3373
50 Units, pets OK. Continental breakfast. Rooms come with phones and cable TV. AAA/Senior discount. Credit cards: AE, DS, MC, V.

GENEVA-ON-THE-LAKE
Surf Motel
$40-50*
5276 Lake Road • 440.466.3283
18 Units, pets OK. Continental breakfast. Rooms come with A/C and cable TV. Major credit cards.
*Summer rates higher.

GIRARD
Econo Lodge
$35-50
1615 E. Liberty Street • 330.759.9820
56 Units, no pets. Continental breakfast. Rooms come with phones and cable TV. Wheelchair accessible. Major credit cards.

Knights Inn
$33-43
1600 Motor Inn Drive • 330.759.7833
125 Units, pets OK. Pool. Laundry facility. Rooms come with phones, A/C and cable TV. Wheelchair accessible. Credit cards: AE, CB, DC, DS, MC, V.

GROVE CITY
Cross Country Inn
$43-50
4055 Jackpot Road • 614.871.9617
120 Units, no pets. Heated pool. Laundry facility. Rooms come with phones and cable TV. AAA/Senior discount. Major credit cards.

Heritage Inn
$36
1849 Stringtown Road • 614.871.0440
120 Units, no pets. Pool. Laundry facility. Rooms come with phones and cable TV. Some rooms have microwaves and refrigerators. AAA/Senior discount. Major credit cards.

Knights Inn
$29-50
3131 Broadway • 614.871.0065
99 Units, no pets. Pool. Rooms come with phones and cable TV. Wheelchair accessible. AAA/Senior discount. Major credit cards.

HEATH
Hometown Inn
$40
1266 Hebron Road • 740.522.6112
58 Units, pets OK. Pool. Rooms come with phones and cable TV. Some rooms have microwaves and refrigerators. AAA discount. Major credit cards.

HEBRON
Red Roof Inn
$45-50
10668 Lancaster Road • 740.467.2020
16 Units, no pets. Restaurant on premises. Laundry facility. Rooms come with phones and cable TV. AAA discount. Major credit cards.

HILLIARD
Motel 6
$36-46
3950 Parkway Lane • 614.771.1500
106 Units, pets OK. Pool. Rooms come with phones, A/C and cable TV. Wheelchair accessible. Credit cards: AE, CB, DC, DS, MC, V.

HILLSBORO
Greystone Motel
$30-40
8190 US 50E • 937.393.1966
37 Units, no pets. Restaurant on premises. Rooms come with phones and cable TV. Major credit cards.

HOLLAND
Cross Country Inn
$40-47
1201 E. Mall Drive • 419.866.6565
128 Units, no pets. Heated pool. Rooms come with phones and cable TV. AAA/Senior discount. Credit cards: AE, DC, DS, MC, V.

Red Roof Inn
$37-59
1214 Corporate Drive • 419.866.5512
108 Units, pets OK. Rooms come with phones and cable TV. Credit cards: AE, CB, DC, DS, MC, V.

HUBER HEIGHTS
Super 8 Motel
$48
8110 Old Troy Pike • 937.237.1888
63 Units, no pets. Heated pool. Laundry facility. Rooms come with phones and cable TV. AAA/Senior discount. Wheelchair accessible. Major credit cards.

Travelodge
$50*
7911 Brandt Pike • 937.236.9361
51 Units, pets OK. Pool. Rooms come with phones and cable TV. Some rooms have refrigerators. Senior discount. Major credit cards.
*AAA discounted rate.

HURON
Gull Motel
$45-50*
45 Cleveland Road E. • 419.433.4855
25 Units, no pets. Rooms come with phones and cable TV. Wheelchair accessible. Major credit cards.
*Rates as high as $85/night.

Plantation Motel
$37-49 (49-69)*
2815 Cleveland Road E. • 419.433.4790
26 Units, pets OK ($7). Pool. Rooms come with phones and cable TV. AAA/Senior discount. Major credit cards.
*Higher rates effective during summer months. Closed November through March.

INDEPENDENCE
Days Inn
$40-50
5555 Brecksville Road • 216.524.3600
68 Units, pets OK. Restaurant on premises. Continental breakfast. Laundry facility. Meeting room. Airport transportation. Rooms come with phones and cable TV. Wheelchair accessible. AAA discount. Major credit cards.

IRONTON — *see South Point*

JACKSON
Knights Inn
$40-53
404 Chillicothe Street • 740.286.2135
35 Units, pets OK ($20 dep. req.). Rooms come with A/C, phones and cable TV. AAA/Senior discount. Credit cards: AE, DS, MC. V.

LANCASTER
Lancaster Motel
$50
533 S. Columbus Street • 740.653.5706
36 Units, no pets. Rooms come with phones and cable TV. Major credit cards.

LIMA
Days Inn
$40-60
1250 Neubrecht Road • 419.227.6515
123 Units, pets OK. Continental breakfast. Restaurant on premises. Pool. Playground. Rooms come with phones and cable TV. AAA discount. Credit cards: AE, CB, DC, DS, JCB, MC, V.

Econo Lodge
$46
1201 Neubrecht Road • 419.222.0596
130 Units, pets OK. Restaurant on premises. Continental breakfast. Pool. Fitness facility. Rooms come with phones and cable TV. Major credit cards.

Motel 6
$36-40*
1800 Harding Hwy. • 419.228.0456
97 Units, pets OK. Laundry facility. Data ports. Rooms come with phones, A/C and cable TV. Wheelchair accessible. Credit cards: AE, CB, DC, DS, MC, V.
*Prices higher during weekends and special events.

LOGAN
Shawnee Inn
$45-55
30916 Lake Logan Rd. • 740.385.5674
22 Units, pets OK ($5). Rooms come with phones and cable TV. AAA/Senior discount. Credit cards: AE, DS, MC. V.

MACEDONIA
Motel 6
$36-50 (60)*
311 E. Highland Road • SR 8 & I-271
330.468.1670
123 Units, pets OK. Pool. Laundry facility. Data ports. Rooms come with phones, A/C and cable TV. Wheelchair accessible. Credit cards: AE, CB, DC, DS, MC, V.
*Higher rate effective summer weekends.

MANSFIELD
Knights Inn
$45-60
555 N. Trimble Road • 419.529.2100
88 Units, pets OK. Continental breakfast. Pool. Meeting rooms. Rooms come with phones and cable TV. AAA/Senior discount. Major credit cards.

Super 8 Motel
$45-55
2425 Interstate Circle • 419.756.8875
69 Units, pets OK ($50 dep. req.). Continental breakfast. Rooms come with phones and cable TV. Senior discount. Major credit cards.

MARIETTA
Knights Inn
$42-53
506 Pike Street • 740.373.7373
110 Units, pets OK. Continental breakfast. Pool. Laundry facility. Meeting rooms. Rooms come with phones and cable TV. AAA/Senior discount. Major credit cards.

Super 8 Motel
$43-49*
46 Acme Street Washington Center
740.374.8888
62 Units, no pets. Meeting room. Rooms come with phones and cable TV. Wheelchair accessible. AAA/Senior discount. Credit cards: AE, DC, DS, MC, V.
*Rates may increase slightly during special events and some weekends.

MARION
Travelodge
$50
1952 Marion-Mt. Gilead Rd. • 740.389.4671
92 Units, pets OK. Pool. Laundry facility. Rooms come with phones and cable TV. Some rooms have microwaves and refrigerators. Major credit cards.

MARYSVILLE
Super 8 Motel
$38-44
10220 US 42 • 614.873.4100
30 Units, pets OK ($5). Rooms come with phones and cable TV. Senior discount. Major credit cards.

MASSILLON
Red Carpet Inn
$40
412 Lincoln Way E. • 330.832.1538
48 Units, no pets. Meeting rooms. Rooms come with phones and cable TV. Senior discount. Major credit cards.

MAUMEE
Cross Country Inn
$36-43
1704 Tollgate Drive • 419.891.0880

120 Units, no pets. Heated pool. Rooms come with phones and cable TV. AAA/Senior discount. Credit cards: AE, DC, DS, MC, V.

Knights Inn
$40-46
1520 S. Holland-Sylvania Rd.
419.865.1380
161 Units, pets OK. Pool. Meeting rooms. Laundry facility. Rooms come with phones and cable TV. AAA/Senior discount. Credit cards: AE, CB, DC, DS, MC, V.

Red Roof Inn
$37-57
1570 Reynolds Road • 419.893.0292
110 Units, pets OK. Data ports. Rooms come with phones and cable TV. AAA discount. Credit cards: AE, CB, DC, DS, MC, V.

MEDINA
Cross County Inn
$39-46
5021 Eastpoint Drive • 330.725.1395
120 Units, no pets. Heated pool. Rooms come with phones and cable TV. AAA/Senior discount. Major credit cards.

MENTOR
Motel 6
$36-52 (60)*
8370 Broadmoor Road • I-90, Exit 193
440.953.8835
103 Units, pets OK. Pool. Laundry facility. Data ports. Rooms come with phones, A/C and cable TV. Wheelchair accessible. Credit cards: AE, CB, DC, DS, MC, V.
*Higher rates effective summer weekends.

MIAMISBURG
Knights Inn
$40-50
185 Byers Road • 937.859.8797
104 Units, no pets. Continental breakfast. Pool. Laundry facility. Meeting rooms. Rooms come with phones and cable TV. Wheelchair accessible. Senior discount. Major credit cards.

MIDDLEBURG HEIGHTS
Cross Country Inn
$46-53
7233 Engle Road • I-71, Exit 235
440.243.2277
112 Units, no pets. Pool. Meeting rooms. Rooms come with phones and cable TV. AAA/Senior discount. Major credit cards.

Motel 6
$40-50 (56-58)*
7219 Engle Road • I-71, Exit 235
440.234.0990
95 Units, pets OK. Pool. Laundry facility. Data ports. Rooms come with phones, A/C and cable TV. Wheelchair accessible. Credit cards: AE, CB, DC, DS, MC, V.
*Higher rates effective summer weekends.

MIDDLETOWN
Park Way Inn
$30-36
2425 N. Verity Parkway • 513.423.9403
55 Units, pets OK. Pool. Game room. Rooms come with phones and cable TV. Major credit cards.

MORAINE
Super 8 Motel
$47*
2450 Dryden Road • 937.298.0380
72 Units, no pets. Pool. Copy and fax service. Rooms come with phones and cable TV. Senior discount. Credit cards: AE, CB, DC, DS, MC, V.
*Rates may increase slightly during weekends, special events and holidays.

MOUNT GILEAD
Knights Inn
$40-50
5898 SR 95 • 419.946.6010
47 Units, pets OK ($15). Laundry facility. Meeting rooms. Rooms come with phones and cable TV. AAA/Senior discount. Credit cards: AE, CB, DC, DS, MC, V.

NEWARK
University Inn
$40*
1225 W. Church Street • 740.344.2136
36 Units, pets OK. Restaurant on premises. Rooms come with phones and cable TV. Major credit cards.
*Summer rates may be higher.

NEW PHILADELPHIA — *see also Dover*
Motel 6
$30-46*
181 Bluebell Drive S.W. • I-77, Exit 81
330.339.6446
83 Units, pets OK. Pool. Laundry facility. Rooms come with phones, A/C and cable TV. Wheelchair accessible. Credit cards: AE, CB, DC, DS, MC, V.
*Prices higher during weekends and special events.

NEWTON FALLS
Rodeway Inn
$39-50*
4248 SR 5 • 330.872.0988
36 Units, pets OK ($5). Continental breakfast. Pool. Rooms come with phones and cable TV. AAA/Senior discount. Major credit cards.
*Rates higher during special events and holidays.

NORTH LIMA
Comfort Lodge
$26-38
10145 Market Street • 330.549.3224
43 Units, no pets. Pool. Meeting room. Rooms come with phones and cable TV. AAA discount. Major credit cards.

NORTH OLMSTEAD
Days Inn
$50-60
24399 Lorain Road, I-480, Exit 6B
440.777.4100
73 Units, no pets. Restaurant on premises. Continental breakfast. Pool. Airport transportation. Rooms come with phones and cable TV. Wheelchair accessible. AAA discount. Major credit cards.

NORTH RIDGEVILLE
Super 8 Motel
$39-52*
32801 Lorain Road • 440.327.0500
55 Units, no pets. Continental breakfast. Game room. Rooms come with phones and cable TV. Wheelchair accessible. Senior discount. Credit cards: AE, CB, DC, DS, MC, V.
*Higher rates effective Memorial Day through Labor Day.

Travelers Inn
$40*
32751 Lorain Road • 440.327.6311
86 Units, pets OK. Laundry facility. Rooms come with phones and cable TV. Major credit cards.
*Summer rates may be higher.

NORWALK
Norwalk Inn
$36 (50-54)*
283 Benedict Avenue • 419.668.8255
20 Units, pets OK. Rooms come with phones and cable TV. Major credit cards.
*Higher rates effective May through September.

NORWICH
Baker's Motel
$28-50
8855 E. Pike • I-70, Exit 164
740.872.3232
57 Units, pets OK. Restaurant on premises. Laundry facility. Meeting room. Rooms come with phones and cable TV. Major credit cards.

NORWOOD
Red Roof Inn
$39-51
5300 Kennedy Avenue • 513.531.6589
80 Units, pets OK. Fitness facility. Rooms come with phones and cable TV. AAA discount. Major credit cards.

OXFORD
Scottish Inns
$37-47
5235 College Corner Rd • 513.523.6306
30 Units, pets OK. Restaurant on premises. Continental breakfast. Pool. Playground. Rooms come with phones and cable TV. Major credit cards.

PERRYSBURG
Howard Johnson Inn
$34-49
I-280, Exit 1B • 419.837.5245
142 Units, pets OK. Restaurant on premises. Heated pool. Rooms come with phones and cable TV. AAA/Senior discount. Major credit cards.

Red Carpet Inn
$35-45
26054 N. Dixie Hwy. • 419.872.2902
37 Units, pets OK ($5). Rooms come with phones and cable TV. Some rooms have microwaves and refrigerators. AAA/Senior discount. Credit cards: AE, DS, MC, V.

PIQUA
Red Carpet Inn
$34-40
9060 Country Club Road • I-75, Exit 83
937.773.6275
50 Units, pets OK. Restaurant on premises. Meeting rooms. Rooms come with phones and cable TV. Senior discount. Major credit cards.

PORTSMOUTH — *see also Wheelersburg*
Four Keys Inn
$30
2302 Scioto Trail • 740.354.2844

39 Units, pets OK ($10 dep. req.). Pool. Rooms come with phones and cable TV. Major credit cards.

REYNOLDSBURG
Cross County Inn
$45-52
2055 Brice Road • 614.864.3880
120 Units, no pets. Heated pool. Fitness facility. Rooms come with A/C, phones and cable TV. AAA/Senior discount. Major credit cards.

RIVERSIDE
Microtel Inn & Suites
$40-50
4500 Linden Avenue • I-675, Exit 14
937.252.9700
53 Units, no pets. Continental breakfast. Rooms come with phones and cable TV. Wheelchair accessible. Major credit cards.

ROSSFORD
Knights Inn
$43-48*
1120 Buck Road • 419.661.6500
148 Units, no pets. Continental breakfast. Pool. Meeting rooms. Laundry facility. Rooms come with A/C, phones and TV. AAA/Senior discount. Major credit cards.
*Rates could climb as higher as $69/night.

Rossford Inn
$38*
1135 Buck Road • 419.666.4515
50 Units, no pets. Rooms come with phones and cable TV. Wheelchair accessible. Senior discount. Credit cards: AE, CB, DC, DS, MC, V.
*Rates may increase slightly during weekends, special events and holidays.

ST. CLAIRSVILLE
Knights Inn
$39-45
51260 National Road • 740.695.5038
104 Units, pets OK. Continental breakfast. Picnic area. Pool. Laundry facility. Rooms come with phones and cable TV. Some rooms have microwaves, jacuzzis and refrigerators. AAA/Senior discount. Major credit cards.

Red Roof Inn
$38-49
68301 Red Roof Lane, I-70, Exit 218
740.695.4057
108 Units, no pets. Rooms come with phones, A/C and cable TV. Major credit cards.

SANDUSKY
Best Budget Inn
$28-48 (58-98)*
2027 Cleveland Road • 419.626.3610 or 419.627.9770
47 Units, no pets. Continental breakfast. Pool. Game room. Rooms come with phones and TV. Some rooms have jacuzzis. AAA discount. Major credit cards.
*Higher rates effective Memorial Day through Labor Day.

Best Budget Inn South
$34-40 (59-149)*
5918 Milan Road • 419.625.7252
54 Units, no pets. Pool. Laundry facility. Game room. Rooms come with phones and TV. Some rooms have jacuzzis. Wheelchair accessible. AAA/Senior discount. Major credit cards.
*Higher rates effective Memorial Day through Labor Day.

SHARONVILLE
Motel 6
$34-50
3850 Hauck Road • I-275, Exit 46
513.563.1123
110 Units, pets OK. Pool. Laundry facility. Data ports. Rooms come with phones, A/C and cable TV. Wheelchair accessible. Credit cards: AE, CB, DC, DS, MC, V.

Motel 6
$30-40
2000 E. Kemper Road • Junction of I-75 and I-275 • 513.772.5944
123 Units, pets OK. Pool. Laundry facility. Data ports. Rooms come with phones, A/C and cable TV. Wheelchair accessible. Credit cards: AE, CB, DC, DS, MC, V.

SIDNEY
Econo Lodge
$36-40
2009 W. Michigan St. • 937.492.9164
98 Units, no pets. Restaurant on premises. Pool. Meeting rooms. Laundry facility. Rooms come with phones and cable TV. Some rooms have refrigerators. Senior discount. Credit cards: AE, CB, DC, DS, JCB, MC, V.

SOUTH POINT
Best Western Southern Hills Inn
$45
803 Solida Road • 740.894.3391
49 Units, pets OK ($6). Continental breakfast. Pool. Rooms come with phones and cable TV. AAA discount. Major credit cards.

SPRINGDALE
Cross Country Inn
$42-49
330 Glensprings Drive • 513.671.0556
120 Units, no pets. Heated pool. Meeting rooms. Rooms come with A/C, phones and cable TV. AAA/Senior discount. Major credit cards.

SPRINGFIELD
Executive Inn
$40
325 W. Columbia Avenue • I-70, Exit 54
937.324.5601
74 Units, pets OK. Playground. Rooms come with phones and cable TV. Wheelchair accessible. Major credit cards.

Knights Inn
$36-52
2207 W. Main Street • I-70, Exit 52B
937.325.8721
39 Units, pets OK ($10). Continental breakfast. Pool. Laundry facility. Rooms come with A/C, phones and cable TV. Senior discount. Major credit cards.

Super 8 Motel
$44-55*
2 W. Leffel Lane • I-70, Exit 54
937.324.5501
100 Units, no pets. Continental breakfast. Rooms come with phones and cable TV. Senior discount. Major credit cards.
*Rates higher during weekends, special events and holidays.

STRONGSVILLE
Days Inn
$40-50
9029 Pearl Road • I-71, Exit 234
440.234.3575
40 Units, pets OK ($5). Continental breakfast. Laundry facility. Rooms come with phones and cable TV. Some rooms have microwaves and refrigerators. AAA discount. Credit cards: AE, DS, MC, V.

TOLEDO — *see also Maumee and Rossford*
Motel 6
$30-42
5335 Heatherdowns Blvd.
I-80/90, Exit 59 • 419.865.2308
100 Units, pets OK. Laundry facility. Rooms come with phones, A/C and cable TV. Wheelchair accessible. Credit cards: AE, CB, DC, DS, MC, V.

TROY
Econo Lodge
$30-45
1210 Brukner Drive • 937.335.0013
81 Units, pets OK. Rooms come with phones, A/C and cable TV. Wheelchair accessible. Credit cards: AE, CB, DC, DS, MC, V.

Knights Inn
$45-55
30 Troy Town Drive • I-75, Exit 74
937.339.1515
84 Units, pets OK. Laundry facility. Airport transportation. Rooms come with phones and cable TV. Some rooms have microwaves and refrigerators. Wheelchair accessible. AAA discount. Major credit cards.

Super 8 Motel
$45*
1330 Archer Drive • 937.339.6564
70 Units, no pets. Pool. Continental breakfast. Meeting room. Rooms come with phones and cable TV. Wheelchair accessible. Senior discount. Credit cards: AE, CB, DC, DS, MC, V.
*Rates may increase slightly during weekends, special events and holidays.

VANDALIA
Cross Country Inn
$40-47
550 E. National Road • 937.898.7636
94 Units, no pets. Heated pool. Meeting rooms. Rooms come with phones and cable TV. AAA/Senior discount. Major credit cards.

Crossroads Motel
$32
845 E. National Road • 937.898.5871
84 Units, no pets. Pool. Rooms come with phones and cable TV. Wheelchair accessible. Major credit cards.

WAPAKONETA
Days Inn
$40-50
1659 Wapak Fisher Rd. • 419.738.2184
95 Units, pets OK ($5). Restaurant on premises. Pool. Rooms come with phones and cable TV. AAA discount. Major credit cards.

Super 8 Motel
$46
1011 Lunar Drive • I-75, Exit 111
419.738.8810
38 Units, pets OK. Continental breakfast. Rooms come with phones and cable TV. AAA/Senior discount. Wheelchair accessible. Major credit cards.

WASHINGTON COURT HOUSE
Knights Inn
$40-53
1820 Columbus Avenue • 740.335.9133
56 Units, pets OK. Meeting rooms. Rooms come with phones and cable TV. Some rooms have microwaves and refrigerators. Wheelchair accessible. AAA/Senior discount. Credit cards: AE, CB, DC, DS, MC, V.

WESTLAKE
Cross Country Inn
$44-51
25200 Sperry Drive • 440.871.3993
115 Units, no pets. Heated pool. Rooms come with phones and cable TV. AAA/Senior discount. Major credit cards.

WESTERVILLE
Cross Country Inn
$43-50
909 S. State Street • I-270, Exit 29
614.890.1244
152 Units, no pets. Heated pool. Rooms come with phones and cable TV. AAA/Senior discount. Major credit cards.

Knights Inn
$50
32 Heatherdown Drive • I-270, Exit 29
614.890.0426
105 Units, pets OK. Continental breakfast. Pool. Rooms come with phones and cable TV. AAA/Senior discount. Major credit cards.

WILLOUGHBY
Days Inn
$37-44
4145 SR 306 • I-90, Exit 193
440.946.0500
113 Units, pets OK ($35). Continental breakfast. Pool. Laundry facility. Rooms come with phones and cable TV. Some rooms have microwaves and refrigerators. AAA/Senior discount. Major credit cards.

WINCHESTER
Budget Host Inn
$45
18760 SR 136 • 937.695.0381
19 Units, no pets. Data ports. Rooms come with phones and cable TV. Some rooms have microwaves and refrigerators. AAA/Senior discount. Credit cards: AE, DS, MC, V.

WOOSTER
Super 8 Motel
$45-49
969 Timken Road • 330.264.6211
43 Units, pets OK ($2). Rooms come with phones and cable TV. Senior discount. Major credit cards.

WORTHINGTON
Econo Lodge
$40-46
50 E. Wilson Bridge Rd. • 614.888.3666
45 Units, no pets. Rooms come with phones and cable TV. Some rooms have refrigerators. AAA/Senior discount. Major credit cards.

XENIA
Allendale Inn
$38-48
6 Allison Avenue • 937.376.8124
88 Units, no pets. Meeting rooms. Rooms come with phones and cable TV. Some rooms have microwaves and refrigerators. AAA discount. Credit cards: AE, DS, MC, V.

Best Western Regency Inn
$43-46
600 Little Main Street • 937.372.9954
19 Units, pets OK. Rooms come with phones and cable TV. AAA/Senior discount. Major credit cards.

YOUNGSTOWN — *see also Austintown, Boardman and Girard*

Days Inn
$35-50
1610 Motor Inn Drive • 330.759.3410
136 Units, pets OK ($5). Continental breakfast. Pool.. Laundry facility. Rooms come with phones and cable TV. Some rooms have microwaves and refrigerators. AAA/Senior discount. Major credit cards.

Econo Lodge
$39-52
1615 E. Liberty Street • I-80, Exit 229
330.759.9820
56 Units, no pets. Rooms come with phones and cable TV. AAA/Senior discount. Major credit cards.

Super 8 Motel
$42-48*
4250 Belmont Avenue • 330.759.0040
48 Units, pets OK. Jacuzzi. Rooms come with phones and cable TV. Senior discount. Major credit cards.
*Rates higher during special events, weekends and holidays.

ZANESVILLE — *see also Norwich*

Travelodge
$40-50 (55-70)*
68 North 6th Street • I-70, Exit 155
740.453.0611
54 Units, no pets. Laundry facility. Rooms come with phones and cable TV. Major credit cards.
*Higher rates effective April through September.

oklahoma

ADA
Economy Inn
$33
1017 N. Broadway • 580.332.3883
46 Units, no pets. Pool. Rooms come with phones and cable TV. Major credit cards.

ALTUS
Days Inn
$40-49
3202 N. Main • 580.477.2300
39 Units, pets OK. Continental breakfast. Laundry facility. Data ports. Rooms come with phones and cable TV. Some rooms have refrigerators. AAA/Senior discount. Credit cards: AE, CB, DC, DS, MC, V.

Friendship Inn
$30
1800 N. Main Street • 580.482.7300
50 Units, pets OK. Restaurant on premises. Pool. Rooms come with phones and cable TV. Major credit cards.

ARDMORE
Days Inn
$31-34
2614 W. Broadway • 580.226.1761
50 Units, pets OK. Continental breakfast. Rooms come with phones and cable TV. AAA discount. Major credit cards.

Motel 6
$30-32
120 Holiday Drive • 580.226.7666
126 Units, pets OK. Pool. Laundry facility. Data ports. Rooms come with phones, A/C and cable TV. Wheelchair accessible. Credit cards: AE, CB, DC, DS, MC, V.

BARTLESVILLE
Green Country Inn
$40
3910 Nowata Road • 918.333.0710
45 Units, pets OK. Restaurant on premises. Pool. Rooms come with phones and cable TV. Major credit cards.

Super 8 Motel
$43-46
211 S.E. Washington Blvd.
918.335.1122
40 Units, pets OK. Restaurant on premises. Continental breakfast. Jacuzzi. Rooms come with phones and cable TV. Senior discount. Major credit cards.

BIG CABIN
Super 8 Motel
$40-44
I-44, Exit 283 • 918.783.5888
40 Units, pets OK. Laundry facility. Data ports. Rooms come with phones and cable TV. Senior discount. Credit cards: AE, DS, MC, V.

BLACKWELL
Days Inn
$50
4302 W. Doolin • 580.363.2911
50 Units, pets OK. Continental breakfast. Pool. Rooms come with refrigerators, phones and cable TV. Some rooms have microwaves. AAA/Senior discount. Credit cards: AE, CB, DC, DS, MC, V.

Super 8 Motel
$36*
1014 W. Doolin • 580.363.5945
43 Units, no pets. Rooms come with phones and cable TV. Wheelchair accessible. Senior discount. Credit cards: AE, CB, DC, DS, MC, V.
*Rates may increase slightly during weekends, holidays and special events.

BOISE CITY
Townsman Motel
$34
On US 287E • 580.544.2506
40 Units, pets OK. Rooms come with phones and cable TV. Major credit cards.

BROKEN ARROW
Luxury Inn & Suites
$43
1401 E. Elm Place • 918.258.6617
30 Units, pets OK ($5). Continental breakfast. Data ports. Rooms come with phones and cable TV. Some rooms have microwaves and refrigerators. AAA/Senior discount. Credit cards: AE, DS, MC, V.

BROKEN BOW
Charles Wesley Motorlodge
$25-46
302 N. Park Drive • 580.584.3303
50 Units, pets OK. Pool. Rooms come with phones and cable TV. Major credit cards.

CATOOSA
Super 8 Motel
$33-53
19250 Timbercrest Cir. • 918.266.7000
113 Units, no pets. Heated pool. Spa. Laundry facility. Data ports. Rooms come with phones and cable TV. Senior discount. Wheelchair accessible. Major credit cards.

CHANDLER
Econo Lodge
$40-49
600 N. Price • 405.258.2131
41 Units, pets OK ($5). Restaurant on premises. Pool. Rooms come with phones and cable TV. Wheelchair accessible. AAA discount. Major credit cards.

CHECOTAH
Lake Eufaula Inn
$35-63*
I-40, Exit 259 • 918.473.2376
48 Units, pets OK. Continental breakfast. Laundry facility. Pool. Rooms come with phones and cable TV. Senior discount. Major credit cards.
*AAA discounted rates.

CHICKASHA
Days Inn
$45-50
2701 S. 4th Street • 405.222.5800
95 Units, pets OK. Restaurant on premises. Laundry facility. Rooms come with phones and cable TV. Some rooms have microwaves and refrigerators. AAA discount. Major credit cards.

Deluxe Inn
$40-45
2728 S. Fourth Street • 405.222.3710
50 Units, pets OK. Continental breakfast. Pool. Rooms come with phones and cable TV. Senior discount. Credit cards: AE, CB, DC, DS, MC, V.

CLAREMORE
Claremore Motor Inn
$35
1709 N. Lynn Riggs • 918.342.4545
29 Units, pets OK. Continental breakfast. Rooms come with phones and cable TV. Some rooms have microwaves and refrigerators. AAA discount. Major credit cards.

CLINTON
Super 8 Motel
$41-45
1120 S. 10th Street • 580.323.4979
27 Units, no pets. Continental breakfast. Data ports. Rooms come with phones and cable TV. Wheelchair accessible. AAA/Senior discount. Credit cards: AE, CB, DC, DS, MC, V.

DUNCAN
Days Inn
$39-44
2535 N. Hwy. 81 • 580.252.0810
65 Units, no pets. Pool. Laundry facility. Rooms come with phones and cable TV. AAA/Senior discount. Major credit cards.

Duncan Inn
$28-32
3402 N. US 81 • 580.252.5210
92 Units, pets OK. Pool in summer. Laundry facility. Rooms come with phones and cable TV. Major credit cards.

DURANT
Budget Inn
$35-38
2301 W. Main Street • 580.920.0411
60 Units, pets OK ($5). Continental breakfast. Pool. Rooms come with phones and cable TV. Senior discount available ($1). Major credit cards.

ELK CITY
Budget Host Inn
$35
2000 W. Third • 580.225.1811
23 Units, pets OK. Restaurant on premises. Laundry facility. Meeting rooms. Rooms come with phones and cable TV. Senior discount. Credit cards: AE, DS, MC, V.

Econo Lodge
$38-42
108 Meadow Ridge • 580.225.5120
44 Units, pets OK. Continental breakfast. Rooms come with phones and cable TV. AAA/Senior discount. Credit cards: AE, CB, DC, DS, JCB, MC, V.

Super 8 Motel
$40-42
2801 E. Hwy. 66 • 580.225.9430
45 Units, pets OK ($5). Pool. Rooms come with phones and cable TV. Wheelchair accessible. AAA/Senior discount. Credit cards: AE, DS, MC, V.

EL RENO
Regency Inn
$35
2640 S. Country Club Road
405.262.1526 or 800.251.1962
30 Units, pets OK. Continental breakfast. Pool. Rooms come with phones and cable TV. Major credit cards.

Super 8 Motel
$37-43
2820 Hwy. 81S. • 405.262.8240
50 Units, pets OK ($5). Continental breakfast. Pool. Laundry facility. Fax service. Rooms come with phones and cable TV. Wheelchair accessible. AAA/Senior discount. Credit cards: AE, CB, DC, DS, MC, V.

ENID
Motel 6
$38
2523 Mercer Drive • 580.237.3090
69 Units, pets OK. Data ports. Rooms come with phones, A/C and cable TV. Wheelchair accessible. Credit cards: AE, CB, DC, DS, MC, V.

Stratford House Inn
$40
2713 W. Owen K. Garriott
580.242.6100
40 Units, no pets. Continental breakfast. Rooms come with phones and cable TV. Credit cards: AE, DS, MC, V.

ERICK
Days Inn
$47
I-40 & Hwy. 30 • 580.526.3315
32 Units, pets OK ($3). Continental breakfast. Rooms come with phones and cable TV. AAA discount. Credit cards: AE, CB, DC, DS, JCB, MC, V.

FREDERICK
Scottish Inns
$35-50
1015 S. Main Street
580.335.2129 or 800.251.1962
21 Units, pets OK. Pool. Data ports. Rooms come with phones and cable TV. Senior discount. Major credit cards.

GUYMON
Econo Lodge
$36-45
923 Hwy. 54E • 580.338.5431
40 Units, pets OK ($3). Rooms come with phones and cable TV. AAA/Senior discount. Major credit cards.

HEAVENER
Green Country Inn
$50
North end of town on SR 59
918.653.7801
28 Units, pets OK ($10). Data ports. Rooms come with phones and cable TV. AAA/Senior discount. Credit cards: AE, DC, DS, MC, V.

HENRYETTA
Gateway Inn
$28-35
Hwy. 75 & Trudgeon St • 918.652.4448
34 Units, pets OK ($25 dep. req.). Continental breakfast. Pool. Data ports. Rooms come with phones and cable TV. Senior discount. Credit cards: AE, CB, DC, DS, MC, V.

Super 8 Motel
$37-46
I-40 & Dewey Bartlett Road
918.652.2533
50 Units, pets OK. Continental breakfast. Rooms come with phones and cable TV. Senior discount. Credit cards: AE, CB, DC, DS, MC, V.

IDABEL
Americana Motor Lodge
$34
Highway 70E • 580.286.6526
40 Units, pets OK ($5). Hot tub and sauna. Rooms come with phones and cable TV. Senior discount. Major credit cards.

LAWTON
Motel 6
$35
202 S.E. Lee Blvd. • 580.355.9765
105 Units, pets OK. Pool. Laundry facility. Data ports. Rooms come with phones, A/C and cable TV. Wheelchair accessible. Credit cards: AE, CB, DC, DS, MC, V.

Super 8 Motel
$45-50
2202 N.W. Hwy. 277 • 580.353.0310
124 Units, pets OK ($6). Continental breakfast. Laundry facility. Data ports. Rooms come with phones and cable TV. AAA/Senior discount. Major credit cards.

McALESTER
Highway Inn & Suites
$35
On George Nigh Expsswy. S. 918.423.7170
48 Units, no pets. Pool. Restaurant on premises. Pool in summer. Rooms come with phones and cable TV. Major credit cards.

Super 8 Motel
$49-56
2400 S. Main • 918.426.5400
32 Units, no pets. Pool. Laundry facility. Rooms come with phones and cable TV. Some rooms have refrigerators. Senior discount. Credit cards: AE, CB, DC, DS, MC, V.

MIAMI
Super 8 Motel
$46-50
2120 E. Steve Owens Blvd.
918.542.3382
50 Units, no pets. Continental breakfast. Heated indoor pool. Sauna. Rooms come with phones and cable TV. Wheelchair accessible. Senior discount. Credit cards: AE, CB, DC, DS, MC, V.

MIDWEST CITY
Motel 6
$30-35
6166 Tinker Diagonal • 405.737.6676
93 Units, pets OK. Pool. Laundry facility. Data ports. Rooms come with phones, A/C and cable TV. Wheelchair accessible. Credit cards: AE, CB, DC, DS, MC, V.

Super 8 Motel
$41
6821 S.E. 29th Street • 405.737.8880
41 Units, pets OK. Meeting room. Rooms come with phones and cable TV. Senior discount. Credit cards: AE, CB, DC, DS, MC, V.

MOORE
Days Inn Moore
$36-50
1701 N. Moore Avenue • 405.794.5070
49 Units, pets OK ($10). Pool. Rooms come with phones and cable TV. Some rooms have refrigerators. AAA/Senior discount. Credit cards: AE, CB, DC, DS, MC, V.

Motel 6
$32-33
1417 N. Moore Avenue • 405.799.6616
121 Units, pets OK. Pool. Laundry facility. Data ports. Rooms come with phones, A/C and cable TV. Wheelchair accessible. Credit cards: AE, CB, DC, DS, MC, V.

Super 8 Motel
$44
1520 N. Service Road • 405.794.4030
40 Units, pets OK ($8). Continental breakfast. Data ports. Rooms come with phones, jacuzzis and cable TV. AAA/Senior discount. Major credit cards.

MUSKOGEE
Days Inn
$42-50
900 S. 32nd Street • 918.683.3911
43 Units, pets OK ($5). Continental breakfast. Pool. Data ports. Rooms come with phones and cable TV. Some rooms have microwaves and refrigerators. AAA/Senior discount. Major credit cards.

Motel 6
$30-35
903 S. 32nd Street • 918.683.8369
81 Units, pets OK. Pool. Laundry facility. Data ports. Rooms come with phones, A/C and cable TV. Wheelchair accessible. Credit cards: AE, CB, DC, DS, MC, V.

Muskogee Inn
$36-45
2300 E. Shawnee • 918.683.6551
122 Units, pets OK. Restaurant on premises. Pool. Meeting rooms. Rooms come with phones and cable TV. AAA/Senior discount. Major credit cards.

Super 8 Motel
$47*
2240 S. 32nd • 918.683.8888
56 Units, pets OK. Rooms come with phones and cable TV. Wheelchair accessible. Senior discount. Credit cards: AE, CB, DC, DS, MC, V.
*Rates may increase slightly during special events, holidays and weekends.

NORMAN

Days Inn
$40-45
609 N. Interstate Drive • 405.360.4380
70 Units, pets OK. Rooms come with phones and cable TV. Some rooms have microwaves and refrigerators. AAA discount. Major credit cards.

Thunderbird Lodge
$40-45
1430 24th Avenue S.W. • 405.329.6990
93 Units, pets OK. Laundry facility. Meeting rooms. Data ports. Rooms come with phones and cable TV. Some rooms have microwaves and refrigerators. Major credit cards.

OKLAHOMA CITY

Courtesy Inn
$30-35
1307 S.E. 44th Street • 405.672.4533
70 Units, no pets. Restaurant on premises. Pool. Fax service. Rooms come with phones and cable TV. Wheelchair accessible. Major credit cards.

Motel 6—Airport
$35-47
820 S. Meridian Avenue • 405.946.6662
128 Units, pets OK. Pool. Laundry facility. Data ports. Rooms come with phones, A/C and cable TV. Wheelchair accessible. Credit cards: AE, CB, DC, DS, MC, V.

Motel 6
$29-43
12121 N.E. Expressway • I-35, Exit 137
405.478.4030
99 Units, pets OK. Pool. Laundry facility. Data ports. Rooms come with phones, A/C and cable TV. Wheelchair accessible. Credit cards: AE, CB, DC, DS, MC, V.

Motel 6
$39-51
4200 W. Interstate 40 • 405.947.6550
119 Units, pets OK. Pool. Jacuzzi. Game room. Data ports. Rooms come with phones, A/C and cable TV. Wheelchair accessible. Credit cards: AE, CB, DC, DS, MC, V.

Super 8 Motel—Medical Center
$37-41*
1117 N.E. 13th Street • 405.232.0404
25 Units, no pets. Continental breakfast. Data ports. Rooms come with phones and cable TV. Some rooms have refrigerators. Credit cards: AE, DS, MC, V.
*AAA discounted rates.

Super 8 Motel
$38-42
3030 I-35S • 405.766.1000
101 Units, no pets. Data ports. Rooms come with jacuzzi tubs, phones and cable TV. Wheelchair accessible. Senior discount. Credit cards: AE, CB, DC, DS, MC, V.

Travelodge
$35-45
11900 N. I-35 • I-35, Exit 137
405.478.8668
101 Units, pets OK. Continental breakfast. Rooms come with phones and cable TV. Wheelchair accessible. AAA/Senior discount. Major credit cards.

OKMULGEE

Days Inn
$50
1221 S. Wood Drive • 918.758.0660
62 Units, pets OK ($25 dep. req.). Rooms come with phones and cable TV. AAA/Senior discount. Major credit cards.

PAULS VALLEY

Relax Inn
$26
From I-35, Exit 72, east on SR 19
405.238.7545
29 Units, no pets. Rooms come with phones and cable TV. AAA discount. Credit cards: AE, DS, MC, V.

PERRY

Best Western
$45-48
I-35, Exit 185 • 580.336.2218
88 Units, pets OK. Restaurant on premises. Heated pool. Laundry facility. Meeting rooms. Data ports. Rooms come with phones and cable TV. Senior discount. Major credit cards.

PONCA CITY

Econo Lodge
$35-40
212 S. 14th Street • 580.762.3401
88 Units, no pets. Continental breakfast. Pool. Meeting rooms. Rooms come with phones and cable TV. Major credit cards.

Super 8 Motel
$39-49*
301 S. 14th Street • 580.762.1616
40 Units, no pets. Continental breakfast. Jacuzzi. Rooms come with phones and cable TV. Senior discount. Credit cards: AE, CB, DC, DS, MC, V.
*Rates may increase slightly during special events.

PRYOR
Days Inn
$40-50
3.2 miles south on US 69
918.825.7600
55 Units, pets OK ($5). Pool. Airport transportation. Data ports. Rooms come with phones and cable TV. Some rooms have refrigerators and microwaves. AAA/Senior discount. Major credit cards.

PURCELL
Econo Lodge
$45-50
2500 Hwy. 74S. • 405.527.5603
32 Units, pets OK ($4). Rooms come with phones and cable TV. Some rooms have refrigerators. AAA/Senior discount. Credit cards: AE, DC, DS, MC, V.

SALLISAW
Econo Lodge
$37-40
2403 E. Cherokee • 918.775.7981
42 Units, pets OK. Continental breakfast. Meeting rooms available. Rooms come with phones and cable TV. Wheelchair accessible. Senior discount. Credit cards: AE, DC, DS, MC, V.

Super 8 Motel
$37-40
924 S. Kerr, Hwy. 59/I-40
918.775.8900
97 Units, pets OK ($5). Continental breakfast. Pool. Meeting room. Rooms come with phones and cable TV. Wheelchair accessible. Senior discount. Credit cards: AE, CB, DC, DS, MC, V.

SAPULPA
Super 8 Motel
$44-49
1505 New Sapulpa Rd. • 918.227.3300
61 Units, pets OK. Pool. Meeting room. Rooms come with phones and cable TV. Wheelchair accessible. Senior discount. Credit cards: AE, CB, DC, DS, MC, V.

SAVANNA
Travelodge
$33
US Hwy. 69 (in town) • 918.548.3506
54 Units, pets OK. Laundry facility. Meeting rooms. Rooms come with phones and cable TV. AAA/Senior discount. Credit cards: AE, CB, DC, DS, MC, V.

SEMINOLE
Rexdale Inn
$36
2151 Hwy. 9W. • 405.382.7002
20 Units, pets OK. Rooms come with phones and cable TV. Senior discount. Credit cards: AE, CB, DC, DS, JCB, MC, V.

SHAWNEE
Motel 6
$37-49
4981 N. Harrison Street • 405.275.5310
64 Units, pets OK. Pool. Data ports. Rooms come with phones, A/C and cable TV. Wheelchair accessible. Credit cards: AE, CB, DC, DS, MC, V.

Super 8 Motel
$38-43
4900 N. Harrison • 405.275.0089
36 Units, no pets. Rooms come with phones and cable TV. Wheelchair accessible. Senior discount. Credit cards: AE, CB, DC, DS, MC, V.

STILLWATER
Motel 6
$30-35
5122 W. 6th Avenue • 405.624.0433
87 Units, pets OK. Pool. Laundry facility. Data ports. Rooms come with phones, A/C and cable TV. Wheelchair accessible. Credit cards: AE, CB, DC, DS, MC, V.

Relax Inn
$35
2313 W. Sixth Street • 405.372.2425
58 Units, pets OK. Rooms come with phones and cable TV. Major credit cards.

SULPHUR
Super 8 Motel
$48-55*
2110 W. Broadway • 580.622.6500
40 Units, pets OK. Laundry facility. Meeting

room. Rooms come with phones and cable TV. Wheelchair accessible. Senior discount. Credit cards: AE, CB, DC, DS, MC, V.
*Rates may increase slightly during special events, holidays and weekends.

TAHLEQUAH
Tahlequah Motor Lodge
$45-50*
2501 S. Muskogee • 918.456.2350
53 Units, pets OK ($5 and $20 dep. req.). Restaurant on premises. Continental breakfast. Pool. Meeting rooms. Data ports. Rooms come with phones and cable TV. Some rooms have refrigerators. Credit cards: AE, DC, DS, MC, V.
*AAA discounted rates.

TONKAWA
Western Inn
$32-38
I-35 & US 60 • 580.628.2577
28 Units, pets OK. Rooms come with phones and cable TV. AAA discount. Credit cards: AE, DS, MC. V.

TULSA — *see also Catoosa*
Econo Lodge (Airport)
$38-52
11620 E. Skelly Drive
I-44, Exit 235 • 918.437.9200
120 Units, no pets. Restaurant on premises. Continental breakfast. Indoor pool. Laundry facility. Airport transportation. Rooms come with phones and cable TV. AAA discount. Major credit cards.

Motel 6
$32-38
5828 W. Skelly Drive • 918.445.0223
128 Units, pets OK. Pool. Laundry facility. Data ports. Rooms come with phones, A/C and cable TV. Wheelchair accessible. Credit cards: AE, CB, DC, DS, MC, V.

Motel 6
$34-38
1011 S. Garnett Road • 918.234.6200
153 Units, pets OK. Pool. Laundry facility. Data ports. Rooms come with phones, A/C and cable TV. Wheelchair accessible. Credit cards: AE, CB, DC, DS, MC, V.

Super 8 Motel—Airport
$40-50
6616 E. Archer Street • 918.836.1981
55 Units, no pets. Continental breakfast. Pool. Rooms come with phones and cable TV. Wheelchair accessible. AAA/Senior discount. Credit cards: AE, CB, DC, DS, MC, V.

Super 8 Motel—I-44
$39
1347 E. Skelly Drive • 918.743.4431
75 Units, pets OK ($5 and $20 dep. req.). Pool. Rooms come with phones and cable TV. Wheelchair accessible. Senior discount. AAA discount. Credit cards: AE, CB, DC, DS, MC, V.

VINITA — *see also Big Cabin*
Super 8 Motel
$40-46*
30954 S. Hwy. 69 • 918.783.5888
40 Units, pets OK. Continental breakfast. Laundry facility. Fax service. Rooms come with phones and cable TV. Wheelchair accessible. Senior discount. Credit cards: AE, CB, DC, DS, MC, V.
*Rates may increase slightly during special events.

WAGONER
Sleepy Traveler
$32
805 S. Dewey • 918.485.4818
40 Units, pets OK. Rooms come with phones and cable TV. Wheelchair accessible. Senior discount. Credit cards: AE, CB, DC, DS, MC, V.

WEATHERFORD
Econo Lodge
$37-48
US 54 & I-40 • 580.722.7711
44 Units, no pets. Pool. Fax service. Rooms come with phones and cable TV. Major credit cards.

WEBBERS FALLS
Knights Inn
$32-36
I-40 & Hwy. 100 • 918.464.2272
40 Units, pets OK. Rooms come with phones and cable TV. Wheelchair accessible. Senior discount. Credit cards: AE, CB, DC, DS, MC, V.

WOODWARD
Red Country Inn
$32-40
2314 8th Street • 580.254.9147
54 Units, pets OK. Continental breakfast.

Pool. Laundry facility. Data ports. Rooms come with phones and cable TV. Some rooms have microwaves and refrigerators. AAA/Senior discount. Major credit cards.

Wayfarer Inn
$35-47
2901 Williams Avenue • 580.256.5553
90 Units, pets OK. Continental breakfast. Pool. Playground. Laundry facility. Rooms come with phones and cable TV. Some rooms have microwaves and refrigerators. AAA discount. Major credit cards.

oregon

ALBANY

Budget Inn
$34-45
2727 E. Pacific Blvd. • 541.926.4246
48 Units, pets OK. Restaurant on premises. Laundry facility. Rooms come with cable TV, A/C and phones. Some rooms have kitchenettes. Wheelchair accessible. Major credit cards.

Motel 6
$47-50
2735 E. Pacific Blvd. • 541.926.4233
41 Units, pets OK. Airport transportation. Laundry facility. Rooms come with cable TV, A/C and phones. Major credit cards.

Relax Inn & Suites
$43
1212 S.E. Price Road • 541.926.0170
76 Units, pets OK. Pool. Laundry facility. Rooms come with cable TV, A/C and phones. Some rooms have kitchenettes. Major credit cards.

ASHLAND

Traveler Advisory: Beware that accommodations in Ashland become very pricey during the Shakespeare Festival which begins at the end of February and runs through October.

Ashland Motel
$39-49
1145 Siskiyou Blvd.
541.482.2261 or 800.460.8858
27 Units, pets OK. Pool. Laundry facility. Playground. Rooms come with cable TV, A/C and phones. Major credit cards.

Knights Inn
$44-59 (68-78)*
2359 Ashland Street • 541.482.5111
40 Units, pets OK ($10). Hot tub and heated pool. Rooms come with phones and cable TV. AAA discount. Major credit cards.
*Higher rates effective mid-May through mid-October.

Regency Inn
$43-48
50 Lowe Road • 541.482.4700
44 Units, no pets. Heated pool. Rooms come with cable TV, A/C and phones. AAA discount. Major credit cards.

ASTORIA

Columbia Inn
$32 (48-52)*
495 Marine Drive • 503.325.4211
22 Units, no pets. Rooms come with phones and cable TV. Major credit cards.
*Higher rates effective during summer months.

Lamplighter Motel
$50
131 W. Marine Drive • 503.325.4051
29 Units, pets OK. Continental breakfast. Laundry facility. Rooms come with phones and cable TV. Major credit cards.

BAKER CITY

Eldorado Inn
$33-53
695 Campbell Street • 541.523.6494
56 Units, pets OK. Pool. Rooms come with phones, A/C and cable TV. Major credit cards.

Oregon Trail Motel & Restaurant
$39-48
211 Bridge Street
541.523.5844 or 800.628.3982
54 Units, pets OK. Restaurant on premises. Continental breakfast. Laundry facility. Sauna and pool. Meeting rooms. Rooms come with A/C, cable TV and phones. Major credit cards.

BANDON

Shooting Star Motel
$45-55
1640 Oregon Avenue (US 101)
541.347.9192
15 Units, pets OK. Rooms come with phones and cable TV. Wheelchair accessible. Major credit cards.

Table Rock Motel
$45
840 Beach Loop Road • 541.347.2700
19 Units, pets OK. Playground. Data ports.

Rooms come with phones and cable TV. Major credit cards.

BEAVERTON
Lamplighter Motel
$40-55
10307 S.W. Parkway • 503.297.2211
56 Units, no pets. Laundry facility. Data ports. Rooms come with A/C, cable TV and phones. Wheelchair accessible. Major credit cards.

BEND
Bend Holiday Motel
$30-45
880 S.E. 3rd Street (Hwy 97)
541.382.4620 or 800.252.0121
25 Units, pets OK. Continental breakfast provided. Spa pool. Rooms come with A/C, kitchens, cable TV, fireplaces and phones. Major credit cards.

Rainbow Motel
$30-50
154 N.E. Franklin Ave. • 541.382.1821
50 Units, no pets. Continental breakfast. Rooms come with A/C, cable TV and phones. Wheelchair accessible. Major credit cards.

Westward Ho Motel
$35-45*
904 S.E. 3rd Street
541.382.2111 or 800.999.8143
65 Units, pets OK. Pool. Rooms come with phones and cable TV. Major credit cards.
*Rates increase during special events.

BOARDMAN
Dodge City Inn
$43-45
First and Front Streets • 541.481.2441
40 Units, pets Ok. Restaurant on premises. Rooms come with phones and cable TV. Wheelchair accessible. Major credit cards.

Econo Lodge
$50
105 S.W. Front Street • 541.481.2375
51 Units, pets OK. Pool. Rooms come with phones and cable TV. Major credit cards.

BROOKINGS
Pacific Sunset Inn
$35-50
1144 Chetco Avenue • 541.469.2141
40 Units, pets OK. Playground. Rooms come with phones and cable TV. Major credit cards.

Spindrift Motor Inn
$42-52
1215 Chetco Avenue • 541.469.5345
35 Units, no pets. Rooms come with refrigerators, phones and cable TV. No A/C in rooms. AAA/Senior discount. Major credit cards.

BURNS
Best Inn
$42-50 (53-60)*
999 Oregon Avenue
On US 395/20 • 541.573.1700
38 Units, pets OK ($20 dep. req.). Continental breakfast. Indoor pool. Laundry facility. Rooms come with phones and cable TV. AAA/Senior discount. Major credit cards.
*Higher rates effective May through October.

Days Inn Ponderosa Motel
$48-52
577 W. Monroe Street • 541.573.7047
52 Units, pets OK. Continental breakfast. Pool. Rooms come with A/C, phones and cable TV. Wheelchair accessible. AAA discount. Major credit cards.

CANYONVILLE
Leisure Inn
$40-45
554 S.W. Pine Street • 541.839.4278
37 Units, pets OK. Pool. Rooms come with A/C, phones and cable TV. Wheelchair accessible. Major credit cards.

CHEMULT
Crater Lake Motel
$42
On US 97 • 541.365.2241
20 Units, pets OK. Meeting room. Rooms come with A/C, kitchens, cable TV, fireplaces and phones. Wheelchair accessible. Credit cards: MC, V.

COOS BAY — *see also North Bend*
Motel 6
$38-50 (56)*
1445 Bayshore Drive • 541.267.7171
94 Units, pets OK. Laundry facility. Data ports. Rooms come with A/C, phones and cable TV. Wheelchair accessible. Credit cards: AE, CB, DC, DS, MC, V.
*Higher rate effective summer weekends.

CORVALLIS
Econo Lodge
$42-50
345 N.W. 2nd Street • 541.752.9601 or 800.553.2666
61 Units, pets OK. Hot tub. Laundry facility. Rooms come with A/C, kitchens, phones and cable TV. Credit cards: MC, V.

Jason Inn
$36-48
800 N.W. 9th Street
541.753.7326 or 800.346.3291
51 Units, pets OK. Restaurant on premises. Pool. Rooms come with phones and cable TV. Major credit cards.

Towne House Motor Inn
$35-45
350 S.W. 4th Street • 541.753.4496
50 Units, pets OK. Restaurant on premises. Continental breakfast. Laundry facility. Meeting rooms. Rooms come with phones and cable TV. Major credit cards.

CRATER LAKE AREA
Holiday Village Motel
$35-40
Mile Post 209 on US 97 • 541.365.2394
8 Units, pets OK. Rooms come with kitchens and cable TV. Credit cards: DS, MC, V.

Whispering Pines Motel
$35
Diamond Lake Junction (Hwys. 138 & 97)
541.365.2259
11 Units, pets OK. Rooms come with phones, kitchens and cable TV. Wheelchair accessible. Credit cards: MC, V.

CRESCENT
Woodsman Country Lodge
$37-39
P.O. Box 54 (midtown on US 97)
541.433.2710
15 Units, pets OK ($5). Rooms come with phones and cable TV. Some rooms have microwaves and refrigerators. AAA discount. Credit cards: DS, MC, V.

CRESWELL
Creswell Garden Inn
$46-61
345 E. Oregon
541.895.3341 or 800.626.1900
70 Units, no pets. Continental breakfast. Pool. Meeting rooms. Rooms come with A/C, kitchens, cable TV and phones. Some rooms have microwaves and refrigerators. AAA/credit discount available. Credit cards: AE, CB, DC, DS, MC, V.

ENTERPRISE
Wilderness Inn
$46-55
301 W. North Street • 541.426.4535
29 Units, pets OK ($5). Sauna. Rooms come with phones and cable TV. Some rooms have refrigerators. Senior discount. Major credit cards.

EUGENE
Classic Residence Inn
$34-45
1140 W. 6th Avenue • 541.343.0730
33 Units, pets OK. Laundry facility. Rooms come with A/C, kitchens, phones and cable TV. Wheelchair accessible. Credit cards: MC, V.

Motel 6
$40-52
3690 Glenwood Drive • 541.687.2395
59 Units, pets OK. Pool. Laundry facility. Data ports. Rooms come with A/C, phones and cable TV. Wheelchair accessible. Credit cards: AE, CB, DC, DS, MC, V.

Timbers Motel
$39-49
1015 Pearl Street
541.343.3345 or 800.643.4167
57 Units, no pets. Sauna. Rooms come with A/C, phones and cable TV. Credit cards: DS, MC, V.

FLORENCE
Economy Inn of Florence
$42-50
3829 Hwy. 101 • 541.997.7115
29 Units, no pets. Indoor pool. Jacuzzi. Rooms come with cable TV and phones. Some rooms have kitchenettes. Major credit cards.

Le Chateau Motel
$32-50
1084 Hwy. 101 • 541.997.3481
49 Units, no pets. Heated pool. Sauna. Jacuzzi. Laundry facility. Rooms come with cable TV and phones. No A/C in rooms. AAA/Senior discount. Major credit cards.

Park Motel
$42-64 (59-75)*
85034 US 101 (1.5 miles south on US 101)
541.997.2634
15 Units, pets ($5). Units set back in quiet, wooded area. Rooms come with cable TV. No A/C. Some rooms have radios. Credit cards: AE, CB, DC, DS, MC, V.
*Higher rates effective mid-June through September.

GARIBALDI
Harbor View Inn
$45
302 S. 7th Street • 503.322.3251
20 Units, pets OK. Rooms come with cable TV and phones. Wheelchair accessible. Major credit cards.

GOLD BEACH
City Center Motel
$45*
94200 Harlow Street • 541.247.6675
21 Units, pets OK. Laundry facility. Playground. Rooms come with phones and cable TV. Major credit cards.
*Summer rates may be higher.

Drift In Motel
$45*
94250 Port Drive • 541.247.4547 or 800.424.3833
23 Units, no pets. Rooms come with phones and cable TV. Major credit cards.
*Summer rates may be higher.

Motel 6
$36-43 (68)*
94433 Jerry's Flat Road • (On US 101 at Mile Post 328) • 541.247.4533
50 Units, pets OK. Laundry facility. Rooms come with A/C, phones and cable TV. Wheelchair accessible. Credit cards: AE, CB, DC, DS, MC, V.
*Higher rate effective July through September.

GRANTS PASS
Knights Inn
$38-45
104 S.E. 7th Street • 541.479.5595
32 Units, pets OK. Restaurant on premises. Laundry facility. Rooms come with phones and cable TV. Wheelchair accessible. Major credit cards.

Motel 6
$40-50
1800 N.E. 7th Street • 541.474.1331
122 Units, pets OK. Pool. Laundry facility. Data ports. Rooms come with A/C, phones and cable TV. Wheelchair accessible. Credit cards: AE, CB, DC, DS, MC, V.

Regal Lodge
$35-40
1400 N.W. 6th Street • 541.479.3305
30 Units, pets OK. Pool. Rooms come with A/C, phones and cable TV. Some rooms have refrigerators. Wheelchair accessible. Credit cards: MC, V.

GRESHAM
Best Inn & Suites
$49-55
121 N.E. 181st Avenue • I-84, Exit 13
503.661.5100
44 Units, pets OK ($10). Continental breakfast. Laundry facility. Jacuzzi. Meeting rooms. Data ports. Rooms come with phones and cable TV. AAA/Senior discount. Major credit cards.

Travelodge
$44-55
23705 N.E. Sandy Blvd. • 503.666.6623
44 Units, no pets. Restaurant on premises. Laundry facility. Rooms come with phones and cable TV. Major credit cards.

HERMISTON
Oxford Inn
$50
655 N. 1st Street • 541.567.7777
90 Units, pets OK. Restaurant on premises. Continental breakfast. Pool. Rooms come with phones and cable TV. Wheelchair accessible. Major credit cards.

The Way Inn
$44-46
635 S. Hwy. 395
541.567.5561 or 888.564.8767
30 Units, pets OK. Pool. Playground. Rooms come with A/C, phones and cable TV. Major credit cards.

HILLSBORO
Travelodge
$41-52*
622 S.E. 10th Avenue • 503.640.4791
58 Units, pets OK ($20). Continental breakfast. Laundry facility. Data ports.

Rooms come with refrigerators, cable TV and phones. Senior discount. Credit cards: AE, DS, MC, V.
*AAA discounted rates.

HOOD RIVER
Meredith Gorge Motel
$49*
4300 Westcliff Drive • 541.386.1515
21 Units, pets OK. Rooms come with A/C, cable TV and phones. Some rooms have kitchenettes. Major credit cards.
*Rates as high as $79/night.

Sunset Motel
$50
2300 W. Cascade Ave. • 541.386.6098
14 Units, no pets. Rooms come with A/C, cable TV and phones. Wheelchair accessible. Major credit cards.

JOHN DAY
Budget 8 Motel
$40-50
711 W. Main Street • 541.575.2155
14 Units, pets OK. Restaurant on premises. Pool. Laundry facility. Rooms come with A/C, cable TV and phones. Major credit cards.

Little Pine Inn
$41
250 E. Main Street • 541.575.2100
14 Units, pets OK. Restaurant on premises. Pool. Rooms come with A/C, cable TV and phones. Major credit cards.

JORDAN VALLEY
Sahara Motel
$37-44
607 Main Street (Hwy. 95) • 541.586.2500
22 Units, pets OK. Rooms come with A/C, phones and cable TV. Wheelchair accessible. Credit cards not accepted.

KLAMATH FALLS
Maverick Motel
$39-45
1220 Main Street • 541.882.6688 or 800.404.6690
49 Units, pets OK. Continental breakfast. Pool. Rooms come with A/C and phones. Wheelchair accessible. Credit cards: MC, V.

Motel 6
$36-50
5136 S. 6th Street • 541.884.2110
61 Units, pets OK. Restaurant on premises. Laundry facility. Pool. Data ports. Rooms come with A/C, phones and cable TV. Wheelchair accessible. Credit cards: AE, CB, DC, DS, MC, V.

Oregon Motel 8
$44-58
5225 Hwy 97 North • 541.883.3431
29 Units, pets OK ($5). Heated pool. Rooms come with phones and cable TV. Some rooms have kitchens. AAA/Senior discount. Credit cards: AE, DC, DS, MC, V.

LA GRANDE
Royal Motor Inn
$28-37
1510 Adams Avenue • 541.963.4154
44 Units, no pets. Rooms come with phones and cable TV. AAA/Senior discount. Credit cards: AE, CB, DC, DS, MC, V.

Travelodge
$44
2215 E. Adams Avenue • 541.963.7116
34 Units, pets OK. Continental breakfast. Indoor pool. Fitness facility. Rooms come with phones and cable TV. Major credit cards.

LAKEVIEW
Interstate 8 Motel
$38-48
354 N. "K" Street • 541.947.3341
32 Units, pets OK. Continental breakfast. Laundry facility. Rooms come with A/C, phones and cable TV. Credit cards: MC, V.

LA PINE
Timbercrest Inn
$33-50
52560 Hwy. 97 • 541.536.1737
21 Units, pets OK. Rooms come with A/C, phones and cable TV. Wheelchair accessible. Credit cards: MC, V.

LEBANON
Shanico Inn
$40-46
1840 Main Street • 541.259.2601
40 Units, no pets. Rooms come with phones and cable TV. Wheelchair accessible. Major credit cards.

LINCOLN CITY
Budget Inn—Lincoln City
$35-55
1713 N.W. 21st • 541.994.5281

50 Units, pets OK. Rooms come with TV and phones. Some rooms have kitchenettes. Wheelchair accessible. Major credit cards.

MADRAS
Budget Inn
$45
133 N.E. 5th Street • 541.475.3831
30 Units, pets OK. Continental breakfast. Laundry facility. Rooms come with phones and cable TV. Major credit cards.

Juniper Motel
$35-50
414 N. Hwy. 26
541.473.6186 or 800.244.1399
22 Units, pets OK. Playground. Rooms come with A/C, phones and cable TV. Major credit cards.

McMINNVILLE
Paragon Motel
$45-48
2065 S. Hwy. 99W • 503.472.9493 or 800.525.5469
55 Units, pets OK. Continental breakfast. Pool. Laundry facility. Rooms come with phones, A/C and cable TV. Major credit cards.

MEDFORD
Cedar Lodge Motor Inn
$43-52
518 N. Riverside Avenue
541.773.7361 or 800.282.3419
79 Units, pets OK ($20 dep. req.). Continental breakfast. Heated pool. Meeting rooms. Rooms come with A/C, cable TV and phones. Some rooms have kitchenettes. Major credit cards.

Knight's Inn
$36-40
500 N. Riverside Drive • 541.773.3676 or 800.626.1900
84 Units, pets OK ($100 dep. req.). Pool. Laundry facility. Rooms come with A/C, phones and cable TV. Wheelchair accessible. AAA discount. Major credit cards.

Motel 6—South
$40-48
950 Alba Drive • I-5, Exit 27
541.773.4290
101 Units, pets OK. Pool. Laundry facility. Data ports. Rooms come with A/C, phones and cable TV. Wheelchair accessible. Credit cards: AE, CB, DC, DS, MC, V.

Red Carpet Inn
$39-49
525 S. Riverside Avenue • I-5, Exit 27
541.772.6133
37 Units, no pets. Continental breakfast. Laundry facility. Rooms come with phones and cable TV. Credit cards: AE, DS, MC, V.

MILWAUKIE
Milwaukie Inn
$32-40
14015 S.E. McLoughlin Blvd.
503.659.2125 or 800.255.1553
40 Units, pets OK. Restaurant on premises. Laundry facility. Rooms come with A/C, cable TV and phones. Some rooms have kitchenettes. Wheelchair accessible. Major credit cards.

MYRTLE POINT
Myrtle Trees Motel
$47-52
1010 8th Street (Hwy. 42) • 541.572.5811
29 Units, pets OK. Rooms come with cable TV and phones. No A/C. AAA/Senior discount. Credit cards: AE, DS, MC, V.

NEWPORT
City Center Motel
$40-55
538 S.W. Coast Hwy.
541.265.7381 or 800.628.9665
30 Units, pets OK. Rooms come with A/C, cable TV and phones. Some rooms have kitchenettes. Wheelchair accessible. Major credit cards.

Newport Motor Inn
$24-48
1311 N. Coast Hwy. • 541.265.8516
39 Units, pets OK. Continental breakfast. Laundry facility. Rooms come with cable TV and phones. Major credit cards.

Puerto Nuevo Inn
$38-55
544 S.W. Coast Hwy • 541.265.5767
32 Units, no pets. Continental breakfast. Jacuzzi. Rooms come with cable TV and phones. No A/C in rooms. AAA/Senior discount. Major credit cards.

NORTH BEND—see also Coos Bay
City Center Motel
$28-40
750 Connecticut at US 101 • 541.756.5118
78 Units, pets OK. Continental breakfast.

Rooms come with phones and cable TV. Credit cards: AE, CB, DC, DS, MC, V.

ONTARIO
Carlile Motel
$38
589 N. Oregon Street
541.889.8658 or 800.640.8658
17 Units, pets OK ($5). Rooms come with A/C, kitchens, phones and cable TV. Some rooms have microwaves and refrigerators. AAA/Senior discount. Credit cards: AE, DC, DS, MC, V.

Holiday Motor Inn
$38-42
615 E. Idaho • 541.889.9188
72 Units, pets OK. Restaurant on premises. Heated pool. Rooms come with cable TV. AAA/Senior discount. Credit cards: AE, CB, DC, DS, MC, V.

Motel 6
$36-40
275 N.E. 12th Street • 541.889.6617
103 Units, pets OK. Pool. Laundry facility. Rooms come with A/C, phones and cable TV. Wheelchair accessible. Credit cards: AE, CB, DC, DS, MC, V.

PENDLETON
Econo Lodge
$45-49
620 S.W. Tutuilla • 541.276.8654
51 Units, pets OK ($5). Rooms come with phones and cable TV. Some rooms have kitchenettes. Wheelchair accessible. AAA/Senior discount. Major credit cards.

Motel 6
$36-40
325 S.E. Nye Avenue • 541.276.3160
89 Units, pets OK. Restaurant on premises. Pool. Laundry facility. Data ports. Rooms come with A/C, phones and cable TV. Wheelchair accessible. Credit cards: AE, CB, DC, DS, MC, V.

Tapadera Budget Inn
$41
105 S.E. Court Avenue • 541.276.3231
47 Units, pets OK ($5). Restaurant on premises. Rooms comes with cable TV, A/C and phones. Major credit cards.

PORTLAND — *see also Gresham, Hillsboro, Tigard, Troutdale, Tualatin and Wilsonville*

Aladdin Motor Inn
$42-50
8905 S.W. 30th Avenue • 503.246.8241
54 Units, pets OK. Laundry facility. Rooms come with phones and cable TV. Some rooms have kitchenettes. Wheelchair accessible. Major credit cards.

Chestnut Tree Inn
$45-60
9699 S.E. Stark • I-205, Exit 21A (southbound) or Exit 20 (northbound)
503.255.4444
58 Units, no pets. Rooms come with phones and cable TV. Some rooms have refrigerators. Major credit cards.

Econo Lodge Expo Center
$38-45
405 N.E. Columbia Blvd • 503.289.9999
58 Units, no pets. Continental breakfast. Rooms come with phones and cable TV. Wheelchair accessible. Major credit cards.

Motel 6
$40-50 (56)*
3104 S.E. Powell Blvd.
I-205 at Powell Blvd. • 503.238.0600
69 Units, pets OK. Pool. Data ports. Rooms come with A/C, phones and cable TV. Wheelchair accessible. Credit cards: AE, CB, DC, DS, MC, V.
*Higher rate effective summer weekends.

Motel 6
$47-54
1125 N. Schmeer Road
I-5, Exit 306B • 503.466.8356
65 Units, pets OK. Indoor pool. Laundry facility. Data ports. Rooms come with A/C, phones and cable TV. Wheelchair accessible. Credit cards: AE, CB, DC, DS, MC, V.

Travelodge
$42-48
10450 S.W. Barbur Blvd.
I-5, Exit 296A • 503.244.0151
42 Units, pets OK ($10). Heated pool. Data ports. Rooms come with A/C, phones and cable TV. AAA/Senior discount. Major credit cards.

PORT ORFORD
Sea Crest Motel
$42-48 (52-74)*
44 Hwy. 101 (1 mile south of town)
541.332.3040

18 Units, pets OK. Rooms come with phones and cable TV. No A/C in rooms. Credit cards: AE, DS, MC, V.
*Higher rates effective mid-June through mid-September.

PRINEVILLE
Executive Inn
$35-50
1050 E. 3rd Street • 541.447.4152
26 Units, pets OK. Continental breakfast. Laundry facility. Rooms come with A/C, kitchens, phones and cable TV. Wheelchair accessible. Credit cards: MC, V.

Ochoco Inn & Motel
$38-50
123 E. 3rd Street • 541.447.6231
47 Units, pets OK. Restaurant on premises. Meeting rooms. Rooms come with A/C, phones and cable TV. Kitchenettes available. Major credit cards.

REDMOND
Hub Motel & Restaurant
$38-48
1128 N. Hwy. 97
541.548.2101 or 800.7.THEHUB
30 Units, pets OK. Restaurant on premises. Rooms come with A/C, kitchens, phones and cable TV. Credit cards: MC, V.

REEDSPORT — *see also Winchester Bay*
Economy Inn
$29-45
1593 Highway Avenue 101
541.271.3671 or 800.799.9920
41 Units, pets OK ($3). Continental breakfast. Pool. Rooms come with cable TV. Some rooms have refrigerators, microwaves and kitchens. No A/C. AAA/ Senior discount. Credit cards: AE, CB, DC, DS, MC, V.

Fir Grove Motel
$38-45
2178 Winchester Ave. • 541.271.4848
19 Units, pets OK. Continental breakfast. Pool. Rooms come with kitchens, phones and cable TV. Credit cards: MC, V.

ROSEBURG
Budget 16 Motel
$32-50
1067 N.E. Stephens St. • I-5, Exit 125
541.673.5556
48 Units, pets OK. Pool. Rooms come with A/C, kitchens, phones and cable TV. Some rooms have kitchenettes. Major credit cards.

Howard Johnson Express Inn
$39-49
978 N.E. Stephens St. • I-5, Exit 125
541.673.5082
31 Units, pets OK ($7). Laundry facility. Rooms come with A/C, phones and cable TV. Senior discount. Major credit cards.

SALEM
Holiday Lodge
$38-50
1400 Hawthorne Avenue N.E.
I-5, Exit 256 • 503.585.2323
54 Units, pets OK ($5). Heated pool. Rooms come with A/C, kitchens, phones and cable TV. AAA discount. Major credit cards.

Motel 6
$38-50
1401 Hawthorne Avenue N.E.
I-5, Exit 256 • 503.371.8024
115 Units, pets OK. Pool. Laundry facility. Data ports. Rooms come with A/C, phones and cable TV. Wheelchair accessible. Credit cards: AE, CB, DC, DS, MC, V.

Tiki Lodge Motel
$33-55
3705 Market Street N.E.
503.581.4441 or 800.438.8458
50 Units, pets OK. Pool and sauna. Laundry facility. Rooms come with A/C, kitchens, phones and cable TV. Wheelchair accessible. Major credit cards.

SEASIDE
Hostelling International
$15-16
930 N. Holladay Drive • 503.738.7911
48 Beds, Office hours: 8 am - 11 pm
Facilities: 24-hour access, out-door decks and lawn on river, barbecue, equipment storage area, information desk, kitchen, laundry facilities, linen rentals, espresso and pastry bar. Private rooms available. Open year-round. Reservations advisable summer weekends. Credit cards: MC, V.

Night Cap Inn
$45-55
241 Avenue "U" • 503.738.7473
19 Units, no pets. Rooms come with A/C, phones and cable TV. Wheelchair accessible. Credit cards: AE, CB, DC, DS, MC, V.

SPRINGFIELD
Motel 6—North
$38-47
3752 International Court
I-5, Exit 195/195A • 541.741.1105
131 Units, pets OK. Pool. Laundry facility. Data ports. Rooms come with A/C, phones and cable TV. Wheelchair accessible. Credit cards: AE, CB, DC, DS, MC, V.

Travelodge
$39-53
3550 Gateway Street
I-5, Exit 195A • 541.726.9266
119 Units, no pets. Continental breakfast. Laundry facility. Heated pool. Rooms come with A/C, phones and cable TV. Wheelchair accessible. AAA discount. Credit cards: DS, MC, V.

ST. HELENS
Village Inn Motel
$44-51
535 S. Hwy. 30 • 503.397.1490
52 Units, pets OK. Restaurant on premises. Meeting rooms. Rooms come with A/C, kitchens, phones and cable TV. Wheelchair accessible. Major credit cards.

SWEET HOME
Sweet Home Inn
$45-49 (50-57)*
805 Long Street • 541.367.5137
28 Units, pets OK ($5-10). Pool. Sauna and jacuzzi. Rooms come with phones and cable TV. Some rooms have microwaves and refrigerators. Major credit cards.
*AAA discounted rates. Higher rates effective June through September.

THE DALLES
American Hospitality Inns
$38
200 W. 2nd Street • 541.296.9111
54 Units, pets OK. Restaurant on premises. Pool. Rooms come with phones and cable TV. Major credit cards.

The Inn at The Dalles
$30-55
3550 S.E. Frontage Road
541.296.1167 or 800.982.3496
44 Units, pets OK. Indoor and outdoor pool. Rooms come with A/C, kitchens, cable TV and phones. Major credit cards.

Super 8 Motel
$46-53*
609 Cherry Heights Road
541.296.6888
73 Units, pets OK. Continental breakfast. Laundry facility. Heated pool. Meeting rooms. Rooms come with phones and cable TV. Some rooms have jacuzzis. Wheelchair accessible. Major credit cards.
*Rates as high as $73/night.

TIGARD
Motel 6
$38-50
17950 S.W. McEwan Road
I-5, Exit 290 • 503.620.2066
117 Units, pets OK. Pool. Laundry facility. Rooms come with A/C, phones and cable TV. Wheelchair accessible. Credit cards: AE, CB, DC, DS, MC, V.

TILLAMOOK
Western Royal Inn
$45-55 (65-75)*
1125 N. Main Street • 503.842.8844
40 Units, pets OK. Rooms come with phones and cable TV. Some rooms have kitchenettes. AAA/Senior discount. Major credit cards.
*Higher rates effective summers.

TROUTDALE
Motel 6
$38-48
1610 N.W. Frontage Rd • 503.665.2254
123 Units, pets OK. Pool. Laundry facility. Data ports. Rooms come with A/C, phones and cable TV. Wheelchair accessible. Credit cards: AE, CB, DC, DS, MC, V.

Travelodge
$44-54*
23705 N.E. Sandy Blvd. • 503.666.6623
44 Units, pets OK ($30 dep. req.). Restaurant on premises. Continental breakfast. Laundry facility. Rooms come with phones and cable TV. Credit cards: AE, DS, MC, V.
*AAA discounted rates.

TUALATIN
Ramada Limited
$49-54
17993 Lower Boones Ferry Road,
I-5, Exit 290 • 503.620.2030
68 Units, pets OK ($10). Continental breakfast. Heated pool. Sauna and jacuzzi. Laundry facility. Fitness facility. Meeting

rooms. Data ports. Rooms come with A/C, kitchens, phones and cable TV. AAA/Senior discount. Major credit cards.

UMATILLA
Tillicum Inn
$39-41
1481 6th Street • 541.922.3236
79 Units, no pets. Pool. Rooms come with A/C, kitchens, phones and cable TV. Some rooms have kitchenettes. Major credit cards.

WILSONVILLE
Best Inn & Suites
$49
8815 S.W. Sun Place • 503.682.3184 or 800.626.1900
74 Units, no pets. Continental breakfast. Pool. Jacuzzi. Laundry facility. Rooms come with A/C, phones and cable TV. Wheelchair accessible. AAA discount. Major credit cards.

SnoozInn
$39-42
30245 Parkway Avenue
503.682.2333 or 800.343.1553
58 Units, pets OK. Restaurant on premises. Pool. Meeting rooms. Rooms come with A/C, phones and cable TV. Major credit cards.

WINCHESTER BAY
Winchester Bay Inn
$48 (65)*
390 Broadway • 541.271.4871
51 Units, pets OK ($2). Continental breakfast. Rooms come with phones and cable TV. No A/C in rooms. Some rooms have microwaves, refrigerators and jacuzzis. Senior discount. Major credit cards.
*Higher rate effective summers.

WOODBURN
Woodburn Inn
$40-55
1025 N. Pacific Hwy. • 503.982.9741
20 Units, no pets. Rooms come with A/C, kitchens, phones and cable TV. Some rooms have kitchenettes. Wheelchair accessible. Major credit cards.

pennsylvania

Traveler Advisory: If you are planning to travel to the Poconos/Stroudsburg area or to the Pennsylvania Dutch region (including Lancaster, Strasburg, Bird-in-Hand, New Holland and Honey Brook), be prepared to encounter higher-than-average room rates for motels. These areas are popular tourist destinations and local innkeepers have raised their rates accordingly. The average single room rate is around $50/night in the winter and slightly more in the summertime, although rooms can be found in the $45-$50 range.

AKRON
Motel Akron
$40-50*
116 S. 7th Street • 717.859.1654
23 Units, no pets. Rooms come with phones and cable TV. AAA discount. Credit cards: DS, MC, V.
*Rates as high as $89/night.

ALLENTOWN
Allenwood Motel
$45-55*
1058 Hausman Road • 610.395.3707
22 Units, pets OK ($6). Data ports. Rooms come with phones and cable TV. AAA/Senior discount. Credit cards: AE, DS, MC. V.
*Rates as high as $120/night.

ALTOONA
Econo Lodge
$49-55
2906 Pleasant Valley Blvd.
814.944.3555
69 Units, pets OK. Continental breakfast. Laundry facility. Rooms come with phones and cable TV. AAA/Senior discount. Major credit cards.

Motel 6
$40-48
1500 Sterling Street
I-99, Exit Plank Road • 814.946.7601
113 Units, pets OK. Pool. Laundry facility. Rooms come with phones, A/C and cable TV. Wheelchair accessible. Major credit cards.

Super 8 Motel
$43-56
3535 Fairway Drive • 814.942.5350
63 Units, pets OK. Continental breakfast. Rooms come with phones and cable TV. Wheelchair accessible. AAA/Senior discount. Major credit cards.

AVALON — *see Pittsburgh*

BARKEYVILLE
Super 8 Motel
$50*
On Route 8 • I-80, Exit 29 • 814.786.8375
50 Units, no pets. Continental breakfast. Laundry facility. Rooms come with phones, refrigerators and cable TV. Major credit cards.
*Rates higher during special events, weekends and holidays.

BEAVER FALLS
Beaver Valley Motel
$50
7257 Big Beaver Blvd. • 724.843.0630
27 Units, no pets. Rooms come with phones, refrigerators and cable TV. AAA/Senior discount. Major credit cards.

Lark Motel
$45
On SR 18, half mile north of turnpike, Exit 2 • 724.846.6507
12 Units, no pets. Rooms come with phones and cable TV. Some rooms have refrigerators. Credit cards: AE, DS, MC, V.

BEDFORD
Budget Host Inn
$32-50
On US 220 Bus. (Exit 11 from I-70 & I-76)
814.623.8107
33 Units, pets OK. Pool. Rooms come with phones and cable TV. Some rooms have microwaves and refrigerators. AAA discount. Credit cards: AE, CB, DC, DS, MC, V.

Janey Lynn Motel
$35-50
On US 220 Bus. (Exit 11 from I-70 & I-76)

814.623.9515
21 Units, pets OK. Rooms come with cable TV. Some rooms have microwaves, refrigerators and phones. AAA discount. Credit cards: AE, CB, DC, DS, MC, V.

Motel Town House
$30-42
200 S. Richard Street (I-70/76, Exit 146)
814.623.5138
17 Units, pets OK ($6). Continental breakfast. Data ports. Rooms come with phones and cable TV. AAA/Senior discount. Major credit cards.

BELLE VERNON
Best Val-U Motel
$33
975 Rostraver Road • 724.929.8100
89 Units, no pets. Pool. Rooms come with phones and cable TV. Credit cards: AE, CB, DC, DS, MC, V.

Sleeper Inn
$30
Jct. I-70 & Rte. 51 (Exit 22B)
724.929.4501
94 Units, no pets. Continental breakfast. Pool. Meeting rooms. Game rooms. Laundry facility. Rooms come with phones and cable TV. Senior discount available (10%). Major credit cards.

BERWICK
Red Maple Inn
$45*
Bloomsburg-Berwick Hwy. • From I-80, Exit 36N, 1.5 mi. N on Rte 11. • 570.752.6220
18 Units, pets OK ($5 and $50 dep. req.). Rooms come with A/C, refrigerators, phones and cable TV. Credit cards: DS, MC. V.
*Rates as high as $60/night.

BLOOMSBURG
Budget Host Patriot Inn
$50-55
6305 Columbia Blvd.
I-80, Exit 241A • 570.387.1776
48 Units, no pets. Restaurant on premises. VCRs and movie rentals. Laundry facility. Meeting rooms. Rooms come with A/C, refrigerators, phones and cable TV. AAA/ Senior discount. Major credit cards.

BLUE MOUNTAIN
Kenmar Motel
$40-50
17788 Cumberland Hwy.
I-76, Exit 15 • 717.423.5915
15 Units, pets OK ($3). Continental breakfast. Pool. Rooms come with A/C, refrigerators, phones and cable TV. AAA/ Senior discount. Major credit cards.

BREEZEWOOD
Best Western Plaza Motor Lodge
$44-54*
On US 30 (Exit 12 from I-76)
814.735.4352
89 Units, no pets. Continental breakfast. Pool. Rooms come with phones and cable TV. Senior discount. Credit cards: AE, CB, DC, DS, MC, V.
*AAA discounted rates. Rates as high as $75/night.

BRIDGEVILLE
Knights Inn
$45
111 Hickory Grade Rd. • 412.221.8110
104 Units, pets OK. Pool. Laundry facility. Rooms come with phones and cable TV. Some rooms have microwaves and refrigerators. Wheelchair accessible. AAA/ Senior discount. Major credit cards.

BROOKVILLE
Budget Host Gold Eagle Inn
$34-55
250 W. Main Street • 814.849.7344
29 Units, pets OK. Continental breakfast. Restaurant on premises. Rooms come with phones and cable TV. Some rooms have refrigerators. Credit cards: AE, DS, MC, V.

Howard Johnson
$38-44
245 Allegheny Blvd. • I-80, Exit 78
814.849.3335
40 Units, pets OK. Restaurant on premises. Rooms come with phones and cable TV. Senior discount. Major credit cards.

Super 8 Motel
$45-55
251 Allegheny Blvd.
I-80, Exit 78 • 814.849.8840
57 Units, pets OK. Continental breakfast. Rooms come with phones and cable TV. AAA/Senior discount. Major credit cards.

BUTLER
Super 8 Motel
$47-53
138 Pittsburgh Road • 2 miles south on SR 8 from town • 724.287.8888

66 Units, pets OK ($20 dep. req.). Continental breakfast. Rooms come with phones and cable TV. Senior discount. Major credit cards.

CAMBELLTOWN
Village Motel
$30-50*
On US 322 (half mile west of town)
717.838.4761
32 Units, no pets. Pool. Tennis court. Playground. Laundry facility. Rooms come with cable TV. Some rooms have phones. Credit cards: AE, DS, MC, V.
*Higher rates effective Memorial Day through August.

CAMP HILL
Hampton Inn Camp Hill/Mechanicsburg
$42
3721 Market Street • 717.737.6711
58 Units, no pets. Restaurant on premises. Airport transportation. Rooms come with phones and cable TV. AAA/Senior discount. Credit cards: AE, CB, DC, MC, V.

CANONSBURG
Super 8 Motel
$50
8 Curry Avenue • 724.873.8808
50 Units, pets OK. Meeting rooms. Rooms come with phones and cable TV. Senior discount. Wheelchair accessible. Major credit cards.

CARLISLE
Motel 6
$30-44
1153 Harrisburg Pike
I-76 & US 11, Exit 16 • 717.249.7622
118 Units, pets OK. Pool. Laundry facility. Data ports. Rooms come with phones, A/C and cable TV. Wheelchair accessible. Major credit cards.

Super 8 Motel
$40-50
1800 Harrisburg Pike • 717.249.7000
112 Units, no pets. Continental breakfast. Laundry facility. Rooms come with phones and cable TV. Wheelchair accessible. Senior discount. Major credit cards.

CHAMBERSBURG
Econo Lodge
$45-55
1110 Sheller Avenue • 717.264.8005
61 Units, pets OK ($10). Continental breakfast. Laundry facility. Rooms come with phones and cable TV. Some rooms have microwaves and refrigerators. Major credit cards.

Travelodge
$30-45
565 Lincoln Way E. • I-81, Exit 16
717.264.4187
49 Units, pets OK. Restaurant on premises. Continental breakfast. Laundry facility. Rooms come with phones and cable TV. AAA/Senior discount. Credit cards: AE, DS, MC, V.

CLARION
Super 8 Motel
$39-55
135 Hotel Road
I-80, Exit 62 • 814.226.4550
99 Units, pets OK. Continental breakfast. Pool. Laundry facility. Rooms come with phones and cable TV. Senior discount. Major credit cards.

CLARKS SUMMIT
Summit Inn
$50
649 Northern Blvd. • 570.586.1211
32 Units, pets OK ($5). Continental breakfast. Rooms come with phones and cable TV. Senior discount. Major credit cards.

CLEARFIELD
Rodeway Inn
$35-55
814.765.7587 • I-80, Exit 19, 1.5 mi. west on SR 879, 1 mi. east on US 322
34 Units, pets OK. Continental breakfast. Rooms come with refrigerators, phones and cable TV. Some rooms have microwaves and refrigerators. AAA discount. Major credit cards.

CORAOPOLIS
Motel 6—Airport
$38-43
1170 Thorn Run Road • 412.269.0990
95 Units, no pets. Laundry facility. Airport transportation. Rooms come with A/C, phones and cable TV. Wheelchair accessible. Major credit cards.

Red Roof Inn
$44-54
1454 Beers School Rd. • 412.264.5678
119 Units, pets OK. Laundry facility. Game

rooms. Airport transportation. Meeting rooms. Rooms come with A/C, phones and cable TV. AAA discount. Major credit cards.

Super 8 Motel
$50*
1465 Beers School Rd. • 412.264.7888
60 Units, pets OK. Continental breakfast. Airport transportation. Rooms come with phones and cable TV. Senior discount. Wheelchair accessible. Major credit cards.
*Rates higher weekends, special events and holidays.

DELMONT
Super 8 Motel
$48
180 Sheffield Drive • 724.468.4888
46 Units, pets OK ($5). Data ports. Rooms come with phones and cable TV. Wheelchair accessible. Senior discount. Major credit cards.

DUBOIS
DuBois Manor Motel
$35-42
525 Liberty Blvd. • 814.371.5400
45 Units, pets OK. Rooms come with phones and cable TV. Senior discount. Credit cards: AE, DS, MC, V.

DUNCANSVILLE
Wye Motor Lodge
$40-50
200 North 220 Bus. Rte.
I-99, Exit 31 • 814.895.4407
38 Units, no pets. Laundry facility. Rooms come with phones and cable TV. Some rooms have microwaves and refrigerators. Credit cards: AE, DS, MC, V.

EAST STROUDSBURG
Budget Motel
$49*
I-80, Exit 51 • 570.424.5451
115 Units, pets OK ($20). Restaurant on premises. Rooms come with phones and cable TV. Major credit cards.
*Rates as high as $84/night.

ERIE
Microtel Erie
$36-44 (59-63)*
8100 Peach Street • 814.864.1010
101 Units, pets OK. Continental breakfast. Laundry facility. Rooms come with phones and cable TV. Wheelchair accessible. Senior discount. Credit cards: AE, CB, DC, DS, MC, V.
*Higher rate effective May through August.

Motel 6
$45 (60-70)*
7875 Peach Street
I-90, Exit 6 • 814.864.4811
83 Units, pets OK. Restaurant on premises. Indoor pool. Laundry facility. Airport transportation. Rooms come with A/C, phones and cable TV. Wheelchair accessible. Major credit cards.
*Higher rate effective Memorial Day through Labor Day.

Red Roof Inn
$34-49*
7865 Perry Hwy. • 814.868.5246
110 Units, pets OK. Rooms come with A/C, phones and cable TV. AAA discount. Major credit cards.
*Rates as high as $76/night.

Super 8 Motel
$40-45 (70)*
8040 Perry Hwy.
I-90, Exit 27 • 814.864.9200
93 Units, pets OK. Laundry facility. Airport transportation. Meeting rooms. Rooms come with phones and cable TV. AAA/Senior discount. Major credit cards.
*Higher rate effective Memorial Day through Labor Day.

ETTERS
Super 8 Motel
$42-56*
70 Robinhood Drive • 717.938.6200
95 Units, no pets. Continental breakfast. Meeting room. Copy and fax service. Rooms come with phones and cable TV. Wheelchair accessible. Senior discount. Major credit cards.
*Rates may increase slightly on weekends.

FAYETTEVILLE
Rite Spot Motel
$30-45
5651 Lincoln Way E. • 717.352.2144
20 Units, pets OK ($3). Data ports. Rooms come with phones and cable TV. AAA/Senior discount. Credit cards: AE, DS, MC. V.

FRACKVILLE
Granny's Motel & Restaurant
$43-46
Jct. I-81 & Rte. 61 (Exit 36W)

570.874.0408
34 Units, pets OK. Restaurant on premises. Meeting rooms. Rooms come with A/C, phones and cable TV. AAA discount. Major credit cards.

Motel 6
$42-43
Jct. Rte. 61 & I-81 • 570.874.1223
55 Units, pets OK. Rooms come with A/C, phones and cable TV. Wheelchair accessible. Major credit cards.

GALETON
Pine Log Motel
$50
5156 US 6W • 814.435.6400
10 Units, pets OK. Rooms come with phones and cable TV. No A/C in rooms. Senior discount. Credit cards: AE, DS, MC. V.

GETTYSBURG
Blue Sky Motel
$44-55
2585 Biglerville Road • 717.677.7736
16 Units, no pets. Pool. Playground. Rooms come with phones and cable TV. Some rooms have microwaves and refrigerators. AAA discount. Credit cards: AE, CB, DC, DS, MC, V.

Budget Host Motor Lodge
$40-50 (69)*
205 Steinwehr Avenue • 717.334.3168
29 Units, no pets. Pool. Laundry facility nearby. Rooms come with phones and cable TV. Senior discount. Major credit cards.
*Higher rate effective late June through late August.

GREENCASTLE
Rodeway Inn
$45
10835 John Wayne Dr. • 717.597.7762
36 Units, no pets. Restaurant on premises. Laundry facility. Rooms come with phones and cable TV. AAA discount. Credit cards: AE, DS, MC. V.

HARBOR CREEK
Rodeway Inn
$40-50
4050 Depot Road
I-90, Exit 35 • 814.899.1919
36 Units, no pets. Restaurant on premises. Continental breakfast. Laundry facility. Rooms come with phones and cable TV. AAA/Senior discount. Major credit cards.

HARMARVILLE
Valley Motel
$40-50
I-76, Exit 5, 1 miles south on Freeport Road • 412.828.7100
28 Units, no pets. Rooms come with phones and cable TV. Some rooms have refrigerators. AAA/Senior discount. Credit cards: AE, DS, MC. V.

HARRISBURG — *see also Etters and New Cumberland*
Daystop
$50
7848 Linglestown Road • 717.652.9578
31 Units, no pets. Restaurant on premises. Laundry facility. Data ports. Rooms come with phones and cable TV. Some rooms have microwaves and refrigerators. AAA/ Senior discount. Credit cards: AE, DS, MC. V.

Red Roof Inn North
$40-55
400 Corporate Circle • I-81, Exit 24
717.657.1445
110 Units, pets OK. Rooms come with A/C, phones and cable TV. AAA discount. Major credit cards.

Super 8 Motel
$44-55*
4131 Executive Park Dr. • 717.564.7790
48 Units, no pets. Continental breakfast. Pool. Rooms come with phones and cable TV. Wheelchair accessible. AAA/Senior discount. Credit cards: AE, CB, DC, DS, MC, V.
*Rates as high as $79/night.

HAZLETON — *see also West Hazleton*
Hazleton Motor Inn
$35-40
615 E. Broad Street • 570.459.1451
25 Units, pets OK. Rooms come with phones and cable TV. Some rooms have microwaves and refrigerators. Senior discount. Credit cards: AE, CB, DC, DS, MC, V.

HONESDALE
Fife & Drum Motor Inn
$46*
100 Terrace Street • 570.253.1392
28 Units, pets OK ($6 and $6 dep. req.). Rooms come with phones and cable TV. Major credit cards.
*Rates as high as $59/night.

HOPWOOD — *see Uniontown*

HUNTINGDON
Huntingdon Motor Inn
$41-55
Jct. Rtes. 22 & 26 • 814.643.1133
48 Units, pets OK ($5). Restaurant on premises. Rooms come with phones and cable TV. Major credit cards.

INDIANA
Super 8 Motel
$45-55
111 Plaza Drive • 724.349.4600
70 Units, pets OK. Continental breakfast. Rooms come with phones and cable TV. Wheelchair accessible. AAA/Senior discount. Major credit cards.

JOHNSTOWN
Motel 6
$42-52
430 Napoleon Place • 814.536.1114
47 Units, pets OK. Laundry facility. Data ports. Rooms come with phones, A/C and cable TV. Wheelchair accessible. Credit cards: AE, CB, DC, DS, MC, V.

Super 8 Motel
$39-43
627 Solomon Run Rd. • 814.535.5600
65 Units, pets OK. Rooms come with phones and cable TV. Senior discount. Wheelchair accessible. Major credit cards.

KITTANNING
Rodeway Inn
$44-49*
SR 28, Exit 19A • 724.543.1100
20 Units, no pets. Laundry facility. Rooms come with phones and cable TV. Some rooms have microwaves and refrigerators. AAA discount. Major credit cards.
*AAA discounted rates.

LANCASTER — *see also Manheim*
Travel Inn
$30-59
2151 Lincoln Hwy. E
4.5 miles east on US 30 • 717.299.8971
66 Units, pets OK ($10). Pool. Rooms come with phones and cable TV. AAA/Senior discount. Credit cards: AE, DS, MC, V.

MANHEIM
Rodeway Inn
$42-48 (58)*
2931 Lebanon Road • 717.665.2755
39 Units, pets OK ($10). Pool (seasonal). Rooms come with phones and cable TV. AAA/Senior discount. Credit cards: AE, DS, MC, V.
*Higher rate effective April through Labor Day.

MANSFIELD
West's Deluxe Motel
$40-50
On US 15 (3.5 miles south of town)
570.659.5141
20 Units, pets OK. Pool. Rooms come with phones and cable TV. Some rooms have refrigerators. AAA discount. Credit cards: AE, DS, MC, V.

MAPLETON DEPOT — *see Mount Union*

MARKLEYSBURG

National Trail Motel
$45
On US 40 • 724.329.5531
89 Units, no pets. Pool. Rooms come with phones and cable TV. Credit cards: AE, CB, DC, DS, MC, V.

MARS
Motel 6
$38-50
I-76, Ex. 3/I-79, Ex. 25 • 724.776.4333
120 Units, pets OK. Laundry facility. Rooms come with phones, A/C and cable TV. Wheelchair accessible. Credit cards: AE, CB, DC, DS, MC, V.

MEADVILLE
Motel 6
$45 (55-90)*
11237 Shaw Avenue
I-79, Exit 36A • 814.724.6366
63 Units, pets OK. Restaurant on premises. Laundry facility. Data ports. Rooms come with phones, A/C and cable TV. Wheelchair accessible. Credit cards: AE, CB, DC, DS, MC, V.
*Higher rates effective Memorial Day through August.

Super 8 Motel
$45-55
845 Conneaut Lake Rd. • 814.333.8883
62 Units, pets OK ($50 dep. req.). Continental breakfast. Rooms come with phones and cable TV. Major credit cards.

MECHANICSBURG
Amber Inn
$45-55
1032 Audubon Road • 717.766.9006
15 Units, no pets. Continental breakfast. Rooms come with phones and cable TV. Some rooms have microwaves and refrigerators. AAA/Senior discount. Credit cards: AE, DS, MC, V.

Econo Lodge
$45-55
650 Gettysburg Road • 717.766.4728
41 Units, no pets. Pool. Rooms come with phones and cable TV. AAA and Senior discount. Credit cards: AE, DC, DS, MC, V.

MIFFLINVILLE
Super 8 Motel
$46
450 3rd Street
I-80, Exit 37 • 570.759.6778
30 Units, pets OK. Fax service. Rooms come with phones and cable TV. Wheelchair accessible. Senior discount. Credit cards: AE, CB, DC, DS, MC, V.
*Rates may increase slightly during special events and weekends.

MILFORD
Milford Motel
$45-55*
591 Rte. 6 & 209 • 570.296.6411
19 Units, pets OK. Pool. Playground. Rooms come with phones and cable TV. AAA/Senior discount. Credit cards: AE, DS, MC, V.
*Rates as high as $75/night.

Scottish Inns
$47-53
US 6 & 209 (I-84, Exit 11, one mile south)
570.491.4414
18 Units, pets OK. Laundry facility. Rooms come with phones and cable TV. Some rooms have refrigerators and kitchenettes. Major credit cards.

MONROEVILLE
Super 8 Motel
$49-51
1807 Rte. 286 • I-76, Exit 57; I-376,
[illegible]it 14A • 724.733.8008
[illegible]nits, pets OK ($5). Continental breakfast. [illegible]nd movie rentals. Data ports. Rooms [illegible]ith phones and cable TV. AAA/Senior [illegible] Major credit cards.

MONTGOMERY
Northwood Motel
$40-44
On US 15 (8 miles south of Williamsport)
570.547.6624
10 Units, pets OK. Pool. Rooms come with microwaves, refrigerators, phones and cable TV. AAA discount. Credit cards: AE, DS, MC, V.

MORGANTOWN
Red Carpet Inn & Suites
$40
Rte. 23 (quarter mile from Exit 22 of PA Tpk.) • 610.286.5061
27 Units, pets OK. Rooms come with phones, A/C and cable TV. Major credit cards.

MOUNT UNION/MAPLETON DEPOT
Motel 22
$40-50
On US 22 (3.3 miles west of junction US 522) • 814.542.2571
32 Units, no pets. Pool. Rooms come with phones and TV. Senior discount. Credit cards: AE, DC, DS, MC, V.

NEW CUMBERLAND
Motel 6
$32-42*
200 Commerce Drive • 717.774.8910
124 Units, pets OK. Pool. Data ports. Rooms come with phones, A/C and cable TV. Wheelchair accessible. Credit cards: AE, CB, DC, DS, MC, V.
*Prices higher during weekends and special events.

NEW SMITHVILLE
Super 8 Motel
$50*
2160 Golden Key Road
I-78, Exit 13 • 610.285.4880 or
866.285.4800
38 Units, no pets. Continental breakfast. Rooms come with phones and cable TV. Some rooms have microwaves and refrigerators. Wheelchair accessible. Senior discount. Major credit cards.
*AAA discounted rates.

NORTH EAST
Super 8 Motel
$45-55
11021 Sidehill Road • 814.725.4567
45 Units, no pets. Meeting room. Rooms

come with phones and cable TV. AAA/Senior discount. Credit cards: AE, CB, DC, DS, MC, V.

OAKDALE — *see Pittsburgh*

PENNSYLVANIA DUTCH REGION — *see Lancaster, Manheim and Ronks*

PHILADELPHIA — *see also Trevose*

Traveler Advisory: If you are planning to spend the night in Philadelphia, you will need to plan on spending a little more than $50/night. With the exception of youth hostels, you would be very fortunate to find accommodations in downtown Philadelphia for less than $60/night. The following are a few recommendations to suit your budget in-town:

In-Town

Shippen Way Inn ($80-100)
418 Bainbridge Street
215.627.7266

Philadelphia Metro Area

Days Inn ($70**)
4200 Roosevelt Blvd. (Philadelphia)
215.289.9200

Econo Lodge ($57-66)
600 SR 291 (Lester)
610.521.3900

Extended Stay America ($69-79)
9000 Tinicum Blvd. (I-95, Ex. 10)

(Philadelphia)
215.492.6766
McIntosh Inn/Bensalem ($59-75)
3671 "E" Street Road (Bensalem)
215.245.0111

McIntosh Inn ($65-82)
260 N. Gulph Road (King of Prussia)
610.768.9500

Microtel Inn & Suites ($64-74)
500 Willowbrook Lane (West Chester)
US 202, Exit Matlock Street
610.738.9111

Motel 6 ($50-66)
43 Industrial Hwy (Essington, Airport)
(I-95, Exit 9A)
610.521.6650

Motel 6 ($56-60)
815 W. Dekalb Pike (King of Prussia)
I-76, Exit 26A
610.265.7200

Red Roof Inn ($49-69)
3100 Lincoln Hwy. (Trevose)
215.244.9422

Nearby NJ

Days Inn ($65-75)
525 Rte. 38E (I-295, Exit 34B)
(Cherry Hill)
856.663.0100

Econo Lodge ($45-80)
611 Fellowship Road (Mt. Laurel)
New Jersey Tpke., Exit 4
856.722.1919

McIntosh Inn ($55-75)
1132 Rte. 735 (Mt. Laurel)
New Jersey Tpke., Exit 4/
I-295, Exit 36A
856.234.7194

Red Roof Inn ($49-69)
603 Fellowship Road (Mt. Laurel)
New Jersey Tpke., Exit 4
856.234.5589

***Additional discount with AAA membership.**

Hostelling International
$18
32 S. Bank Street • 215.922.0222 or 800.392.4678
70 Beds, Office hours: 8-10 am & 4:30-midnight. Facilities: common room with TV, pool table, kitchen, lockers, A/C and vending machines. Open year-round. Reservations recommended July, August and September. Credit cards not accepted.

Hostelling International
$13
Chamounix Drive, West Fairmount Park
215.878.3676
44 Beds, Office hours: 8-11 am & 4:30-midnight. Facilities: information desk, kitchen, laundry facility, lockers, parking, A/C, TV/VCR lounge, picnic area. Private rooms available. Closed mid-December through mid-January. Reservations essential. Credit cards: MC, V.

PHILIPSBURG
Main Liner Motel
$31-39
On US 322 (1.2 miles west of town)
814.342.2004
21 Units, pets OK. Rooms come with phones and cable TV. Some rooms have refrigerators. AAA/Senior discount. Credit cards: AE, DS, MC, V.

PITTSBURGH — *see also Belle Vernon, Bridgeville, Coraopolis, Harmarville and Mars*
Econo Lodge
$39-55
4800 Steubenville Pike
I-79, Exit 16 • 412.922.6900
105 Units, pets OK. Continental breakfast. Pool. Rooms come with phones and cable TV. Wheelchair accessible. Major credit cards.

Motel 6
$34-36
211 Beecham Drive • 412.922.9400
126 Units, pets OK. Laundry facility. Rooms come with phones, A/C and cable TV. Wheelchair accessible. Credit cards: AE, CB, DC, DS, MC, V.

Super 8 Motel
$50
8 Landings Drive
I-76, Exit 5 • 412.828.8900
60 Units, no pets. Rooms come with phones and cable TV. Senior discount. Wheelchair accessible. Major credit cards.

PITTSTON
Knights Inn
$35-40
310 SR 315 • 570.654.6020
64 Units, pets OK. Continental breakfast. Rooms come with phones and cable TV. Some rooms have microwaves, refrigerators and jacuzzis. AAA/Senior discount. Credit cards: AE, DC, DS, JCB, MC, V.

POCONO MOUNTAIN AREA — *see East Stroudsburg and Milford*

POTTSTOWN
Days Inn
[illegible]39-55
[illegible]igh Street • 610.970.1101
[illegible]nits, pets OK. Continental breakfast. [illegible] come with phones and cable TV. [illegible]oms have refrigerators. AAA/Senior discount. Credit cards: AE, CB, DC, DS, MC, V.

POTTSVILLE
Pottsville Motor Inn
$35-55
On SR 61N • 570.622.4917
27 Units, pets OK ($5). Picnic area. Rooms come with phones and cable TV. Wheelchair accessible. Major credit cards.

PUNXSUTAWNEY
Country Villa Motel
$35
On US 119 (1.5 miles south of town)
814.938.8330
27 Units, pets OK. Restaurant on premises. Rooms come with phones and cable TV. AAA discount. Credit cards: AE, DS, MC, V.

READING
Econo Lodge
$42-46*
2310 Fraver Drive • 610.378.1145
48 Units, pets OK. Continental breakfast. Rooms come with phones and cable TV. Major credit cards.
*Rates as high as $60/night.

RIDGWAY
The Royal Inn
$39-45
1 miles south of town on US 219
814.773.3153
45 Units, pets OK. Restaurant on premises. Continental breakfast. Rooms come with phones and cable TV. Some rooms have refrigerators. AAA discount. Major credit cards.

RONKS
Quiet Haven Motel
$48-55 (62)*
2556 Siegrist Road • 717.397.6231
15 Units, no pets. Rooms come with phones and cable TV. Major credit cards.
*Higher rate effective mid-June through October.

Red Carpet Inn
$48 (68)*
2884 Lincoln Hwy. E. • 717.687.8020
26 Units, pets OK ($5). Rooms come with phones and cable TV. Major credit cards.
*Higher rate effective weekends.

SCRANTON — *see Clarks Summit*

SHAMOKIN DAM
Golden Arrow Diner & Motel
$34-37
On Rtes. 11 & 15 • 717.143.1611 or 800.537.4380
30 Units, pets OK ($5). Restaurant on premises. Rooms come with A/C, phones and color TV. Major credit cards.

SHIPPENSBURG
Budget Host Shippensburg Inn
$33-35
10 Hershey Road
I-81, Exit 10 • 717.530.1234
38 Units, pets OK. Restaurant on premises. Continental breakfast. Laundry facility. Rooms come with phones and cable TV. Credit cards: AE, DS, MC, V.

SLIPPERY ROCK
Evening Star Motel
$40-46
On SR 106 • I-79, Exit 30 • 724.794.3211
18 Units, pets OK. Rooms come with phones and cable TV. Senior discount. Credit cards: AE, DS, MC, V.

SOMERSET
Budget Host Inn
$30-60
799 N. Center Avenue • 814.445.7988
27 Units, pets OK ($5). Continental breakfast. Rooms come with phones and cable TV. Some rooms have microwaves and refrigerators. Senior discount available (10%). Major credit cards.

Knights Inn
$36
585 Ramada Road
I-70/76, Exit 110 • 814.445.8933
112 Units, pets OK. Laundry facility. VCR and movie rentals. Data ports. Rooms come with phones and cable TV. Some rooms have refrigerators. AAA/Senior discount. Major credit cards.

SOUTH WILLIAMSPORT
Kings Inn
$35-50*
590 Montgomery Pike • 570.322.4707
48 Units, pets OK. Continental breakfast. Rooms come with phones and cable TV. Some rooms have refrigerators. AAA/Senior discount. Major credit cards.
*Rates as high as $59/night.

STATE COLLEGE
Happy Valley Motor Inn
$45-55
1245 S. Atherton Street • 814.238.8461
35 Units, no pets. Restaurant on premises. Data ports. Rooms come with phones and cable TV. AAA/Senior discount. Major credit cards.

Motel 6
$40-50 (54-64)*
1274 N. Atherton Street • 814.234.1600
98 Units, pets OK. Restaurant on premises. Laundry facility. Data ports. Rooms come with phones, A/C and cable TV. Wheelchair accessible. Credit cards: AE, CB, DC, DS, MC, V.
*Higher rates effective weekends.

TOWN HILL
Days Inn
$48-55
9648 Old Rte. 126
I-70, Exit 156 • 814.735.3860
64 Units, pets OK. Restaurant on premises. Continental breakfast. Rooms come with phones and cable TV. AAA/Senior discount. Major credit cards.

TREVOSE
Knights Inn
$40-50*
2707 US 1N • 215.639.4900
103 Units, pets OK. Rooms come with phones and cable TV. AAA/Senior discount. Major credit cards.
*Rates as high as $80/night.

UNIONTOWN
Hopwood Motel
$35-49
On SR 40 (half mile west of town)
724.437.7591
15 Units, no pets. Rooms come with phones and cable TV. Some rooms have refrigerators. AAA/Senior discount. Credit cards: AE, DS, MC, V.

WASHINGTON
Motel 6
$34-48
1283 Motel 6 Drive
I-70/I-79, Exit 7A • 724.223.8040
102 Units, pets OK. Pool. Laundry facility. Rooms come with phones and cable TV. Wheelchair accessible. Credit cards: AE, CB, DC, DS, MC, V.

Red Roof Inn
$39-59
1399 W. Chestnut St. • 724.228.5750
110 Units, pets OK. Data ports. Rooms come with phones and cable TV. AAA discount. Major credit cards.

WAYNESBURG
Econo Lodge
$40-50
350 Miller Lane
I-79, Exit 14 • 724.627.5544
60 Units, pets OK. Rooms come with phones and cable TV. AAA/Senior discount. Wheelchair accessible. Major credit cards.

Super 8 Motel
$46*
80 Miller Lane
I-79, Exit 14 • 724.627.8880
56 Units, pets OK. Rooms come with phones and cable TV. Senior discount. Wheelchair accessible. Major credit cards.
*Rates higher weekends, special events and holidays.

WELLSBORO
Colton Point Motel
$35-45
13 miles west on US 6 • 750.724.2155
14 Units, pets OK ($5). Restaurant on premises. Playground. Rooms come with phones and cable TV. No A/C in rooms. AAA/Senior discount. Credit cards: AE, DS, MC, V.

Sherwood Motel
$35-55
2 Main Street • 570.724.3424
32 Units, no pets. Continental breakfast. Pool. Rooms come with refrigerators, microwaves, phones and cable TV. AAA discount. Credit cards: AE, CB, DC, DS, MC, V.

WEST HAZLETON
Forest Hill Inn
$50
I-81, Exit 41 (on SR 93) • 717.459.2730
40 Units, pets OK. Laundry facility. Rooms come with phones and cable TV. AAA/Senior discount. Major credit cards.

...ES-BARRE
...nn
...*
... Street • I-81, Exit 170B, then Exit 1 • 570.826.0111
75 Units, pets OK ($10). Continental breakfast. Rooms come with phones and cable TV. Some rooms have microwaves and refrigerators. AAA/Senior discount. Major credit cards.
*Rates as high as $59/night.

Econo Lodge
$45-53*
1075 Wilkes-Barre Township Blvd.
570.823.0600
104 Units, no pets. Continental breakfast. Laundry facility. Rooms come with phones and cable TV. Some rooms have microwaves and refrigerators. AAA discount. Major credit cards.
*Rates as high as $63/night.

Red Roof Inn
$39-51
1035 Hwy. 315
I-81, Exit 170B • 570.829.6422
115 Units, pets OK. Data ports. Rooms come with phones and cable TV. AAA discount. Major credit cards.

WILLIAMSPORT — *see also South Williamsport*
Ridgemont Motel
$45-49
On US 15 (2 miles south of town)
570.321.5300
8 Units, pets OK. Rooms come with refrigerators, microwaves, phones and cable TV. Credit cards: DS, MC, V.

WIND GAP
Travel Inn of Wind Gap
$40-50
499 E. Moorestown Rd. • 610.863.4146
35 Units, pets OK ($5). Rooms come with phones and cable TV. AAA/Senior discount. Credit cards: AE, DS, MC, V.

YORK
Budget Host Inn Spirit of 76
$30-37
1162 Haines Road • 717.755.1068
40 Units, pets OK. Rooms come with phones and cable TV. Some rooms have refrigerators. Credit cards: AE, DS, MC, V.

Motel 6
$34-48
125 Arsenal Road • 717.846.6260
100 Units, pets OK. Rooms come with

phones, A/C and cable TV. Wheelchair accessible. Credit cards: AE, CB, DC, DS, MC, V.

Red Roof Inn
$39-51*
323 Arsenal Road • 717.843.8181
103 Units, pets OK. Rooms come with phones and cable TV. Credit cards: AE, CB, DC, DS, MC, V.
*Rates as high as $59/night.

rhode island

JOHNSTON
Sky-View Motor Inn
$50 (65)*
2880 Hartford Avenue • 401.934.1188
31 Units, no pets. Rooms come with phones and cable TV. Major credit cards.
*Higher rate effective weekends.

MIDDLETOWN
Bay Willows Inn
$49 (69)*
1225 Aquidneck Avenue • 401.847.8400
21 Units, pets OK ($50 dep. req.). Rooms come with phones and cable TV. Some rooms have microwaves and refrigerators. AAA discount. Major credit cards.
*Higher rate effective weekends.

NEWPORT
Motel 6
$40-50 (60-76)*
249 J.T. Connell Hwy. (Rte. 114 at Coddington Hwy) • 401.848.0600
77 Units, pets OK. Data ports. Rooms come with phones, A/C and cable TV. Wheelchair accessible. Credit cards: AE, CB, DC, DS, MC, V.
*Higher rates effective mid-June through mid-October.

NORTH KINGSTOWN
Kingstown Motel
$50 (60-80)*
6530 Post Road • 401.884.1160
20 Units, no pets. Rooms come with phones, refrigerators and cable TV. Some rooms have microwaves. Wheelchair accessible. Credit cards: AE, MC, V.
*Higher rates effective weekends and May through Labor Day.

NORTH SMITHFIELD
Hilltop Inn
$50-55
797 Eddie Dowling Hwy • 401.762.9631
21 Units, no pets. Rooms come with phones and cable TV. Wheelchair accessible. Major credit cards.

PROVIDENCE — *see Johnston and Warwick*

WARWICK
Open Gate Motel
$50-60
840 Quaker Lane • 401.884.4490
23 Units, no pets. Rooms come with phones and cable TV. Major credit cards.

WEST GREENWICH
Classic Motor Lodge
$45
859 Victory Hwy. (Rte. 102)
401.397.6280
28 Units, no pets. Rooms come with phones and cable TV. Wheelchair accessible. Major credit cards.

WOONSOCKET
Woonsocket Motor Inn
$51-58*
333 Clinton Street • 401.762.1224
38 Units, no pets. Rooms come with phones and cable TV. Wheelchair accessible. Major credit cards.
*AAA discounted rates.

south carolina

AIKEN
Days Inn
$38
2654 Columbia Hwy. • 803.642.5692
78 Units, no pets. Pool. Laundry facility. Rooms come with phones and cable TV. Some rooms have microwaves and refrigerators. AAA/Senior discount. Major credit cards.

Days Inn Downtown
$38-42
1204 Richland Ave. W. • 803.649.5524
42 Units, pets OK ($10). Continental breakfast. Pool. Meeting rooms. Rooms come with microwaves, refrigerators, phones and cable TV. AAA/Senior discount. Credit cards: AE, CB, DC, DS, MC, V.

ANDERSON
Cape Cod Inn
$37
4020 Clemson Blvd. • 864.224.4464
40 Units, no pets. Continental breakfast. Fitness facility. Laundry facility. Rooms come with phones and cable TV. Wheelchair accessible. AAA/Senior discount. Major credit cards.

Royal American Motor Inn
$42
4515 Clemson Blvd.
I-85, Exit 19A • 864.226.7236
52 Units, pets OK. Rooms come with phones and cable TV. Some rooms have refrigerators. AAA/Senior discount. Credit cards: AE, MC, V.

Super 8 Motel
$45
3302 Cinema Avenue • 864.225.8384
62 Units, pets OK ($25). Continental breakfast. Rooms come with phones and cable TV. Senior discount. Wheelchair accessible. Major credit cards.

BEAUFORT
Atlantic Inn
$45
2249 Boundary Street • 843.524.6024
29 Units, no pets. Rooms come with phones and cable TV. Major credit cards.

BENNETTSVILLE
Marlboro Inn
$36
US 15 & 401 Bypass • 843.479.4051
56 Units, no pets. Continental breakfast. Meeting rooms. Rooms come with phones and cable TV. AAA/Senior discount. Credit cards: AE, CB, DC, DS, MC, V.

BISHOPVILLE
Econo Lodge
$31-40
1135 Sumter Hwy.
I-20, Exit 116 • 803.428.3200
48 Units, pets OK. Continental breakfast. Rooms come with phones and satellite TV. AAA/Senior discount. Major credit cards.

Howard Johnson Express Inn
$45
I-20 & Hwy. 341 • 803.428.5001
32 Units, no pets. Continental breakfast. Rooms come with phones and satellite TV. Wheelchair accessible. Major credit cards.

CAMDEN
Colony Inn
$49-52
2020 W. DeKalb Street • 803.432.5508
72 Units, pets OK ($10). Restaurant on premises. Pool. Laundry facility. Rooms come with phones and cable TV. Senior discount. Credit cards: AE, CB, DC, DS, MC, V.

Knights Inn
$30-50
322 DeKalb St. (US 1) • 803.432.2453
35 Units, no pets. Restaurant on premises. Pool. Rooms come with phones and cable TV. Major credit cards.

CAYCE
Knights Inn
$37-48
1987 Airport Blvd. • 803.794.0222
117 Units, pets OK ($10 dep. req.).

Continental breakfast. Pool. Laundry facility. Meeting rooms. Rooms come with refrigerators, microwaves, phones and cable TV. AAA/Senior discount. Credit cards: AE, DC, DS, MC, V.

Masters Economy Inn
$29-40
2125 Commerce Drive • I-26, Exit 113
803.791.5850
112 Units, pets OK ($5). Pool. Rooms come with phones and cable TV. Senior discount. Credit cards: AE, CB, DC, DS, MC, V.

CHARLESTON — *see also Mount Pleasant and North Charleston*
Econo Lodge
$45-60
6155 Fain Blvd.
I-26, Exit 211A • 843.747.7691
100 Units, pets OK. Restaurant on premises. Continental breakfast. Pool. Fitness facility. Meeting rooms. Rooms come with phones and cable TV. Some rooms have refrigerators. Senior discount. Major credit cards.

Motel 6
$35-43*
2551 Ashley Phosphate Rd. • 843.572.6590
125 Units, pets OK. Pool. Laundry facility. Rooms come with phones, A/C and cable TV. Wheelchair accessible. Credit cards: AE, CB, DC, DS, MC, V.
*Prices higher during weekends and special events.

Motel 6—South
$36-52*
2058 Savannah Hwy. • 843.556.5144
111 Units, pets OK. Pool. Laundry facility. Rooms come with phones, A/C and cable TV. Wheelchair accessible. Credit cards: AE, CB, DC, DS, MC, V.
*Prices higher during weekends and special events.

Super 8 Motel
$44
4620 Dorchester Road • 843.747.7500
100 Units, no pets. Continental breakfast. Pool. Copy and fax service. Laundry facility. Rooms come with phones and cable TV. Some rooms have microwaves and refrigerators. Wheelchair accessible. Senior discount. Credit cards: AE, CB, DC, DS, MC, V.

CHERAW
Days Inn
$45
820 Market Street • 843.537.5554
50 Units, pets OK ($5). Continental breakfast. Pool. Laundry facility. Rooms come with phones and cable TV. Some rooms have microwaves and refrigerators. AAA discount. Major credit cards.

CLINTON
Days Inn
$42-55
12374 Hwy. 56N
I-26, Exit 52 • 864.833.6600
58 Units, pets OK ($10). Continental breakfast. Pool. Laundry facility. Sauna. Meeting rooms. Rooms come with phones and TV. Wheelchair accessible. AAA discount. Major credit cards.

COLUMBIA
Days Inn—Northeast
$36-53
7128 Parklane Road (I-20, Exit 74)
803.736.0000
135 Units, pets OK. Restaurant on premises. Continental breakfast. Pool. Rooms come with phones and cable TV. Some rooms have microwaves and refrigerators. AAA discount. Credit cards: AE, DC, DS, MC, V.

Motel 6
$30-40
1776 Burning Tree Rd. • 803.798.9210
97 Units, pets OK. Pool. Rooms come with phones, A/C and cable TV. Wheelchair accessible. Credit cards: AE, CB, DC, DS, MC, V.

Knights Inn
$35-46
1803 Bush River Road • 803.772.0022
105 Units, pets OK ($5). Continental breakfast. Pool. Meeting rooms. Rooms come with phones and cable TV. Some rooms have refrigerators. AAA discount. Major credit cards.

Red Roof Inn—West
$35-46
10 Berryhill Road • 803.798.9220
109 Units, pets OK. Rooms come with phones and cable TV. AAA discount. Credit cards: AE, CB, DC, DS, MC, V.

DILLON
Best Value Inn
$29-45
904 Radford Blvd. • 843.774.5111
79 Units, pets OK. Continental breakfast. Pool. Rooms come with phones and cable TV. Credit cards: AE, DS, MC. V.

Super 8 Motel
$40-60
I-95 (Exit 193) & SR 9 • 843.774.4161
100 Units, pets OK. Continental breakfast. Pool. Wading pool. Meeting room. Copy and fax service. Rooms come with phones and cable TV. Wheelchair accessible. AAA/Senior discount. Credit cards: AE, CB, DC, DS, MC, V.

DUNCAN
Days Inn
$45-50
1386 E. Main Street
I-85, Exit 63 • 864.433.1122
80 Units, no pets. Pool. Laundry facility. Meeting rooms. Rooms come with phones and cable TV. Wheelchair accessible. AAA/Senior discount. Major credit cards.

Microtel Inn
$45-55
1534 E. Main Street
I-85, Exit 63 • 864.433.1000
60 Units, no pets. Continental breakfast. Rooms come with phones and cable TV. Wheelchair accessible. Senior discount. Major credit cards.

EASLEY
Days Inn
$45-48
121 Days Inn Drive
I-85, Exit 40 • 864.859.9902
72 Units, pets OK ($6). Continental breakfast. Pool. Fitness facility. Meeting rooms. Rooms come with phones and cable TV. Wheelchair accessible. AAA discount. Major credit cards.

FLORENCE
Days Inn South
$35-55
I-95 (Exit 157), on US 76
843.665.8550
181 Units, pets OK ($6). Restaurant on premises. Pool. Jacuzzi. Playground. Rooms come with phones and cable TV. AAA discount. Credit cards: AE, CB, DC, DS, MC, V.

Motel 6
$30-35*
1834 W. Lucas Road • 843.667.6100
109 Units, pets OK. Pool. Rooms come with phones, A/C and cable TV. Wheelchair accessible. Credit cards: AE, CB, DC, DS, MC, V.
*Prices higher during weekends and special events.

Park Inn International
$39
831 S. Irby Street • 843.662.9421
106 Units, pets OK. Restaurant on premises. Continental breakfast. Pool. Meeting rooms. Laundry facility. Rooms come with phones and cable TV. Some rooms have refrigerators. AAA/Senior discount. Credit cards: AE, CB, DC, DS, JCB, MC, V.

Young's Plantation Inn
$36
US 76 & I-95 (Exit 157) • 843.669.4171
120 Units, pets OK ($4). Restaurant on premises. Pool. Wading pool. Jacuzzi. Meeting rooms. Rooms come with phones and cable TV. AAA/Senior discount. Credit cards: AE, CB, DC, DS, MC, V.

FORT MILL
Motel 6
$34-46 (60)*
255 Carowinds Blvd. • 803.548.9656
122 Units, pets OK. Restaurant on premises. Pool. Laundry facility. Rooms come with phones, A/C and cable TV. Wheelchair accessible. Credit cards: AE, CB, DC, DS, MC, V.
*Higher rate effective summer weekends.

GREENVILLE
Motel 6
$28-34
224 Bruce Road • 864.277.8630
102 Units, pets OK. Pool. Laundry facility. Rooms come with phones, A/C and cable TV. Wheelchair accessible. Credit cards: AE, CB, DC, DS, MC, V.
*Prices higher during weekends and special events.

Red Roof Inn
$36-48
2801 Laurens Road • I-85, Exit 48A
864.297.4458
108 Units, pets OK. Rooms come with phones and cable TV. AAA discount. Major credit cards.

Super 8 Motel
$37-47
536 Wade Hampton Blvd. • 864.232.6416
48 Units, pets OK. Rooms come with phones and cable TV. Senior discount. Major credit cards.

GREENWOOD
Econo Lodge
$42-50
719 Bypass 25 N.E. • 864.229.5329
50 Units, no pets. Continental breakfast. Pool. Rooms come with phones and cable TV. AAA discount. Major credit cards.

HARDEEVILLE
Howard Johnson Lodge
$35-50*
On US 17 (I-95, Exit 5) • 843.784.2271
128 Units, pets OK ($5). Restaurant on premises. Pool. Wading pool. Rooms come with phones and cable TV. AAA discount. Credit cards: AE, CB, DC, DS, MC, V.
*AAA discounted rates.

Scottish Inn
$33*
On US 17 (I-95, Exit 5) • 843.784.2151
94 Units, pets OK ($2). Pool. Meeting rooms. Laundry facility. Rooms come with phones and cable TV. Senior discount. Credit cards: AE, CB, DC, DS, MC, V.
*Rates increase to $55/night during first three weeks of March.

HARTSVILLE
Comfort Inn
$47
US 15 & Washington St. • 843.383.0110
68 Units, no pets. Continental breakfast. Pool. Jacuzzi. Rooms come with phones and cable TV. Wheelchair accessible. AAA discount. Major credit cards.

HILTON HEAD
Motel 6
$50 (56-62)*
830 Wm. Hilton Pkwy. • 843.785.2700
116 Units, pets OK. Pool. Laundry facility. Rooms come with phones, A/C and cable TV. Wheelchair accessible. Credit cards: AE, CB, DC, DS, MC, V.
*Higher rates effective weekends and summer months.

LANCASTER
Best Western
$47-50*
1201 Hwy. 9 Bypass • 803.283.1200
60 Units, no pets. Continental breakfast. Pool. Laundry facility. Rooms come with phones and cable TV. Wheelchair accessible. Senior discount. Major credit cards.
*AAA discounted rates.

MANNING
Guesthouse Inn & Suites
$48 (58)*
Jct. I-95 & SR 261 (Exit 119)
803.473.4021
57 Units, pets OK. Pool. Rooms come with phones and cable TV. Senior discount. Credit cards: AE, DS, MC, V.
*Higher rate effective weekends.

MONCKS CORNER
Berkeley Motel
$50
399 Hwy. 52N • 843.761.8400
98 Units, pets OK. Laundry facility. Rooms come with phones and cable TV. Major credit cards.

MOUNT PLEASANT
Masters Economy Inn
$36-46
300 Wingo Way • 843.884.2814
120 Units, pets OK ($6 dep. req.). Continental breakfast. Pool. Meeting rooms. Laundry facility. Rooms come with phones and cable TV. AAA discount. Major credit cards.

MYRTLE BEACH
El Dorado Motel
$26-61
2800 S. Ocean Blvd. • 843.626.3559
41 Units, pets OK ($5-10). Heated pool. Jacuzzi. Sauna. Laundry facility. Rooms come with phones and cable TV. Senior discount. Credit cards: DS, MC, V.

Hurl Rock Motel
$23-55*
2010 S. Ocean Blvd. • 843.626.3531
55 Units, no pets. Heated pool. Jacuzzi. Laundry facility. Rooms come with phones and cable TV. Some rooms have microwaves and refrigerators. AAA discount. Credit cards: AE, MC, V.
*Rates as high as $98/night.

The Ocean Front Viking Motel
$19-50*
1811 S. Ocean Blvd. • 843.448.4335
75 Units, no pets. Heated Pool. Laundry facility. Rooms come with phones and cable TV. Some rooms have microwaves and refrigerators. AAA discount. Major credit cards.
*Rates as high as $88/night.

Tradewinds Motel
$31 (60-70)*
2201 Withers Drive • 843.448.5441
40 Units, no pets. Heated pool. Laundry facility. Rooms come with refrigerators, phones and cable TV. Some rooms have kitchens. Credit cards: MC, V.
*Higher rates effective June through mid-August.

NEWBERRY
Best Western Newberry Inn
$47-60
11701 S. Carolina Hwy. • 803.276.5850
116 Units, pets OK. Restaurant on premises. Continental breakfast. Pool. Meeting rooms. Fitness facility. Playground. Laundry facility. Rooms come with phones and cable TV. Some rooms have microwaves and refrigerators. Senior discount. Credit cards: AE, CB, DC, DS, MC, V.

Days Inn
$46-49
50 Thomas Griffin Road • 803.276.2294
58 Units, pets OK ($4). Continental breakfast. Heated pool. Rooms come with phones and cable TV. Some rooms have microwaves and refrigerators. Wheelchair accessible. AAA discount. Major credit cards.

NORTH CHARLESTON
Budget Inn of Charleston
$37
6155 Fain Street • 843.747.7691
102 Units, no pets. Restaurant on premises. Pool. Laundry facility. Continental breakfast. Rooms come with phones and cable TV. Some rooms have microwaves and refrigerators. Senior discount. Credit cards: AE, MC, V.

Masters Economy Inn
$35-50
I-26 & Aviation Avenue (Exit 211B)
843.744.3530
150 Units, no pets. Meeting rooms. Fax service. Rooms come with phones and cable TV. Wheelchair accessible. Senior discount. Major credit cards.

Motel 6
$35-37
2551 Ashley Phosphate Road
843.572.6590
128 Units, pets OK. Pool. Laundry facility. Rooms come with phones, A/C and cable TV. Wheelchair accessible. Credit cards: AE, CB, DC, DS, MC, V.

Red Roof Inn
$39-59
7480 Northwoods Blvd. • 843.572.9100
109 Units, pets OK. Laundry facility. Fitness facility. Rooms come with phones and cable TV. AAA discount. Credit cards: AE, CB, DC, DS, MC, V.

NORTH MYRTLE BEACH
Days Inn
$35-49
3209 Hwy. 17S • 843.272.6196
44 Units, pets OK ($10). Pool. Rooms come with phones and cable TV. Some rooms have microwaves and refrigerators. AAA/ Senior discount. Major credit cards.

ORANGEBURG
Ramada Limited
$40-50
826 John C. Calhoun Dr. • 803.534.7630
104 Units, pets OK. Continental breakfast. Pool. Laundry facility. Rooms come with phones and cable TV. Some rooms have microwaves and refrigerators. Senior discount. Major credit cards.

Super 8 Motel
$38
610 John C. Calhoun Dr. • 803.531.1921
46 Units, pets OK. Continental breakfast. Pool. Rooms come with phones and cable TV. Some rooms have refrigerators. AAA/ Senior discount. Credit cards: AE, DC, DS, MC, V.

POINT SOUTH
Days Inn
$36-58
I-95, Exit 33 • 803.726.8156
117 Units, pets OK ($5). Restaurant on premises. Pool. Laundry facility. Rooms come with phones and cable TV. Wheelchair

accessible. AAA discount. Major credit cards.

RICHBURG
Super 8 Motel
$49
3085 Lancaster Hwy.
I 77, Exit 65 • 803.789.7888
58 Units, pets OK ($3). Continental breakfast. Pool. Rooms come with phones and cable TV. Some rooms have microwaves and refrigerators. Senior discount. Major credit cards.

RIDGELAND
Econo Lodge
$42-52
516 E. Main Street • 843.726.5553
77 Units, pets OK. Rooms come with phones and cable TV. Some rooms have microwaves and refrigerators. Wheelchair accessible. Major credit cards.

ROCK HILL
Days Inn
$45-55
914 Riverview Road
I-77, Exit 82B • 803.329.6581
113 Units, no pets. Restaurant on premises. Continental breakfast. Pool. Rooms come with phones and cable TV. Wheelchair accessible. AAA discount. Major credit cards.

ST. GEORGE
Econo Lodge
$33-43
5971 W. Jim Bilton Blvd • 843.563.4195
92 Units, pets OK ($3). Continental breakfast. Pool. Rooms come with phones and cable TV. Wheelchair accessible. Credit cards: AE, CB, DC, DS, MC, V.

Economy Inns of America
$36
5971 W. Jim Bilton Blvd • 843.563.4195
68 Units, pets OK ($2). Pool. Rooms come with phones and cable TV. AAA/Senior discount. Credit cards: AE, CB, DC, DS, MC, V.

Super 8 Motel
$38-54
From I-95, Exit 77 (On US 78)
843.563.5551
60 Units, pets OK ($5). Continental breakfast. Pool. Rooms come with phones and cable TV. Credit cards: AE, CB, DC, DS, JCB, MC, V.

ST. STEPHEN
Econo Lodge
$40*
3986 Byrnes Drive • 843.567.7397
50 Units, pets OK. Restaurant on premises. Pool. Rooms come with phones and cable TV. Wheelchair accessible. Major credit cards.
*Rates as high as $76/night.

SANTEE
Days Inn
$43-50
9074 Old Hwy. 6 • 803.854.2175
119 Units, pets OK ($6). Pool. Playground. Laundry facility. Rooms come with phones and cable TV. AAA/Senior discount. Major credit cards.

Super 8 Motel
$34-38
On SR 6 (I-95, Exit 98) • 803.854.3456
43 Units, pets OK. Continental breakfast. Rooms come with phones and cable TV. Some rooms have jacuzzis. Senior discount. Credit cards: AE, CB, DC, DS, MC, V.

SENECA
Town & Country Motel
$35-40
320 Hwy. 123 Bypass • 864.882.3376
21 Units, no pets. Rooms come with refrigerators, phones and cable TV. Some rooms have kitchenettes. Credit cards: AE, CB, DC, DS, MC, V.

SPARTANBURG
Motel 6
$30-35*
105 Jones Road • 864.573.6383
124 Units, pets OK. Pool. Laundry facility. Rooms come with phones, A/C and cable TV. Wheelchair accessible. Credit cards: AE, CB, DC, DS, MC, V.
*Prices higher during weekends and special events.

Sunset Inn
$25-35
1355 Boiling Springs Rd • 864.585.2413
120 Units, pets OK. Continental breakfast. Pool. Rooms come with phones and cable TV. Some rooms have microwaves and refrigerators. Credit cards: AE, CB, DC, DS, JCB, MC, V.

Super 8 Motel
$35-55
1350 Boiling Springs Road
I-85, Exit 75 • 864.585.5890
68 Units, no pets. Continental breakfast. Pool. Jacuzzi. Rooms come with phones and cable TV. Senior discount. Major credit cards.

SUMMERTON
Knights Inn
$22-45
I-95, Exit 108 • 803.485.2895
140 Units, pets OK. Restaurant on premises. Laundry facility. Rooms come with phones and cable TV. Wheelchair accessible. Major credit cards.

TIMMONSVILLE
Travelodge
$38-45
2200 Yarborough Hwy.
1-85, Exit 150 • 843.346.9696
40 Units, no pets. Continental breakfast. Rooms come with phones and cable TV. Senior discount. Major credit cards.

TURBEVILLE
Days Inn
$37
On Hwy. 378
1-95, Exit 135 • 843.659.8060
58 Units, pets OK ($5). Continental breakfast. Pool. Rooms come with phones and cable TV. AAA/Senior discount. Major credit cards.

UNION
Palmetto Motor Inn
$30
1235 S. Duncan Bypass • 864.427.5682
62 Units, pets OK. Continental breakfast offered at restaurant next door. Rooms come with phones and cable TV. Major credit cards.

WALTERBORO
Budget Inn
$40-49
1305 Bells Hwy. • 843.538.3272
61 Units, no pets. Pool. Rooms come with phones and cable TV. AAA/Senior discount. Credit cards: AE, DS, MC, V.

Rice Planters Inn
$26-31
Jct. I-95 & SR 63 (Exit 53)
843.538.8964
76 Units, pets OK. Pool. Rooms come with phones and cable TV. AAA/Senior discount. Credit cards: AE, DS, MC, V.

Super 8 Motel
$37-50*
I-95 (Exit 57), on Hwy. 64 843.538.5383
45 Units, pets OK. Pool. Rooms come with phones and cable TV. Senior discount. AAA/Senior discount. Credit cards: AE, CB, DC, DS, MC, V.
*Rates may increase slightly on weekends.

WEST COLUMBIA
Villager Lodge
$27-31
1617 Charleston Hwy. • 803.796.3714
48 Units, no pets. Rooms come with phones and cable TV. Some rooms have microwaves and refrigerators. Senior discount. Major credit cards.

WINNSBORO
Days Inn
$36-44
Junction US 321, SR 34 & 213
803.635.1447
45 Units, pets OK ($5). Continental breakfast. Pool. Rooms come with phones and cable TV. Some rooms have microwaves and refrigerators. AAA/Senior discount. Credit cards: AE, DS, MC, V.

YEMASSEE
Knights Inn
$27-43
Rte. 1, P.O. Box 52E • I-95, Exit 33 on Hwy. 17 • 843.726.8488
70 Units., pets OK. Pool. Rooms come with phones and cable TV. Wheelchair accessible. AAA/Senior discount. Major credit cards.

Super 8 Motel
$33*
Hwy. 68 & I-95 • 843.589.2177
49 Units, pets OK. Pool. Rooms come with phones and cable TV. Wheelchair accessible. Senior discount. Credit cards: AE, CB, DC, DS, MC, V.
*Rates may increase slightly during special events, holidays and weekends.

south dakota

ABERDEEN
Super 8 Motel
$38-48
770 N.W. Hwy. 281 • 605.226.2288
25 Units, pets OK. Continental breakfast. Airport transportation. Rooms come with phones and cable TV. Wheelchair accessible. AAA/Senior discount. Credit cards: AE, CB, DC, DS, MC, V.

Super 8 Motel
$38-48
714 S. Hwy. 281 • 605.225.1711
39 Units, pets OK. Continental breakfast. Airport transportation. Laundry facility. Rooms come with phones and cable TV. Wheelchair accessible. Senior discount. Credit cards: AE, CB, DC, DS, MC, V.

The White House Inn
$39-50
500 6th Ave. S.W. • 605.225.5000
96 Units, pets OK. Continental breakfast. Meeting rooms. Rooms come with phones and cable TV. Some rooms have refrigerators. AAA/Senior discount. Credit cards: AE, CB, DC, DS, MC, V.

ARLINGTON
Super 8 Motel
$41-46 (51-56)*
704 S. Hwy 81 • 605.983.4609
21 Units, no pets. Continental breakfast. Meeting rooms. Rooms come with phones and cable TV. AAA/Senior discount. Credit cards: AE, CB, DC, DS, JCB, MC, V.
*Higher rates effective mid-October through November 3.

BADLANDS NATIONAL PARK
Badlands Budget Host Motel
$46-52*
HC54, Box 115 • 605.433.5335
17 Units, pets OK ($2). Pool. Playground. Laundry facility. Rooms come with A/C, phones and cable TV. AAA/Senior discount. Credit cards: DS, MC, V.
*Closed mid-September through April.

Cedar Pass Lodge
$40-50*
605.433.5460 • I-90, Exit 131, 8 miles to Visitor's Center on SR 240.
25 Units, pets OK. Lodge consists of individual cabins. Meeting rooms. Dining room on premises. Rooms come with A/C. No phones or televisions in cabins. Credit cards: AE, DC, DS, MC, V.
*Lodge is closed November through March.

BELLE FOURCHE
Motel Lariat
$25-35
1033 Elkhorn • 605.892.2601
11 Units, pets OK ($3). Nicely decorated and comfortable rooms come with phones, A/C and cable TV. Senior discount. Credit cards: AE, DS, MC, V.

Motel 6
$40-50 (60-100)*
1815 5th Avenue • 605.892.6663
51 Units, pets OK. Indoor pool. Laundry facility. Rooms come with phones and cable TV. Wheelchair accessible. Credit cards: AE, CB, DC, DS, MC, V.
*Higher rates effective June through mid-August.

BERESFORD
Super 8 Motel
$46-56
1410 W. Cedar • 605.763.2001
39 Units, pets OK. Continental breakfast. Indoor pool and hot tub. Rooms come with phones and cable TV. Senior discount. Wheelchair accessible. Major credit cards.

BLACK HILLS — *see Custer, Keystone and Rapid City*

BROOKINGS
Super 8 Motel
$48
3034 Lefevre Drive • 605.692.6920
46 Units, pets OK. Continental breakfast. Pool. Meeting rooms. Game room. Rooms come with phones and cable TV. Wheelchair

accessible. Senior discount. Major credit cards.

BUFFALO
Tipperary Lodge
$36-40
605.375.3721 • On US 85, half mile north from town.
20 Units, pets OK. Continental breakfast. Airport transportation. Rooms come with phones and cable TV. AAA/Senior discount. Credit cards: AE, DC, DS, MC, V.

CANISTOTA
Best Western U-Bar Motel
$32-50*
130 Ash Street • 605.296.3466
28 Units, pets OK. Continental breakfast. Laundry facility. Rooms come with phones and cable TV. Some rooms have refrigerators and microwaves. AAA discount. Credit cards: AE, CB, DC, DS, JCB, MC, V.
*Rates as high as $66/night.

CHAMBERLAIN
Bel Aire Motel
$35-54*
312 E. King Street • 605.734.5595
35 Units, pets OK ($5). Rooms come with A/C and cable TV. Some rooms have phones. AAA/Senior discount. Credit cards: AE, DS, MC, V.
*Closed November through March.

Hillside Motel
$35
502 E. King Street • 605.734.5591 or 800.435.5591
35 Units, no pets. Rooms come with phones, A/C and cable TV. Some rooms have kitchenettes. Major credit cards. Senior discount.

CUSTER
Custer Motel
$19-59*
109 Mt. Rushmore Rd • 605.673.2876
31 Units, no pets. Pool. Laundry facility. Rooms come with phones and cable TV. AAA discount. Credit cards: AE, DS, MC, V.
*Motel is closed December through mid-April.

Mile Hi Motel
$30-55*
244 Mt. Rushmore Rd • 605.673.4048
15 Units, no pets. Playground. Rooms come with phones and cable TV. AAA/Senior discount. Credit cards: AE, DS, MC, V.
*Motel is closed mid-October through April.

DEADWOOD
Budget Host Jackpot Inn
$29-50 (59-70)*
Hwy 385 at south city limits • 605.578.7791
47 Units, pets OK ($5). Continental breakfast. Heated pool. Picnic area. Jacuzzi. Rooms come with phones and cable TV. AAA/Senior discount. Major credit cards.
*Higher rate effective late June through August.

Hostelling International
$13
818 Upper Main Street • 605.578.1842 or 877.565.8140
20 Beds, Hours: 8 am until 10 pm
Facilities: Bicycle rental, laundry facility, parking, luggage storage and kitchen. Free bagels. Closed August 7-15. Reservations recommended. Credit cards: AE, DS, MC, V.

Terrace Motel
$39 (64-74)*
250 Main Street • 605.578.2351 or 800.851.5699
20 Units, pets OK. Rooms come with A/C and cable TV. Major credit cards.
*Higher rates effective June through August.

FAITH
Prairie Vista Inn
$45-50*
On US 212 • 605.967.2343
27 Units, pets OK ($50 dep. req.). Sauna and jacuzzi. Fitness facility. Meeting rooms. Rooms come with phones, A/C and cable TV. Wheelchair accessible. Senior discount. Major credit cards.
*AAA discounted rates.

FAULKTON
Super 8 Motel
$37-53
700 Main Street • 605.598.4567
20 Units, pets OK ($10). Laundry facility. Meeting rooms. Rooms come with phones and cable TV. Some rooms have refrigerators and jacuzzis. Senior discount. Credit cards: AE, CB, DC, DS, MC, V.

FORT PIERRE
Fort Pierre Motel
$40-44
211 S. First Street • 605.223.3111
21 Units, pets OK. Continental breakfast. Airport transportation. Rooms come with phones and cable TV. Some rooms have microwaves and refrigerators. AAA/Senior discount. Credit cards: AE, DS, MC, V.

GETTYSBURG
Super 8 Motel
$39-46
719 E. Hwy. 212 • 605.765.2373
24 Units, pets OK. Continental breakfast. Laundry facility. Copy machine. Rooms come with phones and cable TV. Wheelchair accessible. Senior discount. Credit cards: AE, CB, DC, DS, MC, V.

HOT SPRINGS
Bison Motel
$34 (55-65)*
On US 385S • 605.745.5191
18 Units, pets OK. Rooms come with phones, A/C and cable TV. Major credit cards.
*Higher rates effective during summer months.

Skyline Motel
$35-50*
Three blocks east of Evans Plunge on US 385 • 605.745.6980 or 800.380.8494
22 Units, pets OK. Laundry facility. Rooms come with phones, kitchenettes and cable TV. Credit cards: DS, MC, V.
*Summer rates higher. Closed November through April.

HURON
Dakota Inn
$35-50
From I-90, Exit 150 • 605.837.2151
36 Units, pets OK. Pool. Laundry facility. Rooms come with phones and cable TV. Credit cards: DS, MC, V.

INTERIOR — *see Badlands National Park*

KADOKA
Best Value Dakota Inn
$30-50
I-90, Exit 150 • 605.837.2151
34 Units, pets OK. Heated pool. Laundry facility. Rooms come with phones, A/C and color TV. Wheelchair accessible. AAA/ Senior discount. Credit cards: DS, MC, V.

West Motel
$33-42*
306 W. Hwy 16 • 605.837.2427
18 Units, pets OK ($3). Rooms come with phones and cable TV. Credit cards: DS, MC, V.
*Closed November through March.

KENNEBEC
Budget Host Inn
$26-36
From I-90, Exit 235 • 605.869.2210
16 Units, no pets. Restaurant on premises. Continental breakfast. Shuttle to casino. Laundry facility. Rooms come with cable TV. Some rooms have refrigerators. Senior discount available ($3). Credit cards: AE, MC

KEYSTONE
Brookside Motel
$35*
605.666.4496 or 800.551.9381
In town just three blocks east of stoplight on Hwy 40.
9 Units, no pets. Continental breakfast. Pool. Rooms come with A/C and cable TV. Major credit cards.
*Summer rates higher.

KIMBALL
Travelers Motel
$32-53
From I-90, Exit 284 • 605.778.6215
27 Units, no pets. Rooms come with phones and cable TV. AAA discount. Credit cards: AE, DS, MC, V.

LEMMON
Lemmon Country Inn
$42
HCR 63 Box 15 • 605.374.3711 or 800.591.3711
31 Units, no pets. Continental breakfast. Rooms come with phones and cable TV. Credit cards: AE, DC, DS, MC, V.

MADISON
Lake Park Motel
$39-49
605.256.3524 • One mile west from jct of US 81 and SR 34.
40 Units, pets OK. Heated pool. Rooms come with cable TV. Some rooms have microwaves and refrigerators. Senior discount. Credit cards: AE, CB, DC, DS, MC, V.

Super 8 Motel
$43-50
Jct. SR 34 and US 81 • 605.256.6931
34 Units, pets OK. Continental breakfast. Rooms come with phones and cable TV. Wheelchair accessible. AAA discount. Credit cards: AE, CB, DC, DS, MC, V.

MARTIN
Best Value Crossroads Inn
$42-48
Jct. Hwys. 18 & 73 • 605.685.1070
34 Units, no pets. Meeting rooms. Rooms come with phones and cable TV. Wheelchair accessible. AAA/Senior discount. Major credit cards.
*AAA discounted rate.

MILBANK
Manor Motel
$37
On US 12E (0.8 miles east of town)
605.432.4527
30 Units, pets OK. Heated indoor pool, sauna and jacuzzi. Rooms come with phones and cable TV. Some rooms have microwaves and refrigerators. AAA discount. Credit cards: AE, CB, DC, DS, MC, V.

Super 8 Motel
$40-49
On US 12E (one mile from town)
605.432.9288
39 Units, no pets. Meeting rooms, sauna, jacuzzi and fitness facility. Laundry facility. Rooms come with phones and cable TV. Some rooms have microwaves, refrigerators, radios and kitchens. AAA/Senior discount. Credit cards: AE, CB, DC, DS, MC, V.

MILLER
Super 8 Motel
$38-41
605.853.2721 • Jct. US 14 & SR 45 N.
21 Units, no pets. Airport transportation. Rooms come with phones and cable TV. Senior discount. Credit cards: AE, CB, DC, DS, MC, V.

MITCHELL
Anthony Motel
$45-50
1518 W. Havens Street • 605.996.7518
34 Units, no pets. Heated pool and miniature golf. Airport transportation. Laundry facility. Rooms come with cable TV. Some rooms have refrigerators. AAA discount. Credit cards: AE, DS, MC, V.

Motel 6
$34-49
1309 S. Ohlman Street • 605.996.0530
122 Units, pets OK. Pool. Laundry facility. Rooms come with phones and cable TV. Wheelchair accessible. Credit cards: AE, CB, DC, DS, MC, V.

MOBRIDGE
Super 8 Motel
$40-55
On Hwy 12 W. • 605.845.7215
31 Units, pets OK. Continental breakfast. Rooms come with phones and cable TV. Senior discount. Credit cards: AE, CB, DC, DS, MC, V.

MOUNT RUSHMORE — *see Rapid City*

MURDO
Super 8 Motel
$43-48 (61-71)*
605 E. 5th • 605.669.2437
50 Units, pets OK (call ahead for permission, $5). Rooms come with phones and cable TV. Wheelchair accessible. Credit cards: AE, CB, DC, DS, MC, V.
*Higher rates effective June through Labor Day.

PIERRE
Budget Host Inn/State Motel
$33-40
640 N. Euclid Avenue • 605.224.5896
36 Units, pets OK. Continental breakfast. Heated pool, sauna, jacuzzi and fitness facility. Rooms come with phones and cable TV. Some rooms have microwaves and refrigerators. AAA/Senior discount. Credit cards: AE, CB, DC, DS, MC, V.

Capitol Inn
$33
815 Wells Avenue • 605.224.6387 or 800.658.3055
102 Units, pets OK. Continental breakfast. Pool. Laundry facility. Rooms come with phones and cable TV. Wheelchair accessible. Credit cards: AE, DC, DS, MC, V.

Super 8 Motel
$37-50
320 W. Sioux • 605.224.1617
78 Units, pets OK. Continental breakfast.

Laundry facility. Copy machine. Rooms come with phones and cable TV. Wheelchair accessible. AAA/Senior discount. Credit cards: AE, CB, DC, DS, MC, V.

PRESHO

Hutch's Motel
$35-44
830 E. 9th Street • 605.895.2591
29 Units, pets OK ($5). Rooms come with phones and cable TV. AAA/Senior discount. Credit cards: AE, DS, MC, V.

RAPID CITY

Traveler Advisory: Rapid City, the hub of western South Dakota, is a popular summertime destination. Because of its proximity to Mt. Rushmore, the Black Hills and Badlands National Park, local innkeepers raise their rates substantially to match the demand for rooms in the summer. Increasing the demand for rooms, thousands of motorcycle enthusiasts from around the country converge in Sturgis, South Dakota, just 20 miles west of Rapid City, in early August of each year. If you are traveling through western South Dakota between June and August, you will have a difficult time finding a room for less than $50 per night, particularly without advance reservations, in Rapid City or any of the surrounding communities (Deadwood, Wall, Lead, Keystone, Spearfish, Sturgis and Custer). Be sure to call ahead and make reservations if you know well enough ahead of time that you will be in Rapid City. If you are just passing through and have not made reservations, **Kadoka, South Dakota**, located about 100 miles east of Rapid City on I-90, offers a number of inexpensive lodgings during the summer. Beware, however, that these rooms go quickly in the summertime, so it is advisable to get there early in the evening to get your room. Likewise, **Belle Fourche, South Dakota** (50 miles northwest of Rapid City on US 85), and **Sundance, Wyoming** (80 miles west of Rapid City on I-90) offer a selection of inexpensive lodgings.

Big Sky Motel
$33-48*
4080 Tower Road • 605.348.3200 or 800.318.3208
31 Units, pets OK. Playground and picnic area. No phones in rooms. Rooms come with A/C. AAA discount. Credit cards: DS, MC, V.
*Closed November through April.

Lamplighter Inn
$28-58
27 St. Joseph Street • I-90, Exit 58
605.342.3385
27 Units, no pets. Heated pool. Rooms come with phones, A/C and cable TV. AAA/Senior discount. Credit cards: AE, DS, MC, V.

Motel 6
$34-50 (60-70)*
620 E. Latrobe Street • 605.343.3687
150 Units, pets OK. Pool. Laundry facility. Data ports. Rooms come with phones, A/C and cable TV. Wheelchair accessible. Credit cards: AE, CB, DC, DS, MC, V.
*Higher rate effective mid-June through mid-August.

Stardust Motel
$40-60*
520 E. North Street • 605.343.8844 or 800.456.0084
37 Units, no pets. Heated pool and small casino. Rooms come with phones, A/C and cable TV. Some rooms have refrigerators. AAA discount. Major credit cards.
*Higher rate effective July through late August.

Townhouse Motel
$24-49 (39-59)*
210 St. Joseph Street • 605.342.8143
40 Units, no pets. Heated pool. Rooms come with phones and cable TV. Some rooms have radios. AAA/Senior discount. Credit cards: AE, DS, MC, V.
*Higher rates effective June through mid-August.

REDFIELD

Super 8 Motel
$45
Junction US 212 & 281 • 605.472.0720
31 Units, pets OK. Continental breakfast. Rooms come with phones and cable TV. Senior discount. Credit cards: AE, CB, DC, DS, MC, V.

SELBY

Super 8 Motel
$45
5000 US Hwys. 12 & 83 • 605.649.7979
34 Units, pets OK (additional charge).

Continental breakfast. Laundry facility. Rooms come with phones and cable TV. Wheelchair accessible. Senior discount. Credit cards: AE, CB, DC, DS, MC, V.

SIOUX FALLS
Empire Inn
$42
4208 W. 41st Street • 605.361.2345
84 Units, no pets. Continental breakfast. Heated pool, sauna and jacuzzi. Rooms come with phones and cable TV. Some rooms have refrigerators, mini bars, microwaves, radios and kitchens. AAA discount. Credit cards: AE, CB, DC, DS, MC, V.

Exel Inn of Sioux Falls
$41-55
1300 W. Russell Street • 605.331.5800 or 800.291.4414
105 Units, pets OK in smoking rooms only. Continental breakfast. Laundry facility. Some rooms have refrigerators, microwaves and jacuzzis. Senior discount. Credit cards: AE, CB, DC, DS, MC, V.

Motel 6
$34-45
3009 W. Russell Street • 605.336.7800
87 Units, pets OK. Pool. Laundry facility. Data ports. Rooms come with phones, A/C and cable TV. Wheelchair accessible. Credit cards: AE, CB, DC, DS, MC, V.

Select Inn
$38-50
3500 S. Gateway Blvd.
605.361.1864 or 800.641.1000
100 Units, pets OK ($25 dep. req.). Continental breakfast. Laundry facility. Meeting rooms, heated indoor pool and jacuzzi. Rooms come with phones and cable TV. Senior discount. Credit cards: AE, CB, DC, DS, JCB, MC, V.

Super 8 Motel
$34-50*
1508 W. Russell • 605.339.9330
95 Units, pets OK. Rooms come with phones and cable TV. Senior discount. Credit cards: AE, CB, DC, DS, MC, V.
*Rates as high as $90/night.

SPEARFISH
Royal Rest Motel
$25-45*
444 Main Street • 605.642.3842
12 Units, pets OK. Heated pool. Laundry facility. Rooms come with phones and cable TV. AAA discount. Credit cards: AE, CB, DC, DS, MC, V.
*Closed late November through February.

STURGIS
National 9 Junction Inn
$36-50
1802 S. Junction Ave. • 605.347.5675
50 Units, pets OK ($5). Airport transportation. Rooms come with phones and cable TV. Some rooms have refrigerators. Senior discount. Credit cards: AE, CB, DC, DS, MC, V.

National 9 Star Lite Inn
$32-50 (55-60)*
2426 Junction Avenue • 605.347.2506
20 Units, pets OK ($5). Laundry facility. Rooms come with phones and cable TV. Some rooms have refrigerators. Senior discount. Credit cards: AE, CB, DC, DS, MC, V.
*Higher rates effective mid-June through mid-August.

VERMILLION
Super 8 Motel
$41-45
1208 E. Cherry Street • 605.624.8005
39 Units, pets OK ($5). Continental breakfast. Indoor heated pool, spa and jacuzzi. Rooms come with phones and cable TV. Wheelchair accessible. Senior discount. Credit cards: AE, CB, DC, DS, MC, V.

WAGNER
Super 8 Motel
$36-50
Jct. Hwys. 46 & 50 • 605.384.5464
78 Units, no pets. Coffee and doughnuts offered. Meeting rooms, heated indoor pool, sauna and jacuzzi. Rooms come with phones and cable TV. AAA/Senior discount. Credit cards: AE, DC, DS, MC, V.

WALL
Knights Inn
$35-50 (75)*
In town on South Blvd. • 605.279.2127
47 Units, pets OK. Pool. Rooms come with phones and cable TV. Credit cards: AE, CB, DC, DS, MC, V.
*Higher rate effective summer months.

WATERTOWN
Budget Host Inn
$30-35*
309 8th Avenue S.E. • 605.886.6248
41 Units, pets OK. Picnic area. Rooms come with phones and cable TV. Credit cards: AE, MC, V. Senior discount available ($1).
*Rates slightly higher during hunting season, typically October 15 through November 15.

Traveler's Inn Motel
$42
920 14th Street S.E. • I-29, Exit 177
605.882.2243
49 Units, pets OK ($6). Continental breakfast. Laundry facility. Rooms come with phones and cable TV. AAA/Senior discount. Major credit cards.

WEBSTER
Super 8 Motel
$40-50*
605.345.4701 • On US 12, just W of SR 25
27 Units, pets OK with permission. Rooms come with phones and cable TV. Senior discount. Major credit cards.
*Rates higher during special events and weekends.

WINNER
Buffalo Trail Motel
$40-42*
950 W. 1st • 605.842.2212
31 Units, pets OK. Continental breakfast. Airport transportation. Heated pool. Rooms come with phones and cable TV. AAA discount. Credit cards: AE, CB, DC, DS, MC, V.
*Rates jump to $100 between October 15 and November 15.

Super 8 Motel
$37-43*
902 E. Hwy. 44 • 605.842.0991
25 Units, pets OK with permission . Pastries offered. Laundry facility. Rooms come with phones and cable TV. Wheelchair accessible. Senior discount. Credit cards: AE, DC, DS, MC, V.
*Rates higher during special events and weekends.

YANKTON
Colonial Inn Motel
$32
1509 Broadway • 605.665.3647
20 Units, pets OK ($5 per night). Rooms come with phones, cable TV and A/C. Kitchenettes, microwaves and refrigerators are available. Credit cards: DS, MC, V.

Super 8 Motel
$40-44
605.665.6510 • On SR 50, just E of US 81
58 Units, pets OK with permission. Rooms come with phones and cable TV. Senior discount. Credit cards: AE, CB, DC, DS, MC, V.

tennessee

Traveler's Advisory: The communities of **Sevierville**, **Pigeon Forge** and **Gatlinburg** are popular family travel destinations and offer a number of hotel and motel accommodations. You should be aware that summertime rates are quite high ($50-70) for a single accommodation in these communities. If you're looking for budget accommodations in this area, you'll have better luck in neighboring **Knoxville** and **Asheville, NC**.

ATHENS
Homestead Inn West
$33-34
2808 Decatur Pike • 423.745.9002
41 Units, pets OK ($5). Pool. Rooms come with phones and cable TV. Some rooms have jacuzzis. Senior discount. Credit cards: AE, CB, DC, DS, MC, V.

Knights Inn
$33-40
2620 Decatur Pike • 423.744.8200
90 Units, pets OK ($4). Continental breakfast. Pool. Playground. Rooms come with phones and cable TV. AAA/Senior discount. Credit cards: AE, DS, MC, V.

Super 8 Motel
$34-45
2539 Decatur Pike • 423.745.4500
55 Units, pets OK. Pool. Rooms come with phones and cable TV. Some rooms have jacuzzis, microwaves and refrigerators. Senior discount. Credit cards: AE, CB, DC, DS, JCB, MC, V.

BOLIVAR
Aristocrat Motor Inn
$35
108 Porter Street (Hwy. 64W)
731.658.6451
30 Units, no pets. Meeting room. Rooms come with phones and cable TV. Some rooms have kitchenettes. Senior discount. Major credit cards.

The Bolivar Inn
$35
626 W. Market Street • 731.658.3372
39 Units, pets OK ($5 and $5 dep. req.). Laundry facility. Rooms come with phones and cable TV. AAA/Senior discount. Credit cards: AE, CB, DC, DS, MC, V.

BRISTOL
Days Inn
$38-48
536 Volunteer Parkway • 423.968.2171
63 Units, no pets. Continental breakfast. Pool. Jacuzzi. Rooms come with phones and cable TV. AAA discount. Major credit cards.

Scottish Inns
$40-45
1403 Bluff City Hwy. • 423.764.4145
33 Units, no pets. Restaurant on premises. Rooms come with phones and cable TV. Senior discount. Major credit cards.

BROWNSVILLE/BELLS
Comfort Inn
$39-57
2600 Anderson Avenue • 731.772.4082
52 Units, no pets. Continental breakfast. Pool. Laundry facility. Rooms come with phones and cable TV. Senior discount. Major credit cards.

Motel 6
$32-36
9740 US 70E • I-40, Exit 66
731.772.9500
43 Units, pets OK. Restaurant on premises. Laundry facility. Rooms come with phones and cable TV. Wheelchair accessible. Credit cards: AE, CB, DC, DS, MC, V.

BUCKSNORT
Travel Inn
$26-30
111 E. Rte. 1 • 931.729.5450
34 Units, pets OK ($10 dep. req.). Continental breakfast. Rooms come with phones and cable TV. Senior discount. Credit cards: AE, CB, DC, DS, MC, V.

BUFFALO/HURRICANE MILLS
Super 8 Motel
$37-45

I-40 (Exit 143) • 931.296.2432
45 Units, pets OK. Continental breakfast. Pool. Rooms come with phones and cable TV. Senior discount. Wheelchair accessible. Credit cards: AE, DC, DS, MC, V.

CAMDEN
Days Inn
$39-45
On US 70E • 731.584.3111
41 Units, pets OK. Continental breakfast. Pool. Rooms come with phones and cable TV. Wheelchair accessible. AAA discount. Major credit cards.

CARYVILLE
Budget Host Inn
$25-29
101 Tennessee Drive • 423.562.9595
22 Units, pets OK. Playground. Picnic area. Airport transportation. Rooms come with phones and cable TV. Credit cards: AE, CB, DC, DS, MC, V.

Super 8 Motel
$36-44
I-75, Exit 134 • 423.562.8476
97 Units, pets OK. Continental breakfast. Pool. Rooms come with phones and cable TV. Senior discount. Wheelchair accessible. Major credit cards.

CENTERVILLE
Days Inn
$45-55
634 David Street (On Hwy. 100)
931.729.5600
40 Units, pets OK ($5). Restaurant on premises. Continental breakfast. Pool. Meeting rooms. Rooms come with phones and cable TV. Wheelchair accessible. AAA/ Senior discount. Major credit cards.

CHATTANOOGA
Days Inn East Ridge
$30-45
6510 Ringgold Road • 423.894.0911
146 Units, no pets. Pool. Rooms come with phones and cable TV. Senior discount. Major credit cards.

Microtel Inn
$39-43
7014 McCutcheon Road • 423.510.0761
100 Units, pets OK. Continental breakfast. Laundry facility. Rooms come with phones and cable TV. Wheelchair accessible. Major credit cards.

Motel 6
$30-36
7707 Lee Hwy. • 423.892.7707
97 Units, pets OK. Pool. Laundry facility. Data ports. Rooms come with phones, A/C and cable TV. Wheelchair accessible. Credit cards: AE, CB, DC, DS, MC, V.

Motel 6—Downtown
$36-50
2440 Williams Street • I-24, Exit 178
423.265.7300
59 Units, pets OK. Data ports. Rooms come with phones, A/C and cable TV. Wheelchair accessible. Credit cards: AE, CB, DC, DS, MC, V.

CLARKSVILLE
Days Inn
$35-60
130 Westfield Court • I-24, Exit 4
931.552.1155
76 Units, no pets. Continental breakfast. Pool. Laundry facility. Meeting rooms. Rooms come with phones and cable TV. Some rooms have microwaves and refrigerators. Wheelchair accessible. AAA discount. Major credit cards.

Motel 6
$37
254 Holiday Drive • I-24/US 79, Exit 4
931.552.2663
59 Units, pets OK. Pool. Rooms come with phones, A/C and cable TV. Wheelchair accessible. Credit cards: AE, CB, DC, DS, MC, V.

CLEVELAND
Days Inn of Cleveland
$30-55
2550 Georgetown Road • 423.476.2112
57 Units. Continental breakfast. Pool. Rooms come with phones and cable TV. Some rooms have jacuzzis and refrigerators. AAA/Senior discount. Credit cards: AE, CB, DC, DS, MC, V.

COLUMBIA
James K. Polk Motel
$30-40
1111 Nashville Hwy. • 931.388.4913
50 Units, pets OK. Continental breakfast. Pool. Rooms come with phones and cable TV. Some rooms have refrigerators. AAA/ Senior discount. Credit cards: AE, DS, MC, V.

COOKEVILLE
Best Western Thunderbird Motel
$36-41
900 S. Jefferson • 931.526.7115
60 Units, pets OK. Pool. Laundry facility. Rooms come with phones and cable TV. Some rooms have refrigerators. AAA/Senior discount. Credit cards: AE, CB, DC, DS, MC, V.

Econo Lodge
$40-60
1100 S. Jefferson • 931.526.9521
69 Units, no pets. Continental breakfast. Pool. Rooms come with phones and cable TV. Some rooms have microwaves and refrigerators. AAA/Senior discount. Major credit cards.

Executive Inn
$33-40
897 S. Jefferson • 931.526.9521
83 Units, no pets. Continental breakfast. Heated pool. Wading pool. Meeting rooms. Laundry facility. Rooms come with phones and cable TV. Some rooms have microwaves and refrigerators. AAA discount. Credit cards: AE, CB, DC, DS, MC, V.

CORNERSVILLE
Econo Lodge
$45-55
3731 Pulaski Hwy. • 931.293.2111
41 Units, pets OK ($5 dep. req.). Pool. Rooms come with phones and color TV. AAA discount. Major credit cards.

CROSSVILLE
Village Inn
$31
70 Burnett Street (I-40, Exit 317)
931.484.7561
147 Units, pets OK. Restaurant on premises. Meeting room. Rooms come with phones and cable TV. Major credit cards.

DICKSON
Knights Inn
$30-50*
2328 Hwy. 465 • 615.446.3766
49 Units, pets OK. Pool. Rooms come with phones and cable TV. AAA/Senior discount. Major credit cards.
*Rates can climb as high as $60/night.

DYERSBURG
Days Inn
$50
2600 Lake Road • 731.287.0888
59 Units, pets OK. Continental breakfast. Laundry facility. Rooms come with phones and cable TV. AAA/Senior discount. Major credit cards.

ELKTON — *see Pulaski*

ERWIN
Super 8 Motel
$32-46
1101 N. Buffalo Street • 423.743.0200
49 Units, no pets. Continental breakfast. Rooms come with phones and cable TV. Senior discount. Major credit cards.

FAYETTEVILLE
Days Inn
$49
1651 Huntsville Hwy. • 931.433.6121
48 Units, pets OK. Restaurant on premises. Continental breakfast. Pool. Rooms come with phones and cable TV. AAA discount. Major credit cards.

GATLINBURG
Highland Motor Inn
$25-40
131 Parkway • 865.436.4110
46 Units, pets OK ($5). Pool. Rooms come with phones and cable TV. Some rooms have microwaves and refrigerators. AAA/Senior discount. Credit cards: AE, DS, MC, V.

GOODLETTSVILLE
Econo Lodge
$35-60
320 Long Hollow Pike • 615.859.4988
107 Units, pets OK. Pool. Meeting rooms. Rooms come with phones and cable TV. AAA/Senior discount. Major credit cards.

Motel 6
$32-38
323 Cartwright Street • 615.859.9674
94 Units, pets OK. Pool. Laundry facility. Data ports. Rooms come with phones, A/C and cable TV. Wheelchair accessible. Credit cards: AE, CB, DC, DS, MC, V.

Rodeway Inn
$30-40
650 Wade Circle • 615.859.1416
30 Units, pets OK. Pool. Rooms come with phones and cable TV. AAA/Senior discount. Credit cards: AE, DS, MC, V.

GREENEVILLE
Andrew Johnson Inn
$40
2145 E. Andrew Johnson Hwy.
423.638.8124
44 Units, pets OK. Pool. Rooms come with phones and cable TV. Some rooms have refrigerators. AAA/Senior discount. Credit cards: AE, CB, DC, DS, JCB, MC, V.

HARRIMAN
Best Western Sundancer Motor Lodge
$42
I-40 & Hwy. 27 • 865.882.6200
50 Units, pets OK ($2). Continental breakfast. Pool. Rooms come with phones and cable TV. Senior discount. Credit cards: AE, CB, DC, DS, MC, V.

Super 8 Motel
$46
1867 S. Roane Street • 865.882.6600
48 Units, pets OK. Pool. Rooms come with phones and cable TV. Senior discount. Major credit cards.

HERMITAGE
Hermitage Inn
$30-42
4144 Lebanon Road • 615.883.7444
70 Units, pets OK. Pool. Rooms come with phones and cable TV. Some rooms have microwaves and refrigerators. AAA discount. Credit cards: AE, DS, MC, V.

HUMBOLDT
Regal Inn
$32
618 N. 22nd Avenue • 731.784.9693
53 Units, no pets. Restaurant on premises. Meeting room. Rooms come with phones and cable TV. Some rooms have kitchenettes. Senior discount. Major credit cards.

JACKSON
Days Inn—West
$32-40
2239 Hollywood Drive • 731.668.4840
95 Units, pets OK. Continental breakfast. Meeting rooms. Pool. Rooms come with phones and cable TV. Some rooms have refrigerators. AAA discount. Credit cards: AE, CB, DC, DS, MC, V.

Days Inn
$32-50
1919 US 45 Bypass • 731.668.3444
120 Units, pets OK. Continental breakfast. Pool. Laundry facility. Rooms come with phones and cable TV. AAA/Senior discount. Credit cards: AE, CB, DC, DS, MC, V.

Super 8 Motel
$37-39
2295 N. Highland • 731.668.1145
95 Units, pets OK. Continental breakfast. Pool. Meeting room. Fitness facility. Rooms come with phones and cable TV. Wheelchair accessible. Senior discount. Credit cards: AE, CB, DC, DS, MC, V.

JELLICO
Best Western
$36-40
I-75 (Exit 160) • 423.784.7241
50 Units, pets OK. Restaurant on premises. Pool. Rooms come with phones and cable TV. AAA discount. Credit cards: AE, DC, DS, MC, V.

Days Inn
$36-51
I-75N (Exit 160) • 423.784.7281
128 Units, pets OK ($4). Restaurant on premises. Pool. Playground. Rooms come with phones and cable TV. AAA discount. Credit cards: AE, DC, DS, MC, V.

The Jellico Motel
$44
I-75 & 25W (Exit 160) • 423.784.7211 or 800.251.9498
92 Units, pets OK. Restaurant on premises. Pool. Meeting room. Rooms come with phones and cable TV. Senior discount. Major credit cards.

JOHNSON CITY
Super 8 Motel
$40-45
108 Wesley Street • 423.282.8818
60 Units, pets OK. Laundry facility. Rooms come with phones and cable TV. Some rooms have microwaves and refrigerators. Major credit cards.

KIMBALL

Budget Host Inn
$33-36
395 Main Street • 423.837.7185
64 Units, no pets. Continental breakfast. Heated pool. Laundry facility. Rooms come with phones and cable TV. Major credit cards.

KINGSPORT

Microtel
$37-50
1708 E. Stone Drive • 423.378.9220
87 Units, no pets. Continental breakfast. Meeting rooms. Fitness facility. Rooms come with phones and cable TV. Wheelchair accessible. Credit cards: AE, DC, DS, MC, V.

Super 8 Motel
$47
1238 Shipley Ferry Rd • 423.239.9137
55 Units, no pets. Continental breakfast. Pool. Meeting rooms. Rooms come with phones and cable TV. Some rooms have refrigerators. Credit cards: AE, CB, DC, DS, MC, V.

KINGSTON

Days Inn
$40-42
495 Gallaher Road • 865.376.2069
42 Units, pets OK ($5). Continental breakfast. Pool. Rooms come with phones and cable TV. AAA/Senior discount. Major credit cards.

Knights Inn
$30-45
1200 N. Kentucky St • 865.376.3477
30 Units, no pets. Continental breakfast. Pool. Rooms come with phones and cable TV. Major credit cards.

KNOXVILLE

Knights Inn
$34-37
11320 Outlet Drive • 865.966.7500
100 Units, no pets. Pool. Rooms come with phones and color TV. Senior discount. Credit cards: AE, DS, MC, V.

Motel 6
$32-36
402 Lovell Road • 865.675.7200
113 Units, pets OK. Pool. Laundry facility. Data ports. Rooms come with phones, A/C and cable TV. Wheelchair accessible. Credit cards: AE, CB, DC, DS, MC, V.

Motel 6—North
$30-36
5640 Merchant Center Blvd.
I-75, Exit 108 • 865.689.7100
84 Units, pets OK. Data ports. Rooms come with phones, A/C and cable TV. Wheelchair accessible. Credit cards: AE, CB, DC, DS, MC, V.

Scottish Inns North
$40-50
301 Callahan Drive • I-75, Exit 110
865.689.7777
85 Units, pets OK. Continental breakfast. Pool. Rooms come with phones and cable TV. Wheelchair accessible. AAA/Senior discount. Major credit cards.

LAKE CITY

The Lamb's Inn
$29-39
620 N. Main Street • 865.426.2171
34 Units, pets OK. Continental breakfast. Pool. Rooms come with phones and cable TV. AAA/Senior discount. Credit cards: AE, DS, MC, V.

LAKELAND

Super 8 Motel
$46-50
9779 Huff-n-Puff Road • 901.372.4575
75 Units, no pets. Continental breakfast. Pool. Jacuzzi. Rooms come with phones and cable TV. AAA discount. Credit cards: AE, DC, DS, MC, V.

LAWRENCEBURG

David Crockett Motel
$40
503 E. Gaines Street • 931.762.7191
40 Units, no pets. Rooms come with phones and cable TV. Senior discount. Major credit cards.

Richland Inn
$47*
2125 N. Locust Avenue • 931.762.0061
56 Units, no pets. Continental breakfast. Rooms come with phones and cable TV. Some rooms have jacuzzis, A/C and refrigerators. Credit cards: AE, CB, DC, DS, MC, V.
*AAA discounted rates.

LEBANON
Days Inn
$30-50
I-40, Exit 238 • 615.444.5635
50 Units, pets OK ($5). Continental breakfast. Pool. Laundry facility. Rooms come with phones and cable TV. Some rooms have jacuzzis and refrigerators. AAA/ Senior discount. Credit cards: AE, CB, DC, DS, JCB, MC, V.

LENOIR CITY
Days Inn
$42-50
1110 Hwy. 321N • 865.986.2011
90 Units, no pets. Restaurant on premises. Pool. Wading pool. Playground. Meeting room. Rooms come with phones and cable TV. Some rooms have refrigerators. AAA/ Senior discount. Credit cards: AE, DS, MC, V.

Econo Lodge
$40-54*
1211 Hwy. 321N • 865.986.0295
42 Units, no pets. Continental breakfast. Pool. Rooms come with phones and cable TV. Some rooms have jacuzzis and refrigerators. Senior discount. Credit cards: AE, DS, MC, V.
*AAA discounted rates.

LOUDON
Knights Inn
$33-50*
15100 Hwy. 72 • 865.456.4855
44 Units, pets OK. Pool. Continental breakfast. Rooms come with phones and cable TV. AAA/Senior discount. Credit cards: AE, DS, MC, V.
*Rates can climb as high as $60/night.

MANCHESTER
Scottish Inn
$36-43
2457 Hillsboro Hwy. • 931.728.0506
92 Units, pets OK. Continental breakfast. Heated pool. Rooms come with phones and cable TV. Some rooms have microwaves and refrigerators. AAA/Senior discount. Credit cards: AE, DS, MC, V.

Super 8 Motel
$35-40
2430 Hillsboro Hwy. • 931.728.9720
50 Units, pets OK. Continental breakfast. Pool. Rooms come with phones and cable TV. Some rooms have refrigerators. Credit cards: AE, CB, DC, DS, JCB, MC, V.

McKENZIE
Briarwood Inn of McKenzie
$50
635 N. Highland Drive • 731.352.1083
27 Units, no pets. Continental breakfast. Rooms come with phones and cable TV. Some rooms have microwaves and refrigerators. Credit cards: AE, CB, DC, DS, MC, V.

McMINNVILLE
Best Value Inn
$35-40
508 Sunnyside Heights • 931.473.4446
61 Units, pets OK. Continental breakfast. Pool. Laundry facility. Rooms come with phones and cable TV. Some rooms have microwaves and refrigerators. Major credit cards.

MEMPHIS — *see also Horn Lake (MS) and West Memphis (AR)*
Graceland Inn
$35-40
3280 Elvis Presley Blvd. • 901.345.1425
120 Units, pets OK ($5). Continental breakfast. Pool. Meeting room. Fax service. Rooms come with phones and cable TV. Wheelchair accessible. AAA/Senior discount. Credit cards: AE, CB, DC, DS, MC, V.

The Memphis Inn
$38-46
4879 American Way • I-240, Exit 18
901.794.8300
109 Units, no pets. Pool. Laundry facility. Rooms come with phones and cable TV. Senior discount. Major credit cards.

Motel 6—East
$34-46
1321 Sycamore View Rd • 901.382.8572
100 Units, pets OK. Pool. Laundry facility. Data ports. Rooms come with phones, A/C and cable TV. Wheelchair accessible. Credit cards: AE, CB, DC, DS, MC, V.

Motel 6
$36-47
1117 E. Brooks Road • 901.346.0992
125 Units, pets OK. Pool. Laundry facility. Data ports. Rooms come with phones, A/C and cable TV. Wheelchair accessible. Credit cards: AE, CB, DC, DS, MC, V.

Red Roof Inn—Medical Center
$40-48
From I-240S, Exit 29, 210 S. Pauline
901.528.0650
120 Units, pets OK. Rooms come with phones and cable TV. AAA discount. Credit cards: AE, CB, DC, DS, MC, V.

Travelodge
$40-45
1360 Spring Brook Ave. • 901.396.3620
100 Units, no pets. Pool. Rooms come with phones and cable TV. Major credit cards.

MONTEAGLE
Budget Host Inn
$26-55
I-24, Exit 134 • 931.924.2221
115 Units, pets OK ($5). Continental breakfast. Meeting rooms. Rooms come with phones and cable TV. Wheelchair accessible. Senior discount. Credit cards: AE, DS, MC, V.

MILLINGTON
Magnolia Inn
$42-49
8193 Hwy. 51N • 901.873.4400
55 Units, pets OK ($3). Pool. Rooms come with phones and cable TV. Some rooms have microwaves and refrigerators. AAA/ Senior discount. Major credit cards.

MORRISTOWN
Days Inn
$35-49
2512 E. Andrew Johnson Hwy.
423.587.2200
40 Units, pets OK. Continental breakfast. Rooms come with phones and cable TV. Some rooms have microwaves and refrigerators. AAA discount. Credit cards: AE, CB, DC, DS, MC, V.

Motel 6
$35-46
5984 W. Andrew Johnson Hwy.
423.586.4666
49 Units, pets OK. Pool. Laundry facility. Rooms come with phones, A/C and cable TV. Wheelchair accessible. Credit cards: AE, CB, DC, DS, MC, V.

MURFREESBORO
Motel 6
$28-36
148 Chaffin Place • 615.890.8524
85 Units, pets OK. Pool. Laundry facility. Rooms come with phones, A/C and cable TV. Wheelchair accessible. Credit cards: AE, CB, DC, DS, MC, V.

Scottish Inns
$41-50 (51-58)*
2029 S. Church Street • 615.896.3211
100 Units, pets OK. Pool. Rooms come with phones and cable TV. Senior discount. Major credit cards.
*Higher rates effective weekends.

NASHVILLE — *see also Goodlettsville and Madison*
Econo Lodge
$32-55
110 Maplewood Lane • 615.262.9193
38 Units, no pets. Pool. Continental breakfast. Rooms come with phones and cable TV. AAA/Senior discount. Credit cards: AE, DC, DS, MC, V.

Executive Inn & Suites
$29-40
323 Harding Place • 615.834.0570
110 Units, pets OK ($10). Continental breakfast. Pool. Meeting rooms. Laundry facility. Rooms come with phones and cable TV. Some rooms have refrigerators. Credit cards: AE, CB, DC, DS, MC, V.

Hallmark Inns of America IV
$38
309 W. Trinity Lane (I-65, Exit 87)
615.228.2624
130 Units, no pets. Continental breakfast. Pool. Meeting rooms. Rooms come with phones and cable TV. Senior discount. Credit cards: AE, DC, DS, MC, V.

Motel 6—North
$30-40
311 W. Trinity Lane (I-65, Exit 87)
615.227.9696
125 Units, pets OK. Pool. Laundry facility. Data ports. Rooms come with phones, A/C and cable TV. Wheelchair accessible. Credit cards: AE, CB, DC, DS, MC, V.

Motel 6—Airport
$30-40
420 Metroplex Drive • I-24, Exit 56
615.833.8887
87 Units, pets OK. Pool. Laundry facility. Data ports. Rooms come with phones, A/C

and cable TV. Wheelchair accessible. Credit cards: AE, CB, DC, DS, MC, V.

NEWPORT
Motel 6
$34-44 (64)*
255 Heritage Blvd. • I-40, Exit 435
423.623.1850
65 Units, pets OK. Pool. Laundry facility. Data ports. Rooms come with phones, A/C and cable TV. Wheelchair accessible. Credit cards: AE, CB, DC, DS, MC, V.
*Higher rate effective summer weekends.

OOLTEWAH
Super 8 Motel
$40
5111 Hunter Road • 423.238.5951
63 Units, pets OK. Heated pool. Rooms come with phones and cable TV. Some rooms have jacuzzis. Senior discount. Credit cards: AE, CB, DC, DS, MC, V.

PARIS
Payless Travelers Inn
$35
1297 E. Wood Street • 731.642.8881
98 Units, pets OK. Continental breakfast. Pool. Laundry facility. Rooms come with phones and cable TV. Major credit cards.

Super 8 Motel
$36*
1309 E. Wood Street • 731.644.7008
49 Units, no pets. Continental breakfast. Jacuzzi. Laundry facility. Meeting room. Rooms come with phones and cable TV. Wheelchair accessible. Senior discount. Credit cards: AE, CB, DC, DS, MC, V.
*Rates may increase slightly during special events, holidays and weekends.

PIGEON FORGE
Briarstone Inn
$34-48
3626 Parkway • 865.453.3050
57 Units, no pets. Pool. Rooms come with refrigerators, phones and cable TV. Some rooms have kitchens and jacuzzis. AAA/Senior discount. Credit cards: AE, CB, DC, DS, MC, V.

Motel 6
$30-35 (60-80)*
336 Henderson Chapel Rd • 865.908.1244
82 Units, pets OK. Pool. Laundry facility. Rooms come with phones, A/C and cable TV. Wheelchair accessible. Credit cards: AE, CB, DC, DS, MC, V.
*Higher rate effective April through August.

River Lodge South
$39
3251 Parkway • 865.453.0783
77 Units, no pets. Heated pool. Rooms come with refrigerators, phones and cable TV. Some rooms have kitchens and jacuzzis. AAA/Senior discount. Credit cards: AE, DC, DS, MC, V.

PORTLAND
Budget Host Inn
$30-33
5339 Long Road • 615.325.2005
50 Units, pets OK ($5). Pool. Laundry facility. Rooms come with phones and cable TV. Some rooms have microwaves and refrigerators. Senior discount available (10%). Credit cards: AE, CB, DC, DS, MC, V.

PULASKI/ELKTON
Motel 6
$25-35
I-65 & Bryson Rd. (Exit 6) • 931.468.2594
40 Units, pets OK. Rooms come with phones, A/C and cable TV. Wheelchair accessible. Credit cards: AE, CB, DC, DS, MC, V.

Super 8 Motel
$40-47
I-65, Exit 14 • 931.363.4501
40 Units, pets OK ($5). Restaurant on premises. Continental breakfast. Pool. Rooms come with phones and cable TV. Senior discount. Major credit cards.

ROGERSVILLE
Sandman Motor Lodge
$50
4319 Hwy. 66S • 423.272.6800
40 Units, no pets. Rooms come with phones and cable TV. Wheelchair accessible. Major credit cards.

SAVANNAH
Shaws Komfort Motel
$30
2302 Wayne Road • 731.925.3977
31 Units, pets OK. Restaurant on premises. Rooms come with phones and cable TV. Senior discount. Major credit cards.

SELMER
Super 8 Motel
$50
644 Mulberry Avenue (on US 45S)
731.645.8880
35 Units, no pets. Continental breakfast. Pool. Rooms come with phones and cable TV. Wheelchair accessible. Senior discount. Major credit cards.

SWEETWATER
Budget Host Inn
$30-60
207 Hwy. 68 • 423.337.9357
60 Units, pets OK ($3). Restaurant on premises. Laundry facility. Rooms come with phones and cable TV. Some rooms have microwaves and refrigerators. Senior discount. Credit cards: AE, CB, DC, DS, MC, V.

Super 8 Motel
$35
720 S. Main Street • I-75, Exit 60
423.337.3585
50 Units, no pets. Continental breakfast. Pool. Rooms come with phones and cable TV. Some rooms have microwaves, jacuzzis and refrigerators. Senior discount. Major credit cards.

TAZEWELL
Tazewell Motor Lodge
$36-41
2140 Hwy. 25E • 423.626.7229
26 Units, no pets. Rooms come with refrigerators, phones and cable TV. Some rooms have microwaves. AAA/Senior discount. Credit cards: AE, CB, DC, DS, MC, V.

UNION CITY
Super 8 Motel
$43-55*
1400 Vaden Avenue • 731.885.4444
62 Units, pets OK. Rooms come with phones and cable TV. Wheelchair accessible. Senior discount. Credit cards: AE, CB, DC, DS, MC, V.
*Rates may increase slightly during special events, holidays and weekends.

WHITE HOUSE
Days Inn
$35-47
1009 Hwy. 79 • I-65, Exit 108
615.672.3746
112 Units, pets OK ($3). Continental breakfast. Pool. Rooms come with phones and cable TV. AAA/Senior discount. Major credit cards.

WILDERSVILLE
Best Western
$40
210 S. Hwy. 22W • 731.968.2532
40 Units, pets OK ($5). Continental breakfast. Heated pool. Playground. Rooms come with phones and cable TV. AAA/Senior discount. Credit cards: AE, DC, DS, MC, V.

WINCHESTER
Best Western Inn
$48
1602 Dinah Shore Blvd. • 931.967.9444
51 Units, no pets. Pool. Rooms come with refrigerators, microwaves, phones and cable TV. Some rooms have kitchens and jacuzzis. AAA discount. Credit cards: AE, DC, DS, MC, V.

Winchester Inn
$32-36
700 S. College Street • 931.967.3846
30 Units, pets OK. Restaurant on premises. Pool. Rooms come with refrigerators, phones and cable TV. Some rooms have kitchens. AAA/Senior discount. Credit cards: AE, MC, V.

texas

ABILENE
Antilley Inn
$40-50
6550 S. Hwy. 83-84 • 325.695.3330
52 Units, pets OK ($5-10). Continental breakfast. Pool. Laundry facility. Data ports. Rooms come with phones and cable TV. Credit cards: AE, CB, DC, DS, MC, V.

Econo Lodge
$35-40
1633 W. Stamford • I-20, Exit 285
325.673.5424
34 Units, pets OK ($10 dep. req.). Continental breakfast. Data ports. Rooms come with phones and cable TV. AAA/Senior discount. Credit cards: AE, CB, DC, DS, JCB, MC, V.

Executive Inn
$35-40
1650 IH-20 E. • I-20, Exit 288
325.677.2200
41 Units, pets OK. Continental breakfast. Pool. Rooms come with phones and cable TV. Some rooms have microwaves and refrigerators. Major credit cards.

Motel 6
$30
4951 W. Stamford St. • 325.672.8462
100 Units, pets OK. Pool. Laundry facility. Data ports. Rooms come with phones, A/C and cable TV. Wheelchair accessible. Credit cards: AE, CB, DC, DS, MC, V.

ALICE
Scottish Inn
$49
815 Hwy. 281 S. • 361.664.4351
100 Units, pets OK. Breakfast buffet. Pool. Rooms come with phones and cable TV. Wheelchair accessible. Credit cards: AE, CB, DC, DS, JCB, MC, V.

ALPINE
Antelope Lodge
$31-50
2310 W. Hwy. 90 • 432.837.3881
27 Units, pets OK. Laundry facility. Rooms come with phones and cable TV. Major credit cards.

Siesta Country Inn
$31
1200 E. Holland Avenue, Hwy 90E
432.837.2503
15 Units, pets OK. Pool. Laundry facility. Rooms come with phones and cable TV. Wheelchair accessible. Credit cards: AE, CB, DC, DS, MC, V.

AMARILLO
Amarillo West Travelodge
$29-50
2035 Paramount Blvd. • I-40, Exit 68A
806.353.0201
100 Units, pets OK. Continental breakfast. Heated pool. Laundry facility. Fitness facility. Rooms come with phones and cable TV. Some rooms have refrigerators. Senior discount. Major credit cards.

Motel 6—Central
$30-40
2032 Paramount Blvd. (I-40, Exit 68A)
806.355.6554
117 Units, pets OK. Pool. Laundry facility. Data ports. Rooms come with phones, A/C and cable TV. Wheelchair accessible. Credit cards: AE, CB, DC, DS, MC, V.

Motel 6—East
$32-40
3930 I-40E (Exit 72B) • 806.374.6444
110 Units, pets OK. Pool. Laundry facility. Data ports. Rooms come with phones, A/C and cable TV. Wheelchair accessible. Credit cards: AE, CB, DC, DS, MC, V.

Red Roof Inn
$40-50
1620 I-40 E. (Frontage Road)
I-40, Exit 71 • 806.374.2020
114 Units, pets OK. Continental breakfast. Heated pool. Laundry facility. Rooms come with phones and cable TV. AAA discount. Major credit cards.

ANTHONY
Super 8 Motel
$42
100 Park North Drive (I-10, Exit 0)
915.886.2888

49 Units, pets OK ($10). Continental breakfast. Laundry facility. Rooms come with refrigerators, phones and cable TV. Wheelchair accessible. AAA discount. Major credit cards.

ARANSAS PASS
Homeport Inn
$30-45
1515 Wheeler Avenue • 361.758.3213
78 Units, pets OK. Laundry facility. Rooms come with phones and cable TV. Major credit cards.

Travelodge
$38-58
545 N. Commercial St. • 361.758.5305
46 Units, pets OK. Rooms come with phones and cable TV. Wheelchair accessible. Major credit cards.

ARLINGTON
Homestead Studio Suites
$45
1221 N. Watson Road
I-30, Hwy. 360 Exit • 817.633.7588
137 Units, pets OK ($75). Laundry facility. Data ports. Rooms come with microwaves, refrigerators, phones and cable TV. AAA discount. Credit cards: AE, DC, DS, MC, V.

Motel 6
$38-50
2626 E. Randol Mill Rd. • 817.649.0147
121 Units, pets OK. Pool. Laundry facility. Data ports. Rooms come with phones, A/C and cable TV. Wheelchair accessible. Credit cards: AE, CB, DC, DS, MC, V.

Park Inn Limited
$38-40
703 Benge Drive • 817.860.2323
58 Units, pets OK ($10 dep. req.). Continental breakfast. Rooms come with phones, A/C and cable TV. AAA/Senior discount. Major credit cards.

ATHENS
Motel 6
$35-40
205 Dallas Hwy. • 903.675.7511
70 Units, pets OK. Pool. Data ports. Rooms come with phones, A/C and cable TV. Wheelchair accessible. Credit cards: AE, CB, DC, DS, MC, V.

ATLANTA
The Butler's Inn
$39
1100 W. Main Street • 903.796.8235
58 Units, pets OK. Continental breakfast. Pool. Rooms come with phones, refrigerators and cable TV. AAA discount. Credit cards: AE, CB, DC, DS, MC, V.

AUSTIN — *see also Round Rock*
Homestyle Inn
$28-35
9220 N. IH-35 • 512.837.7372
150 Units, no pets. Restaurant on premises. Pool. Rooms come with phones and cable TV. Major credit cards.

Motel 6—Central
$40-46
8010 N. Interstate 35 • 512.837.9890
112 Units, pets OK. Pool. Data ports. Rooms come with phones, A/C and cable TV. Wheelchair accessible. Credit cards: AE, CB, DC, DS, MC, V.

Motel 6—South
$38-50*
2707 Interregional Hwy. S. • 512.444.5882
109 Units, pets OK. Restaurant on premises. Pool. Rooms come with phones, A/C and cable TV. Wheelchair accessible. Credit cards: AE, CB, DC, DS, MC, V.
*Higher rate effective weekends mid-February through mid-May.

Motel 6—North
$40-48
9420 N. Interstate 35 (Exit 241)
512.339.6161
158 Units, pets OK. Pool. Laundry facility. Data ports. Rooms come with phones, A/C and cable TV. Wheelchair accessible. Credit cards: AE, CB, DC, DS, MC, V.

Red Roof Inn
$39-54
8210 N. IH-35 • I-35, Exit 241
512.835.2700
143 Units, pets OK. Pool. Meeting rooms. Data ports. Rooms come with phones and cable TV. AAA discount. Major credit cards.

BASTROP
Bastrop Inn Motel
$48
102 Childers Drive • 512.321.3949
32 Units, no pets. Pool. Laundry facility.

Rooms come with phones and cable TV. Some rooms have microwaves and refrigerators. AAA/Senior discount. Major credit cards.

BAY CITY
Cattlemen's Motel & Restaurant
$45-55
905 Avenue "F" • 979.245.1127 or 800.551.6056
90 Units, pets OK. Restaurant on premises. Pool. Rooms come with phones and cable TV. Major credit cards.

Econo Lodge
$39-55
3712 7th Street • 979.245.5115
57 Units, pets OK. Continental breakfast. Pool. Laundry facility. Rooms come with phones and cable TV. Major credit cards.

BAYTOWN
Motel 6
$33-34
8911 Hwy. 146 • 281.576.5777
124 Units, pets OK. Pool. Rooms come with phones, A/C and cable TV. Wheelchair accessible. Credit cards: AE, CB, DC, DS, MC, V.

BEAUMONT — *see also Nederland*
Interstate Inn
$30-50
1295 N. 11th Street • 409.892.6537
120 Units, pets OK. Pool. Rooms come with A/C, phones and cable TV. Wheelchair accessible. Major credit cards.

Motel 6
$38-41
1155 I-10 South • 409.835.5913
93 Units, pets OK. Pool. Laundry facility. Rooms come with phones, A/C and cable TV. Wheelchair accessible. Credit cards: AE, CB, DC, DS, MC, V.

Super 8 Motel
$39-46
2850 I-10E (Exit 853B) • 409.899.3040
80 Units, no pets. Continental breakfast. Data ports. Rooms come with phones and cable TV. Some rooms have refrigerators. Wheelchair accessible. AAA/Senior discount. Credit cards: AE, CB, DC, DS, MC, V.

BEDFORD
Super 8 Motel
$45-55
1800 Airport Frwy. • 817.545.8845
113 Units, pets OK. Continental breakfast. Rooms come with phones and cable TV. Wheelchair accessible. Major credit cards.

BEEVILLE
Beeville Executive Inn
$40
1601 N. St. Marys St. • 361.358.0022
72 Units, no pets. Continental breakfast. Pool. Meeting rooms. Laundry facility. Rooms come with phones and cable TV. Wheelchair accessible. Major credit cards.

BELLMEAD
Motel 6
$36-40
1509 Hogan Lane • 254.799.4957
112 Units, pets OK. Pool. Laundry facility. Data ports. Rooms come with phones, A/C and cable TV. Wheelchair accessible. Credit cards: AE, CB, DC, DS, MC, V.

BELTON
Budget Host Inn
$39
1520 I-35S • 254.939.0744
50 Units, pets OK. Pool. Rooms come with phones and cable TV. Some rooms have microwaves and refrigerators. Wheelchair accessible. AAA/Senior discount. Credit cards: AE, DS, MC, V.

BENBROOK
Motel 6
$42-45
8601 Hwy 377S • I-20/I-820, Exit 429A
817.249.8885
63 Units, pets OK. Pool. Laundry facility. Data ports. Rooms come with phones, A/C and cable TV. Wheelchair accessible. Credit cards: AE, CB, DC, DS, MC, V.

BIG BEND NATIONAL PARK — *see Alpine and Terlingua*

BIG SPRING
Days Inn
$45-55
2701 S. Gregg Street • 432.267.5237
33 Units, pets OK. Restaurant on premises. Pool. Rooms come with phones and cable TV. Wheelchair accessible. AAA discount. Credit cards: AE, CB, DC, DS, MC, V.

Great Western Inn
$40-45
2900 I-20E (Exit 179) • 432.267.4553
64 Units, pets OK ($50 dep. req.). Continental breakfast. Pool. Meeting rooms. Data ports. Rooms come with phones, A/C and cable TV. Some rooms have refrigerators. AAA/Senior discount. Major credit cards.

Motel 6
$32
600 I-20W (Exit 177) • 432.267.1695
92 Units, pets OK. Pool. Laundry facility. Data ports. Rooms come with phones, A/C and cable TV. Wheelchair accessible. Credit cards: AE, CB, DC, DS, MC, V.

BONHAM
Days Inn
$42-50*
1515 Old Ector Road • 903.583.3121
53 Units, pets OK. Continental breakfast. Pool. Meeting rooms. Rooms come with phones and cable TV. Some rooms have refrigerators. Senior discount. Major credit cards.
*AAA discounted rates.

BORGER
Nendels Inn
$30-50
100 Bulldog Blvd. • 806.273.9556
89 Units, pets OK. Laundry facility. Meeting rooms. Rooms come with phones and cable TV. Some rooms have microwaves and refrigerators. Senior discount. Major credit cards.

BOWIE
Days Inn
$45-50
Jct. Hwys. 287 and 59 • 940.872.5426
60 Units, pets OK ($5). Continental breakfast. Pool. Data ports. Rooms come with phones, A/C and cable TV. Some rooms have refrigerators. AAA/Senior discount. Major credit cards.

Park's Inn
$30-45
708 W. Wise Street • 940.872.1111
40 Units, pets OK ($5). Pool. Rooms come with phones and cable TV. Some rooms have microwaves and refrigerators. AAA/Senior discount. Credit cards: AE, DS, MC, V.

BRADY
Days Inn
$36-50
2108 S. Bridge • 915.597.0789
44 Units, pets OK. Continental breakfast. Pool. Laundry facility. Data ports. Rooms come with refrigerators, phones and cable TV. AAA/Senior discount. Credit cards: AE, DC, DS, MC, V.

BROWNSVILLE
Motel 6
$34-42
2255 N. Expressway • 956.546.4699
190 Units, pets OK. Pool. Laundry facility. Data ports. Rooms come with phones, A/C and cable TV. Wheelchair accessible. Credit cards: AE, CB, DC, DS, MC, V.

Red Roof Inn
$50
2377 N. Expressway 83 • 956.504.2300
124 Units, no pets. Laundry facility. Rooms come with phones and cable TV. Some rooms have microwaves and refrigerators. AAA discount. Major credit cards.

Super 8 Motel
$40
55 E. Sam Perl Blvd. • 956.546.0381
100 Units, no pets. Continental breakfast. Pool. Meeting rooms. Rooms come with phones and cable TV. Some rooms have microwaves and refrigerators. Senior discount. Major credit cards.

BROWNWOOD
Days Inn
$44-49
515 E. Commerce St. • 325.646.2551
137 Units, pets OK ($15). Restaurant on premises. Heated pool. Laundry facility. Fitness facility. Jacuzzi. Meeting rooms. Airport transportation provided. Rooms come with phones, A/C and cable TV. Some rooms have microwaves and refrigerators. Senior discount. Major credit cards.

CANADIAN
Canadian Motel and Restaurant
$35
502 N. 2nd Street • 806.323.6402
64 Units, pets OK. Restaurant on premises. Pool in summer. Rooms come with phones and cable TV. Major credit cards.

CARROLLTON
Red Roof Inn—Carrollton
$31-49
1720 S. Broadway • I-35, Exit 442
972.245.1700
137 Units, pets OK. Meeting rooms. Rooms come with phones and cable TV. AAA discount. Credit cards: AE, CB, DC, DS, MC, V.

CHANNELVIEW
Best Value Budget Inn
$50
15545 I-10E • 281.457.3000
31 Units, no pets. Continental breakfast. Rooms come with phones, A/C and cable TV. Some rooms have microwaves and refrigerators. AAA/Senior discount. Major credit cards.

Best Western Houston East
$42 (65-80)*
15919 I-10E • 281.452.1000
98 Units, pets OK ($20 dep. req.). Restaurant on premises. Pool. Rooms come with phones and cable TV. AAA/Senior discount. Credit cards: AE, CB, DC, DS, MC, V.
*Higher rates effective mid-March through mid-April.

CHILDRESS
Econo Lodge
$35-52*
1612 Avenue "F" N.W. (US 287)
940.937.3695
28 Units, pets OK ($5). Restaurant on premises. Pool. Rooms come with phones and cable TV. Senior discount. Major credit cards.
*AAA discounted rates.

CLEBURNE
American Inn
$45-50
1836 N. Main Street • 817.641.3451
39 Units, pets OK ($30 dep. req.). Pool. Data ports. Rooms come with phones and cable TV. Some rooms have microwaves and refrigerators. AAA/Senior discount. Credit cards: AE, DS, MC, V.

CLUTE
Motel 6
$35-37
1000 SR 332 • 979.265.4764
76 Units, pets OK. Pool. Laundry facility. Data ports. Rooms come with phones, A/C and cable TV. Wheelchair accessible. Credit cards: AE, CB, DC, DS, MC, V.

COLDSPRING
San Jacinto Inn
$36-42
936.653.3008 • 1.5 miles W on SR 150
13 Units, pets OK. Pool. Rooms come with phones and TV. Credit cards: AE, CB, DC, DS, MC, V.

COLLEGE STATION
E-Z Travel Motor Inn
$36
2007 S. Texas Avenue • 979.693.5822
71 Units, pets OK ($15). Pool. Rooms come with phones and cable TV. Major credit cards.

Motel 6
$38-44
2327 S. Texas Avenue • 979.696.3379
110 Units, pets OK. Pool. Laundry facility. Rooms come with phones, A/C and cable TV. Wheelchair accessible. Credit cards: AE, CB, DC, DS, MC, V.

COLORADO CITY
Days Inn
$40-43
I-20, Exit 216 • 325.728.2638
52 Units, no pets. Continental breakfast. Pool. Rooms come with phones and cable TV. Wheelchair accessible. AAA discount. Major credit cards.

Villa Inn
$34
2310 Hickory Street • 325.728.5217
40 Units, pets OK ($4). Continental breakfast. Pool. Rooms come with phones and cable TV. AAA/Senior discount. Credit cards: AE, DC, DS, MC, V.

COLUMBUS
Columbus Inn
$40-45
2208 Hwy. 71 • 979.732.5723
72 Units, pets OK ($10). Laundry facility. Rooms come with phones and cable TV. Major credit cards.

CONROE
Days Inn
$40-55
900 1-45S (Exit 85) • 936.756.7771
75 Units, no pets. Continental breakfast.

Pool. Laundry facility. Rooms come with phones, A/C and cable TV. AAA discount. Major credit cards.

Motel 6
$34-40
820 I-45S • 936.760.4003
123 Units, pets OK. Pool. Laundry facility. Rooms come with phones, A/C and cable TV. Wheelchair accessible. Credit cards: AE, CB, DC, DS, MC, V.

CONWAY
Budget Host S&S Motor Inn
$35-45
806.537.5111 • Three-tenths of a mile south from junction of I-40 and SR 207.
24 Units, pets OK. Rooms come with phones and cable TV. AAA/Senior discount. Credit cards: AE, DS, MC, V.

CORPUS CHRISTI
Days Inn
$40-50
901 Navigation Blvd. • 361.888.8599
121 Units, pets OK ($10). Pool. Laundry facility. Playground. Data ports. Rooms come with phones and cable TV. Some rooms have microwaves and refrigerators. AAA/Senior discount. Major credit cards.

Motel 6
$37-54
8202 S. Padre Island Dr • 361.991.8858
126 Units, pets OK. Pool. Laundry facility. Data ports. Rooms come with phones, A/C and cable TV. Wheelchair accessible. Credit cards: AE, CB, DC, DS, MC, V.

Motel 6
$33-40
845 Lantana Street • I-37, Exit 4B
361.289.9397
124 Units, pets OK. Pool. Laundry facility. Data ports. Rooms come with phones, A/C and cable TV. Wheelchair accessible. Credit cards: AE, CB, DC, DS, MC, V.

Red Roof Inn
$36-53
6805 S. Padre Island Drive • 361.992.9222
121 Units, pets OK. Continental breakfast. Pool. Jacuzzi. Laundry facility. Rooms come with phones, A/C and cable TV. AAA/ Senior discount. Major credit cards.

CUERO
Sands Motel and RV Park
$35
2117 N. Esplanade • 361.275.3437
34 Units, pets OK. Restaurant on premises. Pool. Playground. Rooms come with phones and cable TV. Wheelchair accessible. Credit cards: AE, CB, DC, DS, MC, V.

DALHART
Econo Lodge
$40-50
123 Liberal Street • 806.249.6464
46 Units, pets OK ($20 dep. req.). Rooms come with phones and cable TV. AAA/Senior discount. Credit cards: AE, DS, MC, V.

Western Skies Motor Inn
$30-36
623 Denver Avenue • 806.249.4538
48 Units, pets OK ($20 dep. req.). Restaurant on premises. Heated pool. Rooms come with phones and cable TV. Credit cards: AE, CB, DC, DS, JCB, MC, V.

DALLAS — *see also Arlington, Desoto, Duncanville, Euless, Farmers Branch, Garland, Grand Prairie, Irving, Lewisville, Mesquite and Plano*
Delux Inn Express & Suites
$40
2144 California Crossing • 972.373.9555
38 Units, no pets. Laundry facility. Rooms come with phones, A/C and cable TV. Some rooms have microwaves and refrigerators. Senior discount. Major credit cards.

Motel 6
$36-42
2660 Forest Lane • I-635, Exit 26
972.484.9111
117 Units, pets OK. Pool. Laundry facility. Rooms come with phones, A/C and cable TV. Wheelchair accessible. Credit cards: AE, CB, DC, DS, MC, V.

Motel 6
$34-40
2753 Forest Lane • I-635, Exit 26
972.620.2828
100 Units, pets OK. Pool. Laundry facility. Data ports. Rooms come with phones, A/C and cable TV. Wheelchair accessible. Credit cards: AE, CB, DC, DS, MC, V.

Motel 6
$40-50
8108 E. R.L. Thornton Fwy.
I-30, Exit 51 • 214.388.8741
109 Units, pets OK. Rooms come with phones, A/C and cable TV. Wheelchair accessible. Credit cards: AE, CB, DC, DS, MC, V.

Motel 6
$33-40
4220 Independence Dr • 972.296.3331
129 Units, pets OK. Pool. Laundry facility. Data ports. Rooms come with phones, A/C and cable TV. Wheelchair accessible. Credit cards: AE, CB, DC, DS, MC, V.

Red Roof Inn—Dallas Market Center
$40-60
1550 Empire Central Dr • 214.638.3920
111 Units, pets OK. Rooms come with phones and cable TV. AAA discount. Credit cards: AE, CB, DC, DS, MC, V.

Red Roof Inn—Northwest
$35-49
10335 Gardner Road • 972.506.8100
112 Units, pets OK. Rooms come with phones and cable TV. AAA discount. Credit cards: AE, CB, DC, DS, MC, V.

DECATUR
Motel 6
$40-52
1600 South US 81/287 • 940.627.0250
56 Units, pets OK. Pool. Rooms come with phones, A/C and cable TV. Wheelchair accessible. Credit cards: AE, CB, DC, DS, MC, V.

DEL RIO
Days Inn
$47*
3808 Avenue "F" • 830.775.0585 or 800.682.0555
85 Units, pets OK. Continental breakfast. Pool. Jacuzzi. Laundry facility. Rooms come with phones and cable TV. Wheelchair accessible. AAA/Senior discount. Major credit cards.
*Rates higher during special events.

Economy Inn
$29-33
3811 Hwy. 90W • 830.775.7414
41 Units, no pets. Pool. Laundry facility. Rooms come with phones and cable TV. Credit cards: AE, CB, DC, DS, JCB, MC, V.

Motel 6
$30-38
2115 Avenue "F" • 830.774.2115
122 Units, pets OK. Pool. Laundry facility. Data ports. Rooms come with phones, A/C and cable TV. Wheelchair accessible. Credit cards: AE, CB, DC, DS, MC, V.

DENISON
Motel 6
$40-42
615 N. Hwy. 75 • 903.465.4446
60 Units, pets OK. Pool. Laundry facility. Rooms come with phones, A/C and cable TV. Wheelchair accessible. Credit cards: AE, CB, DC, DS, MC, V.

DENTON
Exel Inn of Denton
$36-54
4211 I-35E North • 940.383.1471
114 Units, pets OK. Continental breakfast. Pool. Laundry facility. Meeting rooms. Rooms come with phones and cable TV. AAA/Senior discount. Credit cards: AE, CB, DC, DS, MC, V.

Motel 6
$37-46
4125 Interstate 35N • 940.566.4798
85 Units, pets OK. Pool. Laundry facility. Data ports. Rooms come with phones, A/C and cable TV. Wheelchair accessible. Credit cards: AE, CB, DC, DS, MC, V.

DESOTO
Red Roof Inn
$44-52
1401 N. Beckley • I-35, Exit 416
972.224.7100
108 Units, pets OK. Meeting rooms. Rooms come with phones and cable TV. AAA discount. Major credit cards.

DUMAS
Econo Lodge
$35-50
1719 S. Dumas • 806.935.9098
41 Units, pets OK ($3). Continental breakfast. Heated pool. Jacuzzi. Laundry facility. Rooms come with phones and cable TV. Some rooms have microwaves and refrigerators. AAA/Senior discount. Credit cards: AE, CB, DC, DS, JCB, MC, V.

DUNCANVILLE
Motel 6
$36-48
202 Jellison Road • I-20, Exit 462A
972.296.0345
76 Units, pets OK. Pool. Laundry facility. Data ports. Rooms come with phones, A/C and cable TV. Wheelchair accessible. Credit cards: AE, CB, DC, DS, MC, V.

EAGLE PASS
Super 8 Motel
$41-48*
2150 N. Hwy. 277 • 830.773.9531
56 Units, pets OK. Restaurant on premises. Pool. Meeting rooms. Rooms come with phones and cable TV. Wheelchair accessible. AAA discount. Major credit cards.
*AAA discounted rates.

EASTLAND
Budget Host Inn
$35-37
2001 I-20W • 254.629.3324
46 Units, pets OK. Continental breakfast. Pool. Game room. Rooms come with phones and cable TV. Some rooms have refrigerators. AAA/Senior discount. Credit cards: AE, DC, DS, MC, V.

Super 8 Motel & RV Park
$49
3900 I-20E • 254.629.3336
30 Units, pets OK ($2). Pool. Data ports. Rooms come with phones and cable TV. Some rooms have microwaves and refrigerators. AAA/Senior discount. Credit cards: AE, CB, DC, DS, JCB, MC, V.

EL PASO
Americana Inn
$37
14387 Gateway W. • 915.852.3025
50 Units, pets OK ($10). Pool. Laundry facility. Rooms come with phones and cable TV. AAA discount. Credit cards: AE, CB, DC, DS, MC, V.

Executive Inn
$35
500 Executive Ctr. Blvd. • 915.532.8981
99 Units, no pets. Restaurant on premises. Heated pool. Laundry facility. Rooms come with phones and cable TV. Some rooms have refrigerators. Credit cards: AE, CB, DC, DS, MC, V.

Motel 6
$36-40
4800 Gateway Blvd. E. • 915.533.7521
200 Units, pets OK. Restaurant on premises. Pool. Laundry facility. Data ports. Rooms come with phones, A/C and cable TV. Wheelchair accessible. Credit cards: AE, CB, DC, DS, MC, V.

Motel 6
$35-43
1330 Lomaland Drive • 915.592.6386
121 Units, pets OK. Pool. Data ports. Rooms come with phones, A/C and cable TV. Wheelchair accessible. Credit cards: AE, CB, DC, DS, MC, V.

Travelodge
$36-46
7815 N. Mesa Street • 915.833.2613
127 Units, pets OK ($25 dep. req.). Heated pool. Laundry facility. Jacuzzi. Data ports. Rooms come with phones and cable TV. Some rooms have refrigerators. AAA/Senior discount. Major credit cards.

EULESS
Motel 6
$36
110 W. Airport Freeway • 817.545.0141
120 Units, pets OK. Pool. Data ports. Rooms come with phones, A/C and cable TV. Wheelchair accessible. Credit cards: AE, CB, DC, DS, MC, V.

FAIRFIELD
Sam's Motel Inc.
$47
I-45 & US Hwy. 84 • 903.389.2172
72 Units, no pets. Rooms come with phones and cable TV. Credit cards: AE, DS, MC, V.

FALFURRIAS
Falfurrias Executive Inn
$45
On US 281 • 361.325.5661
24 Units, no pets. Pool. Rooms come with phones and cable TV. Wheelchair accessible. Major credit cards.

FARMERS BRANCH
Econo Lodge
$38-42
2275 Valley View Lane • 972.243.5500
108 Units, pets OK. Laundry facility. Rooms come with phones and cable TV. Some rooms have microwaves and refrigerators. Major credit cards.

FORT HANCOCK
Fort Hancock Motel
$39
I-10, Exit 72 • 915.769.3981
27 Units, pets OK. Heated pool. Laundry facility. Rooms come with phones and cable TV. Some rooms have refrigerators. AAA discount. Major credit cards.

FORT STOCKTON
Econo Lodge
$40-50
800 E. Dickinson Blvd. • 432.336.9711
86 Units, pets OK ($8). Continental breakfast. Pool. Laundry facility. Rooms come with phones and cable TV. Some rooms have microwaves and refrigerators. AAA/Senior discount. Major credit cards.

Motel 6
$32-34
3001 W. Dickinson Blvd • 432.336.9737
139 Units, pets OK. Pool. Laundry facility. Data ports. Rooms come with phones, A/C and cable TV. Wheelchair accessible. Credit cards: AE, CB, DC, DS, MC, V.

FORT WORTH — *see also Bedford*
Days Inn
$32-49
8500 I-30 & Las Vegas Trail
817.246.4961
121 Units, pets OK. Continental breakfast. Pool. Meeting rooms. Rooms come with phones and cable TV. AAA discount. Major credit cards.

Motel 6—East
$40
1236 Oakland Blvd. • I-30, Exit 18
817.834.7361
96 Units, pets OK. Restaurant on premises. Pool. Data ports. Rooms come with phones, A/C and cable TV. Wheelchair accessible. Credit cards: AE, CB, DC, DS, MC, V.

Motel 6—North
$36-40
3271 Interstate 35W • I-35, Exit 54B
817.625.4359
106 Units, pets OK. Pool. Data ports. Rooms come with phones, A/C and cable TV. Wheelchair accessible. Credit cards: AE, CB, DC, DS, MC, V.

Motel 6
$36-40
7804 Bedford Euless Road
I-820, Exit 22A • 817.485.3000
84 Units, pets OK. Pool. Data ports. Rooms come with phones, A/C and cable TV. Wheelchair accessible. Credit cards: AE, CB, DC, DS, MC, V.

Motel 6—South
$36-40
6600 S. Freeway • I-35W, Exit 44
817.293.8595
148 Units, pets OK. Pool. Laundry facility. Data ports. Rooms come with phones, A/C and cable TV. Wheelchair accessible. Credit cards: AE, CB, DC, DS, MC, V.

Motel 6—West
$34-40
8701 Interstate 30W • I-30, Exit 6
817.244.9740
118 Units, pets OK. Restaurant on premises. Pool. Data ports. Rooms come with phones, A/C and cable TV. Wheelchair accessible. Credit cards: AE, CB, DC, DS, MC, V.

FREDERICKSBURG
Sunset Inn
$47-55
900 S. Adams Street • 830.997.9581
26 Units, pets OK. Restaurant on premises. Laundry facility. Rooms come with phones and cable TV. AAA discount. Major credit cards.

GAINESVILLE
Best Western Southwinds Motel
$45
2103 N I-35 • 940.665.7737
35 Units, pets OK. Continental breakfast. Pool. Rooms come with phones and cable TV. Some rooms have microwaves and refrigerators. Senior discount. Credit cards: AE, CB, DC, DS, JCB, MC, V.

Budget Host Inn
$36-40
From I-35, Exit 499 • 940.665.2856
24 Units, pets OK. Rooms come with phones and cable TV. AAA/Senior discount. Credit cards: AE, DC, DS, MC, V.

GALVESTON
Motel 6
$36-48 (54-56)*
7404 Avenue "J" Broadway • 409.740.3794
114 Units, pets OK. Pool. Laundry facility. Rooms come with phones, A/C and cable TV. Wheelchair accessible. Credit cards: AE, CB, DC, DS, MC, V.

*Higher rate weekends Memorial Day through Labor Day.

GARLAND
Days Inn
$47
6222 Belt Line Road • 972.226.7621
120 Units, pets OK ($10). Continental breakfast. Pool. Rooms come with phones and cable TV. AAA/Senior discount. Major credit cards.

Motel 6
$34-44
436 I-30W & Beltline Rd • 972.226.7140
110 Units, pets OK. Pool. Laundry facility. Data ports. Rooms come with phones, A/C and cable TV. Wheelchair accessible. Credit cards: AE, CB, DC, DS, MC, V.

GATESVILLE
Regency Motor Inn
$45-50*
2307 Main Street • 254.865.8405
30 Units, no pets. Pool. Jacuzzi. Data ports. Rooms come with phones and cable TV. Senior discount. Credit cards: AE, CB, DC, DS, MC, V.
*AAA discounted rates.

GIDDINGS
Giddings Sands Motel
$37
1600 Hwy. 290E • 979.542.3111
51 Units, pets OK. Continental breakfast. Pool. Jacuzzi. Airport transportation. Laundry facility. Rooms come with phones and cable TV. Some rooms have refrigerators. AAA discount. Credit cards: AE, CB, DC, DS, MC, V.

Ramada Limited
$45-54
On US 290, 2.5 miles east from town
979.542.9666
60 Units, pets OK. Pool. Rooms come with phones and cable TV. AAA/Senior discount. Credit cards: AE, CB, DC, DS, MC, V.

GRAHAM
Gateway Inn
$41
1401 Hwy. 165 • 940.549.0222
77 Units, pets OK. Restaurant on premises. Pool. Rooms come with phones and cable TV. Wheelchair accessible. Major credit cards.

GRAND PRAIRIE
Motel 6
$34-46
406 E. Safari Blvd. • 972.642.9424
119 Units, pets OK. Pool. Laundry facility. Data ports. Rooms come with phones, A/C and cable TV. Wheelchair accessible. Credit cards: AE, CB, DC, DS, MC, V.

GREENVILLE
Motel 6
$34
5109 Interstate 30 • 903.455.0515
94 Units, pets OK. Pool. Laundry facility. Rooms come with phones, A/C and cable TV. Wheelchair accessible. Credit cards: AE, CB, DC, DS, MC, V.

American Inn
$30-34
5000 I-30 • 903.455.9600
60 Units, pets OK. Full breakfast offered. Pool. Wading pool. Rooms come with phones and cable TV. Credit cards: AE, CB, DC, DS, MC, V.

GROESBECK
Limestone Inn
$40
300 S. Ellis Street • 254.729.3017
110 Units, pets OK. Pool. Meeting rooms. Rooms come with phones, A/C and cable TV. Some rooms have kitchenettes. Wheelchair accessible. Major credit cards.

GROVES
Motel 6
$36
5201 E. Parkway • 409.962.6611
124 Units, pets OK. Pool. Laundry facility. Data ports. Rooms come with phones, A/C and cable TV. Wheelchair accessible. Credit cards: AE, CB, DC, DS, MC, V.

HAMILTON
Western Inn
$35-45
1208 S. Rice Street • 254.386.3141
25 Units, pets OK ($20 dep. req.). Pool. Rooms come with phones and cable TV. Some rooms have microwaves and refrigerators. Senior discount. Major credit cards.

HARLINGEN
Motel 6
$40-44

205 N. Expressway 77 • 956.423.9292
61 Units, pets OK. Pool. Laundry facility. Rooms come with phones, A/C and cable TV. Wheelchair accessible. Credit cards: AE, CB, DC, DS, MC, V.

Scottish Inns & Suites
$35-50
1800 W. Harrison • 956.425.1212
87 Units, pets OK ($6). Pool. Meeting rooms available. Rooms come with phones and cable TV. Wheelchair accessible. Major credit cards.

HEREFORD
Best Western Red Carpet Inn
$47-51
830 W. First Street • 806.364.0540
90 Units, pets OK. Continental breakfast. Pool. Rooms come with phones and cable TV. AAA/Senior discount. Major credit cards.

HILLSBORO
Motel 6
$43
1506 Hillview Drive • I-35, Exit 368A
254.580.9000
45 Units, pets OK ($10). Pool. Rooms come with phones, A/C and cable TV. Wheelchair accessible. Credit cards: AE, CB, DC, DS, MC, V.

HONDO
Whitetail Lodge
$45
US 90 at Jct. Hwy. 173 • 830.426.3031
52 Units, pets OK ($10). Continental breakfast. Pool. Rooms come with phones and cable TV. AAA/Senior discount. Major credit cards.

HOUSTON — *see also Baytown, Channelview, Conroe, Humble, Katy, Richmond, Spring and Webster*
Days Inn
$39
9430 S. Main Street • 713.668.0691 or 800.323.4550
51 Units, no pets. Restaurant on premises. Fitness facility. Rooms come with A/C, phones and cable TV. AAA discount. Major credit cards.

Days Inn—North
$42-51
9025 N. Freeway • 281.820.1500
100 Units, pets OK ($20 dep. req.). Continental breakfast. Pool. Laundry facility. Rooms come with phones and cable TV. Some rooms have microwaves and refrigerators. AAA/Senior discount. Major credit cards.

Econo Lodge
$47-49
6630 Hoover Street • US 290, Exit Bingle Road • 713.956.2828
32 Units, no pets. Continental breakfast. Data ports. Rooms come with phones and cable TV. Some rooms have microwaves and refrigerators. AAA/Senior discount. Major credit cards.

Interstate Motor Lodge
$40
13213 I-10E (Exit 780) • 713.453.6353
76 Units, pets OK ($20 dep. req.). Restaurant on premises. Laundry facility. Rooms come with phones and cable TV. AAA discount. Credit cards: AE, DS, MC, V.

Motel 6
$38-50
3223 S. Loop W. • 713.664.6425
111 Units, pets OK. Pool. Laundry facility. Rooms come with phones, A/C and cable TV. Wheelchair accessible. Credit cards: AE, CB, DC, DS, MC, V.

Motel 6—Northwest
$40-45
5555 W. 34th Street • I-610, US 290W to 34th Street • 713.682.8588
118 Units, pets OK. Pool. Laundry facility. Rooms come with phones, A/C and cable TV. Wheelchair accessible. Credit cards: AE, CB, DC, DS, MC, V.

Motel 6—Hobby Airport
$38-44
8800 Airport Blvd. (I-45, Exit 36)
713.941.0990
124 Units, pets OK. Pool. Laundry facility. Rooms come with phones, A/C and cable TV. Wheelchair accessible. Credit cards: AE, CB, DC, DS, MC, V.

Motel 6—Southwest
$38
9638 Plainfield Road • US 59, Bissonnett Road Exit • 713.778.0008
205 Units, pets OK. Pool. Laundry facility. Rooms come with phones, A/C and cable TV.

Wheelchair accessible. Credit cards: AE, CB, DC, DS, MC, V.

Super 8 Motel
$34-40
4045 North Freeway • 713.691.6671
168 Units, no pets. Pool. Rooms come with phones and cable TV. Senior discount. Credit cards: AE, CB, DC, DS, MC, V.

HUMBLE
Budget Host Inn
$50
7815 N. Sam Houston Pkwy. E.
281.441.9800
29 Units, no pets. Rooms come with microwaves, refrigerators, phones and cable TV. Some rooms have jacuzzis. Senior discount. Credit cards: AE, DS, MC, V.

HUNTSVILLE
Econo Lodge
$39-50
112 N. IH-45 • 936.295.6401
57 Units, pets OK ($10 dep. req.). Continental breakfast. Pool. Rooms come with phones and cable TV. Senior discount. Credit cards: AE, CB, DC, DS, MC, V.

Motel 6
$30-40
122 I-45 • 936.291.6927
122 Units, pets OK. Restaurant on premises. Pool. Laundry facility. Rooms come with phones, A/C and cable TV. Wheelchair accessible. Credit cards: AE, CB, DC, DS, MC, V.

IRVING
Microtel Inn & Suites
$45-55
3232 W. Irving Blvd.
SR 183, Exit S. Belt Lane • 972.986.8700
47 Units, no pets. Continental breakfast. Data ports. Rooms come with phones, A/C and cable TV. Wheelchair accessible. AAA/Senior discount. Major credit cards.

Motel 6
$36-40
510 S. Loop 12 • 972.438.4227
76 Units, pets OK. Laundry facility. Data ports. Rooms come with phones, A/C and cable TV. Wheelchair accessible. Credit cards: AE, CB, DC, DS, MC, V.

Motel 6—Airport
$38-46
7800 Heathrow Drive • 972.915.3993
120 Units, pets OK. Pool. Laundry facility. Airport transportation. Data ports. Rooms come with phones, A/C and cable TV. Wheelchair accessible. Credit cards: AE, CB, DC, DS, MC, V.

Red Roof Inn/DFW Airport North
$41-55
8150 Esters Blvd. • SR 114, Exit Esters Blvd. • 972.929.0020
156 Units, pets OK. Laundry facility. Airport transportation. Meeting rooms. Data ports. Rooms come with phones, A/C and cable TV. Some rooms have microwaves and refrigerators. AAA discount. Major credit cards.

JACKSBORO
Jacksboro Inn
$34-42
704 S. Main Street • 940.567.3751
49 Units, pets OK. Pool. Rooms come with phones and cable TV. Some rooms have refrigerators. AAA discount. Senior discount. Credit cards: AE, CB, DC, DS, MC, V.

JASPER
Chateau Inn
$34-42
612 W. Gibson • 409.384.2511
72 Units, no pets. Restaurant on premises. Pool. Rooms come with phones and cable TV. Wheelchair accessible. Senior discount. Credit cards: AE, DS, MC, V.

Days Inn
$34-43
1730 S. Wheeler • 409.384.6816
31 Units, pets OK. Continental breakfast. Pool. Rooms come with phones and cable TV. AAA discount. Major credit cards.

JUNCTION
The Hills Motel
$32-34
1520 Main Street • 325.446.2567
27 Units, pets OK. Restaurant on premises. Pool. Rooms come with phones and cable TV. Some rooms have refrigerators. Senior discount. Major credit cards.

Legends Inn Motel
$35-38
1908 N. Main Street • 325.443.8444
30 Units, pets OK. Heated pool. Rooms come with phones and cable TV. Some rooms have refrigerators. AAA discount. Credit cards: AE, CB, DC, DS, MC, V.

KATY
Motel 6
$38-40
14833 Katy Fwy. (I-10, Exit 751)
281.497.5000
135 Units, pets OK. Restaurant on premises. Pool. Laundry facility. Rooms come with phones, A/C and cable TV. Wheelchair accessible. Credit cards: AE, CB, DC, DS, MC, V.

Super 8 Motel
$50
22157 Katy Fwy. (I-10, Exit 743)
281.395.5757
30 Units, pets OK. Continental breakfast. Rooms come with phones and cable TV. Senior discount. Major credit cards.

KENEDY
Days Inn
$35-50
453 N. Sunset Strip • 830.583.2521
30 Units, pets OK. Rooms come with phones and cable TV. Some rooms have refrigerators. AAA discount. Major credit cards.

KERRVILLE
Budget Inn
$40-55
1804 Sidney Baker St. • 830.896.8200
45 Units, pets OK. Restaurant on premises. Continental breakfast. Pool. Laundry facility. Rooms come with phones and cable TV. AAA/Senior discount. Credit cards: AE, CB, DC, DS, MC, V.

Sands Motel
$35-45
1145 Junction Hwy. • 830.896.5000
28 Units, no pets. Continental breakfast. Pool. Playground. Rooms come with refrigerators, phones and cable TV. Credit cards: AE, CB, DC, DS, MC, V.

KILLEEN
Rodeway Inn
$40-50
517 W. Veterans Mem. Bl. • 254.634.1001
42 Units, no pets. Continental breakfast. Rooms come with phones and cable TV. Wheelchair accessible. Major credit cards.

Super 8 Motel
$43-50
606 E. Central Texas Expwy.
254.634.6868
40 Units, no pets. Continental breakfast. Pool. Rooms come with phones and cable TV. Some rooms have kitchenettes. Senior discount. Major credit cards.

KILGORE
Days Inn
$45-50
3505 Hwy. 259N • I-20, Exit 589
903.983.2975
49 Units, no pets. Continental breakfast. Data ports. Rooms come with phones and cable TV. Some rooms have microwaves and refrigerators. AAA/Senior discount. Major credit cards.

KINGSVILLE
Howard Johnson
$47-53
105 US 77 • 361.592.6471
86 Units, pets OK. Continental breakfast. Pool. Laundry facility. Rooms come with phones and cable TV. AAA discount. Major credit cards.

Motel 6
$34-35
101 N. US 77 • 361.592.5106
86 Units, pets OK. Pool. Laundry facility. Data ports. Rooms come with phones, A/C and cable TV. Wheelchair accessible. Credit cards: AE, CB, DC, DS, MC, V.

LAKE JACKSON
Super 8 Motel
$50
915 Hwy. 332 • 979.297.3031
109 Units, pets OK ($5). Continental breakfast. Wading pool. Laundry facility. Rooms come with phones and cable TV. Some rooms have microwaves and refrigerators. AAA/Senior discount. Major credit cards.

LAMESA
Budget Host Inn
$30-32
901 S. Dallas Avenue • 806.872.2118
30 Units, pets OK. Pool. Laundry facility.

Rooms come with phones and cable TV. AAA/Senior discount. Credit cards: AE, DS, MC, V.

Shiloh Inn
$37-42
1707 Lubbock Hwy. • 806.872.6721
50 Units, pets OK. Pool. Rooms come with phones and cable TV. AAA discount. Credit cards: AE, DS, MC, V.

LAREDO
Gateway Inn
$37
4910 San Bernardo • 956.722.5272
142 Units, no pets. Restaurant on premises. Pool. Meeting room. Rooms come with phones and cable TV. Major credit cards.

Motel 6
$42-45
5310 San Bernardo Avenue (I-35, Exit 3B)
956.725.8187
94 Units, pets OK. Pool. Laundry facility. Data ports. Rooms come with phones, A/C and cable TV. Wheelchair accessible. Credit cards: AE, CB, DC, DS, MC, V.

LEWISVILLE
Microtel Inns & Suites
$45
881 S. Stemmons Fwy. • I-35E, Exit 451
972.434.0447
51 Units, pets OK ($10). Continental breakfast. Data ports. Rooms come with phones and cable TV. Wheelchair accessible. AAA/Senior discount. Major credit cards.

Motel 6
$35-40
1705 Lakepointe Drive • I-35E, Exit 449
972.436.5008
119 Units, pets OK. Pool. Laundry facility. Data ports. Rooms come with phones, A/C and cable TV. Wheelchair accessible. Credit cards: AE, CB, DC, DS, MC, V.

Super 8 Motel
$45
1305 S. Stemmons Fwy. • 972.221.7511
86 Units, pets OK ($5 and $20 dep. req.). Pool. Laundry facility. Fitness facility. Rooms come with phones and cable TV. Senior discount. Major credit cards.

LIVINGSTON
Econo Lodge
$40-45
117 US 59 at Loop S and US 190
936.327.2451
55 Units, no pets. Continental breakfast. Pool. Laundry facility. Rooms come with phones and cable TV. Some rooms have refrigerators. AAA/Senior discount. Credit cards: AE, CB, DC, DS, MC, V.

LLANO
Best Western
$47 (63)*
901 W. Young Street • 325.247.4101
41 Units, pets OK. Continental breakfast. Pool. Rooms come with phones and cable TV. Some rooms have microwaves and refrigerators. AAA/Senior discount. Major credit cards.
*Higher rate effective weekends.

LONGVIEW — *see also Kilgore*
Econo Lodge
$49
3120 Estes Parkway (I-20, Exit 595)
903.753.4884
79 Units, pets OK. Continental breakfast. Laundry facility. Rooms come with phones and cable TV. Some rooms have refrigerators. Major credit cards.

Executive Inn & Suites
$39
1905 E. Marshall Ave. • 903.234.2920
31 Units, no pets. Continental breakfast. Data ports. Rooms come with phones, A/C and cable TV. AAA/Senior discount. Credit cards: AE, DS, MC, V.
*AAA discounted rates.

Motel 6
$34-37
110 W. Access Road • 903.758.5256
78 Units, pets OK. Pool. Laundry facility. Data ports. Rooms come with phones, A/C and cable TV. Wheelchair accessible. Credit cards: AE, CB, DC, DS, MC, V.

LUBBOCK
Days Inn
$40-50
6025 Avenue "A" • 806.745.5111
75 Units, no pets. Restaurant on premises. Indoor heated pool. Rooms come with phones and cable TV. AAA discount. Major credit cards.

Econo Lodge
$39-50
910 Avenue "Q" • 806.765.6307
28 Units, no pets. Continental breakfast. Rooms come with phones and cable TV. Wheelchair accessible. Major credit cards.

Howard Johnson Motel
$35-50
4801 Avenue "Q" • 806.747.1671
58 Units, no pets. Continental breakfast. Data ports. Rooms come with phones and cable TV. AAA/Senior discount. Major credit cards.

Motel 6
$36-42
909 66th Street • 806.745.5541
169 Units, pets OK. Pool. Laundry facility. Data ports. Rooms come with phones, A/C and cable TV. Wheelchair accessible. Credit cards: AE, CB, DC, DS, MC, V.

LUFKIN
Lufkin Inn
$30
308 N. Timberland • 936.634.6626
45 Units, pets OK. Restaurant on premises. Pool. Rooms come with phones and cable TV. Credit cards: AE, DS, MC, V.

Motel 6
$34-38
1110 S. Timberland Dr. • 936.637.7850
107 Units, pets OK. Pool. Laundry facility. Data ports. Rooms come with phones, A/C and cable TV. Wheelchair accessible. Credit cards: AE, CB, DC, DS, MC, V.

MARFA
Holiday Capri Inn
$40-45
On Hwy. 90 (in town) • 432.729.4326
46 Units, pets OK. Pool in summer. Rooms come with phones and cable TV. Major credit cards.

Riata Inn
$40
On Hwy. 90 (east end) • 432.729.3800
30 Units, pets OK ($5). Pool. Data ports. Rooms come with phones and cable TV. Major credit cards.

MARLIN
Relax Inn
$34-44
Hwy. G Bypass • 254.883.2581
62 Units, pets OK. Restaurant on premises. Pool. Rooms come with phones and cable TV. Wheelchair accessible. Major credit cards.

MARSHALL
Motel 6
$34-40
300 I-20E • 903.935.4393
121 Units, pets OK. Pool. Laundry facility. Data ports. Rooms come with phones, A/C and cable TV. Wheelchair accessible. Credit cards: AE, CB, DC, DS, MC, V.

Super 8 Motel
$45-52
6002 E. End Blvd. S. • 903.935.1184
40 Units, pets OK ($5). Continental breakfast. Pool. Rooms come with phones and cable TV. Some rooms have microwaves and refrigerators. Credit cards: AE, DC, DS, MC, V.

McALLEN
Deluxe Inn—Airport
$35-55
3201 S. 10th Street • 956.682.3111
50 Units, pets OK. Pool. Rooms come with phones and cable TV. Major credit cards.

Motel 6
$40-43
700 W. Expressway 83 • 956.687.3700
93 Units, pets OK. Pool. Laundry facility. Rooms come with phones, A/C and cable TV. Wheelchair accessible. Credit cards: AE, CB, DC, DS, MC, V.

McKINNEY
Motel 6
$40-43
2125 White Avenue • US 75, Exit 40B
972.542.8600
58 Units, pets OK. Laundry facility. Rooms come with phones, A/C and cable TV. Wheelchair accessible. Credit cards: AE, CB, DC, DS, MC, V.

McKinney Inn
$35
1431 N. Tennessee St. • 972.542.4469
38 Units, pets OK. Pool. Rooms come with phones and cable TV. AAA discount. Credit cards: AE, CB, DC, DS, MC, V.

MEMPHIS
Executive Inn
$45-50
Hwy. 287N • 806.259.3583
37 Units, pets OK. Restaurant on premises. Pool. Rooms come with phones and cable TV. AAA/Senior discount. Major credit cards.

MESQUITE
Microtel Inn & Suites
$45-50
317 U.S. 80E • 972.216.4418
40 Units, no pets. Continental breakfast. Meeting rooms. Rooms come with phones and cable TV. Wheelchair accessible. AAA/Senior discount. Credit cards: AE, DS, MC, V.

Super 8 Motel
$44-55
121 Grand Junction • 972.289.5481
118 Units, no pets. Continental breakfast. Heated pool. Laundry facility. Rooms come with phones and cable TV. AAA/Senior discount. Major credit cards.

MIDLAND
Motel 6
$29
1000 S. Midkiff Road • 432.697.3197
87 Units, pets OK. Pool. Rooms come with phones, A/C and cable TV. Wheelchair accessible. Credit cards: AE, CB, DC, DS, MC, V.

Super 8 Motel
$41-51*
1000 I-20W • 432.684.8888
55 Units, pets OK. Continental breakfast. Pool. Copy and fax service. Rooms come with phones and cable TV. Wheelchair accessible. AAA/Senior discount. Credit cards: AE, CB, DC, DS, MC, V.
*Rates may increase slightly during special events.

MINERAL WELLS
Budget Host Mesa Motel
$40
3601 E. Hwy. 180 • 940.325.3377
40 Units, pets OK. Pool. Playground. Picnic and playground area. Laundry facility. Rooms come with phones and cable TV. Senior discount. Credit cards: AE, CB, DC, DS, MC, V.

MONAHANS
Best Western Colonial Inn
$42-52
702 W. I-20 • 432.943.4345
90 Units, pets OK. Restaurant on premises. Pool. Laundry facility. Data ports. Rooms come with phones and cable TV. AAA/Senior discount. Major credit cards.

MOUNT PLEASANT
Super 8 Motel
$45-55
204 Lakewood Drive • 903.572.9808
65 Units, pets OK ($5). Continental breakfast. Pool. Rooms come with phones and cable TV. AAA/Senior discount. Credit cards: AE, DC, DS, MC, V.

MOUNT VERNON
Super 8 Motel
$45-55
I-30, Exit 146 or 147 • 903.588.2882
44 Units, pets OK ($5). Continental breakfast. Picnic area. Data ports. Rooms come with phones and cable TV. Wheelchair accessible. AAA/Senior discount. Major credit cards.

NACOGDOCHES
Best Western Inn of Nacogdoches
$45-50*
3428 South Street • 936.560.4900
60 Units, no pets. Continental breakfast. Pool. Laundry facility. Data ports. Rooms come with phones and cable TV. AAA/Senior discount. Major credit cards.
*AAA discounted rates.

Victorian Inn & Suites
$41-50
3612 North Street • 936.560.6038 or 800.935.0676
41 Units, pets OK. Pool. Rooms come with phones and cable TV. Wheelchair accessible. Major credit cards.

NEW BOSTON
Best Western Inn of New Boston
$49
1024 N. Center • 903.628.6999
49 Units, pets OK ($20 dep. req.). Pool. Laundry facility. Meeting rooms. Rooms come with phones and cable TV. AAA/Senior discount. Major credit cards.

ODEM
Days Inn
$45
1505 Voss Ave. (US 77) • 361.368.2166
24 Units, pets OK. Continental breakfast. Pool. Jacuzzi. Rooms come with phones and cable TV. Some rooms have refrigerators. AAA discount. Credit cards: AE, CB, DC, DS, MC, V.

ODESSA
Deluxe Inn
$32
1518 S. Grant • 432.333.1486
38 Units, pets OK ($20 dep. req.). Continental breakfast. Rooms come with phones and cable TV. Some rooms have refrigerators and microwaves. Senior discount. Credit cards: AE, DC, DS, MC, V.

Executive Inn
$38
2505 E. Business 20 • 432.333.1528
44 Units, no pets. Rooms come with phones and cable TV. Credit cards: AE, CB, DC, DS, MC, V.

Motel 6
$32
200 I-20E Service Road • 432.333.4025
125 Units, pets OK. Pool. Laundry facility. Data ports. Rooms come with phones, A/C and cable TV. Wheelchair accessible. Credit cards: AE, CB, DC, DS, MC, V.

Parkway Inn
$30-34
3071 E. Hwy. 80 • 432.332.4224 or 800.926.6760
84 Units, no pets. Continental breakfast. Pool. Rooms come with phones and cable TV. Credit cards: AE, CB, DC, DS, MC, V.

ORANGE
Days Inn
$35-50
2900 IH-10W • 409.883.9981
80 Units, pets OK. Pool. Laundry facility. Data ports. Rooms come with phones and cable TV. Wheelchair accessible. AAA discount. Major credit cards.

Motel 6
$36
4407 27th Street • 409.883.4891
126 Units, pets OK. Pool. Laundry facility. Data ports. Rooms come with phones, A/C and cable TV. Wheelchair accessible. Credit cards: AE, CB, DC, DS, MC, V.

OZONA
Best Value Inn
$39-45
820 11th Street (Loop 466W)
325.392.2631
24 Units, pets OK. Laundry facility. Rooms come with phones and cable TV. AAA/Senior discount. Major credit cards.

Hillcrest Motor Inn/Thrift Inn
$28-37
On US 290W • I-10, Exit 363
325.392.5515
32 Units, pets OK. Restaurant on premises. Continental breakfast. Laundry facility. Rooms come with phones and cable TV. Senior discount. Major credit cards.

PALESTINE
Best Western Palestine Inn
$45-50
1601 W. Palestine Ave. • 903.723.4655
66 Units, pets OK. Restaurant on premises. Continental breakfast. Pool. Laundry facility. Airport transportation. Meeting rooms. Rooms come with phones and cable TV. AAA/Senior discount. Major credit cards.

Super 8 Motel
$50
2300 W. Oak Street • 903.731.9495
50 Units, no pets. Continental breakfast. Pool. Spa. Meeting rooms. Rooms come with phones and cable TV. Wheelchair accessible. Major credit cards.

PANHANDLE — *see Conway*

PARIS
Best Western Inn of Paris
$48-50
3755 N.E. Loop 286 • 903.785.5566
80 Units, pets OK. Laundry facility. Jacuzzi. Data ports. Rooms come with phones and cable TV. AAA/Senior discount. Credit cards: AE, CB, DC, DS, JCB, MC, V.

Victorian Inns
$44-50
425 N.E. 35th at Loop 286N • 903.785.3871 or 800.935.0863
40 Units, pets OK. Rooms come with phones and cable TV. Wheelchair accessible. Major credit cards.

PASADENA
Great Western Inn
$36-40
4709 Spencer Hwy. • 281.998.8888
85 Units, no pets. Pool. Rooms come with phones and cable TV. Major credit cards.

PEARSALL
Budget Inn
$35
Jct. of I-35 and FM 140 (Exit 101) • 830.334.9466
42 Units, no pets. Restaurant on premises. Rooms come with phones and cable TV. Credit cards: AE, DS, MC, V.

Executive Inn
$36-42
613 North Oak • 830.334.3693
19 Units, pets OK ($5). Rooms come with microwaves, refrigerators, phones and cable TV. Some rooms have kitchens. AAA/Senior discount. Credit cards: AE, CB, DC, DS, MC, V.

PECOS
Motel 6
$32
3002 S. Cedar Street • 432.445.9034
96 Units, pets OK. Pool. Laundry facility. Rooms come with phones, A/C and cable TV. Wheelchair accessible. Credit cards: AE, CB, DC, DS, MC, V.

PLAINVIEW
Days Inn
$42-50
3600 Olton Road • 806.293.2561
49 Units, pets OK. Continental breakfast. Pool. Laundry facility. Rooms come with phones and cable TV. AAA discount. Major credit cards.

PLANO
Motel 6
$38-40
2550 N. Central Expwy. • 972.578.1626
118 Units, pets OK. Pool. Laundry facility. Data ports. Rooms come with phones, A/C and cable TV. Wheelchair accessible. Credit cards: AE, CB, DC, DS, MC, V.

Red Roof Inn
$38-59
301 Ruisseau Drive • 972.881.8191
123 Units, pets OK. Rooms come with phones and cable TV. Some rooms have microwaves and refrigerators. Wheelchair accessible. AAA discount. Major credit cards.

PLEASANTON
Super 8 Motel
$50
1913 W. Oaklawn • 830.569.5587
47 Units, pets OK. Continental breakfast. Pool. Rooms come with phones and cable TV. Senior discount. Major credit cards.

PORT ARANSAS
Tropic Island Motel
$50*
303 Cutoff Road • 361.749.6128
38 Units, pets OK. Pool. Laundry facility. Rooms come with phones and cable TV. Some rooms have kitchenettes. Major credit cards.
*Rates higher during spring break.

PORT ISABEL
Budget Host Inn
$32-49*
1411 Hwy. 100 • 956.943.7866
58 Units, no pets. Pool. Jacuzzi. Rooms come with phones and cable TV. Senior discount. Credit cards: AE, DS, MC, V.
*Rates as high as $300/night during spring break.

QUANAH
Casa Royale Inn
$47
1500 W. 11th Street • 940.663.6341
40 Units, no pets. Spa. Rooms come with phones and cable TV. Major credit cards.

RANGER
Days Inn
$50
I-20, Exit 349 • 254.647.1176
30 Units, pets OK. Continental breakfast. Pool. Rooms come with phones and cable TV. Wheelchair accessible. AAA discount. Major credit cards.

REFUGIO
Inns of Texas
$40
920 Victoria Hwy. • 361.526.5351
44 Units, no pets. Continental breakfast. Pool. Rooms come with phones and cable TV. Wheelchair accessible. Credit cards: AE, CB, DC, DS, MC, V.

RICHMOND
Executive Inn
$40
26035 Southwest Freeway (US 59)
281.342.5387
50 Units, pets OK ($5). Continental breakfast. Pool. Meeting rooms. Laundry facility. Rooms come with phones and cable TV. Credit cards: AE, DS, MC, V.

ROBSTOWN
Days Inn
$45-55
320 Hwy. 77S • 361.387.9416
24 Units, pets OK ($2). Pool. Jacuzzi. Rooms come with phones and cable TV. Some rooms have refrigerators. Credit cards: AE, CB, DC, DS, MC, V.

ROCKPORT
Sea View Motel
$35-45
1155 Hwy. 35N • 361.729.9112
23 Units, pets OK. Pool. Rooms come with phones and cable TV. Wheelchair accessible. Major credit cards.

ROUND ROCK
Red Roof Inn
$40-55
1990 I-35 N (I-35, Exit 254)
512.310.1111
107 Units, pets OK. Pool. Laundry facility. Rooms come with phones and cable TV. AAA/Senior discount. Major credit cards.

SALADO
Super 8 Motel
$50*
290 N. Robertson Road • 254.947.5000
42 Units, no pets. Continental breakfast. Pool. Data ports. Rooms come with phones and cable TV. Some rooms have microwaves and refrigerators. AAA/Senior discount. Major credit cards.
*Weekends add $10.

SAN ANGELO
Days Inn
$45-55
4613 S. Jackson • 325.658.6594
113 Units, pets OK. Continental breakfast. Pool. Meeting rooms. Rooms come with phones and cable TV. AAA/Senior discount. Major credit cards.

Motel 6
$32-40
311 N. Bryant • 325.658.8061
98 Units, pets OK. Pool. Laundry facility. Data ports. Rooms come with phones, A/C and cable TV. Wheelchair accessible. Credit cards: AE, CB, DC, DS, MC, V.

SAN ANTONIO
Motel 6—East
$30-46
138 N. WW White Road • I-10, Exit 580
210.333.1850
101 Units, pets OK. Pool. Laundry facility. Data ports. Rooms come with phones, A/C and cable TV. Wheelchair accessible. Credit cards: AE, CB, DC, DS, MC, V.

Motel 6—Northeast
$30-46
4621 E. Rittiman Road • I-410/I-35, Rittman Rd. Exit • 210.653.8088
112 Units, pets OK. Pool. Rooms come with phones, A/C and cable TV. Wheelchair accessible. Credit cards: AE, CB, DC, DS, MC, V.

Motel 6
$30-46
5522 N. Pan Am Expressway • I-410/I-35, Rittman Rd. Exit • 210.661.8791
156 Units, pets OK. Pool. Laundry facility. Data ports. Rooms come with phones, A/C and cable TV. Wheelchair accessible. Credit cards: AE, CB, DC, DS, MC, V.

Motel 6—North
$30-46
9503 Interstate Hwy. 35N • I-35, Exit 167B
210.650.4419
113 Units, pets OK. Pool. Laundry facility. Data ports. Rooms come with phones, A/C and cable TV. Wheelchair accessible. Credit cards: AE, CB, DC, DS, MC, V.

Motel 6—West
$36-50 (57)*
2185 S.W. Loop 410 • 210.673.9020
122 Units, pets OK. Pool. Laundry facility. Data ports. Rooms come with phones, A/C and cable TV. Wheelchair accessible. Credit cards: AE, CB, DC, DS, MC, V.
*Higher rate effective summer weekends.

Red Roof Inn
$35-55
6861 Hwy. 90W • 210.675.4120

157 Units, no pets. Pool. Laundry facility. Data ports. Rooms come with phones and cable TV. Some rooms have refrigerators. AAA/Senior discount. Major credit cards.

Super 8 Motel—Downtown
$35-50*
3617 N. Pan Am Expwy • 210.227.8888
62 Units, pets OK (not in summer). Pool. Copy and fax service. Rooms come with phones and cable TV. Wheelchair accessible. AAA/Senior discount. Credit cards: AE, CB, DC, DS, MC, V.
*Rates may increase slightly during special events, holidays and weekends.

SAN AUGUSTINE
San Augustine Inn
$34-45
1009 Hwy. 21W • 936.275.3452
57 Units, pets OK. Restaurant on premises. Pool. Rooms come with phones and cable TV. Wheelchair accessible. Major credit cards.

SAN BENITO
Days Inn
$40-50
1451 W. Expwy. 83 & 77 • 956.399.3891
31 Units, no pets. Continental breakfast. Pool. Rooms come with phones and cable TV. Wheelchair accessible. AAA discount. Major credit cards.

SAN MARCOS
Econo Lodge
$40-50
811 S. Guadalupe St. • 512.353.5300
57 Units, no pets. Continental breakfast. Pool. Rooms come with phones, A/C and cable TV. Some rooms have microwaves and refrigerators. AAA discount. Major credit cards.

Motel 6
$34-50
1321 I-35N • 512.396.8705
126 Units, pets OK. Pool. Laundry facility. Rooms come with phones, A/C and cable TV. Wheelchair accessible. Credit cards: AE, CB, DC, DS, MC, V.

SCHULENBERG
Oakridge Motor Inn
$48
I-10 and Hwy. 77 • 979.743.4192
71 Units, pets OK. Restaurant on premises. Pool. Rooms come with phones and cable TV. Wheelchair accessible. Major credit cards.

SEALY
Rodeway Inn
$35-50
2021 SR 36 South • 979.885.7407
50 Units, pets OK. Continental breakfast. Pool. Rooms come with phones and cable TV. Wheelchair accessible. Major credit cards.

SEMINOLE
Raymond Motor Inn
$37-40
301 W. Avenue "A" • 432.758.3653
37 Units, pets OK ($5). Rooms come with refrigerators, phones and cable TV. Some rooms have microwaves. AAA/Senior discount. Credit cards: AE, DS, MC, V.

Seminole Inn
$36-39
2200 Hobbs Hwy. • 432.758.9881
40 Units, pets OK ($5). Pool. Rooms come with phones and cable TV. Some rooms have microwaves and refrigerators. AAA discount. Credit cards: AE, DS, MC, V.

SHAMROCK
Budget Host Blarney Inn
$25-29
402 E. 12th Street • 806.256.2101
20 Units, pets OK. Continental breakfast. Pool. Playground. Rooms come with phones and cable TV. Senior discount. Credit cards: AE, DS, MC, V.

Econo Lodge
$40-50
1006 E. 12th Street • 806.256.2111
78 Units, pets OK. Restaurant on premises. Continental breakfast. Pool. Meeting rooms. Rooms come with phones and cable TV. AAA/Senior discount. Major credit cards.

SHERMAN
Days Inn
$40-50
1831 Texoma Pkwy. • 903.892.0433
86 Units, pets OK. Restaurant on premises. Pool. Fitness facility. Rooms come with phones and cable TV. AAA discount. Credit cards: AE, CB, DC, DS, MC, V.

Super 8 Motel
$40-46
111 E. Hwy. 1417 • 903.868.9325
47 Units, no pets. Rooms come with phones and cable TV. Wheelchair accessible. Senior discount. Credit cards: AE, CB, DC, DS, MC, V.

SNYDER
Days Inn
$42-54
800 E. Coliseum Drive • 325.573.1166
56 Units, no pets. Restaurant on premises. Pool. Data ports. Rooms come with phones and cable TV. Some rooms have microwaves and refrigerators. AAA/Senior discount. Credit cards: AE, DC, DS, MC, V.

Purple Sage Motel
$46-56
1501 E. Coliseum Drive • 325.573.5491 or 800.545.5792
45 Units, pets OK. Continental breakfast. Pool. Rooms come with phones and cable TV. Wheelchair accessible. AAA/Senior discount. Major credit cards.

SONORA
Days Inn Devil's River Motel
$40-50
I-10 & Golf Course Road (Exit 400)
325.387.3516
99 Units, pets OK ($2). Restaurant on premises. Continental breakfast. Laundry facility. Data ports. Rooms come with phones and cable TV. AAA/Senior discount. Credit cards: AE, DC, DS, MC, V.

Twin Oaks Motel
$35-40
907 Crockett Avenue • 325.387.2551
53 Units, pets OK. Rooms come with phones and cable TV. AAA discount. Credit cards: AE, CB, DC, DS, MC, V.

SOUTH PADRE ISLAND
Motel 6
$36-50 (56-70)*
4013 Padre Blvd. • 956.761.7911
52 Units, pets OK. Pool. Laundry facility. Rooms come with phones, A/C and cable TV. Wheelchair accessible. Credit cards: AE, CB, DC, DS, MC, V.
*Higher rates effective late January through early April and then again Memorial Day through Labor Day.

SPRING
Budget Host Spring Lodge
$36
20543 I-45 N • 281.353.3547
86 Units, no pets. Continental breakfast. Pool. Laundry facility. Meeting rooms. Rooms come with phones, A/C and cable TV. Wheelchair accessible. Senior discount. Credit cards: AE, DS, MC, V.

Motel 6
$40
19606 Cypresswood Ct. • 281.350.6400
108 Units, pets OK. Pool. Laundry facility. Rooms come with phones, A/C and cable TV. Wheelchair accessible. Credit cards: AE, CB, DC, DS, MC, V.

SURFSIDE BEACH
Anchor Motel
$30-40
1302 Bluewater Hwy. • 979.239.3543
32 Units, pets OK. Laundry facility. Rooms come with phones and cable TV. Wheelchair accessible. Credit cards: AE, CB, DC, DS, JCB, MC, V.

SWEETWATER
Motel 6
$29
510 N.W. Georgia St. • 325.235.4387
121 Units, pets OK. Pool. Laundry facility. Rooms come with phones, A/C and cable TV. Wheelchair accessible. Credit cards: AE, CB, DC, DS, MC, V.

Ranch House Motel
$39-54
301 S.W. Georgia St. • 325.236.6341
49 Units, pets OK. Restaurant on premises. Continental breakfast. Pool. Wading pool. Rooms come with phones and cable TV. Senior discount. Credit cards: AE, DC, DS, MC, V.

TAYLOR
Regency Inn
$49
2007 N. Main • 512.352.2666
25 Units, pets OK ($50 dep. req.). Data ports. Rooms come with phones and cable TV. Some rooms have microwaves and refrigerators. AAA/Senior discount. Major credit cards.

TEMPLE
Howard Johnson Lodge
$44
1912 S. 31st Street • 254.778.5521
48 Units, pets OK. Continental breakfast. Laundry facility. Rooms come with phones and cable TV. Some rooms have refrigerators. AAA discount. Major credit cards.

Motel 6
$30-38
1100 N. General Bruce Dr • 254.778.0272
95 Units, pets OK. Restaurant on premises. Pool. Data ports. Rooms come with phones, A/C and cable TV. Wheelchair accessible. Credit cards: AE, CB, DC, DS, MC, V.

TERLINGUA
Chisos Mining Co. Motel
$35-55
Hwy. 170 (one mile from Hwy. 188 junction) • 432.371.2254
28 Units, pets OK. Rooms come with phones and cable TV. Some rooms have kitchenettes. Credit cards: AE, DS, MC, V.

TERRELL
Best Inn
$36-55
309 IH-20E • I-20, Exit 501
972.563.2676
60 Units, pets OK ($5). Continental breakfast. Pool. Laundry facility. Data ports. Rooms come with phones and cable TV. AAA/Senior discount. Major credit cards.

Motel 6
$40-43
101 Mira Place (I-20, Exit 501)
972.524.6066
49 Units, pets OK. Pool. Rooms come with phones, A/C and cable TV. Wheelchair accessible. Credit cards: AE, CB, DC, DS, MC, V.

TEXARKANA — *see also Texarkana (AR)*
Econo Lodge
$34-40
4505 N. State Line Ave. • 903.793.5546
54 Units, no pets. Jacuzzi. Rooms come with phones and cable TV. Wheelchair accessible. Credit cards: AE, CB, DC, DS, MC, V.

Motel 6
$33-38
1924 Hampton Road • 903.793.1413
100 Units, pets OK. Pool. Laundry facility. Data ports. Rooms come with phones, A/C and cable TV. Wheelchair accessible. Credit cards: AE, CB, DC, DS, MC, V.

THE WOODLANDS
Red Roof Inn
$42
24903 I-45N • 281.367.5040
85 Units, pets OK. Pool. Rooms come with phones and cable TV. Major credit cards.

TYLER
Econo Lodge
$40
3209 W. Gentry Pkwy. • 903.593.0103
50 Units, no pets. Pool. Rooms come with phones and cable TV. Senior discount. Major credit cards.

Motel 6
$30-37
3236 Brady Gentry Pkwy • 903.595.6691
103 Units, pets OK. Restaurant on premises. Pool. Laundry facility. Data ports. Rooms come with phones, A/C and cable TV. Wheelchair accessible. Credit cards: AE, CB, DC, DS, MC, V.

UVALDE
Amber Sky Motel
$31
2005 E. Main Street • 830.278.5602
40 Units, pets OK. Rooms come with phones and TV. Some rooms have refrigerators and microwaves. Major credit cards.

VAN HORN
Days Inn
$41-55
600 E. Broadway • 432.283.1007
59 Units, pets OK ($8-10). Restaurant on premises. Continental breakfast. Pool. Rooms come with phones and cable TV. Some rooms have microwaves and refrigerators. AAA/Senior discount. Credit cards: AE, DS, MC, V.

Motel 6
$39
1805 W. Broadway • 432.283.2992
40 Units, pets OK. Pool. Rooms come with phones and cable TV. Senior discount.

Wheelchair accessible. Credit cards: AE, DC, DS, MC, V.

Super 8 Motel
$40-42
I-10 & Golf Course Rd. • 432.283.2282
41 Units, pets OK. Continental breakfast. Rooms come with phones and cable TV. Wheelchair accessible. AAA/Senior discount. Credit cards: AE, CB, DC, DS, MC, V.

VERNON
Greentree Inn
$45-49
3029 Morton Street • 940.552.5421
30 Units, pets OK. Continental breakfast. Pool. Data ports. Rooms come with phones and cable TV. AAA/Senior discount. Major credit cards.

Super 8 Motel
$40-44
1829 Exp. Hwy. 287 • 940.552.9321
34 Units, no pets. Rooms come with phones and cable TV. AAA/Senior discount. Credit cards: AE, CB, DC, DS, MC, V.

VICTORIA
Days Inn
$45-49
2605 Houston Hwy. • 361.578.9911
104 Units, no pets. Continental breakfast. Pool. Laundry facility. Rooms come with phones and cable TV. AAA/Senior discount. Major credit cards.

Motel 6
$34-40
3716 Houston Hwy. • 361.573.1273
80 Units, pets OK. Pool. Laundry facility. Rooms come with phones, A/C and cable TV. Wheelchair accessible. Credit cards: AE, CB, DC, DS, MC, V.

WACO
Knights Inn
$39-49
1510 I-35N • 254.799.0244
53 Units, pets OK. Pool in summer. Rooms come with phones and cable TV. Senior discount. Major credit cards.

Motel 6
$38-44
3120 Jack Kultgen Fwy • 254.662.4622
110 Units, pets OK. Pool. Laundry facility. Data ports. Rooms come with phones, A/C and cable TV. Wheelchair accessible. Credit cards: AE, CB, DC, DS, MC, V.

WAXAHACHIE
Ramada Limited
$40-50
792 S. I-35E (Exit 401A) • 972.937.4982
90 Units, pets OK ($25 dep. req.). Continental breakfast. Meeting rooms. Jacuzzi. Laundry facility. Rooms come with phones and cable TV. AAA/Senior discount. Major credit cards.

WEATHERFORD
Super 8 Motel
$37-40*
111 I-20W • 817.594.8702
80 Units, pets OK ($5). Continental breakfast. Pool. Laundry facility. Rooms come with phones and cable TV. Senior discount. Major credit cards.
*Rates may increase slightly during special events and holidays.

WEBSTER
Motel 6
$38-48
1001 W. NASA Road 1 (I-45, Exit 25)
281.332.4581
122 Units, pets OK. Pool. Laundry facility. Rooms come with phones, A/C and cable TV. Wheelchair accessible. Credit cards: AE, CB, DC, DS, MC, V.

WESLACO
Deluxe Inn & Suites
$35-50
601 N. Westgate Dr. • 956.968.0606 or 800.804.9957
50 Units, pets OK. Restaurant on premises. Pool. Rooms come with phones and cable TV. Some rooms have refrigerators and microwaves. Wheelchair accessible. Major credit cards.

WICHITA FALLS
Best Western Towne Crest Inn
$37-47
1601 8th Street • 940.322.1182
42 Units, pets OK. Rooms come with phones and cable TV. AAA/Senior discount. Credit cards: AE, CB, DC, DS, JCB, MC, V.

Motel 6
$34-46
1812 Maurine Street • 940.322.8817
82 Units, pets OK. Pool. Laundry facility.

Data ports. Rooms come with phones, A/C and cable TV. Wheelchair accessible. Credit cards: AE, CB, DC, DS, MC, V.

YOAKUM
Budget Host La Mancha Inn
$45
606 S. US 77A • 361.293.5211
48 Units, pets OK. Restaurant on premises. Pool. Laundry facility. Meeting rooms. Rooms come with phones and cable TV. Major credit cards.

ZAPATA
Executive Inn
$42
On US 83S • 956.765.6982
24 Units, no pets. Pool. Rooms come with phones and cable TV. Wheelchair accessible. Major credit cards.

utah

ARCHES NATIONAL PARK — *see Green River and Moab*

BEAVER
Country Inn
$33-38
1450 N. 300 W. • 435.438.2484
37 Units, pets OK. Gas station on premises. Rooms come with phones and cable TV. AAA discount. Credit cards: AE, CB, DC, DS, MC, V.

Motel 6
$34-50
1345 N. 450 West • I-15, Exit 112
435.438.1666
42 Units, pets OK. Restaurant on premises. Indoor pool. Laundry facility. Data ports. Rooms come with phones, A/C and cable TV. Wheelchair accessible. Credit cards: AE, CB, DC, DS, MC, V.

Super 8 Motel
$48-53
626 W. 1400 N. • 435.438.3888
50 Units, no pets. Continental breakfast. Rooms come with phones and cable TV. Senior discount. Major credit cards.

BICKNELL
Aquarius Inn
$25-42
240 W. Main Street • 435.425.3835
27 Units, pets OK ($5 and $25 dep. req.). Laundry facility. Restaurant open 6 a.m. to 10 p.m. Rooms come with phones and cable TV. Credit cards: AE, CB, DC, DS, MC, V.

BLANDING
Four Corners Inn
$36-45
131 E. Center Street • 435.678.3257
32 Units, pets OK ($5). Continental breakfast. Rooms come with phones and cable TV. Some rooms have microwaves and refrigerators. AAA discount. Credit cards: AE, DS, MC. V.

Prospector Motor Lodge
$30-40
591 S. Main Street • 435.678.3231
19 Units, no pets. Rooms come with phones and cable TV. Some rooms have A/C, kitchens and refrigerators. AAA discount. Credit cards: AE, DS, MC, V.

BLUFF
Kokopelli Inn
$48*
On Hwy. 191 • 435.762.2322 or 800.541.8854
26 Units, pets OK. Rooms come with phones, A/C and cable TV. AAA discount. Major credit cards.
*Closed in winter.

Recapture Lodge
$34-50
202 E. Main Street • 435.672.2281
28 Units, pets OK. Laundry facility. Rooms come with A/C and cable TV. No phones in rooms. Some rooms have kitchenettes, microwaves and refrigerators. AAA discount. Major credit cards.

BRIGHAM CITY
Galaxie Motel
$29-35
740 S. Main Street • 435.723.3439
29 Units, no pets. Restaurant on premises. Rooms come with phones and TV. Some rooms have kitchenettes. Major credit cards.

BRYCE CANYON NATIONAL PARK — *see Panguitch*

CEDAR CITY
Motel 6
$37-49
1620 West 200 N • I-15, Exit 59
435.586.9200
79 Units, pets OK. Laundry facility. Rooms come with phones, A/C and cable TV. Wheelchair accessible. Credit cards: AE, CB, DC, DS, MC, V.

Valu-Inn
$25-40*
344 S. Main Street • 435.586.9114
29 Units, pets OK ($10). Rooms come with phones and cable TV. Some rooms have refrigerators. Senior discount. Credit cards:

AE, CB, DC, DS, MC, V.
*Rates $30-40 April through September.

Zion Inn
$35 (45)*
222 S. Main Street • 435.586.9487
24 Units, no pets. Rooms come with phones and cable TV. Credit cards: AE, CB, DC, DS, MC, V.
*Summer weekend rates.

CLEARFIELD
Super 8 Motel
$43-55
572 N. Main Street • 801.825.8000
58 Units, pets OK ($20 dep. req.). Rooms come with phones and cable TV. Some rooms have microwaves and refrigerators. Senior discount. Major credit cards.

DELTA
Budget Motel
$25-30
75 South 350 E. • 435.864.4533
29 Units, pets OK. Rooms come with phones and cable TV. Some rooms have kitchens and refrigerators. Senior discount. Credit cards: AE, DS, MC, V.

ESCALANTE
Moqui Motel & RV Park
$25-35*
480 W. Main Street • 435.826.4210
10 Units, no pets. Rooms come with TV. Some rooms have kitchenettes. Major credit cards.
*Closed mid-December through January 5.

FILLMORE
Fillmore Motel
$33
61 N. Main Street • 435.743.5454
20 Units, pets OK. Rooms come with phones and cable TV. Some rooms have microwaves and refrigerators. AAA discount. Credit cards: AE, DS, MC, V.

GREEN RIVER
Green River Inn
$30
456 W. Main Street • 435.564.8237
30 Units, pets OK. Rooms come with phones and cable TV. Wheelchair accessible. Major credit cards.

Motel 6
$30-50
846 E. Main Street • 435.564.3436
103 Units, pets OK. Pool. Laundry facility. Rooms come with phones, A/C and cable TV. Wheelchair accessible. Credit cards: AE, CB, DC, DS, MC, V.

HANKSVILLE
Best Value Inn
$40-45
264 East 100 North • 435.542.3471
22 Units, pets OK. Restaurant on premises. Pool. Meeting room. Rooms come with cable TV. No phones in rooms. Major credit cards.

HATCH
Riverside Motel
$38-45
594 US 89 • 435.735.4223
13 Units, pets OK ($50 dep. req.). Playground and recreation room. Restaurant on premises. Laundry facility. Rooms come with cable TV. No phones in rooms. AAA discount. Credit cards: DS, MC, V.

HEBER CITY
Hylander Motel
$45
425 S. Main Street • 435.654.2150
22 Units, no pets. Continental breakfast. Pool. Rooms come with microwaves, refrigerators, phones and cable TV. AAA/ Senior discount. Credit cards: AE, DC, DS, MC, V.

HURRICANE
Days Inn
$29-49
40 N. 2600 W. • 435.635.0500
40 Units, no pets. Continental breakfast. Jacuzzi. Rooms come with phones and cable TV. Some rooms have microwaves, jacuzzi and refrigerators. AAA discount. Major credit cards.

Motel 6
$45
650 West State Street • 435.635.4010
53 Units, pets OK. Pool. Laundry facility. Rooms come with phones, A/C and cable TV. Wheelchair accessible. Credit cards: AE, CB, DC, DS, MC, V.

KANAB
Kanab Mission Inn
$37-42*
386 E. 300 South • 435.644.5373
65 Units, pets OK. Rooms come with phones

and TV. AAA discount. Major credit cards. *Closed November through mid-April.

National 9 Aikens Lodge
$38-45
79 W. Center Street • 435.644.2625
32 Units, pets OK ($20 dep. req.). Lodge closed January and February. Pool. Some rooms have A/C, phones and cable TV. Credit cards: AE, CB, DC, DS, MC, V.

LEHI
Days Inn
$40-47
280 North 850 East • I-15, Exit 282
801.768.8322
46 Units, no pets. Continental breakfast. Indoor pool. Spa. Rooms come with phones, A/C and cable TV. Wheelchair accessible. AAA discount. Credit cards: AE, CB, DC, DS, MC, V.

Motel 6
$36
210 S. 1200 E. (I-15, Exit 282)
801.768.2668
112 Units, pets OK. Pool. Laundry facility. Rooms come with phones, A/C and cable TV. Wheelchair accessible. Credit cards: AE, CB, DC, DS, MC, V.

LOGAN
Days Inn
$42-52
364 S. Main Street • 435.753.5623
64 Units, no pets. Continental breakfast. Laundry facility. Rooms come with phones and cable TV. Some rooms have kitchenettes and refrigerators. AAA/Senior discount. Major credit cards.

Super 8 Motel
$40-57
865 S. Hwy 89/91 • 435.753.8883
61 Units, no pets. Continental breakfast. Rooms come with phones and cable TV. Senior discount. Major credit cards.

MEXICAN HAT
Burch's Trading Co. & Motel
$33 (55)*
Hwy. 163 (Main Street) • 435.683.2221
41 Units, pets OK. Restaurant on premises. Rooms come with phones and TV. Major credit cards.
*Summer rates.

MIDVALE
Motel 6
$40
496 N. Catalpa Street • I-15, Exit 301
801.561.0058
128 Units, pets OK. Pool. Laundry facility. Rooms come with phones, A/C and cable TV. Wheelchair accessible. Credit cards: AE, CB, DC, DS, MC, V.

National 9 Discovery Inn
$40-50
380 W. 7200 S. • I-15, Exit 301
801.561.2256
85 Units, pets OK. Continental breakfast. Pool. Laundry facility. Spa. Rooms come with phones, A/C and cable TV. Wheelchair accessible. Credit cards: AE, CB, DC, DS, MC, V.

MOAB
Adventure Inn
$50
512 N. Main • 435.259.6122
22 Units, no pets. Rooms come with phones and cable TV. Credit cards: DS, MC. V.

Inca Inn Motel
$41
570 N. Main Street • 435.259.7261
23 Units, no pets. Rooms come with cable TV. No A/C or phones in rooms. Credit cards: DS, MC, V.

MONTICELLO
Navajo Trail National 9 Inn
$30-42
248 N. Main Street • 435.587.2251
28 Units, no pets. Restaurant on premises. Rooms come with phones and TV. Some rooms have kitchenettes. Major credit cards.

Triangle H Motel
$34-42
164 E. US 666 • 435.587.2274
26 Units, no pets. Rooms come with phones and cable TV. Some rooms have microwaves and refrigerators. AAA/Senior discount. Credit cards: AE, CB, DC, DS, MC, V.

MOUNT CARMEL JUNCTION
Golden Hills Motel
$33-45
125 E. State Street • 435.648.2268
31 Units, pets OK. Pools. Restaurant on premises. Pool. Laundry facility. Rooms

come with phones. Credit cards: AE, DS, MC, V.

NEPHI
Motel 6
$34-50
2195 S. Main Street • 435.623.0666
43 Units, pets OK. Restaurant on premises. Indoor pool. Laundry facility. Rooms come with phones, A/C and cable TV. Wheelchair accessible. Credit cards: AE, CB, DC, DS, MC, V.

Roberta's Cove Motor Inn
$40
2250 S. Main Street • 435.623.2629
43 Units, no pets. Picnic tables. Laundry facility. Rooms come with phones and cable TV. Major credit cards.

Super 8 Motel
$35-55
1901 S. Frontage Road • I-15, Exit 222
435.623.0888
41 Units, no pets. Continental breakfast. Rooms come with phones and cable TV. Wheelchair accessible. Senior discount. Major credit cards.

OGDEN — *see also Sunset*
Motel 6
$36-40
1455 Washington Blvd. • 801.627.4560
70 Units, pets OK. Pool. Laundry facility. Rooms come with phones, A/C and cable TV. Wheelchair accessible. Credit cards: AE, CB, DC, DS, MC, V.

Red Roof Inn
$40
1500 W. Riverdale Rd. • 801.627.2880
110 Units, pets OK. Restaurant on premises. Pool. Laundry facility. Rooms come with phones, A/C and cable TV. Wheelchair accessible. Credit cards: AE, CB, DC, DS, MC, V.

Super 8 Motel
$39
1508 W. 2100 S. • 801.731.7100
60 Units, pets OK with permission (dep. req.). Convenience store and gas station on premises. Copy machine. Laundry facility. Rooms come with phones and cable TV. Wheelchair accessible. Senior discount. Credit cards: AE, CB, DC, DS, MC, V.

PANGUITCH
Bryce Way Motel
$35-45
429 N. Main Street • 435.676.2400
26 Units, no pets. Heated indoor pool. Restaurant on premises (closed November through February). Rooms come with phones and cable TV. Some rooms have refrigerators. Senior discount. Credit cards: AE, DC, DS, MC, V.

Color Country Motel
$35
526 N. Main Street • 435.676.2386
26 Units, pets OK ($4). Pool (open June through September). Rooms come with phones and cable TV. Credit cards: AE, DC, DS, MC, V.

PRICE
Budget Host Inn
$35-39
145 N. Carbonville Rd. • 435.637.2424
33 Units, pets OK ($10). Continental breakfast. Heated pool. Laundry facility. Rooms come with phones and cable TV. Some rooms have microwaves, kitchens and refrigerators. AAA/Senior discount. Credit cards: AE, DS, MC, V.

National 9 Price River Inn
$35-40
641 W. Price River Dr. • 435.637.7000
94 Units, pets OK ($4 and $10 dep. req.). Playground. Rooms come with phones and cable TV. Some rooms have microwaves and refrigerators. Senior discount. Credit cards: AE, DS, MC, V.

PROVO
National 9 Colony Inn Suites
$38-48
1380 S. University Ave. • 801.374.6800
80 Units, pets OK ($4 and $15 deposit require). Pool. Laundry facility. Rooms come with phones and cable TV. AAA/Senior discount. Major credit cards.

Motel 6
$36
1600 S. University Ave. • 801.375.5064
119 Units, pets OK. Pool. Laundry facility. Rooms come with phones, A/C and cable TV. Wheelchair accessible. Credit cards: AE, CB, DC, DS, MC, V.

Travelodge
$38-59
124 S. University Ave. • 801.373.1974
59 Units, no pets. Pool. Rooms come with phones and cable TV. Senior discount. Major credit cards.

RICHFIELD
Budget Host Nights Inn
$30-44
69 S. Main Street • 435.896.8228
50 Units, pets OK. Restaurant on premises. Heated pool. Rooms come with phones, refrigerators, microwaves and cable TV. AAA/Senior discount. Major credit cards.

Romanico Inn
$28-36
1170 S. Main Street • 435.896.8471
29 Units, pets OK ($3). Jacuzzi. Laundry facility. Rooms come with phones and cable TV. Some rooms have microwaves and refrigerators. AAA/Senior discount. Credit cards: AE, DC, DS, MC, V.

ROOSEVELT
Frontier Motel
$44
75 S. 200 E. • 435.722.2201
54 Units, pets OK. Restaurant on premises. Pool. Meeting room. Hot tub. Rooms come with phones and cable TV. Some rooms have kitchenettes. Major credit cards.

ST. GEORGE
Ambassador Inn
$43-53
1481 S. Sunland Drive • 435.673.7900
68 Units, no pets. Continental breakfast. Pool. Rooms come with phones and cable TV. AAA/Senior discount. Major credit cards.

Budget 8 Motel
$39-49
1230 S. Bluff • 435.628.5234
53 Units, no pets. Restaurant on premises. Pool. Hot tub. Rooms come with phones and cable TV. Some rooms have kitchenettes. Wheelchair accessible. Major credit cards.

Budget Inn & Suites
$34-44
1221 S. Main Street • 435.673.6661
77 Units, pets OK. Restaurant on premises. Pool. Hot tub. Rooms come with phones and cable TV. Some rooms have kitchenettes. Wheelchair accessible. Major credit cards.

Motel 6
$30-40
205 N. 1000 E. Street • 435.628.7979
103 Units, pets OK. Pool. Laundry facility. Rooms come with phones, A/C and cable TV. Wheelchair accessible. Credit cards: AE, CB, DC, DS, MC, V.

SALINA
Henry's Hideaway
$30-38
60 N. State Street • 435.529.7467
32 Units, pets OK ($20 dep. req.). Meeting rooms. Pool. Indoor jacuzzi. Laundry facility. Rooms come with phones and cable TV. AAA/Senior discount. Credit cards: AE, DS, MC, V.

SALT LAKE CITY — *see also Lehi, Midvale and Woods Cross*
Travel Advisory: In Salt Lake City you'll have a difficult time finding rooms at or below $50/night, particularly in the summertime. Below are listed a few of the places where you'll find the most reasonably-priced rooms in the Salt Lake City area.

Econo Lodge ($49-65)
715 W. North Temple
801.363.0062

Howard Johnson Express Inn
($49-69)
121 N. 300 West
801.521.3450

Ramada Inn Downtown ($40-60*)
230 W. 600 South
801.364.5200

Super 8 Motel ($50-58)
616 S. 200 West
801.534.0808

***Additional AAA discount.**

Motel 6
$38-46
1990 W. North Temple Street (I-80, Exit 118) • 801.364.1053
104 Units, pets OK. Pool. Laundry facility. Rooms come with phones, A/C and cable TV.

Wheelchair accessible. Credit cards: AE, CB, DC, DS, MC, V.

Motel 6—Downtown
$40-46
176 W. 600 South • 801.531.1252
109 Units, pets OK. Pool. Laundry facility. Rooms come with phones, A/C and cable TV. Wheelchair accessible. Credit cards: AE, CB, DC, DS, MC, V.

SUNSET — *see also Ogden*
Crystal Cottage Inn
$40
815 N. Main Street • 801.825.9500
37 Units, no pets. Continental breakfast. Meeting rooms. Indoor jacuzzi. Rooms come with phones and cable TV. Some rooms have jacuzzis. Credit cards: AE, CB, DC, DS, MC, V.

TORREY
Boulder View Inn
$45
385 W. Main Street • 435.425.3800
12 Units, no pets. Continental breakfast. Rooms come with cable TV. Some rooms have phones, microwaves and refrigerators. AAA discount. Major credit cards.

TREMONTON
Sandman Motel
$42
585 W. Main Street • 435.257.7149
38 Units, pets OK ($20 dep. req.). Rooms come with phones and cable TV. Senior discount. Credit cards: AE, CB, DC, DS, MC, V.

VERNAL
Motel 6
$50
1092 W. US 40 • 435.789.0666
63 Units, pets OK. Indoor pool. Laundry facility. Airport transportation. Rooms come with phones, A/C and cable TV. Wheelchair accessible. Credit cards: AE, CB, DC, DS, MC, V.

Rodeway Inn
$36-56
590 W. Main Street • 435.789.8172
42 Units, pets OK. Restaurant on premises. Rooms come with phones and cable TV. Major credit cards.

Sage Motel & Restaurant
$30-37
54 W. Main Street • 435.789.1442
26 Units, no pets. Restaurant on premises. Continental breakfast. Rooms come with phones and cable TV. Credit cards: AE, DS, MC. V.

WELLINGTON
National 9 Inn
$30-45
50 South 700 East • 435.637.7980 or 800.524.9999
47 Units, pets OK ($5 and $15 dep. req.). Restaurant on premises. Pool. Rooms come with phones and cable TV. Major credit cards.

WENDOVER
Bonneville Motel
$35
375 Wendover Blvd. W. • 435.665.2500
87 Units, no pets. Restaurant on premises. Rooms come with cable TV. No phones in rooms. Major credit cards.

Motel 6
$22-50
561 E. Wendover Blvd. • 435.665.2267
130 Units, pets OK. Pool. Laundry facility. Airport transportation. Rooms come with phones, A/C and cable TV. Wheelchair accessible. Credit cards: AE, CB, DC, DS, MC, V.

WOODS CROSS
Motel 6
$40-46
2433 S. 800 W. • I-15, Exit 318
801.298.0289
125 Units, pets OK. Pool. Laundry facility. Rooms come with phones, A/C and cable TV. Wheelchair accessible. Credit cards: AE, CB, DC, DS, MC, V.

ZION NATIONAL PARK — *see Hurricane and Mount Carmel Junction*

vermont

BARRE
Motel Pierre
$42-52 (69-79)*
362 N. Main Street • 802.476.3188
20 Units, no pets. Continental breakfast. Rooms comes with phones and cable TV. Major credit cards.
*Higher rates effective mid-September through mid-October.

BENNINGTON
Apple Valley Inn & Cafe
$39-55 (59-75)*
979 US 7 • 802.442.6588
18 Units, pets OK. Restaurant on premises. Pool. Rooms comes with phones and cable TV. Some rooms have refrigerators. AAA/ Senior discount. Credit cards: AE, DS, MC, V.
*Higher rates effective mid-September through late October.

Mid-Town Motel
$45-50 (58-72)*
107 W. Main Street • 802.447.0189
17 Units, no pets. Rooms comes with phones and cable TV. Some rooms have refrigerators. AAA/Senior discount. Major credit cards.
*Higher rates effective mid-June through late October.

BRATTLEBORO
Molly Stark Motel
$40-48 (70-80)*
829 Marlboro Road, 3 miles west of I-91, Exit 2 • 802.254.2440
14 Units, pets OK ($5). Rooms come with phones and cable TV. Credit cards: AE, DS, MC. V.
*Higher rates effective late September through October.

Motel 6
$40-52
1254 Putney Road (Rte. 5N), I-91, Exit 3
802.254.6007
59 Units, pets OK. Rooms come with phones, A/C and cable TV. Wheelchair accessible. Credit cards: AE, CB, DC, DS, MC, V.

BURLINGTON — *see also South Burlington*
Bel-Aire Motel
$45-50 (69-99)*
111 Shelburne Road • 802.863.3116
14 Units, pets OK. Continental breakfast. Rooms come with phones and cable TV. AAA discount. Major credit cards.
*Higher rates effective July through October.

Colonial Motor Inn
$50 (58)*
462 Shelburne Road • 802.862.5754
34 Units, no pets. Rooms come with phones and cable TV. Major credit cards.
*Higher rate effective April through October.

Motel 6
$40-52 (60-70)*
I-89, Exit 16 • 802.654.6860
106 Units, pets OK. Pool. Laundry facility. Rooms come with phones, A/C and cable TV. Wheelchair accessible. Credit cards: AE, CB, DC, DS, MC, V.
*Higher rates effective summer weekends.

COLCHESTER — see Burlington

LONDONDERRY
Magic View Motel
$35-49 (60-65)*
1.6 miles east on SR 11 • 802.824.3793
19 Units, no pets. Continental breakfast. Rooms comes with phones and cable TV. No A/C in rooms. AAA discount. Major credit cards.
*Higher rates effective late September through mid-October.

LYNDONVILLE
Colonnade Inn
$50-55 (60-65)*
I-91, Exit 23 • 802.626.9316
40 Units, no pets. Rooms come with phones and cable TV. Senior discount. AAA/Senior discount. Major credit cards.
*Higher rates effective mid-September through mid-October.

Lynburke Motel
$40-50 (60)*
US 5 & 114 • 802.626.3346

24 Units, pets OK ($10). Pool. Rooms come with phones and cable TV. Credit cards: AE, DS, MC, V.
*Higher rate effective autumn weekends.

MARLBORO
Golden Eagle Motel
$35-50
Rte. 9 • 802.464.5540
18 Units, pets OK. Rooms come with phones and cable TV. Major credit cards.

NEWPORT
Newport City Motel
$59-55 (60-65)*
444 E. Main Street • 802.334.6558
64 Units, no pets. Heated pool. Laundry facility. Fitness facility. Jacuzzi. Meeting rooms. Rooms come with phones and cable TV. AAA discount. Major credit cards.
*Higher rates effective September and October.

Super 8 Motel
$49-56 (54-67)*
4412 US 5 • 802.334.1775
52 Units, no pets. Rooms come with phones and cable TV. Wheelchair accessible. Major credit cards.
*Higher rates effective September and October.

NORTH CLARENDON
Country Squire Motel
$30-40
Rtes. 7B & 103 • 802.773.3805
12 Units, no pets. Continental breakfast. Rooms come with phones and cable TV. Credit cards: MC, V.

RUTLAND
Greenmont Motel
$37-59 (52-95)*
138 N. Main Street • 802.775.2575 or 800.774.2575
29 Units, pets OK. Pool. Rooms come with phones and cable TV. Some rooms have microwaves and refrigerators. AAA discount. Major credit cards.
*Higher rates effective leaf-viewing season.

ST. JOHNSBURY
Aime's Motel
$36-60 (45-75)*
I-93, Exit 1, Junction US 2 & SR 18 (half mile north) • 802.748.3194
16 Units, pets OK. Rooms come with phones and cable TV. Credit cards: AE, DS, MC. V.
*Higher rates effective mid-September through late October.

Changing Seasons Motor Lodge
$36-42
I-91 (Exit 23) • 802.626.5832
From Fwy exit, 1.3 miles south on US 5
22 Units, no pets. Restaurant on premises. Pool. Sauna. Steam room. Rooms come with phones and cable TV. Credit cards: AE, DS, MC, V.

SHAFTSBURY
Hillbrook Motel
$50 (70)*
Rte. 7A • 802.447.7201
17 Units, pets OK. Pool. Rooms come with phones and cable TV. Some rooms have microwaves and refrigerators. Credit cards: MC. V.
*Higher rates effective autumn.

Serenity Motel
$45-55 (55-60)*
3.3 miles north on SR 7A from SR 67 Junction • 802.442.6490
8 Units, pets OK. Rooms come with phones and cable TV. AAA discount. Credit cards: AE, DS, MC. V.
*AAA discounted rates. Higher rates effective mid-September through October. Closed November through April.

SHELBURNE
Dutch Mill Motel
$28-55 (70-80)*
Rte. 7, 2056 Shelburne Rd • 802.985.3568
15 Units, pets OK ($25). Restaurant on premises. Pool. Rooms come with phones and cable TV. Major credit cards.
*Open May through October. Higher rates effective autumn.

SOUTH BURLINGTON
Super 8
$50 (70)*
1016 Shelburne Road • 802.862.6421
53 Units, pets OK. Pool Laundry facility. Rooms come with phones and cable TV. Senior discount. Major credit cards.
*Higher rate effective during leaf-viewing season.

Town & Country Motel
$49 (59)*
490 Shelburne Road • 802.862.5786

12 Units, pets OK. Rooms come with phones and cable TV. Major credit cards.
*Higher rates effective May through October.

WELLS RIVER
Wells River Motel
$50 (60)
Main Street (Rtes. 5 & 302)
802.757.2191
11 Units, pets OK. Rooms come with A/C, phones and cable TV. Major credit cards.
*Higher rate effective mid-September through mid-October.

WHITE RIVER JUNCTION
Pleasant View Motel
$46 (89)*
65 Woodstock Road • 802.295.3485
15 Units, pets OK. Rooms come with phones and cable TV. Major credit cards.
*Higher rate effective autumn.

Super 8 Motel
$50 (77)*
On US 5 west of I-89/91 • 802.295.7577
83 Units, no pets. Pool. Rooms come with phones and cable TV. Major credit cards.
*Higher rate effective late September through late October.

WOODFORD
Whispering Pines Motel
$40-55
5135 SR 9 • 802.447.7149
16 Units, no pets. Pool. Rooms come with phones and cable TV. Senior discount. Credit cards: DS, MC, V.

virginia

ABINGDON
Empire Motor Lodge
$40-45
887 Empire Drive S.W. • 276.628.7131
105 Units, pets OK. Continental breakfast. Rooms come with phones and cable TV. AAA/Senior discount. Major credit cards.

ALEXANDRIA — *see District of Columbia*

APPOMATTOX
Budget Inn
$42
714 W. Confederate Blvd. • 434.352.7451
20 Units, pets OK. Pool. Rooms come with phones and cable TV. Some rooms have refrigerators. AAA/Senior discount. Credit cards: AE, DS, MC, V.

ARLINGTON — *see District of Columbia*

ASHLAND
Super 8 Motel
$45-49
806B England Street • 804.752.7000
150 Units, no pets. Continental breakfast. Pool. Rooms come with phones and cable TV. Senior discount. Wheelchair accessible. Major credit cards.

ATKINS
Days Inn
$49-53
Exit 50, I-81 (on US 11) • 540.783.2144
50 Units, no pets. Continental breakfast. Rooms come with phones and cable TV. AAA/Senior discount. Major credit cards.

BIG STONE GAP
Country Inn Motel
$40
627 Gilley Avenue • 276.523.0374
42 Units, pets OK. Rooms come with phones and cable TV. Major Credit cards.

BLACKSBURG
Red Carpet Inn
$50
1615 S. Main Street • 540.552.4011
44 Units, no pets. Pool. Rooms come with phones and cable TV. Some rooms have microwaves and refrigerators. Major credit cards.

BRISTOL
Budget Host Inn
$31-50*
1209 W. State Street • 276.669.5187
24 Units, no pets. Rooms come with phones and cable TV. AAA/Senior discount available (15%). Credit cards: AE, DS, MC.
*Rates as high as $115/night.

Motel 6
$43-49
21561 Clear Creek Road • I-81, Exit 7
276.466.6060
53 Units, pets OK. Laundry facility. Rooms come with phones, A/C and cable TV. Wheelchair accessible. Credit cards: AE, CB, DC, DS, MC, V.

Scottish Inns
$40-49
15589 Lee Hwy. • 276.669.4148
30 Units, no pets. Rooms come with phones and cable TV. AAA/Senior discount. Credit cards: AE, DC, DS, MC, V.

Super 8 Motel
$45
I-81, Exit 5, 2139 Lee Hwy • 540.466.8800
62 Units, pets OK ($10). Rooms come with phones and cable TV. Senior discount. Major credit cards.

CHARLOTTESVILLE
Budget Inn
$49*
140 Emmet Street S. • 434.293.5141
40 Units, no pets. Rooms come with phones and cable TV. Major credit cards.
*AAA discounted rates.

Knights Inn
$41-60
1300 Seminole Trail • On US 29 North
434.973.8133
115 Units, pets OK. Pool Meeting rooms. Rooms come with phones and cable TV. Some rooms have microwaves and

refrigerators. Wheelchair accessible. Major credit cards.

CHESAPEAKE
Motel 6
$33-50
701 Woodlake Drive • 757.420.2976
80 Units, pets OK. Laundry facility. Rooms come with phones, A/C and cable TV. Wheelchair accessible. Credit cards: AE, CB, DC, DS, MC, V.

Red Roof Inn
$38-47
724 Woodlake Drive • 757.523.0123
108 Units, pets OK. Laundry facility. Rooms come with phones and cable TV. Some rooms have microwaves and refrigerators. Credit cards: AE, CB, DC, DS, MC, V.

CHESTERFIELD
Chester Inn
$34
2201 Ruffin Mill Road • 804.526.4611
60 Units, pets OK ($5). Restaurant on premises. Pool. Laundry facility. Rooms come with phones and cable TV. Some rooms have microwaves and refrigerators. AAA discount. Credit cards: AE, CB, DC, DS, JCB, MC, V.

CHILHOWIE
Knights Inn
$39-59
I-81 (Exit 35) • 540.646.8981
42 Units, pets OK. Laundry facility. Rooms come with phones and cable TV. AAA discount. Credit cards: AE, DC, DS, MC, V.

CHINCOTEAGUE
Sunrise Motor Inn
$37-46 (68)*
4491 Chicken City Road • 757.336.6671
24 Units, no pets. Pool. Rooms come with phones and cable TV. Major credit cards. *Higher rate effective mid-June through Labor Day. Closed December through mid-March.

CHRISTIANSBURG
Econo Lodge
$43-58
2430 Roanoke Street • 540.382.6161
72 Units, pets OK. Pool. Rooms come with phones and cable TV. AAA discount. Credit cards: AE, CB, DC, DS, MC, V.

Howard Johnson Express Inn
$40-55
100 Bristol Drive • 540.381.0150
68 Units, pets OK ($3). Continental breakfast. Rooms come with phones and cable TV. Some rooms have microwaves and refrigerators. Senior discount. Credit cards: AE, CB, DC, DS, MC, V.

COLLINSVILLE
Knights Inn
$45-54
2357 Virginia Avenue • 540.647.3716
40 Units, no pets. Continental breakfast. Pool. Rooms come with phones and cable TV. Some rooms have microwaves and refrigerators. Wheelchair accessible. Major credit cards.

COLONIAL HEIGHTS
Interstate Inns
$32-40
2201 Indian Hill Road • I-95, Exit 58
804.526.4772
100 Units, no pets. Pool. Playground. Rooms come with phones and cable TV. Major credit cards.

CULPEPER
Super 8 Motel
$49-55
889 Willis Lane • 540.825.8088
61 Units, pets OK. Laundry facility. Rooms come with phones and cable TV. Wheelchair accessible. Senior discount. Major credit cards.

DANVILLE
Budget Host Inn
$38-40
127 Neal Court • 434.792.2200
21 Units, no pets. Rooms come with phones and cable TV. Some rooms have microwaves and refrigerators. Wheelchair accessible. Credit cards: AE, DS, MC, V.

Travel Inn
$30
3500 W. Main Street • 434.799.4600
50 Units, pets OK. Pool in summer. Rooms come with phones and cable TV. Senior discount. Major credit cards.

DUMFRIES — *see District of Columbia*

EMPORIA
Knights Inn
$25-50
3173 Sussex Drive • 804.535.8535
64 Units, pets OK. Pool. Rooms come with phones and cable TV. Some rooms have microwaves and refrigerators. Credit cards: AE, CB, DC, DS, JCB, MC, V.

Red Carpet Inn
$31-40
1586 Skipper Road • 804.634.4181
42 Units, pets OK. Restaurant on premises. Pool in summer. Rooms come with phones and TV. Senior discount. Major credit cards.

FAIRFAX — *see District of Columbia*

FANCY GAP
Days Inn
$40 (70)*
I-77, Exit 8 • 276.728.5101
60 Units, no pets. Continental breakfast. Rooms come with phones and cable TV. AAA discount. Major credit cards.
*Higher rate effective during October.

FRANKLIN
Days Inn
$45-55
1660 Armory Drive • 757.562.2225
84 Units, no pets. Continental breakfast. Pool. Rooms come with phones and cable TV. Some rooms have microwaves and refrigerators. AAA discount. Major credit cards.

FREDERICKSBURG
Best Western—Central Plaza
$48-53
3000 Plank Road • 540.786.7404
76 Units, pets OK. Continental breakfast. Laundry facility. Rooms come with phones and cable TV. AAA discount. Credit cards: AE, CB, DC, DS, JCB, MC, V.

Econo Lodge Central
$39-53
I-95 & SR 3 (Exit 130B) • 540.786.8374
96 Units, pets OK ($25 dep. req.). Rooms come with phones and cable TV. AAA discount. Credit cards: AE, DS, MC, V.

Heritage Inn
$30-37
5308 Jefferson Davis Hwy. • 540.898.1000
100 Units, pets OK ($5). Continental breakfast. Pool. Laundry facility. Rooms come with phones and cable TV. AAA discount. Credit cards: AE, CB, DC, DS, MC, V.

Motel 6
$30-44
401 Warrenton Road • 540.371.5443
119 Units, pets OK. Pool. Rooms come with phones, A/C and cable TV. Wheelchair accessible. Credit cards: AE, CB, DC, DS, MC, V.

FRONT ROYAL
Budget Inn
$43
1122 N. Royal Street • 540.635.2196
21 Units, pets OK ($3 and $5 dep. req.). Rooms come with phones and cable TV. AAA/Senior discount. Credit cards: AE, CB, DC, DS, MC, V.

Twin Rivers Motel
$39-44
1801 Shenandoah Avenue • 540.635.4101
20 Units, no pets. Pool. Rooms come with phones and cable TV. AAA discount. Credit cards: AE, MC, V.

GALAX
Knights Inn
$35-61
312 W. Stuart Drive • 276.236.5117
50 Units, no pets. Continental breakfast. Pool. Rooms come with phones and cable TV. Some rooms have refrigerators. AAA/ Senior discount. Credit cards: AE, DS, MC, V.

Super 8 Motel
$47
303 N. Main Street • 276.236.5127
60 Units, pets OK. Continental breakfast. Laundry facility. Rooms come with phones and cable TV. Senior discount. Wheelchair accessible. Major credit cards.

GLADE SPRING
Swiss Inn
$40-45
33361 Lee Hwy., I-81, Exit 29 • 276.429.5191
32 Units, no pets. Restaurant on premises. Rooms come with phones and cable TV. AAA discount. Credit cards: AE, MC, V.

Travelodge
$35-40
12412 Maple Street • 276.429.5131
53 Units, pets OK. Restaurant on premises. Rooms come with phones and cable TV. AAA discount. Credit cards: AE, CB, DC, DS, MC, V.

HAMPTON
Arrow Inn
$46-56
7 Semple Farm Road • 757.865.0300
I-64, Exit 261B (eastbound), Exit 262B (westbound)
58 Units, pets OK ($5). Laundry facility. Meeting rooms. Rooms come with refrigerators, phones and cable TV. Some rooms have kitchenettes. Senior discount. Major credit cards.

Econo Lodge
$35-50
2708 W. Mercury Blvd. • 757.826.8970
72 Units, pets OK ($5). Pool. Laundry facility. Rooms come with phones and cable TV. Some rooms have microwaves and refrigerators. Major credit cards.

HARRISONBURG
Motel 6
$37-45
10 Linda Lane • I-81, Exit 247A, east on US 33E • 540.433.6939
113 Units, pets OK. Pool. Laundry facility. Rooms come with phones, A/C and cable TV. Wheelchair accessible. Credit cards: AE, CB, DC, DS, MC, V.

Red Carpet Inn
$45
3210 S. 9th Street • 540.434.6704
160 Units, pets OK. Continental breakfast. Pool. Rooms come with phones and cable TV. Senior discount. Major credit cards.

LEXINGTON
Econo Lodge
$41-55
I-64, Exit 55 • 540.463.7371
48 Units, pets OK. Continental breakfast. Rooms come with phones and cable TV. Wheelchair accessible. Major credit cards.

LYNCHBURG — *see also Madison Heights*

Timberlake Motel
$43-47
11222 Timberlake Road • 434.525.2160
41 Units, no pets. Heated pool. Jacuzzi. Laundry facility. Rooms come with refrigerators, phones and cable TV. Some rooms have jacuzzis. AAA/Senior discount. Credit cards: AE, CB, DC, DS, MC, V.

MADISON HEIGHTS
Knights Inn
$42-52
3642 S. Amherst Hwy. • 434.929.6506
50 Units, no pets. Restaurant on premises. Continental breakfast. Pool. Meeting rooms. Rooms come with phones and cable TV. Major credit cards.

MARION
Budget Host Marion Motel
$28-60
435 S. Main Street • I-81, Exit 44
276.783.8511
15 Units, pets OK ($5). Laundry facility. Rooms come with phones and color TV. Senior discount. Major credit cards.

Virginia House Motor Inn
$38-43
1419 N. Main Street • 276.783.5112
38 Units, pets OK ($2-5). Continental breakfast. Pool. Rooms come with phones and cable TV. AAA discount. Major credit cards.

MARTINSVILLE – *see also Collinsville*
Super 8 Motel
$49 (59)*
960 N. Memorial Blvd. • 276.666.8888
54 Units, pets OK. Rooms come with phones and cable TV. Major credit cards.
*Higher rate effective June through September.

NATURAL BRIDGE
Budget Inn
$50*
I-81 (Exit 180), on US 11 • 540.291.2896
21 Units, pets OK ($5). Rooms come with phones and cable TV. Some rooms have refrigerators. AAA/Senior discount. Credit cards: AE, DC, DS, MC, V.
*Weekend, special event and holiday rates could be higher.

NEW MARKET
Blue Ridge Inn
$40-50*
2251 Old Valley Pike • 540.740.4136
18 Units, no pets. Playground. Rooms come

with phones, refrigerators and cable TV. Major credit cards.
*Rates as high as $60/night weekends May through October.

Budget Inn
$30-45
2192 Old Valley Pike • 540.740.3105 or 800.296.6835
14 Units, pets OK ($4 and $5 dep. req.). Playground. Rooms come with refrigerators, phones and cable TV. AAA/Senior discount. Credit cards: AE, CB, DC, DS, MC, V.

NEWPORT NEWS
Econo Lodge—Oyster Point
$40-60
11845 Jefferson Ave. • 757.599.3237
110 Units, no pets. Playground. Meeting room. Laundry facility. Rooms come with refrigerators, phones and cable TV. Some rooms have microwaves. AAA discount. Credit cards: AE, CB, DC, DS, JCB, MC, V.

Host Inn
$40-45
985 J. Clyde Morris Blvd • 757.599.3303
50 Units, pets OK ($3 and $15 dep. req.). Pool. Rooms come with phones and cable TV. Some rooms have microwaves and refrigerators. AAA discount. Credit cards: AE, DC, DS, MC, V.

Motel 6
$36-52
797 J. Clyde Morris Blvd • 757.595.6336
117 Units, pets OK. Pool. Laundry facility. Rooms come with phones, A/C and cable TV. Wheelchair accessible. Credit cards: AE, CB, DC, DS, MC, V.

Relax Inn
$40
12340 Warwick Blvd. • 757.599.6035
52 Units, no pets. Rooms come with phones and cable TV. Some rooms have microwaves and refrigerators. AAA/Senior discount. Credit cards: AE, CB, DC, DS, MC, V.

NORFOLK
International Inn
$40-60
1850 E. Little Creek Road • I-64, Exit 276, then east • 757.588.8888
62 Units, no pets. Pool. Laundry facility. Rooms come with phones and cable TV. Some rooms have microwaves and refrigerators. AAA discount. Major credit cards.

Motel 6
$40-48 (58)*
853 N. Military Hwy. • I-64, Exit 281
757.461.2380
151 Units, pets OK. Pool. Laundry facility. Rooms come with phones, A/C and cable TV. Wheelchair accessible. Credit cards: AE, CB, DC, DS, MC, V.
*Higher rate effective summer weekends.

Tides Inn
$40-45
7950 Shore Drive • 757.587.8781
100 Units, no pets. Laundry facility. Rooms come with phones and cable TV. Some rooms have microwaves and refrigerators. AAA discount. Major credit cards.

PETERSBURG
Global Inn
$30
622 E. Wythe Street • 804.732.1194
48 Units, pets OK. Rooms come with phones and cable TV. Some rooms have kitchenettes. AAA/Senior discount. Wheelchair accessible. Major credit cards.

Super 8 Motel
$45-50*
555 Wythe Street E. • 804.861.0793
48 Units, pets OK. Continental breakfast. Meeting room. Laundry facility. Rooms come with phones and cable TV. Wheelchair accessible. Senior discount. Credit cards: AE, CB, DC, DS, MC, V.
*Rates may increase slightly during special events, holidays and weekends.

PORTSMOUTH
Super 8 Motel
$46-59
925 London Blvd. • 757.398.0612
56 Units, no pets. Rooms come with phones and cable TV. Senior discount. Wheelchair accessible. Major credit cards.

PULASKI
Days Inn
$45-60
3063 Old Rte. 100 Road • I-81, Exit 94
540.980.2230
55 Units, pets OK ($10). Continental breakfast. Rooms come with phones and

cable TV. AAA/Senior discount. Major credit cards.

RICHMOND — *see also Chesterfield, Sandston (Airport)*

Days Inn

$45-55

1600 Robin Hood Road • 804.353.1287
99 Units, pets OK ($3). Pool. Rooms come with phones and cable TV. AAA discount. Major credit cards.

Motel 6—Chippenham

$36-42

100 Greshamwood Pl. • 804.745.0600
100 Units, pets OK. Rooms come with phones, A/C and cable TV. Wheelchair accessible. Credit cards: AE, CB, DC, DS, MC, V.

Red Roof Inn

$32-55

4350 Commerce Road • 804.271.7240
108 Units, pets OK. Rooms come with phones and cable TV. Some rooms have microwaves and refrigerators. Credit cards: AE, CB, DC, DS, MC, V.

ROANOKE — *see also Salem and Troutville*

Econo Lodge

$40-53

308 Orange Avenue • 540.343.2413
48 Units, no pets. Rooms come with phones and cable TV. AAA discount. Credit cards: AE, CB, DC, DS, MC, V.

Knights Inn

$32-42

7120 Williamson Road • I-81, Exit 146 to Rte. 115 • 540.366.7681
72 Units no pets. Pool. Rooms come with phones and cable TV. Some rooms have kitchenettes. Wheelchair accessible. Major credit cards.

Rodeway Inn

$35-50

526 Orange Avenue N.E. • I-581, Exit 4E
540.981.9341
102 Units, pets OK. Continental breakfast. Meeting rooms. Laundry facility. Rooms come with phones and cable TV. Some rooms have microwaves and refrigerators. AAA discount. Major credit cards.

ROCKY MOUNT

Budget Host Inn

$38

Hwy. 220N • 2 miles north of town
540.483.9757
18 Units, pets OK ($5). Picnic area. Playground. Meeting rooms. Laundry facility. Rooms come with phones and cable TV. AAA/senior discount available (10%). Major credit cards.

SALEM

Blue Jay Budget Host Inn

$25-45

5399 W. Main Street • I-81, Exit 132 •
540.380.2080
14 Units, pets OK ($5). Pool. Picnic area. Airport transportation. Rooms come with phones and cable TV. AAA/Senior discount. Credit cards: AE, DS, MC, V.

Knights Inn

$30-60

301 Wildwood Road • I-81, Exit 137
540.389.0280
66 Units, pets OK. Rooms come with phones and cable TV. Some rooms have microwaves and refrigerators. Wheelchair accessible. AAA discount. Credit cards: AE, DS, MC, V.

Super 8 Motel

$46

300 Wildwood Road • 540.389.0297
62 Units, pets OK. Rooms come with phones and cable TV. Some rooms have microwaves and refrigerators. Credit cards: AE, DC, DS, MC, V.

SANDSTON

Best Western Airport Inn

$44

5700 Williamsburg Rd • 804.222.2780
122 Units, pets OK ($25 dep. req.). Pool. Rooms come with phones and cable TV. Some rooms have refrigerators. Major credit cards.

Legacy Inn

$35-40

5252 Airport Square Ln • 804.226.4519
138 Units, pets OK. Pool. Meeting rooms. Laundry facility. Rooms come with phones and cable TV. Some rooms have refrigerators. Credit cards: AE, CB, DC, DS, MC, V.

Motel 6
$36-48
5704 Williamsburg Road (US 60) (I-64, Exit 197A) • 804.222.7600
120 Units, pets OK. Pool. Rooms come with phones, A/C and cable TV. Wheelchair accessible. Credit cards: AE, CB, DC, DS, MC, V.

SOUTH BOSTON
Days Inn
$40-55
On US 58 • 1.5 miles west of town
434.572.4941
76 Units, no pets. Pool. Rooms come with phones and cable TV. Some rooms have microwaves and refrigerators. AAA/Senior discount. Major credit cards.

SOUTH HILL
Econo Lodge
$40-45
623 Atlantic Street • 434.447.7116
53 Units, pets OK. Pool. Rooms come with phones and cable TV. Some rooms have microwaves and refrigerators. AAA discount. Major credit cards.

SPRINGFIELD — *see District of Columbia*

STAUNTON
Budget Host Inn
$37-45
I-81/64, Exit 213 • 540.337.1231
32 Units, pets OK ($5). Restaurant on premises. Continental breakfast. Pool. Rooms come with phones and cable TV. Wheelchair accessible. Major credit cards.

Days Inn
$45
273 Bells Lane • 540.248.0888
100 Units, pets OK ($6). Restaurant on premises. Continental breakfast. Rooms come with phones and cable TV. Wheelchair accessible. Senior discount. Major credit cards.

SUFFOLK
Regal Inn Motel
$40
2361 Pruden Blvd. • 757.925.4770
18 Units, pets OK. Rooms come with phones and cable TV. Major credit cards.

Super Inn
$37-40*
633 N. Main Street • 757.925.0992
51 Units, pets OK. Meeting rooms. Rooms come with phones and cable TV. Senior discount. Wheelchair accessible. Major credit cards.
*Rates higher weekends, special events and holidays.

TAPPAHANNOCK
Days Inn
$50
On US 17 & 360, 1 mile south of town
804.443.9200
60 Units, no pets. Continental breakfast. Rooms come with phones and cable TV. Wheelchair accessible. AAA/Senior discount. Major credit cards.

TROUTVILLE
Travelodge
$38-45
2444 Lee Hwy. S. • I-81, Exit 150A
540.992.6700
108 Units, pets OK ($6). Continental breakfast. Pool. Playground and picnic area. Rooms come with phones and cable TV. AAA discount. Major credit cards.

VIRGINIA BEACH
Econo Lodge
$40-55
5819 Northampton Blvd • 757.460.1000
104 Units, pets OK ($25 dep. req.). Continental breakfast. Laundry facility. Rooms come with phones and cable TV. Some rooms have microwaves and refrigerators. AAA discount. Major credit cards.
*Rates can climb as high as $72/night.

Red Roof Inn
$40-47*
195 Ballard Court • Half mile east of Jct. I-64 & SR 44 • 757.490.0225
108 Units, pets OK. Rooms come with phones and cable TV. Credit cards: AE, CB, DC, DS, MC, V.
*Rates as high as $86/night.

Wayside Motor Inn
$40-45
400 S. Military Hwy. • 757.420.1130
108 Units, no pets. Pool. Rooms come with phones and cable TV. Some rooms have

refrigerators. Credit cards: AE, CB, DS, MC, V.

WILLIAMSBURG
Econo Lodge Colonial
$35-55
216 Parkway Drive • 757.253.6450
48 Units, no pets. Continental breakfast. Pool. Picnic area. Rooms come with phones and cable TV. Some rooms have microwaves and refrigerators. AAA discount. Credit cards: AE, DS, MC, V.

Governor Spottswood Motel
$40 (58)*
1508 Richmond Road • 757.229.6944 or 800.368.1244
78 Units, no pets. Pool. Rooms come with phones and cable TV. Major credit cards.
*Higher rate effective May through October.

Motel 6
$30-50 (60)*
3030 Richmond Road • I-64, Exit 234
757.565.3433
169 Units, pets OK. Pool. Laundry facility. Rooms come with phones, A/C and cable TV. Wheelchair accessible. Credit cards: AE, CB, DC, DS, MC, V.
*Higher rate effective summer weekends.

WINCHESTER
Days Inn
$44-50*
2951 Valley Avenue • 540.667.1200
66 Units, pets OK. Restaurant on premises. Pool. Rooms come with phones and cable TV. Some rooms have microwaves and refrigerators. Credit cards: AE, DC, DS, MC, V.
*AAA discounted rates.

Howard Johnson Express Inn
$40-55
2649 Valley Ave. (US 11) • 540.662.2521
70 Units, no pets. Continental breakfast. Pool. Rooms come with phones and cable TV. Some rooms have microwaves and refrigerators. AAA/Senior discount. Credit cards: AE, DC, DS, MC, V.

WOODBRIDGE — *see District of Columbia*

WOODSTOCK
Budget Host Inn
$38
1290 S. Main Street • 540.459.4086
43 Units, pets OK. Restaurant on premises. Pool. Laundry facility. Rooms come with phones and cable TV. AAA/Senior discount. Credit cards: AE, CB, DC, DS, MC, V.

WYTHEVILLE
Motel 6
$30-42
220 Lithia Road • I-77/81, Exit 73
276.228.7988
109 Units, pets OK. Pool. Laundry facility. Rooms come with phones, A/C and cable TV. Wheelchair accessible. Credit cards: AE, CB, DC, DS, MC, V.

Super 8 Motel
$49*
130 Nye Circle • 276.228.6620
95 Units, no pets. Continental breakfast. Rooms come with phones and cable TV. Credit cards: AE, CB, DC, DS, MC, V.
*AAA discounted rates.

YORKTOWN
Yorktown Motor Lodge
$50*
8829 George Washington Hwy.
757.898.5451
42 Units, no pets. Pool. Playground. Rooms come with microwaves, refrigerators, phones and cable TV. AAA discount. Credit cards: AE, CB, DC, DS, MC, V.
*Rates can climb as high as $55/night.

washington

ABERDEEN
Thunderbird Motel
$45
410 W. Wishkah • 360.532.3153
36 Units, pets OK. Rooms come with phones and cable TV. Some rooms have microwaves and refrigerators. Wheelchair accessible. Major credit cards.

ANACORTES
San Juan Motel
$40
1103 6th Street • 360.293.5105
29 Units, pets OK. Rooms come with phones and cable TV. Wheelchair accessible. Major credit cards.

AUBURN — *see Seattle*

BELLINGHAM
Bay City Motor Inn
$42
116 N. Samish Way • 360.676.0332
50 Units, no pets. Continental breakfast. Rooms come with phones and cable TV. Some rooms have microwaves and refrigerators. AAA discount. Credit cards: AE, DS, MC. V.

Motel 6
$38-50 (56)*
3701 Byron • I-5, Exit 252 • 360.671.4494
60 Units, pets OK. Pool. Laundry facility. Data ports. Rooms come with A/C, phones and cable TV. Wheelchair accessible. Credit cards: AE, CB, DC, DS, MC, V.
*Higher rate effective summer weekends.

BLAINE
Bayside Motor Inn
$40-50
340 Alder Street • 360.332.5288
24 Units, no pets. Pool. Rooms come with phones and cable TV. Senior discount. Major credit cards.

BREMERTON
Dunes Motel
$45-50
3400 11th Street • 360.377.0093
64 Units, pets OK ($20 dep. req.). Continental breakfast. Jacuzzi and swim spa. Laundry facility. Rooms come with phones and cable TV. Some rooms have kitchenettes, refrigerators and microwaves. Credit cards: AE, CB, DC, DS, MC, V.

BURLINGTON
Sterling Motor Inn
$38-47
866 S. Burlington Blvd. • 360.757.0071
35 Units, no pets. Restaurant on premises. Rooms come with cable TV. Some rooms have efficiencies, microwaves, refrigerators. Credit cards: AE, DS, MC, V.

CASHMERE
Village Inn Motel
$39-45 (49-58)*
229 Cottage Avenue • 509.782.3522
21 Units, pets OK ($5). Rooms come with phones and cable TV. Some rooms have microwaves and refrigerators. AAA discount. Major credit cards.
*Higher rates effective weekends between May and December.

CASTLE ROCK
Mt. St. Helens Motel
$50
1340 Mt. St. Helens Way N.E. (I-5, Exit 49)
360.274.7721
32 Units, pets OK. Fitness facility. Laundry facility. Rooms come with phones and cable TV. Wheelchair accessible. Senior discount. Major credit cards.

CENTRALIA
Ferryman's Inn
$35-45
1003 Eckerson Road • 360.330.2094
84 Units, pets OK ($5). Continental breakfast. Rooms come with phones and cable TV. Major credit cards.

Motel 6
$36-44
1310 Belmont Avenue • I-5, Exit 82
360.330.2057
123 Units, pets OK. Pool. Laundry facility. Rooms come with A/C, phones and cable TV.

Wheelchair accessible. Credit cards: AE, CB, DC, DS, MC, V.

Peppertree West Motor Inn & RV Park
$41
1208 Alder Street • 360.736.1124
26 Units, pets OK ($5). Restaurant on premises. Laundry facility. Rooms come with phones and cable TV. Some rooms have kitchenettes and refrigerators. Credit cards: MC, V.

CHEHALIS
Relax Inn
$50
550 S.W. Parkland Dr. • 360.748.8608
29 Units, pets OK ($5 dep. req.). Rooms come with phones and cable TV. Some rooms have microwaves and refrigerators. AAA discount. Credit cards: AE, DS, MC, V.

CHELAN
Apple Inn Motel
$35-39 (49-59)*
1002 E. Woodin Avenue • 509.682.4044
41 Units, no pets. Some rooms have kitchens and refrigerators. AAA discount. Credit cards: AE, DC, DS, MC, V.
*Higher rates effective late May through mid-September.

Midtowner Motel
$40-50
721 E. Woodin Avenue • 509.682.4051
45 Units, pets OK. Pool. Rooms come with phones and cable TV. Wheelchair accessible. Senior discount. Major credit cards.

CHENEY
Willow Springs Motel
$46
5 "B" Street • 509.235.5138
42 Units, pets OK ($5). Continental breakfast. Laundry facility. Rooms come with phones and cable TV. AAA/Senior discount. Credit cards: AE, DC, DS, MC, V.

CLARKSTON
Motel 6
$38-40*
222 Bridge Street • 509.758.1631
85 Units, pets OK. Restaurant on premises. Pool. Laundry facility. Data ports. Rooms come with A/C, phones and cable TV. Wheelchair accessible. Credit cards: AE, CB, DC, DS, MC, V.
*Rates higher during special events.

CLE ELUM
Cle Elum Travelers Inn
$36-55
1001 E. First Street • 509.674.5535
33 Units, pets OK ($5). Rooms come with phones and cable TV. Some rooms have refrigerators and microwaves. AAA discount. Credit cards: AE, DS, MC. V.

Timber Lodge Inn
$45
301 W. First Street • I-90, Exit 84
509.674.5966
35 Units, pets OK ($10). Continental breakfast. Jacuzzi. Laundry facility. Meeting rooms. Rooms come with phones and cable TV. AAA/Senior discount. Credit cards: AE, MC. V.

CONNELL
M&M Motel
$42
730 S. Columbia Ave. • 509.234.8811
40 Units, pets OK. Rooms come with phones and cable TV. Wheelchair accessible. Senior discount. Major credit cards.

COPALIS BEACH
Echoes of the Sea
$40-50 (50-65)*
3208 Hwy. 109 • 360.289.3358
8 Units, pets OK. Rooms come with cable TV. Senior discount. Major credit cards.
*Higher rates effective during summer months.

DES MOINES — *see also Seattle*
Motel 6
$40-48 (54-56)*
20651 Military Road (I-5, Exit 151)
206.824.9902
124 Units, pets OK. Pool. Laundry facility. Data ports. Rooms come with A/C, phones and cable TV. Wheelchair accessible. Credit cards: AE, CB, DC, DS, MC, V.
*Higher rates effective summer weekends.

EDMONDS — *see also Seattle*
K&E Motor Inn
$40-50
23921 Hwy. 99 • I-5, Exit 177
425.778.2181
32 Units, pets OK. Laundry facility. Rooms come with phones and cable TV. AAA discount. Major credit cards.

ELLENSBURG
Harolds Motel
$32-38
601 N. Water • 509.925.4141
60 Units, pets OK ($3 and $20 deposit). Heated pool. Rooms come with cable TV. Some rooms have efficiencies and refrigerators. Senior discount. Credit cards: AE, CB, DC, DS, MC, V.

I-90 Inn Motel
$40-52
1390 Dollar Way Road • 509.925.9844
72 Units, pets OK. Laundry facility. Rooms come with phones and cable TV. Some rooms have microwaves and refrigerators. Credit cards: AE, DS, MC, V.

Thunderbird Motel
$40
403 W. 8th Avenue • 509.962.9856
72 Units, pets OK. Pool. Rooms come with cable TV. Wheelchair accessible. Senior discount. Major credit cards.

ENUMCLAW
Kings Motel
$35-50
1334 Roosevelt Ave. E. • 360.825.1626
44 Units, pets OK. Restaurant on premises. Pool. Rooms come with phones and cable TV. Some rooms have microwaves and refrigerators. Wheelchair accessible. Major credit cards.

EPHRATA
Travelodge
$45-50
31 Basin S.W. • 509.754.4651
28 Units, no pets. Heated pool. Data ports. Rooms come with phones and cable TV. AAA discount. Major credit cards.

EVERETT
Motel 6
$40-50
10006 Evergreen Way • 425.347.2060
119 Units, pets OK. Pool. Laundry facility. Airport transportation. Data ports. Rooms come with A/C, phones and cable TV. Wheelchair accessible. Credit cards: AE, CB, DC, DS, MC, V.

Motel 6
$40-50
224 128th Street S.W. (I-5, Exit 186)
425.353.8120
100 Units, pets OK. Restaurant on premises. Laundry facility. Data ports. Rooms come with A/C, phones and cable TV. Wheelchair accessible. Credit cards: AE, CB, DC, DS, MC, V.

Royal Motor Inn
$38-45
952 N. Broadway • 425.259.5177
35 Units, pets OK. Pool. Rooms come with phones and cable TV. Some rooms have microwaves and refrigerators. Major credit cards.

Welcome Motor Inn
$47
1205 N. Broadway • 425.252.8828
42 Units, pets OK ($5/$20 dep. req.). Rooms come with phones and cable TV. Senior discount. Major credit cards.

FEDERAL WAY
Federal Way Motel
$38-50
29815 Pacific Hwy. S. • 253.941.6996
28 Units, no pets. Rooms come with phones and cable TV. Some rooms have microwaves and refrigerators. Wheelchair accessible. Major credit cards.

FERNDALE
Scottish Lodge Motel
$35
5671 Riverside Drive • 360.384.4040
97 Units, pets OK. Pool. Rooms come with phones and cable TV. Senior discount. Major credit cards.

FIFE
Days Inn
$45-55
3021 Pacific Hwy. E. • I-5, Exit 136
253.922.3500
186 Units, no pets. Continental breakfast. Heated pool. Laundry facility. Meeting rooms. Rooms come with phones and cable TV. AAA/Senior discount. Major credit cards.

Econo Lodge
$45-59
3518 Pacific Hwy. E. • 253.922.0550
81 Units, pets OK ($10). Continental breakfast. Laundry facility. Rooms come with phones and cable TV. Some rooms have refrigerators and microwaves. Wheelchair accessible. AAA discount. Major credit cards.

Motel 6
$35-47
5201 20th Street E. • I-5, Exit 137
253.922.1270
120 Units, pets OK. Restaurant on premises. Pool. Laundry facility. Data ports. Rooms come with A/C, phones and cable TV. Wheelchair accessible. Credit cards: AE, CB, DC, DS, MC, V.

FORKS
Pacific Inn Motel
$47-55
352 Hwy. 101 • 360.374.9400
34 Units, no pets. Restaurant on premises. Rooms come with phones and cable TV. Wheelchair accessible. Major credit cards.

GOLDENDALE
Ponderosa Motel
$45-55
775 E. Broadway • 509.773.5842
28 Units, pets OK ($7-12). Rooms come with phones, refrigerators and cable TV. Some rooms have microwaves. Senior discount. Credit cards: AE, DS, MC. V.

GRAND COULEE
Trail West Motel
$28-39
108 Spokane Way • 509.633.3155
26 Units, pets OK. Pool. Rooms come with phones and cable TV. Major credit cards.

GRANDVIEW
Apple Valley Motel
$40
903 W. Wine Country Rd • 509.882.3003
16 Units, no pets. Pool. Rooms come with phones and cable TV. Major credit cards.

GRAYLAND
Walsh Motel
$38-45*
1593 Hwy. 105 • 360.267.2191
24 Units, pets OK. Rooms come with phones and cable TV. Wheelchair accessible. Major credit cards.
*Summer rates higher.

HOQUIAM
Timberline Inn
$45-50
415 Perry Avenue • 360.533.8048
25 Units, pets OK. Rooms come with phones and cable TV. Senior discount. Major credit cards.

ISSAQUAH — *see Seattle*

KALAMA
Best Value Kalama River Inn
$40-55
602 N.E. Frontage Road • 360.673.2855
42 Units, pets OK. Restaurant on premises. Continental breakfast. Meeting rooms. Rooms come with phones and cable TV. Some rooms have microwaves and refrigerators. Major credit cards.

KELSO
Best Value Inn
$35-40
505 N. Pacific • 360.636.4610
51 Units, pets OK ($5). Rooms come with phones and cable TV. Some rooms have microwaves and refrigerators. AAA discount. Credit cards: AE, DS, MC, V.

Motel 6
$38-52
106 Minor Road (I-5, Exit 39)
360.425.3229
63 Units, pets OK. Pool. Laundry facility. Data ports. Rooms come with A/C, phones and cable TV. Wheelchair accessible. Credit cards: AE, CB, DC, DS, MC, V.

KENNEWICK
Motel 6
$38-46
1751 Fowler Street (SR 240, Columbia Center Blvd. Exit) • 509.783.1250
94 Units, pets OK. Restaurant on premises. Pool. Laundry facilities. Data ports. Rooms come with A/C, phones and cable TV. Wheelchair accessible. Credit cards: AE, CB, DC, DS, MC, V.

Tapadera Inn
$45-55
300A N. Ely Street (on US 395 and Clearwater Avenue)
509.783.6191
61 Units, pets OK ($5). Restaurant on premises. Continental breakfast. Rooms come with phones and cable TV. Senior discount. Credit cards: AE, DS, MC, V.

Travelodge
$50*
321 N. Johnston Street (off Clearwater Avenue) • 509.735.6385
47 Units, pets OK. Continental breakfast. Rooms come with phones and cable TV.

Senior discount. Major credit cards.
*Rate discounted with AAA membership

KENT — *see Seattle*

KETTLE FALLS
Kettle Falls Best Value Inn
$46-51
205 E. Third Street • 509.738.6514 or 888.315.2378
26 Units, pets OK. Indoor pool. Laundry facility. Rooms come with phones, A/C and cable TV. Some rooms have microwaves and refrigerators. Major credit cards.

LEAVENWORTH
Ingalls Creek Lodge
$45
3003 US 97 (toward Blewett Pass)
509.548.6281
4 Units, no pets. Restaurant on premises. Rooms come with phones and cable TV. Major credit cards.

LONG BEACH
Our Place on the Beach
$42-47 (54-86)*
1309 S. Boulevard • 360.642.3793
25 Units, pets OK ($5). Sauna and jacuzzi. Rooms come with phones, refrigerators and cable TV. Some rooms have microwaves and kitchenettes. No A/C in rooms. AAA discount. Major credit cards.
*Higher rates effective mid-June through mid-October.

LONGVIEW
Hudson Manor Motel
$32-42
1616 Hudson Street • 360.425.1100
25 Units, pets OK ($25 dep. req.). Rooms come with phones, refrigerators and cable TV. Some rooms have kitchenettes and microwaves. AAA discount. Credit cards: AE, DS, MC, V.

The Townhouse Motel
$32-42
744 Washington Way • 360.423.7200
28 Units, pets OK ($15 dep. req.). Seasonal heated pool. Rooms come with phones and cable TV. Some rooms have microwaves and refrigerators. Credit cards: AE, DS, MC, V.

Travelodge
$42-55
838 15th Avenue • 360.423.6460
32 Units, no pets. Data ports. Rooms come with phones and cable TV. Some rooms have microwaves, refrigerators and kitchenettes. AAA discount. Major credit cards.

MERCER ISLAND — *see Seattle*

MONROE
Fairgrounds Inn
$50
18950 SR 2 • 360.794.5401
60 Units, pets OK. Rooms come with phones and cable TV. Wheelchair accessible. AAA/Senior discount. Major credit cards.

MORTON
Stiltner Motel
$40
250 Hwy 7N • 360.496.5103
10 Units, pets OK. Rooms come with phones and cable TV. Some rooms have microwaves and refrigerators. Major credit cards.

MOSES LAKE
Maples Motel
$40-45
1006 W. Third • 509.765.5665
44 Units, pets OK. Pool. Rooms come with phones and cable TV. Wheelchair accessible. Senior discount. Major credit cards.

Motel 6
$30-52
2822 Wapato Drive • I-90, Exit 176
509.766.0250
89 Units, pets OK. Pool. Laundry facility. Data ports. Rooms come with A/C, phones and cable TV. Wheelchair accessible. Credit cards: AE, CB, DC, DS, MC, V.

Sage 'n' Sand Motel
$27-50
1011 S. Pioneer Way • 509.765.1755 or 800.336.0454
38 Units, pets OK. Pool. Rooms come with cable TV. Senior discount. Major credit cards.

MOUNTLAKE TERRACE
Studio 6
$52
6017 244th Street S.W. • I-5, Exit 177
425.771.1656
100 Units, pets OK. Laundry facility. Data ports. Rooms come with A/C, phones and cable TV. Wheelchair accessible. Credit cards: AE, CB, DC, DS, MC, V.

MOUNT RAINIER NATIONAL PARK —
see Packwood and Randle

MOUNT VERNON
West Winds Motel
$40
2020 Riverside Drive • 360.424.4224
40 Units, pets OK. Rooms come with phones and cable TV. Senior discount. Major credit cards.

NEWPORT
Golden Spur Motor Inn
$35-40
924 W. Hwy. 2 • 509.447.3823
24 Units, pets OK. Restaurant on premises. Rooms come with refrigerators, microwaves, phones and cable TV. Wheelchair accessible. Senior discount. Major credit cards.

OAK HARBOR
Acorn Motor Inn
$44-52 (68-94)*
31530 SR 20 • 360.675.6646
32 Units, pets OK. Continental breakfast. Rooms come with phones and cable TV. Wheelchair accessible. AAA discount. Major credit cards.
*Higher rates effective weekends.

OCEAN SHORES
Silver King Motel
$45 (55-65)*
1070 Discovery Ave. SE • 360.289.3386 or 800.562.6001
50 Units, pets OK. Rooms come with cable TV. Wheelchair accessible. Senior discount. Major credit cards.
*Higher rates effective during summer months.

OKANOGAN
Ponderosa Motor Lodge
$41-45
1034 S. 2nd Avenue • 509.422.0400
25 Units, pets OK. Pool. Laundry facility. Rooms come with phones and cable TV. Some rooms have kitchens, microwaves, radios and refrigerators. AAA discount. Credit cards: AE, CB, DC, DS, MC, V.

OLYMPIA — *see also Tumwater*
Bailey Motor Inn
$35-40
3333 Martin Way • 360.491.7515
48 Units, pets OK. Rooms come with phones and cable TV. Major credit cards.

Golden Gavel Motor Hotel
$43-50
909 Capitol Way • 360.352.8533
27 Units, no pets. Rooms come with phones and cable TV. No A/C. AAA discount. Credit cards: AE, DS, MC, V.

OMAK
Leisure Village Motel
$30-35
630 Okoma Drive • 509.826.4442
33 Units, pets OK ($5). Heated indoor pool, whirlpool and sauna. Rooms come with phones, refrigerators and cable TV. Some rooms have kitchens and microwaves. AAA/ Senior discount. Credit cards: AE, DS, MC, V.

Rodeway Inn & Suites
$44
122 N. Main Street • 509.826.0400
60 Units, pets OK ($5). Pool. Rooms come with phones and cable TV. Wheelchair accessible. Senior discount. Credit cards: AE, DS, MC, V.

OROVILLE
Red Apple Inn
$30-45
Hwy. 97 and 18th • 509.476.3694
37 Units, pets OK. Pool. Rooms come with phones and cable TV. Major credit cards.

OTHELLO
Cabana Motel
$35-45
665 E. Windsor Street • 509.488.2605 or 800.442.4581
55 Units, pets OK. Pool. Rooms come with cable TV. Senior discount. Major credit cards.

PACKWOOD
Inn of Packwood
$45-55
13032 US 12 • 360.494.5500
33 Units, no pets. Heated pool. Jacuzzi. Rooms come with phones and cable TV. No A/C in rooms. Senior discount. Credit cards: AE, DS, MC, V.

Mountain View Lodge Motel
$37-55
13163 Hwy 12 • 360.494.5555
21 Units, pets OK on ground level only ($3 and $20 dep. req.). Seasonal pool and jacuzzi. Some rooms have kitchens, B/W

cable TV and refrigerators. Credit cards: AE, DC, DS, MC, V.

PASCO
Plantation Inn
$30
1232 S. 10th Street • 509.547.2451 or 800.391.9188
32 Units, pets OK. Pool. Rooms come with cable TV. Wheelchair accessible. Senior discount. Major credit cards.

PORT ANGELES
Aircrest Motel
$42-54
1006 E. Front Street • 360.452.9255
24 Units, no pets. Rooms come with phones and cable TV. AAA discount. Credit cards: AE, DS, MC, V.

Royal Victoria Motel
$34-56*
521 E. 1st Street • 360.452.2316
20 Units, no pets. Rooms come with phones and cable TV. Some rooms have A/C, microwaves and refrigerators. Credit cards: AE, DS, MC, V.
*Summer rates as high as $80/night.

PORT TOWNSEND
Hostelling International
$14
Fort Worden State Park, #272 Battery Way 360.385.0655
24 Beds, Hours: 7:30-9:30a & 5-10 pm
Facilities: information desk, kitchen, linen rental (sleeping bags allowed). Private rooms available. Serves pancakes for $1.00. Open year-round. Reservations recommended. Credit cards: MC, V.

PROSSER
The Barn Motor Inn
$50
490 Wine Country Road • 509.786.2121
30 Units, no pets. Meeting rooms and pool. Rooms come with cable TV. Some rooms have refrigerators and jacuzzis. Credit cards: AE, DC, DS, MC, V.

PULLMAN
American Travel Inn
$45
5155 Grand Street • 509.334.3500
35 Units, pets OK. Heated pool. Rooms come with phones and cable TV. Some rooms have refrigerators. AAA discount. Major credit cards.

Cougar Land Motel
$36-50
W. 120 Main • 509.334.3535
43 Units, no pets. Pool. Rooms come with phones and cable TV. Senior discount. Major credit cards.

PUYALLUP
Northwest Motor Inn
$44-49*
1409 S. Meridian • 253.841.2600
51 Units, pets OK ($5). Continental breakfast. Rooms comes with phones and cable TV. Major credit cards.
*Rates increase during first three weeks of September.

RANDLE
Woodland Motel
$35-40
11890 US 12 • 360.494.6766
6 Units, pets OK ($3). Set in wooded area. Rooms come with refrigerators and efficiencies. No A/C or phones. Credit cards: MC, V.

RAYMOND
Maunu's Mountcastle Motel
$36-40
524 Third Street • 360.942.5571
28 Units, pets OK ($4). Rooms come with phones and cable TV. No A/C in rooms. Some rooms have microwaves and refrigerators. Major credit cards.

RENTON — *see Seattle*

REPUBLIC
Northern Inn
$45
852 S. Clark • 509.775.3371
25 Units, pets OK. Continental breakfast. Rooms come with phones and cable TV. Senior discount. Wheelchair accessible. Major credit cards.

Prospector Inn
$46
979 S. Clark Avenue • 509.775.3361
33 Units, pets OK. Continental breakfast. Rooms come with cable TV. Wheelchair accessible. Senior discount. Major credit cards.

RICHLAND
Bali Hi Motel
$46
1201 Geo. Washington Wy • 509.943.3101
44 Units, pets OK ($5). Heated pool and jacuzzi. Rooms come with phones, refrigerators, microwaves and cable TV. Credit cards: AE, CB, DC, DS, MC, V.

Economy Inn
$39
515 Geo. Washington Wy • 509.946.6117
41 Units, pets OK ($5). Continental breakfast. Heated pool (seasonal). Rooms come with phones and cable TV. Some rooms have microwaves, refrigerators and kitchenettes. AAA discount. Major credit cards.

RITZVILLE
Colwell Best Value Inn
$43-55 (52-60)*
501 W. First Street • 509.659.1620
25 Units, pets OK ($4). Heated pool. Laundry facility. Rooms come with phones and cable TV. AAA/Senior discount. Major credit cards.
*Higher rates effective mid-June through mid-September.

SEA-TAC
Motel 6
$40-50*
18900 47th Avenue S. • I-5, Exit 152
206.241.1648
145 Units, pets OK. Pool. Laundry facility. Data ports. Rooms come with A/C, phones and cable TV. Wheelchair accessible. Credit cards: AE, CB, DC, DS, MC, V.
*Higher rate mid-June thru late October.

Motel 6
$38-54*
16500 Pacific Hwy S. • 206.246.4101
111 Units, pets OK. Rooms come with A/C, phones and cable TV. Wheelchair accessible. Credit cards: AE, CB, DC, DS, MC, V.
*Higher rate mid-June thru late October.

SEATTLE — *see also Des Moines, Kent, Mountlake Terrace, Renton, Sea-Tac, Shoreline and Tukwila*
Travel Advisory: There are many reasonably-priced rooms in Seattle, and some are even below $50/night. Below are listed a few of the best bargains in the Seattle metro area.

Auburn
Val-U Inn ($54-65)
9 14th Street N.W.
(SR 167, Exit 15th St. N.W.)
253.735.9600

Issaquah
Motel 6 ($50-60)
1885 15th Place N.W.
I-90, Exit 15
425.392.8405

Kent
Days Inn ($65)
1711 W. Meeker Street
253.854.1950

Kirkland
Motel 6 ($50-60)
12010 120th Place N.E.
425.821.5618

Mercer Island
Travelodge ($49-79)
7645 Sunset Hwy.
206.232.8000

Renton
Travelers Inn ($49-64)
4710 Lake Washington Blvd.
(I-405, Exit 7)
425.228.2858

Travelodge ($50-65)
3700 E. Valley Road
(SR 167, E. Valley Rd. Exit)
425.251.9591

Seattle
La Hacienda Motel ($60)
5414 First Avenue S.
206.762.2460

Marco Polo Motel ($58-66)
4114 Aurora Avenue N.
206.633.4090

Seattle Inn ($59-79)
225 Aurora Avenue N.
206.728.7666

Villager Lodge Everspring Inn
$49 (59)*
8201 Aurora Avenue N. • 206.789.1888

33 Units, pets OK. Laundry facility. Rooms come with phones, A/C and cable TV. Some rooms have microwaves and refrigerators. Major credit cards.
*Higher rate effective weekends.

SEDRO WOOLLEY
Skagit Motel
$40-45
1977 Hwy. 20 • 360.856.6001
47 Units, pets OK. Rooms come with phones and cable TV. Senior discount. Major credit cards.

SHORELINE
Days Inn
$49 (59)*
19527 Aurora Avenue N. (Hwy. 99)
I-5, Exit 176 • 206.542.6300
56 Units, no pets. Continental breakfast. Rooms comes with phones, A/C and cable TV. Wheelchair accessible. AAA discount. Major credit cards.
*Higher rate effective weekends.

Quest Inn
$49
14817 Aurora Avenue N. (Hwy. 99)
I-5, Exit 175 • 206.367.7880
44 Units, no pets. Continental breakfast. Rooms comes with phones, A/C and cable TV. Some rooms have microwaves and refrigerators. Wheelchair accessible. Major credit cards.

SPOKANE
Motel 6—Airport
$37-50
1508 S. Rustle Street
I-90, Exits 277/277A • 509.459.6120
121 Units, pets OK. Pool. Laundry facility. Data ports. Rooms come with A/C, phones and cable TV. Wheelchair accessible. Credit cards: AE, CB, DC, DS, MC, V.

Rodeway Inn
$42-48
W. 901 First Avenue • 509.747.1041
36 Units, no pets. Continental breakfast. Fitness facility. Jacuzzi. Rooms come with phones and cable TV. Major credit cards.

Trade Winds Motel
$35-45
907 W. 3rd Avenue • I-90, Exit 280
509.838.2091
59 Units, pets OK ($20 dep. req.). Sauna. Jacuzzi. Laundry facility. Data ports. Rooms come with phones and cable TV. Senior discount. Major credit cards.

West Wynn Motel
$30-40
W. 2701 Sunset Blvd. • 509.747.3037
33 Units, no pets. Pool. Jacuzzi. Sauna. Rooms come with refrigerators, phones and cable TV. Laundry facility. Wheelchair accessible. Senior discount. Major credit cards.

SUNNYSIDE
Sun Valley Inn
$36
724 Yakima Hwy. • 509.837.4721
40 Units, pets OK. Pool. Rooms come with phones and cable TV. Senior discount. Major credit cards.

TACOMA — *see also Fife, Lakewood and Puyallup*
Knights Inn
$35-40
9325 S. Tacoma Way • 253.582.7550
77 Units, no pets. Indoor pool. Laundry facility. Meeting rooms. Rooms come with phones and cable TV. Wheelchair accessible. Major credit cards.

Motel 6
$40-48 (54)*
1811 S. 76th Street, I-5, Exit 128/129
253.473.7100
120 Units, pets OK. Restaurant on premises. Pool. Laundry facility. Data ports. Rooms come with A/C, phones and cable TV. Wheelchair accessible. Credit cards: AE, CB, DC, DS, MC, V.
*Higher rate effective summer weekends.

TONASKET
Red Apple Inn
$37-45
Jct. Hwy. 97 & First St. • 509.486.2119
21 Units, pets OK ($2, no cats). Rooms come with phones and cable TV. Some rooms have microwaves and refrigerators. Major credit cards.

TOPPENISH
Oxbow Motor Inn
$45
511 S. Elm Street • 509.865.5800
44 Units, pets OK. Rooms come with phones and cable TV. Senior discount. Major credit cards.

TRI CITIES — *see Kennewick, Pasco and Richland*

TUMWATER
Motel 6
$36-44
400 W. Lee Street • I-5, Exit 102
360.754.7320
119 Units, pets OK. Pool. Laundry facility. Data ports. Rooms come with A/C, phones and cable TV. Wheelchair accessible. Credit cards: AE, CB, DC, DS, MC, V.

VANCOUVER — *see also Portland (OR)*
Vancouver Lodge
$45-55
601 Broadway • 360.693.3668
45 Units, pets OK. Continental breakfast. Rooms come with phones and cable TV. Wheelchair accessible. Major credit cards.

VASHON ISLAND
Hostelling International
$13
12119 S.W. Cove Road • 206.463.2592
36 Beds, Hours: 8 a.m. to 10 p.m. Facilities: equipment storage, kitchen, linen rental, lockers/baggage storage, free bicycles, on-site parking. Private rooms available. Free pancake breakfast. Closed November through April. Reservations recommended. Credit cards: MC, V.

WALLA WALLA
Tapadera Budget Inn
$40
211 N. 2nd Street • 509.529.2580 or 800.722.8277
30 Units, pets OK. Pool. Continental breakfast. Rooms come with cable TV. Senior discount. Major credit cards.

WENATCHEE
Avenue Motel
$43-50
720 N. Wenatchee Ave. • 509.663.7161 or 800.733.8981
39 Units, pets OK. Pool. Rooms come with phones and cable TV. Senior discount. Credit cards: AE, DS, MC, V.

Travelodge
$45-49
1004 N. Wenatchee Ave. • 509.662.8165
49 Units, no pets. Continental breakfast. Sauna. Jacuzzi. Heated pool. Laundry facility. Rooms come with phones and cable TV. Some rooms have microwaves, radios, refrigerators and jacuzzis. Major credit cards.

WESTPORT
Windjammer Motel
$30-50
461 E. Pacific Avenue • 360.268.9351
12 Units, no pets. Rooms come with cable TV. No A/C or phones. Some rooms have refrigerators. Credit cards: DS, MC, V.

YAKIMA
Motel 6
$34-42
1104 N. 1st Street • 509.454.0080
95 Units, pets OK ($5). Pool. Laundry facility. Data ports. Rooms come with A/C, phones and cable TV. Wheelchair accessible. Credit cards: AE, CB, DC, DS, MC, V.

Red Apple Motel
$35-43
416 N. First Street • 509.248.7150
60 Units, pets OK. Pool. Rooms come with phones and cable TV. Senior discount. Major credit cards.

Red Carpet Motor Inn
$30-37
1608 Fruitvale Blvd. • 509.457.1131
29 Units, pets OK ($5). Heated pool and sauna. Laundry facility. Rooms come with phones and cable TV. Some rooms have microwaves and refrigerators. AAA/Senior discount. Credit cards: DS, MC, V.

west virginia

BARTOW
The Hermitage Motel
$43
On Route 250 • 304.456.4808 or 877.456.4884
50 Units, no pets. Restaurant on premises. Rooms come with cable TV. Credit cards: MC, V.

BECKLEY
Best Western Four Seasons Inn
$48-54*
1939 Harper Road • I-77, Exit 44
304.252.0671
80 Units, pets OK ($5). Continental breakfast. Jacuzzi. Rooms come with phones and cable TV. Major credit cards. *AAA discounted rates.

Budget Inn
$42
223 S. Heber Street • 304.253.8318
27 Units, pets OK. Rooms come with A/C, phones and cable TV. Some rooms have kitchenettes. Credit cards: AE, DS, MC, V.

BERKELEY SPRINGS
Berkeley Springs Motel
$43
402 Wilkes Street • 304.258.1776
14 Units, no pets. Rooms come with cable TV. No phones in rooms. Wheelchair accessible. Credit cards: AE, DS, MC, V.

BLUEFIELD
Econo Lodge
$36-56
3400 E. Cumberland Rd • 304.327.8171
48 Units, pets OK ($5). Continental breakfast. Rooms come with phones and cable TV. Senior discount. Major credit cards.

Economy Inn
$30
3206 E. Cumberland Rd • 304.325.9111
65 Units, pets OK. Rooms come with A/C, phones and cable TV. Some rooms have kitchenettes. Wheelchair accessible. Credit cards: AE, DS, MC, V.

BRIDGEPORT
Knights Inn
$47
1235 W. Main Street • 304.842.7115
116 Units, pets OK. Pool. Laundry facility. Rooms come with A/C, phones and cable TV. Some rooms have refrigerators. AAA discount. Major credit cards.

BUCKHANNON
Bicentennial Motel
$50
88 E. Main Street • I-70, Exit 99
304.472.5000 or 800.762.5137
54 Units, pets OK. Restaurant on premises. Rooms come with phones and cable TV. Wheelchair accessible. AAA discount. Major credit cards.

Budget Host Baxa Inn
$42-48
21 N. Kanawha • 304.472.2500 or 800.356.5623
18 Units, pets OK. Rooms come with A/C, phones and cable TV. Major credit cards.

BURNSVILLE
Motel 79
$32-37
102 S. Main Street • 304.853.2918
28 Units, pets OK. Rooms come with A/C, phones and cable TV. Some rooms have kitchenettes. Wheelchair accessible. Credit cards: AE, DS, MC, V.

CHAPMANVILLE
Rodeway Inn
$48-50
On SR 10 • 304.855.7182
44 Units, pets OK ($5). Continental breakfast. Laundry facility. Meeting rooms. Rooms come with A/C, phones and cable TV. AAA/Senior discount. Major credit cards.

CHARLESTON — *see also Nitro and South Charleston*
Budget Host Inn
$31-45
3313 E. Kanawha Blvd. • 304.925.2592
26 Units, no pets. Restaurant on premises.

Rooms come with phones and cable TV. AAA/Senior discount. Credit cards: AE, DS, MC, V.

Knights Inn
$40-51
6401 MacCorkle Ave SE • 304.925.0451
133 Units, pets OK. Pool. Laundry facility. Rooms come with phones and cable TV. Some rooms have refrigerators and microwaves. AAA/Senior discount. Credit cards: AE, CB, DC, DS, MC, V.

Motel 6
$36-48
6311 MacCorkle Ave SE • 304.925.0471
104 Units, pets OK. Rooms come with phones, A/C and cable TV. Wheelchair accessible. Credit cards: AE, CB, DC, DS, MC, V.

Red Roof Inn
$38-49
6305 S.E. MacCorkle Avenue
I-71, Exit 95 • 304.925.6953
108 Units, pets OK. Laundry facility. Meeting rooms. Rooms come with A/C, phones and cable TV. AAA discount. Major credit cards.

CHARLES TOWN
Towne House Motor Lodge
$40-45
549 E. Washington St • 304.725.8441
115 Units, no pets. Restaurant on premises. Pool. Rooms come with A/C, phones and cable TV. Some rooms have kitchenettes. Wheelchair accessible. Credit cards: AE, CB, DC, DS, MC, V.

Turf Motel
$42 (66)*
608 E. Washington Street • 304.725.2081 or 800.422.8873
46 Units, pets OK. Restaurant on premises. Pool. Rooms come with A/C, phones and cable TV. Some rooms have kitchenettes. Wheelchair accessible. Credit cards: AE, CB, DC, DS, MC, V.
*Higher rate effective weekends.

CLARKSBURG — *see also Bridgeport*
Towne House Motor Lodge
$36
On Route 50W • 304.623.3716
75 Units, no pets. Restaurant on premises. Pool. Rooms come with A/C, phones and cable TV. Credit cards: MC, V.

CROSS LANES
Motel 6
$37-42
330 Goff Mountain Rd • 304.776.5911
112 Units, pets OK. Pool. Laundry facility. Rooms come with phones, A/C and cable TV. Wheelchair accessible. Credit cards: AE, CB, DC, DS, MC, V.

ELKINS
Super 8 Motel
$49
350 Beverly Pike • 304.636.6500
44 Units, pets OK. Meeting room. Rooms come with phones and cable TV. Senior discount. Wheelchair accessible. Major credit cards.

FAIRLEA
Rodeway Inn
$37-45
107 W. Fair Street • 304.645.7070
27 Units, pets OK. Laundry facility. Rooms come with phones and cable TV. Some rooms have microwaves and refrigerators. AAA discount. Major credit cards.

FAIRMONT
Colonial Inn
$37
1117 Fairmont Avenue • 304.363.0100
50 Units, no pets. Pool. Meeting rooms. Rooms come with phones and cable TV. AAA discount. Credit cards: AE, CB, DC, DS, MC, V.

Red Roof Inn
$37-49
50 Middletown Road • 304.366.6800 or 800.843.7663
109 Units, pets OK. Data ports. Rooms come with A/C, phones and cable TV. Wheelchair accessible. AAA discount. Credit cards: AE, CB, DC, DS, MC, V.

FRANKLIN
Thompson's Motel
$27
Jct. US 220 & 33 • 304.358.2331 or 800.338.3351
39 Units, no pets. Restaurant on premises. Rooms come with A/C, phones and cable TV. Wheelchair accessible. Credit cards: AE, CB, DC, DS, MC, V.

HUNTINGTON
Econo Lodge
$39-56
3325 US 60E • 304.529.1331
112 Units, pets OK ($10). Restaurant on premises. Continental breakfast. Pool. Meeting rooms. Fitness facility. Rooms come with phones and cable TV. AAA discount. Credit cards: AE, CB, DC, DS, MC, V.

Red Roof Inn
$39-52
5190 US 60E • I-64, Exit 15
304.733.3737
108 Units, pets OK. Laundry facility. Data ports. Rooms come with A/C, phones and cable TV. AAA discount. Major credit cards.

HURRICANE
Days Inn
$45-55
Putnam Village Drive • I-64, Exit 39 • 304.757.8721
89 Units, no pets. Pool. Laundry facility. Rooms come with phones and cable TV. Some rooms have refrigerators. Wheelchair accessible. AAA discount. Credit cards: AE, DC, DS, MC, V.

Red Roof Inn
$39-53
Putnam Village Drive • I-64, Exit 39
304.757.6392
79 Units, pets OK. Data ports. Rooms come with phones and cable TV. AAA discount. Credit cards: AE, CB, DC, DS, MC, V.

JUSTICE
The Justonian Motel
$34
On Hwy. 52 • 304.664.3239
45 Units, pets OK. Restaurant on premises. Rooms come with A/C, phones and cable TV. Credit cards: AE, DS, MC, V.

KINGWOOD
Heldreth Motel & Restaurant
$36
On Route 265 • 304.329.1145
70 Units, no pets. Restaurant on premises. Rooms come with A/C, phones and cable TV. Wheelchair accessible. Credit cards: AE, CB, DC, DS, MC, V.

LEWISBURG
Brier Inn
$44-49
540 N. Jefferson Street • I-64, Exit 169
304.645.7722
162 Units, pets OK ($10). Restaurant on premises. Pool. Laundry facility. Rooms come with phones and cable TV. Some rooms have microwaves and refrigerators. AAA discount. Major credit cards.

MARTINSBURG
Economy Inn
$33-45
1193 Winchester Ave. • 304.267.2994
22 Units, pets OK ($5). Restaurant on premises. Pool. Rooms come with A/C, phones and cable TV. Some rooms have refrigerators. AAA discount. Credit cards: AE, CB, DC, DS, JCB, MC, V.

Knights Inn
$46
1997 Edwin Miller Blvd. • I-81, Exit 16E
304.267.2211
59 Units, pets OK ($5). Rooms come with A/C, phones and cable TV. AAA/Senior discount. Major credit cards.

Scottish Inns
$38-45
1024 Winchester Ave. • 304.267.2935
18 Units, pets OK ($5). Pool. Rooms come with phones and cable TV. Some rooms have refrigerators. Senior discount. AAA discount. Credit cards: AE, DC, DS, MC, V.

MORGANTOWN
Friends Inn
$47
452 Country Club Road • 304.599.4850
30 Units, pets OK. Rooms come with phones and cable TV. Wheelchair accessible. Major credit cards.

Morgantown Motel
$42
US 119 & SR 73S • 304.292.3374
49 Units, no pets. Rooms come with A/C, phones and cable TV. Some rooms have kitchenettes. Credit cards: AE, MC, V.

MOUNDSVILLE
Plaza Motel
$39
1400 Lafayette Avenue • 304.845.9650
17 Units, no pets. Restaurant on premises.

Rooms come with A/C, phones and cable TV. Wheelchair accessible. Credit cards: AE, DS, MC, V.

MOUNT NEBO
Days Inn
$44-49
On Route 19S • 304.872.5151
102 Units, pets OK. Restaurant on premises. Jacuzzi. Meeting rooms. Rooms come with phones and cable TV. Wheelchair accessible. AAA discount. Major credit cards.

PARKERSBURG
Expressway Motor Inn
$43-48
6333 Emerson Avenue • I-77, Exit 179
304.485.1851
48 Units, pets OK. Rooms come with A/C, phones and cable TV. Some rooms have refrigerators. AAA discount. Major credit cards.

Motel 6
$36-50 (55)*
3604 7th Street • 304.424.5100
95 Units, pets OK. Pool. Laundry facility. Data ports. Rooms come with A/C, phones and cable TV. Major credit cards.
*Higher rate effective summer weekends.

Red Roof Inn
$37-54*
3714 E. 7th Street • I-77, Exit 176
304.485.1741
107 Units, pets OK. Laundry facility. Meeting rooms. Data ports. Rooms come with A/C, phones and cable TV. Major credit cards.
*Higher rate effective summer weekends.

PETERSBURG
Hermitage Motor Inn
$46-48
203 Virginia Avenue • 304.257.1711
39 Units, no pets. Jacuzzi. Rooms come with phones and cable TV. Some rooms have microwaves and refrigerators. AAA/Senior discount. Major credit cards.

Homestead Inn & Motel
$43-45
1.5 miles W on SR 55/28 • 304.257.1049
12 Units, no pets. Continental breakfast. Data ports. Rooms come with A/C, phones and cable TV. AAA/Senior discount. Major credit cards.

PRINCETON
Super 8 Motel
$38-48*
901 Oakvale Road • 304.487.6161
69 Units, no pets. Pool. Rooms come with phones and cable TV. AAA/Senior discount. Credit cards: AE, CB, DC, DS, MC, V.
*Rates may climb as high as $58/night.

Town-N-Country Motel
$33-42
805 Oakvale Road • 304.425.8156
37 Units, pets OK ($10). Heated pool. Wading pool. Rooms come with phones and cable TV. AAA/Senior discount. Credit cards: AE, DS, MC, V.

RAVENSWOOD
Scottish Inns
$29
Rte. 2, Box 33 • 304.273.2830
24 Units, pets OK. Restaurant on premises. Rooms come with A/C, phones and cable TV. Credit cards: AE, CB, DC, DS, MC, V.

RIPLEY
Super 8 Motel
$46
102 Duke Drive • I-77, Exit 138
304.372.8880
44 Units, pets OK. Continental breakfast. Meeting rooms. Rooms come with A/C, phones and cable TV. Wheelchair accessible. Major credit cards.

SAINT ALBANS
Days Inn
$46-53
6210 MacCorkle Avenue • 304.766.6231
185 Units, pets OK. Restaurant on premises. Pool. Rooms come with phones and cable TV. AAA/Senior discount. Major credit cards.

Rustic Motel
$30
5910 MacCorkle Avenue • 304.768.7386
32 Units, no pets. Rooms come with A/C, phones and cable TV. Some rooms have kitchenettes. Credit cards: DS, MC, V.

SOUTH CHARLESTON
Microtel
$39-50
600 Second Avenue • 304.744.4900 or 800.248.8879
102 Units, pets OK. Continental breakfast.

Rooms come with A/C, phones and cable TV. Wheelchair accessible. Credit cards: AE, CB, DC, DS, MC, V.

SUMMERSVILLE — *see also Mt. Nebo*
Mountain State Motel
$36
US 19, Exit to SR 41S • 304.872.2702
50 Units, no pets. Rooms come with A/C, phones and cable TV. Some rooms have kitchenettes. AAA discount. Credit cards: MC, V.

Super 8 Motel
$48*
306 Merchants Walk • 304.872.4888
56 Units, pets OK. Continental breakfast. Laundry facility. Rooms come with A/C, phones and cable TV. Some rooms have kitchenettes. Wheelchair accessible. Senior discount. Major credit cards.
*Rates as high as $58/night.

SUTTON
Elk Motor Court
$38
35 Camden Avenue • 304.765.7351
28 Units, no pets. Restaurant on premises. Game room. Rooms come with A/C, phones and cable TV. Credit cards: DS, MC, V.

TEAYS
Days Inn
$42-56
I-64, Exit 39 • 304.757.8721
89 Units, no pets. Pool. Rooms come with phones and cable TV. AAA/Senior discount. Major credit cards.

TRIADELPHIA
Days Inn
$40-54
I-70, Exit 11 (Dallas Pike) • 304.547.0610
106 Units, pets OK. Restaurant on premises. Continental breakfast. Pool. Laundry facility. Meeting rooms. Rooms come with phones and cable TV. Wheelchair accessible. AAA discount. Major credit cards.

WESTON
Weston Motor Inn
$38
On US 19S • 304.269.1975
49 Units, pets OK. Restaurant on premises. Rooms come with A/C, phones and cable TV. Some rooms have kitchenettes. Wheelchair accessible. Credit cards: AE, DC, DS, MC, V.
WHEELING — ***see Triadelphia and St. Clairsville (OH)***

WHITE SULPHUR SPRINGS
Old White Motel
$30-45
865 E. Main Street • 304.536.2441
26 Units, pets OK. Heated pool. Rooms come with phones and cable TV. Credit cards: AE, CB, DC, DS, MC, V.

WILLIAMSTOWN
Days Inn
$40-49
I-77, Exit 185 • 304.375.3730
110 Units, no pets. Continental breakfast. Pool. Laundry facility. Meeting rooms. Rooms come with phones and cable TV. AAA/Senior discount. Major credit cards.

wisconsin

ABBOTSFORD
Abby Inn
$40-50
1201 E. Spruce Street • 715.223.3332 or 888.422.2946
24 Units, no pets. Jacuzzi. Meeting rooms. Fitness facility. Rooms come with phones and cable TV. Major credit cards.

ALGOMA
River Hills Motel
$45
820 N. Water Street • 920.487.2031
30 Units, pets OK. Rooms come with phones and cable TV. Major credit cards.

Scenic Shore Inn
$36-49*
2221 Lake Street • 920.487.3214
14 Units, no pets. Rooms come with phones and cable TV. Some rooms have refrigerators, kitchens and jacuzzis. Credit cards: AE, CB, DC, DS, MC, V.
*AAA discounted rate.

ANTIGO
Super 8 Motel
$49-51
535 Century Avenue • 715.623.4188
52 Units, no pets. Continental breakfast. Pool. Rooms come with phones and cable TV. Major credit cards.

APPLETON
Exel Inn
$36-52
210 Westhill Blvd. • 920.733.5551
104 Units, pets OK. Continental breakfast. Laundry facility. Fitness facility. Rooms come with phones and cable TV. AAA/Senior discount. Major credit cards.

Microtel Inn & Suites
$47
321 Metro Drive • 920.997.3121
79 Units, pets OK ($10). Continental breakfast. Rooms come with phones and cable TV. Wheelchair accessible. Major credit cards.

ASHLAND
Anderson's Chequamegon Motel
$26-56
2200 W. Lakeshore Dr. • 715.682.4658
18 Units, pets OK. Rooms come with phones and cable TV. Some rooms have microwaves and refrigerators. AAA discount. Credit cards: AE, CB, DC, DS, MC, V.

Ashland Motel
$25-50
2300 W. Lakeshore Dr. • 715.682.5503
34 Units, pets OK ($5). Rooms come with phones and cable TV. AAA/Senior discount. Credit cards: AE, DS, MC, V.

BAYFIELD
Seagull Bay Motel
$35-45 (50-60)*
Hwy 13 & S. 7th St. • 715.779.5558
25 Units, pets OK. Rooms come with phones and cable TV. Kitchenettes available. Major credit cards.
*Higher rates effective during summer months.

BEAVER DAM
Super 8 Motel
$46-49
711 Park Avenue • US 151, Exit 132
920.887.8880
50 Units, pets OK ($50 dep. req.). Laundry facility. Data ports. Rooms come with phones and cable TV. AAA/Senior discount. Major credit cards.

BLOOMER
Bloomer Inn & Suites
$40 (56)*
2407 Woodard Drive • 715.568.3234
30 Units, pets OK ($25). Rooms come with phones and cable TV. Some rooms have refrigerators. Senior discount. Credit cards: AE, DS, MC, V.
*Higher rate effective weekends.

BROOKFIELD
Motel 6
$34-52
20300 W. Bluemound Road • I-94, Exit 297

262.786.7337
146 Units, pets OK. Pool. Laundry facility. Rooms come with phones, A/C and cable TV. Wheelchair accessible. Credit cards: AE, CB, DC, DS, MC, V.

CAMERON
Viking Motel
$50
201 S. First Street • 715.458.2111
20 Units, pets OK. Rooms come with phones and cable TV. Senior discount. Credit cards: AE, DS, MC, V.

CHIPPEWA FALLS
Country Villa Motel
$42
10765 County Hwy. Q • 715.288.6376
23 Units, pets OK. Playground. Rooms come with phones and cable TV. Kitchenettes available. Major credit cards.

Indianhead Motel
$38-55
501 Summit Avenue • 715.723.9171
27 Units, pets OK ($3). Rooms come with phones and cable TV. Some rooms have microwaves and refrigerators. AAA discount. Credit cards: AE, CB, DC, DS, MC, V.

CRANDON
Four Seasons Motel
$38-42
304 W. Glen • 715.478.3377
20 Units, no pets. Rooms come with phones and cable TV. Some rooms have microwaves and refrigerators. AAA discount. Credit cards: AE, DS, MC, V.

DOOR COUNTY — *see Sister Bay and Sturgeon Bay*

EAGLE RIVER
Traveler's Inn Motel
$36-40*
309 Wall Street • 715.479.4403
26 Units, no pets. Continental breakfast. Rooms come with phones and cable TV. Some rooms have kitchens and refrigerators. AAA/Senior discount. Credit cards: AE, DS, MC, V.
*Rates as high as $75/night.

White Eagle Motel
$40
4948 Hwy. 70W • 715.479.4426
22 Units, pets OK ($10). Heated pool. Sauna. Jacuzzi. Boat dock. Rooms come with phones and cable TV. No A/C in rooms. Some rooms have kitchens and refrigerators. Senior discount. Credit cards: DS, MC, V.

EAU CLAIRE
Exel Inn
$35-55
2305 Craig Road • 715.834.3193
100 Units, pets OK. Continental breakfast. Laundry facility. Fitness facility. Rooms come with A/C, phones and cable TV. AAA/Senior discount. Major credit cards.

Maple Manor Motel
$35-40
2507 S. Hastings Way • 715.834.2618 or 800.624.3763
34 Units, pets OK. Restaurant on premises. Continental breakfast. Rooms come with phones and cable TV. Some rooms have microwaves and refrigerators. AAA discount. Credit cards: AE, DC, DS, MC, V.

Roadstar Inn
$32-38
1151 W. MacArthur Ave • 715.832.9731
62 Units, pets OK. Continental breakfast. Rooms come with phones and cable TV. Some rooms have refrigerators. AAA/Senior discount. Credit cards: AE, CB, DC, DS, MC, V.

ELLISON BAY
Hillside Inn
$38-50
11934 Hwy. 42 • 920.854.2928
16 Units, no pets. Restaurant on premises. Rooms come with phones and cable TV. Major credit cards.

FOND DU LAC
Knights Inn
$35
738 W. Johnson Street • 920.923.6990
79 Units, pets OK. Continental breakfast. Pool. Rooms come with phones, A/C and cable TV. Wheelchair accessible. Credit cards: AE, CB, DC, DS, MC, V.

Microtel Inn & Suites
$46
US 41 & US 151 • 920.929.4000
79 Units, pets OK ($10). Continental breakfast. Rooms come with phones and cable TV. Wheelchair accessible. AAA discount. Major credit cards.

Northway Motel
$35-55*
301 S. Pioneer Road • 414.921.7975
19 Units, pets OK ($7). Continental breakfast offered in the summer and on weekends. Rooms come with refrigerators, phones and cable TV. Credit cards: AE, DS, MC, V.
*Rates as high as $80/night.

GRANTSBURG
Wood River Inn
$45-55
703 W. SR 70 • 715.463.2541
21 Units, pets OK. Fitness facility. Meeting rooms. Laundry facility. Rooms come with phones and cable TV. Some rooms have refrigerators and jacuzzis. AAA discount. Credit cards: AE, DS, MC, V.

GREEN BAY
Bay Motel
$40-50
1301 S. Military Avenue • 920.494.3441
53 Units, pets OK ($5). Rooms come with phones and cable TV. Some rooms have refrigerators. AAA discount. Credit cards: AE, DS, MC, V.

Exel Inn
$40-52
2870 Ramada Way • US 41, Exit 164
920.499.3599
104 Units, pets OK. Continental breakfast. Laundry facility. Fitness facility. Rooms come with phones and cable TV. AAA/Senior discount. Major credit cards.

Motel 6
$36-40*
1614 Shawano Avenue • 920.494.6730
103 Units, pets OK. Pool. Rooms come with phones, A/C and cable TV. Wheelchair accessible. Credit cards: AE, CB, DC, DS, MC, V.
*Prices higher during special events.

GREENFIELD
The Golden Key
$38-55
3600 S. 108th Street • 414.543.5300
23 Units, no pets. Pool. Rooms come with phones and cable TV. AAA/Senior discount. Credit cards: AE, DS, MC. V.

HUDSON
Royal Inn
$41-55
1509 Coulee Road • 715.386.2366
30 Units, pets OK ($3). Rooms come with phones and cable TV. Senior discount. Credit cards: AE, DS, MC, V.

JANESVILLE
Microtel Inn
$44-54
3121 Wellington Place • 608.752.3121
61 Units, pets OK. Continental breakfast. Rooms come with phones and cable TV. Wheelchair accessible. AAA/Senior discount. Credit cards: AE, CB, DC, DS, MC, V.

Motel 6
$28-34*
3907 Milton Avenue • 608.756.1742
119 Units, pets OK. Laundry facility. Data ports. Rooms come with phones, A/C and cable TV. Wheelchair accessible. Credit cards: AE, CB, DC, DS, MC, V.
*Prices higher during special events.

Select Inn
$37-53
3520 Milton Avenue • 608.754.0251
63 Units, pets OK ($25 dep. req.). Rooms come with phones and cable TV. Some rooms have kitchens and refrigerators. AAA/ Senior discount. Credit cards: AE, DS, MC, V.

KENOSHA
Knights Inn
$45-60
7221 122nd Avenue • 262.857.2622
113 Units, pets OK. Rooms come with phones and cable TV. Senior discount. Major credit cards.

LA CROSSE
Exel Inn
$39-59
2150 Rose Street • I-90, Exit 3
608.781.0400
101 Units, pets OK. Continental breakfast. Laundry facility. Rooms come with phones and cable TV. AAA/Senior discount. Major credit cards.

Guest House Motel
$45-54*
810 S. 4th Street • 608.784.8840
39 Units, no pets. Restaurant on premises.

Heated pool. Rooms come with phones and cable TV. Some rooms have refrigerators. Credit cards: DC, DS, MC, V.
*AAA discounted rate.

Roadstar Inn
$50 (60)*
2622 Rose Street • 608.781.3070
110 Units, pets OK ($25 dep. req.). Continental breakfast. Meeting rooms. Rooms come with phones and cable TV. Some rooms have refrigerators. Credit cards: AE, CB, DC, DS, MC, V.
*Higher rate effective weekends.

LAKE DELTON — *see Wisconsin Dells*

MADISON
Budget Host Aloha Inn
$38-54
3177 E. Washington • 608.249.7667
39 Units, no pets. Indoor heated pool. Sauna. Jacuzzi. Rooms come with phones and cable TV. Credit cards: AE, CB, DC, DS, MC, V.

Exel Inn of Madison
$40-55
4702 E. Towne Blvd. • 608.241.3861
100 Units, pets OK. Continental breakfast. Laundry facility. Fitness facility. Data ports. Rooms come with refrigerators, phones and cable TV. AAA/Senior discount. Major credit cards.

Motel 6—North
$40-50
1754 Thierer Road • I-94/90, Exit 135A
608.241.8101
91 Units, pets OK. Indoor pool. Laundry facility. Data ports. Rooms come with phones, A/C and cable TV. Wheelchair accessible. Credit cards: AE, CB, DC, DS, MC, V.

Select Inn
$41-54
4845 Hayes Road • 608.249.1815
96 Units, pets OK in smoking rooms only ($25 dep. req.). Meeting rooms. Rooms come with phones and cable TV. Some rooms have refrigerators. AAA/Senior discount. Credit cards: AE, DC, DS, MC, V.

MANITOWOC
Birch Creek Inn
$36
4626 Calumet Avenue • 920.684.3374
20 Units, pets OK. Meeting rooms. Copy and fax service. Laundry facility. Rooms come with phones and cable TV. Major credit cards.

Super 8 Motel
$45-55
4004 Calumet Avenue • 920.684.7841
80 Units, no pets. Continental breakfast. Rooms come with phones and cable TV. Senior discount. Major credit cards.

MARINETTE
Super 8 Motel
$44-49
1508 Marinette Avenue • 715.735.7887
68 Units, pets OK. Continental breakfast. Meeting rooms. Rooms come with phones and cable TV. Senior discount. Wheelchair accessible. Major credit cards.

MARSHFIELD
Park Motel
$35-39
1806 Roddis Avenue • 715.387.1741
20 Units, no pets. Rooms come with phones and cable TV. AAA discount. Credit cards: AE, DS, MC, V.

MAUSTON
Alaskan Motor Inn
$30-45
I 90-94/Hwy. 82 • 608.847.5609 or 800.835.8268
48 Units, pets OK. Restaurant on premises. Playground. Meeting rooms. Rooms come with phones and cable TV. Kitchenettes available. Major credit cards.

MEDFORD
Medford Inn
$38-47
321 N. 8th Street • 715.748.4420
23 Units, pets OK. Continental breakfast. Rooms come with phones and cable TV. Senior discount. Credit cards: AE, CB, DC, DS, MC, V.

MENOMONIE
Motel 6
$38-45
2100 Stout Street • I-94, Exit 41
715.235.6901
63 Units, pets OK. Laundry facility. Data ports. Rooms come with phones, A/C and cable TV. Wheelchair accessible. Credit cards: AE, CB, DC, DS, MC, V.

MEQUON
Fort Zedler Motel
$44*
10036 N. Port Washington Road
262.241.5850
16 Units, pets OK ($5). Rooms come with phones and cable TV. Some rooms have microwaves and refrigerators. Senior discount. Credit cards: AE, DS, MC, V.
*Rates as high as $70/night.

MERRILL
Pine Ridge Inn
$40-54
200 S. Pine Ridge Road • 715.536.9526
40 Units, no pets. Rooms come with phones and cable TV. Some rooms have kitchens, microwaves and refrigerators. Senior discount. Credit cards: AE, CB, DC, DS, MC, V.

MILWAUKEE — *see also Greenfield, Mequon, Oak Creek, Waukesha and West Allis*
Motel 6
$32-50*
5037 S. Howell Avenue • I-94, Exit 318
414.482.4414
117 Units, pets OK. Pool. Rooms come with phones, A/C and cable TV. Wheelchair accessible. Major Credit cards.
*Prices higher during special events.

MINERAL POINT
Redwood Motel
$37-55
One mile north on US 151 from town
608.987.2317
28 Units, no pets. Miniature golf. Rooms come with phones and cable TV. Some rooms have microwaves and refrigerators. Senior discount. Credit cards: DS, MC, V.

MONROE
Alphorn Inn
$30-50
250 N. 18th Avenue • 608.325.4138
63 Units, no pets. Rooms come with phones and cable TV. Some rooms have microwaves and refrigerators. AAA discount. Credit cards: AE, CB, DC, DS, MC, V.

Gasthaus Motel
$34-42
685 30th Street • 608.328.8395
18 Units, no pets. Horseshoe pits. Rooms come with phones and cable TV. AAA discount. Credit cards: AE, DS, MC, V.

NEENAH
Twin City Motel
$31-36
375 S. Green Bay Road • 920.725.3941
17 Units, no pets. Continental breakfast. Putting green. Rooms come with phones and cable TV. Some rooms have microwaves and refrigerators. Credit cards: AE, DS, MC, V.

OAK CREEK
Exel Inn of Milwaukee South
$40-60
1201 W. College Avenue • I-94, Exit 319
414.764.1776
109 Units, pets OK. Continental breakfast. Laundry facility. Fitness facility. Rooms come with A/C, phones and cable TV. AAA/ Senior discount. Major credit cards.

Red Roof Inn
$35-55
6360 S. 13th Street • I-94, Exit 319
414.764.3500
108 Units, pets OK. Data ports. Rooms come with A/C, phones and cable TV. AAA discount. Major credit cards.

ONALASKA
Microtel Inn
$38-59
3240 N. Kinney Coulee Road • I-90, Exit 5
608.783.0833
63 Units, pets OK ($5). Continental breakfast. Laundry facility. Data ports. Rooms come with refrigerators, phones and cable TV. Wheelchair accessible. AAA/ Senior discount. Major credit cards.

Shadow Run Lodge
$34
710 2nd Avenue N. • 608.783.0020
20 Units, pets OK. Rooms come with refrigerators, phones and cable TV. Some rooms have kitchens. Credit cards: AE, CB, DC, DS, MC, V.

OSSEO
Budget Host Ten-Seven Inn
$31-33
1994 E. 10th • 715.597.3114
19 Units, pets OK. Rooms come with phones and cable TV. Senior discount. Credit cards: AE, CB, DC, DS, MC, V.

PLATTEVILLE
Super 8 Motel
$47-55
100 Hwy. 80-81S • 608.348.8800
46 Units, pets OK ($10). Continental breakfast. Laundry facility. Jacuzzi and sauna. Rooms come with phones and cable TV. Senior discount. Wheelchair accessible. Major credit cards.

PORTAGE
Porterhouse Motel
$30
Hwy. 51N • 608.742.2186
35 Units, pets OK. Restaurant on premises. Rooms come with phones and TV. Major credit cards.

PRAIRIE DU CHIEN
Holiday Motel
$30-55
1010 S. Marquette Rd. • 608.326.2448
18 Units, no pets. Rooms come with phones and cable TV. Some rooms have refrigerators and jacuzzis. Credit cards: AE, DS, MC, V.

PRENTICE
Countryside Motel
$38-55
Granberg Road • 715.428.2333
23 Units, pets OK. Rooms come with phones and cable TV. Credit cards: AE, DC, DS, MC, V.

RACINE
Knights Inn
$40-55
1149 Oakes Road • 262.886.6667
107 Units, pets OK. Continental breakfast. Laundry facility. Rooms come with phones and cable TV. Some rooms have microwaves and refrigerators. AAA discount. Major credit cards.

RICE LAKE
Microtel Inn & Suites
$50-55
2771 Decker Drive • US 53, Exit 140
715.736.2010
56 Units, pets OK ($10). Continental breakfast. Rooms come with phones and cable TV. Some rooms have kitchenettes. Wheelchair accessible. Major credit cards.

Super 8 Motel
$45-50
2401 S. Main Street • 715.234.6956
47 Units, pets OK ($10). Continental breakfast. Laundry facility. Data ports. Rooms come with phones and cable TV. Some rooms have kitchenettes. AAA/Senior discount. Major credit cards.

SHEBOYGAN
Fountain Park Motel
$45
930 W. 8th Street • 920.458.4641
53 Units, pets OK ($25 dep. req.). Continental breakfast. Rooms come with phones and cable TV. AAA discount. Major credit cards.

SISTER BAY
Edge of Town Motel
$42-52 (62)*
11092 Hwy. 42 • 920.854.2012
9 Units, pets OK ($8). Rooms come with phones and cable TV. Credit cards: DS, MC, V.
*Higher rate effective mid-June through October.

SPARTA
Scottish Inn
$30-36
509 S. Water Street • 608.269.3138
20 Units, pets OK. Rooms come with phones and cable TV. Senior discount. Credit cards: DS, MC, V.

Budget Host Heritage Motel
$35-39
704 W. Wisconsin St. • 608.269.6991
22 Units, pets OK. Heated pool. Jacuzzi. Rooms come with phones and cable TV. Senior discount. Credit cards: AE, DS, MC, V.

STEVENS POINT
Point Motel
$36-42
209 Division Street • 715.344.8312
44 Units, pets OK ($6). Continental breakfast. Meeting rooms. Rooms come with phones and cable TV. Some rooms have refrigerators. AAA/Senior discount. Credit cards: AE, DC, DS, MC, V.

STURGEON BAY
Chal-A Motel
$29-59*
3910 Hwy. 42-57 • 920.743.6788
20 Units, pets OK. Rooms come with phones and cable TV. Credit cards: MC, V.
*Higher rates July through August and weekends during September and October.

Nightingale Motel
$27-55
1547 Egg Harbor Road • 920.743.7633
34 Units, pets OK. Rooms come with phones and cable TV. Major credit cards.

SUN PRAIRIE
McGovern's Motel & Suites
$46*
820 W. Main Street • 608.837.7321
56 Units, pets OK. Restaurant on premises. Meeting room. Rooms come with phones and cable TV. Kitchenettes available. AAA discount. Major credit cards.
*Rates as high as $78/night.

Super 8 Motel
$47
1033 Emerald Terrace • 608.837.8889
59 Units, no pets. Continental breakfast. Rooms come with phones and cable TV. Senior discount. Wheelchair accessible. Major credit cards.

SUPERIOR — *see also Duluth (MN)*
Driftwood Inn
$24-50*
2200 E. 2nd Street • 715.398.6661
12 Units, pets OK ($4). Rooms come with refrigerators, phones and cable TV. Credit cards: MC, V.
*AAA discounted rates.

TOMAH
Villager Lodge
$32-50
Hwys. 12 & 16 • 608.372.5946
32 Units, pets OK. Meeting rooms. Rooms come with phones and cable TV. AAA/Senior discount. Major credit cards.

VIROQUA
Doucette's Hickory Hill Motel
$40
608.637.3104 • 1.8 miles SE on US 14, SR 27 & 82.
25 Units, pets OK. Continental breakfast. Heated pool. Rooms come with phones and cable TV. Some rooms have refrigerators. Senior discount. Credit cards: AE, DS, MC, V.

WASHBURN
Redwood Motel & Chalets
$33-50
26 W. Bayfield Street • 715.373.5512
18 Units, pets OK ($3). Rooms come with phones and cable TV. Some rooms have refrigerators. AAA discount. Credit cards: AE, DC, DS, MC, V.

WAUKESHA
Super 8 Motel
$40-55*
2501 Plaza Court • 262.785.1590
109 Units, no pets. Continental breakfast. Meeting rooms. Rooms come with phones and cable TV. Some rooms have kitchenettes. Wheelchair accessible. Senior discount. Major credit cards.
*Rates as high as $80/night in summer.

WAUSAU
Exel Inn
$39-49
116 S. 17th Avenue • I-39, Exit 192
715.842.0641
122 Units, pets OK. Continental breakfast. Laundry facility. Fitness facility. Rooms come with phones and cable TV. AAA/Senior discount. Major credit cards.

Marjon Motel
$35-39
512 S. Third Avenue • 715.845.3125
26 Units, pets OK. Meeting room. Rooms come with phones and cable TV. Kitchenettes available. Major credit cards.

WEST ALLIS
Days Inn
$47-55
1673 S. 108th Street
I-94, Exit Hwy. 100 S • 414.771.3399
85 Units, no pets. Restaurant on premises. Continental breakfast. Fitness facility. Meeting rooms. Rooms come with phones and cable TV. AAA/Senior discount. Major credit cards.

WINDSOR
Super 8 Motel
$46
I-90/94 & Hwy. 19 • 608.846.3971
56 Units, pets OK. Continental breakfast. Laundry facility. Rooms come with phones and cable TV. Senior discount. Major credit cards.

WISCONSIN DELLS
Coachlight Motel
$38-50 (75)*
827 Cedar Street • 608.254.7917
15 Units, no pets. Rooms come with cable

TV. No phones in rooms. Major credit cards.
*Higher rates effective July and August. Closed November through April.

River Road Motel
$36-50*
828 River Road • 608.254.8252
25 Units, no pets. Local transportation available. Rooms come with phones and cable TV. Some rooms have microwaves and refrigerators. Credit cards: AE, DS, MC, V.
*Open April through October. Rates as high as $60/night peak summer months.

Travelodge
$40-50*
S 2275A Hwy. 12 • 608.254.5000
101 Units, pets OK. Pool. Jacuzzi. Meeting rooms. Rooms come with phones and cable TV. Some rooms have microwaves and refrigerators. Senior discount. Major credit cards.
*Summer rates higher.

WISCONSIN RAPIDS
Camelot Motel
$35-48
9210 Hwy. 13S • 715.325.5111
43 Units, pets OK. Rooms come with refrigerators, phones and cable TV. Senior discount. Credit cards: AE, DS, MC, V.

Econo Lodge
$40-45
3300 8th Street S. • 715.423.7000
55 Units, pets OK ($25 dep. req.). Restaurant on premises. Rooms come with phones and cable TV. Major credit cards.

wyoming

AFTON
Mountain Inn
$50
83542 US 89 (1.5 miles south of town)
307.886.5424
20 Units, pets OK ($3). Rooms come with phones and cable TV. No A/C in rooms. Major credit cards.

BUFFALO
Historic Mansion House Inn
$36-45
313 N. Main Street • 307.684.2218
17 Units, no pets. Continental breakfast. Rooms come with cable TV. No phones in rooms. Some rooms have refrigerators. AAA discount. Credit cards: DS, MC, V.

Z-Bar Motel
$34-50
626 Fort Street • 307.684.5535
20 Units, pets OK ($4). Rooms come with phones, refrigerators and cable TV. Senior discount. Credit cards: AE, DC, DS, MC, V.

CASPER
Motel 6
$36-42
1150 Wilkins Circle • 307.234.3903
130 Units, pets OK. Pool. Laundry facility. Data ports. Rooms come with A/C, phones and cable TV. Wheelchair accessible. Credit cards: AE, CB, DC, DS, MC, V.

National 9 Inn Showboat
$34-46
100 West "F" Street • 307.235.2711
45 Units, pets OK ($5 and $10 dep. req.). Continental breakfast. Rooms come with phones and cable TV. Some rooms have refrigerators and radios. AAA/Senior discount. Credit cards: AE, CB, DC, DS, MC, V.

Super 8 Motel
$50
3838 Cy Avenue • 307.266.3480
66 Units, pets OK ($2). Continental breakfast. Meeting rooms. Laundry facility. Rooms come with phones and cable TV. Senior discount. Credit cards: AE, CB, DC, DS, MC, V.

Westridge Motel
$28-42
955 Cy Avenue • I-25, Exit 188B
307.234.8911
28 Units, pets OK ($5). Rooms come with phones and cable TV. AAA/Senior discount. Major credit cards.

CHEYENNE
Fleetwood Motel
$39-52
3800 E. Lincolnway • 307.638.8908
21 Units, pets OK ($3). Heated pool in season. Rooms come with phones and cable TV. AAA discount. Major credit cards.

Lincoln Court Motel
$40-55
1720 W. Lincolnway • I-25, Exit 9
307.638.3302
65 Units, pets OK. Heated pool. Miniature golf and playground. Airport transportation. Rooms come with phones and cable TV. AAA/Senior discount. Major credit cards.

Luxury Inn
$29-50
1805 Westland Road • I-25, Exit 9
307.638.2550
32 Units, no pets. Continental breakfast. Rooms come with phones and cable TV. AAA/Senior discount. Major credit cards.

Motel 6
$34-50
1735 Westland Road • 307.635.6806
108 Units, pets OK. Pool. Laundry facility. Data ports. Rooms come with A/C, phones and cable TV. Wheelchair accessible. Credit cards: AE, CB, DC, DS, MC, V.

CHUGWATER
Super 8 Motel
$40-57*
100 Buffalo Drive (I-25, Exit 54)
307.422.3248
23 Units, pets OK ($4). Restaurant on premises. Pool. Laundry facility. Rooms come with phones and cable TV. Credit cards: AE, DS, MC. V.
*AAA discounted rates.

CODY

Big Bear Motel

$34-40 (65)*

139 W. Yellowstone Hwy • 307.587.3117
42 Units, pet OK. Heated pool. Rooms come with phones, A/C and cable TV. Senior discount. Credit cards: DS, MC, V.
*Open April through October. Higher rate effective mid-June through mid-August.

Rainbow-Park Motel

$28-38 (54-57)*

1136 17th Street • 307.587.6251 or 800.341.8000
39 Units, no pets. Laundry facility. Rooms come with phones and cable TV. Some rooms have refrigerators and kitchens. AAA discount. Credit cards: AE, CB, DC, DS, MC, V.
*Higher rates mid-June thru late August.

Skyline Motor Inn

$28-52

1919 17th Street • 307.587.4201 or 800.843.8809
46 Units, pets OK. Restaurant on premises. Pool. Rooms come with phones and cable TV. Major credit cards.

DIAMONDVILLE

Energy Inn

$38-48 (58-68)*

307.877.6901 • Jct. US 30 & 189
43 Units, pets OK ($75 dep. req.). Horseshoe pits. Rooms come with phones and cable TV. Some rooms have refrigerators, radios and kitchens. Senior discount. Credit cards: AE, CB, DC, DS, MC, V. Senior discount.
*Higher rates effective May through mid-August.

DOUGLAS

Alpine Inn

$35-50

2310 E. Richards • 307.358.4780
40 Units, pets OK ($5). Laundry facility. Rooms come with phones and cable TV. AAA discount. Major credit cards.

First Interstate Inn

$36-45

2349 E. Richards • 307.358.2833
43 Units, pets OK ($5). Airport transportation. Laundry facility. Rooms come with cable TV. Credit cards: AE, CB, DC, DS, MC, V. Senior discount.

Super 8 Motel

$40-50

314 Russell Avenue • I-25, Exit 140
307.358.6800
37 Units, pets OK ($5). Rooms come with phones and cable TV. Some rooms have refrigerators. AAA/Senior discount. Major credit cards.

DUBOIS

Branding Iron Motel

$29-49

401 W. Ramshorn • 307.455.2893
23 Units, pets OK. Rooms come with phones and cable TV. No A/C. Some rooms have kitchenettes and refrigerators. AAA/Senior discount. Credit cards: AE, CB, DC, DS, MC, V.

Stagecoach Motor Inn

$36-52

103 Ramshorn • 307.455.2303
50 Units, pets OK ($5). Heated pool. Playground. Horseshoe pits. Laundry facility. Rooms come with phones and cable TV. No A/C. Some rooms have refrigerators and kitchens. AAA discount. Credit cards: AE, DC, DS, MC, V.

Super 8 Motel

$47-51 (56-71)*

1414 Warm Springs Dr. • 307.455.3694
32 Units, pets OK ($5). Rooms come with phones and cable TV. Major credit cards.
*Higher rates effective June through September.

EVANSTON

Motel 6

$35-40

261 Bear River Drive • I-80, Exit 6
307.789.0791
90 Units, pets OK. Pool. Laundry facility. Rooms come with A/C, phones and cable TV. Wheelchair accessible. Credit cards: AE, CB, DC, DS, MC, V.

Prairie Inn

$40-50

264 Bear River Drive • I-80, Exit 6
307.789.2920
31 Units, pets OK ($5). Continental breakfast. Data ports. Rooms come with phones and cable TV. AAA discount. Major credit cards.

Super 8 Motel
$42-55*
70 Bear River Drive • 307.789.7510
89 Units, pets OK. Continental breakfast. Game room. Rooms come with phones and cable TV. Wheelchair accessible. Senior discount. Credit cards: AE, CB, DC, DS, MC, V.
*Summer rates may be higher.

Weston Super Budget Inn
$45
1936 Harrison Drive • 307.789.2810
115 Units, pets OK. Restaurant on premises. Pool. Rooms come with phones and cable TV. Major credit cards.

GILLETTE
Motel 6
$36-50
2105 Rodgers Drive (I-90, Exit 124)
307.686.8600
74 Units, pets OK. Laundry facility. Airport transportation. Data ports. Rooms come with A/C, phones and cable TV. Wheelchair accessible. Credit cards: AE, CB, DC, DS, MC, V.

Super 8 Motel
$35-50*
208 S. Decker Court • 307.682.8078
60 Units, pets OK ($5). Continental breakfast. Rooms come with phones and cable TV. Wheelchair accessible. Senior discount. Major credit cards.
*Rates as high as $80/night in summer.

GRAND TETON NATIONAL PARK — *see Alpine and Jackson*

GREEN RIVER
Super 8 Motel
$37-47
280 W. Flaming Gorge Way
307.875.9330
37 Units, pets OK ($25 dep. req.). Rooms come with phones and cable TV. AAA discount. Credit cards: AE, CB, DC, DS, MC, V.

Western Inn
$36
890 W. Flaming Gorge Way
307.875.2840
31 Units, pets OK ($25 dep. req.). Rooms come with phones and cable TV. Some rooms have refrigerators. AAA discount. Credit cards: AE, CB, DC, DS, MC, V.

GREYBULL
Antler Motel
$35
1116 N. 6th Street • 307.765.4404
14 Units, pets OK. Playground. Rooms come with microwaves, refrigerators, phones and cable TV. Credit cards: AE, DS, MC, V.

Yellowstone Motel
$40-50 (52-62)*
247 Greybull Avenue • 307.765.4456
34 Units, pets OK ($5). Putting green and heated pool. Rooms come with phones and cable TV. AAA/Senior discount. Credit cards: AE, DC, DS, MC, V.
*Higher rates June through August.

JACKSON
Motel 6
$36-40 (64-88)*
600 S. Hwy 89 • 307.733.1620
155 Units, pets OK. Pool. Laundry facility. Data ports. Rooms come with A/C, phones and cable TV. Wheelchair accessible. Credit cards: AE, CB, DC, DS, MC, V.
*Higher rates Memorial Day through September.

KEMMERER
Antler Motel
$37
419 Coral Street • 307.877.4461
58 Units, pets OK. Rooms come with phones and cable TV. Major credit cards.

LANDER
Budget Host Pronghorn Lodge
$42-56*
150 E. Main Street • 307.332.3940
55 Units, pets OK ($10). Airport transportation. Hot tub and picnic area. Laundry facility. Rooms come with phones and cable TV. Wheelchair accessible. Senior discount. Credit cards: AE, CB, DC, DS, MC, V.
*AAA discounted rates.

Holiday Lodge National 9
$36-50
210 McFarlane Drive • 307.332.2511
40 Units, pets OK ($5). Continental breakfast. Jacuzzi. Rooms come with cable TV. AAA/Senior discount. Credit cards: AE, CB, DC, DS, MC, V.

Silver Spur Motel
$30-42
340 N. 10th • 307.332.5189

25 Units, pets OK ($3). Heated pool. Child-care services available. Rooms come with phones and cable TV. Some rooms have microwaves and refrigerators. AAA discount. Credit cards: AE, DC, DS, MC, V.

LARAMIE
Motel 6
$34-44
621 Plaza Lane • 307.742.2307
100 Units, pets OK. Pool. Laundry facility. Data ports. Rooms come with A/C, phones and cable TV. Wheelchair accessible. Credit cards: AE, CB, DC, DS, MC, V.

Motel 8
$43
501 Boswell Drive • 307.745.4856
143 Units, pets OK. Pool. Rooms come with phones and cable TV. Major credit cards.

Travel Inn
$38-55
262 N. Third Street • I-80, Exit 313
307.745.4853
28 Units, no pets. Heated pool. Rooms come with phones and cable TV. AAA discount. Major credit cards.

LOVELL
Horseshoe Bend Motel
$39-49
357 E. Main Street • 307.548.2221
22 Units, pets OK. Heated pool. Rooms come with phones and cable TV. Some rooms have microwaves and refrigerators. AAA/Senior discount. Credit cards: AE, CB, DC, DS, MC, V.

Super 8 Motel
$35-50
595 E. Main Street • 307.548.2725
34 Units, pets OK. Continental breakfast. Laundry facility. Rooms come with phones and cable TV. Senior discount. Credit cards: AE, CB, DC, DS, MC, V.

LUSK
Town House Motel
$30-55*
525 S. Main Street • 307.334.2376
20 Units, pets OK ($5). Rooms come with phones and cable TV. AAA/Senior discount. Credit cards: AE, DS, MC. V.
*Closed January through April.

Trail Motel
$42-52 (52-67)*
305 W. 8th Street • 307.334.2530 or 800.333.5875
22 Units, pets OK. Continental breakfast. Playground. Heated pool. Airport transportation. Rooms come with phones and cable TV. Senior discount. Major credit cards.
*Closed mid-October through April. Higher rates mid-June through mid-August.

NEWCASTLE
Pines Motel
$34-50
248 E. Wentworth • 307.746.4334
11 Units, pets OK. Jacuzzi. Rooms come with phones and refrigerators and cable TV. AAA/Senior discount. Credit cards: AE, CB, DC, DS, MC, V.

PINEDALE
Sundance Motel
$40-60
148 E. Pine Street • 307.367.4336
19 Units, pets OK. Rooms come with phones and cable TV. Some rooms have refrigerators. No A/C in rooms. AAA discount. Credit cards: AE, DS, MC. V.

POWELL
Park Motel
$32-45 (52-59)*
737 E. Second Street • 307.754.2233
18 Units, no pets. Rooms come with phones and cable TV. Some rooms have microwaves, refrigerators and jacuzzis. Major credit cards.
*Higher rates mid-June thru mid-August.

Super 8 Motel
$44-50 (63-69)*
845 E. Coulter • 307.754.7231
35 Units, pets OK. Continental breakfast. Laundry facility. Rooms come with phones and cable TV. Wheelchair accessible. Senior discount. Credit cards: AE, CB, DC, DS, MC, V.
*Higher rate effective mid-June through August.

RAWLINS
First Choice Inn
$46
1904 E. Cedar • 307.328.1401
50 Units, pets OK. Rooms come with phones and cable TV. Major credit cards.

Rawlins Motel
$35
905 W. Spruce Street • 307.324.3456
25 Units, pets OK ($5). Airport transportation. Rooms come with cable TV. Some rooms have microwaves and refrigerators. Credit cards: AE, DS, MC, V. Senior discount.

RIVERTON
Super 8 Motel
$40-50
1040 N. Federal Blvd. • 307.857.2400
32 Units, pets OK ($5). Continental breakfast. Airport transportation. Rooms come with phones and cable TV. Some rooms have refrigerators. Credit cards: AE, CB, DC, DS, JCB, MC, V.

Thunderbird Motel
$34-46
302 E. Fremont • 307.856.9201
48 Units, pets OK ($4). Rooms come with phones and cable TV. Some rooms have microwaves and refrigerators. AAA discount. Credit cards: AE, DS, MC, V.

Tomahawk Motor Lodge
$42-50
208 E. Main Street • 307.856.9205
32 Units, no pets. Fitness facility and Airport transportation. Rooms come with phones and cable TV. Some rooms have refrigerators. Senior discount. Credit cards: AE, DC, DS, MC, V.

ROCK SPRINGS
Budget Host Inn
$35-45
1004 Dewar Drive • 307.362.6673
32 Units, pets OK. Continental breakfast. Rooms come with phones and cable TV. Some rooms have microwaves and refrigerators. AAA/senior discount available (10%). Major credit cards.

Motel 6
$34-48
2615 Commercial Way • 307.362.1850
99 Units, pets OK. Pool. Laundry facility. Data ports. Rooms come with A/C, phones and cable TV. Wheelchair accessible. Credit cards: AE, CB, DC, DS, MC, V.

Motel 8
$34-38
108 Gateway Blvd. • 307.362.8200
92 Units, pets OK. Rooms come with phones and cable TV. Major credit cards.

SHERIDAN
Guest House Motel
$35-55
2007 N. Main Street • 307.674.7496
44 Units, pets OK ($5). Laundry facility. Rooms come with phones and cable TV. Some rooms have refrigerators. AAA/Senior discount. Credit cards: AE, DC, DS, MC, V.

Rock Trim Motel
$32-54
449 Coffeen Avenue • 307.672.2464
18 Units, pets OK. Laundry facility. Rooms come with phones cable TV. Some rooms have microwaves, A/C and refrigerators. AAA discount. Credit cards: AE, DS, MC. V.

SUNDANCE
Bear Lodge Motel
$44-50 (56)*
218 Cleveland • 307.283.1611
33 Units, pets OK. Jacuzzi. Rooms come with phones and cable TV. Major credit cards.
*Higher rate effective July and August.

Budget Host Arrowhead Motel
$36-45 (50-58)*
214 Cleveland • 307.283.3307
12 Units, no pets. Laundry facility. Airport transportation. Rooms come with phones and cable TV. Major credit cards.
*Higher rates effective mid-May through mid-September.

THERMOPOLIS
Rainbow Motel
$40-50
408 Park • 307.864.2129 or 800.554.8815
17 Units, pets OK. Rooms come with phones and cable TV. Some rooms have microwaves and refrigerators. Major credit cards.

TORRINGTON
Maverick Motel
$38-40
Rt. 1, Box 354 • 307.532.4064
1.5 miles west from town on US 26/85.
11 Units, pets OK. Rooms come with phones and cable TV. Some rooms have refrigerators and kitchens. AAA discount. Credit cards: AE, CB, DC, DS, MC, V.

WAPITI
Wise Choice Inn
$35-40 (50-57)*
2908 Yellowstone Hwy. • 307.587.5004
2.8 miles west of town on US 14/16/20.
17 Units, pets OK ($3). Playground. Rooms come with TVs. No phones in rooms. Some rooms have A/C. AAA discount. Credit cards: AE, DS, MC, V.
*Closed mid-November through mid-April. Higher rates early June through August.

WHEATLAND
Motel 6
$35-41*
95 16th Street • 307.322.1800
47 Units, pets OK. Rooms come with A/C, phones and cable TV. Wheelchair accessible. Credit cards: AE, CB, DC, DS, MC, V.
*Rates higher during special events.

WORLAND
Days Inn
$42-55
500 N. 10th • 307.347.4251
42 Units, pets OK. Laundry facility. Continental breakfast. Rooms come with phones and cable TV. Wheelchair accessible. AAA/Senior discount. Major credit cards.

Super 8 Motel
$36-50*
2500 Big Horn Avenue • 307.347.9236
36 Units, pets OK ($5). Continental breakfast. Airport transportation. Rooms come with phones and cable TV. Some rooms have refrigerators and safes. Credit cards: AE, CB, DC, DS, JCB, MC, V.
*Rates as high as $60/night in summer.

YELLOWSTONE NATIONAL PARK — *see Cody, Wapiti, West Yellowstone (MT) and Gardiner (MT)*

index

A

B

D

G

M

T

U

V

W

X

Y

Z